NIXON

The First Year of His Presidency

CONGRESSIONAL   QUARTERLY

1735 K STREET, N.W. WASHINGTON, D.C.

Library of Congress Catalog Card Number: 71-114440
Standard Book Number: 87187-007-X

Editor and President: Nelson Poynter
Executive Editor: Richard N. Billings
Book Service Editor: Merrill T. McCord
Contributing Staff: Judy Aldock, Gail Bensinger, Barbara Coleman, T. G. Hayes, Carole Horn, Charles W. Riesz, Margaret Thompson, Elder Witt
Publisher: Buel F. Weare
Sales Manager: Robert C. Hur

Congressional Quarterly Service

CONGRESSIONAL QUARTERLY, founded in 1945, is a privately owned news research service which provides the full facts on Congress, the Government and politics. The CQ Service consists of 52 Weekly Reports; the accumulative Quarterly Indexes; the annual 1,200-page Almanac, which distills, reorganizes and cross-indexes the complete year's coverage; and a Query Service. The Service is sold by annual subscription. Rates will be furnished on request.

Congressional Quarterly also is the publisher of various background paperbacks on Congress and politics; the CQ Guide to Current American Government, published twice a year; and Congress and the Nation Vol. I (1945-64) and Vol. II (1965-68), a detailed review of the Government and politics in the postwar years.

The CQ student service consists of either 10 or 13 consecutive issues of the CQ Weekly Report mailed in bulk every Friday night with the current issue of the CQ Guide, an optional inclusion. The CQ Guide is published twice a year, in early January and late August.

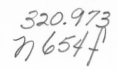

Table of Contents

1970 STATE OF THE UNION

Nixon Stresses Control of Pollution, Inflation, Crime

Focusing on the nation's unfinished business—issues that he described as being above partisanship—President Nixon presented his first State of the Union message to a joint session of the 91st Congress and a nationwide television audience Jan. 22.

He called for the "creation of a new American experience, an experience richer and deeper and more truly a reflection of the goodness and grace of the human spirit." *(For text, see p. 5.)*

The President received a lengthy ovation as he appeared before the Democratic-controlled Legislative Branch. Members of the Cabinet, the Supreme Court other dignitaries and Mr. Nixon's family heard the 36-minute address.

The tenor of the message was somewhat philosophical in content, emphasizing broad priorities and long-range objectives rather than more concrete legislative proposals. It treated in a general way questions concerning the "quality of American life."

Mr. Nixon had said (Jan. 21) that his message would not contain a "laundry list" of specific legislative proposals; moreover, the nature of the message seemed to coincide with his view of the Presidency as "a place where priorities are set and goals determined" which he described as a candidate for the office in 1968.

In his State of the Union message, Mr. Nixon addressed difficult issues in a general and rather non-controversial way. The message both reflected and drew on a growing awareness of the need to begin to solve these problems, but sharp conflicts were likely to develop on methods to deal with them.

Emphasis of the Nixon message was on long-term goals. In it, the President sought to harness the energy of all Americans in bettering their society and environment. Throughout the address ran the theme of reappraisal: "The critical question is not whether we will grow, but how we will use that growth." The President said:

"Our purpose (in the next decade) should not be simply better management of the programs of the past. The time has come for a new quest—a quest not for a greater quantity of what we have—but for a new quality of life in America."

Although the President stressed at the outset of his remarks that the first priority of Americans "must always be peace," most of the message dealt with broad domestic issues facing the nation, not only in the coming year, but also during the next decade.

Mr. Nixon, however, did touch briefly on the Administration's efforts to wind down the war in Vietnam and its determination to avoid future military involvements. His comments on both were enthusiastically applauded. The President was to amplify his thoughts on foreign policy in a "State of the World" message he would submit to Congress early in February. That message, which the President said he would not deliver in person, would review the Administration's international efforts in 1969 and outline future foreign policy directions.

Part of the Jan. 22 message dealt with issues confronting the Administration when it assumed office—particularly the war in Vietnam and the spiraling inflation.

While the Administration had had only partial success in both areas, the President had been able to win wide approval for his Vietnam policy, and his critics had muted their voices considerably.

The fight on inflation had received a more mixed assessment (although recent economic indicators showed some downswing in growth) and was likely to figure prominently in the 1970 political campaigns. To these unresolved problems the President added new challenges Jan. 22.

In doing so, he took the opportunity to remind the assembled lawmakers that "more than two-score legislative proposals which I sent to the Congress last year... still await enactment."

"At least a dozen" pieces of major legislation would be submitted to the second session of the 91st Congress. (To avoid repeating the backlog of the first session, Congressional leaders pledged early action on items left over from the 1969 agenda. The Administration promised to submit its new proposals more promptly—at the rate of one or two a week.) *(For action not completed in 1969, see p. 9, 40.)*

Emphasis on volunteerism and on restructuring national programs rather than "putting good money into bad programs" reflected the President's continuing concern with private initiatives and increased Government effectiveness. It also was reminiscent of the themes of his inaugural address. But it reflected as well the Administration's dilemma of coping with rising demands for a reordering of national priorities while at the same time wrestling with inflation.

These conflicting pressures would be particularly strong in an election year. Democrats had already launched a political offensive by criticizing the President on both counts.

Illustrative also of these problems was the fact that, as the President was drafting his State of the Union message (largely written during a three-day visit to the Presidential retreat at Camp David), he had simultaneously been hard at work on paring down the federal Budget, scheduled for presentation Jan. 30.

Caught between the inflation/budget squeeze and the need to respond to increasing demands for major initiatives in environment and social welfare, Mr. Nixon warned on Jan. 21, "Some needed federal programs

---

State of the Union. Article II, Section 3, of the Constitution provides: "He (the President) shall from time to time give the Congress information on the State of the Union, and recommend to their consideration such measures as he shall judge necessary and expedient." There is no set date for the message; but normally it is delivered shortly after Congress convenes. President Johnson gave his sixth and final message Jan. 14, 1969.

simply will have to be postponed so that we live within our means." And in his Jan. 22 address, he called on Congress to join him in a bipartisan effort to combat inflation.

He said he would present a balanced budget for 1971, but added, "To present but stay within a balanced budget requires some very hard decisions. It means rejecting spending programs which would benefit some of the people when their net effect would result in price increases for all the people."

Against the background of Senate passage (Jan. 20, 1970) of the $19.7-billion Labor-HEW appropriations bill, which Mr. Nixon later vetoed, the President said he recognized "the political popularity of spending programs, particularly in an election year. But unless we stop the rise in prices, the cost of living for millions of American families will become unbearable and the government's ability to plan programs for progress for the future will become impossible."

The President listed three areas in which, he said, "urgent priorities demand that we move":

• Total reform of the welfare system (the Administration's legislation was pending before Congress). *(See p. 55.)*

• An assessment and reform of government institutions at all levels (the Administration in 1969 submitted a wide-ranging proposal for revenue sharing between federal and state governments). *(See p. 66.)*

• "Reforms which will expand the range of opportunities for all Americans" in the fields of voting rights, employment and property ownership. *(See p. 49.)*

He touched briefly on the need for reforms in health, education, housing and transportation before turning to the crime problem, stating, "We must declare and win the war against the criminal elements which increasingly threaten our cities, our homes and our lives." (The President's remarks on crime were enthusiastically applauded.)

Law enforcement programs, he said, would be the major exception to budget cuts, with proposed Government spending to aid local law enforcement for fiscal 1971 double that budgeted for 1970. In this area, few new Administration proposals were foreseen, with the President requesting action on his previous proposals.

In the final third of his message, devoted to the American environment, the President joined the growing ranks of politicians, students and other citizens concerned to halt pollution, rebuild American cities and preserve the nation's open spaces.

Calling on all Americans to do their share in making their country more livable, the President asked, "Shall we surrender to our surroundings, or shall we make our peace with nature and begin to make reparations for the damage we have done to our air, to our land and to our water?"

As with the inflation issue, the President said, "Restoring nature to its natural state is a cause beyond party and beyond factions."

He pledged to submit "the most comprehensive and costly program in this field in America's history," a program which he said could not be for one year only but should look ahead to the next 5 or 10 years. More specifically, he mentioned:

Congressional Reaction

Both Republicans and Democrats generally praised the President's speech, although a few Democrats said they thought it did not contain enough specific legislative proposals.

Senate Majority Leader Mike Mansfield (D Mont.) called the speech "hopeful" and "impressive," and said, "I would hope specific recommendations will be sent up shortly so that Congress can get to work."

Senate Minority Leader Hugh Scott (R Pa.) said the message was "excellent...an upbeat speech which appealed to the very best in the American mood which is for a better and cleaner environment." His counterpart in the House, Gerald R. Ford (R Mich.), called it "great and inspiring" and expressed the hope that Congress would work with the President in a bipartisan spirit.

House Majority Leader Carl Albert (Okla.) was more critical, forecasting possible recession. "Regrettably the President appears oblivious to both our current national economic stagnation and what that portends for the future," he said.

Sen. J.W. Fulbright (D Ark.), chairman of the Foreign Relations Committee, said it was an "impressive statement" but the Vietnam war was "passed over lightly." "We're all for peace," he commented.

"I don't see how anyone can find fault with the goals and objectives," said Sen. Henry M. Jackson (D Wash.). "What it boils down to is how are we going to implement it."

Asked whether the message might have an impact on 1970 political campaigns, GOP National Chairman Rep. Rogers C.B. Morton (Md.) said he thought it would. "He set a tone, a spirit of leadership within the party to move the nation ahead. He stressed sound fiscal management and addressed himself to the environment problem."

• A $10-billion nationwide clean water program.

• New financing methods for purchasing open space and park lands.

• Increased research on automobile pollution, combined with more strict standards and strengthened enforcement procedures.

• New regulations concerning the use of air and water.

• The development of a "national growth policy" on population redistribution in an effort to redirect both the rural-urban exodus and the decay of major cities.

In all these areas, he said, "The answer is not to abandon growth, but to redirect it. For example, we should turn toward ending congestion and eliminating smog the same reservoir of inventive genius that created them in the first place."

Foreign Policy

Although the President planned to submit a separate foreign policy message early in February, he declared at the outset of his State of the Union address that the first priority of the nation "must always be peace for America and the world." He said that the major immediate goal of the Administration's foreign policy was to end the war in Vietnam in a way that would bring lasting peace—a theme he has repeatedly stressed in Vietnam policy statements.

On Vietnam, the President referred to Congressional support for a "just peace" (through passage of H Res 613 Dec. 2) and said, "You have completely demolished the enemy's hopes that they can gain in Washington the victory our fighting men have denied them in Vietnam." The phrase was applauded by Republican Members, while some Democratic doves remained silent. *(For stories on H Res 613, see p. 23; for other Vietnam developments, see p. 11 and 19.)*

Applause came from both sides of the aisle when the President, paraphrasing what has become known as the Nixon Doctrine, said, "Neither the defense nor the development of other nations can be exclusively or primarily an American undertaking....We shall be faithful to our treaty commitments, but we shall reduce our involvement and our presence in other nations' affairs."

The President said the new policy was based on "an evaluation of the world as it is, rather than as it was 25 years ago" when the United States had to assume the major burden of the free world's defense. The new emphasis on partnership had strengthened American alliances with the countries of Europe, Latin America and Asia, the President said. He mentioned in particular the development of "an historic new basis for Japanese-American friendship." *(For story on NATO, see p. 19; for Latin America, see p. 24; for Asia, see p. 17; for Okinawa, see p. 18.)*

Turning to East-West relations, the President repeated a theme of his inaugural address, stating, "We are moving with precision and purpose...to an era of negotiation." He said that negotiations on strategic arms and other subjects would have a greater chance for success if motivated by "mutual self-interest rather than naive sentimentality." In this context, he mentioned the recent renewal of the Warsaw talks with Communist China. *(For story on strategic arms limitation talks, see p. 24.)*

New Federalism

President Nixon urged Congress to act on a set of programs he had proposed in mid-1969—programs he had packaged together at that time under the title "New Federalism."

The New Federalism programs, the President had said in an Aug. 8 message to Congress, offered "a new and drastically different approach to the way in which government cares for those in need, and to the way the responsibilities are shared between the state and federal governments." *(See p. 4, 56, 66.)*

Although the President failed in his State of the Union address to list details of new programs he said he would propose in 1970, he specifically urged Congress to act on his New Federalism proposals. These included welfare reform and federal-state relationships—two out of three areas in which, he said, "urgent priorities demand that we move." The third priority, he said, was the adoption of reforms to expand the range of opportunities for all Americans.

Welfare. "We cannot delay longer in accomplishing a total reform of our welfare," the President said. The Administration had been critical of Congressional Democrats recently for not moving faster on the President's welfare reform program, called the Family Assistance Plan. Secretary of Health, Education and Welfare Robert H. Finch said Jan. 13 that the program was threatened with "death by inaction" in a Congress which had failed "even to offer alternative reform proposals."

The proposal called for a national minimum benefit of $1,600 annually for a family of four with no income. Blind, elderly and disabled persons were to be assured of a minimum monthly income of $90.

The plan also included providing federal benefits for "working poor" families whose income fell below $3,920 annually for a family of four. All recipients of family assistance were to participate in job training and to take jobs under the President's bill. *(See p. 56.)*

Federal-State Relationships. After 190 years of power flowing from the people and local and state governments to Washington, the President said, it was time for the process to be reversed. In his Aug. 8 New Federalism message, the President had specifically proposed turning over to state and local governments the administration of federal job-training programs. He had also recommended that $500 million be returned to state and local governments in fiscal 1971 through a revenue-sharing measure. *(See p. 58, 66.)*

Anti-Inflation Effort

Mr. Nixon confirmed expectations by stressing the importance of controlling inflation and assigning the highest order of priorities to the battle.

"When I speak of actions which would be beneficial to the American people," he said, "I can think of none more important than for the Congress to join this Administration in the battle to stop the rise in the cost of living."

He specifically avoided blaming either business or labor for inflation. The primary cause, he said, was the fact that the Federal Government during the 1960s spent $57 billion more than it took in. By citing deficit Government spending, he placed the blame on the Kennedy and Johnson Administrations and Congress.

"The American people," he said, "paid the bill for that deficit in price increases which raised the cost of living for the average family of four by $200 per month.

"Millions of Americans are forced to go into debt today because the Federal Government decided to go into debt yesterday."

"We had a balanced budget in 1969," he said. "This Administration cut more than $7 billion out of spending plans in order to produce a surplus in 1970.

"In spite of the fact that Congress reduced revenues by $3 billion, I shall present a balanced budget for 1971."

The President sent requests for budget cuts totaling $4 billion to Congress on April 15, 1969. The cuts were to be made from the fiscal 1970 Budget former President Johnson submitted before Mr. Nixon's inauguration. *(See p. 12.)*

On July 22, 1969, Mr. Nixon directed federal agencies to cut an additional $3.5 billion from their spending during fiscal 1970. He cited as the reason a worsening budget situation brought on by rising uncontrollable expenditures and unbudgeted Congressional actions plus failure of Congress to act on some of his recommendations.

War on Crime

Proclaiming again a "war on crime," the President singled out law enforcement agencies as the one area where fiscal 1971 spending would increase.

Mr. Nixon proposed that federal spending for aid to local and state law enforcement agencies in 1971 double the $268 million being spent for such aid in fiscal 1970.

He emphasized expansion of the federal role in partnership with local law enforcement agencies, which he termed "the cutting edge in the effort to eliminate street crime, burglaries and murder."

Reminding Congress that he had sent to it 13 measures to deal with crime, Mr. Nixon said that he expected enactment of the proposals to provide the Government with stronger weapons in the war against crime.

Mr. Nixon said that he hoped the city of Washington, now a "tragic example" of the crime problem, would become an example of respect for law.

Mr. Nixon's crime bills sent to Congress in 1969 include:

• A new witness immunity law (included in the Organized Crime Control Act, S 30, as reported Dec. 16 by the Senate Judiciary Committee).

• A measure to ban the infiltration of racketeers into legitimate businesses (included in S 30 as reported).

• Formal endorsement of S 30, the Organized Crime Control Act.

• A bill to ban use of the mails to deliver obscene material to persons under 18. (HR 11031)

• A comprehensive revision and reform of federal law controlling narcotics and dangerous drugs (incorporated into S 3246, reported by the Senate Judiciary Committee Dec. 16). *(See p. 53.)*

Environment

Criticized in 1969 for showing insufficient concern for the nation's environmental needs, the President devoted major attention to those problems—suffocating smog, poisoned water, deafening noise and abused land. *(See p. 13.)*

Water Pollution. Although his specific proposals were few, the President's remarks indicated that the Nixon Administration recognized the urgency of attacking the problems of environmental pollution. He called his proposed program for a better environment "the most comprehensive and costly program in this field ever in the nation's history."

The President said that he would propose to Congress a $10-billion, nationwide clean water program to construct municipal waste treatment plants within the next five years wherever they are needed.

The clean water proposal indicated the President would not "freeze" the $586 million in extra funds voted by Congress in early December for the fight against water pollution.

The Administration had requested only $214 million in appropriations for fiscal 1970 out of a $1-billion

authorization, although the Interior Department had said it could use at least $600 million to help cities build sewage plants. Congress voted $800 million over Administration objections on Dec. 4. There was conjecture that the President would "freeze" the extra funds because of budgetary pressures.

The Nixon proposal appeared similar to an Interior Department plan to have local governments float $10 million in bonds over the next five years to pay for sewage plants and then commit the Federal Government to pay off the principal in annual $500-million payments over 20 years. (A Congressional spokeman said any financing plan would require approval by Congress.)

Air Pollution. The President said there would be immediate action on setting strict standards, strengthening enforcement procedures and intensifying research. He acknowledged the automobile as "our worst polluter of the air," but indicated no forthcoming legislation. He called for further advances in engine design and fuel composition, thus leaving the problem in the hands of industry.

The President emphasized voluntary individual efforts in cleaning up the environment, stating that "each of us must resolve that each day he will leave his home, his property, and the public places of his city or town a little cleaner...." He also proposed an innovation in waste disposal policy that would involve industry responsibility. "To the extent possible," Mr. Nixon said, "the price of goods should be made to include the costs of producing and disposing of them without damage to the environment."

Other Programs

Education. Mr. Nixon cited education as a program in need of reform, but made no further explanation. The President did not send a message to Congress on education during 1969. U.S. Commissioner of Education James E. Allen Jr. told a House Subcommittee that the goal of the Administration was to eliminate illiteracy during the 1970s.

Civil Rights. Despite listing the need to increase opportunity for all Americans as one of his "urgent priorities," Mr. Nixon made no specific mention of civil rights programs.

He defined the "fair chance" which each American should have as including equal voting rights and equal employment opportunity but made no reference to any specific legislative programs. *(For story on 1969 civil rights developments, see p. 49.)*

Transportation. The President mentioned in passing that in six years he foresaw "faster transportation," but he made no new proposals and did not urge Congressional action on proposals he made in 1969. They included urban mass transit aid, airport development, and merchant marine subsidies.

Housing. Mr. Nixon said the Federal Government must be in a position to assist in building new cities and rebuilding old ones and called for development of a national growth policy. No housing proposals were spelled out.

A Jan. 21 statement issued by the President reiterated the Administration's commitment to control inflationary spending, but promised housing aid to the extent that it did not interfere with that policy.

TEXT OF PRESIDENT NIXON'S STATE OF UNION MESSAGE

Following is a transcript of President Nixon's Jan. 22, 1970, State of the Union Message: (Story p. 1)

Mr. Speaker, Mr. President, my colleagues in the Congress, our distinguished guests and my fellow Americans:

To address a joint session of the Congress in this great chamber, in which I was once privileged to serve, is an honor for which I am deeply grateful.

The State of the Union Address is traditionally an occasion for a lengthy and detailed account by the President of what he has accomplished in the past, what he wants the Congress to do in the future, and, in an election year, to lay the basis for the political issues which might be decisive in the Fall.

Occasionally there comes a time when profound and far-reaching events command a break with tradition.

This is such a time.

I say this not only because 1970 marks the beginning of a new decade in which America will celebrate its 200th birthday. I say it because new knowledge and hard experience argue persuasively that both our programs and our institutions in America need to be reformed.

The moment has arrived to harness the vast energies and abundance of this land to the creation of a new American experience, an experience richer and deeper and more truly a reflection of the goodness and grace of the human spirit.

The seventies will be a time of new beginnings, a time of exploring both on the earth and in the heavens, a time of discovery. But the time has also come for emphasis on developing better ways of managing what we have and of completing what man's genius has begun but left unfinished.

Our land, this land that is ours together, is a great and a good land. It is also an unfinished land and the challenge of perfecting it is the summons of the seventies.

It is in that spirit that I address myself to those great issues facing our nation which are above partisanship.

When we speak of America's priorities the first priority must always be peace for America and the world.

The major immediate goal of our foreign policy is to bring an end to the war in Vietnam in a way that our generation will be remembered, not so much as the generation that suffered in war, but more for the fact that we had the courage and character to win the kind of a just peace that the next generation was able to keep.

We are making progress toward that goal.

The prospects for peace are far greater today than they were a year ago.

A major part of the credit for this development goes to the members of this Congress who, despite their differences on the conduct of the war, have overwhelmingly indicated their support of a just peace. By this action, you have completely demolished the enemy's hopes that they can gain in Washington the victory our fighting men have denied them in Vietnam.

No goal could be greater than to make the next generation the first in this century in which America was at peace with every nation in the world.

I shall discuss in detail the new concepts and programs designed to achieve this goal in a separate report on foreign policy, which I shall submit to the Congress at a later date.

Today, let me describe the directions of our new policies.

We have based our policies on an evaluation of the world as it is, not as it was twenty-five years ago at the end of World War II. Many of the policies which were necessary and right then are obsolete today.

Then, because of America's overwhelming military and economic strength, because of the weakness of other major free world powers and the inability of scores of newly independent nations to defend—or even govern—themselves, America had to assume the major burden for the defense of freedom in the world.

In two wars, first in Korea and now in Vietnam, we furnished most of the money, most of the arms, most of the men to help others defend their freedom.

Today the great industrial nations of Europe, as well as Japan, have regained their economic strength, and the nations of Latin America—and many of the nations who acquired their freedom from colonialism after World War II in Asia and Africa—have a new sense of pride and dignity, and a determination to assume the responsibility for their own defense.

That is the basis of the doctrine I announced at Guam.

Neither the defense nor the development of other nations can be exclusively or primarily an American undertaking.

The nations of each part of the world should assume the primary responsibility for their own well-being; and they themselves should determine the terms of that well-being.

We shall be faithful to our treaty commitments, but we shall reduce our involvement and our presence in other nations' affairs.

To insist that other nations play a role is not a retreat from responsibility, it is a sharing of responsibility.

The result of this new policy has been not to weaken our alliances, but to give them new life, new strength and a new sense of common purpose.

Relations with our European allies are once again strong and healthy, based on mutual consultation and mutual responsibility.

We have initiated a new approach to Latin America, in which we deal with those nations as partners rather than patrons.

The new partnership concept has been welcomed in Asia. We have developed an historic new basis for Japanese-American friendship and cooperation, which is the linchpin for peace in the Pacific.

And if we are to have peace in the last third of the Twentieth Century, a major factor will be the development of a new relationship between the United States and the Soviet Union.

I would not underestimate our differences, but we are moving with precision and purpose from an era of confrontation to an era of negotiation.

Our negotiations on strategic arms limitations and in other areas will have far greater chance for success if both sides enter them motivated by mutual self-interest rather than naive sentimentality.

This is the same spirit with which we have resumed discussions with Communist China in our talks at Warsaw.

Our concern in our relations with both these nations is to avoid a catastrophic collision and to build a solid basis for peaceful settlement of our differences.

I would be the last to suggest that the road to peace is not difficult and dangerous, but I believe our new policies have contributed to the prospect that America may have the best chance since World War II to enjoy a generation of uninterrupted peace and that chance will be enormously increased if we continue to have a relationship between Congress and the Executive in which, despite differences in detail, where the security of America and the peace of mankind are concerned, we act not as Republicans, not as Democrats—but as Americans.

As we move into the decade of the 70s, we have the greatest opportunity for progress at home of any people in world history.

Our Gross National Product will increase by five hundred billion dollars in the next ten years. This increase alone is greater than the entire growth of the American economy from 1790 to 1950.

The critical question is not whether we will grow, but how we will use that growth.

The decade of the sixties was also a period of great growth economically. But in that same ten-year period we witnessed the greatest growth of crime, the greatest increase in inflation, the greatest social unrest in America in 100 years. Never has a nation seemed to have had more and enjoyed it less.

At heart, the issue is the effectiveness of government.

Ours has become as it continues to be—and should remain—a society of large expectations. Government helped to generate these expectations and undertook to meet them. Yet, increasingly, it proved unable to do so.

As a people, we had too many visions—and too little vision.

Now, as we enter the seventies, we should enter also a great age of reform of the institutions of American government.

Our purpose in this period should not be simply better management of the programs of the past. The time has come for a new quest—a quest not for a greater quantity of what we have—but for a new quality of life in America.

A major part of the substance for an unprecedented advance in this nation's approach to its problems and opportunities is contained in more than two-score legislative proposals which I sent to the Congress last year and which still await enactment.

I will offer at least a dozen more major programs in the course of this session.

At this point I do not intend to go through a detailed listing of what I have proposed or will propose, but I would like to mention three areas in which urgent priorities demand that we move and move now:

First, we cannot delay longer in accomplishing a total reform of our welfare system. When a system penalizes work, breaks up homes and robs recipients of dignity, there is no alternative to abolishing that system and adopting in its place the program of income support, job training and work incentives which I recommended to the Congress last year.

Second, the time has come to assess and reform all of our institutions of government at the Federal, state and local level. It is time for a New Federalism, in which, after 190 years of power flowing from the people and local and state governments to Washington, D.C., it will begin to flow from Washington back to the states and to the people of the United States.

We must adopt reforms which will expand the range of opportunities for all Americans. We can fulfill the American dream only when each person has a fair chance to fulfill his own dreams. This means equal voting rights, equal employment opportunity and new opportunities for expanded ownership because in order to be secure in their human rights, people need access to property rights.

I could give similar examples of the need for reform in our programs for health, education, housing, and transportation, as well as other critical areas which directly affect the well-being of millions of Americans.

The people of the United States should wait no longer for these reforms that would so deeply enhance the quality of their life.

When I speak of actions which would be beneficial to the American people, I can think of none more important than for the Congress to join this Administration in the battle to stop the rise in the cost of living.

Now, I realize it is tempting to blame someone else for inflation.

Some blame business for raising prices.

And some blame unions for asking for more wages.

But a review of the stark fiscal facts of the 1960s, clearly demonstrates where the primary blame for rising prices must be placed.

In the decade of the sixties the Federal government spent fifty-seven billion dollars more than it took in in taxes.

In that same decade the American people paid the bill for that deficit in price increases which raised the cost of living for the average family of four by $200 per month in America.

Now, millions of Americans are forced to go into debt today because the Federal government decided to go into debt yesterday. We must balance our Federal budget so that American families will have a better chance to balance their family budgets.

Only with the cooperation of the Congress can we meet this highest priority objective of responsible government.

We're on the right track.

We had a balanced budget in 1969.

This Administration cut more than seven billion dollars out of spending plans in order to produce a surplus in 1970.

And in spite of the fact that Congress reduced revenues by three billion dollars, I shall recommend a balanced budget for 1971.

But I can assure you that not only to present but stay within a balanced budget requires some very hard decisions. It means rejecting spending programs which would benefit some of the people when their net effect would result in price increases for all the people.

It is time to quit putting good money into bad programs. Otherwise we will end up with bad money and bad programs.

I recognize the political popularity of spending programs, particularly in an election year. But unless we stop the rise in prices, the cost of living for millions of American families will become unbearable and government's ability to plan programs for progress for the future will become impossible.

In referring to budget cuts, there is one area where I have ordered an increase rather than a cut and that is—the requests of those agencies with the responsibility for law enforcement.

We have heard a great deal of over-blown rhetoric during the sixties in which the word "war" has perhaps too often been used—the war on poverty, the war on misery, the war on disease, the war on hunger. But if there is one area where the word "war" is appropriate it is in the fight against crime. We must declare and win the war against the criminal elements which increasingly threaten our cities, our homes and our lives.

We have a tragic example of this problem in the nation's Capital, for whose safety the Congress and the Executive have the primary responsibility. I doubt if many members of this Congress who live more than a few blocks from here would dare leave their cars in the Capitol Garage and walk home alone tonight.

This (sic) year this Administration sent to the Congress thirteen separate pieces of legislation dealing with organized crime, pornography, street crime, narcotics, crime in the District of Columbia.

None of these bills has reached my desk for signature.

I am confident that the Congress will act now to adopt the legislation I placed before you last year. We in the Executive have done everything we can under existing law, but new and stronger weapons are needed in that fight.

While it is true that state and local law enforcement agencies are the cutting edge in the effort to eliminate street crime, burglaries, murder, my proposals to you have embodied my belief that the Federal government should play a greater role in working in partnership with these agencies.

That is why 1971 Federal spending for local law enforcement will double that budgeted for 1970.

The primary responsibility for crimes that affect individuals is with local and state rather than with Federal government. But in the field of organized crime, narcotics, pornography, the Federal government has a special responsibility it should fulfill. And we should make Washington, D.C., where we have the primary responsibility, an example to the nation and the world of respect for law rather than lawlessness.

I now turn to a subject which, next to our desire for peace, may well become the major concern of the American people in the decade of the seventies.

In the next ten years we shall increase our wealth by fifty percent. The profound question is—does this mean we will be fifty percent richer in a real sense, fifty percent better off, fifty percent happier?

Or, does it mean that in the year 1980 the President standing in this place will look back on a decade in which seventy percent of our people lived in metropolitan areas choked by traffic, suffocated by smog, poisoned by water, deafened by noise and terrorized by crime?

These are not the great questions that concern world leaders at summit conferences. But people do not live at the summit. They live in the foothills of everyday experience and it is time for us all of us to concern ourselves with the way real people live in real life.

The great question of the seventies is, shall we surrender to our surroundings, or shall we make our peace with nature and begin to make reparations for the damage we have done to our air, to our land and to our water?

Restoring nature to its natural state is a cause beyond party and beyond factions. It has become a common cause of all the people of this country. It is a cause of particular concern to young Americans—because they more than we will reap the grim consequences of our failure to act on programs which are needed now if we are to prevent disaster later.

Clean air, clean water, open spaces—these should once again be the birthright of every American. If we act now—they can be.

We still think of air as free. But clean air is not free, and neither is clean water. The price tag on pollution control is high. Through our years of past carelessness we incurred a debt to nature, and now that debt is being called.

The program I shall propose to Congress will be the most comprehensive and costly program in this field in America's history.

It is not a program for just one year. A year's plan in this field is no plan at all. This is a time to look ahead not a year, but five years or ten years—whatever time is required to do the job.

I shall propose to this Congress a ten billion dollar nation-wide clean waters program to put modern municipal waste treatment plants in every place in America where they are needed to make our waters clean again, and do it now.

We have the industrial capacity, if we begin now, to build them all within five years. This program will get them built within five years.

As our cities and suburbs relentlessly expand, those priceless open spaces needed for recreation areas accessible to their people are swallowed up—often forever. Unless we preserve these spaces while they are still available, we will have none to preserve. Therefore, I shall propose new financing methods for purchasing open space and park lands, now, before they are lost to us.

The automobile is our worst polluter of the air. Adequate control requires further advances in engine design and fuel composition. We shall intensify our research, set increasingly strict standards and strengthen enforcement procedures—and we shall do it now.

We no longer can afford to consider air and water common property, free to be abused by anyone without regard to the consequences. Instead, we should begin now to treat them as scarce resources, which we are no more free to contaminate than we are free to throw garbage into our neighbor's yard. This requires comprehensive new regulations. It also requires that, to the extent possible, the price of goods should be made to include the costs of producing and disposing of them without damage to the environment.

Now I realize that the argument is often made that a fundamental contradiction has arisen between economic growth and the quality of life, so that to have one we must forsake the other.

The answer is not to abandon growth, but to redirect it. For example, we should turn toward ending congestion and eliminating smog the same reservoir of inventive genius that created them in the first place.

Continued vigorous economic growth provides us with the means to enrich life itself and to enhance our planet as a place hospitable to man.

Each individual must enlist in this fight if it is to be won.

It has been said that no matter how many national parks and historical monuments we buy and develop, the truly significant environment for each of us is that in which we spend eighty percent of our time—in our homes, in our places of work, the streets over which we travel.

Street litter, rundown parking strips and yards, dilapidated fences, broken windows, smoking automobiles, dingy working places, all should be the object of our fresh view.

We have been too tolerant of our surroundings and too willing to leave it to others to clean up our environment. It is time for those who make massive demands on society to make some minimal demands on themselves. Each of us must resolve that each day he will leave his home, his property, the public places of his city or town a little cleaner, a little better, a little more pleasant for himself and those around him.

With the help of people we can do anything and without their help we can do nothing. In this spirit, together, we can reclaim our land for ours and generations to come.

Between now and the year 2000, over one-hundred-million children will be born in the United States. Where they grow up—and how—will, more than any one thing, measure the quality of American life in these years ahead.

This should be a warning to us.

For the past thirty years our population has also been growing and shifting. The result is exemplified in the vast areas of rural America emptying out of people and of promise—a third of our counties lost population in the 1960s.

The violent and decayed central cities of our great metropolitan complexes are the most conspicuous area of failure in American life today.

I propose that before these problems become insoluble, the nation develop a national growth policy.

In the future Government decisions as to where to build highways, locate airports, acquire land or sell land should be made with a clear objective of aiding a balanced growth for America.

In particular, the Federal government must be in a position to assist in the building of new cities and the rebuilding of old ones.

At the same time, we will carry our concern with the quality of life in America to the farm as well as the suburb, to the village as well as to the city. What rural America needs most is a new kind of assistance. It needs to be dealt with, not as a separate nation, but as part of an overall growth policy for America. We must create a new rural environment which will not only stem the migration to urban centers but reverse it. If we seize our growth as a challenge, we can make the 1970s an historic period when by conscious choice we transformed our land into what we want it to become.

America, which has pioneered in the new abundance, and in the new technology, is called upon today to pioneer in meeting the concerns which have followed in their wake—in turning the wonders of science to the service of man.

In the majesty of this great chamber we hear the echoes of America's history, of debates that rocked the Union and those that repaired it, of the summons to war and the search for peace, of the uniting of the people, the building of a nation.

Those echoes of history remind us of our roots and our strengths.

They remind us also of that special genius of American democracy, which at one critical turning point after another has led us to spot the new road to the future and given us the wisdom and the courage to take it.

As I look down that new road which I have tried to map out today, I see a new America as we celebrate our two hundredth anniversary six years from now.

I see an America in which we have abolished hunger, provided the means for every family in the nation to obtain a minimum income, made enormous progress in providing better housing, faster transportation, improved health and superior education.

I see an America in which we have checked inflation, and waged a winning war against crime.

I see an America in which we have made great strides in stopping the pollution of our air, cleaning up our water, opening up our parks, continuing to explore in space.

And, most important, I see an America at peace with all the nations of the world.

This is not an impossible dream. These goals are all within our reach.

In times past, our forefathers had the vision but not the means to achieve such goals.

Let it not be recorded that we were the first American generation that had the means but not the vision to make this dream come true.

But let us, above all, recognize a fundamental truth. We can be the best clothed, best fed, best housed people in the world, enjoying clean air, clean water and beautiful parks, but we could still be the unhappiest people in the world without an indefinable spirit—the lift of a driving dream which has made America from its beginning the hope of the world.

Two hundred years ago this was a new nation of three million people, weak militarily, poor economically. But America meant something to the world then which could not be measured in dollars, something far more important than military might. Listen to President Thomas Jefferson in 1802. "We act not for ourselves alone, but for the whole human race." We had a spiritual quality which caught the imagination of millions of people in the world.

Today, when we are the richest and strongest nation in the world, let it not be recorded that we lack the moral and spiritual idealism which made us the hope of the world at the time of our birth. The demands on us in 1976 are even greater than in 1776.

It's no longer enough to live and let live. Now we must live and help live.

We need a fresh climate in America, one in which a person can breathe freely and breathe in freedom.

Our recognition of the truth that wealth and happiness are not the same thing requires us to measure success or failure by new criteria.

Even more than the programs I have described today, what this nation needs is an example from elected leaders in providing the spiritual and moral leadership which no programs for material progress can satisfy.

Above all, let us inspire young Americans with a sense of excitement, a sense of destiny, a sense of involvement in meeting the challenges we face in this great period of our history. Only then are they going to have any sense of satisfaction in their lives.

The greatest privilege an individual can have is to serve in a cause bigger than himself. We have such a cause.

How we seize the opportunities I have described today will determine not only our future, but the future of peace and freedom in this world in the last third of the century.

May God give us the wisdom, the strength and, above all, the idealism to be worthy of that challenge, so that America can fulfill its destiny of being the world's best hope for liberty, for opportunity, for progress and peace for all peoples.

Reference Guide to the Presidency and Executive Departments

Current Documents

The Presidents of the United States 1789-1962—Bibliography compiled annually by the Library of Congress. Includes books on the Presidency, Vice Presidency, elections, published writings and papers of Presidents and biographical books and articles on Presidents. (Available from Government Printing Office, $1.00.)

Weekly Compilation of Presidential Documents—Includes transcripts of President's news conferences, messages to Congress, speeches and statements and other White House releases. (Available from GPO, $9 per year.)

Federal Register—Published five times weekly, includes Presidential Executive Orders, proclamations and reorganization plans, and rules and regulations issued by executive departments and agencies. (Available from GPO, $25 per year.)

Treaties in Force—Contains a list of treaties and other international agreements to which the U.S. has become a party. Bilateral treaties are arranged by country, multilateral treaties by subject. (Available from GPO, $1.75.)

The Budget of the U.S.—Includes the budget message of the President. A second volume of the Budget, the Appendix, contains detailed estimates of federal receipts and expenditures by Departments, agencies, functions and object. (Available from GPO: Budget, $2.75; Appendix, between $6-$8.50.)

Economic Report of the President—The President's annual report on the state of the economy and the economic outlook. Also includes the report of the Council of Economic Advisers. (Available from GPO, $1.50.)

Other Reports—Annual reports of Executive Departments and agencies, special reports of Presidential commissions and committees are available from GPO. Prices vary.

U.S. Code Congressional and Administrative News—This biweekly service gives the full text of all public laws and some committee reports on legislation. Executive Orders and Proclamations are also included. (Available from West Publishing Co., St. Paul, $60 per year, including bound volumes at end of year.)

U.S. Government Organization Manual—Published annually in July, the Manual describes the current organization and functions of the departments and agencies that make up the Executive Branch. (Available from GPO, $3.00.)

Congressional Quarterly Weekly Report—Includes texts of President's messages to Congress, news conferences, vetoes, etc. Gives President's position on all major legislation and on roll-call votes in Congress. Also includes annual report on status of President's program in Congress.

Historical Documents

Inaugural Addresses of the Presidents—From George Washington to Richard M. Nixon. (Available from GPO, $1.25.)

The Public Papers of the Presidents—This continuing series, published under the direction of the Office of the Federal Register, begins with a 1945 volume of papers and messages of President Truman. Volumes are currently available through 1967. *(Available from GPO.)*

Microfilm of Papers of 23 Presidents—The Manuscript division of the Library of Congress contains the papers of 23 Presidents from George Washington to Calvin Coolidge. An index is available in book form.

Congress and the Nation, Vol. I (1945-64), Vol. II (1965-68), Congressional Quarterly. The 3,100-page, two-volume set documents all major legislative actions and national political campaigns in postwar period. Vol. 1, $27.50; Vol. II, $35; both $55.

Congressional Quarterly Almanacs—Published each year since 1945, the Almanac presents a thorough review of each session of Congress' legislative and political activity. (Available with regular CQ Service.)

Code of Federal Regulations—Since 1938, supplements to Title 3 of the Code of Federal Regulations contain the text of proclamations, Executive Orders, reorganization plans, trade agreements, letters, and certain administrative orders issued by the President. (Available from GPO.)

United States Treaties and Other International Agreements—This series includes texts of all trade agreements and Executive agreements made by the President with other nations since 1952. (Available from GPO.)

1969 REVIEW

Nixon Wrestles with Problems of War, Inflation

President Nixon ended his first year in office confronted with the two overriding problems he had faced when he was sworn in Jan. 20—the war in Vietnam and the inflationary growth of the economy.

Against this backdrop, Mr. Nixon during 1969 was faced with the difficulties inherent in turning campaign slogans and promises into real policies, programs and proposals. He had to restaff the top echelons of the Government while ensuring that the huge federal bureaucracy kept moving. He had to give direction to the Republican party and make peace with the Democratic-controlled Congress. And he had to perform the duties and make the decisions that American citizens and the rest of the world expect from a President of the United States.

As 1969 drew to a close, the news media and other "President watchers" attempted to assess Mr. Nixon's first year in the Presidency. Throughout their comments, there seemed to run two recurrent thoughts: the President increasingly was trying to isolate his critics by broad appeals to "middle America"—to the "silent majority" which he conceived of as his real constituency; the President had miscalculated the level of opposition to his policies in Congress and had failed to listen either seriously or regularly to the views of Members of Congress.

Critics acknowledged that Mr. Nixon in 1969 faced some unusual and some largely uncontrollable problems—he was the first President in over a century to face a Congress dominated by the opposition party in his first term, and he entered office with the burdens of an unpopular war affecting every facet of domestic life.

Mr. Nixon's first year brought him both a reassuring victory and a stunning defeat on Capitol Hill. His foremost victory came with Congressional approval of the controversial Safeguard antiballistic missile (ABM) system. His worst defeat was the Senate's refusal to confirm his nominee for the United States Supreme Court, Clement F. Haynsworth Jr.

The President received other victories with Congressional approval of his requests to institute a draft lottery system and to extend the surtax. Also at the President's request, Congress raised the debt-limit ceiling, and the Senate ratified the nuclear nonproliferation treaty. Action was not completed on Administration requests dealing with electoral college reform, manpower training, revenue sharing, crime, postal reform, unemployment insurance and changes in the welfare programs. The Senate passed an Administration-opposed "commitments resolution" designed to reassert a Congressional voice in decisions committing the United States to the defense of other nations.

The War and the Economy. Mr. Nixon's major legacies from his predecessor—the war and the economy —continued to plague him as they had President Johnson.

The new President came into the office committed to ending the war and obtaining an honorable peace. But through 1969 the results were disappointing. The Paris peace talks remained virtually stalemated. After six months of withholding criticism, opponents of American policy in Vietnam began speaking out again by midsummer. Congressional criticism began to get harsh, and Sen. J. W. Fulbright (D Ark.), chairman of the Senate Foreign Relations Committee and one of Congress' most vocal opponents of the war, threatened to call public hearings on American involvement in Vietnam. The sentiments of Congressional doves were further aroused by a prolonged Senate debate over the Administration's Safeguard antiballistic missile (ABM) system. The ABM debate climaxed in a cliff-hanging 50-50 victory for the President.

Student dissenters and the antiwar sector of the public became active again in the summer and organized two major peace demonstrations for the fall. The Vietnam moratorium staged protests throughout the country on Oct. 15. The next month, on Nov. 15, more than 250,000 people assembled in Washington, D.C., for the largest demonstration in the history of the nation's capital. The rallies were organized by the New Mobilization to End the War in Vietnam.

Finally, the President outlined his policies in a major address Nov. 3. Responsibility for conducting the war would gradually be shifted from the Americans to the South Vietnamese, he said. U.S. combat troops would be withdrawn according to an unspecified timetable in coordination with the South Vietnam takeover of war duties. He called on the silent majority of Americans to support his aims.

Although the doves continued to criticize policy, public opinion polls showed that the President's popularity took a sharp jump after the speech. By the end of 1969, about 65,000 American troops had been withdrawn from Vietnam. Between inauguration day and the end of the year, 9,414 American servicemen died there.

The Administration's drive to slow down the economy resulted in less success than Mr. Nixon had hoped for. The President and his advisers feared turning the inflation into a recession with overly stringent measures and pursued a course of "gradualism." They trimmed Government expenditures, ordered a cutback in federal construction projects and tried to encourage businessmen to postpone large capital investments. They also sought to use persuasion in getting industry to hold down prices and labor to hold down wage-increase demands.

Domestic Programs. The new Administration's most dramatic proposal was a major reform of the welfare system to set minimum annual payments for recipients. Welfare reform would be linked to job training or employment, and for the first time it would benefit the working poor.

Along with welfare reform were two other proposed programs which together the President referred to as "New Federalism." These were manpower training reform, which would gradually shift responsibility for job training to the states, and revenue sharing, which would return a portion of federal tax revenues to the states.

Throughout the year Mr. Nixon spoke often of returning power from Washington to the state and local governments. The manpower and revenue-sharing proposals were prime examples of such a shift.

Law and order was a major theme of the election campaign, and the President spoke often of the need for new crime control measures. His Administration submitted to Congress a patchwork collection of proposals, but few were enacted into law.

Civil rights leaders took little solace in the Administration's actions during 1969. The Justice Department for the first time since the 1954 Supreme Court desegregation case asked for a delay in the pace of school desegregation. The Supreme Court denied the request. Enforcement of desegregation plans was shifted from the Department of Health, Education and Welfare (HEW) to the courts, which traditionally had moved more slowly in the field.

The President's voting rights proposal would liquidate most of the landmark Voting Rights Act of 1965, which had produced massive voter registration of black voters in the South. On the other hand, the Administration devised and fought for the "Philadelphia Plan" for hiring minority workers on federal construction projects.

The Silent Majority. Mr. Nixon's appeal to the silent majority to support his Vietnam policies seemed to strike a responsive chord across the nation. A Gallup Poll showed that 56 percent of the public approved of the way he handled his job in late October. By mid-November, the positive rating jumped to 68 percent.

Vice President Spiro T. Agnew's biting speeches criticizing dissenters and the national news media, given at about the same time, also were well received by the public, despite criticism from Congressional Democrats and civil libertarians.

In exchange for the support of the silent majority, Mr. Nixon risked alienating antiwar dissenters and members of minority groups. His November speech on the war gave little hope to Americans who felt the Administration should speed up its disengagment from Vietnam. The President said he would not be influenced at all by the October moratorium, although shortly before that date he announced that Gen. Lewis Hershey—a long-time target of the war critics—would be relieved of his duties as head of the Selective Service System.

The White House. The President relied heavily on his staff to handle policy matters. Few of his top aides had previous Government experience, and many were friends of long standing from previous campaigns and the days of his New York law practice. Four were on the staff of the same Los Angeles advertising firm.

Three of his aides were given Cabinet ranking: Arthur F. Burns, later named to head the Federal Reserve Board starting in 1970; Daniel P. Moynihan, an urban affairs specialist; and Bryce N. Harlow, the chief White House lobbyist.

The President relied on Attorney General John N. Mitchell as one of his closest advisers. Mitchell's authority ranged far beyond his duties at the Justice Department. He often recommended action on foreign affairs and domestic programs. Mitchell was given credit for helping to shape the "southern strategy" and for selecting Haynsworth for the Supreme Court vacancy.

Early in the year, the President beefed up the National Security Council to advise him on foreign affairs. Put at the head of this group was former Harvard University Prof. Henry A. Kissinger. Mr. Nixon also established an Urban Affairs Council under Moynihan. Other

White House policy groups included a Rural Affairs Council, an Environmental Quality Council and a Cabinet Committee on Economic Policy.

Later, when Moynihan and Harlow were elevated to the positions of counsellor to the President, John D. Ehrlichman was named as top assistant for domestic matters.

Under other members of the White House staff, Mr. Nixon also organized a number of task forces and project groups to study major programs and problems.

Relations with Congress

President Nixon experienced numerous difficulties in working with a Congress controlled by the other political party. He frequently called on Democratic leaders in the House and Senate to push his legislative programs, although he interspersed his criticism with pleas for co-operation. President Nixon was doubly troubled by Congress; not only was it Democratic, it was also abnormally sluggish in acting on most bills.

At times the President had trouble in keeping the members of his own party in line. Particularly in the Senate, Republican lawmakers opposed him on a number of major issues. These included the 50-50 vote on an amendment to kill the Safeguard ABM system, his narrowest victory of the year, and the rejection of federal Judge Clement F. Haynsworth Jr. as a Supreme Court Justice, Mr. Nixon's major defeat. On increasing income tax exemptions and raising spending levels for education, a number of Republicans also opposed the President.

Congress and the President engaged in a running debate over priorities. Moderates and liberals on Capitol Hill wanted to spend less for defense and more for education, health and pollution control than the President had requested.

Throughout the year, the President had difficulty establishing good liaison with Congress, especially with Senate Republican liberals.

Sen. Hugh Scott (R Pa.), then the Senate Minority Whip, June 27 voiced opposition to Administration policy on civil rights and school desegregation guidelines and the dropping of the nomination of Dr. John H. Knowles for the top federal health post. He hinted that the GOP liberals were nearing rebellion.

All three of the Senate GOP leaders voted against Mr. Nixon's Haynsworth nomination. Sen. Ernest F. Hollings (D S.C.), Haynsworth's chief sponsor, said the White House let Haynsworth opponents take the initiative.

Scott Dec. 4 criticized the Administration for its lack of strategy on the tax exemption amendment to the tax reform bill. "I do hope that the responsible people in the Treasury, in my Administration, will listen the next time we try to advise them," Scott said. "We understand more about tactics and strategy than they do."

Sen. Jacob K. Javits (R N.Y.), said the Vietnam war and speeches by Vice President Spiro T. Agnew had introduced problems between Congress and the Executive Branch. "I would hope that the White House would come to a realization of that and buttress its liaison machinery."

Sen. Charles McC. Mathias Jr. (R Md.), calling the President's advisers "the Prussians," said, "I suppose they are bright in their way. But they just don't understand this body. They just haven't found any way to communicate effectively."

In a feud over the Congressional pace, Democrats criticized the Administration on a variety of counts: delays in submitting specific program proposals, further delays in sending up specific legislative requests to back up the President's general messages and failure to provide witnesses to testify on the Administration's position when hearings were scheduled early in the session.

The Administration and its leaders on Capitol Hill pointed out a political situation in Washington unique in this century. Not since Zachary Taylor became President in 1849 had a President come into office facing opposition majorities in both houses of Congress.

This extraordinary division created a "slowdown" in activity in both branches because both sides exercised caution on new programs or broad changes in existing ones. Committee hearings and floor debate on military procurement, tax reform and extension of the surtax consumed much time.

The White House also pointed out that the 91st Congress was running at about half the working hours of some of its predecessors during the Kennedy and Johnson Administrations. The White House admitted that the figures excluded committee time but maintained that Congress was working about 60 percent as long as normal.

On the matter of delays in transmitting proposals to the Hill, White House officials admitted that the President's requests had been released later than usual, but said that Mr. Nixon preferred to work that way.

Republican Senate and House leaders, meeting with President Nixon Sept. 16, suggested it was time to charge the Democrats with running a "do-nothing" Congress. Scott, then the acting Senate Minority Leader, Sept. 14 charged the Democratic leaders with "foot-dragging."

House Democrats voted Sept. 17 to compile a record of instances in which the Nixon Administration declined committee invitations to take a stand on pending issues. The Democratic caucus urged the committee chairmen to move ahead on legislation anyhow.

House Majority Leader Carl Albert (D Okla.) Sept. 22 told a news conference that "Congress has moved as fast as it could under the circumstances. It has not received reports and estimates from the Administration as fast as it could have."

In a message to Congress, President Nixon Oct. 13 said legislative action was imperative on 12 "reform" measures to serve "the needs of a nation in distress," and called for renewed consideration on more than a score of other issues stalled or pending on Capitol Hill.

The President, in a subdued yet urgent statement, did not accuse Congress alone of laxity, saying "neither the Democratic Congress nor the Republican Administration is without fault for the delay of vital legislation."

He urged that "political posturing" be set aside in order to expedite legislation, much of which the White House ranked as top priority. Mr. Nixon said the watchword of his Administration was "reform," and he called for action in 1969 on a dozen measures aimed at reformation of existing programs.

"The country is not interested in what we say, but in what we do—let us roll up our sleeves and go to work," he said.

First on Mr. Nixon's list of reforms was the draft, followed by the welfare system, tax structure, revenue sharing, post office, manpower training, Social Security, grant-in-aid system, Electoral College, District of Columbia government, Office of Economic Opportunity and foreign aid.

Democratic Congressional leaders were pleasantly suprised by the tone of the message, unexpectedly mild and lacking in partisan criticism of Congress. Some Democrats had been anticipating an attack seeking to place a "do-nothing" label on Congress in anticipation of the 1970 elections.

However, the President later criticized the Congress for not acting on his crime proposals and for its slow pace on appropriations bills. He threatened to call Congress back into special session after Christmas if it did not complete action on the appropriations. At a Dec. 8 news conference, the President said the 1969 session had "the worst record in terms of appropriations of any Congress in history."

Nine of the 13 regular appropriations bills were not cleared until the last month of Congress; while final action on two others (foreign aid and Labor-Health, Education and Welfare Departments) was postponed until 1970. The fiscal year began July 1.

The President also called on Congress to help hold down federal spending and threatened to veto tax reform, Social Security increase, federal pay increase and Labor-Health, Education and Welfare appropriations legislation as inflationary. Congress delayed action on the federal pay bill and the Labor-HEW appropriations. The Social Security increase became part of the final version of the tax reform bill, which the President signed.

Vietnam and Foreign Policy

The Nixon Administration in 1969 attempted to shape a policy on Vietnam which would gradually shift responsibility for fighting the war from Washington to Saigon.

In an address to the nation on Nov. 3, the President said that virtually no progress had been made at the Paris peace talks, where representatives of the United States, both North and South Vietnam and the National Liberation Front had been meeting formally since January 1969. Mr. Nixon said that U.S. policy would stress "Vietnamization" of the war. The South Vietnamese forces would assume more military responsibility for conducting the war as American combat troops were withdrawn according to an "orderly scheduled timetable."

Mr. Nixon restated the eight-point peace proposal, first outlined in a May 14 speech, which had included mutual withdrawal of all non-South Vietnamese troops and internationally supervised elections in the South. He also put on the record his so-called Asian Doctrine, first described in a July 25 news conference in Guam. The doctrine maintained that the United States should continue its alliances in the Pacific but should not become involved in future wars on the Asian mainland.

In the Nov. 3 speech, President Nixon appealed to the "silent majority" to support his proposal for ending the war. By Dec. 15, more than 60,000 U.S. troops had actually been withdrawn from Vietnam, leaving nearly half a million American servicemen on duty there.

Asian Doctrine. In stating his Asian Doctrine to reporters in Guam at the beginning of a five-day Far East tour in July, Mr. Nixon insisted that the United States would honor its commitments to its allies. Greater stress would be placed on self-help and on economic development of the region, he said.

Understanding of the doctrine was complicated by the manner in which the President presented it: reporters were forbidden to quote him directly and the Administration's interpretation of the doctrine remained unclear. In his Nov. 3 speech, Mr. Nixon said that the nation would "furnish military and economic assistance when requested in accordance with our treaty commitments" but that the threatened nation should assume "primary responsibility" for its own defense.

One result of the policy was an agreement between the United States and Japan for the return of Okinawa to Japan by 1972. The agreement was announced on Nov. 21.

Other Developments. The United States and the Soviet Union since early 1969 engaged in bilateral talks on ending the Middle East conflict. The U.S. proposals presented in those talks were outlined in a major foreign policy address on Dec. 9 by Secretary of State William P. Rogers. The Secretary called on Israel to withdraw from Arab territories it had occupied since the June 1967 war in return for Arab assurances of a binding commitment to a Middle East peace. Rogers said detailed peace provisions should be worked out between Israel and the Arab states under United Nations auspices.

On Nov. 17 the United States and the Soviet Union met in Helsinki, Finland, to begin preliminary discussions on strategic arms limitation.

The President took two trips abroad: to Europe in late February and early March and to several Asian nations and Rumania in late July and early August.

The Economy

The Nixon Administration's drive to slow down the pace of the economy's inflationary growth met with little tangible success in 1969. The President and his financial advisers pursued a policy of "gradualism" in an attempt to halt inflation without bringing on a recession. But by the end of the year, their actions showed—at best—limited success in holding down Government expenditures and the wage-price spiral within the private sector.

When he submitted his revised Budget to Congress in April, Mr. Nixon promised to hold down federal spending to $192.9 billion and to produce an anti-inflationary surplus for fiscal 1970 of nearly $6 billion.

But actions and inactions of Congress, coupled with increases in uncontrollable spending such as interest on the national debt, cast doubt upon the likelihood of so large a surplus by the end of fiscal 1970. Congress's moves to increase Social Security benefits by 15 percent and to reduce tax revenues in conjunction with the tax reform bill helped throw the Budget out of alignment.

Congress did cut $5.6 billion from Budget requests for defense spending, but it added unrequested funds for numerous other programs, such as nearly $600 million for water pollution control. Failure to enact Presidential requests on items like postal rate increases and adjustment of credit programs of the Veterans Administration and the Farmers Home Administration also cut down on new revenues that the President had figured into his Budget estimates.

As 1969 ended, Congress and the President were involved in a dispute about more than $1 billion added by the House and Senate for various education and health programs onto requests for the Department of Health, Education and Welfare (HEW). President Nixon threatened repeatedly to veto the Labor-HEW appropriations bill despite conference action to cut $1.6 billion out of the final Senate version. Final action on the bill was put off until the beginning of the 1970 session.

Outside of Congress, the Administration took a number of actions involving the economy which resulted in only limited success in slowing growth. However, unlike previous Administrations, President Nixon maintained an official hands-off policy toward labor and industry concerning wage and price increases.

The unemployment level crept upward through the year, although rates of increase in industrial production and retail sales did not turn downward until the end of 1969. Growth of personal and corporate income also slowed toward the end of the year, with the prospect of affecting tax revenues obtained from those sources. The Federal Reserve Board had maintained a program of tight money and high credit.

Domestic Programs

During his first year in office, Mr. Nixon proposed few new major programs for solving domestic problems. Unlike President Johnson, whose Great Society programs focused chiefly on urban blight and poor city dwellers, President Nixon stressed a balance between urban and nonurban needs and greater emphasis on state and local action instead of an expanded federal role. Rather than stressing the special needs of the very poor, he emphasized "the quality of life" of all Americans.

The Nixon Administration's most dramatic new proposal was a complete overhaul of the federal welfare program. The President Aug. 8 advocated setting minimum annual payments for those eligible to receive aid and linking aid with either employment or job training for recipients. He recommended extending aid to the "working poor" who were employed but earned wages classified within the poverty level. Mr. Nixon said his new "family assistance system" would do away with inequities in welfare benefits between states and ease the financial burdens made by welfare programs on state budgets.

Along with welfare reform, Mr. Nixon recommended reform in two other areas: manpower training and revenue sharing. Together, the President said, they represented "a New Federalism in which power, funds and responsibility will flow from Washington to the states and to the people."

In manpower training, Mr. Nixon asked Congress to enact legislation which ultimately would allocate most responsibility for programs with state and local governments. Existing federal programs, which were spread among a number of agencies, would be coordinated by a single federal agency which would be responsible for planning. States would gradually assume control of administration and funds for the manpower programs.

The President's revenue sharing proposal would turn about $5 billion in federal tax revenues back to the states by fiscal 1976. The returned funds would be divided among the states by a formula based upon each state's share of national population adjusted for the state's effort to raise revenue. A "pass through" formula would ensure that cities and counties would receive funds in proportion to their relative tax effort within the state.

The House Ways and Means Committee held hearings on the welfare proposal in October but took no further action on the measure.

In the same New Federalism message, Mr. Nixon proposed a reorganization of the Office of Economic Opportunity (OEO) aimed at turning it into a research-oriented agency stressing innovation and experimentation to bring people out of poverty.

Early in the year, the President asked for a one-year extension of the OEO authorization. But after he appointed a Republican Representative, Donald Rumsfeld of Illinois, as director of OEO, he asked for a two-year extension instead. Late in the year the Administration successfully opposed a proposal to switch the administration of a number of the poverty agency's programs over to the states. The two-year extension bill cleared Congress shortly before adjournment.

Social Security. Congress enacted a 15-percent increase in basic Social Security payments but adopted none of the other reforms requested by Mr. Nixon in a Sept. 25 message. The President had asked for a 10-percent increase, automatic cost-of-living adjustment, changes in Medicare tax rates and provisions for recipients with outside earnings, widows and aged parents of retired and disabled workers.

Hunger. The new Administration was involved in a number of hunger issues. The President proposed a $270-million increase in spending for fiscal 1970 for the food stamp program, bringing the total authorization to $610 million. For fiscal 1971, he requested a $1-billion increase in the authorization, and he asked that families with incomes of less than $30 a month receive free food stamps. Congress passed legislation raising the fiscal 1970 authorization but did not complete action on broad reforms in the program.

In his Budget requests for the Agriculture Department, the President asked for appropriations of more than $1.73 billion for food stamps and other food assistance programs. This was an increase of nearly $500 million over fiscal 1969 levels. Congress cleared a bill appropriating about $90 million more than the President requested. Mr. Nixon had asked that the school milk program be eliminated—as had President Johnson—but it was put back into the bill on the House floor.

At a White House Conference on Food, Nutrition and Health in early December, President Nixon called for enactment of his welfare and food stamp proposals and establishment of a Commission on Population Growth and the American Future. Such action, he said, would "virtually eliminate the problem of poverty as a cause of malnutrition."

Two weeks after the conference, the Administration made reforms in the food stamp program, reducing cost of the stamps to guarantee that a poor family would not have to spend more than 25 percent of its income on food.

Crime. During the 1968 election campaign and after taking office, President Nixon and his aides spoke on numerous occasions of the need to increase efforts to eliminate crime in the nation. The Administration submitted proposals aimed at curbing organized crime, halting the illegal traffic in dangerous drugs and narcotics, curbing obscenity in the mails and increasing funds available for local, state and federal law enforcement agencies. Mr. Nixon submitted to Congress a series of proposals dealing with law enforcement in the District of Columbia

that he said would make the city a model for the rest of the nation.

Numerous hearings were held on the Administration's bills, and the Senate Judiciary Committee included a number of the President's recommendations in its organized crime and narcotics control bills, reported late in December. In District matters, the Senate passed Administration bills on court reform, juvenile code revision, criminal law revision and establishment of a legal defender system. The Senate did not act on the President's bail reform bill, which contained a controversial preventive detention section.

Consumer Affairs. President Nixon's first action on consumer affairs turned out to be an embarrassment for the new Administration. On Feb. 11 he appointed Willie Mae Rogers, director of the Good Housekeeping Institute, as a part-time consultant on consumer affairs. She resigned four days later, following criticism for potential conflicts of interest between her public and private roles. On April 9 Mr. Nixon named Virginia H. Knauer, director of the Pennsylvania Bureau of Consumer Protection, as full-time assistant for consumer affairs.

On Oct. 30 the President sent to Congress a message calling for a "buyer's bill of rights." He requested legislation establishing a statutory office of consumer affairs in the White House and a consumer protection division in the Justice Department. He also requested a bill allowing class action suits in which consumers could sue in groups for damages resulting from certain fraudulent trade practices. The legislation was criticized in Congress by some Democrats who said it did not go far enough in protecting consumers.

The Administration was involved in other controversies over the protection of consumers. Secretary of HEW Robert H. Finch in October banned the use of cyclamates, certain low-calorie artificial sweeteners used widely in diet foods and soft drinks, because laboratory animals given large daily doses showed a high incidence of tumors. In November, Finch rescinded the order for all products except soft drinks.

On Nov. 20 Secretary of Agriculture Clifford M. Hardin announced limitations on the use of the pesticide DDT would be in effect in 30 days. A total ban on the widely-used substance would be announced in early 1970, he said. The Department planned to investigate other controversial pesticides if studies showed such action was warranted.

Environment. Despite a great deal of public concern over water and air pollution, the Nixon Administration took few actions in this area. After an offshore oil well near Santa Barbara, Calif., began leaking and caused extensive damage to the seashore, the Interior Department tightened the restrictions for granting leases on federally owned property for offshore drilling.

Congress substantially increased the President's $214-million Budget request for sewage treatment—the same amount President Johnson had recommended in the Budget he submitted before leaving office. As cleared by Congress, the public works appropriations bill contained $800 million for the program.

Post Office. The President May 27 asked Congress to pass legislation converting the Post Office Department into an independent, Government-owned corporation. He called the request "one of the most significant proposals that will be made during the entire period of this Administration." The corporation proposal was killed by the House Post Office and Civil Service Committee, but other elements of the Administration's reform bill were still under consideration by the end of the year.

In an unusual move for a new President whose party had been out of power for eight years, Mr. Nixon early in the year called for the elimination of political patronage in the selection of postmasters. Postmaster General Winton M. Blount took administrative action to select candidates on the basis of merit tests, and the President asked Congress to eliminate the statutory requirement for Senate confirmation of postmasters.

Mass Transit. Mr. Nixon Aug. 7 recommended establishment of a $10-billion, 12-year program to develop and improve public transportation in local communities. He said that the nation should have a "truly balanced system" in which use of automobiles was "complemented by adequate public transportation."

Mine Safety. In a March 3 mine safety message, the President called for new mine health and safety legislation. But the final version of the bill enacted by Congress also contained a provision granting federal compensation for miners suffering from black lung disease, which had not been included in the Administration's request. The White House estimated that the compensation could cost between $150 million and $300 million and at one point hinted that the President might veto it because of those costs.

SST. President Nixon decided to go ahead with federal funding for the controversial supersonic transport (SST) plane despite the recommendation of an interdepartmental committee to withdraw from the program. Opponents of the project claimed the plane would be too noisy and too expensive and that funds should be spent on more pressing domestic needs.

The Arts. Mr. Nixon asked Congress to double federal subsidies of the arts in fiscal 1971 and to extend for three years the National Foundation on the Arts and the Humanities, due to expire June 30, 1970. In a Dec. 10 message, he said that increasing appropriations to $40 million might seem extravagant in a time of budgetary strain. "However, I believe that the need for a new impetus to the understanding and expression of the American idea has a compelling claim on our resources."

Civil Rights

President Nixon was elected to office with little support from Negroes and other non-white minorities. Although he promised early in his Presidency "to rectify" his reputation of indifference to black aspirations, the new Administration took few actions in 1969 to back up the promise.

The Administration's long-awaited policy statement on school desegregation guidelines, made public July 3, stated that plans for dismantling dual school systems must be carried out by September unless "bona fide educational and administrative problems" warrant delay. But in late August, HEW Secretary Finch asked a federal court to delay implementation of HEW-approved desegregation plans scheduled to go into effect in September. Later, the Justice Department aligned itself with southern school officials and against civil rights advocates in defending the delay request before the Supreme Court. This

was the first split in the Justice Department-civil rights partnership since the 1954 Supreme Court decision which declared that segregated schools were illegal. The Court refused to delay desegregation plans.

In June Attorney General Mitchell presented the Administration's voting rights bill, which sought to extend the provisions of the 1965 Voting Rights Act throughout the entire nation rather than limit them to states with histories of discriminating against black voters. In a surprise vote, the House Dec. 11 substituted the Administration bill for a five-year extension of the existing law by a 234-179 roll-call vote.

The Labor Department in June drew up the "Philadelphia Plan," a scheme for increasing employment of black laborers in the highly segregated construction industry. A dispute with Congress over the legality of the plan ensued, and in December the Administration engineered a campaign to save the life of the Philadelphia Plan.

When the House was considering an anti-desegregation amendment to the Labor-HEW appropriations bill in July, some Republican Members asked for help from the White House in an attempt to kill the provision. They did not get it. When the matter came up in the Senate, the Administration lobbied successfully to add language to the amendment to make it ineffective.

President Nixon appointed few Negroes or other minority representatives to high positions. Most of his proposals on crime were opposed by civil rights leaders, who claimed that the bills were preying upon white fears of black crimes.

Controversy over the President's so-called "southern strategy" for rebuilding the Republican party also damaged the President's reputation on civil rights. Although the Administration claimed that the southern strategy was a myth, a number of actions appeared to reinforce the view that the party was trying to attract conservative southern Democrats and 1968 supporters of George C. Wallace into the GOP ranks. Among the actions were the school desegregation and voting rights policies and the controversial nomination of Clement F. Haynsworth Jr., a federal judge from South Carolina, to be a Supreme Court Justice despite his history of decisions in civil rights cases viewed as inimical to Negroes.

National Security

The Nixon Administration and Congress engaged in a protracted debate over the weight that should be given to national security needs which compete for funds with domestic programs.

In a strongly worded speech June 4 at the U.S. Air Force Academy, President Nixon criticized some critics of defense policies as "isolationists" and advocates of "unilateral disarmament." He defended patriotism and military strength and said the United States would never become a police state as critics had charged.

The most dramatic fight came in the Senate over the Administration's Safeguard antiballistic missile system (ABM). Senators debated the issue for two months before defeating by a 50-50 vote a proposal to block any work on the Safeguard system. The Aug. 6 vote was a central, if shaky, victory for the Nixon Administration, which had extensively revised former President Johnson's Sentinel ABM system before launching a campaign for acceptance of its own Safeguard system.

In an attempt to shave funds from defense spending, the Administration dropped requests for the Manned Orbiting Laboratory (MOL), the Cheyenne helicopters and the controversial F-111 plane which had been involved in several well-publicized crashes. In a response to mounting criticism from Congress and the public, the President announced near the end of the year a halt to military biological aspects of chemical-biological warfare (CBW). The President told the Defense Department to plan for the destruction of stockpiled biological weapons and reaffirmed U.S. renunciation of the first use of lethal or incapacitating chemical weapons. He also stated he would submit for Senate ratification a 1925 treaty banning the first use of CBW weapons.

Another major Administration request was a bill granting the President authority to establish a draft lottery. Future reforms in the system of drafting young men for military service were put off until 1970.

ABM. As the Vietnam war momentarily waned in intensity following the Presidential election and the Nixon Administration's early transition period, reaction to the deployment of an antiballistic missile system replaced it as the defense operation most frequently criticized.

Once the Army began locating sites for nuclear warheads for the system near major cities in late 1968, a new group of homeowner protesters joined the ranks of the defense critics. The ABM urban protesters tended to be articulate and middle class, with a political muscle which eventually was felt. First, Members of Congress responded to pressure from constituents. Feeling the pressure in turn, President Nixon ordered a delay of construction pending a review of the program. Following the review, Mr. Nixon March 14 ordered a modified system to be set up away from population centers. But foes continued their campaign, picturing the program as a prime example of wasteful military spending detrimental to U.S. security and disarmament efforts.

After an emotional, hard-fought Senate debate of two months over the bill authorizing the ABM system, moves to cut funds for the ABM system were defeated in August by 50-50 and 549-51 votes. Support was also registered in the House by a wider margin.

Further attempts to block the ABM system were made late in the year during consideration of the defense appropriations bill. However, amendments to cut back funds for the program were defeated by a 25-78 standing vote in the House Dec. 8 and by a 36-49 roll-call vote in the Senate Dec. 15.

Other Administration Action

The President on his own authority reorganized the Office of Economic Opportunity and manpower programs in the Labor Department and closed 59 Job Corps centers around the country. By Executive Order authorized by existing law, he raised the pay of 2.3 million federal employees and nearly 3 million military personnel as of July 1.

Following up campaign statements on the law-and-order theme, the President nominated for Chief Justice of the United States a man known in legal circles for his conservative stance on questions of criminal law. The nominee, Warren Earl Burger, was quickly confirmed.

The Administration supported Congressional action extending existing housing and urban programs, cut back spending on Model Cities programs and initiated a program called Operation Breakthrough aimed at encouraging the development of new housing technologies.

The President on several occasions spoke out against student disorders. However, he said it was the responsibility of the schools and not the Federal Government to maintain campus peace.

The Administration, in addition to sending Congress a comprehensive bill to revise and modernize the system for federal control of narcotics and other dangerous drugs, also imposed an intensified inspection program, Operation Intercept, in September to police the Mexican-American border and halt the flow of drugs there.

The Administration proposed legislation to aid airport and airway development and the merchant marine, the establishment of a Commission on Population Growth and the American Future and an expanded budget for family planning.

President Nixon's first legislative request was for extension of Presidential authority to submit executive reorganization plans to Congress. The authority was first contained in the Reorganization Act of 1949, which allowed the President to reorganize executive agencies unless Congress vetoed the actions within 60 calendar days. President Johnson in 1968 requested extension of the authority, but Congress did not complete action on the request. However, Congress in 1969 granted Mr. Nixon's request for extension.

Under the renewed authority, President Nixon sent one reorganization plan to Congress during 1969. The plan permitted the President to designate the chairman of the Interstate Commerce Commission from among its members and went into effect Oct. 11.

In other 1969 action, President Nixon rescinded a controversial decision of former President Johnson allocating new Pacific air routes among U.S. commercial airlines and later reassigned the routes. Mr. Nixon invoked the Railway Labor Act to delay a threatened nationwide railroad strike for 60 days. He established a Council for Urban Affairs, a Cabinet Committee on Economic Policy, an Office of Intergovernmental Relations, an Office of Minority Business Enterprises and a Cabinet Committee on Voluntary Action. He also set up 10 common regions and regional centers for federal departments and agencies engaged in social or economic programs.

Politics

President Nixon faced many problems all new chief executives must tackle and others unique to his Presidency. He was faced with the task of assuring that the Federal Government operated smoothly during the transition from one administration to another. At the same time he had to pick appointees to fill most of the top positions in every department and agency.

He had to put together a personal staff to help seek solutions to problems and work out details of programs. He had to establish accord with Congress in the hope of getting favorable action on his legislative proposals. He had to give leadership to his political party, and to perform the ceremonial duties of being President.

Despite some early blunders, notably in connection with appointments, the Nixon Administration by late 1969 apparently had weathered the transition fairly smoothly and in most areas seemed well along in its tasks of running the Government.

Republican Party. On Feb. 26 President Nixon named Rep. Rogers C.B. Morton of Maryland as chairman of the Republican National Committee. Morton replaced Ray C. Bliss, who resigned Feb. 18 reportedly because of White House insistence that he name as his deputy Murray Chotiner, manager of Nixon's early political campaigns. Picked as Morton's assistant was James N. Allison Jr., a former Texas newspaper publisher who had managed Republican Senatorial campaigns in Texas and Florida.

Together they managed to satisfy most factions of the Republican party, which was recovering from the disarray it suffered following the defeat of Sen. Barry Goldwater in the 1964 Presidential election. When Morton announced he would remain as chairman rather than run for the Senate against Democrat Joseph D. Tydings in 1970, Mr. Nixon said: "Morton has unified the party as no chairman in my memory has been able to do it in recent years."

By the end of 1969, the Committee was in good financial shape and had begun extensive preparations for the 1970 Congressional elections and the 1972 Presidential election.

Southern Strategy. Republicans in 1969, according to some observers, looked to the southern and border states as an area of great potential for party growth. In 1968, for the first time since the Civil War, a substantial majority of the electoral votes were withheld from the Democratic Presidential candidate. Mr. Nixon carried seven states in the region, and five more went for American Independent party candidate George C. Wallace.

Although GOP officials denied that a southern strategy existed, the Administration took a number of actions that attracted support in the South. The Nixon proposal on the voting rights bill, which narrowly passed the House in December, was designed to eliminate the "regional" nature of the original Voting Rights Act. The Administration's success in shifting school desegregation enforcement from the Department of Health, Education and Welfare to the courts put the onus on the Supreme Court instead of the President. And the nomination of South Carolina federal judge Clement F. Haynsworth Jr. was warmly received in the South.

The President named as one of his chief political aides Harry S. Dent, former chairman of the South Carolina Republican party and a former assistant to Sen. Strom Thurmond (R S.C.). Dent was active in seeking to build GOP strength in the South. Chief targets were Wallace supporters and conservative Democrats dissatisfied with the national leadership of their party.

Largely as a result of his actions in the South, blacks and members of other minority groups gave the President little support. Civil rights leaders were highly critical of President Nixon's first year in office.

Relations with GOP Members. Relations with Republican Members of Congress were strained on a number of occasions. Early in the year the President recommended that the political patronage system of appointing local postmasters be ended. Republicans on the House Post Office and Civil Service Committee complained that they were not consulted beforehand.

Even after the election of Hugh Scott (R Pa.), to be Minority Leader following the death of Everett McKinley Dirksen of Illinois, moderate Republican Senators complained that their views were not being heard at the White House.

The President had particular difficulty commanding loyalty from six freshman GOP Senators: Marlow W. Cook of Kentucky, Charles McC. Mathias Jr. of Maryland, William B. Saxbe of Ohio, Richard S. Schweiker of Pennsylvania, Robert W. Packwood of Oregon and Charles E. Goodell of New York. All but Packwood opposed Mr. Nixon on the antiballistic missile (ABM) program; all but Cook voted against the Haynsworth nomination. Goodell was one of the most persistent critics of the President's Vietnam policy; and Cook, Mathias and Schweiker broke with the President to support an amendment to increase personal income tax exemptions.

The President Dec. 10 sent his top aides to meet with a group of moderate and liberal GOP Senators after reports circulated that the group was irritated over poor liaison with the White House. An aide to one of the Senators said the group was especially upset at the strict discipline demanded by the White House once policy had been set.

Appointments. President Nixon began his term with about 2,000 patronage jobs to distribute, and by the end of the year most of them were filled. Most of the appointees were white, male Republicans. The President came under fire at various times throughout the year for failing to appoint many members of minority groups, women or people whose party affiliation was not easily identifiable.

The *Baltimore Sun* estimated that 85 percent of all patronage jobs had gone to Republicans, 5 percent to Negroes and the remainder to independents or people whose party affiliation was unknown. It noted that a higher number of Southerners had received patronage appointments under President Nixon than ever before.

Over two dozen defeated GOP candidates for high-ranking offices were given assignments in the new Administration.

The most significant defeat suffered by the President in 1969 was the rejection of Haynsworth by the Senate. The nomination of U.S. District Court Judge Warren E. Burger to be Chief Justice, on the other hand, encountered little difficulty.

Other controversial appointments early in Mr. Nixon's tenure were Interior Secretary Walter J. Hickel and Deputy Defense Secretary David Packard. Willie Mae Rogers, head of the Good Housekeeping Institute, his part-time adviser on consumer matters, resigned after four days amid charges of conflict of interest.

Appointments which were never made also created controversy. Dr. John H. Knowles was slated to get the job of Assistant Secretary of HEW for health and scientific affairs, but the nomination was blocked after opposition was heard from Sen. Dirksen and the American Medical Association. Franklin Long, vice president for research of Cornell University, reportedly was rejected for appointment as head of the National Science Foundation because of his opposition to the ABM system.

The President lost a traditional source of patronage when he moved to eliminate the political advisory system of selecting postmasters. Although Congress never enacted the Administration bill to end Presidential appointment and Senate confirmation of postmasters, the Post Office Department adopted regulations which required nominees to be chosen from competitive examinations.

WAR, DEFENSE COMMITMENTS DOMINATE FOREIGN AFFAIRS

U.S. involvement in Vietnam and the nation's global defense commitments provided the focus of Administration and Congressional concern in foreign affairs in 1969. These issues were, in turn, closely related to mounting criticism of the defense establishment and a desire to curb military and foreign expenditures.

While discontent with the war in Vietnam gave principal impetus to Congressional debate on American military commitments and expenditures, the war in Vietnam did not itself become a subject of prolonged controversy on Capitol Hill until the fall of 1969. Until that time, the attention of Congress had focused on investigating the Pentagon's programs and budget, national priorities and other defense issues.

One result of Congressional dissatisfaction with the direction of U.S. foreign policy was an attempt to reassert the legislature's prerogatives in the foreign policy field through the overwhelming passage of a two-year-old "national commitments" resolution (S Res 85) by the Senate June 25. By declaring that the Executive-Legislative "balance" should be restored in the field of foreign policy decisions, it was hoped that future Vietnams could be avoided and the U.S. global defense role scaled down. Although the resolution was simply a declaration by the Senate without the force of law, its passage characterized the tenor of the first session of the 91st Congress.

National Commitments Issue

Since 1961, Americans had been laying down their lives and paying higher taxes to honor a commitment which the Kennedy, Johnson and Nixon Administrations maintained this nation owed to the government and people of South Vietnam. The accumulating costs, casualties and frustrations of this sacrifice led to a rising tide of protest, dissent and reappraisal—on the campus, in Congress and within the Johnson Administration. President Nixon, picking up from where his predecessor left off, sought to disengage the United States from the conflict in Vietnam.

The scope of the reappraisal was not confined to Vietnam. Increasingly, Americans asked whether U.S. commitments to other nations could lead to other costly military involvements. The Nixon Administration, alert to this concern, indicated that in the future the United States would avoid using its own combat troops in wars of civil insurgency.

The most striking expression of Congressional concern over the scope of U.S. military commitments abroad was the adoption by the Senate on June 25, 1969, of a "national commitments" resolution (S Res 85) by an overwhelming 70-16 vote. The announced purpose of the resolution was to restore what many Senators regarded as a constitutional imbalance resulting from continued Congressional abnegation in the field of foreign affairs. For too long, many Senators argued, Congress had simply followed the Executive Branch's lead in foreign policy with the result that the United States had found itself drawn into military engagements or war without Congressional action.

The resolution sought to reverse a trend of Congressional delegation of wide discretionary power to the President to deal with foreign policy crises. On five occasions since 1955, Congress had overwhelmingly delegated this power. In the last of these instances, in August 1964, the Senate adopted by an 88-2 vote a resolution (known as the Tonkin Gulf resolution) which gave the Johnson Administration what was widely interpreted as a blank check to escalate the Vietnam war. Demonstrative of the change in attitude from 1964 to 1969, 45 Senators who voted for the Tonkin Gulf resolution in 1964 voted for the national commitments resolution in 1969.

In addition to the national commitments resolution, Congress also started questioning U.S. military agreements and defense policies. During the summer of 1969, under the continued prodding of Sen. J.W. Fulbright (D Ark.), chairman of the Foreign Relations Committee, the Administration acknowledged the existence since 1964 of a "contingency plan" with Thailand under which U.S. troops reportedly could be involved in combatting insurgency against the Thai government. This disclosure and Fulbright's demand that the Foreign Relations Committee be shown the document led to the Administration's announcement in September that the United States and Thailand had begun talks on the reduction of the 49,000-man U.S. military contingent in that country.

In another Southeast Asian country, Laos, reports began surfacing in 1969 on the extent of U.S. involvement in the Laotian civil war. While the Administration maintained there were no U.S. ground "combat troops" in Laos, it acknowledged that U.S. bombers were flying combat missions against the Ho Chi Minh trail, which runs through Laos; and it was widely known that U.S. Air Force planes had flown bombing and logistical missions in support of Laotian government armed forces. Senate Majority Leader Mike Mansfield (D Mont.), who returned in September from a two-week trip to Southeast Asia, reported that American "reinvolvement" in Laos had attained "disturbing proportions."

Nixon Position. The Nixon Administration was responsive to the growing pressure to scale down U.S. military activities abroad. Emerging was a commitments policy intended to avoid involvements like the Vietnam war by emphasizing the firmness of existing U.S. defense pledges (thereby deterring would-be aggressors) while at the same time eschewing direct and immediate involvement of American troops in areas faced with non-nuclear aggression or internal subversion.

In a March 4, 1969, news conference, President Nixon said, "...As far as commitments are concerned, the United States has a full plate. I first do not believe we should make new commitments around the world unless our national interests are very vitally involved. Secondly, I do not belive we should become involved in the quarrels of nations in other parts of the world unless we are asked to become involved and unless also we are vitally involved."

Asia and the Far East. U.S. activities in Asia, more than in any other region, planted the seeds of anxiety about the nature and repercussions of American commitments abroad. Accordingly, the Nixon Administration focused its attention on reassessing U.S. policy in the Far East.

During 1969, Mr. Nixon frequently repeated his desire to mute the U.S. military presence in Asia and to push back the moment when the United States felt obliged to intervene militarily. A statement by the President in Guam July 25, 1969, was widely heralded as a first step in a reassessment of U.S. policy in order to avoid future Vietnams. The President said that future U.S. policy in Asia would aim to avoid military intervention which could involve the country in situations like Vietnam, would encourage Asian nations to assume greater defense responsibilities and would place increasing emphasis on the concept of self-help and the creation of a partnership between the United States and Asian nations for the region's economic development. During his July Asian trip, however, the President emphasized that as long as turmoil in Asia posed a significant threat to world peace, the United States would continue to play a major (though no longer front-line) role there and would abide by its existing defense arrangements (though they might be interpreted more strictly).

Mr. Nixon restated the self-help concept when South Korean President Chung Hee Park visited the United States Aug. 21-22.

During an address on Vietnam Nov. 3, the President put on record the so-called "Nixon Doctrine " (first outlined in the Guam statement). The three key principles as explained by the President were:

• "The United States will keep all of its treaty commitments."

• "We shall provide a shield if a nuclear power threatens the freedom of a nation allied with us or of a nation whose survival we consider vital to our security."

• "In cases involving other types of aggression, we shall furnish military and economic assistance when requested in accordance with our treaty commitments. But we shall look to the nation directly threatened to assume the primary responsibility of providing the manpower for its defense." *(For text, see p. 94-A.)*

Many observers considered the Administration's Vietnamization program as the first test of the viability of the policy of a low-level U.S. Asian profile.

Mansfield Report. Senate Majority Leader Mike Mansfield (D Mont.) Sept. 21 urged the Administration to take immediate steps to reduce the U.S. military presence in Asia. The Senator made his recommendations in a report to the Foreign Relations Committee after submitting a confidential report to the President Aug. 27. The recommendations were based on a two-week trip to Asia in August at Mr. Nixon's request.

Okinawa Negotiations. Six months of almost continuous U.S.-Japanese negotiations over the political administration of the Okinawa Islands culminated in the Nov. 19-21 visit of Japanese Premier Eisaku Sato to Washington.

The future status of U.S. military bases on Okinawa was a related and controversial issue. Some observers had argued that if the Nixon Administration was aiming toward a more cautious and low-level military posture, it should then be willing to agree to Japanese demands for restrictions on the use of Okinawa facilities (as long as the island was under U.S. political administration, the United States had completely free use of its vast military facilities there).

The Okinawa issue provided an opportunity for the first concrete application of the Senate's "national com-

mitments" resolution. An amendment to the State-Justice Departments appropriations bill (HR 12964) Nov. 5 instructed the President to obtain the Senate's advice and consent on any agreement or understanding which changed the status of Okinawa.

Despite the Senate declaration (which was later deleted from the conference report on the bill), the two governments Nov. 21 announced reversion of the islands to Japanese administration by the end of 1972. Under the terms of the arrangement, the United States agreed to extend the provisions of the 1960 U.S.-Japanese mutual security treaty to American military bases on Okinawa at the time of reversion, making their use for offensive combat missions dependent on prior consultation with the Japanese government, as had applied to U.S. bases in Japan.

The two governments agreed on the need to retain the extensive U.S. facilities on Okinawa, but the United States, heeding widespread Japanese antinuclear sentiment, indicated it would remove nuclear weapons from the island by the time of reversion and would reintroduce them only after consulting the Japanese government. In return for these concessions, the Japanese government stated that it considered the safety of Nationalist China and South Korea as important to its own national security and indicated that it would allow free use of the Okinawa bases to counter attacks on those countries.

Mathias Resolution. Sen. Charles McC. Mathias Jr. (R Md.) Dec. 8 introduced a resolution (S J Res 166) to rescind four Congressional measures which delegated far-reaching emergency powers to the Executive to use U.S. armed forces in repelling Communist threats around the world. The four were: the 1955 Formosa resolution, the 1957 Middle East resolution, the 1962 Cuba resolution on Latin America and the 1964 Tonkin Gulf resolution on Vietnam. All gave formal Congressional endorsement to any future military actions considered by the Executive as necessary to combat Communist aggression in those regions. S J Res 166 also would terminate the state of national emergency declared by President Truman Dec. 16, 1950, at the outbreak of the Korean war.

Mathias termed these measure "cold war enactments" which were "based on an essentially negative view of the American world mission. In each instance, we imply the principle that military containment of international Communism is the chief function of our foreign policy."

The Senator's action won endorsement from both Majority Leader Mansfield and Minority Leader Hugh Scott (R Pa.). The Administration opposed repeal of the Tonkin Gulf resolution but said it had no objections to repeal of the three other measures.

Prohibition on U.S. Combat Troops. The Senate Dec. 16, in an unusual secret floor session, voted by a roll call of 73-17 to prohibit a commitment of U.S. ground combat troops to Laos and Thailand. The prohibition was added to the defense appropriations bill (HR 15090) and retained in the House-Senate conference report. The amendment stated, "In line with the expressed intention of the President of the United States, none of the funds appropriated by this act shall be used to finance the introduction of American ground combat troops into Laos or Thailand." The amendment was approved by the White House, which regarded it as an "endorsement" of its Asian policy. Sen. Frank Church (D Idaho), a principal sponsor of the amendment, said it was a "reassertion of Congressional prerogatives" in foreign policy—in keeping with the national commitments resolution.

NATO. The North Atlantic Treaty Organization (NATO), the oldest and frequently the most troublesome of the United States' military commitments, completed its 20th year in 1969. After Aug. 24, any of the 15 allied nations could withdraw by giving a year's notice that it wished to pull out of the defensive grouping.

Until the Soviet Union's August 1968 Czechoslovakia intervention instilled a new sense of purpose in the alliance and President Nixon began to promote Atlantic cooperation in 1969, it seemed likely that wholesale revisions would mark NATO's 20th anniversary. Although these factors eased the possibility of a NATO breakup, they did not completely halt continuing problems and differences of policy.

President Nixon underscored the importance of the NATO commitment (which, he said March 28, "remains firm and vital") by visiting member nations in late February. During that trip, however, he urged a greater defense contribution on the part of other participants.

At the annual meeting of the North Atlantic assembly in Brussels Oct. 21, Sen. John Sherman Cooper (R Ky.) warned that Congressional pressures to reduce U.S. troop strength in Europe could grow, unless other members increased their contribution.

Senate Majority Leader Mansfield Dec. 1 reintroduced a resolution (S Res 292) he had proposed in 1966 calling for a "substantial reduction" of U.S. troops in Europe. Noting that there were 550,000 Americans associated with the military in Europe, Mansfield said the net U.S. foreign exchange gap with West Germany alone was about $965 million annually as a result of U.S. military outlays. Mansfield predicted the resolution would be approved.

At a three-day semiannual meeting of NATO foreign, economic and defense ministers Dec. 3-5, representatives approved political guidelines for the use of tactical nuclear weapons, agreeing on faster political consultation regarding the use of the weapons and outlining situations and geographical areas in which they might be employed.

A formal communique issued at the close of the conference Dec. 5 stated that the members were "receptive" to Communist bloc (Warsaw Pact) overtures for an all-European security conference. The cautious response had been urged by Secretary of State William P. Rogers, who emphasized the need for "skillful and thorough preparatory work." Members of the alliance also formally praised West German efforts to normalize its relations with East European countries, declaring that such efforts represented "constructive steps toward relaxation of tension in Europe."

Spanish Bases. Concern was expressed by some Senators in 1969 that the United States had committed itself to the defense of Spain in return for leasing military bases in the country. Members of the Senate Foreign Relations Committee, which investigated the relation, questioned whether the value of the bases was worth their price and argued that any commitment to Spain should take the form of a treaty, requiring Senate advice and consent.

The panel also expressed concern that the U.S. presence alone constituted a *de facto* commitment to support the Franco regime, particularly in light of reports of joint U.S.-Spanish maneuvers to suppress a theoretical internal revolt there.

The United States and Spain June 20 signed an agreement which would extend U.S. military base rights in the country to Sept. 26, 1971, in return for $50 million of military equipment and a loan from the Export-Import Bank for the purchase of an additional $35 million of American equipment.

Congressional criticism resulted in Administration assurances that the U.S. commitment to Spain had not been upgraded by the Nixon Administration.

Thai Contingency Plan. A four-month attempt to obtain a copy of a U.S. military contingency plan with Thailand was capped Nov. 7 in an unannounced, executive session of the Senate Foreign Relations Committee when Pentagon officials brought the text of the plan for members to examine. The controversy had surfaced July 8, when Committee Chairman J.W. Fulbright (D Ark.) charged that the plan (known as COMUSTAF Plan 1/64), negotiated in 1964-65, went far beyond U.S. treaty commitments to Thailand. Subsequently, the Defense Department had offered to show the plan to members of the panel who were willing to go over to the Pentagon to examine it. Following the Nov. 7 session, Fulbright said "there were really no surprises" and that he continued to believe the plan "comprised more of a treaty than just a 'contingency plan.' " Frank Church (D Idaho), a member of the Committee, said he thought the decision to produce the document before the panel "reaffirms the constitutional authority of the Senate to be fully informed on matters that could vitally affect the country abroad."

Subcommittee Investigations. A Senate Ad Hoc Foreign Relations Subcommittee on U.S. Security Agreements and Commitments Abroad, chaired by Stuart Symington (D Mo.), was organized in February 1969, with a two-year life span. Its purpose: "To make a detailed review of the international military commitments of the United States and their relationship to foreign policy." Closed hearings before the Subcommittee on U.S. commitments to the Philippines were held Sept. 30-Oct. 3, after which an unclassified version of the testimony was published.

A similar procedure was followed with U.S. involvement in Laos, on which closed hearings began Oct. 20. The staff also played a major role in bringing the Spanish base and Thai contingency plan issues to the Senate's attention.

Vietnam Developments

As a Presidential candidate and after assuming office, Mr. Nixon repeatedly pledged to end U.S. involvement in the Vietnam war. While the sincerity of his desire for peace was seldom questioned, debate began to grow on whether the President's policies would achieve this objective. The timetable for withdrawal became a focal point of controversy between the President and his critics.

The first year of the Nixon Administration saw a gradual scaling down of the U.S. military presence in the country. The President also abandoned the concept of a "purely military victory" in Vietnam. He responded to the public's weariness with sustained involvement in remote regions by outlining a policy (the "Nixon Doctrine") aimed at avoiding future Vietnams. And, according to some observers, President Nixon sought to isolate his critics by broad appeals to "middle America"—to the "silent majority" which he conceived of as his real constituency.

Situation in January and December 1969. When the new Administration came into office, U.S. troop strength stood at 542,500. A U.S. halt on bombing of North Vietnam had been in effect since November 1968. On Jan. 16, the United States and North Vietnam agreed on the shape of the negotiating table in Paris; and all four parties announced agreement to begin substantive negotiations in Paris.

By mid-December, U.S. troop strength stood at 472,500, having dipped to its lowest level since late 1967. Despite secret peace probes, no progress had been made in Paris, but battlefield activities and U.S. casualties had decreased compared with the previous year.

On April 1, 1969, U.S. deaths in Vietnam reached 33,630, surpassing the Korean war toll.

Nixon Policies. The Administration's program in Vietnam involved measures on both the diplomatic and military fronts to end the war. In his first nationwide policy address on Vietnam, the President May 14 offered an 8-point proposal to bring about a settlement, which included: mutual withdrawal of all non-South Vietnamese forces to designated bases over a 12-month period, after which remaining troops would be totally withdrawn from the South; creation of an international body to supervise and verify the withdrawal and ceasefire; internationally supervised free elections in the South; and agreement by all parties to observe the 1954 Geneva Accords regarding Vietnam and Cambodia and the 1962 Laos Accords. *(For text, see p. 104-A.)*

The President's speech was viewed as a public reply to a 10-point peace proposal offered in Paris May 8 by the National Liberation Front (NLF) and endorsed by Hanoi. The Communist proposal reiterated demands for a unilateral unconditional withdrawal of all U.S. forces.

Mr. Nixon restated his proposals and programs in a Nov. 3 nationally televised address, during which he asked for support from "the great silent majority" and stated the U.S. position as "anything is negotiable except the right of the people of South Vietnam to determine their own future. *(For text, see p. 94-A.)*

Troop Withdrawals. In a June 19 news conference, the President expressed the hope that most U.S. troops could be withdrawn by the end of 1970. On Oct. 12, he predicted that the war would be over "in just three years."

In his Nov. 3 address, the President said he had an "orderly scheduled timetable" for the complete withdrawal of all U.S. combat forces. Throughout the year, however, the President refused to detail his withdrawal schedule.

Mr. Nixon and Administration officials repeatedly ruled out a "precipitous" or immediate total withdrawal, and declared that the rate of U.S. troop reductions would depend on events in one or all of three fronts: progress in the Paris negotiations; a decline in the level of enemy military activity; and the rate at which South Vietnamese forces were trained and equipped to assume major combat responsibilities.

By Dec. 15, 1969, over 60,000 U.S. combat troops had been withdrawn from Vietnam. The first withdrawal of 25,000 was announced June 8 by Mr. Nixon and South Vietnamese President Nguyen Van Thieu, who met on

Midway Island. The second withdrawal of 35,000 was announced Sept. 16, after having been deferred Aug. 23 following outbreak of major enemy fighting Aug. 10-11. *(For text, see p. 111-A.)*

The President, in a brief televised report to the nation Dec. 15, announced a reduction by April 15, 1970, of 50,000 more U.S. troops from the authorized level. Actual troop reductions could vary from that figure, however. In his Sept. 16 announcement of a 35,000 cutback by Dec. 15, the President established the authorized troop ceiling at 484,000. His December announcement would reduce the ceiling to 434,000 by April 15. However, by Dec. 15 the actual number of troops in Vietnam had fallen below the September ceiling.

In his Dec. 15 address, the President said he based his decision on progress in the Vietnamization program but said he could not report favorably on the two other factors which he had previously singled out as affecting troop withdrawal decisions.

Concerning developments in the Paris peace negotiations, Mr. Nixon said "no progress whatever" had been made since Nov. 3. Turning to the second factor—level of enemy activity—the President noted the "disturbing new development" of substantially increased enemy infiltration, and restated his Nov. 3 warning to Hanoi that he would "not hesitate to take strong and effective measures" to counter renewed enemy offensives.

Vietnamization Program. As U.S. troops were being scaled down, the Administration launched what became known as the "Vietnamization" program—the centerpiece of its plan to end direct U.S. involvement in the war. During a trip to Saigon in early March, Defense Secretary Melvin R. Laird said he would ask Congress for a $70-million increase in the Vietnam budget to carry out the program.

On Oct. 9, Laird confirmed reports that U.S. commanders had received new orders to give "highest priority" to the program. At that time, he said the Vietnamization plan had "achieved a real momentum."

Administration officials continued to point to successes in the program, but it was difficult to assess results with certainty. Following a July 30 briefing by Gen. Earle G. Wheeler, chairman of the Joint Chiefs of Staff, who had recently returned from Saigon, Sen. John Stennis (D Miss.) said it appeared it would take several years before South Vietnamese combat troops could assume most of the fighting.

In his Nov. 3 address, Mr. Nixon stressed that the Vietnamization program was a means of ending the war "regardless of what happens on the negotiating front."

Costs of the War. As of Dec. 1, 1969, 39,642 Americans had been killed in action in Vietnam; 8,618 had been killed between Jan. 1 and Nov. 1, 1969, compared with 13,843 in the same period in 1968. At the beginning of 1969, the Defense Department put the cost of the war at about $28 billion per year, approximately the Pentagon's original Budget request for Vietnam war funds for fiscal 1970. Between 1946 and 1968, Vietnam ranked sixth among major recipients of U.S. economic and military aid, having received about $5.6 billion.

On Dec. 4, 1969, total U.S. casualties in the nine years of war in Vietnam surpassed 300,000. The toll approached that of World War I (320,710 casualties).

Congress appropriated for fiscal 1970 $2.2 billion to support Vietnamese and other free-world forces in Vietnam and local forces in Laos and Thailand (1969 appropriation, $1.7 billion). Of that amount, $651.8 million was for modernization of the South Vietnamese armed forces.

Military Activity. During 1969, battlefield activity was characterized by intermittent lulls, broken by renewed enemy offensives which increased toward the end of the year. But enemy attacks never reached the intensity of the 1968 Tet offensive. U.S. casualties during the week of Oct. 6 (numbering 64) were the lowest since Dec. 1966. Secretary of State William P. Rogers Oct. 12 said there had been a net reduction of North Vietnamese troop strength in the South of "roughly 25 to 30 thousand" over the previous 6-7 months.

On July 27, Laird said U.S. military tactics had been modified in accordance with shifts in enemy operations. Mr. Nixon Nov. 3 pointed to a reduction of U.S. air operations of "over 20 percent" compared with the previous year.

A survey released by the Administration in October showed that more than 90 percent of the South Vietnamese population was under Saigon government control, an increase of 11.3 percent since the beginning of the year.

Paris Negotiations. On March 25, the President predicted that progress in Paris would be made through private rather than public talks; on Nov. 3, he revealed that secret meetings had been held, but without success. South Vietnam President Nguyen Van Thieu's offer (March 25) of private unconditional talks with the NLF was rejected. North Vietnam scorned a proposal by U.S. Chief negotiator Henry Cabot Lodge to hold private talks outside the large formal sessions.

Frustrations in Paris led Secretary Rogers Oct. 12 to suggest that the conflict could gradually "fade away" without ever being formally resolved at the negotiating table.

Lodge Resignation. The U.S. chief negotiator, Henry Cabot Lodge, and his deputy, Lawrence E. Walsh, Nov. 20 announced their resignations effective Dec. 8. Both expressed pessimism concerning the course of the negotiations. President Nixon Nov. 20 named Philip C. Habib, formerly chief advisor to Lodge, as acting head of the U.S. delegation. At the same time, the White House formally discounted any intention of down-grading the talks.

Ho Chi Minh Death. The most important political event related to the Vietnam war was the death Sept. 3 of North Vietnamese President Ho Chi Minh, the 79-year-old leader of the nationalist-Communist movement in Southeast Asia. For three days following his death, Communist and U.S. forces observed a de facto cease-fire, which was rejected by Saigon. Ho's death did not appear to alter the North Vietnamese position in Paris or the nation's desire to pursue its objectives.

Criticism of Saigon. A South Vietnamese cabinet reorganization announced Sept. 1 elicited a critical reaction from some observers, who charged that the government had narrowed rather than broadened its popular base and was continuing to prohibit participation of other political groups. President Nixon also came under some attack for his apparently firm support of the Saigon government in a July 30 visit to South Vietnam during his trip to Asia.

Green Beret Case. Controversy erupted over the activities of U.S. Special Forces (or Green Berets) in Vietnam, when the Army charged 6 Green Berets with allegedly murdering a South Vietnamese double intel-

ligence agent June 20. The Army dropped the charges Sept. 29, offering little explanation. Some Members of Congress indicated their dissatisfaction and said they would pursue an investigation.

U.S. Massacre of Vietnam Civilians. Horror, incredulity and dismay were registered in Congress and among the public with the revelation in 1969 of an alleged massacre of Vietnamese civilians by U.S. forces in March 1968. The Army Nov. 24 announced the court-martial of First Lt. William L. Calley on charges of the premeditated murder of at least 109 Vietnamese civilians "of various ages and sexes." Calley, 26, a platoon leader involved in the alleged massacre at May Lai village in Quang Ngai Province, was ordered to be tried at Fort Benning, Ga., on a "capital" basis, meaning that the death sentence could be imposed.

The White House Nov. 26 declared that the alleged massacre was "in direct violation not only of U.S. military policy but is also abhorrent to the conscience of the American public." The House and Senate Armed Services Committtees held closed hearings on the incident, as numerous other Members called for a full Congressional investigation.

Related Laos Activities. U.S. military operations in Laos came under Congressional scrutiny during closed Senate subcommittee hearings in the fall of 1969. The President, who had said that Laos must be included in any settlement of the Vietnam war, Sept. 26 acknowledged that the United States maintained "aerial reconnaissance" over Laos and added, "we do have perhaps some other activities," which he declined to clarify. He pointed to the importance of Laos in the Vietnam war by citing North Vietnam's use of the Ho Chi Minh trail to infiltrate men and supplies through Laos into South Vietnam, Secretary of State Rogers, speaking to reporters Oct. 29 after testifying before the Senate Subcommittee on the U.S. role in Laos, said, "I thought Congress was familiar with what we are doing there."

Prisoners of War. North Vietnam's repeated refusal to disclose the names of American prisoners or to allow Red Cross inspection was a matter of considerable concern both to Congress and the Administration. The President Nov. 6 signed a joint resolution (H J Res 910) declaring Nov. 9 a national day of prayer for American servicemen held prisoner in North Vietnam. More than 275 Members sponsored resolutions on the prisoners-of-war issue, which were the subject of House Foreign Affairs Subcommittee hearings Nov. 13 and 14. H Con Res 454, calling for humane treatment and release of U.S. prisoners, was passed by the House Dec. 15, as was another resolution (H Res 661) commending American servicemen and veterans of Vietnam for their efforts and sacrifices.

The House Dec. 2 added an amendment to a resolution on Vietnam (H Res 613) requesting the President to continue to press North Vietnam on complying with the 1949 Geneva Conventions on prisoners of war.

War Protests and Debate

Congress and the public generally adopted a "wait and see" attitude during the first nine months of 1969, reflecting a widespread feeling that the new Administration should be given time to work out its policies and carry out its pledges. Only one major antiwar demonstration occurred (April 5-6), while Congressional criticism was infrequent and relatively mild. When Sen. George McGovern (D S.D.) launched the first major attack on the President's Vietnam policy March 17, his remarks were given a cool reception by other Congressional doves.

By May, however, several Members—including Sens. George D. Aiken (R Vt.), Mike Mansfield (D Mont.), Jacob K. Javits (R N.Y.), Edward M. Kennedy (D Mass.), Charles H. Percy (R Ill.) and Hugh Scott (R Pa.)—were beginning to call for substantial reductions of U.S. troops.

Reaction on Capitol Hill to the President's May 14 proposals was generally favorable, but Sen. Frank Church (D Idaho), a leading dove, called the speech a "bitter disappointment."

The Midway meeting between Presidents Nixon and Thieu, combined with the 25,000 troop withdrawal, encountered a more mixed reaction. Some Members criticized the size of the withdrawal as only a "token pullout" and expressed dissatisfaction with U.S. support of the Thieu regime. Nonetheless, the announcement of the initial troop pullout raised expectations that the President was committed to a U.S. withdrawal and consequently dampened criticism for a time.

Although the summer was relatively quiet, some restlessness in Congress and among the public began to be evident by August and early September, particularly following the Administration's Aug. 23 announcement that a decision on additional troop withdrawals would be deferred. During the temporary cease-fire observed at Ho Chi Minh's death Sept. 3, Sens. Mansfield, John Sherman Cooper (R Ky.) and Gaylord Nelson (D Wis.) were among those urging the President to use the military halt as an opportunity for new peace initiatives.

Vietnam Moratorium. The desire for peace, frustration with an apparent impasse in reaching any settlement and a wish to see the President move more quickly in extricating the United States from Vietnam culminated in the "Vietnam moratorium" Oct. 15, when an estimated million Americans participated in antiwar demonstrations, protest rallies and peace vigils across the nation.

The moratorium against "business as usual," organized primarily by the Vietnam Moratorium Committee and the more radical New Mobilization Committee to End the War in Vietnam, captured the attention and endorsement of Congressional war critics. More than 80 Members announced support of the Oct. 15 moratorium as a "peaceful demonstration for peace." Over 50 actively participated in the protest. But at least as many Members objected that the demonstration appeared as a gesture of support for Hanoi. A minority urged the President to end the war by stepped-up military operations. Many Members who endorsed the protest did not agree with the organizers' demands for immediate, unconditional withdrawal of all U.S. forces, however.

The moratorium was conducted in what was described as a generally peaceful and dignified manner.

Considerable debate arose over Vice President Spiro T. Agnew's Oct. 19 characterization of antiwar protesters as an "effete corps of impudent snobs." Agnew's charges—"if the moratorium had any use whatever, it served as an emotional purgative for those who feel the need to cleanse themselves of their lack of ability to offer a constructive solution to the problem"—met with vigorous counter-criticism in the press and among Congressional doves.

Activities in Congress. Meanwhile, a number of Congressional resolutions were introduced on the Vietnam issue. They ranged from a bill proposed Sept. 25 by Sen. Charles E. Goodell (R N.Y.), setting a statutory deadline for a troop pullout by Dec. 1970, to resolutions calling on the Communists to demonstrate flexibility at the peace talks. A number of resolutions urging immediate or more rapid troop withdrawals were introduced by doves, while Sen. Harold E. Hughes (D Iowa) and Thomas F. Eagleton (D Mo.) introduced a resolution calling for a termination of aid to Saigon unless the regime undertook political reforms. Although Members tried to avoid turning the war into a partisan issue, the debate did produce a tendency for a Republican-Democratic split on assessment of the President's efforts. Doves rejected a call by Senate Minority Leader Scott and House Minority Leader Gerald R. Ford (Mich.) for a 60-day halt to Vietnam debate. However, a bipartisan group of 109 Representatives introduced a resolution commending Mr. Nixon's troop withdrawals and urging him to continue the policy.

Congressional debate was capped on the eve of the Oct. 15 moratorium, when war opponents kept the House in session into the night, during which they engaged in a spirited contest with supporters of the Nixon Administration's war policy.

On another aspect of the Vietnam controversy in Congress, Fulbright revealed Sept. 12 that he had written a letter to Secretary of State Rogers on May 12, 1969, asking for copies of any request from South Vietnam for U.S. intervention with combat troops.

After four months, the Department replied (Sept. 2) that there had been no such request, but that "the initial decisions to deploy U.S. combat troops to South Vietnam in the spring and summer of 1965 resulted from a continuing analysis of a constantly changing situation...The process of analyzing the situation by the two governments, and the consultation and agreement thereon, were such as to be regarded by our Government as constituting a request from the government of Vietnam." The request was confirmed by a communique issued by the government of Vietnam on March 7, 1965, concerning the arrival of two U.S. Marine battalions.

Commenting on the absence of a formal request, Fulbright said, "It is shocking to realize that Congress was not asked for specific authority for the sending of American soldiers to South Vietnam and, indeed, that the government of South Vietnam itself did not make a written formal request for those troops."

Administration Response. The President said he recognized the right of all Americans to express their opinions, but he said that to abandon policies "based on exhaustive study of all available evidence...because of a public demonstration would...be an act of gross irresponsibility on my part." Nonetheless, a series of Vietnam policy consultations among high-level officials took place in the days preceding the moratorium, and Administration spokesmen sought to deflate criticism by pointing to the successes of the President's policy. In other moves, the White House Oct. 10 announced the planned replacement of Lt. Gen. Lewis B. Hershey, chief of the Selective Service for 28 years and a target of antidraft and antiwar protesters. The Administration also took the unusual step of announcing three weeks in advance that the President would address the nation on Vietnam Nov. 3.

Lull in Debate. Between the Oct. 15 moratorium and the President's Nov. 3 address, the Vietnam controversy died down and was replaced by a mood of expectation. The Senate Foreign Relations Committee postponed Vietnam hearings it had scheduled for Oct. 27 to await the President's speech. Although the Administration tried to dampen widespread speculation that further troop reductions, a cease-fire (advocated by Mansfield and Scott) or a specific withdrawal timetable might be announced Nov. 3, it circulated on Capitol Hill a fact sheet enumerating steps it had taken to de-escalate the war.

Reaction to Nov. 3 Address. While some doves expressed disappointment that the President had offered no new peace initiatives or major policy shifts in his Nov. 3 address, the predominant Congressional reaction was one of support for the Administration and a conviction that the President was "on the right track." The leadership of both parties introduced resolutions supporting the President's withdrawal policy. They were sponsored by about 350 Members.

Complicating Congressional feeling on Vietnam was the fact that many doves and Members who had endorsed the Oct. 15 moratorium dissociated themselves from the Nov. 13-15 protest because they feared possible violence under more radical organization. Consequently, many of them muted their own criticism, arguing that debate should be responsible and should avoid inflaming an already sensitive issue. The Foreign Relations Committee decided to hold closed, rather than public, hearings on Vietnam and postponed them until after the Nov. 13-15 protests.

November Demonstrations. An estimated 250,000 antiwar protesters converged in Washington in mid-November to participate in a 40-hour "march against death," capped by a mass march and rally. Although violence had been predicted by some, the demonstration was generally peaceful. However, considerably fewer Members of Congress participated in the November Vietnam activities than in October, and only two Senators—Goodell and McGovern—spoke at the rally. The war demonstrations were concentrated in the capital, with fewer activities across the nation than had occurred in October.

At the same time, however, supporters of the Administration's policy held numerous "unity rallies" throughout the United States, the largest of which was held at the Washington Monument on Veterans' Day Nov. 11.

The Administration again publicly ignored the antiwar protest, and White House spokesmen again declared that the President's Vietnam policy would not be affected by public demonstrations. Meanwhile, the Administration continued to invoke the attitude of the "silent majority of Americans"—to whom the President had appealed in his Nov. 3 speech—as evidence of support for its Vietnam policy.

Foreign Relations Committee Hearings. The Senate Foreign Relations Committee, meeting in executive session, heard testimony from Secretary of State Rogers (Nov. 18) and Defense Secretary Laird (Nov. 19) on Vietnam. The Committee decided Nov. 20 to hold public hearings on Vietnam, but did not plan to open them until early in 1970.

House Vietnam Resolution. The House Dec. 2 by a 334-55 roll-call vote passed a resolution (H Res 613) supporting the President's efforts to achieve "peace with

justice" in Vietnam. Although the resolution was overwhelmingly approved, considerable debate focused on its interpretation. Numerous doves, voting for and against the measure, said the resolution should not be construed as conveying support for the President's policies outlined in his Nov. 3 address. But the President, referring to the resolution in his Dec. 15 address, said he considered it to be evidence of overwhelming Congressional support for his policy and "plan" of Nov. 3.

Summary. Unlike 1968, the 1969 debate on Vietnam did not occur primarily in the political arena or the voting booths but took place in the streets and in the halls of Congress. It reached a peak in early October and focused around the Oct. 15 moratorium and mass rally in November. But the effect of those protests was made more indeterminate because they captured the support of persons with widely varying opinions on how to end the war. The subsequent protests in December attracted far less public attention and Congressional support.

Despite a dramatic downswing in the debate toward the end of 1969, the Administration had to contend with a steadily growing weariness with the war. The possibility of rising opposition to its policy of pacing troop withdrawals on events occurring in Hanoi or South Vietnam was also a factor to be taken into account. Increasingly, Americans were beginning to express the opinion that if there were to be no military victory, the Government should "bring the boys home" regardless of factors which many considered beyond U.S. control.

Nixon Steps To End War

In news conferences and addresses during his first year in office, President Nixon repeatedly referred to his plans to end the Vietnam war. But he also refused to detail his "plan for peace" and consistently ruled out an "immediate, precipitate" withdrawal. While some critics challenged the Administration to produce specific evidence of the plan and questioned whether the objective of the Nixon policy was an eventual total U.S. withdrawal, Administration officials insisted the plan was in operation and was succeeding.

In 1969, Mr. Nixon:

• Publicly abandoned a "military victory."

• Committed the Administration to gradual troop withdrawal.

• Made specific political proposals for internationally supervised elections, with participation by the NLF in a coalition supervisory government.

• Obtained public endorsement by South Vietnamese President Thieu on NLF political participation as well as an offer of unconditional secret talks.

• Emphasized "Vietnamization"—preparing South Vietnam forces to assume a larger combat role. (Assessment of progress has been mixed.)

• Altered U.S. combat orders to limit offensive operations and focus on training South Vietnamese.

• Called for mutual troop withdrawal over a 12-month period.

• Said U.S. withdrawals would depend not only on progress in Paris and reaching formal political settlement but also on enemy activity and South Vietnamese readiness, indicating that the war could gradually dissipate without formal agreement.

• Declared U.S. policy was firm only on the issue of self-determination and was not committed to a particular government or form of political settlement.

U.S.-Soviet Relations

"After a period of confrontation, we are entering an era of negotiation," the President declared in his inaugural address. Although the Vietnam war continued to be a major source of friction in East-West relations, the United States and Soviet Union agreed to hold bilateral talks on the Middle East situation and to open preliminary negotiations on strategic arms limitation.

Nonproliferation Treaty. The Senate March 13 ratified a treaty (Exec H, 90th Congress, 2nd Session) banning the spread of nuclear weapons. Senate action on the pact had been held up in 1968 at the request of Mr. Nixon in reaction to the Soviet invasion of Czechoslovakia in August. President Nixon Feb. 5 requested the Senate's prompt consideration and approval of the treaty. By December 1969, 24 of the 40 states required to effect the treaty had ratified it, including the major sponsors (Britain, the Soviet Union and the United States). President Nixon Nov. 24 formally completed U.S. action on the treaty by signing it in a ceremony which coincided with ratification by the Presidium of the Supreme Soviet and signature by Soviet President Nikolai V. Podgorny.

SALT Talks. The United States and Soviet Union Nov. 17 began preliminary discussions on the long-awaited strategic arms limitation talks (SALT) in Helsinki, Finland. On Dec. 22, they agreed to open full-scale talks April 16, 1970, in Vienna. President Johnson in late 1966 and early 1967 had focused on the need to begin such discussions. But the Soviet invasion of Czechoslovakia and the arrival of a new Administration which wanted to review the U.S. strategic position led to delays. Early in 1969, the Senate Foreign Relations Committee began prodding the Administration to set a date for the talks. During hearings on the nonproliferation treaty, Committee members reminded Administration officials that Art. VI of the pact pledged the nuclear signatories to undertake negotiations on arms control "at an early date."

Controversy over the antiballistic missile system (ABM) and development of multiple independently targeted re-entry vehicles (MIRV) was closely related to the arms control issue, since it was argued that development of these weapons could create instability and spur the arms race onto a new level.

Mr. Nixon on June 19, 1969, invited the Soviet Union to begin negotiations on arms limitations. But the U.S.S.R. withheld an answer until Oct. 25. The long delay in accepting was attributed to Soviet preoccupation with the Chinese border conflict, Soviet annoyance over U.S. policy in the Middle East, U.S. overtures to Communist China and Mr. Nixon's Aug. 2 visit to Romania (on his return from Asia) and internal Kremlin disputes over bargaining positions and strategy.

Geneva Conference. Meanwhile, the Geneva arms control conference continued to discuss multilateral disarmament. These talks were expanded to 25 nations in 1969. During the session, the United States and Soviet Union agreed on a draft proposal to ban nuclear weapons from the seabed. Attention also focused on a British proposal to ban the possession and manufacture of offensive biological weapons.

U.S. chemical and biological warfare (CBW) programs had received much critical attention in Congress during 1969. Responding to the buildup of sentiment against these programs, President Nixon Nov. 25 ordered the Defense Department to halt its participation in the military biological aspects of CBW. He renounced the use of lethal biological, or germ, weapons as well as the first use of lethal chemical, or gas, weapons. Mr. Nixon said the United States would support efforts by Great Britain and other nations at the Geneva conference to ban the use of biological warfare. Finally, he said he would resubmit to the Senate a 1925 treaty banning all signers from being the first to use CBW.

The President's actions were widely praised in Congress, but Senate ratification of the 1925 Geneva Protocol was not expected until early in 1970.

Export Control. The Export Control Act of 1949, which gave the President authority to curb U.S. exports to Communist nations, expired June 30, 1969. The Act was temporarily extended for short periods (the last being through Dec. 31) while Congress debated liberalizing the controls. The Administration had requested simple four-year extension of the existing Act, arguing that political factors did not warrant a more liberal bill and that the existing Act was flexible enough to be modified if the situation changed.

The House Oct. 16 passed a bill (HR 4293) extending the existing authorization for two years, with some modifications. The Senate, however, Oct. 22 passed HR 4293 with substitute language designed to relax the trade controls. The bill then went to House-Senate conference, where conferees accepted the Senate language (some liberalizing aspects of the bill were omitted). The Senate Nov. 14 accepted the conference report (H Rept 91-681), but the House Dec. 10 took the unusual action of rejecting a conference report, sending the bill back to the Senate with an amendment which would tighten up Presidential authority to control exports. The Senate disagreed with the House amendment, and HR 4293 was again sent to conference.

In its last legislative act before adjournment, Congress Dec. 23 accepted a second conference report on the bill, thus clearing HR 4293 for the President's signature. The legislation represented a compromise but still contained provisions designed to liberalize the trade restrictions and eliminate nonstrategic items on the export control list.

U.S.-Latin American Relations

U.S. relations with Latin America were exacerbated by a number of crises during 1969. Latin American dissatisfaction with U.S. policies was intensified by a mood of nationalism in the region, while Congressional discontent with the foreign aid program led to cuts in Alliance for Progress funds.

Expropriation. President Nixon March 11 named John N. Irwin II special envoy to negotiate a settlement between the U.S.-owned International Petroleum Co. and the Peruvian military government, following the regime's expropriation of the firm in October 1968. Agreement to talk about compensation avoided a cutoff of U.S. aid to the country under the terms of the "Hickenlooper amendment," but little progress toward a settlement was made. U.S.-Peru relations further deteriorated with the latter's seizure of U.S. vessels fishing off Peru's coast.

Bolivia followed the Peruvian example one year later, in October 1969, when the new military regime moved to expropriate the U.S.-owned Gulf Oil Corp.

Envoy Kidnapped. Leftist opponents of the Brazilian military regime held U.S. Ambassador C. Burke Elbrick captive for three days, releasing him Sept. 7 after the Brazilian government had agreed to free 15 political prisoners.

Rockefeller Mission, Report. Gov. Nelson A. Rockefeller (R N.Y.) undertook a series of four fact-finding missions to Latin American nations during the spring and summer of 1969. He encountered several anti-American demonstrations and was barred from visiting Peru, Chile and Venezuela. Most of the Rockefeller report—"The Quality of Life in the Americas"—was made public Nov. 10. Soon afterward, Rockefeller appeared before Senate and House subcommittees to explain the report. The President's new Latin American policy proposals were based in part on the report's recommendations.

Nixon Policy. President Nixon, in his first major Latin American policy address, Oct. 31 called for a new "more mature partnership" between the United States and Latin America. He offered a number of more specific policy proposals, some of which had been suggested by Latin American governments on June 11, when they had presented the Administration with a statement (the "Consensus of Vina del Mar") demanding changes in U.S. aid and trade policies. Major Nixon proposals included: giving increased responsibility for development assistance decisions to multilateral agencies, establishing an Under Secretary of State for Inter-American Affairs, a commitment to lead a vigorous effort to reduce nontariff barriers and to press for a liberal system of generalized tariff preferences for all developing nations and an immediate untying of U.S. aid to purchases in the United States. *(For text, see p. 112-A.)*

Previously (in June), the Administration had eliminated the controversial aid policy of "additionality," which required recipient countries to purchase in the United States specific items that they probably would otherwise not buy or would buy elsewhere.

Alliance for Progress Hearings. The House Foreign Affairs Subcommittee on Inter-American Affairs conducted a series of hearings on the Alliance during March-May 1969, which formed the basis of a report calling for new directions in the Alliance.

Foreign Aid

Congress in 1969 continued the downward trend in U.S. foreign assistance, passing Dec. 19 a bill (HR 14580) authorizing $1.6 billion in economic assistance and $350 million in military assistance. The Administration had requested $2.63 billion (the lowest request in the history of the aid program).

Legislation (HR 15149) making appropriations for the foreign aid program, Peace Corps, international lending banks and Foreign Military Credit Sales Program was one of the last regular appropriations bills to be acted on by Congress in 1969. The House Dec. 9 approved a $1.6 billion appropriation for the economic and military aid program; and the Senate Dec. 18 voted a $2.2 billion appropriation for the program. But because the Senate tabled the conference report on the bill, final action on the appropriations was delayed until 1970. Continuing appropriations for the foreign aid programs at the fiscal 1969 level were made pending final action on HR 15149.

Congress approved establishment of a semiautonomous Overseas Private Investment Corporation to stimulate private initiatives in development activities. The agency was a principal new feature of the Administration's foreign aid legislation, as was increased emphasis on technical assistance programs through creation of a new Technical Assistance Bureau.

Debate on the foreign aid program on the floor of both houses was concentrated on a House addition of $50 million in military aid to South Korea and $54.5 million to Nationalist China. The Senate had opposed the additions (which had not been requested by the Administration), and had omitted them in the authorization bill. Senate objection to the Taiwan funds was the principal reason for rejection of the conference report on the appropriations bill.

Foreign Aid Reviews. The President Sept. 24 appointed a high-level task force of private citizens to review U.S. foreign aid policies and present its findings by February 1970. Mr. Nixon said the panel was instructed to take into account the recommendations of the Pearson Commission, established in August 1968, and headed by former Canadian Prime Minister Lester B. Pearson. In its Oct. 1 report to the World Bank, the Commission had strongly urged greater development assistance efforts by industrialized nations.

IDA Funds. Congress in 1969 authorized a $480 million U.S. share of a $1.2 billion replenishment of the loan fund of the International Development Association (IDA), the soft-loan window of the World Bank Group. The legislature had failed to act on a request for replenishment in 1968, but the Nixon Administration resubmitted the request, reflecting the new President's desire to channel U.S. aid increasingly through multilateral agencies. Early in 1969, Congress appropriated $160 million for fiscal 1969; appropriations for fiscal 1970 were contained in the foreign operations bill (HR 15149). Action on HR 15149 was not completed in 1969.

Peace Corps. Congress authorized $98,450,000 (HR 11039) for Peace Corps operations in fiscal 1970, less than the $101.1 million requested by the Administration. No final action on appropriations was taken. The new Peace Corps director, Joseph H. Blatchford, Sept. 23 announced several changes in the agency to remedy what he said were defects in the program. Among the changes: recruitment of volunteers with special skills and training, more vigorous recruitment of minority groups and a decision to allow 200 volunteers with dependents to enter the program.

Trade Policy, Quotas

The Administration had to contend with conflicting trade demands during 1969. On the one hand, it faced increasing Congressional pressures to restrict imports of such goods as textiles, footwear, dairy products, meat and iron and steel products. At the same time, it had to deal with major trade partners which were reluctant to agree to voluntary export controls.

Administration trade officials focused their efforts on obtaining a voluntary textile trade arrangement with principal exporters—particularly Japan—as well as on pressing the Japanese to eliminate quotas on over 100 products of interest to U.S. exporters. Before the end of the year, Japan had agreed to liberalize many of its quotas by 1972 and to discuss possible action on the remaining restrictions. No final agreement was reached on extending and expanding the voluntary international textile trade agreement, however.

Several Members introduced bills which would establish statutory quotas on textiles and other products, but Congress took no action on them until late in the year in order to give the Administration an opportunity to negotiate voluntary arrangements with other nations. Congressional impatience was finally registered by inclusion in the Senate version of the tax reform bill (HR 13270) an amendment authorizing the President to impose import restrictions to protect American industries and requiring him to remove those restrictions on goods from countries which did not have such restrictions on U.S. goods. The provision, however, was omitted in the final bill.

The predominant attitude in Congress, as well as the major theme of Administration policy, was to emphasize "fair trade" rather than "free trade." This change in emphasis from the era of the Kennedy Round of tariff cuts was demonstrated by Congressional controversy over the nomination of Carl J. Gilbert, an advocate of free trade policies, to be U.S. Special Representative for Trade Negotiations.

President Nixon Nov. 18 sent the Administration's trade bill to Congress, but no action was taken on the measure in 1969. *(For text, see p. 101-A.)*

In his message, Mr. Nixon declared that the legislation was "modest in scope but significant in its impact." The President requested:

- Authority to make modest reductions in tariffs (previous authority lapsed in 1967 with expiration of the 1962 Trade Expansion Act).
- Repeal of the American Selling Price System of fixing duties, which primarily affected chemical imports.
- Changes in current escape-clause provisions which would make it easier for industries that could show injury from imports to gain relief through temporary import restrictions.
- Liberalization of adjustment-assistance provisions to allow workers and individual firms to receive financial aid if they demonstrated injury from imports.
- Expansion of Presidential authority to retaliate against nations that erected "unfair" barriers against U.S. exports (the authority would include the imposition of duties).

The President also announced establishment of a commission to review U.S. trade policies.

The President's trade message had a generally favorable reception on Capitol Hill, but controversy was expected to arise over repeal of the American Selling Price.

In addition to the trade message, the President announced he would seek legislation modifying U.S. trade policies to Latin America and other developing regions.

Other Developments

Recognition Policy. The Senate Sept. 25 passed a resolution (S Res 205) declaring that "when the United States recognizes a foreign government and exchanges diplomatic representatives with it, this does not of itself imply that the United States approves of the form, ideology or policy of that foreign government." Sponsors

of the resolution said it was designed to clarify U.S. recognition policy but was not aimed specifically at laying the groundwork for recognizing Communist China. Administration officials endorsed the resolution, stating that it simply reflected established U.S. policy on recognizing foreign governments.

U.S. Relations with Communist China. U.S. relations with Communist China remained substantially unchanged during 1969, despite some attempts by the Administration to improve the situation. The Chinese Feb. 18 canceled an agreement to resume bilateral talks with the United States in Warsaw. The Administration continued to oppose seating Communist China at the United Nations, although several Members—including Sens. Javits, Kennedy and Henry M. Jackson (D Wash.)—urged the Administration to adopt a less rigid policy.

The State Department extended for two six-month periods the ban on travel to Communist China, North Vietnam, North Korea and Cuba, but July 21 announced a relaxation of U.S. restrictions on China travel, which would apply to scholars, students, scientists, physicians and journalists. However, the effect of the relaxation was weakened by the fact that travellers still had to obtain entry visas from Chinese authorities, who had granted no visas to Americans since 1966.

In his first news conference Jan. 27, Mr. Nixon said that "until some changes occur on (the Chinese) side...I see no immediate prospect of any change in our policy." Secretary of State Rogers, speaking in Australia Aug. 8, said the United States would like to resume the Warsaw "dialogue" with China. He said that none of the U.S. initiatives to normalize relations with the country had met with a positive response. *(For text, see p. 1-A.)*

Soviet-Chinese border tension which flared during the summer of 1969 gave rise to considerable U.S. concern, expressed by Under Secretary of State Elliot L. Richardson in a Sept. 5 speech. Richardson emphasized that the United States would not intervene or associate with either side against the other. When tensions subsequently subsided, Secretary Rogers noted (Oct. 12), "I think if they are successful in eliminating their very severe tension on the border that it might give us an opportunity to develop closer relationships both with the Soviet Union and with China."

Toward the end of 1969, there was some indication that a breakthrough in the impasse in U.S.-Chinese relations might be forthcoming. The U.S. ambassador to Poland, Walter J. Stoessel Jr., met briefly Dec. 11 with Chinese charge d'affaires Lei Yang Chen in Warsaw, paving the way for resumption of the bilateral talks Jan. 20, 1970.

On Dec. 19, the State Department announced a relaxation of trade restrictions. Effective Dec. 22, subsidiaries and affiliates of U.S. firms abroad were permitted to sell nonstrategic goods to Communist China and buy Communist Chinese products for resale in foreign markets. Individuals (including art collectors) and museums could bring products of Communist Chinese origin into the United States for noncommercial purposes without a limit on the value (a $100 ceiling had been in effect since July 21). Previous restrictions limiting imports to "accompanied baggage" were also removed.

Middle East. As the Middle East situation continued to be explosive, the Administration, in a departure from previous U.S. policy, agreed early in 1969 to a series of bilateral talks with the Soviet Union, as well as four-power talks which included Britain and France. But the President repeatedly emphasized that a lasting solution could only be negotiated by the parties directly involved.

Mr. Nixon conferred with King Hussein of Jordan (April 8) and Israeli Premier Golda Meir (Sept. 25) when the two leaders visited Washington.

The United States began in September to deliver the first of 50 Phantom jet planes to Israel in accordance with a Congressional directive in the form of an amendment to the 1968 Foreign Assistance Act.

Despite a year of sporadic high-level talks, during which the U.S. and Soviet positions seemed at times more closely aligned, prospects for a settlement continued to appear remote.

In a major foreign policy address Dec. 9, Secretary of State Rogers called on Israel to withdraw from Arab territories occupied in the June 1967 war in return for Arab assurances of a binding commitment to a Middle East peace. He also put on record for the first time the peace proposals made by the United States Oct. 28 during bilateral talks with the Soviet Union:

• A "binding commitment" to peace by the parties directly involved, "including the obligation to prevent hostile acts originating from their respective territories" (a reference particularly to Arab guerrilla terrorist attacks).

• Detailed provisions for peace should be worked out between the parties under the auspices of UN Ambassador Gunnar Jarring (who had been attempting to mediate a settlement in the region).

• "In the context of peace and agreement on specific security safeguards, withdrawal of Israeli forces from Egyptian territory would be required."

Rogers said the Soviet Union had not yet replied to the proposals. He said four-power talks had been resumed. The Secretary also called on Jordan and Israel to negotiate a settlement making Jerusalem a unified and free city.

The Secretary's remarks encountered a cool reception in Israel, Egypt and the Soviet Union.

Espionage Plane. North Korea April 14 announced that it had downed "with a single shot" an unescorted propeller-driven U.S. EC-121 reconnaissance plane. The President responded four days later by terming the act "unprovoked, deliberate and without warning." At no time, he stated, had the plane been within North Korean territorial limits.

He said that although he had discontinued such flights immediately after the incident they had been resumed and would continue with protection in the future. "This is not a threat," he said. "This is simply a statement of fact." *(For text, see p. 17-A.)*

The United States asked the Soviet Union, Japan and South Korea for assistance in locating the crewmen, but no survivors were found. A sharply worded U.S. protest was delivered to North Korean representatives during a meeting at Panmunjom April 17.

Numerous Members of Congress praised the President for his deliberate but firm response to the attack.

Pueblo. North Korea Dec. 22, 1968, released the crew of the U.S. intelligence ship *Pueblo*, captured off the Korean coast Jan. 22, 1968. A special Subcommittee of the House Armed Services Committee held hearings on the Pueblo case during 1969. In its report, released July

28, the Subcommittee stated that a serious deficiency existed in the organizational and administrative military command structure of both the Departments of Defense and Navy.

Foreign Affairs Reorganization. President Nixon March 20 issued an Executive Order (11460) re-establishing the President's Foreign Intelligence Advisory Board, created in 1956 to review foreign intelligence activities of the Central Intelligence Agency and other Government Departments.

Secretary of State Rogers announced May 7 the reactivation of the Board of the Foreign Service and named as its chairman Under Secretary of State Elliot L. Richardson. The Board began a thorough review of the entire foreign affairs personnel structure.

Sen. J. W. Fulbright (D Ark.) Oct. 7 introduced a joint resolution (S J Res 157) to create a Presidential panel to make recommendations on State Department reorganization and reform.

Biafra Aid. As the civil war between the federal government of Nigeria and the secessionist state of Biafra entered its third year, Congressional concern about the prospects of massive starvation in the war-torn region intensified. The issue also captured the attention of the public. Members received thousands of letters from constituents calling for increased U.S. humanitarian relief efforts. Fifty-two Senators Jan. 22 introduced a resolution (S Con Res 3) urging the Nixon Administration to "increase significantly" U.S. assistance.

President Nixon responded to Congressional pressures Feb. 22 by naming Clarence C. Ferguson Jr. as special coordinator for Biafran relief. The Administration also increased U.S. contributions to international relief agencies, including the Red Cross. Like his predecessor, however, Mr. Nixon firmly rejected U.S. military involvement or direct political intervention, despite suggestions by some Members to use diplomatic measures in seeking an immediate cease-fire. Administration witnesses restated their opposition to any military involvement in testimony July 15 before the Senate Judiciary Subcommittee on Refugees and Escapees, whose chairman, Edward M. Kennedy (D Mass.), had urged the United States "to assume some leadership in this area."

Foreign Policy Psychology. The Senate Foreign Relations Committee examined the psychological problems involved in conducting U.S. foreign policy in three days of hearings, during which the panel received testimony from noted scholars in the field of social sciences.

U.S. Rhodesian Policy. The House Foreign Affairs Subcommittee on Africa held a series of hearings during the fall of 1969 on U.S. policy toward Southern Rhodesia In particular, the panel examined the impact of U.S. economic sanctions against the country and whether they should be continued.

U.S. Trade, Aid and Investment Policies. A Joint Economic Subcommittee Dec. 2 began a year-long investigation of U.S. foreign economic policies, with the objective of establishing guidelines for the 1970s.

Treaties. In addition to the nonproliferation treaty, the Senate in 1969 consented to the ratification of seven other treaties.

NIXON WON 74 PERCENT OF TEST ROLL-CALL VOTES

President Nixon won on 74 percent of the 119 Congressional roll-call votes that presented clear-cut tests of support for his views in 1969.

The figures represented a 1-percent decline from the 75-percent support score for 1968, the final year of Lyndon Johnson's Presidency. Mr. Johnson that year took a public stand on 267 of 514 roll-call votes. Mr. Nixon took a position on 119 of 422 roll-call votes.

Mr. Nixon ranked lower in over-all support during his first year in office than did any other President since 1953, when *Congressional Quarterly* Presidential support studies began. A Republican Congress endorsed the opinions of Republican President Dwight D. Eisenhower on 89 percent of test votes. President John F. Kennedy scored 81 percent in 1961, and President Johnson in 1964 —the year after Kennedy's assassination—was backed by Congress on 88 percent of test votes. In his first year after election to a full term, Mr. Johnson was supported on 93 percent of test votes. But Democrats Kennedy and Johnson both had Democratic majorities in Congress.

President Nixon, a Republican, was supported on 72 percent of test votes in the Democratic-controlled House and on 75 percent in the Democratic-controlled Senate. On 47 test votes in the House, Mr. Nixon lost 13. On 72 test votes in the Senate, he lost 17.

But on *CQ* key votes in the Senate, the President lost five out of nine on which he expressed an opinion. In the House, he lost only two of seven on which his views were made public.

Mr. Nixon's over-all score was determined in large part from bipartisan support in Congress. Of the 278 roll-call votes in which bipartisanship occurred in both Houses, President Nixon took stands on 79. He won on 63 of his positions and lost on 16.

Eastern Members of Congress in both parties gave the President slightly more support than any other regional group, although support was generally evenly divided among the nation's four geographical areas. (*See regional breakdown below.*)

Foreign Policy. Large majorities in both parties in 1969 gave broad backing to President Nixon on legislation affecting foreign affairs. In the House, the President won approval of 80 percent of those bills on which he took a stand. In the Senate, his positions were supported on 75 percent of test votes.

Domestic Policy. On internal matters, however, Mr. Nixon ran into obstacles, particularly on tax reform, civil rights and Social Security increases. The House endorsed the President's views on 71 percent of the votes, while the Senate gave Mr. Nixon support on 68 percent of votes on domestic matters.

Ground Rules

CQ's 1969 Presidential support study was based on 119 test votes on which there was a clear indication, as revealed in President Nixon's own messages and public statements, that he would have supported or opposed the proposals put to a vote. (*See box p. 30.*)

Nixon Victories and Defeats

Supreme Court. The most publicized issue on which the Senate did not consent to President Nixon's recommendation was its failure to confirm the nomination of Clement F. Haynsworth Jr. as Supreme Court Justice. Seventeen Republicans were among those who voted against confirmation in the 45-55 vote.

ABM. The Senate's refusal, by a 50-50 vote, to cut defense funding authority for an antiballistic missile system was Mr. Nixon's most notable victory during the first session of Congress.

Draft. Most significant long-range victory for the President was winning his appeal for reform of the Selective Service System. The House approved his recommendation Oct. 30 by a 383-12 vote. The Senate Nov. 19 approved it by voice vote.

Tax Reform. Realigning the tax structure was an issue on which the President suffered a long series of setbacks. On 13 test votes on tax reform in the Senate, Mr. Nixon lost 10, including questions on oil depletion allowances, personal exemptions and passage of the Senate version of the tax reform bill. A conference committee changed the bill to make it more acceptable to Mr. Nixon.

Social Security. Both houses rejected the President's plea to hold Social Security payment increases to 10 percent, voting instead for 15-percent hikes.

Vietnam Resolution. The House, by a 334-55 vote, passed a resolution (H Res 613) commending President' Nixon's efforts to achieve "peace with justice" in Vietnam.

Minority Hiring. The House, by a 156-208 vote, sided with the Administration in rejecting an amendment which would have killed the President's minority hiring plan for federal contractors.

Other. The President also won partial or compromise victories in the general areas of school desegregation, extension of the surtax, voting rights and farm subsidies.

Average Scores

Composites of Republican and Democratic scores for over-all support and opposition for 1969 and the 90th Congress (1967-68):

	Nixon 1969		Johnson 90th Congress	
	DEM.	REP.	DEM.	REP.
SUPPORT				
Senate	47%	66%	55%	50%
House	48	57	56	48
OPPOSITION				
Senate	39%	23%	24%	33%
House	38	31	18	40

Nixon support scores on 24 foreign policy roll calls in 1969 (19 in the Senate, 5 in the House), compared with 90th Congress scores:

	Nixon 1969 DEM.	Nixon 1969 REP.	Johnson 90th Congress DEM.	Johnson 90th Congress REP.
SUPPORT				
Senate	66%	72%	59%	57%
House	63	51	66	44
OPPOSITION				
Senate	21%	16%	21%	24%
House	19	33	18	43

Nixon support scores on 95 domestic policy roll calls in 1969 (53 in the Senate, 42 in the House), compared with 90th Congress scores:

	Nixon 1969 DEM.	Nixon 1969 REP.	Johnson 90th Congress DEM.	Johnson 90th Congress REP.
SUPPORT				
Senate	40%	64%	53%	47%
House	46	58	67	49
OPPOSITION				
Senate	45%	25%	25%	36%
House	41	31	18	39

Breakdown by Region

Regional over-all support scores for 1969:

	East	West	South	Midwest
DEMOCRATS				
Senate	50%	47%	48%	42%
House	49	48	47	47
REPUBLICANS				
Senate	66%	67%	61%	69%
House	58	55	55	58

Regional over-all opposition scores for 1969:

	East	West	South	Midwest
DEMOCRATS				
Senate	40%	35%	38%	43%
House	40	36	38	38
REPUBLICANS				
Senate	26%	22%	24%	19%
House	30	28	37	31

Individual Highs, Lows

Highest individual scorers in Nixon support—those who voted "with" the President most often in 1969:

Not eligible for all roll calls in 1969.

HIGH SCORERS—OVER-ALL SUPPORT

SENATE

Democrats		Republicans	
Holland (Fla.)	67%	Bennett (Utah)	88%
McGee (Wyo.)	64	Allott (Colo.)	81
Jackson (Wash.)	61	Pearson (Kan.)	81
Dodd (Conn.)	60	Boggs (Del.)	78
Spong (Va.)	60	Cotton (N.H.)	78
Byrd (Va.)	58	Scott (Pa.)	78
Harris (Okla.)	57	Hruska (Neb.)	76
Pastore (R.I.)	57	Bellmon (Okla.)	76
		Packwood (Ore.)	76

HOUSE

Democrats		Republicans	
Boggs (La.)	72%	Frelinghuysen (N.J.)	79%
Hamilton (Ind.)	68	Byrnes (Wis.)	79
Mahon (Texas)	68	Keith (Mass.)	77
McFall (Calif.)	66	Ford (Mich.)	76
Murphy (Ill.)	66	Wilson (Calif.)	74
Jones (Ala.)	64	Mayne (Iowa)	74
Udall (Ariz.)	64	Davis (Wis.)	74
Alexander (Ark.)	64	Schwengel (Iowa)	72
Burke (Mass.)	64	Shriver (Kan.)	72
Stratton (N.Y.)	64	Beall (Md.)	72
Vigorito (Pa.)	64	Robison (N.Y.)	72
		Bow (Ohio)	72

Highest individual scorers in Nixon opposition—those who voted "against" the President most often in 1969:

HIGH SCORERS—OVER-ALL OPPOSITION

SENATE

Democrats		Republicans	
Young (Ohio)	58%	Hatfield (Ore.)	44%
Nelson (Wis.)	57	Cook (Ky.)	36
Allen (Ala.)	56	Williams (Del.)	33
McGovern (S.D.)	53	Case (N.J.)	33
Proxmire (Wis.)	53	Javits (N.Y.)	33
Hartke (Ind.)	49	Schweiker (Pa.)	32
Byrd (W.Va.)	47	Gurney (Fla.)	31
Ervin (N.C.)	46	Smith (Maine)	31

HOUSE

Democrats		Republicans	
Randall (Mo.)	64%	Gross (Iowa)	64%
Hagan (Ga.)	62	Crane (Ill.)*	63
Brinkley (Ga.)	60	Burke (Fla.)	55
Rarick (La.)	60	Harsha (Ohio)	53
Dowdy (Texas)	60	Scott (Va.)	51
Flowers (Ala.)	57	Scherle (Iowa)	49
Henderson (N.C.)	57	Clancy (Ohio)	49
Jones (N.C.)	57	Miller (Ohio)	49
Gaydos (Pa.)	57	McClure (Idaho)	47
Hungate (Mo.)	55	Foreman (N.M.)	47
Daniel (Va.)	55	Duncan (Tenn.)	47

Ground Rules for CQ Presidential Support-Opposition

● **Presidential Issues**—*CQ* analyzes all messages, press conference remarks and other public statements of the President to determine what he personally, as distinct from other Administration spokesmen, does or does not want in the way of legislative action.

● **Borderline Cases**—By the time an issue reaches a vote, it may differ from the original form on which the President expressed himself. In such cases, *CQ* analyzes the measure to determine whether, on balance, the features favored by the President outweigh those he opposes or vice versa. Only then is the vote classified.

● **Important Votes Excluded**—Occasionally, important measures are so extensively amended on the floor that it is impossible to characterize final passage as a victory or defeat for the President.

● **Motions**—Roll calls on motions to recommit, to reconsider or to table often are key tests that govern the legislative outcome. Such votes are necessarily included in the Nixon support tabulations.

● **Rules**—In the House, debate on most significant bills is governed by rules that restrict time and may bar floor amendments. These rules must be adopted by the House before the bills in question may be considered. Members may vote for the rule, in order to permit debate, although they intend to vote against the bill. Generally, however, a vote against a rule is a vote

against the bill, and vice versa, since rejection of the rule prevents consideration of the bill. *CQ* assumes that if the President favored a bill, he favored the rule, unless it was a closed rule that would prevent amendments he wanted.

● **Appropriations**—Generally, roll calls on passage of appropriation bills are not included in this tabulation, since it is rarely possible to determine the President's position on the over-all revisions Congress almost invariably makes in the sums allowed. Votes to cut or increase specific funds requested in the President's Budget, however, are included.

● **Failures to Vote**—In tabulating the Support or Opposition scores of Members on the selected Nixon-issue roll calls, *CQ* counts only "yea" and "nay" votes on the ground that only these affect the outcome. Most failures to vote reflect absences because of illness or official business.

● **Weighting**—All Nixon-issue roll calls have equal statistical weight in the analysis. Any system of differential weighting would make the analysis subjective and less useful.

● **Changed Position**—Presidential Support is determined by the position of the President at the time of a vote even though that position may be different from an earlier position, or may have been reversed after the vote was taken.

Presidential Support Since 1953

Congressional Quarterly began making studies of Presidential support from the House and Senate in 1953. The highest percentage of Congressional backing of an Administration was 93 percent for President Lyndon B. Johnson in 1965. The lowest was 52 percent in 1959 for President Dwight D. Eisenhower.

Following is a year-by-year summary of Congressional support since 1953:

1953—Eisenhower	89%		1962—Kennedy	85%
1954—Eisenhower	83		1963—Kennedy	87
1955—Eisenhower	75		1964—Johnson	88
1956—Eisenhower	70		1965—Johnson	93
1957—Eisenhower	68		1966—Johnson	79
1958—Eisenhower	76		1967—Johnson	79
1959—Eisenhower	52		1968—Johnson	75·
1960—Eisenhower	65		1969—Nixon	74
1961—Kennedy	81			

Senate All Issues—1969 & 90th Congress

1. Over-All Support Score, 1969. Percentage of 72 Nixon-issue roll calls in 1969—both foreign and domestic—on which Senator voted "yea" or "nay" *in agreement* with the President's position. Failures to vote lower both Support and Opposition scores.

2. Over-All Opposition Score, 1969. Percentage of 72 Nixon-issue roll calls in 1969—both foreign and domestic—on which Senator voted "yea" or "nay" *in disagreement* with the President's position. Failures to vote lower both Support and Opposition scores.

3. Over-All Support Score, 90th Congress. Percentage of 329 Johnson-issue roll calls in 1967 and 1968—both foreign and domestic—on which Senator voted "yea" or "nay" *in agreement* with the President's position. Failures to vote lower both Support and Opposition scores.

4. Over-All Opposition Score, 90th Congress. Percentage of 329 Johnson-issue roll calls in 1967 and 1968—both foreign and domestic—on which Senator voted "yea" or "nay" *in disagreement* with the President's position. Failures to vote lower both Support and Opposition scores.

Headnotes
† Not eligible for all roll calls in 1969.
* Not eligible for all roll calls in 90th Congress.
— Not a Member of the 90th Congress.

	1	2	3	4
ALABAMA				
Allen	38	56	—	—
Sparkman	49	22	58	29
ALASKA				
Gravel	49	26	—	—
Stevens	67	15	—	—
ARIZONA				
Fannin	63	29	35	48
Goldwater	39	19	—	—
ARKANSAS				
Fulbright	35	44	31	28
McClellan	47	39	47	42
CALIFORNIA				
Cranston	47	32	—	—
Murphy	67	24	32	35
COLORADO				
Allott	81	11	49	37
Dominick	63	21	43	37
CONNECTICUT				
Dodd	60	38	54	15
Ribicoff	42	38	58	21
DELAWARE				
Boggs	78	19	64	32
Williams	67	33	44	53
FLORIDA				
Holland	67	33	60	38
Gurney	61	31	—	—
GEORGIA				
Russell	42	36	34	37
Talmadge	47	39	40	36
HAWAII				
Inouye	43	36	64	12
Fong	65	21	66	24
IDAHO				
Church	44	44	41	30
Jordan	71	25	49	45
ILLINOIS				
Percy	71	18	58	18
Smith	36†	22†	—	—
INDIANA				
Bayh	47	35	54	21
Hartke	39	49	48	25

	1	2	3	4
IOWA	-			
Hughes	46	39	—	—
Miller	65	22	49	38
KANSAS				
Dole	75	21	—	—
Pearson	81	14	62	33
KENTUCKY				
Cook	44	36	—	—
Cooper	50	25	54	26
LOUISIANA				
Ellender	56	32	43	40
Long	47	31	51	30
MAINE				
Muskie	51	42	68	11
Smith	69	31	61	29
MARYLAND				
Tydings	40	40	61	18
Mathias	57	21	—	—
MASSACHUSETTS				
Kennedy	44	44	53	11
Brooke	57	26	60	22
MICHIGAN				
Hart	44	42	69	18
Griffin	74	13	62	24
MINNESOTA				
McCarthy	29	43	31	07
Mondale	47	42	71	15
MISSISSIPPI				
Eastland	35	44	41	40
Stennis	56	40	49	44
MISSOURI				
Eagleton	47	38	—	—
Symington	44	22	61	27
MONTANA				
Mansfield	44	38	60	16
Metcalf	43	42	64	16
NEBRASKA				
Curtis	69	28	42	50
Hruska	76	19	39	45
NEVADA				
Bible	47	38	54	30
Cannon	42	42	57	29

	1	2	3	4
NEW HAMPSHIRE				
McIntyre	53	38	71	19
Cotton	78	18	40	46
NEW JERSEY				
Williams	51	39	74	15
Case	60	33	72	20
NEW MEXICO				
Anderson	50	13	69	19
Montoya	43	42	55	14
NEW YORK				
Goodell	53	25	74*	4*
Javits	63	33	58	13
NORTH CAROLINA				
Ervin	46	46	41	43
Jordan	47	42	44	34
NORTH DAKOTA				
Burdick	50	36	66	27
Young	72	26	51	43
OHIO				
Young	33	58	60	24
Saxbe	57	25	—	—
OKLAHOMA				
Harris	57	40	63	12
Bellmon	76	17	—	—
OREGON				
Hatfield	50	44	47	27
Packwood	76	21	—	—
PENNSYLVANIA				
Schweiker	68	32	—	—
Scott	78	18	58	23
RHODE ISLAND				
Pastore	57	36	62	14
Pell	51	42	67	20
SOUTH CAROLINA				
Hollings	38	32	39	36
Thurmond	63	26	41	50
SOUTH DAKOTA				
McGovern	40	53	50	27
Mundt	53	11	48	45
TENNESSEE				
Gore	38	38	53	24
Baker	65	17	45	34

PRESIDENTIAL SUPPORT 1969 AND 90th CONGRESS

	1	2	3	4
TEXAS				
Yarborough	46	35	60	18
Tower	69	15	29	32
UTAH				
Moss	40	39	66	22
Bennett	88	11	43	36
VERMONT				
Aiken	67	24	57	26
Prouty	60	25	54	30
VIRGINIA				
Byrd	58	42	49	47
Spong	60	38	57	36
WASHINGTON				
Jackson	61	31	76	16
Magnuson	42	39	64	18
WEST VIRGINIA				
Byrd	46	47	57	36
Randolph	56	40	66	23
WISCONSIN				
Nelson	36	57	58	28
Proxmire	47	53	69	31
WYOMING				
McGee	64	24	63	13
Hansen	72	19	44	44

Democrats in this type; *Republicans in italics*

Senate Domestic Policy—1969 & 90th Congress

1. Domestic Policy Support Score, 1969. Percentage of 53 Nixon-issue roll calls on domestic matters in 1969 on which Senator voted "yea" or "nay" *in agreement* with the President's position. Failures to vote lower both Support and Opposition scores.

2. Domestic Policy Opposition Score, 1969. Percentage of 53 Nixon-issue roll calls on domestic matters in 1969 on which Senator voted "yea" or "nay" *in disagreement* with the President's position. Failures to vote lower both Support and Opposition scores.

3. Domestic Policy Support Score, 90th Congress. Percentage of 249 Johnson-issue roll calls on domestic matters in 1967 and 1968 on which Senator voted "yea" or "nay" *in agreement* with the President's position. Failures to vote lower both Support and Opposition scores.

4. Domestic Policy Opposition Score, 90th Congress. Percentage of 249 Johnson-issue roll calls on domestic matters in 1967 and 1968 on which Senator voted "yea" or "nay" *in disagreement* with the President's position. Failures to vote lower both Support and Opposition scores.

Headnotes

† Not eligible for all roll calls in 1969.
* Not eligible for all roll calls in 90th Congress.
— Not a Member of the 90th Congress.

	1	2	3	4
ALABAMA				
Allen	42	53	—	—
Sparkman	42	30	52	35
ALASKA				
Gravel	42	32	—	—
Stevens	62	17	—	—
ARIZONA				
Fannin	70	23	34	51
Goldwater	43	17	—	—
ARKANSAS				
Fulbright	21	53	25	32
McClellan	53	36	48	41
CALIFORNIA				
Cranston	38	40	—	—
Murphy	72	17	30	35
COLORADO				
Allott	81	13	46	40
Dominick	68	21	45	39
CONNECTICUT				
Dodd	57	40	55	14
Ribicoff	26	49	60	20
DELAWARE				
Boggs	72	25	60	36
Williams	70	30	42	56
FLORIDA				
Holland	64	36	57	41
Gurney	64	28	—	—
GEORGIA				
Russell	47	30	34	40
Talmadge	49	40	37	36
HAWAII				
Inouye	30	45	61	15
Fong	58	28	63	25
IDAHO				
Church	36	53	41	29
Jordan	72	26	49	44
ILLINOIS				
Percy	68	23	53	24
Smith	36†	29†	—	—
INDIANA				
Bayh	34	45	55	22
Hartke	23	62	48	23

	1	2	3	4
IOWA				
Hughes	32	51	—	—
Miller	66	25	45	41
KANSAS				
Dole	77	19	—	—
Pearson	77	15	56	37
KENTUCKY				
Cook	38	40	—	—
Cooper	42	30	52	31
LOUISIANA				
Ellender	51	34	42	40
Long	55	25	51	32
MAINE				
Muskie	38	55	67	11
Smith	62	38	62	29
MARYLAND				
Tydings	30	53	60	20
Mathias	49	26	—	—
MASSACHUSETTS				
Kennedy	30	58	50	14
Brooke	47	34	59	26
MICHIGAN				
Hart	28	57	65	23
Griffin	74	11	58	30
MINNESOTA				
McCarthy	21	53	25	6
Mondale	38	55	65	18
MISSISSIPPI				
Eastland	43	38	41	39
Stennis	57	38	47	46
MISSOURI				
Eagleton	42	47	—	—
Symington	36	26	63	25
MONTANA				
Mansfield	32	43	56	16
Metcalf	32	51	60	18
NEBRASKA				
Curtis	79	19	39	53
Hruska	79	17	37	47
NEVADA				
Bible	49	38	59	28
Cannon	40	47	58	30

	1	2	3	4
NEW HAMPSHIRE				
McIntyre	45	47	71	18
Cotton	75	19	43	45
NEW JERSEY				
Williams	36	53	73	17
Case	49	43	69	23
NEW MEXICO				
Anderson	42	15	69	19
Montoya	38	47	61	13
NEW YORK				
Goodell	49	34	65*	5*
Javits	55	43	54	17
NORTH CAROLINA				
Ervin	53	40	40	41
Jordan	53	40	44	35
NORTH DAKOTA				
Burdick	47	40	68	23
Young	70	28	50	45
OHIO				
Young	21	70	60	24
Saxbe	51	30	—	—
OKLAHOMA				
Harris	45	53	57	13
Bellmon	72	23	—	—
OREGON				
Hatfield	34	58	44	33
Packwood	70	26	—	—
PENNSYLVANIA				
Schweiker	58	42	—	—
Scott	72	23	57	27
RHODE ISLAND				
Pastore	47	45	57	17
Pell	40	55	67	25
SOUTH CAROLINA				
Hollings	40	28	40	35
Thurmond	68	19	39	53
SOUTH DAKOTA				
McGovern	28	64	45	29
Mundt	53	9	47	46
TENNESSEE				
Gore	32	49	53	26
Baker	66	21	44	37

PRESIDENTIAL SUPPORT 1969 AND 90th CONGRESS

	1	2	3	4
TEXAS				
Yarborough	38	45	59	20
Tower	75	9	27	34
UTAH				
Moss	30	51	61	26
Bennett	83	15	40	39
VERMONT				
Aiken	60	30	55	28
Prouty	57	32	50	31
VIRGINIA				
Byrd	58	42	48	49
Spong	53	43	55	38
WASHINGTON				
Jackson	47	42	73	18
Magnuson	30	47	64	18
WEST VIRGINIA				
Byrd	42	49	57	35
Randolph	49	49	65	23
WISCONSIN				
Nelson	23	68	57	30
Proxmire	34	66	67	33
WYOMING				
McGee	57	32	64	16
Hansen	75	17	42	47

Democrats in this type; *Republicans in italics*

Senate Foreign Policy—1969 & 90th Congress

1. Foreign Policy Support Score, 1969. Percentage of 19 Nixon-issue roll calls in the field of foreign policy in 1969 on which Senator voted "yea" or "nay" *in agreement* with the President's position. Failures to vote lower both Support and Opposition scores.

2. Foreign Policy Opposition Score, 1969. Percentage of 19 Nixon-issue roll calls in the field of foreign policy in 1969 on which Senator voted "yea" or "nay" *in disagreement* with the President's position. Failures to vote lower both Support and Opposition scores.

3. Foreign Policy Support Score, 90th Congress. Percentage of 80 Johnson-issue roll calls in the field of foreign policy in 1967 and 1968 on which Senator voted "yea" or "nay" *in agreement* with the President's position. Failures to vote lower both Support and Opposition scores.

4. Foreign Policy Opposition Score, 90th Congress. Percentage of 80 Johnson-issue roll calls in the field of foreign policy in 1967 and 1968 on which Senator voted "yea" or "nay" *in disagreement* with the President's position. Failures to vote lower both Support and Opposition scores.

Headnotes

† Not eligible for all roll calls in 1969.
* Not eligible for all roll calls in 90th Congress.
— Not a Member of the 90th Congress.

	1	2	3	4		1	2	3	4		1	2	3	4					
ALABAMA					**IOWA**					**NEW HAMPSHIRE**					PRESIDENTIAL SUPPORT 1969 AND 90th CONGRESS				
Allen	26	63	—	—	**Hughes**	84	5	—	—	**McIntyre**	74	11	70	23					
Sparkman	68	0	79	11	*Miller*	63	16	61	30	*Cotton*	84	16	30	48					
ALASKA					**KANSAS**					**NEW JERSEY**									
Gravel	68	11	—	—	*Dole*	68	26	—	—	**Williams**	95	0	75	8					
Stevens	79	11	—	—	*Pearson*	89	11	79	20	*Case*	89	5	79	9					
ARIZONA					**KENTUCKY**					**NEW MEXICO**						1	2	3	4
Fannin	42	47	39	38	*Cook*	63	26	—	—	**Anderson**	74	5	71	16					
Goldwater	26	26	—	—	*Cooper*	74	11	61	10	**Montoya**	58	26	39	18	**TEXAS**				
ARKANSAS					**LOUISIANA**					**NEW YORK**					**Yarborough**	68	5	63	13
Fulbright	74	21	49	16	**Ellender**	68	26	46	38	*Goodell*	63	0	100*	0*	*Tower*	53	32	39	28
McClellan	32	47	43	43	**Long**	26	47	51	24	*Javits*	84	5	70	1	**UTAH**				
CALIFORNIA					**MAINE**					**NORTH CAROLINA**					**Moss**	68	5	81	10
Cranston	74	11	—	—	**Muskie**	89	5	69	10	**Ervin**	26	63	43	46	*Bennett*	100	0	55	26
Murphy	53	42	36	34	*Smith*	89	11	59	33	**Jordan**	32	47	45	33	**VERMONT**				
COLORADO					**MARYLAND**					**NORTH DAKOTA**					*Aiken*	84	5	61	19
Allott	79	5	59	29	**Tydings**	68	5	63	11	**Burdick**	58	26	59	38	*Prouty*	68	5	66	25
Dominick	47	21	—	—	*Mathias*	79	5	—	—	**Young**	79	21	53	36	**VIRGINIA**				
CONNECTICUT					**MASSACHUSETTS**					**OHIO**					**Byrd**	58	42	50	43
Dodd	68	32	51	16	**Kennedy**	84	5	65	3	**Young**	68	26	61	25	**Spong**	79	21	64	31
Ribicoff	84	5	51	26	*Brooke*	84	5	60	8	*Saxbe*	74	11	—	—	**WASHINGTON**				
DELAWARE					**MICHIGAN**					**OKLAHOMA**					**Jackson**	100	0	88	11
Boggs	95	5	78	20	**Hart**	89	0	81	3	**Harris**	89	5	79	6	**Magnuson**	74	16	64	20
Williams	58	42	49	45	*Griffin*	74	16	74	5	*Bellmon*	89	0	—	—	**WEST VIRGINIA**				
FLORIDA					**MINNESOTA**					**OREGON**					**Byrd**	58	42	56	41
Holland	74	26	73	28	**McCarthy**	53	16	50	9	*Hatfield*	95	5	58	9	**Randolph**	74	16	70	23
Gurney	53	37	—	—	**Mondale**	74	5	88	6	*Packwood*	95	5	—	—	**WISCONSIN**				
GEORGIA					**MISSISSIPPI**					**PENNSYLVANIA**					**Nelson**	74	26	61	21
Russell	26	53	35	28	**Eastland**	11	63	43	43	*Schweiker*	95	5	—	—	**Proxmire**	84	16	75	25
Talmadge	42	37	49	38	**Stennis**	53	47	55	39	*Scott*	95	5	64	14	**WYOMING**				
HAWAII					**MISSOURI**					**RHODE ISLAND**					**McGee**	84	0	59	5
Inouye	79	11	74	5	**Eagleton**	63	11	—	—	**Pastore**	84	11	78	4	**Hansen**	63	26	51	34
Fong	84	0	76	21	**Symington**	68	11	55	33	**Pell**	84	5	68	5					
IDAHO					**MONTANA**					**SOUTH CAROLINA**									
Church	68	21	39	31	**Mansfield**	79	21	75	15	**Hollings**	32	42	36	39					
Jordan	68	21	48	48	**Metcalf**	74	16	74	10	*Thurmond*	47	47	48	44					
ILLINOIS					**NEBRASKA**					**SOUTH DAKOTA**									
Percy	79	5	74	1	*Curtis*	42	53	50	43	**McGovern**	74	21	65	24					
Smith	38†	0†	—	—	*Hruska*	68	26	46	38	*Mundt*	53	16	50	41					
INDIANA					**NEVADA**					**TENNESSEE**									
Bayh	84	5	53	18	**Bible**	42	37	39	39	**Gore**	53	5	54	18					
Hartke	84	11	48	33	**Cannon**	47	26	55	26	*Baker*	63	5	48	24					

Democrats in this type; *Republicans in italics*

House All Issues—1969 & 90th Congress

1. Over-All Support Score, 1969. Percentage of 47 Nixon-issue roll calls in 1969—both foreign and domestic—on which Representative voted "yea" or "nay" *in agreement* with the President's position. Failures to vote lower both Support and Opposition scores.

2. Over-All Opposition Score, 1969. Percentage of 47 Nixon-issue roll calls in 1969—both foreign and domestic—on which Representative voted "yea" or "nay" *in disagreement* with the President's position. Failures to vote lower both Support and Opposition scores.

3. Over-All Support Score, 90th Congress. Percentage of 230 Johnson-issue roll calls in 1967 and 1968—both foreign and domestic—on which Representative voted "yea" or "nay" *in agreement* with the President's position. Failures to vote lower both Support and Opposition scores.

4. Over-All Opposition Score, 90th Congress. Percentage of 230 Johnson-issue roll calls in 1967 and 1968—both foreign and domestic—on which Representative voted "yea" or "nay" *in disagreement* with the President's position. Failures to vote lower both Support and Opposition scores.

Headnotes

† Not eligible for all roll calls in 1969.
* Not eligible for all roll calls in 90th Congress.
— Not a Member of the 90th Congress.

	1	2	3	4
ALABAMA				
3 Andrews	47	36	35	49
7 Bevill	45	43	48	45
5 Flowers	34	57	—	—
8 Jones	64	28	70	17
4 Nichols	40	47	39	43
6 Buchanan	64	30	43	54
2 Dickinson	60	32	31	50
1 Edwards	60	30	40	53
ALASKA				
AL Pollock	45	28	42	35
ARIZONA				
2 Udall	64	34	79	7
1 Rhodes	66	30	46	41
3 Steiger	51	40	40	52
ARKANSAS				
1 Alexander	64	30	—	—
2 Mills	57	26	60	31
4 Pryor	66	32	65	23
3 Hammerschmidt	66	30	50	47
CALIFORNIA				
5 Burton	47	36	81	13
7 Cohelan	49	40	80	10
9 Edwards	23	38	71	10
34 Hanna	52†	22†	64	8
2 Johnson	60	38	86	10
4 Leggett	45	40	68	7
15 McFall	66	30	88	7
8 Miller	51	28	71	4
3 Moss	38	43	69	7
16 Sisk	53	26	73	7
38 Tunney	23	21	72	6
37 Van Deerlin	49	34	79	10
14 Waldie	38	51	79	12
1 Clausen	62†	31†	43	40
10 Gubser	62	30	52	36
11 McCloskey	62	23	65*	23*
6 Mailliard	67†	20†	63	27
18 Mathias	51	19	52	33
33 Pettis	53	38	50	42
12 Talcott	64	28	46	47
13 Teague	62†	31†	51	43
35 Utt	36	26	22	42
36 Wilson	74	9	42	37

	1	2	3	4
Los Angeles Co.				
17 Anderson	51	47	—	—
29 Brown	17	36	48	15
22 Corman	45	26	65	5
21 Hawkins	36	47	62	7
19 Holifield	47	32	79	4
26 Rees	40	32	70	11
30 Roybal	47	43	75	9
31 Wilson	40	38	63	8
28 Bell	47	21	55	18
23 Clawson	45	45	35	51
27 Goldwater	49†	29†	—	—
32 Hosmer	55	19	50	37
24 Lipscomb	19	9	40	54
20 Smith	57	32	39	49
25 Wiggins	64	30	43	45
COLORADO				
4 Aspinall	64	19	65	10
3 Evans	60	32	78	11
1 Rogers	64	34	80	11
2 Brotzman	66	30	60	34
CONNECTICUT				
1 Daddario	49	26	79	7
3 Giaimo	47	38	76	10
5 Monagan	60	30	80	12
2 St. Onge	49	38	47	5
6 Meskill	53	43	57	37
4 Weicker	60	34	—	—
DELAWARE				
AL Roth	70	30	53	42
FLORIDA				
3 Bennett	51	49	60	40
4 Chappell	38	43	—	—
12 Fascell	32	19	84	7
2 Fuqua	47	45	55	33
6 Gibbons	49	38	75	12
7 Haley	36	53	36	61
11 Pepper	47	26	70	7
9 Rogers	47	51	54	43
1 Sikes	57	30	53	32
10 Burke	45	55	36	52
8 Cramer	60	36	39	44
5 Frey	53	38	—	—

	1	2	3	4
GEORGIA				
3 Brinkley	40	60	50	46
7 Davis	47	38	61	31
6 Flynt	34	30	38	44
1 Hagan	36	62	35	46
9 Landrum	45	36	47	20
2 O'Neal	34	43	40	47
10 Stephens	38	26	54	21
8 Stuckey	38	49	48	41
4 Blackburn	49	38	38	43
5 Thompson	55	40	43	50
HAWAII				
AL Matsunaga	60	36	80	6
AL Mink	53	47	84	10
IDAHO				
2 Hansen, O.	60	30	—	—
1 McClure	40	47	39	52
ILLINOIS				
21 Gray	43	32	68	10
24 Price	60	36	90	7
23 Shipley	57	38	67	22
16 Anderson	62	17	59	32
17 Arends	62	21	50	41
14 Erlenborn	66	26	55	35
20 Findley	64	17	48	42
12 McClory	55	23	51	36
18 Michel	64	28	39	45
19 Railsback	55	34	57	36
15 Reid	64	34	44	54
22 Springer	68	30	56	38
Chicago-Cook Co.				
7 Annunzio	62	30	79	7
1 Dawson	15	6	64	3
5 Kluczynski	47	30	70	6
2 Mikva	40	45	—	—
3 Murphy	66	34	87	5
11 Pucinski	32	40	72	11
6 Vacancy				
8 Rostenkowski	49	26	72	6
9 Yates	53	43	81	10
10 Collier	48†	33†	44	47
13 Crane	38†	63†	—	—
4 Derwinski	51	36	40	44

	1	2	3	4
PRESIDENTIAL SUPPORT 1969 AND 90th CONGRESS				

	1	2	3	4
INDIANA				
3 Brademas	53	40	77	8
9 Hamilton	68	32	83	13
11 Jacobs	57	38	68	10
1 Madden	55	43	73	8
4 Adair	57	40	43	41
6 Bray	55	34	41	47
10 Dennis	57	34	—	—
2 Landgrebe	49	38	—	—
7 Myers	58†	42†	45	48
5 Roudebush	53	40	34	43
8 Zion	53	43	45	49
IOWA				
2 Culver	53	40	80	5
5 Smith	60	36	79	10
3 Gross	36	64	30	67
4 Kyl	45	38	44	47
6 Mayne	74	26	56	37
7 Scherle	47	49	38	59
1 Schwengel	72	28	63	30
KANSAS				
2 Mize	68	28	52	40
1 Sebelius	60	30	—	—
4 Shriver	72	26	55	39
5 Skubitz	62	30	47	46
3 Winn	57	32	43	51
KENTUCKY				
2 Natcher	53	47	77	23
7 Perkins	62	36	88	12
1 Stubblefield	47	47	63	23

	1	2	3	4
6 **Watts**	57	36	55	23
5 **Carter**	62	32	49	38
3 *Cowger*	43†	30†	41	30
4 *Snyder*	40	45	37	50
LOUISIANA				
2 **Boggs**	72	21	79	5
3 **Caffery**	43	49	—	—
7 **Edwards**	45	23	57	24
1 **Hebert**	30	9	29	19
4 **Long**	36	49	25	42
5 **Passman**	45	45	37	42
6 **Rarick**	32	60	19	48
4 **Waggonner**	53	45	46	43
MAINE				
2 **Hathaway**	60	36	86	7
1 **Kyros**	62	32	84	9
MARYLAND				
4 **Fallon**	49	26	68	10
7 **Friedel**	62	38	89	7
3 **Garmatz**	55	36	80	9
2 **Long**	51	47	80	13
6 *Beall*	72	28	—	—
8 *Gude*	57	36	69	23
5 *Hogan*	57	36	—	—
1 *Morton*	70	6	47	38
MASSACHUSETTS				
2 **Boland**	53	40	79	7
11 **Burke**	64	36	89	11
4 **Donohue**	62	38	82	8
6 **Harrington**	36†	45†	—	—
9 **Macdonald**	43	53	60	12
9 **McCormack**				
8 **O'Neill**	53	36	75	6
3 **Philbin**	60	36	80	7
1 *Conte*	66	32	65	22
10 *Heckler*	60	32	56	24
12 *Keith*	77	23	61	33
5 *Morse*	47	30	61	20
MICHIGAN				
12 **O'Hara**	57	36	79	6
18 *Broomfield*	64	26	45	20
3 *Brown*	70	23	53	40
10 *Cederberg*	64	11	41	44
6 *Chamberlain*	62	34	49	46
9 *Esch*	68	28	61	28
5 *Ford*	76	18	56	35
8 *Harvey*	57	30	63	31
4 *Hutchinson*	55	40	44	54
19 *McDonald*	62	30	61	34
7 *Riegle*	49	43	62	31
11 *Ruppe*	56†	22†	55	27
9 *Vander Jagt*	62	23	52	35
Detroit-Wayne Co.				
1 **Conyers**	19	45	49	12
13 **Diggs**	34	36	48	5
16 **Dingell**	49	34	74	11
15 **Ford**	49	45	72	11
17 **Griffiths**	53	28	73	10
14 **Nedzi**	57	40	83	8
MINNESOTA				
8 **Blatnik**	38	36	76	7
5 **Fraser**	49	43	80	8
5 **Karth**	55	38	75	8
7 *Langen*	64	32	43	55
3 *MacGregor*	70	23	54	32
2 *Nelsen*	66	21	41	41
1 *Quie*	60	30	62	33
6 *Zwach*	55	43	53	40
MISSISSIPPI				
1 **Abernethy**	45	47	34	57
5 **Colmer**	43	36	35	53
3 **Griffin**	34	40	55*	39*
4 **Montgomery**	38	40	41	55
2 **Whitten**	45	45	45	47
MISSOURI				
5 **Bolling**	49	23	71	6
10 **Burlison**	51	49	—	—
1 **Clay**	28	38	—	—
6 **Hull**	38†	44†	53	32
9 **Hungate**	40	55	63	17
1 **Ichord**	36	53	48	37
4 **Randall**	34	64	59	40
3 **Sullivan**	53	26	79	10

	1	2	3	4
2 **Symington**	57	38	—	—
7 *Hall*	36	34	33	63
MONTANA				
2 **Melcher**	56†	41†	—	—
1 **Olsen**	51	47	71	10
NEBRASKA				
2 *Cunningham*	51	15	44	39
1 *Denney*	47	36	45	47
3 *Martin*	38	30	38	41
NEVADA				
AL **Baring**	30	45	35	46
NEW HAMPSHIRE				
2 *Cleveland*	57	43	52	42
1 *Wyman*	60	36	54	43
NEW JERSEY				
14 **Daniels**	47	45	88	8
13 **Gallagher**	45	30	70	6
9 **Helstoski**	45	47	78	9
11 **Howard**	43	40	81	9
11 **Minish**	55	45	84	11
15 **Patten**	66	34	93	7
10 **Rodino**	49	38	83	10
8 **Roe**	47†	53†	—	—
4 **Thompson**	45	40	67	6
6 *Cahill*	26	2	61	27
12 *Dwyer*	66	21	62	27
5 *Frelinghuysen*	79	19	57	23
1 *Hunt*	57	36	49	47
2 *Sandman*	55	32	47	38
7 *Widnall*	68	21	62	27
NEW MEXICO				
2 *Foreman*	40	47	—	—
1 *Lujan*	45	30	—	—
NEW YORK				
41 **Dulski**	55	40	82	11
34 **Hanley**	55	43	86	10
5 **Lowenstein**	30	51	—	—
39 **McCarthy**	47	43	81	11
25 **Ottinger**	45	53	77	19
1 **Pike**	57	43	73	23
35 **Stratton**	64	34	63	17
3 **Wolff**	38	53	71	17
29 *Button*	55	36	63	15
37 *Conable*	66	21	59	30
28 *Fish*	62	32	—	—
2 *Grover*	55	34	52	46
38 *Hastings*	43	32	—	—
36 *Horton*	60	36	69	22
30 *King*	57	30	40	50
31 *McEwen*	55	34	40	37
27 *McKneally*	64	26	—	—
32 *Pirnie*	60	23	59	28
26 *Reid*	53	40	76	16
33 *Robison*	72	26	63	30
40 *Smith*	62	23	57	32
4 *Wydler*	53	36	54	33
New York City				
7 **Addabbo**	49	47	83	11
24 **Biaggi**	49	51	—	—
23 **Bingham**	40	43	81	8
11 **Brasco**	45	47	83	8
15 **Carey**	23	28	69	9
10 **Celler**	43	26	62	4
12 **Chisholm**	21	47	—	—
9 **Delaney**	38	40	80	15
19 **Farbstein**	38	43	73	11
22 **Gilbert**	55	43	79	10
17 **Koch**	51	45	—	—
16 **Murphy**	60	28	68	7
13 **Podell**	45	43	61*	7*
18 **Powell**	4	2	—	—
14 **Rooney**	60	34	78	5
8 **Rosenthal**	38	53	77	10
20 **Ryan**	45	53	76	18
21 **Scheuer**	36	47	71	11
6 *Halpern*	49	28	71	16
NORTH CAROLINA				
2 **Fountain**	47	53	38	38
4 **Galifianakis**	60	38	64	31
5 **Henderson**	40	57	49	46
1 **Jones**	36	57	43	44
7 **Lennon**	43	47	39	59
6 **Preyer**	62	34	—	—

	1	2	3	4
11 **Taylor**	45	43	54	41
10 *Broyhill*	60	40	46	53
9 *Jonas*	62†	33†	43	51
5 *Mizell*	57	40	—	—
8 *Ruth*	57	40	—	—
NORTH DAKOTA				
1 *Andrews*	60	21	55	34
2 *Kleppe*	58†	36†	45	46
OHIO				
9 **Ashley**	57	30	74	9
20 **Feighan**	57	36	80	6
18 **Hays**	36	40	63	12
19 **Kirwan**	6	2	73	7
21 **Stokes**	38	51	—	—
22 **Vanik**	55	43	83	10
17 *Ashbrook*	34	43	26	57
14 *Ayres*	70	23	56	31
8 *Betts*	60	36	47	49
16 *Bow*	72	21	40	36
7 *Brown*	66	26	44	44
2 *Clancy*	47	49	38	50
12 *Devine*	43	38	37	53
6 *Harsha*	38	53	41	49
5 *Latta*	51	34	46	44
24 *Lukens*	40	32	38	40
4 *McCulloch*	62	32	54	31
10 *Miller*	51	49	45	55
23 *Minshall*	55	36	39	42
13 *Mosher*	64	28	59	30
11 *Stanton*	70	23	63	31
1 *Taft*	66	19	50*	36*
3 *Whalen*	62	36	72	24
15 *Wylie*	60	36	53	44
OKLAHOMA				
3 **Albert**	62	28	90	8
2 **Edmondson**	43	36	77	16
4 **Jarman**	47	40	48	46
4 **Steed**	43	34	67	25
1 *Belcher*	57	36	42	49
6 *Camp*	47	32	—	—
OREGON				
3 **Green**	57	23	66	14
2 **Ullman**	55	34	74	14
4 *Dellenback*	64	30	59	33
1 *Wyatt*	60	23	48	35
PENNSYLVANIA				
25 **Clark**	42	38	67	13
21 **Dent**	43	36	67	7
11 **Flood**	60	40	77	9
20 **Gaydos**	43	57	—	—
14 **Moorhead**	55	40	77	5
26 **Morgan**	49	43	82	8
15 **Rooney**	57	34	77	10
24 **Vigorito**	64	34	83	11
5 **Yatron**	51	47	—	—
8 *Biester*	62	36	66	31
18 *Corbett*	68	28	60	26
13 *Coughlin*	64	34	—	—
16 *Eshleman*	53	40	49	45
27 *Fulton*	51	45	65	31
19 *Goodling*	51	40	44	54
23 *Johnson*	60	32	51	43
10 *McDade*	70	30	66	26
22 *Saylor*	40	36	44	44
17 *Schneebeli*	66	21	54	45
12 *Whalley*	36	21	44	44
7 *Williams*	53	40	49	43
Philadelphia City				
1 **Barrett**	51	38	77	7
3 **Byrne**	49	38	90	7
4 **Eilberg**	47	40	85	7
5 **Green**	51	45	82	7
2 **Nix**	53	45	79	6
RHODE ISLAND				
1 **St. Germain**	43	47	77	8
2 **Tiernan**	51	47	80*	9*
SOUTH CAROLINA				
3 **Dorn**	51	40	45	40
5 **Gettys**	40	40	51	30
6 **McMillan**	43	30	43	36
4 **Mann**	55	38	—	—

	1	2	3	4
1 **Rivers**	49	26	46	33
2 *Watson*	49	36	33	55
SOUTH DAKOTA				
2 *Berry*	34	17	39	38
1 *Reifel*	36	15	56	38
TENNESSEE				
6 **Anderson**	51	17	68	11
7 **Blanton**	49	34	59	24
4 **Evins**	51†	18†	50*	10*
5 **Fulton**	32	23	69	10
8 **Jones**	33†	44†	—	—
3 *Brock*	57	21	42	45
2 *Duncan*	53	47	46	54
9 *Kuykendall*	64	21	40	43
1 *Quillen*	55†	41†	36*	52*
TEXAS				
9 **Brooks**	49	19	82	8
17 **Burleson**	55	40	49	41
5 **Cabell**	53	38	59	30
22 **Casey**	60	34	63	26
15 **de la Garza**	51	36	70	19
4 **Dowdy**	50	40	43	45
8 **Eckhardt**	47	30	83	10
21 **Fisher**	38	45	42	41
20 **Gonzalez**	62	38	91	9
23 **Kazen**	57	43	84	10
19 **Mahon**	68	26	76	23
1 **Patman**	47	26	70	10
10 **Pickle**	60	36	66	16
11 **Poage**	47	32	56	32
13 **Purcell**	40	38	56	19
4 **Roberts**	47	45	58	32
6 **Teague**	34	34	41	29
16 **White**	62	38	67	25
12 **Wright**	55	23	70	12
14 **Young**	57	30	80	9
7 *Bush*	64	34	53	40
3 *Collins*	57	34	55*	40*
18 *Price*	57	38	39	60
UTAH				
1 *Burton*	55	21	42	41
2 *Lloyd*	64	21	52	38
VERMONT				
AL *Stafford*	70	26	68	25
VIRGINIA				
4 **Abbitt**	32	30	33	47
5 **Daniel**	45	55	—	—
1 **Downing**	55	36	62	31
7 **Marsh**	57	43	52	47
3 **Satterfield**	51	49	42	52
10 *Broyhill*	49	40	45	48
6 *Poff*	62	34	48	50
8 *Scott*	45	51	38	54
9 *Wampler*	51	36	49	45
2 *Whitehurst*	53	38	—	—
WASHINGTON				
7 **Adams**	53	40	75	11
5 **Foley**	55	36	82	8
3 **Hansen**	49	40	71	7
6 **Hicks**	51	43	81	11
4 **Meeds**	53	34	86	7
4 *May*	64	19	50	38
1 *Pelly*	52†	18†	58*	36*
WEST VIRGINIA				
4 **Hechler**	51	49	90	10
5 **Kee**	62	34	83	10
1 **Mollohan**	57	38	—	—
1 **Slack**	60	38	75	17
2 **Staggers**	53	38	78	12
WISCONSIN				
2 **Kastenmeier**	45	51	81	15
5 **Obey**	51†	49†	—	—
5 **Reuss**	49	43	80	8
4 **Zablocki**	53	47	83	8
8 *Byrnes*	79	15	50	42
9 *Davis*	74	21	37	55
10 *O'Konski*	36	45	46	34
1 *Schadeberg*	57	43	45	51
6 *Steiger*	60	26	60	36
3 *Thomson*	66	32	44	50
WYOMING				
AL *Wold*	49	28	—	—

Democrats in this type; *Republicans in italics*

House Domestic Policy—1969 & 90th Congress

1. Domestic Policy Support Score, 1969. Percentage of 42 Nixon-issue roll calls on domestic matters in 1969 on which Representative voted "yea" or "nay" *in agreement* with the President's position. Failures to vote lower both Support and Opposition scores.

2. Domestic Policy Opposition Score, 1969. Percentage of 42 Nixon-issue roll calls on domestic matters in 1969 on which Representative voted "yea" or "nay" *in disagreement* with the President's position. Failures to vote lower both Support and Opposition scores.

3. Domestic Policy Support Score, 90th Congress. Percentage of 190 Johnson-issue roll calls on domestic matters in 1967 and 1968 on which Representative voted "yea" or "nay" *in agreement* with the President's position. Failures to vote lower both Support and Opposition scores.

4. Domestic Policy Opposition Score, 90th Congress. Percentage of 190 Johnson-issue roll calls on domestic matters in 1967 and 1968 on which Representative voted "yea" or "nay" *in disagreement* with the President's position. Failures to vote lower both Support and Opposition scores.

Headnotes

† Not eligible for all roll calls in 1969.
* Not eligible for all roll calls in 90th Congress.
— Not a Member of the 90th Congress.

PRESIDENTIAL SUPPORT 1969 AND 90th CONGRESS

	1	2	3	4
ALABAMA				
3 Andrews	48	33	38	47
7 Bevill	40	48	50	44
5 Flowers	36	57	—	—
8 Jones	62	31	69	19
4 Nichols	40	50	38	42
6 Buchanan	69	29	44	54
2 Dickinson	64	31	34	47
1 Edwards	62	29	42	53
ALASKA				
AL Pollock	50	26	44	33
ARIZONA				
2 Udall	60	38	79	7
1 Rhodes	69	26	47	41
3 Steiger	52	38	42	50
ARKANSAS				
1 Alexander	64	31	—	—
2 Mills	64	24	63	30
4 Pryor	64	33	66	22
3 Hammerschmidt	67	29	54	43
CALIFORNIA				
5 Burton	45	38	81	13
7 Cohelan	45	43	77	11
9 Edwards	19	40	72	10
34 Hanna	51†	24†	65	9
2 Johnson	57	43	86	12
4 Leggett	43	43	66	7
15 McFall	62	33	87	6
8 Miller	45	31	71	4
3 Moss	33	45	71	7
16 Sisk	50	29	73	7
38 Tunney	21	21	68	7
37 Van Deerlin	45	36	78	10
14 Waldie	36	55	79	11
1 Clausen	68†	28†	46	37
10 Gubser	62	33	53	34
11 McCloskey	60	26	67*	23*
6 Mailliard	63†	23†	57	32
18 Mathias	55	19	52	35
33 Pettis	57	36	52	41
12 Talcott	62	31	48	45
13 Teague	60†	33†	49	44
35 Utt	40	29	24	38
36 Wilson	71	10	45	35

	1	2	3	4
Los Angeles Co.				
17 Anderson	48	50	—	—
29 Brown	14	40	51	11
22 Corman	40	29	65	5
21 Hawkins	36	50	63	9
19 Holifield	45	36	78	5
26 Rees	36	36	70	11
30 Roybal	43	45	72	10
31 Wilson	36	43	63	7
28 Bell	50	24	55	17
23 Clawson	48	45	37	48
27 Goldwater	47†	29†	—	—
32 Hosmer	57	19	48	38
24 Lipscomb	19	5	43	51
20 Smith	60	29	42	47
25 Wiggins	67	26	45	44
COLORADO				
4 Aspinall	62	21	63	11
3 Evans	57	36	77	11
1 Rogers	62	36	80	11
2 Brotzman	67	31	62	33
CONNECTICUT				
1 Daddario	45	26	79	8
3 Giaimo	43	43	75	12
5 Monagan	55	33	77	14
2 St. Onge	48	40	45	6
6 Meskill	57	40	60	34
4 Weicker	55	38	—	—
DELAWARE				
AL Roth	69	31	54	42
FLORIDA				
3 Bennett	52	48	59	41
4 Chappell	38	40	—	—
12 Fascell	26	21	84	7
2 Fuqua	50	45	57	31
6 Gibbons	48	43	75	13
7 Haley	38	52	41	56
11 Pepper	48	29	70	8
9 Rogers	48	50	56	42
1 Sikes	60	29	54	31
10 Burke	45	55	38	50
8 Cramer	57	38	40	45
5 Frey	55	36	—	—

	1	2	3	4
GEORGIA				
3 Brinkley	40	60	52	44
7 Davis	43	40	63	29
6 Flynt	36	33	41	42
1 Hagan	36	62	39	44
9 Landrum	43	38	47	17
2 O'Neal	36	48	42	44
10 Stephens	33	29	55	19
8 Stuckey	40	52	51	39
4 Blackburn	50	36	40	39
5 Thompson	60	38	45	46
HAWAII				
AL Matsunaga	55	40	81	6
AL Mink	50	50	83	11
IDAHO				
2 Hansen, O.	60	31	—	—
1 McClure	40	45	39	52
ILLINOIS				
21 Gray	43	33	67	11
24 Price	57	40	88	8
23 Shipley	57	40	70	21
16 Anderson	60	19	59	33
17 Arends	62	21	49	42
14 Erlenborn	67	26	51	38
20 Findley	62	19	48	43
12 McClory	52	26	51	35
18 Michel	62	29	42	45
19 Railsback	55	38	54	39
15 Reid	67	31	48	51
22 Springer	67	31	55	39
Chicago-Cook Co.				
7 Annunzio	57	33	78	6
1 Dawson	12	7	64	3
5 Kluczynski	43	33	71	6
2 Mikva	36	48	—	—
3 Murphy	62	38	87	5
11 Pucinski	33	40	72	12
6 Vacancy				
8 Rostenkowski	45	29	74	6
9 Yates	50	45	80	11
10 Collier	49†	29†	45	46
13 Crane	33†	67†	—	—
4 Derwinski	55	33	42	45

	1	2	3	4
INDIANA				
3 Brademas	48	45	76	8
9 Hamilton	64	36	83	14
11 Jacobs	52	43	68	11
1 Madden	50	48	71	8
4 Adair	60	38	44	39
6 Bray	60	31	44	44
10 Dennis	62	31	—	—
2 Landgrebe	52	33	—	—
7 Myers	60†	40†	47	45
5 Roudebush	55	40	35	41
8 Zion	55	40	47	46
IOWA				
2 Culver	48	45	78	6
5 Smith	57	40	75	13
3 Gross	38	62	35	62
4 Kyl	48	38	46	44
6 Mayne	74	26	53	39
7 Scherle	50	48	42	56
1 Schwengel	69	31	63	32
KANSAS				
2 Mize	69	29	53	41
1 Sebelius	62	26	—	—
4 Shriver	71	26	54	39
5 Skubitz	64	26	49	46
3 Winn	62	29	45	49
KENTUCKY				
2 Natcher	55	45	79	21
7 Perkins	57	40	87	13
1 Stubblefield	50	45	66	21

Democrats in this **type**; Republicans in *italics*

	1	2	3	4
6 Watts	62	33	58	24
5 Carter	67	29	55	33
3 Cowger	41†	32†	43	27
4 Snyder	43	43	38	47
LOUISIANA				
2 Boggs	69	24	78	6
3 Caffery	45	48	—	—
7 Edwards	50	26	57	24
1 Hebert	31	7	29	20
8 Long	38	48	26	38
5 Passman	45	43	39	39
6 Rarick	36	57	22	42
4 Waggonner	55	43	48	42
MAINE				
2 Hathaway	57	38	86	8
1 Kyros	57	36	84	9
MARYLAND				
4 Fallon	48	26	71	11
7 Friedel	57	43	90	7
3 Garmatz	52	40	81	9
2 Long	52	48	83	12
6 Beall	71	29	—	—
8 Gude	52	40	67	25
5 Hogan	60	33	—	—
1 Morton	67	7	46	39
MASSACHUSETTS				
2 Boland	48	45	80	8
11 Burke	60	40	89	11
4 Donohue	57	43	84	8
6 Harrington	33†	47†	—	—
1 Macdonald	40	55	64	12
9 McCormack				
8 O'Neill	50	38	76	6
3 Philbin	55	40	82	7
1 Conte	62	36	62	24
10 Heckler	55	36	54	26
12 Keith	74	26	57	35
5 Morse	43	33	59	22
MICHIGAN				
12 O'Hara	52	40	78	6
18 Broomfield	60	29	41	22
3 Brown	69	24	55	37
10 Cederberg	64	10	41	44
6 Chamberlain	64	31	52	45
8 Esch	69	31	62	30
5 Ford	75	20	55	36
8 Harvey	55	31	62	31
4 Hutchinson	57	40	46	52
19 McDonald	64	31	63	32
7 Riegle	48	45	64	31
11 Ruppe	55†	23†	55	25
9 Vander Jagt	62	24	52	35
Detroit-Wayne Co.				
1 Conyers	19	48	51	12
13 Diggs	29	38	47	5
16 Dingell	48	38	74	13
15 Ford	45	48	71	13
17 Griffiths	50	31	73	11
14 Nedzi	55	43	82	9
MINNESOTA				
8 Blatnik	38	38	77	8
5 Fraser	45	45	82	7
2 Karth	52	40	74	8
7 Langen	67	31	44	54
3 MacGregor	69	26	54	33
2 Nelsen	64	24	42	42
1 Quie	57	33	60	35
6 Zwach	57	43	55	37
MISSISSIPPI				
1 Abernethy	45	52	37	57
5 Colmer	43	36	35	52
3 Griffin	33	45	58†	36*
4 Montgomery	40	40	44	54
2 Whitten	48	43	47	44
MISSOURI				
5 Bolling	43	26	73	7
10 Burlison	52	48	—	—
1 Clay	29	40	—	—
6 Hull	38†	43†	56	28
9 Hungate	43	52	64	16
1 Ichord	36	52	53	31
4 Randall	33	64	63	36
3 Sullivan	48	29	77	11

	1	2	3	4
2 Symington	52	43	—	—
7 Hall	38	31	37	58
MONTANA				
2 Melcher	56	42	—	—
1 Olsen	48	52	71	9
NEBRASKA				
2 Cunningham	55	14	48	36
1 Denney	48	36	47	46
3 Martin	40	26	40	39
NEVADA				
AL Baring	31	43	41	39
NEW HAMPSHIRE				
2 Cleveland	60	40	53	43
1 Wyman	62	33	57	41
NEW JERSEY				
14 Daniels	43	50	88	9
13 Gallagher	40	33	69	7
9 Helstoski	40	50	77	9
3 Howard	40	45	82	9
11 Minish	50	50	83	11
15 Patten	62	38	92	8
10 Rodino	45	43	82	11
8 Roe	40†	60†	—	—
4 Thompson	43	43	66	6
6 Cahill	21	2	63	29
12 Dwyer	64	24	61	28
5 Frelinghuysen	76	21	52	27
1 Hunt	60	33	52	45
2 Sandman	60	29	46	36
7 Widnall	67	24	63	28
NEW MEXICO				
2 Foreman	40	45	—	—
1 Lujan	48	26	—	—
NEW YORK				
41 Dulski	52	43	82	10
34 Hanley	52	45	86	11
5 Lowenstein	29	55	—	—
39 McCarthy	45	45	81	11
25 Ottinger	40	57	74	21
1 Pike	52	48	72	24
35 Stratton	60	38	62	17
3 Wolff	33	57	69	17
29 Button	55	38	66	15
37 Conable	71	21	58	32
28 Fish	60	33	—	—
2 Grover	60	33	56	42
38 Hastings	45	29	—	—
36 Horton	57	40	69	22
30 King	60	29	44	47
31 McEwen	60	31	41	40
27 McKneally	67	21	—	—
32 Pirnie	57	24	56	32
26 Reid	50	43	74	17
33 Robison	69	29	61	33
40 Smith	62	24	55	33
4 Wydler	52	36	54	35
New York City				
7 Addabbo	48	50	84	12
24 Biaggi	45	55	—	—
23 Bingham	36	45	82	8
11 Brasco	43	50	83	8
15 Carey	19	29	71	11
10 Celler	38	29	62	4
12 Chisholm	21	45	—	—
9 Delaney	38	43	81	14
19 Farbstein	36	45	74	12
22 Gilbert	52	45	78	11
17 Koch	48	48	—	—
16 Murphy	57	31	67	7
13 Podell	45	45	59*	8*
18 Powell	0	2	—	—
14 Rooney	55	38	78	5
6 Rosenthal	36	57	78	11
20 Ryan	40	57	74	18
21 Scheuer	36	50	73	11
6 Halpern	43	31	69	17
NORTH CAROLINA				
2 Fountain	45	55	38	38
4 Galifianakis	60	40	64	31
4 Henderson	40	57	49	45
1 Jones	38	57	45	43
7 Lennon	43	45	41	57
6 Preyer	57	38	—	—

	1	2	3	4
11 Taylor	48	40	57	39
10 Broyhill	60	40	48	51
9 Jonas	65†	30†	44	49
5 Mizell	60	38	—	—
8 Ruth	60	38	—	—
NORTH DAKOTA				
1 Andrews	60	24	55	33
2 Kleppe	60†	33†	46	43
OHIO				
9 Ashley	52	33	72	10
20 Feighan	55	40	77	7
18 Hays	33	43	63	12
19 Kirwan	5	2	73	8
21 Stokes	38	55	—	—
22 Vanik	52	45	82	11
17 Ashbrook	36	38	28	55
14 Ayres	69	26	55	32
8 Betts	62	33	49	47
16 Bow	74	21	42	34
7 Brown	69	26	44	45
2 Clancy	50	45	42	49
12 Devine	45	38	42	49
6 Harsha	40	52	45	44
5 Latta	55	31	48	41
24 Lukens	43	29	39	38
4 McCulloch	60	36	57	28
10 Miller	52	48	47	53
23 Minshall	57	33	42	39
13 Mosher	60	31	62	28
11 Stanton	71	24	63	32
1 Taft	64	21	47*	39*
3 Whalen	57	40	70	26
15 Wylie	64	33	58	40
OKLAHOMA				
3 Albert	62	31	91	8
2 Edmondson	40	40	76	17
5 Jarman	50	38	51	43
4 Steed	45	33	69	24
1 Belcher	60	36	45	46
6 Camp	50	31	—	—
OREGON				
3 Green	55	24	65	15
2 Ullman	55	36	72	16
4 Dellenback	64	33	57	35
1 Wyatt	60	24	48	34
PENNSYLVANIA				
25 Clark	38	43	68	13
21 Dent	40	40	67	7
11 Flood	55	45	74	9
20 Gaydos	43	57	—	—
14 Moorhead	55	43	76	6
26 Morgan	43	48	80	9
15 Rooney	52	38	76	10
24 Vigorito	60	38	82	11
6 Yatron	45	52	—	—
8 Biester	60	38	64	33
18 Corbett	69	29	60	26
13 Coughlin	64	33	—	—
16 Eshleman	57	38	51	44
27 Fulton	48	48	64	33
19 Goodling	52	38	47	53
23 Johnson	60	33	52	42
10 McDade	69	31	65	27
22 Saylor	45	33	48	42
17 Schneebeli	64	21	52	47
9 Watkins	43	26	36	45
12 Whalley	36	21	46	44
7 Williams	55	38	52	41
Philadelphia City				
1 Barrett	48	40	75	7
3 Byrne	45	40	91	7
4 Eilberg	45	45	84	7
5 Green	48	48	81	7
2 Nix	48	50	79	7
RHODE ISLAND				
1 St. Germain	38	52	75	9
2 Tiernan	48	52	80*	9*
SOUTH CAROLINA				
3 Dorn	55	38	49	36
5 Gettys	38	45	49	39
6 McMillan	45	33	44	33
4 Mann	57	36	—	—

	1	2	3	4
1 Rivers	50	26	47	33
2 Watson	50	36	34	52
SOUTH DAKOTA				
2 Berry	36	12	39	36
1 Reifel	36	17	61	34
TENNESSEE				
6 Anderson	48	19	67	11
3 Blanton	50	38	60	23
4 Evins	53†	20†	51*	10*
5 Fulton	31	26	68	9
8 Jones	30†	48†	—	—
3 Brock	55	21	42	43
2 Duncan	55	45	51	49
9 Kuykendall	69	19	43	38
1 Quillen	56†	38†	41*	46*
TEXAS				
9 Brooks	45	21	82	9
17 Burleson	57	38	50	41
22 Casey	62	31	65	24
15 de la Garza	48	40	71	18
7 Dowdy	40	60	47	43
8 Eckhardt	43	33	84	10
21 Fisher	40	43	44	39
20 Gonzalez	57	43	91	9
23 Kazen	55	45	84	11
19 Mahon	67	26	75	24
1 Patman	48	29	69	11
10 Pickle	57	38	63	18
11 Poage	43	36	58	31
13 Purcell	40	36	57	18
4 Roberts	50	45	59	29
6 Teague	38	33	41	29
16 White	64	36	67	25
12 Wright	55	26	69	14
14 Young	52	33	80	11
2 Bush	67	31	53	41
3 Collins	60	31	53*	41*
18 Price	60	36	41	58
UTAH				
1 Burton	52	24	44	39
2 Lloyd	64	21	52	38
VERMONT				
AL Stafford	67	29	67	26
VIRGINIA				
4 Abbitt	33	29	35	45
5 Daniel	45	45	—	—
1 Downing	57	33	62	31
7 Marsh	60	40	55	45
3 Satterfield	52	48	44	50
10 Broyhill	52	38	46	47
6 Poff	60	36	47	51
8 Scott	45	50	39	54
9 Wampler	55	33	50	44
2 Whitehurst	55	36	—	—
WASHINGTON				
7 Adams	50	43	72	12
5 Foley	55	40	84	7
3 Hansen	48	45	70	7
6 Hicks	45	48	81	12
6 Meeds	50	38	86	7
4 May	62	21	52	36
1 Pelly	54†	18†	60*	35*
WEST VIRGINIA				
4 Hechler	48	52	90	10
5 Kee	60	38	83	11
1 Mollohan	52	43	—	—
3 Slack	57	40	75	19
2 Staggers	48	43	79	11
WISCONSIN				
2 Kastenmeier	45	55	83	13
7 Obey	48†	53†	—	—
5 Reuss	48	45	79	8
4 Zablocki	48	52	82	9
8 Byrnes	81	17	49	44
9 Davis	74	21	38	55
10 O'Konski	38	43	49	28
1 Schadeberg	60	40	49	48
6 Steiger	62	26	58	36
3 Thomson	69	29	45	48
WYOMING				
AL Wold	52	26	—	—

Democrats in this type; *Republicans in italics*

House Foreign Policy—1969 & 90th Congress

1. Foreign Policy Support Score, 1969. Percentage of 5 Nixon-issue roll calls in the field of foreign policy in 1969 on which Representative voted "yea" or "nay" *in agreement* with the President's position. Failures to vote lower both Support and Opposition scores.

2. Foreign Policy Opposition Score, 1969. Percentage of 5 Nixon-issue roll calls in the field of foreign policy in 1969 on which Representative voted "yea" or "nay" *in disagreement* with the President's position. Failures to vote lower both Support and Opposition scores.

3. Foreign Policy Support Score, 90th Congress. Percentage of 40 Johnson-issue roll calls in the field of foreign policy in 1967 and 1968 on which Representative voted "yea" or "nay" *in agreement* with the President's position. Failures to vote lower both Support and Opposition scores.

4. Foreign Policy Opposition Score, 90th Congress. Percentage of 40 Johnson-issue roll calls in the field of foreign policy in 1967 and 1968 on which Representative voted "yea" or "nay" *in disagreement* with the President's position. Failures to vote lower both Support and Opposition scores.

Headnotes

† Not eligible for all roll calls in 1969.
* Not eligible for all roll calls in 90th Congress.
— Not a Member of the 90th Congress.

	1	2	3	4
ALABAMA				
3 Andrews	40	60	23	55
7 Bevill	80	0	35	53
5 Flowers	20	60	—	—
8 Jones	80	0	75	8
4 Nichols	40	20	45	43
6 Buchanan	20	40	35	58
2 Dickinson	20	40	18	65
1 Edwards	40	40	35	50
ALASKA				
AL Pollock	0	40	33	43
ARIZONA				
2 Udall	100	0	80	8
1 Rhodes	40	60	43	40
3 Steiger	40	60	30	63
ARKANSAS				
1 Alexander	60	20	—	—
2 Mills	0	40	50	35
4 Pryor	80	20	63	25
3 Hammerschmidt	60	40	33	60
CALIFORNIA				
5 Burton	60	20	83	13
7 Cohelan	80	20	98	2
9 Edwards	60	20	70	2
34 Hanna	60	0	60	3
2 Johnson	80	0	90	0
4 Leggett	60	20	78	5
15 McFall	100	0	93	0
8 Miller	100	0	75	5
3 Moss	80	20	65	3
16 Sisk	80	0	75	5
38 Tunney	40	20	93	0
37 Van Deerlin	80	20	85	5
14 Waldie	60	20	78	15
1 Clausen	20	60	33	50
10 Gubser	60	0	48	43
11 McCloskey	80	0	65*	20*
6 Mailliard	100	0	93	3
18 Mathias	20	20	58	20
33 Pettis	20	60	40	48
12 Talcott	80	0	35	50
13 Teague	80	20	60	35
35 Utt	0	0	18	60
36 Wilson	100	0	25	45

	1	2	3	4
Los Angeles Co.				
17 Anderson	80	20	—	—
29 Brown	40	0	40	33
22 Corman	80	0	68	0
21 Hawkins	40	20	55	0
19 Holifield	60	0	83	0
26 Rees	80	0	73	10
30 Roybal	80	20	95	3
31 Wilson	80	0	60	10
28 Bell	20	0	60	23
23 Clawson	20	40	28	60
27 Goldwater	67†	33†	—	—
32 Hosmer	40	20	55	33
24 Lipscomb	20	40	30	65
20 Smith	40	60	30	58
25 Wiggins	40	60	40	48
COLORADO				
4 Aspinall	80	0	80	5
3 Evans	80	0	85	8
1 Rogers	80	20	80	13
2 Brotzman	60	20	55	35
CONNECTICUT				
1 Daddario	80	20	78	3
3 Giaimo	80	0	78	0
5 Monagan	100	0	93	3
2 St. Onge	60	20	58	0
6 Meskill	20	60	43	50
4 Weicker	100	0	—	—
DELAWARE				
AL Roth	80	20	50	43
FLORIDA				
3 Bennett	40	60	63	37
4 Chappell	40	60	—	—
12 Fascell	80	0	90	5
2 Fuqua	20	40	45	43
6 Gibbons	60	0	78	5
7 Haley	20	60	13	87
11 Pepper	40	0	70	5
9 Rogers	40	60	45	53
1 Sikes	40	40	50	38
10 Burke	40	60	25	65
8 Cramer	80	20	33	43
5 Frey	40	60	—	—

	1	2	3	4
GEORGIA				
3 Brinkley	40	60	35	60
7 Davis	80	20	55	38
6 Flynt	20	0	25	55
1 Hagan	40	60	15	55
9 Landrum	60	20	45	30
2 O'Neal	20	0	33	60
10 Stephens	80	0	48	33
8 Stuckey	20	20	33	53
4 Blackburn	40	60	30	60
5 Thompson	20	60	30	68
HAWAII				
AL Matsunaga	100	0	83	3
AL Mink	80	20	93	5
IDAHO				
2 Hansen, O.	60	20	—	—
1 McClure	40	60	38	58
ILLINOIS				
21 Gray	40	20	73	5
24 Price	80	0	100	0
23 Shipley	60	20	50	30
16 Anderson	80	0	58	28
17 Arends	60	20	58	35
14 Erlenborn	60	20	75	15
20 Findley	80	0	50	33
12 McClory	80	0	50	43
18 Michel	80	20	30	43
19 Railsback	60	0	75	18
15 Reid	40	60	28	68
22 Springer	80	20	60	35
Chicago-Cook Co.				
7 Annunzio	100	0	83	5
1 Dawson	40	0	63	3
5 Kluczynski	80	0	68	5
2 Mikva	80	20	—	—
3 Murphy	100	0	90	0
11 Pucinski	20	40	73	5
6 Vacancy				
8 Rostenkowski	80	0	65	0
9 Yates	80	20	90	8
10 Collier	40	60	35	53
13 Crane	100	0	—	—
4 Derwinski	20	60	30	38

PRESIDENTIAL SUPPORT 1969 AND 90th CONGRESS

	1	2	3	4
INDIANA				
3 Brademas	100	0	85	3
9 Hamilton	100	0	88	3
11 Jacobs	100	0	70	5
1 Madden	100	0	83	5
4 Adair	40	60	43	48
6 Bray	20	60	28	58
10 Dennis	20	60	—	—
2 Landgrebe	20	80	—	—
7 Myers	40	60	33	63
5 Roudebush	40	40	28	55
8 Zion	40	60	30	65
IOWA				
2 Culver	100	0	90	0
5 Smith	80	0	100	0
3 Gross	20	80	5	95
4 Kyl	20	40	38	58
6 Mayne	80	20	73	25
7 Scherle	20	60	23	68
1 Schwengel	100	0	63	23
KANSAS				
2 Mize	60	20	50	30
1 Sebelius	40	60	—	—
4 Shriver	80	20	60	38
5 Skubitz	40	60	35	48
3 Winn	20	60	35	55
KENTUCKY				
2 Natcher	40	60	65	35
7 Perkins	100	0	93	7
1 Stubblefield	20	60	48	7

Democrats in this type; Republicans in italics

	1	2	3	4
6 Watts	20	60	45	18
5 Carter	20	60	25	60
3 Cowger	60	20	35	43
4 Snyder	20	60	28	68
LOUISIANA				
2 Boggs	100	0	83	0
3 Caffery	20	60	—	—
7 Edwards	0	0	60	23
1 Hebert	20	20	30	13
8 Long	20	60	20	63
5 Passman	40	60	23	55
6 Rarick	0	80	8	75
4 Waggonner	40	60	35	53
MAINE				
2 Hathaway	80	20	88	0
1 Kyros	100	0	88	8
MARYLAND				
4 Fallon	60	20	55	5
7 Friedel	100	0	85	5
3 Garmatz	80	0	80	5
2 Long	40	40	73	15
6 Beall	80	20	—	—
8 Gude	100	0	80	13
5 Hogan	40	60	—	—
1 Morton	100	0	55	33
MASSACHUSETTS				
2 Boland	100	0	75	3
11 Burke	100	0	93	7
4 Donohue	100	0	78	5
6 Harrington	67†	33†	—	—
7 Macdonald	60	40	40	10
9 McCormack				
8 O'Neill	80	20	75	3
3 Philbin	100	0	73	5
1 Conte	100	0	83	13
10 Heckler	100	0	68	15
12 Keith	100	0	80	18
5 Morse	80	0	70	8
MICHIGAN				
12 O'Hara	100	0	83	0
18 Broomfield	100	0	63	10
3 Brown	80	20	45	55
10 Cederberg	60	20	40	45
6 Chamberlain	40	60	38	48
2 Esch	60	0	63	18
5 Ford	80	0	63	28
8 Harvey	80	20	68	32
4 Hutchinson	40	40	38	62
19 McDonald	40	20	53	43
7 Riegle	60	20	58	33
11 Ruppe	60	20	60	33
9 Vander Jagt	60	20	53	35
Detroit-Wayne Co.				
1 Conyers	20	20	40	13
13 Diggs	80	20	55	5
16 Dingell	60	0	75	0
15 Ford	80	20	80	0
17 Griffiths	80	0	75	3
14 Nedzi	80	20	93	0
MINNESOTA				
8 Blatnik	40	20	75	3
5 Fraser	80	20	75	10
4 Karth	80	20	80	5
7 Langen	40	40	35	65
3 MacGregor	80	0	58	23
2 Nelsen	80	0	43	38
1 Quie	80	0	73	18
6 Zwach	40	40	43	55
MISSISSIPPI				
1 Abernethy	40	0	20	63
5 Colmer	40	40	33	58
3 Griffin	40	0	47*	47*
4 Montgomery	20	40	25	63
2 Whitten	20	60	35	60
MISSOURI				
5 Bolling	100	0	65	0
10 Burlison	40	60	—	—
1 Clay	20	20	—	—
6 Hull	40	60	43	45
8 Hungate	20	80	58	23
8 Ichord	40	60	23	65
4 Randall	40	60	38	60
3 Sullivan	100	0	90	3

	1	2	3	4
2 Symington	100	0	—	—
7 Hall	20	60	8	85
MONTANA				
2 Melcher	67†	33†	—	—
1 Olsen	80	0	73	13
NEBRASKA				
2 Cunningham	20	60	23	55
1 Denney	40	40	33	55
3 Martin	20	60	30	48
NEVADA				
AL Baring	20	60	8	80
NEW HAMPSHIRE				
2 Cleveland	40	60	45	40
1 Wyman	40	60	45	53
NEW JERSEY				
14 Daniels	80	0	90	3
13 Gallagher	80	0	75	0
9 Helstoski	80	20	85	8
3 Howard	60	0	80	5
11 Minish	100	0	93	7
15 Patten	100	0	98	2
10 Rodino	80	0	90	5
8 Roe	100†	0†	—	—
4 Thompson	60	20	70	3
6 Cahill	60	0	55	13
12 Dwyer	80	0	70	20
5 Frelinghuysen	100	0	80	3
1 Hunt	40	60	38	55
2 Sandman	20	60	50	45
7 Widnall	80	0	60	23
NEW MEXICO				
2 Foreman	40	60	—	—
1 Lujan	20	60	—	—
NEW YORK				
41 Dulski	80	20	83	13
34 Hanley	80	20	90	8
5 Lowenstein	40	20	—	—
39 McCarthy	60	20	88	8
25 Ottinger	80	20	90	5
1 Pike	100	0	83	13
35 Stratton	100	0	73	13
3 Wolff	80	20	78	18
29 Button	60	20	53	13
37 Conable	20	20	60	20
28 Fish	80	20	—	—
2 Grover	20	40	35	60
38 Hastings	20	60	—	—
36 Horton	80	0	65	23
30 King	40	40	28	63
31 McEwen	20	60	43	20
27 McKneally	40	60	—	—
32 Pirnie	80	20	73	10
26 Reid	80	20	88	5
33 Robison	100	0	78	15
40 Smith	60	20	65	25
4 Wydler	60	40	58	25
New York City				
7 Addabbo	60	20	83	5
24 Biaggi	80	20	—	—
23 Bingham	80	20	80	8
11 Brasco	60	20	88	5
15 Carey	60	20	63	0
10 Celler	80	0	60	3
12 Chisholm	20	60	—	—
9 Delaney	40	20	83	15
19 Farbstein	60	20	70	8
22 Gilbert	80	20	83	5
17 Koch	80	20	—	—
16 Murphy	80	0	73	5
13 Podell	40	20	71*	0*
18 Powell	40	0	—	—
14 Rooney	100	0	83	3
8 Rosenthal	60	20	73	10
20 Ryan	80	20	85	13
21 Scheuer	40	20	65	10
6 Halpern	100	0	85	8
NORTH CAROLINA				
2 Fountain	60	40	43	33
4 Galifianakis	60	20	63	35
3 Henderson	40	60	48	48
1 Jones	20	60	35	53
7 Lennon	40	60	28	68
6 Preyer	100	0	—	—

	1	2	3	4
11 Taylor	20	60	43	50
10 Broyhill	60	40	38	60
9 Jonas	40	60	38	58
5 Mizell	40	60	—	—
8 Ruth	40	60	—	—
NORTH DAKOTA				
1 Andrews	60	0	58	38
2 Kleppe	40	60	43	57
OHIO				
9 Ashley	100	0	88	3
20 Feighan	80	0	95	5
18 Hays	60	20	65	8
19 Kirwan	20	0	78	0
21 Stokes	40	20	—	—
22 Vanik	80	20	93	3
17 Ashbrook	20	80	13	70
14 Ayres	80	0	63	23
8 Betts	40	60	33	60
16 Bow	60	20	28	48
7 Brown	40	20	48	38
2 Clancy	20	80	15	58
12 Devine	20	40	15	70
6 Harsha	20	60	23	68
5 Latta	20	60	38	55
24 Lukens	20	60	28	50
4 McCulloch	80	0	43	45
10 Miller	40	60	33	67
23 Minshall	40	60	23	55
13 Mosher	100	0	48	38
11 Stanton	60	20	68	28
1 Taft	80	0	68	20
3 Whalen	100	0	85	15
15 Wylie	20	60	33	60
OKLAHOMA				
3 Albert	60	0	88	5
2 Edmondson	60	0	83	8
5 Jarman	20	60	33	60
4 Steed	20	40	60	28
1 Belcher	40	40	25	65
6 Camp	20	40	—	—
OREGON				
3 Green	80	20	70	10
2 Ullman	60	20	90	5
4 Dellenback	60	0	68	25
1 Wyatt	60	20	50	38
PENNSYLVANIA				
25 Clark	80	0	65	10
21 Dent	60	0	65	0
11 Flood	100	0	95	3
20 Gaydos	40	60	—	—
14 Moorhead	60	20	85	0
26 Morgan	100	0	95	0
15 Rooney	100	0	85	8
24 Vigorito	100	0	90	8
6 Yatron	100	0	—	—
8 Biester	80	20	78	22
18 Corbett	60	20	60	20
13 Coughlin	60	40	—	—
16 Eshleman	20	60	43	45
27 Fulton	80	0	68	28
19 Goodling	40	60	33	60
23 Johnson	60	20	45	48
10 McDade	80	20	70	23
22 Saylor	0	60	23	55
17 Schneebeli	80	20	65	33
9 Watkins	40	40	15	58
12 Whalley	40	20	35	43
7 Williams	40	60	38	50
Philadelphia City				
1 Barrett	80	20	88	0
3 Byrne	80	20	93	0
4 Eilberg	60	0	90	5
5 Green	80	20	90	0
2 Nix	100	0	78	0
RHODE ISLAND				
1 St. Germain	80	0	90	3
2 Tiernan	80	0	81*	6*
SOUTH CAROLINA				
3 Dorn	20	60	30	55
6 Gettys	60	0	55	33
6 McMillan	20	0	33	55
4 Mann	40	60	—	—

	1	2	3	4
1 Rivers	40	20	35	40
2 Watson	40	40	23	70
SOUTH DAKOTA				
2 Berry	20	60	38	48
1 Reifel	40	0	38	53
TENNESSEE				
6 Anderson	80	0	75	10
7 Blanton	40	0	58	28
4 Evins	40	0	50	10
5 Fulton	40	0	73	8
1 Jones	67†	0†	—	—
3 Brock	80	20	38	58
2 Duncan	40	60	20	80
9 Kuykendall	20	40	28	68
1 Quillen	40	60	10	80
TEXAS				
9 Brooks	80	0	85	0
17 Burleson	40	60	43	43
5 Cabell	20	40	58	25
22 Casey	40	60	50	38
15 de la Garza	80	0	68	20
2 Dowdy	40	60	23	60
8 Eckhardt	80	0	85	5
21 Fisher	20	60	30	50
20 Gonzalez	100	0	95	5
23 Kazen	80	20	90	5
19 Mahon	80	20	85	13
1 Patman	40	0	70	8
10 Pickle	80	20	83	8
11 Poage	80	0	45	40
13 Purcell	40	60	55	18
4 Roberts	20	40	53	45
6 Teague	0	40	43	30
16 White	40	60	70	23
12 Wright	60	0	80	0
14 Young	100	0	85	0
7 Bush	40	60	55	35
3 Collins	40	60	33*	67*
18 Price	40	60	28	72
UTAH				
1 Burton	80	0	30	55
2 Lloyd	60	20	53	35
VERMONT				
AL Stafford	100	0	73	18
VIRGINIA				
4 Abbitt	20	40	28	53
5 Daniel	40	60	—	—
1 Downing	40	60	60	35
7 Marsh	40	60	38	60
3 Satterfield	40	60	30	65
10 Broyhill	20	60	38	55
6 Poff	80	20	50	50
8 Scott	40	60	30	58
9 Wampler	20	60	45	50
2 Whitehurst	40	60	—	—
WASHINGTON				
7 Adams	80	20	93	5
5 Foley	60	0	75	10
3 Hansen	60	0	75	5
6 Hicks	100	0	85	5
2 Meeds	80	0	85	5
4 May	80	0	43	45
1 Pelly	40	20	50	35
WEST VIRGINIA				
4 Hechler	80	20	90	10
5 Kee	80	0	83	5
1 Mollohan	100	0	—	—
3 Slack	80	0	78	5
2 Staggers	100	0	78	18
WISCONSIN				
2 Kastenmeier	40	20	75	20
7 Obey	100†	0†	—	—
5 Reuss	60	20	88	5
4 Zablocki	100	0	93	6
8 Byrnes	60	0	50	38
9 Davis	80	20	35	53
10 O'Konski	20	60	28	65
1 Schadeberg	40	60	28	60
6 Steiger	40	20	68	32
3 Thomson	40	60	43	53
WYOMING				
AL Wold	20	40	—	—

Democrats in this type; *Republicans in italics*

CONGRESS APPROVES ONE-THIRD OF NIXON'S REQUESTS

President Nixon's honeymoon with Congress didn't last a full year. As 1969 drew to a close, he and his White House aides complained bitterly that Congress was taking no action on his programs. Democratic Congressional leaders retorted that Mr. Nixon had submitted relatively few new programs of any significance to Congress and that those he did submit came to Capitol Hill late in the year.

Whatever the reasons, the first session of the 91st Congress, despite the unusual length of the session, enacted into law only about a third of the President's proposals.

Congress put off until 1970 final action on most of the major requests made by Mr. Nixon: welfare reform, various crime measures, revenue sharing, manpower training, consumer protection, electoral college reform and postal reform. On other issues, notably mine safety, tax reform and Social Security increases, Congress cleared legislation which was substantially different from the President's original requests. In some few cases, the Administration requests were cleared virtually intact, such as the surtax extension and requests for supplemental appropriations.

As measured by *Congressional Quarterly*'s annual Boxscore, Mr. Nixon made 171 requests for new legislation in about 40 messages to Congress. Of these 55—or about 32 percent—were enacted into law. Though the situations were not comparable, Congress enacted 56 percent of former President Johnson's requests in 1968 and 48 percent in 1967.

The Boxscore does not reflect issues unless they were the subject of messages to Congress. For instance, it does not include the nomination of Judge Clement F. Haynsworth Jr. to be an Associate Justice of the Supreme Court, although the Senate vote against confirmation of Haynsworth was the President's most significant defeat in 1969. It does not include extension of the Export Control Act, although the Administration bill differed significantly from the bill enacted by Congress.

Nor does the Boxscore differentiate between major legislation and less significant proposals. (In District of Columbia affairs, however, some minor requests of purely local interest were omitted.) The individual requests are itemized as they were presented in the messages.

Major Proposals

Following is a summary of the major aspects of President Nixon's program and action on it during 1969.

Foreign Policy. The Senate early in the session ratified the Nuclear Nonproliferation Treaty, ending a six-month impasse. Mr. Nixon sent a message to Congress Feb. 5 asking for ratification of the treaty. On Nov. 25, he said he would seek Senate ratification of the 1925 Geneva Protocol banning wartime use of chemical and biological weapons, but by the end of 1969 he still had not submitted it to the Senate.

On Nov. 18, Mr. Nixon sent to Congress a trade message and legislation which would restore Presidential authority to make limited tariff reductions and would liberalize adjustment assistance to industries endangered by foreign competition.

General Government. The Nixon Administration presented to Congress a number of bills attempting to deal with various aspects of crime: organized crime, obscene mail, numerous District of Columbia crime bills and narcotics control. By the end of the 1969 session, few of these requests had been enacted, although Congress did appropriate funds for the Law Enforcement Assistance Administration, the federal judiciary and special crime programs for Washington, D.C.

In an Oct. 30 consumer protection message, the President requested legislation to create a consumer affairs office in the White House and a division of consumer protection in the Justice Department and to allow "class action" suits in consumer grievance cases. The Administration's proposals and other bills were the subject of hearings in the House but no action.

In an electoral college reform message Feb. 20, Mr. Nixon endorsed proportional division of electoral votes for President and Vice President, but, after the House voted for direct popular elections, he endorsed that plan.

Mr. Nixon asked that the Post Office be converted into a Government-owned corporation and that patronage be eliminated in the selection of postmasters. He also requested mail rate increases. No final action was taken on any of these measures, although the corporation proposal was killed by the House Post Office and Civil Service Committee.

Labor and Agriculture. Mr. Nixon requested new manpower training legislation which would ultimately turn control of training programs over to state and local governments. No action was taken on the bill. The House passed the Administration bill to overhaul the federal unemployment insurance program, but it turned down a request to disallow benefits to strikers.

Mr. Nixon on March 3 submitted a coal mine safety message to Congress. Many of his recommendations were included in a mine safety bill which cleared Congress toward the end of 1969. But the final bill (PL 91-173) was far stronger than the original Administration request, and the President threatened at one point to veto it because of the expense of its federal compensation provisions. He did not.

The President asked successfully for higher authorizations for the food stamp program, but final action on other food stamp reforms was held up in the House Agriculture Committee.

National Security. The Senate by a 51-50 vote authorized funds to build an antiballistic missile defense system (ABM), as the President had requested. Funds to begin work on the ABM were subsequently included in the defense appropriations bill.

Congress also agreed to a Presidential request to establish a draft lottery for inducting young men into the armed services. Further reforms of the draft system were put off until 1970.

Taxes and Economic Policy. The President won an early victory when Congress enacted legislation extending the 10-percent surtax through Dec. 31, 1969. Other requests for changes in the tax laws, made in an April 21 message to Congress, were included in the comprehensive tax reform bill cleared by Congress in December. The Administration requests included a low-income allowance and a minimum income tax for citizens at the bottom and the top of the income scale; repeal of the 7-percent investment tax credit; tighter tax controls over private foundations and charitable deductions; elimination of various tax preferences, and extension of the surtax at a 5-percent level through June 30, 1970.

Mr. Nixon requested a number of new aviation taxes, which did not clear Congress, and extension for 18 months of the interest equalization tax, which was enacted into law. He recommended enactment of a revenue-sharing plan to return to the states a percentage of federal revenues derived from personal income taxes. No action was taken on that request.

Welfare and Urban Affairs. The President on Aug. 11 sent to Congress a message to reform federal welfare programs. He proposed establishing a national minimum benefit of $1,600 annually for a family of four and extending benefits to the "working poor" as well as to families with no income. His plan would require eligible adults to undergo job training or get employment in order to receive benefits, and would expand job training and child daycare programs. Hearings were held on his proposals in the House, but further action was put off until 1970.

Mr. Nixon on Sept. 25 asked that Social Security benefits be raised by 10 percent. Included in the tax reform bill was a provision to increase Social Security payments by 15 percent. Other changes in Social Security to adjust cost-of-living and outside income provisions were not acted upon.

In the transportation field, Congress authorized $300 million in fiscal 1971 for public transportation in local communities, as Mr. Nixon requested on Aug. 7. But Congress took no action on a request in the same message for a $10-billion, 12-year public transportation program.

Source Key For President Nixon's 1969 Legislative Requests

On the following pages, the sources of President Nixon's 1969 legislative requests are indicated by the symbols listed below. Messages asking Senate consent to treaty ratifications are excluded from this compilation.

Symbol	Source, Message	Date	Page
A	Reorganization of Executive Branch	Jan. 30	38-A
B	Statement on District of Columbia	Jan. 31	36-A
C	Electoral Reform	Feb. 20	41-A
D	Supplemental Appropriations	Feb. 20	
E	Public Debt Limit	Feb. 24	41-A
F	Postal Reform	Feb. 25	42-A
G	Coal Mine Safety	March 3	43-A
H	Statement on Antiballistic Missile Defense System	March 14	14-A
I	Statement on One-Bank Holding Companies	March 24	44-A
J	Combating Inflation	March 26	43-A
K	Supplemental Appropriations	March 26	
L	Balance of Payments	April 4	116-A
M	Message on Tax Reform	April 21	48-A
N	Organized Crime	April 23	49-A
O	Postal Rate Increases	April 24	47-A
P	District of Columbia	April 28	52-A
Q	Consolidation of Federal Assistance Programs	April 30	54-A
R	Obscene and Pornographic Materials	May 2	55-A
S	Hunger	May 6	56-A
T	Military Draft	May 13	62-A
U	Supplemental Appropriations	May 13	
V	Postal Reform	May 27	58-A
W	Foreign Aid	May 28	59-A
X	Statement on Extension of Office of Economic Opportunity	June 2	
Y	Air Transportation	June 16	65-A
Z	Unemployment Insurance	July 8	68-A
AA	Control of Narcotics and Dangerous Drugs	July 14	63-A
BB	Population Growth	July 18	70-A
CC	Reorganization Plan No. 1	July 22	73-A
DD	Occupational Safety and Health	Aug. 6	74-A
EE	Public Transportation	Aug. 7	84-A
FF	Message on Welfare Reform	Aug. 11	75-A
GG	Manpower Training	Aug. 12	78-A
HH	Revenue Sharing	Aug. 13	79-A
II	Social Security	Sept. 25	87-A
JJ	Statement on Electoral Reform	Sept. 30	106-A
KK	Merchant Marine	Oct. 23	92-A
LL	Consumer Protection	Oct. 30	98-A
MM	Latin America	Oct. 31	112-A
NN	Trade Policy	Nov. 18	101-A
OO	Statement on Chemical and Biological Warfare	Nov. 25	115-A

PRESIDENTIAL BOXSCORE FOR 1969

Following is a list of President Nixon's specific legislative requests to Congress in 1969, together with a summary of the action taken on each request. A letter in parentheses following each item indicates the most definitive source of the request. A key to the sources appears on the preceding page. Each treaty ratification request made during the Nixon Administration is followed by the date the treaty was sent to the Senate.

STATUS KEY

√   Favorable Action
X   Unfavorable Action
H   Hearings Held
Congressional Inaction Constitutes
    Favorable Action

Foreign Policy

GENERAL

	House Committee Action (1)	House Floor Action (2)	Senate Committee Action (3)	Senate Floor Action (4)	Final Outcome (5)	Public Law Number (6)
1. Increase technical and financial assistance to promote Latin American trade expansion. (MM)						
2. Liberalize system of generalized tariff preferences (in conjunction with other industrialized nations) for all developing countries, including Latin America. (MM)						
3. Raise the rank of the Assistant Secretary of State for Inter-American Affairs to Under Secretary. (MM)						
4. Grant President authority to make modest reductions in U.S. tariffs. (NN)						
5. Eliminate the American Selling Price system of customs evaluation. (NN)						
6. Request clear statement of Congressional intent with regard to non-tariff trade barriers to assist U.S. efforts to obtain reciprocal lowering of such barriers. (NN)						
7. Liberalize escape clause and relief clause of 1962 Trade Expansion Act for industries, firms or workers adversely affected by import competition. (NN)						
8. Provide that determination of eligibility under the escape and relief clauses of the Trade Expansion Act of 1962 be made by the President. (NN)						
9. Make adjustment assistance under Trade Expansion Act of 1962 available to units of multiplant companies and groups of workers in them, when injury is not to entire parent firm. (NN)						
10. Extend President's authority to impose duties or other import restrictions on the products of any nation that places unjustifiable restrictions on U.S. agriculture to cover all U.S. products. (NN)						
11. Provide new authority to take appropriate action against nations that practice what amounts to subsidized competition in third-country markets, when that subsidized competition unfairly affects U.S. exports. (NN)						
12. Provide specific authorization for the funding of U.S. participation in the General Agreement on Tariffs and Trade. (NN)						
13. Create the Overseas Private Investment Corporation and authorize its programs for an initial five years. (W)	√	√	√	√	√	175
14. Expand the role of technical assistance overseas under consolidated legislation and grant a two-year authorization. (W)	√	√	√	√	√	175

FOREIGN AID

	House Committee Action (1)	House Floor Action (2)	Senate Committee Action (3)	Senate Floor Action (4)	Final Outcome (5)	Public Law Number (6)
1. Appropriate $20 million in fiscal 1970 for the ordinary capital of the Asian Development Bank. (W)	√	√	√	X		
2. Appropriate $300 million for the U.S. contribution to the Inter-American Development Bank. (W)	√	√	√	X		

	1	2	3	4	5	6
3. Appropriate $25 million for the U.S. contribution to the Special Fund of the Asia Development Bank in Fiscal 1970. (W)						
4. Include a 43-percent increase in the U.S. contribution for multilateral technical assistance through the U.N. Development Program. (W)	X	X	X	X		
5. Appropriate $605 million in economic aid for Latin America; $625 million for the Near East and South Asia; $186 million for Africa; $234 million for East Asia; $400 million for Vietnam. (W)	X	X	X	X		
6. Appropriate $2.2 billion for AID. (W)	X	X	X	X		
7. Appropriate $75 million to augment existing reserves for guaranties to be issued by the proposed Overseas Private Investment Corp. (W)	X	✓	✓	X		
8. Appropriate $425 million for military assistance. (W)	X	X	X	X		
9. Make $275 million available for credit on essential military equipment by nations able to pay all or part of their defense requirements. (W)	✓	✓	X	X		

TREATIES

	1	2	3	4	5	6
1. Treaty on Non-Proliferation of Nuclear Weapons. 2/5/69	—	—	✓	✓	✓	—
2. Paris Convention for the Protection of Industrial Property. 3/12/69			✓			
3. Convention establishing the World Intellectual Property Organization. 3/12/69			✓			
4. Agreement between the U.S. and Canada for additional temporary diversions of the Niagara River for power purposes. 3/14/69			✓	✓	✓	—
5. Two radio broadcasting agreements with the United Mexican states. 3/35/69			✓	✓	✓	—
6. Convention on Conduct of Fishing Operations in the North Atlantic. 4/16/69			✓	✓	✓	—
7. Consular convention dealing with functions, privileges and immunities of consular officers. 10/8/69			✓	✓		
8. Convention relating to the estate and inheritance tax with the Netherlands for the purpose of avoiding double taxation. 10/13/69			✓			
9. Agreements dealing with adjustments in flood control payments to Canada, resulting from early completion of two projects on the Columbia River. 10/14/69			✓	✓		
10. Geneva Protocol of 1925 which prohibits the first use in war of "asphyxiating, poisonous, or other gases and bacteriological methods of warfare." 11/25/69						
11. Vienna Convention on consular relations and Optional Protocol concerning the compulsory settlement of disputes. 5/5/69			✓	✓	✓	—

Taxes and Economic Policy

TAXES

	1	2	3	4	5	6
1. Impose a tax of nine cents a gallon on all fuels used in general aviation. (Y)	✓	✓	✓			
2. Impose a tax of five percent upon air freight waybills. (Y)	✓	✓	✓			
3. Establish a tax of $3 on passenger tickets for most international flights originating in the U.S. (Y)	✓	✓	✓			
4. Establish a tax of eight percent on airline tickets for domestic flights. (Y)	✓	✓	✓			
5. Extend the President's discretionary authority under the interest equalization tax for 18 months beyond its scheduled expiration in July. (L)	✓	✓	✓	✓	✓	128
6. Enact a "minimum income tax" for citizens with substantial incomes. (M)	✓	✓	X	X	X	172
7. Enact a low-income allowance to remove more than two million low-income families from the Federal tax rolls and assure that those in poverty pay no federal income taxes. (M)	✓	✓	✓	✓	✓	172
8. Help workers who change jobs by liberalizing deductions for moving expenses. (L)	✓	✓	✓	✓	✓	172
9. Reduce proportionately nonbusiness deductions of taxpayers who have certain nontaxable income or other preferences. (M)	✓	✓	X	X	X	172
10. Treat certain mineral transactions in a way that would stop artificial creation of net operating losses in mineral industries. (M)	✓	✓	✓	✓	✓	172
11. Impose stricter surveillance of exempt organizations, including private foundations. (M)	✓	✓	✓	✓	✓	172
12. Tighten rules affecting charitable deductions. (M)	✓	✓	✓	✓	✓	172
13. Curb the practice of using multiple subsidiaries and affiliated corporations to take undue advantage of the lower tax rate on the first $25,000 of corporate income. (M)	✓	✓	✓	✓	✓	172

How the Boxscore Works

The items tabulated in the Boxscore include only the specific legislative requests contained in the President's messages to Congress and other public statements.

Excluded from the Boxscore are proposals advocated by Executive Branch officials but not specifically by the President; measures endorsed by the President but not requested by him; nominations; and suggestions that Congress consider or study particular topics, when legislative action is not requested.

Except for major proposals, Presidential requests for District of Columbia legislation also are excluded from the Boxscore tabulation.

Routine appropriation requests, which provide funds for regular, continuing Government operations,

are excluded. Appropriation requests for specific programs, however, which the President indicated in special messages or other communications were important in his over-all legislative program, are included.

Because the Boxscore fundamentally is a tabular checklist of the President's program, presented in neither greater nor less detail than is found in Presidential messages, the individual requests necessarily differ considerably from one another in their scope and importance.

Because Congress does not always vote "yes" or "no" on a proposal, CQ evaluates legislative action to determine whether compromises amount to approval or rejection of the President's requests.

	1	2	3	4	5	6
14. Impose restrictions on farm losses, to be included in the "limitation on tax preferences." (M)						
15. Recommend repeal of the 7-percent investment tax credit. (M)	√	√	√	√	√	172
16. Extend the surtax at 5 percent for the first six months of 1970. (M)	√	√	√	√	√	172
17. Extend the surtax at 10 percent until Dec. 31, 1969. (M)	√	√	√	√	√	172
18. Enact revenue-sharing plan to return percentage of personal income tax to states on basis of each state's share of national population, adjusted for the state's revenue effort. (HH)	√	√	√	√	√	53
			H			

ECONOMIC POLICY

	1	2	3	4	5	6
1. Establish a new public debt limit of $300 billion. (E)	√	√	√	√	√	8
2. Extend federal regulation to one-bank holding companies. (I)	√	√				

National Security

	1	2	3	4	5	6
1. Amend the Military Selective Service Act of 1967, authorizing modifications in call-up procedures. (T)	√	√	√	√	√	124
2. Approve an antiballistic missile defense system. (H)	√	√	√	√	√	121
3. Appropriate $777,000 in supplemental funds for the Office of Emergency Preparedness for telecommunications research. (K)	√	√	√	√	√	47
4. Appropriate $200,000 in supplemental funds for increased staff capability of the National Security Council. (K)	√	√	√	√	√	47

Resources and Public Works

NATURAL RESOURCES

	1	2	3	4	5	6
1. Appropriate $4 million in supplemental funds for the Department of Agriculture and the Department of Interior for fiscal 1970 for the Administration's lumber program. (K)	√	√				
2. Appropriate $14 million in supplemental funds for the Department of Agriculture to liquidate contract authority required to build 500 miles of forest roads. (K)	√	√	√	√	√	98
3. Appropriate $610,000 in supplemental funds for Interior and Agriculture Departments in 1969 to initiate a new lumber program. (K)	√	√	√	√	√	47
4. Appropriate $35 million in supplemental funds for disaster relief. (K)	√	√	√	√	√	47
5. Appropriate $500,000 in supplemental funds for the Department of Interior to repair facilities damaged during California floods. (K)	√	√	√	√	√	47

Welfare and Urban Affairs

TRANSPORTATION

	1	2	3	4	5	6
1. Provide $10 billion out of general fund over 12-year period for developing and improving public transportation in local communities. (EE)			√			
2. Authorize $300 million in fiscal 1971 for public transportation in local communities. (EE)	√	√	√	√	√	168
3. Provide for authorization renewal every two years to provide for longer range contracts. (EE)			√			
4. Increase shipbuilding subsidy from 10 ships a year to new level of 30 ships a year. (KK)						
5. Lower percentage of cost subsidies for shipbuilding to 45 percent for fiscal 1971. (KK)						
6. Provide that shipbuilding subsidies be paid to ship builders rather than ship owners. (KK)						
7. Increase level of federally insured mortgages by raising ceiling from $1 billion to $3 billion. (KK)						
8. Extend merchant marine subsidy coverage to bulk carriers not presently covered. (KK)						
9. Establish a Commission to review status of American shipbuilding and report within three years. (KK)						
10. Appropriate $148,000 in supplemental funds for fiscal 1969 for the National Transportation Board. (K)	√	√	√	√	√	47
11. Provide $180 million in fiscal 1970 in federal aid for airport development, $220 million in fiscal 1971, and continued expansion to a total of $2.5 million in the next 10 years. (Y)	√	√	√			

GENERAL WELFARE

	1	2	3	4	5	6
1. Revise welfare system to provide that the Federal Government pay a basic income to those American families who cannot care for themselves, in whichever state they live. (FF)	H					
2. Allow first $60 a month of income to be exempt from reduction in benefits under new basic income program. (FF)	H					
3. Allow working poor to qualify for additions to income under new basic income program. (FF)	H					
4. Eliminate requirement that household be without a father under new basic income program. (FF)	H					
5. Require persons to accept training or work under new basic income program. (FF)	H					
6. Provide major expansion of job training and daycare facilities under new basic income program. (FF)	H					
7. Provide uniform Federal payment minimums for the present three categories of welfare aid to adults. (FF)	H					
8. Increase Social Security benefits across-the-board by 10 percent. (II)	X	X		X	X	172
9. Provide that future benefits in Social Security system be automatically adjusted to account for increases in the cost of living. (II)	H					
10. Provide additional adjustments to Social Security regulations in regard to outside earning, rate bases and special categories of recipients. (II)	H					

General Government

CRIME

	1	2	3	4	5	6
1. Enact legislation making it a federal crime to send materials dealing with a sexual subject to anyone under 18. (R)	H					
2. Enact legislation making it a federal crime to use the mails for the commercial exploitation of a prurient interest in sex through advertising. (R)	H					
3. Extend existing law to enable a citizen to protect his home from any intrusion of sex-oriented advertising. (R)	H					
4. Appropriate $2.5 million in supplemental funds for the Department of Justice for crime prevention. (K)	√	√	√	√	√	47
5. Appropriate $25 million in fiscal 1970 to fight organized crime. (N)	√	√	√	√	√	153

	1	2	3	4	5	6
6. Appropriate $300 million in fiscal 1970 for the Law Enforcement Assistance Administration. (N)						
7. Enact a witness immunity law to cover cases involving violation of a federal statute. (N)	✓	✓	✓	✓	✓	153
8. Amend the wagering tax laws and increase the federal operator's tax on gamblers from $50 annually to $1000. (N)			✓			
9. Enact the "Organized Crime Control Act of 1969" to improve the investigation and prosecution of organized crime and to provide appropriate sentencing for convicted offenders. (N)			H			
10. Make the systematic corruption of community political leadership and law enforcement officials a federal crime. (N)			✓			
11. Enact legislation making it a federal crime to engage in an illicit gambling operation from which five or more persons derive income, which has been in operation more than 30 days, or from which the daily "take" exceeds $2000. (N)			H			
12. Appropriate $850,000 in supplemental funds for the Judiciary. (Fiscal 1969) (U)	✓	✓	✓	✓	✓	47
13. Tighten regulatory controls on dangerous drugs to ensure greater accountability and guard against illegal diversion. (AA)	H		✓			
14. Modernize law enforcement criteria and procedures for dangerous drugs. (AA)	H		✓			

CONSUMER PROTECTION

	1	2	3	4	5	6
1. Create new Office of Consumer Affairs in the Executive Office of the President with new legislative standing, expanded budget and greater responsibilities. (LL)	H					
2. Create a new Division of Consumer Protection in the Department of Justice to act as consumer advocate before federal regulatory agencies in judicial proceedings and in Government councils. (LL)	H					
3. Enact a new consumer protection law to establish "class action" procedures to allow groups of consumers to sue for damages resulting from certain kinds of fraudulent or deceptive devices. (LL)	H					
4. Expand the powers for a revitalized Federal Trade Commission. (LL)	H		H			
5. Appropriate operating funds for the National Commission on Consumer Finance to investigate and report on the state of consumer credit. (LL)	✓	✓	✓	✓	✓	166

DISTRICT OF COLUMBIA
(Major Requests Only)

	1	2	3	4	5	6
1. Appropriate $1.24 million to acquire site and complete planning for new District courthouse. (B)	✓	✓	✓	✓	✓	155
2. Provide 10 more judgeships for the District of Columbia. (B)			✓	✓		
3. Authorize 40 more assistant district attorneys for the District. (B)			✓	✓		
4. Appropriate $700,000 for the Legal Aid Agency for a staff increase and an offender rehabilitation project. (B)						
5. Authorize 1,000 extra police officers for the District. (B)			✓	✓		
6. Enact legislation authorizing pretrial detention of dangerous criminals. (B)	✓ H	✓	✓ H	✓ H	✓	155
7. Bring the Juvenile Court into the new District of Columbia Court of General Jurisdiction. (B)			✓	✓		
8. Increase funding for the Group Home Rehabilitation project. (B)	✓	✓	✓	✓	✓	155
9. Provide home rule for the District of Columbia. (B)			H			
10. Create a Commission on Self-Government for the District, to submit to Congress and the President a proposal for self-government in the District. (P)			✓	✓		
11. Approve an amendment to the Constitution granting the District at least one representative in the House and such additional representatives as Congress shall approve, and to provide for the possibility of two Senators. (P)			✓	✓		
12. Until such amendment is ratified, enact legislation to provide for a nonvoting House delegate from the District. (P)			✓	✓		
13. Increase the number of supergrade positions available to the District Government. (P)			✓	✓		
14. Authorize a federal payment formula, fixing the federal contribution at 30 percent of local tax and other general fund revenues. (P)	✓ X	✓	✓ X	✓	✓	187
15. Enact authorizing legislation for a 97-mile national capital regional transit system. (P)	✓	✓	✓	✓	✓	143

GOVERNMENT OPERATIONS

	1	2	3	4	5	6
1. Adopt Reorganization Plan No. 1, to give the President authority to designate the chairman of the Interstate Commerce Commission from among its members. (CC)					#	
2. Adopt Reorganization Plan No. 1, to provide that administrative authority of the Interstate Commerce Commission be vested in its chairman. (CC)					#	
3. Adopt the direct election approach to electoral reform. (JJ)	√	√	H			
4. Extend for at least two years the President's authority to transmit reorganization plans to the Congress. (A)	√	√	√	√	√	5
5. Abolish the system of individual electors. (C)	√	√	H			
6. Allocate electoral votes to Presidential candidates to approximate the popular vote. (C)	X					
7. Make a 40-percent electoral vote plurality sufficient to choose a President. (C)	√	√	H			
8. Specify that if a Presidential candidate who received a clear electoral vote plurality dies before the electoral votes were counted, the Vice President-elect should be chosen President. (C)	√	√	H			
9. Provide that in the event of the death of the Vice President-elect, the President-elect should, upon taking office, be required to follow the procedures provided in the 25th Amendment for filling the unexpired term of the Vice President. (C)	√	√	H			
10. Give Congress responsibility, should both the President-elect and the Vice President-elect die or become unable to serve during this interim, to provide for the selection of persons to serve as President and Vice President. (C)	√	√	H			
11. Clarify the situation presented by the death of a Presidential or Vice Presidential candidate prior to the general election. (C)	√	√	H			
12. Eliminate the requirement for Presidential appointment and Senatorial confirmation of postmasters of first-, second- and third-class post offices. (F)	H	√	√			
13. Provide for appointment of all postmasters by the Postmaster General in the competitive civil service. (F)	H	√	√			
14. Prohibit political considerations in the selection or promotion of postal employees. (F)	H	√	√			
15. Increase postal rates for letters and cards (first-class mail) to seven and six cents respectively. (O)	H					
16. Increase postal rates for newspapers and magazines (second-class mail) which circulate outside the county by 12 percent. (O)	H					
17. Increase postal rates for third-class mail to 16 percent above present levels by January 1, 1970, and increase the single piece third-class rate by one cent on July 1, 1969. (O)	H					
18. Create an independent Postal Service wholly owned by the Federal Government. (V)	X		H			
19. Provide for new and extensive bargaining rights for postal employees. (V)	H		H			
20. Authorize bond financing for major improvements in the postal system. (V)	H		H			
21. Provide a fair and orderly procedure for changing postage rates, subject to Congressional review. (V)	H		H			
22. Provide regular reports to Congress to facilitate Congressional oversight of the postal system. (V)	H		H			
23. Enact a Grant Consolidation Act to empower the President to initiate consolidation of closely related federal assistance programs and to place them under a single agency. (Q)	H		H			
24. Approve extension of the authorization for OEO appropriations from June 30, 1969, to June 30, 1971. (X)	√	√	√	√	√	177
25. Appropriate $172,600,000 in supplemental funds for mandatory payments to veterans (fiscal years 1968 and 1969). (U)	√	√	√	√	√	47
26. Appropriate $30,353,000 in supplemental funds for federal agency expenses for recent storms and floods (fiscal 1969). (U)	√	√	√	√	√	47

Health

	1	2	3	4	5	6
1. Create a Commission on Population Growth and the American Future. (BB)	√		√	√		
2. Grant broader and more precise legislative authority and financial support for family planning service activities within HEW. (BB)	H		H			

Labor and Agriculture

LABOR

#	Item	1	2	3	4	5	6
1.	Provide unemployment insurance coverage for 4.8 million additional workers. (Z)	✓	✓				
2.	Require that states permit workers to continue to receive unemployment insurance benefits while in training programs. (Z)	✓	✓				
3.	Set standard of eligibility for unemployment insurance at minimum period of 15 weeks employment rather than exclusively amount earned. (Z)	X	X				
4.	Disallow unemployment insurance benefits to strikers. (Z)	X	X				
5.	Provide for extension of the length of time for unemployment insurance benefits during periods of high unemployment (Z)	✓	✓				
6.	Raise taxable wage base for unemployment insurance over a five-year period to $6,000. (Z)	✓	✓				
7.	Consolidate major manpower development programs under Department of Labor. (GG)			H			
8.	Provide flexible funding for manpower development programs according to local needs. (GG)			H			
9.	Allow for decentralization of administration of manpower training services as states and cities are able to take over. (GG)			H			
10.	Establish a National Computerized Job Bank. (GG)			H			
11.	Authorize the use of the comprehensive manpower training system as an economic stabilizer (increased funding during high unemployment). (GG)			H			
12.	Establish as part of a comprehensive Occupational Safety and Health Act a National Occupational Safety and Health Board to set standards, and a National Advisory Committee on Occupational Safety and Health to advise the Secretary of Labor and the Secretary of Health, Education and Welfare in the administration of the Act. (DD)	H	H				
13.	Modernize a wide range of mandatory coal mine health and safety standards. (G)	✓	✓	✓	✓	✓	173
14.	Authorize the Secretary of Interior to develop and promulgate additional or revised standards for the health and safety of miners. (G)	✓	✓	✓	✓	✓	173
15.	Provide strict deterrents and enforcement measures and establish appeal procedures to remedy any arbitrary and unlawful actions on mine safety. (G)	✓	✓	✓	✓	✓	173
16.	Recruit and train coal mine inspectors to investigate the coal mines and to enforce broad mandatory standards. (G)	✓	✓	✓	✓	✓	173
17.	Improve federal-state mine inspection plans. (G)	✓	✓	✓	✓	✓	173
18.	Substantially increase, by direct action, grants and contracts, research, training and education for the prevention and control of occupational diseases, the improvement of state workmen's compensation systems and the reduction of mine accidents. (G)	✓	✓	✓	✓	✓	173
19.	Appropriate $20 million in supplemental funds for the Department of Labor for unemployment compensation for federal employees and ex-servicemen. (K)	✓	✓	✓	✓	✓	47

AGRICULTURE

#	Item	1	2	3	4	5	6
1.	Provide poor families enough food stamps to purchase a nutritionally complete diet. (S)	✓	✓	✓	✓	✓	116
2.	Provide food stamps at no cost to those in the very lowest income brackets. (S)	H		X	✓		
3.	Provide food stamps to others at a cost of no more than 30 percent of income. (S)	H		✓	✓		
4.	Give the Secretary of Agriculture authority to operate food stamp and direct distribution programs concurrently in individual counties, at the request and expense of local officials. (S)	H					
5.	Appropriate $1 billion for the Commodity Credit Corporation. (D)	✓	✓	✓	✓	✓	7
6.	Appropriate $1,400,000 in supplemental funds for the Department of Agriculture to prevent a mass migration of screwworms. (K)	✓	✓	✓	✓	✓	47

White House Fails To Assess Legislative Accomplishments

For the second straight year, the White House made no formal, post-session evaluation of how Congress treated Mr. Nixon's legislative requests. Aides of former President Johnson adopted the same stance last year, breaking a pattern set in 1961.

Though no formal evaluation of legislative accomplishments was forthcoming from the White House after adjournment of the first session of the 91st Congress, Nixon aides did hold a brief oral backgrounder on the subject for selected newsmen.

NIXON ADMINISTRATION SLOWS CIVIL RIGHTS MOVEMENT

In the first year of the Nixon Administration, White House support for the civil rights movement declined sharply from that of the Kennedy and Johnson Administrations. *(Congress and the Nation Vol. I p. 1596; Vol. II p. 343)*

The Nixon Administration did not obstruct progress in civil rights, but no longer was the prestige and authority of the White House solidly behind the efforts of minority-group citizens for full equality.

As anticipated, Richard M. Nixon, elected President with strong southern support but only a fraction of the Negro vote, moved deliberately to implement existing law, seeking to soften its impact upon the South and consequently relinquishing any leadership role in civil rights.

Observers noted, however, that the frequency of race-related civil disorders in the nation's cities dropped abruptly in 1969—whatever the reason, still a definite break in the steady increase of such disorders since 1961.

The new Administration enunciated no clear civil rights policy. No civil rights message was sent to Congress.

The stance of the Administration on the crucial domestic questions of equal educational, political and economic opportunity for minority groups was described solely by its actions during the year. Reflecting no singleminded direction, the essential impact of its actions was to slow the tempo of civil rights progress.

• The Administration twice requested—and the Supreme Court twice denied—further delay in the desegregation of Deep South school systems.

• The Administration proposed—and the House of Representatives accepted—amendments to the Voting Rights Act of 1965 (PL 89-110) which would extend its effect nationwide, in place of a simple five-year extension of the existing law which affected only certain southern states.

The civil rights record of the Administration was also marked by more positive action, chiefly the introduction of the "Philadelphia Plan" to require building and construction trades unions to accept more minority-group members. Even usually critical civil rights leaders described this program as potentially the most constructive step toward economic equality taken by a President since the 1930s.

Also, in response to statistics showing segregation of public schools as prevalent in some northern and western cities as in the South, the Administration began to focus more attention upon enforcement efforts outside the South.

School Desegregation

In 1969, the first and the last civil rights moves of the Administration dealt with school desegregation. Despite zigs and zags during the year, the basic thrust of Administration actions was directed toward delaying the final desegregation deadline for southern schools.

Twice that stance was rebuffed brusquely by the Supreme Court which observed that the time for delay and for all deliberate speed was past.

• Within a week of taking office, Secretary of Health, Education and Welfare (HEW) Robert H. Finch announced termination of federal funds to five school districts which had refused to comply with desegregation guidelines. Finch added a proviso, however, allowing the districts 60 days to comply and obtain retroactive restoration of funds. (Ultimately only one of those districts lost its funds.)

• The Justice Department Dec. 31 asked the Supreme Court to disregard pending school cases until September 1970, setting that as the final deadline for desegregation of southern schools. The Administration promised an all-out effort to achieve desegregation by that date. The Court Jan. 14 rejected the request—as it had a previous one Oct. 29—and ordered desegregation of 14 school systems on Feb. 1, 1970.

Enforcement Shift

Attorney General John N. Mitchell and HEW Secretary Finch July 3 announced a shift in the mode of enforcing school desegregation. No longer would the Administration rely chiefly upon fund cut-offs by HEW to bring districts into compliance. Instead, major emphasis would shift to the use of lawsuits initiated by the Justice Department against noncomplying school systems. Such a shift would, Finch and Mitchell said, minimize the need for termination of funds, an action which disproportionately penalized the poor and the black students.

The announced shift to litigation was criticized by the U.S. Commission on Civil Rights as a change to a less effective means of bringing desegregation. School desegregation statistics released by HEW showed that areas under court order achieved substantially less desegregation than those under the jurisdiction of HEW. The new emphasis on litigation as the vehicle of the federal enforcement effort, the Commission said, would slow the pace of school desegregation.

The joint statement was also interpreted as implying that the final deadline for school desegregation could be moved from the fall of 1969 to the fall of 1970. Such an interpretation was considered a major factor in the refusal of more than 40 southern districts to carry out agreed-upon desegregation plans in September 1969.

Fund Termination Orders. During the first six months of 1969, Secretary Finch announced termination of funds to 14 districts. Only five of the districts were without funds at the end of the year: one had regained funds by court order; the others through voluntary compliance.

When the Nixon Administration took office, 123 districts had lost federal funds for noncompliance since 1964.

No fund cut-offs were announced after July 1969, but spokesmen for the HEW Office of Civil Rights told *Congressional Quarterly* that the Administration had not abandoned that mode of enforcement.

An August ruling by the 5th Circuit Court of Appeals had necessitated reconsideration of 41 districts which had been ruled in noncompliance with the HEW guidelines. The Court of Appeals had held that HEW could not terminate funds to all of a school system's programs without presenting facts to show that each program was administered in a discriminatory manner or was so affected by discrimination elsewhere in the system that it became discriminatory *(Taylor County (Fla.) Board of Instruction v. Finch).*

Review of the cases was continuing at the end of 1969. Funds would not be terminated in a district until its case had been considered in light of the August decision.

As of Jan. 8, 1970, 97 districts were without federal funds because of their refusal to desegregate. A court order in the suit brought by the Federal Government against Georgia had directed HEW to restore funds to 30 of those districts.

The largest numbers of terminated districts (prior to the court order) were in Georgia (34) and Mississippi (30), with 10 each in South Carolina and Arkansas, five in Louisiana, four in Florida, and two each in Texas and Virginia. (Alabama is under court order and therefore has not had funds terminated.)

Ninety-nine other districts which had lost funds earlier had returned to compliance: 39 of them in 1969. Those 39 included 10 districts in Mississippi, eight in Virginia, seven in South Carolina, six in Georgia, five in Louisiana, and one each in Arkansas, Tennessee and North Carolina.

Also in 1969, HEW initiated its first enforcement proceedings against a nonsouthern school system, citing Ferndale, Mich. for violation of the guidelines.

Administration Suits. During 1969, the Nixon Administration initiated 43 lawsuits against recalcitrant school districts and joined in more than a dozen others brought by private parties. Five other school suits had been filed early in 1969 by the Johnson Administration. In 1968, 41 school suits had been brought by the Justice Department.

The Nixon Administration Aug. 1 filed the first state-wide desegregation suit, charging that Georgia education officials had acted to perpetuate, rather than to eliminate, that state's dual school systems. A federal court Dec. 17 ordered Georgia to obtain final plans from its noncomplying districts for implementation Sept. 1, 1970. The court ordered the state to cut off funds to districts which refused to comply and directed HEW to restore to some 30 terminated districts their eligibility for federal funds.

In 1969, the Justice Department filed suits against the school systems of Madison, Ill., and Waterbury, Conn., bringing to seven the total number of nonsouthern school suits in which the Government was participating. In July, the Justice Department warned the Chicago school system that its faculty assignment policy did not meet federal desegregation standards.

The Justice Department, on the recommendation of HEW, filed suits against more than a dozen districts which had reneged on pledges to desegregate in September 1969.

A Policy of Delay

During its first year, the Nixon Administration severed the longtime alliance of the Federal Government with civil rights advocates in school desegregation cases, twice requesting delays in desegregation. Both requests were rejected by the Supreme Court.

In an unprecedented move, Secretary Finch Aug. 19 intervened in a school suit to withdraw HEW-approved plans for 33 school districts and to ask the court to delay the desegregation of those systems. Lower courts granted the request; and the delay was appealed to the Supreme Court.

The slowdown in enforcement implied in Finch's request sparked a "revolt" among lawyers in the civil

rights division of the Justice Department who protested such delay. Several of the attorneys resigned.

The U.S. Commission on Civil Rights Sept. 12 charged that the Nixon Administration was leading a major retreat in school desegregation. It expressed concern that, for the first time, the Government had actively sought delay in segregation. It also urged defeat of the Whitten amendment to the HEW appropriation bill which would require HEW to accept freedom-of-choice plans, regardless of their effect.

A unanimous Supreme Court, including the Nixon-appointed Chief Justice Warren E. Burger, Oct. 29 flatly rejected the Administration's request for delay.

The Court directed immediate desegregation, stating that maintenance of segregated schools under the guise of "all deliberate speed" was no longer acceptable. A lower court set Dec. 31 as the desegregation deadline for the schools concerned.

Secretary Finch Nov. 16 announced that—in light of the Supreme Court ruling—he was notifying 112 districts that they must produce effective desegregation plans by Dec. 31 or face punitive action.

Again, on Dec. 31, the Administration asked the Supreme Court to delay desegregation until September 1970, setting that as the final deadline for desegregation of southern schools. The Justice Department pledged a massive effort to effect desegregation by that date.

The Supreme Court Jan. 14—for the second, time—rejected such an Administration request. By a 6-2 vote—the first so divided on school desegregation—the Court ordered schools involved to desegregate by Feb. 1, 1970. Chief Justice Burger and Justice Potter Stewart were the dissenters.

The Whitten Amendment

The Administration helped defeat an amendment to the Labor-HEW appropriations bill (HR 13111) which would have forbidden termination of federal funds to any district which had a freedom-of-choice plan, regardless of its effectiveness.

Known as the Whitten amendment after its author, Rep. Jamie L. Whitten (D Miss.), the amendment was accepted by the House in July. Despite pleas from House Republican leaders, the Administration had not opposed the amendment during House consideration of the bill.

Later in the year, appearing before the Senate Appropriations Committee, Secretary Finch announced the opposition of the Administration to the amendment. On Dec. 13 Finch sent nine-page telegrams to all Senators asking them to delete the amendment or insert nullifying language.

The Senate Dec. 17 inserted language into the amendment to nullify its intended restraining effect. The House later voted to accept the Senate language, effectively killing the amendment.

Voting Rights

The most bitter defeat for civil rights in 1969 was House approval of Administration amendments to the Voting Rights Act of 1965, accepted in place of a simple extension of a law under which more than 800,000 Negroes registered as voters in the South.

The force of the law—which the Rev. Theodore M. Hesburgh, chairman of the U.S. Commission on Civil

Rights, described as the most effective civil rights measure ever enacted—would expire August 1970.

Under the Act—which suspended literacy tests and similar voter qualification devices and authorized federal supervision of election procedures in certain areas—Negro registration in the South jumped from 29 percent to 52 percent of those eligible.

The Act took effect in a county or state where a literacy test or device was in effect on Nov. 1, 1964, and where less than 50 percent of the voting-age population was registered or did vote in the 1964 election. As of 1969, the Act covered Alabama, Georgia, Mississippi, South Carolina, Virginia and a number of North Carolina countries. *(Congress and the Nation, Vol. II p. 356)*

A five-year extension of the Act, through August 1975, was urged as necessary to preserve the political gains which Negroes had made under the Act. Such a bill (HR 4249) was introduced in January by House Judiciary Committee Chairman Emanuel Celler (D N.Y.). The Administration delayed stating its position until late in June.

After cancelling five previously scheduled appearances before the House Judiciary Committee, Attorney General Mitchell appeared June 26 to unveil the Administration position. Stating that the Administration could not support the simple five-year extension of "essentially regional legislation," Mitchell proposed that Congress amend the 1965 Act to suspend all literacy tests until Jan. 1, 1974, make the Act effective in all 50 states, delete the requirement that affected areas obtain federal approval of all changes in voting laws, and set a minimum residency requirement for voting in national elections.

Civil rights leaders immediately criticized the proposal as a sophisticated but deadly way to void the 1965 Act, diluting its impact on areas where discrimination was most prevalent by spreading its effect nationwide. The House Judiciary Committee rejected the Administration bill and reported the five-year extension of the unamended Act.

House Minority Leader Gerald R. Ford (R Mich.) urged approval of the Administration bill, saying that the purpose of such "discriminatory legislation" (The 1965 Act) had been accomplished and that the South should not continue to be punished for actions since remedied.

During floor consideration of the Committee bill, the Administration amendments were proposed as a substitute. Over substantial opposition, they were adopted—by a 208-203 roll-call vote—in place of the five-year extension.

Civil rights advocates described the House action as the most severe defeat for civil rights inflicted by the House in a decade.

In the Senate, liberal Senators blocked referral of the bill to the Judiciary Committee until they received assurances that the Committee would be instructed to report it back by March 1, 1970, and that it would then become the pending business of the Senate. The Senate Judiciary Committee, chaired by James O. Eastland (D Miss.), had not been traditionally speedy in acting upon civil rights legislation.

During 1969, federal election observers were sent to 12 counties. The Justice Department reviewed more than 150 statutory changes in voting procedures and objected to 18 of them. The Administration initiated no voting rights suits.

Equal Employment

The Nixon Administration's most innovative civil rights proposal was its introduction of the "Philadelphia Plan"—which civil rights leaders, generally critical of the Administration, praised as potentially the most constructive step toward economic equality taken by any President since 1934.

The "Philadelphia Plan"—so called after the city in which it was first implemented—was announced June 27 by the Department of Labor. Under the plan, every contractor bidding on a federal construction job would be required to pledge himself to a "good-faith effort" to hire a certain level of minority employees.

Labor unions stridently objected to the plan. The late Senate Minority Leader Everett McKinley Dirksen (R Ill.) had labeled it a violation of the 1964 Civil Rights Act (PL 88-252) and was backed by a ruling to that effect by Comptroller General Elmer B. Staats. Secretary of Labor George P. Shultz and Attorney General Mitchell contradicted Staats and held the plan legal. The plan went into effect late in September, and the Labor Department announced that similar plans would be put into effect in New York, Seattle, Boston, Los Angeles, San Francisco, St. Louis, Detroit, Pittsburgh and Chicago.

The issue hit the floor of the Senate in December after the Appropriations Committee had added to the fiscal 1970 supplemental appropriations bill (HR 15209) an amendment forbidding the use of any federal funds as direct aid or through contracts or agreements which the Comptroller General "holds to be in contravention of any federal statute." The Senate in a series of roll-call votes accepted the amendment, which in effect would nullify the plan. However, after a call by the President for the Senate amendment to be killed, the House refused to accept the provision; and the Senate agreed to delete the language. President Nixon had threatened to veto the bill unless the Senate amendment was knocked out.

The Department of Labor's June 27 order set up—for all federal contractors in the Philadelphia area—a nonnegotiable quota system. The order required bidders on federal construction work exceeding $500,000 to meet specific hiring goals set by the Government before bidding on the project.

Assistant Secretary of Labor Arthur Fletcher said that "because of the deployably low rate of employment among members of minority groups" in building and construction trades unions, the Department planned to act immediately to set up quota systems in other major cities.

A spokesman for the building and construction trades department of the AFL-CIO said that such a system was "unworkable in an intermittent employment industry," and that the construction unions were already making a genuine effort to increase minority membership.

Comptroller General Staats ruled Aug. 5 that the Department of Labor program of mandatory quotas for the hiring of minority group members by federal contractors violated the Civil Rights Act of 1964. He cited Titles VI and VII of the 1964 Act which forbade discrimination on the basis of race, color or national origin by any program receiving federal aid or by any employer. Staats dismissed as "largely a matter of semantics" an attempted distinction between a "quota system" (admittedly contrary to the 1964 Act) and a "goal system."

At a news conference Aug. 7, Shultz said that the Department would continue with its plans. Speaking, he said, with the concurrence of Attorney General Mitchell and President Nixon, Shultz said that Staats had overstepped his authority in interpreting the Civil Rights Act to apply to the Philadelphia Plan.

Attorney General Mitchell Sept. 22 issued an opinion which said that nothing in the plan violated the 1964 Act. Mitchell said that to remove any possibility of such violation—that a nonminority worker might be discriminated against so that a minority worker could be hired in order to meet the specified level—the plan stated that the contractor's obligation could not be used to discriminate against any qualified potential employee.

Employment Discrimination Suits. Unions and other discriminatory employers were the targets of 16 suits filed or joined by the Department of Justice in 1969: seven were filed early in the year by the Johnson Administration and nine by the Nixon Administration. Twenty-seven such suits were filed in 1968.

Contract Compliance

Equal employment practices by federal contractors were scrutinized early in 1969 as actions by the Department of Defense and the Department of Transportation (DOT) called into question the commitment of the new Administration to the federal program of contract compliance.

Under that program, federal contractors are required to act affirmatively to provide equal employment opportunities. The Office of Federal Contract Compliance (OFCC) in the Department of Labor administers the program and is authorized to withhold or cancel contracts with companies which failed to meet equal employment standards. No contracts have ever been cancelled for that reason.

Senate hearings in March 1969 examined execution of the program after the Pentagon awarded $9.4 million in contracts to three textile companies which had been ruled in noncompliance with equal employment standards and DOT announced that highway contractors would no longer have to meet equal employment standards before bidding on jobs.

The Departments involved assured Congress that their actions would strengthen, not weaken, the contract compliance program.

Civil Rights Commission Report. In May, the U.S. Commission on Civil Rights released a report charging that the Federal Government was seriously deficient in enforcing the contract compliance program and was therefore using public funds to subsidize discrimination.

Later in the year, the OFCC referred at least one case of alleged employment discrimination by a federal contractor to the Justice Department, which filed suit against him; and the OFCC also warned 17 Chicago contractors that they were not complying with the equal employment standards.

Equal Employment Opportunity Commission

During the March hearings on contract compliance, Dirksen threatened Clifford L. Alexander Jr., then chairman of the Equal Employment Opportunity Commission (EEOC), with loss of his post unless the "punitive harassment" of businesses concerning equal employment ended. Alexander resigned April 9, stating that "a crippling lack of Administration support" rendered his actions as EEOC chairman ineffective. President Nixon May 7 appointed William H. Brown III to succeed Alexander.

The EEOC took little action during the remainder of the year. Its only hearings had been held in March in Los Angeles. At their conclusion the EEOC recommended that the Justice Department file an employment discrimination suit against the entire motion picture and TV film industry. No such suit was filed in 1969.

Debate concerning expanded powers for the EEOC resulted in no action in 1969. The Administration countered proposals which were supported by the majority of Commission members—to grant the EEOC long-sought power to issue cease-and-desist orders—with a bill to authorize the EEOC to take recalcitrant employers to court.

Federal Employment. President Nixon in March directed the heads of all Executive departments and agencies to make "every reasonable effort" to ensure equal employment opportunity within the Government. On August 8 he stiffened the previous directive by Executive Order 11478 ordering the departments and agencies to act affirmatively to end discrimination in all aspects of federal employment.

Fair Housing

Almost four times as many fair housing suits were initiated by the Justice Department in the first year of the Nixon Administration as in 1968—an increase explained in part by the fact that only on Jan. 1, 1969, did one-third of the nation's housing come under the coverage of the 1968 fair housing law (PL 90-284).

During the 1969 calendar year, the Department filed 23 suits under the new law and joined two others.

The Nixon Administration filed the first suit against alleged "blockbusting" tactics and joined Negro homeowners in Chicago in another such suit.

The Justice Department notified 19 major title insurance companies that their practice of including racially restrictive covenants in policies was in violation of the 1968 Act. By the end of the year, 18 of the companies had assured the Government that they would comply with the law by eliminating such covenants.

Other Action

President Nixon March 5 established an Office of Minority Business Enterprise (OMBE) in the Department of Commerce to coordinate existing federal programs to promote minority business enterprise. No new programs were created nor were any actually transferred to the new office.

Under the authority of the 1964 Civil Rights Act, the Justice Department in 1969 filed 45 lawsuits against the owners or operators of various public accommodations for racial discrimination. Ten of the suits were filed during the last days of the Johnson Administration.

The Department in 1969 filed the first two such suits in northern states, one in Rhode Island and one in Connecticut.

ADMINISTRATION PROPOSES BROAD ANTICRIME PROGRAM

As campaign oratory urging law and order and deploring crime in the streets died away and the nation's crime rate continued to spiral upward, Congress in 1969 provided vastly increased funds but no new programs for crime control.

President Nixon's long-promised anticrime program did not reach Capitol Hill until late in the spring, and most of his proposals were still pending on committee agenda at the session's end.

The Administration anticrime program was directed toward four main objectives:

• Increasing funds available for local, state and federal law enforcement agencies.

• Curbing organized crime: its growth, its infiltration into legitimate businesses, and its corruption of local officials.

• Halting the expanding traffic in dangerous drugs and narcotics.

• Slowing the flow of unsolicited obscene material into American homes.

Later proposals which the Nixon Administration might make for federal anticrime legislation were foreshadowed in a "model anticrime package" for the District of Columbia, which Mr. Nixon sent to Congress in July. To combat crime in the nation's capital, which he had described during the 1968 campaign as the "crime capital of the world," Mr. Nixon proposed a three-part program including:

• Bail reform—including provisions to allow pretrial "preventive detention" of criminal suspects who might pose a danger to the community if released on bail.

• Reorganization of the District court system and revision of its criminal code and procedures.

• Creation of a public defender system.

Law Enforcement Funds. At Mr. Nixon's request, Congress quadrupled funds appropriated for the Law Enforcement Assistance Administration (LEAA) in fiscal 1970 over those available in fiscal 1969. (Fiscal 1969: $59.4 million; fiscal 1970 budget request: $296.6 million; fiscal 1970 appropriation: $268.0 million). Most of the LEAA funds were used for action grants for state and local law enforcement agencies.

Organized Crime. President Nixon April 23 urged Congress to enact: *(For text, see p. 49-A.)*

• A general witness immunity law providing that a witness, although immune from prosecution on the basis of his testimony itself, could be prosecuted on the basis of related evidence.

• Wagering tax amendments to increase the federal gambling tax and to enable the Internal Revenue Service to participate more actively in collecting the tax.

• A law to make a federal crime of corrupting local government officials and law enforcement officers.

• A law to make a federal crime of all large-scale illegal gambling operations.

• The "Organized Crime Control Act of 1969" to revise the procedures of federal criminal law for the prosecution of organized crime.

The Senate Judiciary Committee late in the session reported the "Organized Crime Control Act" (S 30) into

which it had incorporated Mr. Nixon's witness immunity, anticorruption and gambling proposals. The Senate took no action on the bill.

The Senate Judiciary Subcommittee on Criminal Laws and Procedures held hearings on the proposed wagering tax amendments, and a House Judiciary Subcommittee conducted hearings on the proposed witness immunity bill; but no further action was taken on the measures.

As part of the Administration's campaign against organized crime, Mr. Nixon, within days of assuming office, ordered use of wiretapping and electronic eavesdropping against organized crime as authorized by Title III of the Omnibus Crime Control and Safe Streets Act of 1968 (PL 90-351.) Attorney General John N. Mitchell July 14 said that the main use of wiretapping by the Nixon Administration was against organized crime and that it had proven very productive.

Drug Traffic. President Nixon July 14 sent Congress a comprehensive bill to revise and modernize the system for federal control of narcotics and other dangerous drugs. The "Controlled Dangerous Substances Act of 1969" (S 2637) proposed: *(For text, see p. 63-A.)*

• Basing federal narcotics laws solely on the power of Congress to regulate interstate commerce. Several federal drug laws, based upon the Congressional power to tax, had been invalidated as unconstitutional.

• Classifying drugs into four categories according to their usefulness and effects, with four sets of control requirements.

• Tightening federal control over drug manufacturers, distributors and dispensers.

• Revising the penalty structure for possession, use and traffic in dangerous drugs.

• Expanding research and education programs concerning drug use.

• Expanding the law enforcement powers of federal narcotics agents.

During hearings, discussions between the Departments of Justice and Health, Education and Welfare (HEW) produced revised penalty structure proposals which were presented to the Subcommittee for inclusion in S 2637. The Administration softened its stance in regard to penalties for the possession of a drug for personal use, eliminating mandatory minimum penalties and treating possession for personal use as a misdemeanor and not as a felony.

The public controversy over drugs and the role which the government should fill in regulating the flow of narcotics was complicated by the jurisdictional problem of whether to consider drug abuse a health problem or a law enforcement issue. Various Congressional Committees —Judiciary, Education and Labor, Crime, and Labor and Public Welfare—held hearings on drug abuse. In the testimony before the various Committees, the disagreement between the Departments of Justice and HEW on the issue was made quite clear.

The Senate Judiciary Committee Dec. 16 reported a clean bill (S 3246) which combined provisions of the Administration bill (S 2637) with those of other proposed bills. Its revised penalty structure contained substantially softened penalties for marijuana offenses. The Senate did not act on the Committee bill before adjournment.

The Justice Department imposed an intensified inspection program, Operation Intercept, Sept. 21 to police the Mexican-American border and halt the flow of drugs there.

Violent protests concerning the delay and inconvenience produced by the car-by-car search by customs officials brought modification of the program Oct. 10 into Operation Cooperation. The United States agreed to adjust its inspection procedures to eliminate the inconvenience, and Mexico promised to act more effectively to halt drug production and the smuggling of drugs into the United States.

Obscenity. Mr. Nixon May 2 asked Congress to enact laws which would prohibit the unsolicited mailing of obscene material to American young people and homes. He asked that Congress: *(For text, see p. 55-A.)*
• Ban the mailing of offensive materials to any person under 18.
• Ban the sending of sex-oriented advertising to American homes.
• Allow citizens to obtain orders forbidding persons from sending further objectionable material to their homes.

Jurisdictional ambiguity again prevented any one committee from assuming the duty of moving ahead on the proposed legislation, despite widespread support in Congress for the measures. The House Judiciary, Post Office and Civil Service, and Government Operations Committees held hearings on the bills, but no further action was taken.

An element of uncertainty concerning the President's proposal to allow persons to obtain orders banning objectionable material from being sent to their homes was injected into the situation Oct. 27 when the Supreme Court agreed to hear arguments on the constitutionality of a 1967 law which authorized such orders on a limited basis *(Rowan v. U.S. Post Office Department).*

District Crime Package. The Administration's most innovative proposals, contained in its anticrime package for the District, drew considerable fire from persons who warned that individual constitutional rights were being disregarded in the effort to combat crime.

Committees in both chambers held hearings on the proposals, but only the Senate took any further action.

After the Senate District of Columbia Committee removed and placed in another bill (S 2869) the more controversial proposals for revising criminal laws and procedure, the Senate approved reorganization of the District courts (S 2601).

The public defender bill (S 2602) and S 2869 were also approved by the Senate. The bail reform bill (S 2600) was ignored by the Senate Judiciary Committee, chiefly because of the vigorous opposition of the Committee's Subcommittee on Constitutional Rights chairman, Sam J. Ervin Jr. (D N.C.), who termed detention a "police state tactic."

The Senate also approved an Administration bill (S 2981) to revise the juvenile code for the District of Columbia, but the House took no action on it.

Related Issues. Various gun control bills—both to tighten and to relax controls on firearms—were introduced in both houses in 1969, but little action aside from Senate hearings was taken.

The Senate did add, and the House concurred in, an amendment to the interest equalization bill (HR 12829) which repealed provisions of the Gun Control Act of 1968 (PL 90-618) which required merchants to keep records of their sales of shotgun and rifle ammunition.

The House May 1 by unanimous vote established its Select Committee on Crime (H Res 17), authorized to investigate all aspects of crime in the United States. The Committee, under its chairman, Claude Pepper (D Fla.), held extensive hearings in Washington and cities throughout the country to obtain an "overview" of the crime problem.

The Senate Juvenile Delinquency Subcommittee investigated conditions in juvenile penal institutions. The Senate Small Business Committee studied the effect of crime on small businesses.

The National Commission on the Causes and Prevention of Violence issued its final report Dec. 12. The report urged a reordering of national priorities and a greater investment of American resources in fulfilling the constitutional goals of establishing justice and insuring domestic tranquility.

The report consisted of the Commission's nine earlier policy statements—on violent crime, group violence, civil disobedience, assassination, law enforcement, firearms, violence in television entertainment, campus disorder and youth—plus chapters on violence in American history, the strengths of America and the relationship of religion to the problem of violence.

Various Congressional committees investigated campus violence and radical groups, including the Students for a Democratic Society. Provisions were included in a number of appropriations bills which prohibited the use of the funds appropriated in that bill for aid to anyone connected with a college or university who had taken part in campus disorder.

The Senate also approved bills which authorized creation of 70 new district judgeships (S 952) and which allowed federal judges, after 20 years of service, to retire with full benefits, regardless of their age (S 1508). The House Judiciary Committee held hearings on S 952, but took no further action.

Related Developments

Prison Reform. President Nixon Nov. 13 announced initiation of a ten-year program to modernize the entire American correctional system, to assist local and state correctional programs and to coordinate all levels of corrections and rehabilitation efforts. *(For text, see p. 122-A.)*

The President made public a 13-point directive which he had issued to Attorney General John N. Mitchell. He asked Mitchell to prepare a 10-year modernization program for the federal correctional system; initiate talks with state and local officials to explore the feasibility of pooling resources to set up regional special treatment facilities; give special emphasis to juveniles, women and mentally disturbed; expand training programs for correction personnel; provide new rehabilitation programs for prisoners and persons on parole.

Burger. Chief Justice Warren E. Burger Aug. 11 said the nation's system of handling convicted criminals needed major overhaul "to make our correctional system better than the revolving door process...of crime, prison and more crime."

ONLY LIMITED CHANGES MADE IN PROGRAMS FOR POOR

Major changes in federal programs for the poor were promised by the Nixon Administration in 1969, but only limited starts had been made by either Congress or the Administration by the year's end.

One of the President's first messages to Congress called for increased spending for federal food programs for the needy. By the end of the year, however, Congress had only increased the fiscal 1970 appropriations for food stamps from $340 million to $610 million. Other reforms proposed by the President, including a recommendation that the neediest of the poor receive free food stamps, were still awaiting final action at the end of the session.

Legislative proposals by the President to reform the welfare system and to increase Social Security benefits by 10 percent were not sent to Congress until mid-summer and early fall. A decision by House Ways and Means Committee Chairman Wilbur D. Mills (D Ark.) to hold combined hearings on the measures delayed final action on the welfare proposals. But Congress did pass a 15-percent across-the-board increase in Social Security benefits as part of the tax reform bill (HR 13270) just before the end of the session.

The President reorganized the Office of Economic Opportunity (OEO), the headquarters of the antipoverty program—a move which did not require Congressional approval. Local community action agencies complained that their organizations were downgraded and reduced in influence by the reorganization. The President stressed, however, that the antipoverty agency was to assume a more innovative, experimental approach in the future.

After some early and unsuccessful Senate efforts to block his proposal to shift the Job Corps from the OEO to the Labor Department and to close 59 Job Corps camps, other changes were made in agency programs without encountering strong Congressional opposition. In one such move, the President sent the popular Head Start program to the Department of Health, Education and Welfare where it became part of a new Child Development Office.

The continuation and funding of the programs under the OEO did, however, provoke considerable Congressional debate, particularly in the House where the bill did not reach the House floor until December. After the defeat of a strong Republican-Southern Democrat move in the House to turn the program over to the states, Congress passed a bill (S 3016) extending the program unchanged for two years.

Hunger

Background

REFERENCES: *Congress and the Nation Vol. I p. 737-40; Congress and the Nation Vol. II p. 556, 778.*

The two main food programs administered by the Department of Agriculture were the commodity distribution and food stamp programs. Commodity distribution was established by Congress in 1949 (PL 81-439). Surplus foods acquired by the Government under price support laws were to be donated to a wide variety of charities and welfare programs. The food stamp program, created by the Food Stamp Act of 1964 (PL 88-525), was designed to increase the food-buying power of low-income families through a Government subsidy. Needy families for a small

amount of money could buy stamps worth a larger amount when presented in local food stores.

The Federal Government also provided subsidized meals to needy children through the National School Lunch Act (PL 79-396), enacted in 1946; the school milk program (PL 83-690), begun in 1954; and the Child Nutrition Act of 1966 (PL 89-642), which extended the lunch and milk programs and added a school breakfast program.

The ability of these programs to meet the needs of the poor was sharply questioned in Congress and by private groups in 1967 and 1968. Congressional investigations and reports by citizens' groups—particularly a report called "Hunger, USA"—called attention to inadequacies in the federal food programs and to the existence of thousands of hungry Americans. Congress responded by increasing funds for the food programs from a total of about $900 million in fiscal 1968 to $1.2 billion in fiscal 1969 and $1.8 billion in fiscal 1970.

The Senate in 1968 also established a 13-member Select Committee on Nutrition and Human Needs, headed by George McGovern (D S.D.), to evaluate Government food programs. In a report issued Aug. 7, 1969, the Committee said the Federal Government would have to spend almost $4 billion more a year more than it was currently spending if it expected to meet the needs of an estimated 25 million undernourished Americans.

1969 Action

Although substantial agreement developed in Congress during 1969 that federal food programs were not reaching enough of the poor, a food stamp reform bill had not cleared Congress by year's end.

President Nixon May 6 recommended that fiscal 1970 funds for food stamps be increased from $340 million to $610 million and that fiscal 1971 spending for the program reach about $1 billion. He also proposed that free stamps be provided for families with monthly incomes under $30 a month.

Hearings throughout the year by the Senate Select Committee on Nutrition and Human Needs highlighted the difficulties faced by the poor in trying to apply for and receive food under the federal programs. Witnesses complained about encountering endless administrative red tape in applying for the stamps, of having to travel miles to pick up their stamps or food under the surplus commodities program and of having the food run out before the end of the month.

The Senate Sept. 24 passed a food stamp bill (S 2547) which provided free stamps to families with incomes under $60 a month and authorized the Secretary of Agriculture to set eligibility standards for participation in the program. The bill also placed a ceiling on the purchase price of stamps so that no family had to spend more than 25 percent of its income for the stamps and permitted the purchase with the stamps of such non-food items as soap.

Passage of the bill marked a major victory for Senate supporters of food stamp reform. The bill was changed considerably on the Senate floor from the version reported by the Senate Agriculture Committee under Chairman Allen J. Ellender (D La.). The Committee bill had authorized $750 million for the fiscal 1970 program and $1.5

billion for the two succeeding fiscal years; as passed, the bill authorized $1.25 billion for fiscal 1970, $2 billion for fiscal 1971 and $2.5 billion for fiscal 1972. The Committee had not provided for free food stamps for the neediest of the poor.

Action in the House on food stamp reform was delayed, however, because of the insistence of Agriculture Chairman W. R. Poage (D Texas) that food stamp reform had to be considered along with hearings on extension of basic farm programs. (Food stamp and farm commodity programs are all administered by the Department of Agriculture.) Poage was known to believe that he would have difficulty getting continuation of farm commodity programs, including subsidy payments to farmers, without trading for the votes of urban Members by use of the food stamp bill. Poage also indicated his opposition to any kind of free stamp program.

But Congress Nov. 6 cleared a bill (H J Res 934) authorizing an increase in the fiscal 1970 food stamp program from $340 million to $610 million, as the President had requested. The Senate June 24 had passed a $750-million fiscal 1970 authorization for food stamps (S J Res 126) but accepted the House-passed bill when it became apparent the House would not approve a higher authorization in 1969.

The agriculture appropriations bill (HR 11612), which was held up pending final action on the food stamp authorization, when passed Nov. 19 included the full $610 million for food stamps. Total fiscal 1970 appropriations for food assistance programs in the bill were $1.8 billion, an increase of $577 million over 1969.

Action was not completed in 1969 on several House-passed bills affecting the school lunch and milk programs. The House March 20 amended the National School Lunch Act and the Child Nutrition Act (HR 515) to establish uniform eligibility standards to ensure that low-income children receive the free or reduced-price meals provided by the programs. The House on July 21 also voted to transfer $100 million in Section 32 customs receipts to the School Lunch program (HR 11651). On May 6 the House passed a bill (HR 5554) to expand and make permanent the special milk program.

The Nixon Budget, like the Johnson Budget, included no request for milk funds. The Administration said it intended to provide milk funds in its expanded school lunch program. Congress, however, appropriated $84 million for the fiscal 1970 milk program in the agriculture appropriations bill and transferred another $20 million in Section 32 funds to the program.

The Senate Dec. 12 extended the life of the Committee on Nutrition and Human Needs through Jan. 31, 1970, so that the Committee would come before the Senate for a one-year renewal at the same time as other committees.

About 2,500 educators, scientists, medical people, food processors, government officials and consumers Dec. 2-4 attended the White House Conference on Food, Nutrition and Health called by President Nixon to advise him on how to end hunger and malnutrition in America.

Welfare and Social Security

Background

REFERENCES: *Congress and the Nation Vol. I p. 1225; Congress and the Nation Vol. II p. 745.*

Social Security Trust Funds

Social Security benefits are paid from three trust funds financed by the proceeds of federal payroll taxes and interest from trust-fund investments in U.S. Government securities.

The Old-Age and Survivors Insurance (OASI) trust fund was set up in 1939. In 1956, when disability insurance was added to the OASI system, Congress set up a separate trust fund from which the disability benefits were to be paid. In 1965, a health insurance trust fund was established to finance health care payments for the elderly (Medicare).

Some experts maintain that income from payroll taxes and investments provides inadequate support to Social Security beneficiaries. They advocate using general revenues to supplement payments from the trust funds.

Retirement benefits and welfare, as the programs are popularly known, were both authorized under the Social Security Act of 1935 (PL 74-271).

The heart of the Social Security Act consisted of five programs: old-age insurance, unemployment insurance, Old-Age Assistance (OAA), Aid to the Blind (AB) and Aid to Dependent Children.

The old-age insurance program (officially called Old-Age, Survivors and Disability Insurance or OASDI) provided retirement benefits to persons who contributed to the system through their working years. Unemployment insurance was financed through a payroll tax on employer and employee.

The programs generally considered "welfare" programs are the three programs of public assistance authorized under the Act—OAA, AB and Aid to Dependent Children (now called Aid to Families with Dependent Children or AFDC). In 1950, a fourth public assistance program was added: Aid to the Permanently and Totally Disabled (APTD) (PL 81-734).

Also included in the welfare category was the Medicaid program, begun in 1960 as Medical Assistance for the Aged (PL 86-778). The program was designed to provide aid to elderly persons not poor enough to qualify for Old-Age Assistance but judged by the states to be "medically needy." In 1965 the medical assistance program was extended to all persons on public assistance.

1969 Action

President Nixon Aug. 8 proposed a major reform of the welfare system to provide a federal minimum welfare payment of $1,600 a year for needy families and to include the working poor among those eligible for assistance payments. *(For text, see p. 75-A, 81-A.)*

The President recommended replacing the Aid to Families with Dependent Children (AFDC) program with a new Family Assistance program. The bulk of welfare recipients were in the AFDC program—6.5 million recipients in March 1969 out of a total of 9.3 million persons on welfare that month.

Two types of families would be covered by the new program: "dependent families" headed by a female or unemployed father, and "working poor" families headed by an employed male whose earnings were below $3,920.

To be eligible for benefits, unemployed fathers and mothers of school-age children would be required to accept job training or employment. Families with earnings would have their $1,600-a-year federal benefit reduced by 50 percent of earnings on money earned above $750 a year.

Two changes were later made in the program as originally proposed by the President. A bill (HR 14173) taken up by the House Ways and Means Committee provided a monthly payment of $90 for blind, elderly and disabled persons rather than the $65 a month originally recommended by the President. The $90 would consist of $63.75 to be paid by the Federal Government and the remainder by the states, with the states ineligible to receive the federal grant unless they guaranteed to increase the total to $90. The Administration also dropped its earlier recommendation that the Family Assistance payments gradually replace food stamps for families eligible for the new welfare payments.

President Nixon Sept. 25 proposed increasing by 10 percent benefits under the OASDI provisions of the Social Security Act. The higher checks were to be mailed in April 1970. The Administration bill (HR 14080) made future increases in OASDI benefits automatic as the cost of living increased.

The President also proposed an increase in the payroll tax that financed hospital insurance (Medicare) to make up for an increasing deficit in the hospital insurance trust fund.

Welfare, Social Security. Hearings before the House Ways and Means Committee began Oct. 15. When Chairman Mills announced that his Committee would hold joint hearings on welfare reform and Social Security benefits, it was assumed that final action on both measures was unlikely in the House in 1969.

Senators and Representatives of both parties proposed bigger and earlier increases than the Presidential recommendation, with a group of House Democrats leading the fight for a 15-percent increase (HR 11349). Mills said he favored raising benefits by 10 percent or more but was opposed to automatic benefit increases. (Congress had increased benefits seven times, with four of the increases being passed in election years.)

Chairman Russell B. Long (D La.) warned that the Senate Finance Committee might act on higher Social Security benefits only if Medicare taxes were not increased and assurance was given of tighter administration of Medicare. Long held two days of hearings in July on the rising costs of the Medicare and Medicaid programs.

Under pressure from many Members who wanted a Social Security benefit increase passed by the end of the year, Congress did enact a 15 percent across-the-board raise in benefits before adjournment. But other changes in the Social Security program were left for possible 1970 action.

Medicaid. One Congressional response to the cost problems which states were facing with the Medicaid program was the passage of a bill (HR 5833—PL 91-56) allowing states to reduce Medicaid services as long as they did not reduce total cash payments. The bill also required a financially distressed state which wished to cut back Medicaid services to demonstrate that it was applying cost-control measures to Medicaid administration.

AFDC Freeze. Congress also saved the states from being faced with even higher welfare increases than they had been experiencing by repealing a freeze on the number of participants in the AFDC program. The freeze, which had been scheduled to go into effect July 1, had been added to the Social Security Amendments of 1967 (PL 90-248) by the House Ways and Means Committee which had sought to trim AFDC costs through more stringent regulations on participation in the program. The freeze set the future proportion of children in each state who could receive AFDC assistance at the percentage of children on the rolls in January 1968.

Unemployment Insurance. President Nixon July 8 proposed that an additional 4.8 million workers be covered by unemployment insurance and that the duration of benefits be extended in periods of high unemployment. Mr. Nixon also urged states to provide unemployed workers with benefits equaling at least 50 percent of their pay when working.

Hearings were held in October by the House Ways and Means Committee on HR 12625 to implement the President's recommendations. The Committee Nov. 10 reported a clean bill (HR 14705) which passed the House Nov. 13.

HR 14705 extended unemployment coverage to 4.5 million additional workers, established a separate fund for extended unemployment benefits during periods of high unemployment and increased the federal payroll tax for unemployment compensation.

No action was taken on the bill in the Senate.

Poverty
Background

REFERENCES; *Congress and the Nation Vol. I, p. 1326-29; Congress and the Nation Vol. II, p. 748-51.*

The Economic Opportunity Act of 1964 (PL 88-452) contained six titles covering a broad range of poverty programs, coordinated by a central Office of Economic Opportunity (OEO). Although the programs were all under the over-all supervision of the OEO (whose appropriation included funds for the various programs), several were delegated to other agencies to be actually administered, such as the Neighborhood Youth Corps delegated to the Department of Labor.

The program met strong opposition from many Members of Congress from its inception through the five turbulent years of its existence. The program was attacked as wasteful, bureaucratic and inefficient at helping the poor to help themselves. Opponents charged that the program had helped to pit black militants against city hall, had supported neighborhood gangs, had reached only a fraction of the poor and had cost more with poorer results than if private enterprise had done the job.

During Mr. Nixon's campaign for the Presidency, he said little about the poverty program in general but indicated that the Job Corps was a failure and probably should be ended and that Head Start was a success and probably should be expanded.

1969 Action

Although the authorization for the antipoverty program expired on June 30, it was not until Dec. 20 that a new two-year authorization for the program was approved by Congress. The program had been caught during the year in a fight between mostly Democratic supporters in the House, including Education and Labor Committee Chairman Carl D. Perkins (D Ky.), and several members of his Committee who wanted to change the program in a number of important details.

Although committee hearings were completed in early summer, the Senate did not pass a bill (S 3016) until Oct. 14. The bill authorized $2.048 billion for fiscal 1970 (the amount requested by the Administration) and $2.732 billion for fiscal 1971 ($584.2 million more than the Administration request). The Senate also approved a controversial amendment which allowed state Governors to veto legal services projects in their states.

The House Dec. 12 passed HR 12321 authorizing $2,343,000,000 for fiscal 1970 and providing an open-ended authorization for fiscal 1971. The House bill did not contain the Governor's veto of legal services projects.

The final bill authorized $2,195,500,000 for fiscal 1970 and $2,831,900,000 for fiscal 1971. Final action came Dec. 20 after the House Dec. 12 had defeated the strongest attempt ever made in the House to turn the program over to state control.

While debate on the program was developing in Congress, the President took a number of actions himself to revamp the program. In his first message to Congress (Feb. 19), the President announced plans to shift four programs from the OEO to other agencies. He proposed delegating Head Start and transferring comprehensive health centers and the foster grandparent programs to the Department of Health, Education and Welfare (HEW). (A delegation which did not require Congressional approval left the program under the over-all supervision of the OEO but administered by another agency. *(See p. 39-A.)*

He also indicated he would delegate Job Corps to the Labor Department. The delegations took place July 1 as planned. Head Start went to a new office of Child Development in the Department of HEW. The Foster Grandparents program was transferred under the Older Americans Act (PL 91-69).

On April 11 the Administration announced that 59 Job Corps centers would be closed on July 1 and in their place 30 urban centers would be established. The Senate May 13 by a 40-52 roll-call vote rejected a resolution (S Res 194) that the Administration defer the closings until Congress had reviewed antipoverty legislation.

On April 21 the President appointed Rep. Donald Rumsfeld (R Ill.) to be director of the OEO. Mr. Nixon Aug. 8 proposed a reorganization of the OEO aimed at turning the agency into an innovator of experimental programs to take people out of poverty. He said the agency's functions would be handled by three main offices: the Office of Planning, Research, and Evaluation; Office of Program Development and the Office of Program Operations. The health program, instead of being transferred to the HEW Department, was to be expanded within the OEO. *(See p. 85-A.)*

Reports. Two reports on poverty were issued during 1969. The General Accounting Office in a report issued March 19 concluded that many of the antipoverty programs suffered from poor administration and attained varying degrees of success. The Senate Labor and Public Welfare Subcommittee on Employment, Manpower and Poverty in October released a report calling for sweeping

programs to eliminate poverty. The report, "Toward Economic Security for the Poor," recommended that income support for the elderly and for families in which the family head could not work be substantially increased.

Poor People's Campaign. The Poor People's Campaign returned to Washington May 12 to urge the President and Congress to initiate and expand programs of aid to the poor. Representatives of the Campaign, led by the Rev. Ralph David Abernathy, president of the Southern Christian Leadership Conference, presented 10 basic demands to Members of Congress, President Nixon and his Urban Affairs Council. The demands ranged from abandonment of the antiballistic missile (ABM) system to extension of the right of collective bargaining to state and federal employees. The 100 representatives of the 1969 Campaign stayed in Washington only for a week in contrast to the six-week stay of several thousand persons during the 1968 Campaign.

Other Developments

Manpower Training. President Nixon Aug. 12 sent Congress a message asking for a new manpower training act which ultimately would place most of the development responsibility in the hands of state and local governments. The President's plan consolidated and expanded job training activites presently under the Office of Economic Opportunity (OEO) and training programs of the Department of Labor. A variety of manpower services, currently separately funded (including on-the-job and institutional training, basic education and counseling and job placement), would be coordinated by a single agency at the federal planning level and its counterpart in the states. *(See p. 78-A.)*

The Senate Labor and Public Welfare Committee Nov. 4 began hearings on the Administration proposals (S 2838). In addition to consolidating manpower programs, the bill: provided incentive for trainees to choose training best suited to them rather than training that paid more, paid welfare recipients $30 a month more if they went into job training, created a comprehensive career development plan for trainees to help them get and keep jobs, and increased manpower spending by 10 percent whenever unemployment reached at least 4.5 percent for three months.

Housing. Final appropriations approved by Congress in the independent offices appropriations bill (HR 12307) included $575 million for the model cities program and $250 million for the urban renewal program. Both projects seek the rehabilitation and renewal of slum areas of cities. The model cities funds were $100 million less than the Administration had requested and $50 million under the fiscal 1969 figure. The urban renewal funds were the total of the Administration request and, when added to $750 million in advance funding appropriated in 1968, provided $1 billion for obligation in fiscal 1970. Supporters of higher spending for the program argued that applications already exceeded $2 billion and could rise to as much as $4 billion during fiscal 1970. *(See p. 59.)*

The appropriations bill also authorized $90 million in contract authority for low-income homeownership assistance, $85 million in contract authority for low-income rental housing assistance and $50 million in contract authority for rent supplements.

ADMINISTRATION DE-EMPHASIZES MODEL CITIES, NDP

The Nixon Administration in 1969 de-emphasized two Johnson Administration urban programs—model cities and Neighborhood Development Project—while initiating a program to use new technological methods to build housing. The President also set up a Council for Urban Affairs.

Congress studied a number of proposals aimed at alleviating the growing problems of the cities but made few major changes in existing programs. Congress focused its attention on extending and funding programs authorized under the Housing and Urban Development (HUD) Act of 1968.

Housing

The House and Senate Dec. 12 cleared a bill (S 2864), the $4.8-billion Housing and Urban Development Act of 1969, which extended major HUD programs through fiscal 1971, required for the first time that each slum dwelling razed as part of an urban development project be replaced by a new low-income dwelling and moved to prevent interference with use of technological innovations (including mass-produced and prefabricated dwelling units) in experimental HUD programs.

Congress Nov. 18 cleared an appropriations bill (HR 12307) which included $1.8 billion for HUD programs for fiscal 1970.

George Romney, Secretary of Housing and Urban Development (HUD), May 8 launched Operation Breakthrough, an attempt to use modern methods of production and management to increase and improve the production of housing, particularly for low-income families. Operation Breakthrough would first create a mass housing market and then encourage mass production of housing by private industry.

The program would involve all levels of government and private industry in an effort to halt rising housing costs. Romney estimated that the first stage of the project would cost $15 million to $20 million. The first stage involved:

- A cooperative effort by Governors and mayors to identify housing needs and possible housing sites and to relax zoning and building codes to allow construction of experimental housing.
- Encouragement of builders and companies interested in the mass production of housing to submit proposed designs.
- Selection of 10 to 12 designs to be built as prototype units at eight locations with HUD assistance in planning and financing the units.

After testing the units, HUD would select the best and encourage their mass production by private industry. Romney said construction should be underway late in 1969 on the first projects, with the first units completed in a year. He said the program would greatly increase housing production and also improve the quality of housing available, particularly for low-income families.

In launching Operation Breakthrough, Romney met May 7 with construction trade union leaders who said they would work with HUD in an advisory capacity on the project, May 8 with mayors and Governors,

and May 9 with representatives of the home-building industry.

The first eight Operation Breakthrough program sites were announced Dec. 16 after a screening process in which 37 of more than 230 industrial bidders were chosen to negotiate further in the planning of mass-produced housing projects. Some 20 federal contracts were to be awarded. Among cities named as program sites were Indianapolis, Ind.; Jersey City, N.J.; Kalamazoo, Mich.; Macon, Ga.; Memphis, Tenn.; Sacramento, Calif.; St. Louis, Mo. and Wilmington, Del.

The Johnson Administration programs were de-emphasized as Operation Breakthrough received increased attention. Decisions to slow down and limit funding of model cities and Neighborhood Development Project grants were announced in October 1969. *(For new Model Cities guidelines, see below.)*

The Nixon Administration signaled a slowdown in the model cities program on Oct. 1 by cutting $215 million from planned expenditures, prompted, according to officials, by the President's call for $3.5 billion in Government-wide budget cuts and by a slow start for the action phase of the 1966 model cities program. HUD officials declared the drop from earlier estimates of expenditures represented procedural delays and not substantive program cuts.

Those cities to be affected were the 34 first-round model cities locations that had not yet signed grant contracts and the 75 second-round choices. Fiscal 1970 was to have been the first year for implementing plans to attack all the causes of poverty and blight within a slum through one integrated plan.

Some Congressional reaction was sharp. Sen. William Proxmire (D Wis.), chairman of the Senate Banking and Currency Subcommittee on Financial Institutions, commented, "Once again the question of priorities is at stake. The 'go ahead' is given for the SST, the C-5A, the ABM and manned space flights; but housing is cut."

Romney announced Oct. 3 that a shortage of money would prevent the HUD Department from approving more than a limited number of Neighborhood Development Program (NDP) grants in 1969. The NDP grants, authorized in the 1968 Housing Act, proved tremendously popular to cities because they could speedily inject urban renewal funds into specific programs and offered local matching fund reductions if public facilities had been constructed no more than three years prior to the proposed projects in the development areas. Romney said the Government could not provide anything like the $1.2 billion requested by 322 communities seeking funds through the program since the first cities were accepted by the Johnson Administration. He said the 35 cities already approved before a December 1968 freeze on approval of new NDP applications would get "less money...than they had hoped for."

Congress, however, endorsed the program. The House, acting on S 2864, reserved $400 million in fiscal 1970 urban renewal funds for NDP programs and stipulated that 35 percent of urban renewal funds during the following two years be applied to such projects. The Senate Banking and Currency Committee criticized the Administration for lack of support for the program.

Because NDP funds were spent over one-year periods rather than over 15- or 20-year periods as with some HUD projects, the NDP program was called inflationary in nature. By April, the Budget Bureau had ordered a freeze in disbursement of NDP funds to approved cities. Assistant Budget Director Richard P. Nathan commented, "This Administration has every intention of avoiding promising more assistance than can be delivered within available resources."

But the 1969 Housing Act provided that not less than 35 percent of urban renewal funds available in fiscal 1970 and 1971 would be used for financing Neighborhood Development Projects. If the Budget Bureau were to refuse to spend the money, the earmarked funds could not be used for other renewal programs, resulting in a reduction in over-all urban renewal spending.

Romney Dec. 4 announced an end to the freeze on Neighborhood Development Project funds, with expenditures of more than $330 million planned in the fiscal year ending June 30, 1970. Participating cities were limited to about 80 of the more than 300 applications. About $175 million would go to the 35 cities that began projects at the start of the program, and the rest would be divided among 45 other cities.

Interest rates, which reached a record high in 1969, continued to plague the housing industry and was the subject of Congressional hearings. Hearings also were held on the rising prices of lumber and their effect on housing costs.

To attract funds to the housing market, the Government raised the interest rate ceiling on Government-backed mortgages from 6-3/4 to 7½ percent in January 1969 and to 8½ in January 1970. The authority for raising the ceiling was provided by S 2864. Pending enactment of S 2864, Congress earlier had provided (S J Res 152) a 90-day extension of the authority, which expired Oct. 1, 1969.

Model Cities Guidelines

Romney April 28 announced revised guidelines for the model cities program.

Describing the program as undeveloped and incomplete at the close of the Johnson Administration, Romney said that its goals were nevertheless sound and could be achieved if "critical deficiencies in its administration" were corrected. He outlined the revisions:

• The Council for Urban Affairs, of which the President was chairman, had assumed responsibility for interdepartmental policy concerning model cities.

• Secretaries of departments involved were to reserve specific program funds for their department's participation in model cities programs. This, Romney said, was to ensure the availability of funds for model cities programs and to enable local officials to estimate better how much money they could expect from various departments.

• Administration of model cities programs was to be reorganized as part of the reorganization of federal regional offices to facilitate interdepartmental coordination at the regional level. *(See p. 92.)*

• State governments were to be involved to a greater degree as advisers.

• The administrative rule restricting the population of the target neighborhood to 10 percent of the model city's population had been voided. Romney explained that the change did not mean the program would be expanded to encompass entire cities but that local officials would have more latitude in drawing program boundaries.

• Cities which enlisted voluntary and private organizations in their programs were to be given priority consideration for further grants.

• Local officials were to plan their model cities proposals so as to move swiftly toward solution of the most urgent problems "rather than dissipating their resources in a vain effort to solve" all their problems at once.

Romney described decentralization as the chief value of the model cities program because it shifted to local officials the task of determining the application of federal and federally funded state programs.

Romney asserted that when citizen groups differ with local officials about the planning and administration of model cities programs local officials retained final authority. However, if they acted capriciously or arbitrarily, he said, the citizens had the power of the vote to remove them from office.

Supplemental grants had not yet been made, Romney said, to the nine model cities approved by the Johnson Administration in December 1968 and January 1969 to enter the execution stage of their programs. Those cities, Romney said, had been approved without complete plans or contracts and with programs in an "embryonic" stage.

Testifying June 6 before the Senate Banking and Currency Subcommittee on Housing and Urban Affairs, Romney said that he hoped to give local governments a larger role in the planning and administration of model cities plans. In reply to a question from Sen. Edmund S. Muskie (D Maine), he said that the Administration had removed the original 10-percent limit on portions of cities which could be included in the program in order to give local officials more authority in choosing the area to be served.

Romney suggested that the model cities program had been oversold as a cure for urban problems. He said that the public and the Subcommittee should not expect "sensational results overnight."

Mass Transit

The President proposed Aug. 7 in his transportation message a $10-billion, 12-year program to improve urban mass transportation. He recommended Congressional authorization of federal-local contracts matched on a two-thirds to one-third basis for capital investments and research and development of mass transit systems.

The project the President recommended would have been financed from general revenues. The bill was opposed, however, by the U.S. Conference of Mayors and the National League of Cities, as well as by Democrats seeking a trust fund approach to mass transit financing to eliminate the uncertainty over continuity of federal support, which had been a major obstacle to cities in building rapid transit systems. The President's Council of Economic Advisers and the Budget Bureau opposed the financing technique because it would limit the President's flexibility in allocating resources.

The Senate Banking and Currency Subcommittee on Housing and Urban Affairs Nov. 18 completed hearings on the Administration proposal (S 2821). Harrison A. Williams Jr. (D N.J.), who called Nixon's bill a "paper promise," offered an amendment to authorize a contractual obligation of all $3.1 billion proposed for the first five years of operation during the program's first year. Under a compromise reached by Williams and Secretary of Transportation John A. Volpe before hearings were completed, the $3.1 billion would be obligated in the program's first year but would be released in small increments. The full Committee Dec. 22 reported a compromise bill (S 3154).

Additional mass transit funds totaling $300 million were authorized in the Housing and Urban Development Act of 1969.

Special appropriations for the District of Columbia mass transit system, on which construction was begun in December, totaled $43,173,000. The 97-mile system was authorized in 1966.

Relocation Assistance

Hearings on S 1, the Uniform Relocation Assistance and Land Acquisition Policies Act of 1969, to establish uniform policy for land acquisition under federal programs and to provide relocation assistance to displaced persons, began in February and were completed in October by the Senate Government Operations Subcommittee on Intergovernmental Relations. The bill passed the Senate Oct. 27 and was sent to the House Public Works Committee, which began hearings in December and was to continue them in 1970.

Other Developments

Congress. The House Committee on Science and Astronautics' Panel on Science and Technology held a seminar on "Science and Technology and the Cities" Feb. 4-6. John W. Gardner, chairman of the Urban Coalition, described modern cities lying "helpless as the multiple waves of crisis roll over them, like half-sunken battleships battered by heavy seas." He pointed to housing as the most urgent of the cities' problems and called upon Congress to realize the promises of the 1968 HUD Act.

He urged easing of monetary policy, reduction of mortgage interest rates and creation of long-term, stable and growing sources of mortgage financing for federally subsidized housing, a public-private institution for testing new systems of building and elimination of "workable program" requirements and local veto provisions attached to federal public housing, rent supplements and other programs.

The Joint Economic Committee April 2 recommended in its annual report on the President's 1969 economic report that Congress and the Administration give "massive" environmental reconstruction the highest priority in urban and rural areas and termed housing "the most outstanding example of the Federal Government's failure to fulfill its own commitment."

The House Banking and Commerce Committee held hearings on national housing goals, at which Romney blamed "backward" housing production methods and inadequate funding for hindering attainment of the 1969 housing goal. He said the "stop and go" aspect of yearly appropriations was a major problem.

The Senate Government Operations Permanent Subcommittee on Investigations held hearings on "The Aftermath of Riots," an investigation of federal and local efforts to rebuild city neighborhoods damaged by riots.

The House Banking and Currency Ad Hoc Subcommittee on Home Financing Practices and Procedures conducted hearings on District of Columbia real estate financing abuses. Preston Martin, chairman of the Federal Home Loan Bank Board, said he was overhauling the board's regulation of savings and loan associations to create a post of coordinator for inner city housing and urban affairs, develop regulations to encourage associations to locate more branches in the inner city and to finance low-cost housing and to make close checks on loans to discourage lending to speculators.

The Senate Banking and Currency Subcommittee on Housing and Urban Affairs held hearings on the progress of model cities.

The Joint Economic Subcommittee on Urban Affairs held hearings on industrialized housing to supplement information in a compendium of expert papers released by the Subcommittee April 28. Harold B. Finger, HUD Assistant Secretary, said the chief barriers to successful industrialization of housing were fragmentation of the housing market, local building codes, land procurement problems, outmoded zoning laws, a scarcity of skilled labor and financing problems.

The House Banking and Currency Ad Hoc Subcommittee on Urban Growth conducted hearings on the problems of growth of urban America.

Administration. The first rural planning grant authorized by the 1968 HUD Act for nondepressed rural areas was announced Jan. 2.

President Johnson Jan. 19 received the Commission on Urban Housing report calling for private enterprise, government and labor to join in "creative and affirmative partnership" to provide decent housing for every American.

A Council for Urban Affairs, the domestic equivalent of the National Security Council, was formally established by President Nixon Jan. 23.

The new Council was to advise and assist the President in developing a national urban policy in the same way as the National Security Council was created to advise the President in developing an integrated national security policy.

The Council was composed of the President as chairman; the Vice President, Spiro T. Agnew; the Attorney General, John N. Mitchell; the Secretary of Agriculture, Clifford M. Hardin; the Secretary of Commerce, Maurice H. Stans; the Secretary of Labor, George P. Shultz; the Secretary of Health, Education and Welfare, Robert H. Finch, the Secretary of Housing and Urban Development, George W. Romney; and the Secretary of Transportation, John A. Volpe. Dr. Daniel P. Moynihan, Presidential advisor on urban affairs, was named executive secretary of the Council.

Signing the Executive Order establishing the Council, Mr. Nixon said that for too long the Government had reacted to urban problems "in a haphazard, fragmented and often woefully shortsighted manner." He said that the Council would shape a "coherent, consistent" urban policy, but warned that such policy was "no more a guarantor of success" in domestic than in foreign affairs.

The Executive Order, careful to state that the Urban Council assumed none of the functions already executed by federal departments and agencies, specified its functions as including:

Assistance to the President in developing a national urban policy with regard to immediate and long-range concerns and priorities.

Coordination of the Federal Government's urban programs.

Encouraging full cooperation between all levels of government "with special concern for the maintenance of local initiative."

Fostering the decentralization of Government to vest major responsibility in state and local governments.

Encouraging involvement of voluntary organizations in urban programs.

President Nixon April 8 announced that $209 million would be channeled immediately to 20 cities across the nation to assist in restoring areas torn by riots during the spring of 1968.

The failure of government to act effectively in the cities to reconstruct and repair the riot damage was graphic evidence, Mr. Nixon stated, of "the impotence of modern government at all levels."

"There can be no more searing symbol of governmental inability to act than those rubble-strewn lots and the desolate, decaying buildings once a vital part of a community's life and now left to rot," Mr. Nixon said. "No wonder our citizens are beginning to question government's ability to perform."

Cities to receive restoration assistance were: Akron, Ohio; Baltimore; Boston; Cleveland; Chicago; Detroit; Kansas City, Kan.; Los Angeles; Louisville, Ky.; Memphis, Tenn.; Nashville, Tenn.; Newark; New Haven; New York; Pittsburgh; Providence; Rochester, N.Y.; Tampa; Washington; and Wilmington, Del.

President Nixon announced April 30 that the HUD Department would establish a clearinghouse for information on voluntary action programs, and Romney would head a Cabinet Committee on Voluntary Action to solve urban living and poverty problems.

The first three model cities contracts were announced May 9; Seattle, Waco, Texas, and Atlanta, Ga., were the first three of 150 cities to have urban reform plans approved by the Department since the program was initiated in November 1968.

The President Sept. 24 named a task force on model cities, to be headed by Edward C. Banfield, to review the current status of the model cities program, evaluate its operation and make recommendations concerning future direction.

The President Oct. 17 named a task force on urban renewal, headed by Miles L. Colean, a consulting economist, to examine the status of the federal urban renewal program and make recommendations.

Mr. Nixon Oct. 10 named a task force on low-income housing, headed by Raymond J. Saulnier, a Columbia University economics professor, to review public and private programs in low-income housing and recommend measures aimed at increasing the number of dwelling units available.

Raymond Lapin, who had been appointed by President Johnson as head of the Federal National Mortgage Association (FNMA), Dec. 2 announced he would fight an attempt by President Nixon to fire him from his post. Two questions arose in the dispute: political patronage in removing Lapin so Mr. Nixon could name his own man and a legal question on Presidential authority over the FNMA, which originally was a fully federal agency but was

directed by Congress in 1968 to become a private organization.

U.S. District Court Senior Judge Matthew F. McGuire Dec. 5 said he lacked authority to countermand the President's order. In a second court test Dec. 17, Judge Burnita Shelton Matthews of the U.S. District Court refused Lapin's request for a preliminary injunction that would have restored him to his post until the case was decided on its merits. She also removed the President from the list of defendants named by Lapin and refused to advance the case on the court calendar.

Reports. A "One Year Later" report released Feb. 27 by the Urban Coalition and Urban America, which studied national policy change after the Kerner Commission report on Civil Disorders, claimed inadequate funding for the 1968 Housing Act and said employment of nonwhites lagged behind whites.

The National Committee on Urban Growth proposed May 24 that the Federal Government develop 110 "new cities" by the 21st Century. The Committee's recommendations were based on population projections and the new town concept developed in Europe. It proposed long-term federal laws and grants and state-authorized community development corporations to stimulate creation of new cities with populations of 1 million each.

Intergovernmental Report. American cities can avert domestic chaos only if drastic changes are made in governmental institutions and procedures, the Advisory Commission on Intergovernmental Relations warned in a report issued Dec. 21.

In a study culminating 10 years of work, the Commission recommended major changes in the fiscal arrangements among local, state and the Federal Governments. All welfare and medicaid costs should be assumed by the Federal Government, the Commission advised, and all local education costs taken over by the states.

The recommendations included revenue sharing with the states, high-yield state-local tax systems and a national policy on financial incentives to industries to locate in poverty areas.

Insurance Industry. The life insurance industry April 15 pledged to invest a second $1 billion in urban core areas to provide housing and job opportunities. The pledge continued a program initiated in September 1967, under which life insurance companies committed themselves to invest a certain share of their assets in core city areas.

Francis E. Ferguson, chairman of the industry's joint committee on urban problems, said that the first $1-billion investment had been completed. He said that $750 million had been directed into providing housing and $250 million into producing jobs.

President Nixon issued a statement of congratulations to the industry for its "sense of responsibility."

Mayors Conference. Criticism of the urban policies of the Nixon Administration and a call for more money for the cities characterized the June 14-18 annual meeting of the U.S. Conference of Mayors in Pittsburgh.

Most of the criticism came from big-city, northern Democratic mayors, such as Jerome P. Cavanagh of Detroit, Kevin H. White of Boston and Arthur Naftalin of Minneapolis. They charged that Administration efforts to solve urban problems were inadequate and often guided by partisan politics.

NIXON REQUESTS MAJOR CHANGES IN POSTAL SYSTEM

President Nixon in 1969 proposed major changes in the country's postal system, but Congress failed to enact any of the President's program. However, both the House and Senate held extensive hearings on Mr. Nixon's proposals and related subjects.

In a major blow to the Nixon Administration's principal proposal, the House Post Office and Civil Service Committee in October voted in effect to kill the President's plan to turn the Post Office Department into a Government-owned corporation.

Background

The Post Office Department was one of the earliest services established by the United States. In the young days of the nation's history, the Post Office was the only link between isolated communities and the Government, and it provided the impetus for much expansion. The post roads, the famed Pony Express and the railway postal system all helped form a continent-wide communications network designed in large part to help deliver the mails.

Because of its interconnection with the country's development, operation of the Post Office historically has been shaped by tradition and a patchwork of changes in the law. Congress retained control of the operating and capital budgets. It dispensed pay raises and set postage rates, controlled appointments of postmasters and rural letter carriers, legislated labor-management relations and even limited the types of transportation available for moving the mails. The money the public spent on postage and other services went back to the U.S. Treasury and not to the Post Office itself.

By the beginning of 1969, the Post Office Department had grown to a point where it employed more than 725,000 employees handling more than 82 billion pieces of mail a year; Post Office appropriations for fiscal 1969 amounted to nearly $7.13 billion.

Postmaster General Lawrence F. O'Brien first proposed converting the Post Office Department into a corporation in a speech made April 3, 1967, to a group of magazine editors and publishers. He outlined a plan in which a board of directors, appointed by the President and confirmed by the Congress, would hire top management officials. The corporation would bargain collectively with employees to set wages and benefits, and it would be empowered to issue bonds to raise money for new buildings and equipment.

Five days later, President Johnson established a 10-man Commission on Postal Organization, headed by Frederick R. Kappel, former chairman of the board of American Telephone and Telegraph Corp. The Commission was given a mandate to review the corporation proposal and other suggestions for reform.

The Kappel Commission, as the panel became known, issued its report, "Towards Postal Excellence," July 16, 1968. The Commission made several major recommendations, the first of which was the establishment of a Government-owned corporation to operate the postal service on a self-supporting basis. "Piecemeal changes to the present system will not do the job: a basic change in direction is necessary," the report stated.

Nixon Proposals

One of President Nixon's first political actions after taking office Jan. 20 was to end the patronage system by which postmasters had been appointed for nearly 200 years. "As you will recall," he said in making the announcement Feb. 5, "during the course of the last campaign, one pledge I made emphatically over and over again was that we were going to take politics out of the Post Office Department and that we were going to improve postal service."

President Nixon and Postmaster General Winton M. Blount said they were ending the patronage system of appointing postmasters and rural letter carriers. Mr. Nixon said that high scores on competitive examinations would be the sole criterion for filling those posts.

Blount said he would seek a change in postal law provisions (PL 86-682), which currently required Senate confirmation of first, second and third class postmasterships.

The system of choosing postmasters from among the three high scorers on competitive exams was already in effect—but under the current system, the preferred candidate of a Member of Congress or party official got to repeat the test again and again until he was among the top three. Under the proposed system, the test would be given only once, and the Postmaster General would select from among the three high scorers. Members of Congress could still be consulted, but their recommendations would not necessarily have to be followed.

Blount outlined the new procedures for selecting postmasters and rural letter carriers for newsmen Feb. 20. He said that the existing lists of applicants for all vacancies had been eliminated, and new lists would be compiled which were based strictly on merit. The new method of filling vacancies, in which impartial panels would make the selections, would not require new legislation. Blount said that until the confirmation provision was removed from the law, the Senate would be requested to act on nominations made through the new merit system. Before the press conference, Blount said, he had met with House Republicans, who gave "overwhelming support" to the proposal.

Mr. Nixon Feb. 25 sent Congress a message urging enactment of legislation which would eliminate Presidential nomination and Senate confirmation of postmasters in first, second and third class post offices, grant to the Postmaster General authority to name postmasters and forbid political consideration in filling vacancies. (For text, see p. 42-A.)

Blount March 4 sent to Capitol Hill a proposed bill to eliminate patronage. The proposed bill would require postmasters to be appointed through civil service procedures. Further, in the appointments and promotion of Post Office Department employees, the measure stated, "no political test or qualification shall be permitted or given consideration.... Any officer or employee of the Department who violates this section shall be removed from office or otherwise disciplined." The only exceptions to this would be the top four positions in the Post Office Department, certain non-career executive posts and "positions of a confidential or policy determining character."

A provision forbidding political intervention was included in the Congressional reform bill (S 355) which passed the Senate in 1967 but died at the end of the 90th Congress. S 844, another reform bill introduced in the 91st Congress, contained the same patronage provision.

Mr. Nixon April 24 sent Congress a message outlining his requests for postal rate increase in first, second and third class mail classifications. *(For text of message, see p. 47-A.)*

President Nixon May 27 asked Congress to create an independent, Government-owned corporation to take over the duties of the Post Office Department. *(For text, see p. 58-A.)*

"Postal reform is not a partisan political issue, it is an urgent national requirement," the President said in his message to Congress. He told reporters at the White House, the same day that his postal recommendation was "one of the most significant proposals that will be made during the entire period of this Administration."

The plan proposed by the President was similar to the general proposals of the Kappel Commission.

Mr. Nixon told Congress that in the current fiscal year, the postal deficit would exceed $1 billion. "It is bad business, bad government, and bad politics to pour this kind of tax money into an inefficient postal service," he said.

There are already more than a dozen Government-owned corporations. The best-known ones are probably the Tennessee Valley Authority, the Federal Deposit Insurance Corp. and the Commodity Credit Corp. But the Postal Service would be a far larger concern that any of the others, and would be the only important one which was converted from an executive department rather than started from scratch.

Reaction. The postal corporation proposal brought mixed reaction on Capitol Hill but was endorsed by a number of organizations, notably in the business community, such as the U.S. Chamber of Commerce and the National Association of Manufacturers.

Opposition to the corporation concept was registered by the labor unions representing postal employees. The unions' position was that if the Post Office became a corporation, union members should be given the right to strike. They also maintained that the new system would mean cuts in mail service, higher rates and the possibility that the board of directors could contract out to private enterprise work currently performed by civil service workers.

Although not spelled out, a main reason the postal workers opposed the proposal was because they wanted their wages to be continued to be set by Congress, where they could apply political pressure.

Major Features

The President's postal reform bill (HR 11750) was introduced May 28. Following are the major features of the plan:

The Corporation

The U.S. Postal Service would replace the present Post Office Department. The Service would have up to a year to prepare for the transition, after enactment of the bill, and would be required to be self-supporting within five years.

The corporation would be headed by a nine-man board of directors. Seven of the directors would be appointed by the President, would be subject to Senate confirmation, and would serve, part-time, for seven-year terms. One term would expire each year. Appointments would be made without regard to politics, and they would represent the public interest rather than specific interests connected in some way with the Postal Service. They could not be federal employees.

The President would designate one member to be chairman of the board. The Presidentially appointed members would receive $5,000 annually plus $300 for each meeting attended.

The seven Presidential appointees would name an eighth director, who would serve as chief executive officer, and the eight would select a ninth to serve as chief operating officer. Maximum salary for any full-time officers would be Executive Level I (Cabinet members); exact levels would be set by the board.

The Postal Service would be charged with operating the mails. It would be able to adopt its own regulations and procedures, sue and be sued, enter into contracts, handle its own funds, acquire and dispose of property, and in general hold all the powers and privileges of other government corporations.

HR 11750 would re-establish a number of laws now on the books, notably all the criminal laws applicable to the mails and to government employees. It also would make specifically applicable to the Postal Service the Civil Service laws regarding employment policies and suitability, security and conduct; provisions of the Government Corporation Control Act; labor standards for government contractors; the equal employment opportunity provisions of the 1964 Civil Rights Act; the government loyalty oath, and the Hatch Act limitations on political activities by federal employees.

The Postal Service would be required to make annual reports on its operations and its budget to the President and to Congress. Within two years it would report to Congress on suggestions for revising the private express statutes (which give the Post Office Department a monopoly on the carriage of mail). Congress would retain the power to alter, amend or repeal any provisions of the corporation's charter—except that it cannot impair the obligation of contracts.

Employees

All present Post Office Department employees (with the exception of the postmaster general, the deputy postmaster general, six assistant postmasters general and the general counsel—all Presidential appointees) would be transferred to the U.S. Postal Service. For a year after the conversion to a corporation, employees could request transfer to other jobs in the Federal Government.

All employees would retain their sick leave, vacation, and other benefits accumulated while working for the Department. Medical, health and life insurance plans would remain in effect until other programs could be established through collective bargaining. The Civil Service Retirement Program would remain in effect—rather than a separate retirement system—but the

Postal Service could set up a supplemental retirement plan through collective bargaining. The Postal Service would establish a merit system of employment, promotion and adverse action proceedings. The Civil Service adverse action proceedings would remain in effect until a new system could be established.

The bill prohibited political tests or qualifications in regard to any personnel actions.

All wages and benefits would be comparable to those in private industry and at least as good as those employees had within the Civil Service system. The policy of giving preference to veterans would continue.

Employees would have the right to join unions, and their unions could enter into collective bargaining on issues of wages, benefits, working conditions and other matters of concern. Employees would not have the right to strike, but unsolvable disputes would be subject to binding arbitration (now forbidden by law).

If labor and management reached an impasse in bargaining, they could work out their own procedures for settling disputes. Or, they could refer the problems to a disputes panel. There would be a standing panel of nine members—three from the Labor Department's Federal Mediation and Conciliation Service (FMCS), three from the American Arbitration Assn. and three selected by the six others. As any dispute arose, a committee of three members would be selected from the nine-man panel to hear the issues. The three could attempt to bring about a settlement in any manner they chose, and if no settlement were reached they could refer the matters under dispute to arbitration.

If the arbitration state were reached, another three-man panel would be convened—one representing labor, one from management and one picked by the two others. If the first two could not decide on a third member, he would be selected by the FMCS. The decisions made by the arbitration panel would be binding and could not be appealed.

Neither employees nor management could demand to go directly to the arbitration stage; this choice would be reserved for the disputes panel.

Finances

The Postal Service would handle its own funds, financing its operations out of revenues and loans. At the outset, the Postal Service and the General Services Administration—with the concurrence of the Budget Bureau—would work out agreements concerning ownership of the properties now used by the Post Office Department. For the transition period, Congress would be authorized to appropriate sufficient funds to assure mail service continues.

The corporation would be able to borrow money and to issue and sell obligations amounting to up to $10 billion in all. For any one fiscal year, new obligations would be limited to $1.5 billion. The Postal Service could require the Treasury Department to purchase up to $2 billion worth of obligations, and the rest would be sold on the open market without the backing of the U.S. Government.

The General Accounting Office would conduct annual audits of the Postal Service's books, and the GAO reports would be made public.

The only funds the Postal Service could receive from Congress would be those which finance the public service categories of mail. The categories are types of mail and services which—by act of Congress—do not have to pay their own way. (Included now are such mailings as classroom publications, charity appeals and materials from book and record clubs. Other costs include losses on certain types of post offices and other services.)

If Congress did not appropriate enough money to cover the public service costs, then the Postal Service could increase rates for the preferred users enough to close the gap.

Rates And Services

The existing rates and services would remain in effect until changed under the procedures outlined in the bill. The Presidentially appointed board members would name a three-member rate commission, chosen from a special Civil Service register. The rate commissioners would deal only with the Presidential appointees, not with the corporation's executive management. The three would be paid at Executive Level V (the chairman would be paid $500 more than the others). They would serve rotating six-year terms, set their own rules and procedures, and have their own staff.

Any change in rates or classifications would be requested by the Postal Service and would be preceded by 30 days' advance notice in the Federal Register. If the commission received any objections, it would be required to hold hearings on the changes. If the proceedings took more than 90 days from the initial request by the Postal Service, the commissioners could institute interim rate changes.

The commissioners' recommendations on rate changes would be forwarded to the Presidentially appointed board members, who could adopt them, reject them or alter them. The Board would then send its recommendations to Congress. The rate changes would go into effect unless both the House and the Senate vetoed the entire proposal within 60 days.

Changes in services on a nationwide or nearly nationwide basis would be preceded by a public notice and an opportunity for witnesses to present testimony. For changes in service of less than nationwide impact, the commission could either follow the same procedures or set up others of its own. The Presidential appointees on the board could overrule the commission's decisions on such matters. The commission also would hear complaints regarding rates and services, and all its proceedings would be subject to judicial review.

Transportation

The Postal Service would be allowed to contract for the transportation of mail on any common carriers, subject to the normal regulations of the Interstate Commerce Commission and the Civil Aeronautics Board.

HR 11750 would continue the legal obligations of railroads and airlines to provide mail transportation services, and would expand this to include motor carriers, freight forwarders and express companies. (Under present law railroads and airlines are obligated by law to carry the mail, but motor carriers are not. For highway transportation, the Post Office Department enters into four-year contracts with "star route" carriers.)

The bill would retain the star-route system but would simplify the regulations.

NIXON SEEKS 'NO-STRINGS-ATTACHED' REVENUE SHARING

A proposal by President Nixon for a "no-strings-attached" program of sharing federal revenues with the states did not receive Congressional action in 1969. (For text, see p. 79-A, 81-A.)

The President's plan, submitted Aug. 13, would make $500 million available for sharing in its first year of operation and $5 billion a year by fiscal 1976. Funds were to be divided among the states according to population adjusted for state revenue-raising efforts. Cities and counties were to receive part of their states' shares according to their own relative fund-raising efforts.

Thus the plan had two major purposes—to pump additional money into states and localities to be spent as they pleased and to encourage local governments to adopt strong tax systems in order to qualify for a greater share of the program's revenues.

The Administration bills, S 2948 and HR 13982, were referred to the Senate Finance Committee and the House Ways and Means Committee respectively. No action was taken on either during the session. However, Sen. Edmund S. Muskie (D Maine), chairman of the Government Operations Subcommittee on Intergovernmental Relations, held six days of hearings on an alternative bill (S 2483) which he and Sen. Charles E. Goodell (R N.Y.) introduced at the request of the Advisory Commission in Intergovernmental Relations.

Background

Revenue sharing, after an 1836 effort in which the Federal Government split most of the surplus in the Treasury among the states, has become a very small part of the federal grants-in-aid system. The revenues, which have come from the sale of federally owned assets such as timber, usually have been given to the jurisdictions in which the assets were located, and the funds normally have been earmarked by the Government for certain uses. The Budget Bureau estimated that these "shared" revenues would amount in fiscal 1969 to $249.4 million, out of total grants-in-aid of $20.3 billion.

Revenue-sharing plans which have been offered in Congress since 1958 usually have provided for an automatic distribution of a portion of federal tax revenues to the states, with virtually no conditions attached. Republicans generally have favored replacing present financing with funds from shared revenues or tax credits while Democrats have most often seen the new proposals as a supplement to existing financing.

Former Rep. Melvin R. Laird (R Wis.), now Secretary of Defense, generally has been credited with having introduced in 1958 the first bill which embodied many of what later were considered the essential principles of revenue sharing. The Laird bill provided for the automatic return of a portion of federal revenues to the states with relatively few conditions attached.

The revenue-sharing idea was expanded in 1960 by Walter W. Heller, who later became chairman of the Council of Economic Advisers (1961-64). Heller's plan was adopted by a task force which recommended a form of revenue sharing in 1964 to President Johnson. Mr. Johnson, though reportedly in favor of the idea, never did announce his support for a plan. One of the key reasons

for his silence, it was thought, was a continuing lack of Budget surpluses, upon which most revenue-sharing plans were based. Mr. Johnson also reportedly was enraged over news accounts that he planned to endorse the proposal.

Johnson Task Force. A Presidential task force on revenue sharing, headed by Joseph A. Pechman, director of economics for the Brookings Institution, recommended in early fall of 1964 a compromise plan. The proposal was said to follow closely a plan offered in June 1960 by Heller which had called for distributing to the states, with few conditions, the "fiscal dividend" of an expanded economy—that is, a percentage of annual federal tax revenue increases due to economic growth.

Nixon Task Force. According to press reports, a task force appointed by President Nixon after his election recommended a revenue-sharing plan which called for the earmarking of 3 percent to 5 percent of federal personal income tax receipts for return to the states to use as they saw fit. Mr. Nixon's actual proposal took a somewhat different form.

Arguments. Proponents of revenue sharing have argued that it would help offset fiscal deficiencies at the local and state levels, would be used to finance needed social programs, would "revitalize" state governments by giving them independence in the spending of the revenue and would relieve the "fiscal drag" on the economy resulting from a higher growth rate of federal tax revenue than of federal expenditures.

President's Program

President Nixon's "no-strings-attached" program of revenue sharing would automatically return to the states a portion of federal revenues each year. The payout would rise from one-sixth of 1 percent of personal taxable income in the second half of fiscal 1971 to 1 percent in fiscal 1976 and thereafter. The estimated return to the states would be $5 billion in fiscal 1976.

The payout could be authorized under a permanent indefinite appropriation, similar to the manner in which interest on the public debt is handled.

The plan would be a supplement to and not a substitute for current categorical federal grants.

Distribution of Funds. The monies would be divided among the states by a formula based upon population adjusted for the state's relative effort to raise revenue.

A "pass-through" formula would ensure that each city and county would receive a part of the funds in proportion to their relative size and revenue-raising effort within the state.

State statistics may lag by a year. County, city and township statistics often are not even that current. However, because these revenue statistics will determine the localities' shares of the funds it likely will spur them to prepare their statistics more rapidly.

Apportionment among states—The first step in distributing funds is to determine the size of each state's share by the following formula:

S equals $\dfrac{P \times R/I}{A}$

S = State percentage share of federal revenue-sharing payout

P = State population

R = General revenues (includes state and all local units of government, including school and special districts but excludes liquor store sales, revenue from public utilities and from insurance trusts.)

I = Total personal income earned by residents of the state

A = Sum of the product of P x R/I for all 50 states and the District of Columbia

For example, Iowa's share of a hypothetical $1-billion distribution would be determined in the following manner, based upon 1966-67 statistics:

$$\frac{\text{P-2,753,000 x R-\$1.131 billion/ I-\$8.258 billion}}{\text{A-25,939,500}}$$

Result—S equals .0146, or 1.46 percent of the federal distribution. Thus Iowa would receive $14.6 million of the first full year payout.

Under a per-capita formula which did not take into consideration tax-raising effort, Iowa would have received $13.9 million.

State and local shares—The amount of each state's share which must be "passed through" to the counties, cities, and townships would be determined by the following formula:

M divided by G equals L.

M = Locally generated monies, excluding levies from school and special districts. However, if a school system is financed by a county, city or township budget, the monies would be included.

G = Locally generated revenues plus state-generated revenues, excluding liquor store sales and revenue from public utilities and insurance trusts.

L = Percentage share to be passed through to the localities.

In the Iowa example, the pass-through would be determined in the following manner:

$$\frac{\text{M - \$288.7 million}}{\text{G - \$1.13 billion}}$$

Result—L is .255 or 25.5 percent to be passed through to the counties, cities and townships. For Iowa, it would be equal to $4.7 million.

Individual locality share—For a specific county, city or township, the share would be determined according to the following formula:

C divided by F equals H.

C = Revenues generated by the specific locality excluding those from business-type operations such as a transit or water system.

F = Total of all locally generated revenues in the state.

H = Specific locality's share.

In the case of Cedar Rapids, Iowa, the distribution would be as follows:

$$\frac{\text{C- \$9.93 million}}{\text{F-\$288.7 million}}$$

Result—H is .034 or 3.4 percent. Thus, Cedar Rapids would receive $159,800 of the localities' total of $4.7 million.

The Treasury Department emphasized that the tax-effort indexes would change as states and localities increased their taxes relative to other states or localities. Illinois, for example, traditionally has been a low-effort state but adopted an income tax in 1969 and, presumably, will show a significantly higher revenue effort in the future. States could change the "pass-through" formula by getting the agreement of two-thirds of the localities, both by number and by share of locally-generated revenues.

Local governments also could challenge a formula or a particular distribution in federal court.

Reaction

Reaction to the President's plan has been mostly favorable though some traditional opponents of revenue sharing have renewed their objections.

The Advisory Commission on Intergovernmental Relations (ACIR), which offered a revenue-sharing plan of its own (HR 13353, S 2483), found little to quarrel with in the Nixon proposal.

"The differences are in detail," said William G. Colman, executive director of the ACIR. He said the Commission favored a cutoff for the pass-through requirement at governmental units below 50,000 population. Distribution to smaller units would be left entirely to the states, he added.

The ACIR plan would weight the revenue-effort ratio by doubling it for cities and counties with populations of more than 100,000. Cities and counties between 50,000 and 99,999 would have their per-capita payout multiplied by a fraction obtained by multiplying its doubled revenue effort ratio by its population ratio within the state.

Walter W. Heller, author of the revenue-sharing plan that was nearly adopted by the Johnson Administration, said his "child" was "fairly recognizable" in the Nixon proposals.

"The combination of per-capita distribution with tax effort is very good as far as it goes," Dr. Heller said. "It could go further by setting aside, say, 10 percent of the whole..., for the (poorest) quarter or third of a state. But I don't regard this (omission) as a fatal defect."

Though different in many significant aspects, the Nixon Administration's proposal is linked in many minds with the "Heller-Pechman plan" of the Democratic years. At a White House reception in April, Mr. Nixon told Heller: "We're about to present your plan to Congress and our people are giving you a lot of credit for it."

"And some of the liberals are going to give me hell for it," Heller replied.

Politically, liberals have been divided. Some question whether suburb-dominated and rural-dominated state legislatures would pass along adequate revenues to the cities.

Fiscal Policy Objections. Chairman Wilbur D. Mills (D Ark.) of the House Ways and Means Committee renewed his longstanding opposition. He believes that the level of government which spends funds should at least share the responsibility for raising them. "I'm unalterably opposed to a block grant to states for just any use the states want," Mills also said.

John W. Byrnes (R Wis.), ranking minority member of the Ways and Means Committee, did not modify his own objections to the revenue-sharing approach.

Heller has cited three main objections to revenue sharing.

1. Some argue that people should raise their own revenue to maximize the pain and thereby encourage pressures to minimize government spending. "I don't think that is the right objective at this time," Heller said.

2. Some say revenue sharing would lead to looseness in government spending since funds would not come from the level of government spending them. "I regard that as a complete misreading of the way people work...," Heller said. "To get responsibility, all one needs to know is that there is a fixed sum available and no more."

3. Some say that the expense of sending the funds to Washington for redistribution to the states is a waste of money. "The round trip to Washington is less costly than the round trip to the city hall or the state house," Heller said.

Norman B. Ture, a principal in Planning Research Corp. of Washington, D.C., and head of President Nixon's post-election task force on tax policy, considers revenue sharing bad public policy. Though the distribution formula will reward states which make a relatively greater tax effort, Ture said, states still will be able to avoid the responsibility of collecting as much in taxes to pay for the same amount of services as they would have had to collect without the federal monies. A better way, he said is for the Federal Government to reduce taxes, giving the states the opportunity to raise their taxes without increasing the overall burden on their residents.

Robert J. Lampman, professor of economics at the University of Wisconsin, objected to what he terms "overselling" of both the problem and the solution.

Lampman, who was on Heller's staff at the CEA and has served as an adviser to state governments, is skeptical about the so-called "revenue gap" between state and local revenues and the demands for services.

Estimates of state revenues have traditionally been very low, Lampman said, and the elasticity of state and local revenue sources in relation to income growth is greater than many think.

Lampman is not alone in his skepticism about the "revenue gap." The Committee for Economic Development found that without any expansion in state and local tax effort, states and localities could provide a 21-percent expansion in services between 1965 and 1975. By expanding their tax effort according to CED recommendations, states and localities could expand services by 33 percent, the private research organization concluded.

On the other hand, a study by the George Washington University, concluded that states would need to borrow $14 billion to $20 billion in 1970 to meet demands for their services.

Even if the situation were as bad as many claim, Lampman said, the Nixon proposals do not go very far in meeting the problems. The real difficulty is getting the money into the right places, he said.

"I'm not too happy with the choices we have," Lampman added, "But I would argue for more categorical grants."

Education. One key problem area will be education. School districts—along with special districts such as those which provide water and irrigation services—were deliberately left off the list of political subdivisions which would share directly in the grants. Murray Weidenbaum, Assistant Secretary of the Treasury and head of the team which drafted the proposal, said the limitation was perhaps the most important compromise reached at a July 8 White House meeting of state and local government officials.

The Administration believes the bulk of the shared funds will go for education in any event. In cases where school financing is part of a city or county budget, the tax effort for education will count toward increasing the unit's share of the localities' pie. On the other hand, independent school districts can be expected to seek and receive a larger state share for their financing from the increased revenues.

Civil rights advocates have raised the question of states' accountability for the shared revenues. If there truly are no strings attached, what is to prevent a recalcitrant state from turning back its education funds—which can be withheld if a school district refuses to follow the law of the land on integration—and using the funds available for revenue sharing to make up the loss?

Though the amount of shared revenues will not be large enough in the beginning to make up for a loss in federal educational grants, the possibility of substitution is there. However, the Administration timetable shows that every school district is expected to have an acceptable desegregation plan by September 1971, three months before the revenue sharing program begins on a modest scale.

Suburbs versus Cities. Some critics said the distribution formula with its emphasis on revenue effort would aid wealthy suburbs at the expense of the core cities.

Suburbs with high-income residents could afford higher taxes with less pain to the taxpayers—and risk to the political leaders—than could most cities and thus could increase their revenue-effort ratio at the expense of the cities, the argument went.

However, a sampling of major cities and selected suburbs indicated that the cities generally made a better revenue effort than their suburbs.

Following is a list of 10 cities and selected suburbs showing general revenues collected per capita.

The figures were based upon 1966-67 revenues and 1960 population. If population rose in the meantime, it would tend to lower the per-capita revenues. In many areas of the nation, the suburban population went up faster than the urban population. Thus, some of the suburban figures below may overstate the actual per-capita revenues in relation to their nearby cities.

Baltimore, $225; Montgomery County, $212.
Boston, $262; Brockton, $215; Cambridge, $237.50.
Chicago, $106; Evanston, $79; Cicero, $63.50.
Cleveland, $101; Cleveland Heights, $67; Lakewood, $132.
Detroit, $127; Ann Arbor, $101.
Minneapolis, $102; Bloomington, $125; Minnetonka, $43.50.
New York City, $373; New Rochelle, $164; Mt. Vernon, $113.
Philadelphia, $162; Haverford, $38; Penn Hills, $39; Upper Darby, $47.
San Francisco, $300; San Mateo, $89; Palo Alto, $141.
Seattle, $115; Mercer Island, $41.

Statistical Tables

The statistical tables that follow on the next four pages contain the latest Bureau of the Census figures on which states' revenue-sharing receipts would be based, according to the Administration's formula.

The figure represented in the formula by R (general revenues of state and local governments) is found in the revenue tables in the fourth column, which is headed "All general revenue from own sources."

Population and Personal Income, by State: 1967-68

State	Population (excluding Armed Forces overseas) July 1, 1968 (provisional estimates)				Personal income calendar year 1967	
	Total	Under 18 years	18 to 64 years	65 years and over	Amount (millions)	Per capita
United States, total.................	199,861,000	70,809,000	109,923,000	19,129,000	625,068	3,159
Alabama............................	3,566,000	1,309,000	1,942,000	306,000	7,656	2,163
Alaska.............................	277,000	120,000	148,000	6,000	1,017	3,738
Arizona............................	1,670,000	650,000	881,000	132,000	4,444	2,720
Arkansas...........................	2,012,000	706,000	1,056,000	224,000	4,130	2,099
California.........................	19,221,000	6,764,000	10,859,000	1,677,000	70,204	3,665
Colorado...........................	2,048,000	741,000	1,123,000	179,000	6,191	3,135
Connecticut........................	2,959,000	1,017,000	1,670,000	276,000	11,609	3,969
Delaware...........................	534,000	198,000	295,000	41,000	1,905	3,642
District of Columbia...............	809,000	282,000	459,000	68,000	3,336	4,123
Florida............................	6,160,000	2,094,000	3,275,000	783,000	17,101	2,853
Georgia............................	4,588,000	1,706,000	2,517,000	344,000	11,458	2,541
Hawaii.............................	778,000	301,000	438,000	41,000	2,415	3,331
Idaho..............................	705,000	264,000	374,000	65,000	1,800	2,575
Illinois...........................	10,974,000	3,860,000	6,035,000	1,096,000	40,850	3,750
Indiana............................	5,067,000	1,840,000	2,740,000	481,000	15,980	3,196
Iowa...............................	2,748,000	972,000	1,456,000	346,000	8,558	3,109
Kansas.............................	2,303,000	795,000	1,239,000	259,000	6,961	3,060
Kentucky...........................	3,229,000	1,140,000	1,734,000	326,000	7,737	2,426
Louisiana..........................	3,732,000	1,465,000	1,967,000	293,000	8,995	2,456
Maine..............................	979,000	347,000	514,000	115,000	2,585	2,657
Maryland...........................	3,757,000	1,375,000	2,106,000	273,000	12,595	3,421
Massachusetts......................	5,437,000	1,850,000	2,997,000	622,000	19,197	3,541
Michigan...........................	8,740,000	3,260,000	4,724,000	755,000	29,151	3,396
Minnesota..........................	3,646,000	1,356,000	1,891,000	400,000	11,162	3,116
Mississippi........................	2,342,000	921,000	1,210,000	213,000	4,453	1,896
Missouri...........................	4,627,000	1,567,000	2,510,000	548,000	13,775	2,993
Montana............................	693,000	261,000	365,000	67,000	1,939	2,765
Nebraska...........................	1,437,000	512,000	750,000	178,000	4,422	3,081
Nevada.............................	453,000	172,000	251,000	26,000	1,591	3,583
New Hampshire......................	702,000	244,000	380,000	78,000	2,094	3,053
New Jersey.........................	7,078,000	2,380,000	4,050,000	663,000	25,686	3,668
New Mexico.........................	1,015,000	431,000	508,000	66,000	2,484	2,477
New York...........................	18,113,000	5,944,000	10,209,000	1,925,000	68,916	3,759
North Carolina.....................	5,135,000	1,845,000	2,886,000	391,000	12,267	2,439
North Dakota.......................	625,000	236,000	326,000	65,000	1,589	2,487
Ohio...............................	10,591,000	3,805,000	5,801,000	982,000	33,605	3,213
Oklahoma...........................	2,518,000	842,000	1,397,000	281,000	6,594	2,643
Oregon.............................	2,008,000	678,000	1,117,000	212,000	6,122	3,063
Pennsylvania.......................	11,712,000	3,880,000	6,614,000	1,234,000	37,065	3,187
Rhode Island.......................	913,000	298,000	518,000	98,000	2,995	3,328
South Carolina.....................	2,692,000	1,018,000	1,467,000	180,000	5,752	2,213
South Dakota.......................	657,000	247,000	330,000	79,000	1,745	2,590
Tennessee..........................	3,976,000	1,383,000	2,227,000	365,000	9,316	2,394
Texas..............................	10,972,000	4,099,000	5,957,000	922,000	29,822	2,744
Utah...............................	1,034,000	432,000	532,000	70,000	2,667	2,604
Vermont............................	422,000	150,000	225,000	49,000	1,178	2,825
Virginia...........................	4,597,000	1,643,000	2,611,000	341,000	12,719	2,804
Washington.........................	3,276,000	1,138,000	1,832,000	306,000	10,871	3,521
West Virginia......................	1,805,000	607,000	1,003,000	192,000	4,197	2,334
Wisconsin..........................	4,213,000	1,546,000	2,217,000	458,000	13,220	3,156
Wyoming............................	315,000	118,000	168,000	30,000	946	3,002

SOURCE: Bureau of the Census

NOTE: The statistical tables on this and the next three pages contain the Bureau of Census figures on which states' revenue-sharing receipts would be based according to the Administration's formula (the figures would be updated from year to year).

The figure represented in the formula by R (general revenues of state and local governments) is found in the revenue tables in the fourth column, which is headed, "All general revenue from own sources."

State and Local General Revenue: 1967-68 (Ala.-Kan.)

State and level of government	Total general revenue	Intergovernmental revenue		All general revenue from own sources	Taxes			Charges and miscella- neous general revenue
		From Federal Government	Other (local-State and State-local)		Total	Property	Other	
UNITED STATES, TOTAL	101 264.3	17 181.3	(¹)	84 083.0	67 571.6	27 747.3	39 824.3	16 511.4
STATE GOVERNMENTS.	59 132.4	15 227.7	707.2	43 197.4	36 400.2	912.0	35 488.2	6 797.3
LOCAL GOVERNMENTS.	63 180.9	1 953.6	20 341.8	40 885.6	31 171.4	26 835.3	4 336.1	9 714.2
ALABAMA.	1 333.8	332.4	(¹)	1 001.3	729.7	120.9	608.8	271.6
STATE GOVERNMENT . . .	954.5	308.3	7.9	638.4	530.7	20.8	509.8	107.7
LOCAL GOVERNMENTS. . .	676.8	24.1	289.7	363.0	199.1	100.1	99.0	163.9
ALASKA	300.7	128.0	(¹)	172.7	92.8	25.3	67.5	79.9
STATE GOVERNMENT . . .	246.3	124.1	0.2	121.9	60.4	-	60.4	61.5
LOCAL GOVERNMENTS. . .	82.8	3.9	28.1	50.8	32.4	25.3	7.1	18.4
ARIZONA.	892.4	184.7	(¹)	707.8	554.6	252.0	302.6	153.2
STATE GOVERNMENT . . ,	562.4	164.0	3.7	394.7	315.9	46.1	269.8	78.8
LOCAL GOVERNMENTS. . .	495.7	20.6	162.0	313.1	238.7	205.9	32.8	74.4
ARKANSAS	706.8	199.1	(¹)	507.7	401.6	105.5	296.1	106.1
STATE GOVERNMENT . . .	518.9	188.3	0.2	330.4	289.6	0.7	289.0	40.7
LOCAL GOVERNMENTS. . .	320.1	10.7	132.0	177.4	112.0	104.9	7.1	65.4
CALIFORNIA	13 686.5	2 394.6	(¹)	11 291.8	9 388.8	4 347.6	5 041.2	1 903.0
STATE GOVERNMENT . . .	7 524.6	2 172.7	110.1	5 241.7	4 664.3	202.3	4 461.9	577.4
LOCAL GOVERNMENTS. . .	9 367.6	221.9	3 095.6	6 050.1	4 724.5	4 145.3	579.3	1 325.6
COLORADO	1 143.8	214.4	(¹)	929.4	721.7	326.7	395.1	207.7
STATE GOVERNMENT . . .	658.4	198.2	1.0	459.1	361.3	1.1	360.1	97.8
LOCAL GOVERNMENTS. . .	695.8	16.1	209.3	470.3	360.5	325.5	35.0	109.9
CONNECTICUT.	1 485.9	240.1	(¹)	1 245.8	1 055.2	551.8	503.4	190.6
STATE GOVERNMENT . . .	809.0	203.6	2.5	602.9	499.8	-	499.8	103.1
LOCAL GOVERNMENTS. . .	826.6	36.5	147.2	642.9	555.3	551.8	3.6	87.6
DELAWARE	306.2	48.1	(¹)	258.1	185.9	39.0	146.9	72.3
STATE GOVERNMENT . . .	233.0	43.6	3.1	186.4	144.8	0.3	144.5	41.6
LOCAL GOVERNMENTS. . .	138.6	4.5	62.4	71.8	41.1	38.7	2.4	30.7
DISTRICT OF COLUMBIA (LOCAL).	542.0	191.3	(1)	350.7	304.2	110.8	193.3	46.6
FLORIDA.	2 759.1	396.9	(¹)	2 362.2	1 778.1	707.9	1 070.2	584.1
STATE GOVERNMENT . . .	1 442.7	327.7	13.8	1 101.2	973.1	23.1	950.1	128.1
LOCAL GOVERNMENTS. . .	1 788.0	69.2	457.9	1 261.0	805.0	684.8	120.2	456.0
GEORGIA.	1 915.3	393.7	(¹)	1 521.6	1 122.7	346.8	775.9	398.9
STATE GOVERNMENT . . .	1 217.3	360.9	9.1	847.4	737.2	3.2	734.0	110.2
LOCAL GOVERNMENTS. . .	1 102.9	32.9	395.8	674.3	385.5	343.6	41.9	288.7
HAWAII	510.4	110.4	(1)	400.1	327.4	64.1	263.3	72.7
STATE GOVERNMENT . . .	402.2	105.3	5.3	291.6	242.7	-	242.7	48.9
LOCAL GOVERNMENTS. . .	138.0	5.0	24.4	108.5	84.7	64.1	20.7	23.8
IDAHO.	352.8	70.9	(¹)	281.9	222.4	83.9	138.5	59.4
STATE GOVERNMENT . . .	229.9	66.5	2.2	161.2	136.8	0.6	136.2	24.4
LOCAL GOVERNMENTS. . .	174.1	4.4	49.1	120.7	85.6	83.3	2.3	35.0
ILLINOIS . . . . ,	5 137.1	831.1	(¹)	4 306.0	3 622.5	1 657.2	1 965.3	683.5
STATE GOVERNMENT . . .	2 673.0	709.7	20.0	1 943.4	1 730.6	1.2	1 729.4	212.8
LOCAL GOVERNMENTS. . .	3 243.4	121.4	759.4	2 362.6	1 891.9	1 656.0	235.9	470.7
INDIANA.	2 256.8	300.4	(¹)	1 956.4	1 543.4	739.6	803.8	413.0
STATE GOVERNMENT . . .	1 328.1	281.9	6.3	1 040.0	819.2	18.8	800.3	220.8
LOCAL GOVERNMENTS. . .	1 345.0	18.5	410.0	916.4	724.3	720.8	3.5	192.2
IOWA	1 460.0	227.7	(¹)	1 232.3	977.8	473.1	504.6	254.5
STATE GOVERNMENT . . .	849.9	214.1	28.2	607.6	502.5	3.8	498.7	105.1
LOCAL GOVERNMENTS. . .	877.9	13.5	239.7	624.7	475.3	469.3	6.0	149.4
KANSAS	1 104.2	168.9	(¹)	935.2	741.6	382.8	358.8	193.7
STATE GOVERNMENT . . .	607.0	152.3	11.4	443.2	357.0	9.1	347.9	86.2
LOCAL GOVERNMENTS. . .	698.6	16.6	190.0	492.0	384.5	373.7	10.8	107.5

State and Local General Revenue: 1967-68 (Ky.-N.C.)

State and level of government	Total general revenue	Intergovernmental revenue		All general revenue from own sources	Taxes			Charges and miscellaneous general revenue
		From Federal Government	Other (local-State and State-local)		Total	Property	Other	
KENTUCKY	1 330.9	354.1	(¹)	976.8	733.0	194.7	538.3	243.8
STATE GOVERNMENT . . .	931.7	319.9	2.4	609.4	509.3	25.3	484.0	100.1
LOCAL GOVERNMENTS. . .	606.3	34.2	204.6	367.4	223.7	169.4	54.3	143.7
LOUISIANA.	1 793.6	373.5	(¹)	1 420.2	1 046.3	*206.9	839.4	373.8
STATE GOVERNMENT . . .	1 348.8	346.5	11.2	991.0	740.7	20.0	720.6	250.3
LOCAL GOVERNMENTS. . .	862.5	26.9	406.4	429.2	305.7	186.9	118.8	123.5
MAINE.	391.9	72.1	(¹)	319.8	270.6	126.0	144.6	49.2
STATE GOVERNMENT . . .	249.9	64.9	3.9	181.1	146.1	3.0	143.2	34.9
LOCAL GOVERNMENTS. . .	184.5	7.1	38.7	138.7	124.4	123.1	1.4	14.3
MARYLAND	1 909.0	272.1	(¹)	1 636.9	1 343.3	514.7	828.6	293.5
STATE GOVERNMENT . . .	1 113.9	231.9	11.5	870.4	753.0	25.8	727.1	117.5
LOCAL GOVERNMENTS. . .	1 320.9	40.2	514.2	766.4	590.4	488.9	101.5	176.1
MASSACHUSETTS.	2 906.0	424.6	(¹)	2 481.4	2 154.3	1 109.3	1 045.0	327.1
STATE GOVERNMENT . . .	1 608.5	367.0	64.7	1 176.7	1 034.9	0.4	1 034.5	141.9
LOCAL GOVERNMENTS. . .	1 993.4	57.6	631.1	1 304.7	1 119.5	1 108.9	10.6	185.2
MICHIGAN	4 664.5	637.6	(¹)	4 026.9	3 205.0	1 320.7	1 884.3	821.9
STATE GOVERNMENT . . .	2 842.5	579.7	36.1	2 226.6	1 885.6	84.6	1 801.1	341.0
LOCAL GOVERNMENTS. . .	2 832.3	57.9	974.2	1 800.3	1 319.3	1 236.1	83.2	480.9
MINNESOTA.	2 185.6	369.6	(¹)	1 816.0	1 428.2	631.2	796.9	387.8
STATE GOVERNMENT . . .	1 357.5	349.5	19.3	988.7	815.1	33.2	781.9	173.6
LOCAL GOVERNMENTS. . .	1 299.5	20.1	452.2	827.3	613.0	598.0	15.0	214.2
MISSISSIPPI.	852.0	212.7	(¹)	639.3	478.7	128.0	350.8	160.6
STATE GOVERNMENT . . .	599.3	203.2	3.9	392.2	322.5	3.6	318.9	69.7
LOCAL GOVERNMENTS. . .	450.0	9.5	193.3	247.1	156.2	124.4	31.9	90.9
MISSOURI	1 910.0	357.1	(¹)	1 552.9	1 257.0	497.6	759.4	295.8
STATE GOVERNMENT . . .	1 077.0	319.0	3.1	754.8	657.0	3.0	653.9	97.9
LOCAL GOVERNMENTS. . .	1 108.8	38.1	272.7	798.0	600.1	494.6	105.5	198.0
MONTANA.	390.9	88.7	(¹)	302.3	235.5	132.8	102.7	66.8
STATE GOVERNMENT . . .	228.7	83.7	2.6	142.3	105.0	7.6	97.3	37.3
LOCAL GOVERNMENTS. . .	203.2	4.9	38.3	160.0	130.5	125.1	5.3	29.5
NEBRASKA	716.8	118.2	(¹)	598.7	466.2	268.0	198.2	132.5
STATE GOVERNMENT . . .	367.1	109.7	10.1	247.3	194.0	11.4	182.6	53.3
LOCAL GOVERNMENTS. . .	438.4	8.5	78.5	351.3	272.2	256.6	15.6	79.1
NEVADA	317.0	58.9	(¹)	258.1	194.4	81.4	113.0	63.7
STATE GOVERNMENT . . .	175.3	52.8	2.4	120.1	103.5	5.7	97.8	16.6
LOCAL GOVERNMENTS. . .	193.2	6.1	49.2	137.9	90.8	75.7	15.2	47.1
NEW HAMPSHIRE.	288.9	55.3	(¹)	233.7	190.0	116.0	74.0	43.7
STATE GOVERNMENT . . .	154.8	49.4	5.0	100.4	75.3	2.8	72.4	25.2
LOCAL GOVERNMENTS. . .	154.1	5.9	14.9	133.3	114.7	113.1	1.6	18.6
NEW JERSEY	3 336.8	405.1	(¹)	2 931.7	2 468.6	1 413.7	1 054.9	463.1
STATE GOVERNMENT . . .	1 559.8	355.2	37.1	1 167.4	954.0	21.7	932.2	213.5
LOCAL GOVERNMENTS. . .	2 235.7	49.9	421.5	1 764.3	1 514.6	1 392.0	122.7	249.7
NEW MEXICO	597.1	173.4	(¹)	423.8	286.6	62.6	224.0	137.2
STATE GOVERNMENT . . .	457.9	148.9	2.7	306.3	217.1	12.5	204.7	89.2
LOCAL GOVERNMENTS. . .	279.0	24.5	137.1	117.4	69.5	50.1	19.4	48.0
NEW YORK	12 321.0	1 417.3	(¹)	10 903.7	9 119.8	3 482.4	5 637.5	1 783.9
STATE GOVERNMENT . . .	6 462.3	1 204.2	80.4	5 177.7	4 447.2	9.4	4 437.7	730.5
LOCAL GOVERNMENTS. . .	9 774.0	213.2	3 834.8	5 726.0	4 672.7	3 473.0	1 199.7	1 053.3
NORTH CAROLINA	1 863.9	328.8	(¹)	1 535.1	1 214.6	325.2	889.4	320.5
STATE GOVERNMENT . . .	1 351.2	297.8	5.4	1 048.1	901.5	21.1	880.4	146.5
LOCAL GOVERNMENTS. . .	1 042.3	31.1	524.2	487.0	313.0	304.1	9.0	174.0

State and Local General Revenue: (N.D.-Wyo.)

State and level of government	Total general revenue	Intergovernmental revenue		All general revenue from own sources	Taxes			Charges and miscellaneous general revenue
		From Federal Government	Other (local-State and State-local)		Total	Property	Other	
NORTH DAKOTA	375.9	72.5	(1)	303.4	197.5	94.8	102.7	105.9
STATE GOVERNMENT . . .	249.8	68.2	5.5	176.0	101.5	1.4	100.1	74.6
LOCAL GOVERNMENTS. . .	174.6	4.3	42.9	127.4	96.1	93.4	2.6	31.3
OHIO	4 378.0	614.3	(1)	3 763.7	2 931.9	1 439.6	1 492.3	831.8
STATE GOVERNMENT . . .	2 251.3	547.4	33.2	1 670.7	1 370.2	57.0	1 313.2	300.5
LOCAL GOVERNMENTS. . .	2 868.2	66.9	708.4	2 093.0	1 561.6	1 382.6	179.1	531.3
OKLAHOMA	1 273.4	334.1	(1)	939.3	670.4	213.4	457.1	268.9
STATE GOVERNMENT . . .	897.0	312.3	3.6	581.2	427.5	-	427.5	153.7
LOCAL GOVERNMENTS. . .	558.5	21.8	178.6	358.2	242.9	213.4	29.6	115.2
OREGON	1 089.7	228.6	(1)	861.1	640.4	305.4	335.0	220.7
STATE GOVERNMENT . . .	631.8	189.8	10.4	431.6	324.8	0.7	324.1	106.8
LOCAL GOVERNMENTS. . .	638.8	38.8	170.4	429.5	315.6	304.7	10.9	113.9
PENNSYLVANIA	5 008.0	805.4	(1)	4 202.6	3 495.6	1 100.2	2 395.4	707.0
STATE GOVERNMENT . . .	2 970.2	678.3	47.0	2 244.8	2 003.8	2.1	2 001.8	241.0
LOCAL GOVERNMENTS. . .	2 873.0	127.1	788.2	1 957.8	1 491.8	1 098.2	393.7	465.9
RHODE ISLAND	449.1	94.2	(1)	354.8	302.4	133.8	168.7	52.4
STATE GOVERNMENT . . .	288.6	85.0	1.4	202.2	166.7	-	166.7	35.5
LOCAL GOVERNMENTS. . .	210.0	9.2	48.2	152.6	135.7	133.8	1.9	16.9
SOUTH CAROLINA	877.9	169.4	(1)	708.5	542.0	121.2	420.9	166.5
STATE GOVERNMENT . . .	653.1	154.3	8.0	490.8	413.4	1.0	412.4	77.4
LOCAL GOVERNMENTS. . .	441.9	15.1	209.1	217.7	128.6	120.1	8.5	89.1
SOUTH DAKOTA	358.6	83.5	(1)	275.1	214.7	119.4	95.2	60.4
STATE GOVERNMENT . . .	206.1	79.7	1.4	125.1	88.0	-	88.0	37.1
LOCAL GOVERNMENTS. . .	182.0	3.8	28.2	150.0	126.7	119.4	7.3	23.3
TENNESSEE.	1 480.2	329.0	(1)	1 151.3	903.8	253.6	650.1	247.5
STATE GOVERNMENT . . .	958.8	289.0	15.8	654.0	577.3	-	577.3	76.7
LOCAL GOVERNMENTS. . .	867.0	40.0	329.8	497.3	326.5	253.6	72.8	170.8
TEXAS.	4 400.9	859.5	(1)	3 541.4	2 665.4	1 215.8	1 449.7	876.0
STATE GOVERNMENT . . .	2 590.1	788.1	7.5	1 794.5	1 438.0	59.7	1 378.2	356.6
LOCAL GOVERNMENTS. . .	2 531.6	71.4	713.3	1 746.8	1 227.4	1 156.0	71.4	519.4
UTAH	550.3	140.3	(1)	410.0	311.2	127.8	183.4	98.8
STATE GOVERNMENT . . .	379.2	130.8	1.3	247.1	183.5	12.5	171.0	63.6
LOCAL GOVERNMENTS. . .	273.7	9.5	101.3	162.9	127.7	115.3	12.4	35.2
VERMONT.	244.3	66.8	(1)	177.4	147.8	58.4	89.4	29.6
STATE GOVERNMENT . . .	175.2	64.4	1.4	109.4	88.2	0.3	87.9	21.2
LOCAL GOVERNMENTS. . .	92.4	2.5	21.9	68.0	59.6	58.1	1.5	8.4
VIRGINIA	1 860.3	323.5	(1)	1 536.8	1 236.4	366.0	870.4	300.3
STATE GOVERNMENT . . .	1 171.2	270.1	12.2	888.9	731.7	10.8	720.8	157.2
LOCAL GOVERNMENTS. . .	1 050.3	53.4	349.0	647.9	504.8	355.2	149.6	143.1
WASHINGTON	1 950.5	326.0	(1)	1 624.5	1 247.0	397.7	849.3	377.5
STATE GOVERNMENT . . .	1 339.3	302.8	5.4	1 031.1	878.6	83.4	795.3	152.4
LOCAL GOVERNMENTS. . .	1 007.1	23.2	390.5	593.4	368.3	314.4	54.0	225.1
WEST VIRGINIA.	776.1	204.7	(1)	571.4	449.5	114.5	334.9	121.9
STATE GOVERNMENT . . .	581.6	197.7	0.6	383.3	320.2	0.3	319.9	63.1
LOCAL GOVERNMENTS. . .	323.3	7.0	128.2	188.0	129.3	114.2	15.1	58.8
WISCONSIN.	2 271.0	303.5	(1)	1 967.5	1 625.4	674.2	951.2	342.1
STATE GOVERNMENT . . .	1 477.2	292.7	24.8	1 159.7	990.5	49.9	940.7	169.1
LOCAL GOVERNMENTS. . .	1 478.6	10.7	660.0	807.9	634.9	624.3	10.6	173.0
WYOMING.	250.4	74.5	(1)	175.9	127.7	65.5	62.2	48.1
STATE GOVERNMENT . . .	168.6	72.5	0.8	95.3	68.7	10.5	58.2	26.6
LOCAL GOVERNMENTS. . .	118.3	2.1	35.7	80.6	59.0	55.0	4.1	21.5

- Represents zero or rounds to zero.
[1] Duplicative transactions between levels of government are excluded.

NIXON CALLS ON SPECIALISTS TO HELP MAKE UP STAFF

To advise him in crucial areas of decision-making, President Nixon called on men regarded as some of the ablest in their fields. On Nov. 4, 1969, almost exactly one year after his election, Mr. Nixon directed the first broad reorganization of his White House staff.

The staff changes were precipitated in part by Mr. Nixon's appointment in October of Dr. Arthur F. Burns, then a counsellor to the President with Cabinet rank, as chairman of the Federal Reserve Board. He would succeed William McChesney Martin, whose 14-year term was to expire Jan. 30, 1970.

Mr. Nixon also elevated two key assistants to Cabinet rank. Daniel Patrick Moynihan, his adviser on urban affairs, and Bryce N. Harlow, his assistant for Congressional relations, were named counsellors to the President. At the same time he named John D. Ehrlichman, his counsel, to a newly created post of assistant to the President for domestic affairs.

The White House announcement of the changes said the two counsellors would provide the President with "long-range vision," while Ehrlichman would be expected to oversee development of specific policy alternatives and programs.

Other key advisers, in addition to Members of the Cabinet, included Presidential Assistants H. R. Haldeman and Peter Flanigan; Henry A. Kissinger, Assistant for National Security Affairs; Lee A. DuBridge, science adviser; Herbert G. Klein, director of communications; Robert P. Mayo, director of the Budget Bureau; Paul McCracken, chairman of the Council of Economic Advisers; Richard M. Helms, director of the Central Intelligence Agency; and Donald Rumsfeld, director of the Office of Economic Opportunity. Rumsfeld, Mayo, McCracken, Helms and Martin primarily were responsible for heading their own offices and were not considered members of the President's personal office staff.

Another major adviser was Vice President Spiro T. Agnew, who, among other duties, was chairman of several Presidential councils (such as the Council on Youth Opportunity and the National Aeronautics and Space Council) and was a member of the Cabinet and the National Security Council.

The chief economic advisers to the President were Secretary of the Treasury David M. Kennedy, McCracken and Mayo. This group was sometimes referred to as the "troika" and was often enlarged to a "quadriad" by the inclusion of the chairman of the Federal Reserve Board. President Nixon in January 1969 announced formation of a Cabinet Committee on Economic Policy to assist in long-range planning and to supplement the work of the "troika" and "quadriad." Mr. Nixon was chairman of the group, which included the Vice President, Burns, the members of the troika and the Secretaries of Agriculture, Commerce and Labor.

The President was advised on national security matters by the National Security Council, made up of himself, the Vice President, the Secretaries of State and Defense, the director of the Office of Emergency Preparedness (George A. Lincoln), the CIA director and the chairman of the Joint Chiefs of Staff (Gen. Earle G. Wheeler).

Office Staff

Not since the 1960 election of John F. Kennedy had a President faced the staff-building task Richard M. Nixon faced in November 1968—that of putting together a White House staff from scratch.

President Johnson, when he was sworn in Nov. 22, 1963, after the assassination of President Kennedy, inherited a staff assembled by Mr. Kennedy. Mr. Johnson kept those who chose to stay, replacing them with his own appointments as the Kennedy men gradually resigned. By late 1968, only one member of the Kennedy staff remained as a Presidential adviser.

Mr. Nixon as Vice President had observed the staff operation of the Eisenhower Administration in which a few men, principally Assistant Sherman Adams, regulated access and the flow of ideas to the President. Mr. Nixon was intent on avoiding this type of staff structure, an aide said, as well as that of the Johnson Administration in which serious governmental matters were often processed through two or three powerful men and persuasive assistants before they reached the President.

Presidential Assistant H. R. Haldeman said in November 1968 that Mr. Nixon planned for a small group of aides who would assist, advise and funnel information to him but who would not dominate or control the major agencies and bureaus of the Government or inhibit direct communication between the Cabinet and the President. The Chief Executive viewed the major responsibility for policymaking as that of his Cabinet and not of the White House staff.

Special assistants' duties included press relations, appointments, speechwriting, politics and liaison with agencies and bureaus. A number of key men, experts in specific fields, were to advise the President under the title of "Assistant," "Adviser" or "Consultant."

The Nixon staff of 25 to 30 men and one woman was larger than those of recent administrations. President Johnson averaged 22 on his staff and Mr. Kennedy had 16 at the time of his death.

Describing his campaign staff, which provided the majority of his White House staff, Mr. Nixon was quoted by The New York Times in September 1968 as saying:

"The first thing they have is brains.... They're not for sale. These are the guys that money can't buy. They like challenge; they want to be in the battle. They are individualists and debate with each other. You talk to the new generation through these fellows."

Mr. Nixon has been said to preside over his staff like a firm schoolmaster.

Other descriptions of the staff by political writers called them a no-nonsense group of men who appear uneasy when not dressed in suit and tie, well groomed, bright, well educated and often handsome, yet who have somewhat anonymous personalities. The corporate ethic pervaded and they rarely discussed their problems with outsiders.

Mr. Nixon assembled a staff whose political views ranged from the social liberalism of Daniel Moynihan to the conservatism of Patrick Buchanan. Political writers maintained that as a group the Nixon men focused slightly right of center.

One of the most striking characteristics was the staff's general lack of government experience. Of the 28 major members of Mr. Nixon's early White House staff, just seven had had previous government experience.

The average age of the Nixon staff was 44.9 years and varied little from the average age of the Johnson staff. The youngest on the Nixon staff was 28 years old; the oldest at the time of his appointment, 67. Three were in their 60s and three in their 20s.

Five Nixon appointees had Ph.D degrees; four others had master's degrees, and three others were lawyers. All were college graduates. The five with Ph.D degrees were all teaching at universities when appointed.

Reflecting Nixon's California and New York ties during the eight years he was out of office was the geographic distribution among his staff. Ten were New Yorkers, and six others were living in California when named to their positions.

Nearly half of the staff were newspaper, advertising or public relations men when chosen by the President to be his advisers.

One woman and one Negro were among the 28 early members of the White House staff.

President Nixon introduced four new titles into the White House staff: director of communications; Counsellor to the President; Special Assistant for Black Capitalism; and Special Assistant for Liaison with Former Presidents. The title of Special Assistant for Black Capitalists, held by Robert J. Brown, a Negro, reflects the President's view that private industry can solve many of the nation's social problems.

Titles Dropped. The two major titles dropped by Mr. Nixon were those of Press Secretary and Appointments Secretary. Ronald Ziegler, Special Assistant for Press Relations, was authorized to report only that which was released by the President. The President frowned on the power held by former appointments secretaries, according to Haldeman, and Special Assistant for Presidential Appointments and Schedules Dwight Chapin operates primarily as a schedule keeper.

Mr. Nixon also dropped two other titles used by Mr. Johnson: Special Assistant for Peaceful Reconstruction in Vietnam and Special Assistant on the Arts.

The position of Special Assistant on Consumer Affairs was the one appointment Mr. Nixon had not made prior to his inauguration. On Feb. 11 the President appointed Miss Willie Mae Rogers, director of the Good Housekeeping Institute, in the midst of criticism from consumer advocates in Congress for not having filled the position. Miss Rogers resigned four days later after accusations of conflict-of-interest, since she intended to continue on the Institute payroll. On April 9 Mrs. Virginia Knauer, director of the Pennsylvania Bureau of Consumer Protection, was named to the post.

Three Nixon aides, Assistant Robert Ellsworth, Gen. Andrew J. Goodpaster, Consultant on Military Security, and Special Assistant Leonard Zartman, left the staff after the President appointed them to other positions. Goodpaster was made Supreme Allied Commander in Europe in March. Ellsworth was named Ambassador to the North Atlantic Treaty Organization in April. Zartman in June became general counsel of the Small Business Administration.

Background. President Nixon's White House staff could be described as a campaign staff. Twenty of the 28 appointees were key people in his 1968 Presidential campaign and 13 of the 20 were veterans of previous campaigns. The seven involved only in the last campaign were Martin Anderson, Harry Flemming, Ray Price, Patrick Buchanan, Kenneth Cole, former aide Robert Ellsworth and Leonard Garment.

Seven of the 20 were long time Nixon associates: Arthur Burns, Peter Flanigan, H. R. Haldeman, Bryce Harlow, James Keogh, Herbert Klein and Leonard Garment.

Seven worked in Nixon campaigns in the 1960s: Roy Ash, Dwight Chapin, John Davies, John Ehrlichman, H. Dale Grubb, Ronald Ziegler and William Safire.

The two who had known Mr. Nixon the longest were Klein and DuBridge, Klein for 23 years and DuBridge for 22.

Former Eisenhower Aides. Nixon went back to the Eisenhower Administration for five appointments—three of them major ones. They were Arthur Burns, chairman of the Council of Economic Advisers from 1953-1956 and a White House Consultant on Economics for Mr. Eisenhower; Dr. Lee DuBridge, chairman of Mr. Eisenhower's Science Advisory Committee; Gen. Andrew Goodpaster, a former staff secretary to Mr. Eisenhower; Bryce Harlow, an Eisenhower White House aide for Congressional liaison; and Brig. Gen. Robert Schulz, military aide to President Eisenhower.

Harlow was a successful Congressional lobbyist for Mr. Eisenhower. But this success was partly attributed to Mr. Eisenhower's having two personal friends in the Democratic leadership, Speaker of the House Sam Rayburn and Senate Majority Leader Lyndon B. Johnson. Mr. Nixon was the first President in 120 years to begin office with both Congressional houses controlled by the opposition party.

Five Nixon appointments had a Horatio Alger-type background: James Keogh, who started his education in a one-room school; Arthur Burns, who worked his way through Columbia University as a house painter; Roy L. Ash, who went to work after graduating from high school because he could not afford college and in 1966 received the Horatio Alger Award; Daniel Moynihan, a one-time Hudson River longshoreman whose family was often on welfare; and Robert Brown, once a policeman in High Point, N.C., who in 1965 received a Most Outstanding Young Men in America award.

Operation. Almost half of the Nixon White House staffers maintained offices in the Executive Office Building. The President also worked there frequently.

The Nixon staff operated generally not as one large team but as several small squads—for domestic policy, foreign policy, political strategy, speechwriting and administration.

Four key aides—Kissinger, Harlow, Haldeman and Ehrlichman—conferred with the President daily as did Special Assistant Ron Ziegler. Others saw Mr. Nixon at the President's discretion.

Mr. Nixon, who during the 1960 campaign was reported reluctant to delegate authority, consulted frequently with his staff. Nevertheless, an aide said, major decisions were made by the President.

NIXON FILLS CHIEF JUSTICE, OTHER TOP POSITIONS

President Nixon in 1969 filled most of the top policy-making positions in the Federal Government with his own appointees, although several holdovers from previous Administrations remained in office at the end of the year. President Nixon placed a new Chief Justice on the Supreme Court, gained Republican control of seven of the 11 major regulatory agencies and filled 26 federal judgeships.

In keeping with tradition, the President appointed members of his party to many of the coveted patronage positions—Cabinet posts, Western European ambassadorships and the Federal Judiciary. In many cases, however, career Government officials were appointed to fill major administrative positions in the Executive departments.

President Nixon Feb. 5 announced that he was ending the patronage system of appointing postmasters and rural letter carriers. He said that high scores on competitive examinations would be the sole criterion for filling the posts.

The system of choosing postmasters from among the three high scorers on competitive exams already was in effect. However, under past practice, the preferred candidate of a Member of Congress or party official was allowed to repeat the test until he was among the top three. Under the new system, the test would be given only once, and the Postmaster General would select from among the three high scorers. Members of Congress would still be consulted, but their recommendations would not necessarily be followed.

The Administration also sought Congressional approval of legislation to end the requirement for Senate confirmation of first, second and third class postmasters. The Senate approved the proposal, while the House held hearings on the proposal but took no further action. *(See p. 63.)*

Controversial Nominations

Haynsworth. The most controversial of President Nixon's nominations for 1969 was that of federal Judge Clement F. Haynsworth Jr. to be an Associate Justice of the Supreme Court. The nomination was rejected by the Senate Nov. 21 by a 45-55 roll-call vote, giving President Nixon his major Congressional defeat of the session.

Haynsworth, chief judge of the 4th Circuit Court of Appeals, was named by President Nixon Aug. 18 to fill the seat left vacant by Abe Fortas, who had resigned May 14 under threat of impeachment.

The controversy over judicial ethics ignited by Fortas' resignation under fire for accepting an outside fee from the family foundation of a convicted stock manipulator was rekindled by opposition to Haynsworth's nomination.

Opponents of the nomination said they did not question Haynsworth's honesty, but questioned his sensitivity to the appearance of ethical impropriety and his judgment regarding participation in cases where his financial interests could be said to be involved. The nomination also was opposed by labor and civil rights leaders. *(See p. 87.)*

Hickel. The Senate Jan. 20, 1969, confirmed by voice vote all except one of the Cabinet nominations—that of Walter J. Hickel to be Secretary of the Interior. On the motion of Edward M. Kennedy (D Mass.), the Senate deferred action on Hickel for one day.

The Hickel nomination became controversial after conservation groups questioned his dedication to natural preservation and others criticized his ties with oil companies. He had said at a December 1968 news conference that he opposed "conservation for conservation's sake" and that high national standards for clean water "might hinder industrial development."

Hickel was criticized for his opposition as Governor of Alaska to plans to create a foreign-trade sub-zone for oil at Machiasport, Maine, that would result in cheaper fuel oil for New England. Another complaint was over his opposition, as Governor, to an Interior Department freeze on Alaskan public lands until Congress settled pending claims to the land by native Alaskans.

At four days of hearings (Jan. 15-18) by the Senate Interior and Insular Affairs Committee, Hickel also was questioned about his having tried to prevent an Eskimo cooperative from selling fish to the Japanese. The Japanese would have paid higher prices than the Eskimos were receiving locally.

Hickel promised the Committee he would sell about $1 million worth of gas pipelines stock.

Many Senators who expressed doubts as to Hickel's qualifications said they nevertheless would vote for him because it was customary to let the President select his first Cabinet members.

Hickel was supported by Democrat Ernest Gruening, former Alaska Governor (1939-53) and U.S. Senator (1959-69).

The Senate confirmed Hickel's nomination Jan. 23 by a 73-16 roll-call vote. He received unanimous Republican support.

Packard. The nomination of David Packard, chief executive officer of the Hewlett-Packard Co., a defense contractor, to be Deputy Secretary of Defense raised questions of conflict of interest because of Hewlett-Packard's role in the defense industry. Packard owned $300 million worth of stock in the company and claimed that the sale of such a large amount of stock would not be practical. He agreed to place his stock into a charitable trust, and the Senate confirmed his nomination Jan. 23 by a roll-call vote of 82-1.

Brown. At a Senate Judiciary subcommittee hearing March 27, called by Sen. Edward M. Kennedy (D Mass.) to examine the equal employment policies of the Nixon Administration, Senate Minority Leader Everett M. Dirksen charged Clifford L. Alexander Jr., chairman of the Equal Employment Opportunity Commission (EEOC), with harassment of Government contractors in enforcing equal employment regulations. Dirksen told Alexander he would "go to the highest authority in the Government to get somebody fired" if what he called "punitive harassment" by EEOC did not stop. The next day White House Press Secretary Ronald Ziegler announced that Alexander would be replaced as EEOC chairman, but Ziegler denied that the decision had been influenced by Dirksen. Alexander announced April 10 that he would resign as chairman but serve out the rest of his five-year board term, which was to expire July 1, 1972. (Alexander Aug. 15 resigned a a member of the EEOC. *(For related story on the Commission, see p. 52.)*

President Nixon then announced his intention to name William H. Brown III, the newest member of the Commission, to replace Alexander as chairman. Brown, a Republican, had been named to the EEOC by President Johnson in October 1968 but had not been confirmed when the Nixon Administration took office. President Nixon resubmitted Brown's name to the Senate March 13. Brown's nomination met no resistance in the Senate until it was announced that he would probably replace Alexander as chairman. Dirksen threatened to block confirmation and on May 1 forced postponement of Senate floor action on the nomination. Brown was supported by a coalition of Democrats and Republicans led by Minority Whip Hugh Scott (Pa.). Dirksen dropped his objection to the nomination on May 5, and Brown was confirmed as a member by voice vote. Nixon subsequently named Brown as chairman of the EEOC.

Allen. Mr. Nixon's appointment of James E. Allen, New York state education commissioner, to head the Office of Education in the Department of Health, Education and Welfare met opposition, led by Sen. Strom Thurmond (R S.C.), who objected to Allen's policy of busing children to achieve racial balance in New York schools.

In a speech on the Senate floor May 5, Thurmond, who led the Presidential campaign for Nixon in the South, said Allen's views on school integration "conflict with those of President Nixon enunciated during the campaign." Nixon had opposed busing in a campaign speech, saying the practice hurt children rather than helped them. Sen. James O. Eastland (D Miss.) during the debate on Allen's confirmation said approval of the nomination would cause a "national calamity" in the public schools.

Allen's supporters, led by Sens. Kennedy and Jacob K. Javits (R N.Y.), contended that the appointee's extensive background in education qualified him for the post. Kennedy said Allen was simply carrying out New York state policy when he approved the busing plans. During the April 15 hearing on his nomination, Allen testified that he intended to abide by the federal statute which prohibits busing for the purpose of overcoming racial imbalance. Allen was confirmed May 5 by a 55-15 roll-call vote.

Knowles. Secretary of Health, Education and Welfare Robert Finch met opposition from Sen. Dirksen and elements of the American Medical Association (AMA) when he announced his intention to nominate Dr. John Knowles as Assistant Secretary for health and scientific affairs. Knowles, director of the Massachusetts General Hospital in Boston, was opposed because of his views on public medicine. Dirksen said at a news conference April 22 that he had told Finch he would prevent confirmation if Knowles' nomination was sent to the Senate. The nomination was not submitted. President Nixon July 12 nominated Dr. Roger O. Egeberg to the post.

Knowles credited "certain political debts" of President Nixon for his failure to be nominated. The AMA's political arm contributed heavily in 1968 to many Congressional candidates, most of them Republicans.

The Knowles controversy produced strong criticism from several members of the Senate, who charged that the Administration had improperly bowed to outside pressure against Knowles. Sen. Edward W. Brooke (R Mass.) called the rejection of Knowles "a calamity for the country and an abuse of political power."

Sen. Edward M. Kennedy (D Mass.) charged that people in high places in public life and organized medicine "conspired" to defeat the nomination. Sen. Charles E. Goodell (R N.Y.) said the post was filled on the basis of politics and not merit.

Long. The National Science Board recommended to the President that he appoint Dr. Franklin Long, vice president for research at Cornell University, to head the National Science Foundation (NSF). Long received strong support from Dr. Lee DuBridge, science adviser to the President and director of the Office of Science and Technology. After several conferences with DuBridge, Long reportedly decided to accept the post and came to Washington April 11 under the impression that he was to meet with President Nixon and that an announcement of the appointment would be made shortly thereafter. When he arrived, however, Long was told that some members of the White House staff opposed the appointment on grounds that Long's opposition to the antiballistic missile system might jeopardize his chances of confirmation in the Senate. At an April 18 news conference, President Nixon said that Long's name had never reached his desk for final approval but that he had approved of his staff's decision not to submit the nomination. Credit for blocking the appointment was claimed by Sen. Dirksen and by Rep. James G. Fulton (R Pa.). Fulton said he opposed the appointment not because of Long's views on the ABM but because "long is a man of controversy and I want to keep the NSF in a scientific atmosphere and not one of controversy."

At a White House meeting April 28 with scientists from the NSF and the National Academy of Sciences, Mr. Nixon conceded that he had been wrong in opposing Long's nomination on the basis of his opposition to the ABM. The President told the scientists that he had contended Dr. Long and had asked him whether he would care to have his name resubmitted for the position. Long reportedly refused the offer because he did not want to see the case reopened.

Driver. The White House announced April 18 that William J. Driver, director of the Veterans Administration since 1964, had resigned. President Nixon had planned to reappoint Driver, but the move was opposed by Dirksen, who charged that Driver had converted the VA into "a political institution." Driver said he had resigned for personal reasons. President Nixon June 9 appointed Donald E. Johnson to head the VA. Johnson was confirmed June 19.

Otepka. President Nixon March 19 appointed Otto F. Otepka, former State Department security evaluator, to the Subversive Activities Control Board (SACB). Otepka had been demoted by Secretary of State Dean Rusk in 1966 for giving classified Department documents to the Senate Judiciary Internal Security Subcommittee during hearings by the Subcommittee on State Department security. Otepka's nomination to the SACB was criticized by some Democrats in Congress but was supported by Sens. Dirksen and Thurmond. On June 24, the nomination was confirmed by the Senate by a 61-28 roll-call vote.

Gilbert. The President April 10 nominated Carl J. Gilbert, former board chairman of the Gillette Co. and president of the Committee for a National Trade Policy, to be U.S. special representative for trade negotiations. Gilbert, a leading advocate of free trade, was opposed by several Senators because of his opposition to import quotas. The Senate confirmed the nomination July 29 by a 61-30 roll call.

Hurd. The White House Aug. 7 announced the nomination of John G. Hurd as U.S. ambassador to Venezuela had been withdrawn at Hurd's request. The announcement followed an Aug. 5 Senate speech by Frank Church (D Idaho), chairman of the Foreign Relations Subcommittee on Western Hemisphere Affairs, in which Church attacked the nomination of Hurd, president of the Independent Oil Producers Association and a Nixon campaign fund raiser.

Church said Hurd had been "actively engaged in the movement for tighter oil import quotas...To send an oil protectionist to Caracas is like sending a Zionist to Cairo. Given our gigantic oil investment in Venezuela, it would be dubious enough to send an oil man there under any circumstances. But to send one who has lobbied for tighter import quotas boggles the imagination."

Church said oil accounted for 90 percent of Venezuela's foreign exchange. "U.S. oil import policy far overshadows any other issue in U.S.-Venezuelan relations," he said. The appointment of Hurd "would be like sending fire to fuel....I shall do everything I can to oppose his confirmation by the Senate."

In a letter to President Nixon asking that his name be withdrawn, Hurd denied any conflict of interest, but he said the appearance of such a conflict "would impair my effectiveness" as ambassador.

Strausz-Hupé. The nomination of Robert Strausz-Hupé as ambassador to Morocco was withdrawn by President Nixon Dec. 22 after it became evident that the nomination would probably never reach the Senate floor. Strausz-Hupé, director of the Foreign Policy Research Institute of the University of Pennsylvania and the author of several books on Communist cold war tactics, was nominated to the Moroccan post on Aug. 5, but Foreign Relations Committee Chairman J. W. Fulbright (D Ark.) refused to hold hearings on the nomination. Fulbright said that diplomatic relations with Morocco were particularly sensitive and that anti-American sentiment in that country made the appointment of an ambassador with Strausz-Hupe's rigid and outspoken anti-Communist views unwise.

President Nixon, following his withdrawal of the nomination, announced his intention to nominate Strausz-Hupé as ambassador to Ceylon.

Other Controversies. Several of President Nixon's appointees were involved in conflict of interest controversies. One, Miss Willie Mae Rogers, resigned as part-time White House consultant on consumer affairs after only four days on the job. The appointment brought on complaints that Miss Rogers, as director of the Good Housekeeping Institute, was directly involved with the Institute's "seal of approval" given to certain commercial products.

Conflict of interest charges also were leveled at Treasury Secretary David M. Kennedy because of his financial ties and former position with the Continental Illinois National Bank & Trust Co., the nation's eighth largest

bank. Kennedy agreed to place his stock in the firm in a "blind" trust.

Securities and Exchange Commission Chairman Hamer H. Budge was criticized for negotiating with a mutual fund company over the offer of a management position. Hearings were held on the matter.

Judgeships as Patronage

The prestige of a federal judgeship is high, and appointment to the judiciary is considered by most attorneys and politicians to be the apex of a legal and public career.

Federal judgeships are lifetime appointments and pay $42,500 in the circuit court and $40,000 in the district court annually. There is no mandatory retirement age, but judges may retire at full salary at age 65 after 15 years or at 70 after 10 years on the bench.

The following list gives the number of confirmed federal circuit and district court judges appointed by President Nixon during his first year in office and by his five immediate predecessors.

	Democrats	Republicans
Roosevelt	188	6
Truman	116	9
Eisenhower	9	165
Kennedy	111†	11
Johnson	159	9
Nixon	2	24

†*One New York Liberal also was appointed.*

Judicial Nominations

The Senate in 1969 confirmed President Nixon's nominations to 26 federal circuit and district judgeships. Sixteen of these nominations filled vacancies in the courts which existed when Nixon took office. At the end of 1969, there were 13 vacancies in the federal courts. There were 5 in the circuit courts and 8 in the district courts. One judge had been nominated to fill a position in the circuit court but had not been confirmed by the time Congress adjourned.

Total Nominations

In the first session of the 91st Congress, the Senate received 73,159 nominations and confirmed 72,635. President Nixon withdrew 465 nominations which had been submitted to the 91st Congress by President Johnson before he left office. One nomination was rejected by the Senate in 1969, and 46 had not been confirmed by the time Congress adjourned.

Regulatory Agencies

By the end of his first term in early 1973, President Nixon will have, through his appointments, nominal control over 9 of 11 federal regulatory agencies.

The President made 17 appointments in 1969 to those independent agencies and commissions that exercise regulatory powers over a broad range of public interests. *(For list of agencies and members, see p. 86.)*

Only the Federal Reserve System Board of Governors and the Federal Trade Commission will retain in 1972 a majority membership appointed by previous Presidents. But if re-elected in 1972, Mr. Nixon will have appointive control over these two agencies as well.

Securities and Exchange Commission. Most of Mr. Nixon's 17 appointments were Republican and generally conservative. The only Democratic appointee was A. Sydney Herlong Jr. to the Securities and Exchange Commission (SEC). The President was required by law to name a Democrat, since no more than three members of the five-man Commission can be from one political party. Herlong, a 60-year-old Floridian, became acquainted with Mr. Nixon when they were colleagues in the House of Representatives, where Herlong served from 1949 to 1969. On the Ways and Means Committee, Herlong became known as a conservative and as a spokesman for oil and cattle interests. He worked in the Nixon campaign and reportedly was a close friend and adviser to Attorney General John N. Mitchell.

The President made two other appointments to the SEC, including that of Hamer H. Budge as chairman. Budge, reappointed to a five-year term, was involved in a possible conflict-of-interest charge during 1969.

James J. Needham, 42-year-old New York City accountant, was Mr. Nixon's third SEC appointment. Needham, who worked for several accounting firms in New York City, dealt mostly with insurance matters and was relatively unknown to the securities industry.

Federal Trade Commission. Another well-publicized appointment was that of Caspar W. Weinberger to the seven-year chairmanship of the Federal Trade Commission (FTC). He was confirmed by the Senate Nov. 19. Weinberger, as California state Republican chairman, led a group of GOP moderates in an unsuccessful attempt to capture the gubernatorial nomination in 1966. After the election, Weinberger, 52, became state finance director in the administration of Ronald Reagan and was an advocate of tight-money policies in the state.

Federal Communications Commission. Among the more controversial appointments were those of Dean Burch and Robert Wells to the Federal Communications Commission (FCC). Both were confirmed by the Senate Oct. 30 after being labeled conservative and management-oriented.

Although the Commission's 4-3 Democratic majority remained unchanged by the President's appointments, a liberal commissioner, Kenneth A. Cox, would leave the agency in June 1970.

Federal Power Commission. New chairman of the Federal Power Commission (FPC) was John Nassikas, 52, a New Hampshire lawyer and former minority counsel of the Senate Commerce Committee. Nassikas, a Republican, was regarded as a conservative, but one Democratic member of the Commerce Committee said after his nomination, "He's no patsy for industry lobbyists." He was confirmed by the Senate June 17.

Civil Aeronautics Board. The Civil Aeronautics Board chairmanship was filled by Secor D. Browne, who was confirmed by the Senate Oct. 3. Browne, 53, was a former associate professor of aeronautics at Massachusetts Institute of Technology (MIT).

Atomic Energy Commission. Two nuclear scientists, Theos J. Thompson and Clarence E. Larson, began new terms on the Atomic Energy Commission. Thompson was a former professor at MIT, and Larson formerly was head of research and development at the Union Carbide Corporation.

Federal Reserve. The President Oct. 17 nominated Arthur F. Burns, a conservative Republican and Mr. Nixon's chief economic adviser, to replace William McC. Martin Jr. as chairman of the Federal Reserve System. Confirmed by the Senate Dec. 18, Burns would take over Feb. 1, 1970.

All members of the Federal Reserve Board were appointed by Democratic Presidents except Martin, who was appointed to an unexpired term by President Truman in 1951 and reappointed to a full 14-year term by President Eisenhower in 1956. Because of the lengthy terms of Board members, Mr. Nixon would have to wait until January 1976 to appoint a Republican majority.

Others. Other agencies that have a regulatory function are the Federal Deposit Insurance Corporation, the Commodity Exchange Administration and the Federal National Mortgage Administration (FNMA).

A partisan dispute arose over the replacement of Raymond Lapin as president of the quasi-public FNMA. The White House announced Dec. 2 it would replace Lapin, a Johnson appointee. Lapin, characterizing the move as "a lawless exercise of raw power," filed suit to prevent the replacement. *(See p. 62.)*

Confirmations of Mr. Nixon's Major 1969 Nominations

Listed below are the names of 298 persons named to major federal posts by President Nixon and confirmed by the Senate in 1969. Information is given in the following order: name of office, salary, appointee, residence, occupation before appointment, date and place of birth, party affiliation (if known) and date of Senate confirmation. Ambassadorial confirmations are listed only if the appointment was of more than routine interest.

Executive Office of the President

COUNCIL OF ECONOMIC ADVISERS

Chairman, $42,500—**Paul W. McCracken**; Ann Arbor, Mich.; Edmund Ezra Day Univ. professor of business administration; Dec. 29, 1915, in Richmond, Iowa; Rep.; Jan. 29.

Member, $38,000—**Herbert Stein**; Silver Spring, Md.; senior fellow, Brookings Institution; Aug. 27, 1916, in Detroit, Mich.; Rep.; Jan. 29.

Member, $38,000—**Hendrik S. Houthakker**; Belmont, Mass.; professor of economics, Harvard Univ.; Dec. 31, 1924, in Amsterdam, the Netherlands; Rep.; Jan. 29.

OFFICE OF ECONOMIC OPPORTUNITY

Director, $42,500—**Donald Rumsfeld**; Evanston, Ill.; Member, U.S. House of Representatives; July 9, 1932, in Evanston; Rep.; May 23.

Deputy Director, $40,000—**Wesley L. Hjornevik**; Dickinson, Texas; associate director, NASA Manned Spacecraft Center; March 22, 1926, in Minneapolis, Minn.; Dec. 18.

OFFICE OF EMERGENCY PREPAREDNESS

Director, $40,000—**George A. Lincoln**; West Point, N.Y.; head of social science dept., U.S. Military Academy; July 20, 1907, in Harbor Beach, Mich.; Jan. 29.

Deputy Director, $38,000—**Fred J. Russell**; Beverly Hills, Calif.; president, Weiser Lock Co.; June 9, 1916, in Edmonton, Alberta, Canada; Feb. 7.

OFFICE OF SCIENCE AND TECHNOLOGY

Director, $42,500—**Lee A. DuBridge**; Pasadena, Calif.; president, California Institute of Technology; Sept. 21, 1901, in Terre Haute, Ind.; Rep.; Feb. 7.

OFFICE OF SPECIAL REPRESENTATIVE FOR TRADE NEGOTIATIONS

U.S. Special Representative for Trade Negotiations, $40,000—**Carl J. Gilbert**; Dover, Mass.; chairman of Executive Committee, Gillette Co.; April 3, 1906, in Bloomfield, N.J.; Rep.; July 29.

CENTRAL INTELLIGENCE AGENCY

Deputy Director, **Lt. Gen. Robert E. Cushman Jr.**, USMC; St. Paul, Minn.; Commander of 3rd Marine Amphibious Force; 1909 in St. Paul; April 22.

Departments

STATE DEPARTMENT

Secretary, $60,000—**William P. Rogers**; Bethesda, Md.; lawyer, June 23, 1913, in Norfolk, N.Y.; Rep.; Jan. 20.

Under Secretary, $42,500—**Elliot L. Richardson**; Brookline, Mass.; Attorney General of Massachusetts; July 20, 1920, in Boston, Mass.; Rep.; Jan. 23.

Under Secretary for Political Affairs, $42,500—**U. Alexis Johnson**; Washington, D.C.; Ambassador to Japan; Oct. 17, 1908, in Falun, Kan.; Feb. 7.

Deputy Under Secretary for Economic Affairs, $40,000—**Nathaniel Samuels**; New York, N.Y.; investment banker; Oct. 20, 1908, in Chicago, Ill.; Rep.; March 27.

Deputy Under Secretary for Administration, $38,000—**William B. Macomber Jr.**; Washington, D.C.; Assistant Secretary of State for Congressional Relations; March 28, 1921, in Rochester, N.Y.; Rep.; Sept. 24.

Assistant Secretary (Public Affairs) $38,000—**Michael Collins**; Houston, Texas; Col., USAF, NASA Astronaut; Oct. 31, 1930, in Rome, Italy; Dec. 12.

Assistant Secretary (International Organization Affairs), $38,000—**Samuel DePalma**; Bethesda, Md.; Foreign Service officer; June 22, 1918, in Rochester, N.Y.; Feb. 7.

Assistant Secretary (European Affairs), $38,000—**Martin J. Hillenbrand**; Washington, D.C.; Ambassador to Hungary; Aug. 1, 1915, in Youngstown, Ohio; Feb. 7.

Counselor, $38,000—**Richard F. Pederson**; New York, N.Y.; Deputy U.S. Representative to UN Security Council; Feb. 21, 1925, in Miami, Ariz.; Rep.; Jan. 23.

Assistant Secretary (Near Eastern and South Asian Affairs), $38,000—**Joseph J. Sisco**; Washington, D.C.; Assistant Secretary for International Organization Affairs; Oct. 31, 1919, in Chicago, Ill.; Feb. 7.

Assistant Secretary (East Asian and Pacific Affairs), $38,000—**Marshall Green**; Washington, D.C.; Ambassador to Indonesia; Jan. 27, 1916, in Holyoke, Mass.; May 1.

Assistant Secretary (Inter-American Affairs), $38,000—**Charles A. Meyer**; Gladwyne Park, Pa.; Sears, Roebuck executive; June 27, 1918, in Boston, Mass.; Rep.; March 27.

Assistant Secretary (African Affairs), $38,000—**David D. Newsom**; Washington, D.C.; Ambassador to Libya; Jan. 6, 1918, in Richmond, Calif.; July 8.

Assistant Secretary (Educational and Cultural Affairs), $38,000—**John Richardson Jr.**; Bronxville, N.Y.; lawyer, investment banker; Feb. 4, 1921, in Boston, Mass.; Rep.; July 8.

Assistant Secretary (Economic Affairs), $38,000—**Philip H. Trezise**; Washington, D.C.; U.S. Representative to Organization for Economic Cooperation and Development; May 27, 1912, in Calumet, Mich.; July 8.

Legal Adviser, $38,000—**John R. Stevenson**; New York, N.Y.; lawyer; Oct. 24, 1921, in Chicago, Ill.; Rep.; July 8.

Ambassadors

(Salaries for ambassadors depend upon seniority and station and range between $36,000 and $42,500 per year. Only those appointments which are of more than routine interest are listed.)

Argentina, **John D. Lodge**; Westport, Conn.; chairman of Foreign Policy Research Institute, University of Pennsylvania; Oct. 20, 1903, in Washington, D.C.; Rep.; May 23.

Australia, **Walter L. Rice**; Richmond, Va.; lawyer; born in Peever, S.D.; Rep.; Aug. 13.

Austria, **John P. Humes**; New York, N.Y.; lawyer; July 21, 1921, in New York; Rep.; Sept. 24.

Belgium, **John S. Eisenhower**; Gettysburg, Pa.; senior editor, Doubleday & Co.; Aug. 23, 1922, in Denver, Colo.; Rep.; March 13.

Bolivia, **Ernest V. Siracusa**; Huntington Beach, Calif.; Foreign Service Officer; Nov. 30, 1918, in Coalinga, Calif.; Nov. 6.

Brazil, **C. Burke Elbrick**; Gilbertsville, N.Y.; Ambassador to Yugoslavia; March 25, 1908, in Louisville, Ky.; May 1.

Canada, **Adolph W. Schmidt**; Ligonier, Pa.; vice president, T. Mellon and Sons; Sept. 13, 1904, in McKeesport, Pa.; Rep.; July 8.

Colombia, **Jack Hood Vaughan**; Alexandria, Va.; Director of Peace Corps; Aug. 18, 1920, in Columbus, Mont.; Rep.; May 23.

Czechoslovakia, **Malcolm Toon**; Sayer, Pa.; Foreign Service Officer, July 4, 1916, in Troy, N.Y.; May 12.

Denmark, **Guilford Dudley Jr.**; Nashville, Tenn.; insurance executive; June 23, 1907, in Nashville; Rep.; May 12.

Finland, **Val Peterson**; Hastings, Nev.; chairman, Investors Growth Industries Inc.; July 18, 1903, in Oakland, Neb.; Rep.; May 1.

Germany, **Kenneth Rush**; Rye, N.Y.; president of Union Carbide Corp.; Jan. 17, 1910, in Walla Walla, Wash.; Rep.; July 8.

Great Britain, **Walter H. Annenberg**; Philadelphia, Pa.; publisher; March 13, 1908, in Milwaukee, Wis.; Rep.; March 13.

Greece, **Henry J. Tasca**; Washington, D.C.; Ambassador to Morocco; Aug. 23, 1912, in Providence, R.I.; Dec. 19.

Haiti, **Clinton E. Knox**; Rochester, N.Y.; Ambassador to Dahomey; May 6, 1908, in New Bedford, Mass.; Oct. 8.

Honduras, **Hewson A. Ryan**; Bethesda, Md.; Associate Director, USIA; June 16, 1922 in New Haven, Conn.; Oct. 8.

Hungary, **Alfred Puhan**; Washington, D.C.; director, Office of German Affairs, U.S. State Department; March 17, 1913, in Marienburg, Germany; May 1.

Iceland, **Luther I. Replogle**; Oak Park, Ill.; vice president, Meredith Corp.; March 2, 1902, in Tyrone, Pa.; Rep.; July 8.

India, **Kenneth B. Keating**; New York, N.Y.; Associate Justice, New York State Court of Appeals; May 18, 1900, in Lima, N.Y.; Rep.; May 1.

Indonesia, **Francis J. Galbraith**; Washington, D.C.; Ambassador to Singapore; Dec. 9, 1913, in Timberlake, S.D.; Rep.; May 23.

Iran, **Douglas MacArthur II**; Washington, D.C.; Ambassador to Austria; July 5, 1909, in Bryn Mawr, Pa.; Sept. 12.

Ireland, **John D. J. Moore**; Short Hills, N.J.; vice president, W. R. Grace Co.; Nov. 10, 1910, in New York, N.Y.; Rep.; April 18.

Italy, **Graham Martin**; Washington, D.C.; Foreign Service Officer; Sept. 22, 1912, in Mars Hill, N.C.; Sept. 24.

Jamaica, **Vincent de Roulet**; North Hills, N.Y.; Mayor of North Hills; Sept. 16, 1925, in Los Angeles, Calif.; Rep.; Sept. 17.

Japan, **Armin H. Meyer**; Fort Wayne, Ind.; Ambassador to Iran; Jan. 19, 1914, in Fort Wayne; May 23.

Kuwait, **John P. Walsh**; Washington, D.C.; Acting Executive Secretary, U.S. State Department; Dec. 21, 1918, in Chicago, Ill.; Sept. 17.

Laos, **G. McMurtrie Godley**; Morris, N.Y.; Foreign Service Officer; Aug. 23, 1917, in New York, N.Y.; June 12.

Liberia, **Samuel Z. Westerfield Jr.**; Washington, D.C.; Deputy Assistant Secretary of State for African Affairs; Nov. 15, 1919, in Chicago, Ill.; July 8.

Libya, **Joseph Palmer II**; Washington, D.C.; Assistant Secretary of State for African Affairs; June 16, 1914, in Detroit, Mich.; Dem.; July 8.

Luxembourg, **Kingdon Gould Jr.**; Washington, D.C.; owner of Parking Management Inc.; Jan. 6, 1924, in New York, N.Y.; Rep.; May 23.

Malta, **John C. Pritzlaff Jr.**; Phoenix, Ariz.; member, Arizona House of Representatives; May 10, 1925, in Milwaukee, Wis.; Rep.; July 8.

Mexico, **Robert H. McBride**; Washington, D.C.; Ambassador to the Congo (Kinshsa); May 25, 1918, in London, England; June 12.

Netherlands, **J. William Middendorf II**; Greenwich, Conn.; investment banker; Sept. 22, 1924, in Baltimore, Md.; Rep.; June 12.

New Zealand, **Kenneth Franzheim**; Houston, Texas; oil dealer; Sept. 12, 1925, in New York, N.Y.; Rep.; Aug. 12.

Norway, **Philip K. Crowe**; Easton, Md.; conservationist; Jan. 7, 1908, in New York, N.Y.; Rep.; May 1.

Pakistan, **Joseph S. Farland**; Morgantown, W.Va.; Career Ambassador; Aug. 11, 1914, in Clarksburg, W.Va.; Sept. 17.

Panama, **Robert M. Sayre**; Falls Church, Va.; Ambassador to Uruguay; Aug. 18, 1924, in Hillsboro, Ore.; Sept. 12.

Peru, **Taylor G. Belcher**; New York, N.Y.; Ambassador to Cyprus; July 1, 1920, in New York; Aug. 13.

Philippines, **Henry A. Byroade**; Washington, D.C.; Foreign Affairs Adviser, Industrial College of the Armed Forces; July 24, 1913, in Allen Co., Ind.; July 22.

Portugal, **Ridgway B. Knight**; New York, N.Y.; Ambassador to Belgium; June 12, 1911, in Paris, France; July 8.

Romania, **Leonard C. Meeker**; Washington, D.C.; State Department Legal Adviser; April 4, 1916, in Montclair, N.J.; July 22.

Spain, **Robert C. Hill**; Littleton, N.H.; chairman of the board, Hillwood Corp.; Sept. 30, 1917, in Littleton; Rep.; May 1.

Switzerland, **Shelby C. Davis**; New York, N.Y.; investment banker; April 1, 1909, in Peoria, Ill.; Rep.; May 12.

Trinidad and Tobago,, **John F. Symington**; Lutherville, Md.; no occupation at time of appointment (retired in 1960 as President of Baltimore County Supply Co.); Aug. 27, 1910 in Baltimore, Md.; Rep; July 8.

Tunisia, **John A. Calhoun**; Washington, D.C.; acting Deputy Assistant Secretary of State for East Asian and Pacific Affairs; Oct. 29, 1918, in Berkeley, Calif.; July 8.

Turkey, **William J. Handley**; Washington, D.C.; Deputy Assistant Secretary of State for Near East and South Asian Affairs; Dec. 17, 1918, in Netherlands Guiana; May 1.

U.S.S.R., **Jacob D. Beam**; Princeton, N.J.; Ambassador to Czechoslovakia; March 24, 1908, in Princeton; March 13.

Yugoslavia, **William Leonhart**; Washington, D.C.; Foreign Service Officer; Aug. 1, 1919, in Parkersburg, W.Va.; May 1.

Ambassador to the United Nations, **Charles W. Yost**; New York, N.Y.; Foreign Service officer, senior fellow, Council of Foreign Relations; Nov. 6, 1907, in Watertown, N.Y.; Jan. 21.

North Atlantic Treaty Organization, **Robert F. Ellsworth**; Washington, D.C.; Special Assistant to the President; June 11, 1926, in Lawrence, Kan.; Rep.; May 12.

Organization of American States, **Joseph J. Jova**; Fort Lauderdale, Fla.; Ambassador to Honduras; Nov. 11, 1916, in Newburgh, N.Y.; July 8.

Peace Corps

Director, $40,000—**Joseph H. Blatchford**; San Pedro, Calif.; executive director, ACCION International; 1935 in Milwaukee, Wis.; Rep.; May 1.

Deputy Director, $38,000—**Thomas J. Houser**; Arlington Heights, Ill.; lawyer; June 28, 1929, in Chicago, Ill.; Rep.; June 12.

Agency for International Development

Administrator, $40,000—**John A. Hannah**; East Lansing, Mich.; president, Michigan State University; Oct. 9, 1902, in Grand Rapids, Mich.; Rep.; March 27.

TREASURY DEPARTMENT

Secretary, $60,000—**David M. Kennedy**; Northfield, Ill.; chairman, Continental Illinois National Bank and Trust Co.; July 21, 1905, in Randolph, Utah; Rep.; Jan. 20.

Under Secretary, $40,000—**Charls E. Walker**; Riverside, Conn.; executive vice president, American Bankers Assn.; Dec. 24, 1923, in Graham, Texas; Rep.; Jan. 23.

Under Secretary for Monetary Affairs, $40,000—**Paul A. Volcker**; Montclair, N.J.; vice president, Chase Manhattan Bank; Sept. 5, 1927, in Cape May, N.J.; Rep.; Jan. 23.

Assistant Secretary (Tax Policy), $38,000—**Edwin S. Cohen**; Charlottesville, Va.; law professor, University of Virginia; Sept. 27, 1914, in Richmond, Va.; March 4.

Assistant Secretary (International Affairs), $38,000—**John R. Petty**; Washington, D.C.; reappointment; April 16, 1930, in Chicago, Ill.; June 19.

Assistant Secretary (Customs, Engraving and Printing, Mint, Law Enforcement), $38,000—**Eugene T. Rossides**; New York, N.Y.; lawyer, Oct. 23, 1927 in New York; Rep.; March 27.

Assistant Secretary (Economic Policy), $38,000—**Murray Weidenbaum**; St. Louis, Mo.; chairman of Economics Dept.; Washington University; June 2.

General Counsel, $38,000—**Paul W. Eggers**; Wichita Falls, Texas; lawyer; April 20, 1919, in Seymour, Ind.; Rep.; March 27.

Commissioner of Internal Revenue, $40,000—**Randolph W. Thrower**; Atlanta, Ga.; lawyer; Sept. 5, 1913, in Tampa, Fla.; Rep.; March 27.

Treasurer of the United States, $33,500—**Dorothy Elston**; McDonough, Del.; farm owner; March 22, 1917, in Wilkes-Barre, Pa.; Rep.; April 25.

Director of the Mint, $33,500—**Mary T. Brooks**; Washington, D.C.; Member, Idaho State Senate; Nov. 1, 1907, in Colby, Kan.; Rep.; Aug. 8.

DEFENSE DEPARTMENT

Secretary, $60,000—**Melvin R. Laird**; Marshfield, Wis.; Member, U.S. House of Representatives; Sept. 1, 1922, in Omaha, Neb.; Rep.; Jan. 20.

Deputy Secretary, $42,500—**David Packard**; Palo Alto, Calif.; chief executive officer, Hewlett-Packard Corp.; Sept. 7, 1912, in Pueblo, Colo.; Rep.; Jan. 23.

Director of Defense Research and Engineering, $40,000—**John S. Foster Jr.**; Falls Church, Va.; reappointment; Sept. 18, 1922, in New Haven, Conn.; Feb. 28.

Assistant Secretary (Administration), $38,000—**Robert F. Froehlke**; Winchester, Mass.; vice president, Sentry Insurance Co.; Oct. 15, 1922, in Neenah, Wis.; Rep.; Jan. 29.

Assistant Secretary (Public Affairs), $38,000—**Daniel Z. Henkin**; Chevy Chase, Md.; Deputy Assistant Secretary of Defense for Public Affairs; May 10, 1923, in Washington, D.C.; May 20.

Assistant Secretary (Manpower and Reserve Affairs), $38,000—**Roger T. Kelley**; Peoria, Ill.; vice president, Caterpillar Tractor Co.; Jan. 14, 1919, in Milwaukee, Wis.; Rep.; Feb. 28.

Assistant Secretary (Comptroller), $38,000—**Robert C. Moot**; Annandale, Va.; reappointment; June 1, 1911, in Orange, N.J.; Dem.; Feb. 28.

Assistant Secretary (International Security Affairs), $38,000—**G. Warren Nutter**; Charlottesville, Va.; chairman of Economics Dept., University of Virginia; March 10, 1923, in Topeka, Kan.; Rep.; March 4.

Assistant Secretary (Installations and Logistics), $38,000—**Barry J. Shillito**; Washington, D.C.; Assistant Secretary of the Navy; Jan. 21, 1921, in Dayton, Ohio; Jan. 29.

Secretary of the Army, $42,500—**Stanley R. Resor**; Washington, D.C.; reappointment; Dec. 5, 1917, in New York, N.Y.; Dem.; March 4.

Under Secretary of the Army, $38,000—**Thaddeus R. Beal**; Chestnut Hill, Mass.; president, Harvard Trust Co.; March 22, 1917, in New York, N.Y.; Rep.; March 4.

Assistant Secretary of the Army (Financial Management), $38,000—**Eugene M. Becker**; Washington, D.C.; reappointment; Sept. 1, 1930, in St. Paul, Minn.; Dem.; March 4.

Assistant Secretary of the Army (Manpower and Reserve Affairs), $38,000—**William K. Brehm**; Fairfax, Va.; reappointment; March 29, 1929, in Dearborn, Mich.; March 4.

Assistant Secretary of the Army (Installations and Logistics), $38,000—**J. Ronald Fox**; Boxford, Mass.; professor, Harvard Business School; Dec. 11, 1929, in Binghamton, N.Y.; June 20.

Assistant Secretary of the Army (Research and Development), $38,000—**Robert L. Johnson**; Newport Beach, Calif.; vice president, McDonnell-Douglas Aircraft Corp.; May 16, 1920, in Winslow, Ariz.; Nov. 3.

Secretary of the Navy, $42,500—**John H. Chafee**; Warwick, R.I.; Governor of Rhode Island, 1963-69; Oct. 22, 1922, in Providence, R.I.; Rep.; Jan. 29.

Under Secretary of the Navy, $38,000—**John W. Warner**; Washington, D.C.; lawyer; Feb. 8, 1927, in Washington, D.C.; Feb. 7.

Assistant Secretary of the Navy (Financial Management), $38,000—**Charles A. Bowsher**; Washington, D.C.; reappointment; May 30, 1931, in Elkhart, Ind.; Feb. 28.

Assistant Secretary of the Navy (Research and Development), $38,000—**Robert A. Frosch**; Bethesda, Md.; reappointment; May 22, 1928, in New York, N.Y.; Dem.; Feb. 28.

Assistant Secretary of the Navy (Manpower and Reserve Affairs), $38,000—**James D. Hittle**; Arlington, Va.; news commentator; June 10, 1915, in Bear Lake, Mich.; Rep.; Feb. 28.

Assistant Secretary of the Navy (Installations and Logistics), $38,000—**Frank Sanders**; Bethesda, Md.; staff member, U.S. House Appropriations Committee; July 30, 1919, in Tarboro, N.C.; Rep.; Feb. 7.

Secretary of the Air Force, $42,500—**Robert C. Seamans Jr.**; Washington, D.C.; Deputy Administrator, NASA, 1965-68; Oct. 30, 1918, in Salem, Mass.; Rep.; Jan. 29.

Under Secretary of the Air Force, $38,000—**John L. McLucas**; Concord, Mass.; president, Mitre Corp.; Aug. 22, 1920, in Fayetteville, N.C.; March 4.

Assistant Secretary of the Air Force (Research and Development), $38,000—**Grant L. Hansen**; El Cajon, Calif.; vice president, General Dynamics Corp.; Nov. 5, 1921, in Bancroft, Idaho; March 4.

Assistant Secretary of the Air Force (Financial Management), $38,000—**Spencer J. Schedler**; Tulsa, Okla.; budget analysis manager, Sinclair Oil Corp.; Oct. 23, 1933, in Manila, Philippine Islands; June 20.

Assistant Secretary of the Air Force (Manpower and Reserve Affairs), $38,000—**Curtis W. Tarr**; Appleton, Wis.; president, Lawrence University; Sept. 18, 1924, in Stockton, Calif.; Rep.; April 22.

Assistant Secretary of the Air Force (Installations and Logistics), $38,000—**Philip N. Whittaker**; Potomac, Md.; assistant administrator for industrial affairs, NASA; Nov. 7, 1918, in Chestnut Hill, Pa.; Rep.; May 5.

Chairman, Joint Chiefs of Staff, for an additional term of one year—**Gen. Earle G. Wheeler**; Ft. Myer, Va.; Jan. 13, 1908, in Washington, D.C.; June 30.

Chief of Staff, U.S. Air Force—**Gen. John D. Ryan**; San Francisco, Calif.; commander-in-chief, PACAF; Dec. 10, 1915, in Cherokee, Iowa; July 25.

JUSTICE DEPARTMENT

Attorney General, $60,000—**John N. Mitchell**; New York, N.Y.; senior partner in law firm of Nixon, Mudge, Rose, Guthrie, Alexander and Mitchell; Sept. 5, 1913, in Detroit, Mich.; Rep.; Jan. 20.

Deputy Attorney General, $40,000—**Richard G. Kleindienst**; Bethesda, Md.; lawyer, Aug. 5, 1923, in Winslow, Ariz.; Rep.; Jan. 31.

Assistant Attorney General (Lands and Natural Resources), $38,000—**Shiro Kashiwa**; Honolulu, Hawaii; lawyer; 1912 in Kahala, Hawaii; May 5.

Assistant Attorney General (Civil Rights), $38,000—**Jerris Leonard**; Milwaukee, Wis.; lawyer, Jan. 17, 1931, in Chicago, Ill.; Rep.; Jan. 31.

Assistant Attorney General (Antitrust), $38,000—**Richard W. McLaren**; Winnetka, Ill.; head of antitrust division, American Bar Assn.; April 21, 1918, in Chicago, Ill.; Rep.; Jan. 31.

Administrator, Law Enforcement Assistance Administration, $38,000—**Charles H. Rogovin**; Newtonville, Mass.; Assistant Attorney General of Massachusetts; Jan. 24, 1931, in Jersey City, N.J.; Dem.; March 26.

Assistant Attorney General (Legal Counsel), $38,000—**William H. Rehnquist**; Phoenix, Ariz.; lawyer; Oct. 1, 1924, in Milwaukee, Wis.; Rep.; Jan. 31.

Assistant Attorney General (Civil), $38,000—**William D. Ruckelshaus**; Indianapolis, Ind.; lawyer; July 24, 1932, in Indianapolis; Rep.; Jan. 31.

Assistant Attorney General (Tax), $38,000—**Johnnie M. Walters**; Greenville, S.C.; tax specialist; Dec. 20, 1919, in Hartsville, S.C.; Rep.; Jan. 31.

Assistant Attorney General (Criminal), $38,000—**Will R. Wilson**; Austin, Texas; lawyer; July 29, 1912, in Dallas, Texas; Rep.; Jan. 31.

Administrator, Law Enforcement Assistance Administration, $38,000—**Charles H. Rogovin**; Newtonville, Mass.; Assistant Attorney General of Massachusetts; Jan. 24, 1931, in Jersey City, N.J.; Dem.; March 26.

Director, Community Relations Service, $38,000—**Benjamin F. Holman**; Washington, D.C.; news producer, NBC; Dec. 18, 1930, in Columbia, S.C.; April 3.

POST OFFICE DEPARTMENT

Postmaster General, $60,000—**Winton M. Blount**; Montgomery, Ala.; president, U.S. Chamber of Commerce; Feb. 1, 1921, in Union Springs, Ala.; Rep.; Jan. 20.

Deputy Postmaster General, $42,500—**Elmer T. Klassen**; New York, N.Y.; president, American Can Co.; Nov. 6, 1908, in Hillsboro, Kan.; Rep.; Feb. 7.

Assistant Postmaster General (Research and Engineering) $38,000—**Harold F. Faught**; Pittsburgh, Pa.; general manager, Westinghouse Astronuclear Laboratory; 1925 in Washington, D.C.; June 18.

Assistant Postmaster General (Finance and Administration), $38,000—**James W. Hargrove**; Houston, Texas; senior vice president, Texas Eastern Transmission Corp.; Oct. 31, 1922, in Shreveport, La.; Rep.; Feb. 7.

Assistant Postmaster General (Personnel), $38,000—**Kenneth A. Housman**; New Canaan, Conn.; manager of public affairs, Union Carbide Corp.; Nov. 16, 1925, in New York, N.Y.; Feb. 7.

Assistant Postmaster General (Planning, Marketing, and Systems Analysis), $38,000—**Ronald B. Lee**; East Lansing, Mich.; director of Center for Urban Affairs, Michigan State University; May 26, 1932, in New York, N.Y.; Dem.; April 29.

Assistant Postmaster General (Facilities), $38,000—**Henry Lehne**; Weston, Mass.; senior vice president, Sylvania Electronic Products Inc.; July 16, 1914, in Pittsburgh, Pa.; Rep.; April 29.

Assistant Postmaster General (Operations), $38,000—**Frank J. Nunlist**; Harrison, N.J.; chief executive officer, Worthington Corp.; Sept. 8, 1913, in Columbus, Ohio; Rep.; April 29.

General Counsel, $38,000—**David A. Nelson**; Lakewood, Ohio; lawyer; Aug. 14, 1932, in Watertown, N.Y.; Feb. 7.

INTERIOR DEPARTMENT

Secretary, $60,000—**Walter J. Hickel**; Anchorage, Alaska; Governor of Alaska; Aug. 18, 1919, in Claflin, Kan.; Rep.; Jan. 23.

Under Secretary, $40,000—**Russell E. Train**; Washington, D.C.; president, The Conservation Foundation; June 4, 1920, in Jamestown, R.I.; Rep.; Feb. 7.

Assistant Secretary (Mineral Resources), $38,000—**Hollis M. Dole**; Portland, Ore.; director, Oregon Dept. of Geology and Mineral Resources; Sept. 4, 1914, in Paonia, Colo.; Rep.; March 20.

Assistant Secretary (Fish and Wildlife), $38,000—**Leslie L. Glasgow**; Baton Rouge, La.; director, Louisiana Wildlife and Fisheries Comm.; 1914, in Portland, Ind.; Rep.; March 20.

Assistant Secretary (Water Quality and Research), $38,000—**Carl L. Klein**; Chicago, Ill.; member, Illinois State Legislature; May 18, 1917, in Butternut, Wis.; Rep.; March 20.

Assistant Secretary (Public Land Management), $38,000—**Harrison Loesch**;. Montrose, Colo.; lawyer; March 10, 1913, in Chicago, Ill.; Rep.; April 1.

Assistant Secretary (Water and Power Development), $38,000—**James R. Smith**; Omaha, Neb.; manager for marketing relations, Northern Natural Gas Co.; 1917, in Sioux Falls, S.D.; Rep.; March 20.

Solicitor, $38,000—**Mitchell Melich**; Salt Lake City, Utah; assistant to Rep. Sherman P. Lloyd (R Utah); Feb. 1, 1912, in Bingham Canyon, Utah; Rep.; March 20.

Commissioner of Fish and Wildlife, $36,000—**Charles H. Meacham**; Juneau, Alaska; Alaska Director of International Fisheries; 1925 in California; Rep.; June 26.

Commissioner of Indian Affairs, $36,000—**Louis R. Bruce**; New York, N.Y.; advertising executive; Dec. 30, 1906, on Onandaga River Indian Reservation, New York; Rep.; Aug. 12.

Director, Geological Survey, $38,000—**William T. Pecora**; Washington, D.C.; reappointment; Feb. 1, 1913, in Belleville, N.J.; May 23.

Governor of the Virgin Islands, $30,000—**Melvin Evans**; St. Thomas, V.I.; Commissioner of Health, Virgin Islands; Aug. 7, 1917, in Christiansted, St. Croix, V.I.; Rep.; June 19.

AGRICULTURE DEPARTMENT

Secretary, $60,000—**Clifford M. Hardin**; Lincoln, Neb.; chancellor, Univ. of Nebraska; Oct. 9, 1915, in Knightstown, Ind.; Rep.; Jan. 20.

Under Secretary, $40,000—**J. Phil Campbell Jr.**; Watkinsville, Ga.; Georgia commissioner of agriculture; April 9, 1917, in Athens, Ga.; Rep.; Jan. 22.

Assistant Secretary (Rural Development and Conservation), $38,000—**Thomas K. Cowden**; East Lansing, Mich.; dean of College of Agriculture and Natural Resources, Michigan State University; June 14, 1908, in Hickory, Pa.; May 8.

Assistant Secretary (Consumer and Marketing Services), $38,000—**Richard E. Lyng**; Sacramento, Calif.; California Director of Agriculture; 1918, in San Francisco, Calif.; Rep.; Feb. 28.

Assistant Secretary (International Affairs & Commodity Programs), $38,000—**Clarence D. Palmby**; Arlington, Va.; executive vice president, U.S. Feed Grains Council; Feb. 22, 1916, in Eagle Bend, Minn.; Rep.; Jan. 22.

Administrator, Farmers Home Administration, $36,000—**James V. Smith**; Chickasha, Okla.; Member, U.S. House of Representatives, 1967-69; July 23, 1926, in Oklahoma City, Okla.; Rep.; March 17.

Administrator, Rural Electrification Administration, $36,000—**David A. Hamil**; Sterling, Colo.; rancher; Dec. 3, 1908, in Proctor, Colo.; Rep.; Feb. 28.

COMMERCE DEPARTMENT

Secretary, $60,000—**Maurice H. Stans**; New York, N.Y.; investment banker; March 22, 1908, in Shakopee, Minn.; Rep.; Jan. 20.

Under Secretary, $40,000—**Rocco C. Siciliano**; San Francisco, Calif.; president, Pacific Maritime Assn.; March 4, 1922, in Salt Lake City, Utah; Rep.; Jan. 31.

Assistant Secretary (Domestic and International Business), $38,000—**Kenneth N. Davis**; Pound Ridge, N.Y.; vice president, IBM; March 26, 1926, in Greenfield, Mass.; Rep.; March 13.

Assistant Secretary (Administration), $38,000—**Larry A. Jobe**; Chicago, Ill.; CPA; Jan. 12, 1940, in Knox City, Texas; Rep.; March 20.

Assistant Secretary (Economic Affairs), $38,000—**Harold C. Passer**; Rochester, N.Y.; economist, Eastman Kodak Co.; Rep.; Oct. 23.

Assistant Secretary (Economic Development), $38,000—**Robert A. Podesta**; Chicago, Ill.; senior vice president, Chicago Corporation; Oct. 7, 1913, in Chicago; Rep.; March 7.

Assistant Secretary (Science and Technology), $38,000—**Myron Tribus**; Hanover, N.H.; dean of Dartmouth College Engineering School; Oct. 30, 1921, in San Francisco, Calif.; Rep.; March 20.

General Counsel, $38,000—**James T. Lynn**; Cleveland, Ohio; corporation lawyer; Feb. 27, 1927, in Cleveland; Rep.; March 13.

Director of the Census, $36,000—**George Hay Brown**; Ann Arbor, Mich.; market research director; Feb. 4, 1910, in Denver, Colo.; Rep.; Aug. 8.

Maritime Administrator, $36,000—**Andrew E. Gibson**; New York, N.Y.; vice president, the Diebold Group; 1922 in Boston, Mass.; March 13.

Commissioner of Patents, $36,000—**William E. Schuyler Jr.**; Washington, D.C.; lawyer; Feb. 3, 1914, in Washington; Rep.; May 5.

Director, Bureau of Standards, $36,000—**Lewis M. Branscomb**; Boulder, Colo.; chief, Laboratory Astrophysics Division, National Bureau of Standards; born in Asheville, N.C.; Aug. 12.

Director, U.S. Travel Service, $36,000—**C. Langhorne Washburn**; Washington, D.C.; public relations specialist; July 14, 1918, in Washington; Rep.; March 13.

Federal Cochairman, Appalachian Regional Commission, $38,000—**John B. Waters Jr.**; Sevierville, Tenn.; lawyer; July 15, 1929, in Sevierville; Rep.; March 26.

Federal Cochairman, Coastal Plains Regional Commission, $38,000—**G. Fred Steele Jr.**; Durham, N.C.; president, Triangle Underwriters Inc.; Oct. 27, 1929, in Columbus, Ga.; April 3.

Federal Cochairman, Four Corners Regional Commission, $38,000—**L. Ralph Mecham**; Washington, D.C.; Special Assistant to the Secretary of Commerce for Regional Economic Coordination; April 23, 1928, in Murray, Colo.; Rep.; Oct. 1.

Federal Cochairman, New England Regional Commission, $38,000—**Stewart Lamprey**; Moultonborough, N.H.; president of New Hampshire State Senate; April 9, 1921, in Dorchester, Mass.; Rep.; April 29.

Federal Cochairman, Ozarks Regional Commission, $38,000—**E. L. Stewart**; Shawnee, Okla.; owner and operator, Sigma Oil and Gas Co.; June 7, 1928, in Ft. Benning, Ga.; Rep.; April 18.

Federal Cochairman, Upper Great Lakes Regional Commission, $38,000—**Alfred E. France**; Duluth, Minn.; member of Minnesota State Legislature; June 5, 1927, in Harrisburg, Pa.; Rep.; May 20.

LABOR DEPARTMENT

Secretary, $60,000—**George P. Shultz**; Stanford, Calif.; dean of Graduate School of Business, Univ. of Chicago; 1920, in New York, N.Y.; Rep.; Jan. 20.

Under Secretary, $40,000—**James D. Hodgson**; Northridge, Calif.; vice president, Lockheed Aircraft Corp.; Dec. 3, 1915, in Dawson, Minn.; Rep.; Feb. 7.

Assistant Secretary (Wage and Labor Standards), $38,000—**Arthur Fletcher**; Pasco, Wash.; aide to Gov. Daniel J. Evans (R Wash.); Dec. 22, 1924, in Phoenix, Ariz., Rep.; May 1.

Assistant Secretary (Policy Development and Research), $38,000—**Jerome M. Rosow**; New York, N.Y.; manager of employee relations, Esso Europe, Inc.; Dec. 2, 1919, in Chicago, Ill.; Rep.; March 26.

Assistant Secretary (Labor-Management Services), $38,000—**William J. Usery Jr.**; Macon, Ga.; chairman, Cape Kennedy Labor-Management Relations Council; Dec. 21, 1923, in Hardwick, Ga.; Rep.; Feb. 7.

Assistant Secretary (Manpower), $38,000—**Arnold R. Weber**; Chicago, Ill.; director of research, Univ. of Chicago Graduate School of Business; Sept. 20, 1929, in New York, N.Y.; Rep.; Feb. 7.

Solicitor, $38,000—**Lawrence H. Silberman**; Washington, D.C.; lawyer, General Counsel's Office, NLRB; Oct. 12, 1935, in York, Pa.; May 1.

Commissioner of Labor Statistics, $36,000—**Geoffrey H. Moore**; North Plainfield, N.J.; vice president, National Bureau of Economic Research; Feb. 28, 1914, in Pequannock, N.J.; March 7.

Director, Women's Bureau, $36,000—**Elizabeth Duncan Koontz**; Salisbury, N.C.; president, National Education Assn.; June 3, 1919, in Salisbury; Dem.; Feb. 7.

Administrator, Wage and Hour Division, $36,000—**Robert D. Moran**; Springfield, Mass.; Massachusetts state labor official; Oct. 25, 1929, in Brewer, Maine; Rep.; May 1.

DEPARTMENT OF HEALTH, EDUCATION AND WELFARE

Secretary, $60,000—**Robert H. Finch**; Pasadena, Calif.; lieutenant governor of California; Oct. 9, 1925, in Tempe, Ariz.; Rep.; Jan. 20.

Under Secretary, $40,000—**John G. Veneman**; Modesto, Calif.; member, California State Legislature; Oct. 31, 1925, in Modesto; Rep.; March 4.

Assistant Secretary (Education) and Commissioner of Education, $38,000—**James E. Allen Jr.**; Londonville, N.Y.; New York State education commissioner; April 25, 1911, in Elkins, W.Va.; May 5.

Assistant Secretary (Legislation), $38,000—**Creed C. Black**; Kenilworth, Ill.; executive editor, Chicago *Daily News*; July 15, 1925, in Harlan, Ky.; Rep.; March 4.

Assistant Secretary (Planning and Evaluation), $38,000—**Lewis Butler**; San Francisco, Calif.; lawyer, urban affairs expert; April 30, 1927, in San Francisco; April 25.

Assistant Secretary (Health and Scientific Affairs), $38,000—**Dr. Roger O. Egeberg**; Los Angeles, Calif.; dean, University of Southern California Medical School; Nov. 13, 1903, in Chicago, Ill.; Rep.; July 11.

Assistant Secretary (Administration), $38,000—**James Farmer**; New York, N.Y.; former National Director, Congress of Racial Equality; Jan. 20, 1920, in Marshall, Texas; Rep.; April 2.

Assistant Secretary (Community and Field Services), $38,000—**Patricia R. Hitt**; Villa Park, Calif.; National Cochairman, Nixon-Agnew Campaign Committee; 1918 in Taft, Calif.; Rep.; March 4.

General Counsel, $38,000—**Robert C. Mardian**; Pasadena, Calif.; vice president and general counsel, Wesco Financial Corp.; Oct. 23, 1923, in Pasadena; Rep.; April 25.

Commissioner on Aging, $36,000—**John B. Martin Jr.**; Grand Rapids, Mich.; lawyer; Oct. 3, 1909 in Grand Rapids, Mich.; Rep.; May 23.

DEPARTMENT OF HOUSING AND URBAN DEVELOPMENT

Secretary, $60,000—**George Romney**; Bloomfield Hills, Mich.; Governor; of Michigan; July 8, 1907, in Chihuahua, Mexico; Rep.; Jan. 20.

Under Secretary, $40,000—**Richard C. Van Dusen**; Detroit, Mich.; legal assistant to Governor of Michigan; July 18, 1925, in Jackson, Mich.; Rep.; Feb. 7.

Secretary (Administration), $38,000—**Lester P. Condon**; Alexandria, Va.; Inspector General, USDA; Oct. 13, 1922, in Mt. Vernon, N.Y.; Rep.

Assistant Secretary (Renewal and Housing Assistance), $38,000—**Lawrence M. Cox**; Norfolk, Va.; executive director, Norfolk Redevelopment and Housing Authority; March 12, 1912, in Norfolk; Rep.; March 4.

Assistant Secretary (Urban Research and Technology), $38,000—**Harold B. Finger**; Bethesda, Md.; associate administrator, NASA; Feb. 18, 1924, in New York, N.Y.; April 25.

Assistant Secretary (Mortgage Credit and Federal Housing Commissioner), $38,000—**Eugene A. Gulledge**; Greensboro, N.C.; president, Superior Construction Co.; 1919 in New Orleans, La.; Sept. 26.

Assistant Secretary (Model Cities and Governmental Relations), $38,000—**Floyd H. Hyde**; Fresno, Calif.; mayor of Fresno; March 18, 1921, in Fresno; Rep.; Feb. 7.

Assistant Secretary (Metropolian Development), $38,000—**Samuel C. Jackson**; Washington, D.C.; vice president, American Arbitration Assn.; May 8, 1929, in Topeka, Kan.; Rep.; Feb. 7.

Assistant Secretary (Equal Opportunity), $38,000—**Samuel J. Simmons**; Washington, D.C.; director of field services division, U.S. Civil Rights Commission, April 13, 1927, in Flint, Mich.; Feb. 7.

General Counsel, $38,000—**Sherman Unger**; Cincinnati, Ohio; lawyer; Oct. 21, 1927, in Harrison, Ohio; Rep.; Feb. 7.

TRANSPORTATION DEPARTMENT

Secretary, $60,000—**John A. Volpe**; Winchester, Mass.; Governor of Massachusetts; Dec. 8, 1908, in Wakefield, Mass.; Rep.; Jan. 20.

Under Secretary, $42,500—**James M. Beggs**; Ellicott City, Texas; associate administrator, NASA; Jan. 9, 1926, in Dallas, Texas; March 13.

Assistant Secretary (Urban Systems and Environment), $38,000—**James D. Braman**; Seattle, Wash.; Mayor of Seattle; Dec. 23, 1901, in Lorimor, Iowa; Rep.; March 13.

Assistant Secretary (Policy and International Affairs), $38,000—**Paul W. Cherington**; Cambridge, Mass.; professor, Harvard University; June 16, 1918, in Cambridge; Rep.; March 13.

Assistant Secretary (Public Affairs), $38,000—**Walter L. Mazan**; Arlington, Va.; acting director of liaison, OEP; June 5, 1921, in Center Rutland, Vt.; Rep.; April 25.

General Counsel, $38,000—**James A. Washington Jr.**; Washington, D.C.; dean of Howard University Law School; 1914, in Asheville, N.C.; Dem.; July 2.

Federal Aviation Administrator, $42,500—**John H. Shaffer**; Washington, D.C.; vice president, TRW Inc.; May 5, 1916, in Bedford, Pa.; Rep.; March 20.

Federal Highway Administrator, $40,000—**Francis C. Turner**; Arlington, Va.; Director, Bureau of Public Roads; Dec. 28, 1908, in Dallas, Texas; March 12.

Director, Bureau of Public Roads, $38,000—**Ralph R. Bartelsmeyer**; Chicago, Ill.; vice president, H. W. Lochner Inc.; Oct. 23, 1909, in Hoyleton, Ill.; Rep.; April 29.

Federal Rail Administrator, $40,000—**Reginald N. Whitman**; Edina, Minn.; Great Northern Railway official; Oct. 5, 1909 in Jasmin, Saskatchewan, Canada; Rep.; March 20.

Urban Mass Transportation Administrator, $40,000—**Carlos C. Villarreal**; Los Angeles, Calif.; vice president, Marquardt Corp.; Nov. 9, 1924, in Brownsville, Texas; Rep.; March 17.

Member, National Transportation Safety Board, for the term expiring Dec. 31, 1974, $38,000—**Isabel A. Burgess**; Phoenix, Ariz.; Arizona State Senator; born in Cleveland, Ohio; Rep.; Oct. 3.

Independent Agencies

ATOMIC ENERGY COMMISSION

Member for the term expiring June 30, 1974, $40,000—**Clarence E. Larson**; Oak Ridge, Tenn.; president, Union Carbide Corp. Nuclear Division; Sept. 20, 1909, in Cloquet, Minn.; Rep.; Aug. 8.

Member for the remainder of the term expiring June 30, 1971, $40,000—**Theos J. Thompson**; Winchester, Mass.; Director of Nuclear Research, MIT, Aug. 30, 1918, in Lincoln, Neb.; Rep.; May 26.

CIVIL AERONAUTICS BOARD

Member for the term expiring Dec. 31, 1974, $40,000—**Secor D. Browne**; Washington, D.C.; Assistant Secretary of Transportation for Research and Technology; 1916 in Chicago, Ill.; Rep.; Oct. 3.

U.S. CIVIL SERVICE COMMISSION

Member for the remainder of the term expiring March 1, 1971, $38,000—**James E. Johnson**; Sacramento, Calif.; director, Calif. Dept. of Veterans Affairs; March 3, 1926, in Madison, Ill.; Rep.; Jan. 29.

Member for the term expiring March 1, 1975, $38,000—**Ludwig J. Andolsek**; Bethesda, Md.; reappointment; Nov. 6, 1910, in Denver, Colo.; Dem.; April 29.

DISTRICT OF COLUMBIA GOVERNMENT

Commissioner for a term expiring Feb. 1, 1973, $40,000—**Walter E. Washington**; Washington, D.C.; held same position previously; April 15, 1915, in Dawson, Ga.; Jan. 31.

EQUAL EMPLOYMENT OPPORTUNITY COMMISSION

Member (chairman) for the term expiring July 1, 1973, $38,000—**William H. Brown III**; Philadelphia, Pa.; lawyer; Jan. 19, 1928, in Philadelphia; Rep.; May 5.

Member for the term expiring July 1, 1974, $36,000—**Luther Holcomb**; Washington, D.C.; reappointment; Dec. 19, 1911, in Yazoo City, Miss.; Dem.; July 2.

EXPORT-IMPORT BANK

President, $40,000—**Henry Kearns**; San Marino, Calif.; corporation executive; April 30, 1911, in Salt Lake City, Utah; Rep.; March 17.

FEDERAL COMMUNICATIONS COMMISSION

Member (chairman) for the term expiring June 30, 1976, $40,000—**Dean Burch;** Tucson, Ariz.; lawyer; Dec. 20, 1927, in Enid, Okla.; Rep.; Oct. 30.

Member for the remainder of the term expiring June 30, 1971, $38,000—**Robert Wells;** Garden City, Kan.; general manager, Harris Radio Group.

FEDERAL HOME LOAN BANK BOARD

Member for the term expiring June 30, 1970, $38,000—**Preston Martin**; Pasadena, Calif.; California state savings and loan commissioner; Dec. 5, 1923, in Los Angeles, Calif.; Rep.; March 13.

Member for the term expiring June 30, 1973, $38,000—**Thomas Hal Clarke**; Atlanta, Ga.; lawyer; Aug. 10, 1914, in Atlanta; Dem.; July 20.

Member for the remainder of the term expiring June 30, 1971, $38,000—**Carl O. Kamp**; Potomac, Md.; president of Conservative Federal Savings and Loan Co., St. Louis, Mo.; Dec. 20, 1914, in St. Louis; Rep.; May 20.

FEDERAL MARITIME COMMISSION

Member (chairman) for the remainder of the term expiring June 30, 1970, $40,000—**Helen D. Bentley**; Baltimore, Md.; maritime editor, Baltimore *Sun*; Nov. 28, 1923, in Ruth, Nev.; Rep.; Oct. 3.

Member for the term expiring June 30, 1974, $38,000—**James V. Day**; Bethesda, Md.; reappointment; Nov. 17, 1914, in South Brewer, Maine; Rep.; Oct. 23.

FEDERAL MEDIATION AND CONCILIATION SERVICE

Director, $40,000—**James J. Counts**; Los Angeles, Calif.; vice president, Douglas Aircraft Corp.; Aug. 2, 1915, in Los Angeles; Rep.; March 7.

FEDERAL POWER COMMISSION

Member (chairman) for the remainder of the term expiring June 22, 1970, $40,000—**John N. Nassikas**; Washington, D.C.; minority counsel, Senate Commerce Committee; 1917 in Manchester, N.H.; Rep.; June 17.

Member for the term expiring June 22, 1974, $38,000—**Albert B. Brooke**; Towson, Md.; reappointment; June 23, 1921, in Paducah, Ky.; Rep.; Oct. 23.

FEDERAL RESERVE SYSTEM

Chairman, Board of Governors, for the term expiring Jan. 31, 1984, $42,500—**Arthur F. Burns**; New York, N.Y.; Counsellor to the President; April 27, 1904, in Stanislau, Austria; Dec. 18.

FEDERAL TRADE COMMISSION

Member (chairman) for the term expiring Sept. 25, 1976, $40,000—**Caspar W. Weinberger**; Hillsborough, Calif.; California director of finance; 1917 in San Francisco, Calif.; Rep.; Nov. 19.

GENERAL SERVICES ADMINISTRATION

Administrator, $40,000—**Robert L. Kunzig**, Harrisburg, Pa.; executive director, Pennsylvania General State Authority; Oct. 31, 1918, in Philadelphia, Pa.; Rep.; March 11.

INTERSTATE COMMERCE COMMISSION

Member for the remainder of the term expiring Dec. 31, 1973, $38,000—**Donald L. Jackson**; Pacific Palisades, Calif.; Member, U.S. House of Representatives, 1946-60; Jan. 23, 1910, in Ipswich, S.D.; Rep.; March 13.

Member for the term expiring Dec. 31, 1974, $38,000—**Robert C. Gresham**; Washington, D.C.; minority staff director, House Appropriations Committee; Nov. 12, 1917, in Booneville, Miss.; Rep.; Nov. 19.

INDIAN CLAIMS COMMISSION

Member for the term expiring April 10, 1973, $36,000—**Brantley Blue**; Kingsport, Tenn.; lawyer; Oct. 11, 1925, in Pembroke, N.C.; Rep.; April 25.

NATIONAL AERONAUTICS AND SPACE ADMINISTRATION

Administrator, $42,500—**Thomas O. Paine**; Washington, D.C., Deputy Administrator, NASA; Nov. 9, 1921, in Berkeley, Calif.; Dem.; March 20.

Deputy Administrator, $38,000—**George M. Low**; Houston, Texas; Manager, Apollo Spacecraft Program Office; June 10, 1926, in Vienna, Austria; Nov. 26.

NATIONAL MEDIATION BOARD

Member for the term expiring July 1, 1972, $38,000—**George S. Ives**; Bethesda, Md.; lawyer; Jan. 10, 1922, in Brooklyn, N.Y.; Rep.; Sept. 17.

NATIONAL SCIENCE FOUNDATION

Director, $42,500—**Dr. William D. McElroy**; Baltimore, Md.; chairman, biology department, the Johns Hopkins University; Jan. 22, 1917, in Rogers, Texas; July 11.

RAILROAD RETIREMENT BOARD

Member for the term expiring Aug. 29, 1974, $38,000—**Neil P. Speirs**; Buffalo, N.Y.; labor union official; Dec. 25, 1912 in Red Deer, Alberta, Canada; Sept. 17.

RENEGOTIATION BOARD

Member, $36,000—**William H. Harrison**; Sheridan, Wyo.; Member, U.S. House of Representatives, 1951-69; Aug. 10, 1896, in Terre Haute, Ind.; Rep.; June 19.

Member, $36,000—**Rex M. Mattingly**; Albuquerque, N.M.; partner, Mattingly Oil Co.; May 25, 1919, in Lucy, N.M.; Rep.; Aug. 13.

Member, $36,000—**D. Eldred Rinehart**; Smithsburg, Md.; dairy farmer, member of Republican National Committee; Nov. 13, 1903, in Smithsburg; Rep.; Sept. 26.

Member, $36,000—**William S. Whitehead**; Arlington, Va.; president, Ives, Whitehead Co. Inc.; May 27, 1907, in Denver, Colo.; Rep.; June 19.

SECURITIES AND EXCHANGE COMMISSION

Member (chairman) for the term expiring June 5, 1974, $40,000—**Hamer H. Budge**; Washington, D.C.; reappointment; Nov. 21, 1910, in Pocatello, Idaho; Rep.; June 2.

Member for the term expiring June 5, 1973, $38,000—**James J. Needham**; Plainview, N.Y.; accountant; Aug. 18, 1926, in Woodhaven, N.Y.; Rep.; June 18.

Member for the term expiring June 5, 1971, $38,000—**A. Sydney Herlong Jr.**; Leesburg, Fla.; Member, U.S. House of Representatives, 1949-69; Feb. 14, 1909, in Manistee, Ala.; Dem.; Sept. 19.

SMALL BUSINESS ADMINISTRATION

Administrator, $40,000—**Hilary J. Sandoval Jr.**; El Paso, Texas; president, Sandoval News Service Inc.; Jan. 29, 1930, in El Paso, Texas; Rep.; March 4.

SUBVERSIVE ACTIVITIES CONTROL BOARD

Member for the term expiring Aug. 9, 1970, $36,000—**Otto F. Otepka**; Washington, D.C.; security evaluator, U.S. State Dept.; 1915 in Chicago, Ill.; Rep.; June 24.

Member for the term expiring Aug. 9, 1974, $36,000—**Paul J. O'Neill**; Miami, Fla.; stock broker; Feb. 16, 1913, in Pleasantville, N.J.; Rep.; Nov. 5.

TENNESSEE VALLEY AUTHORITY

Chairman for the term expiring May 18, 1978, $40,000—**Aubrey J. Wagner**; Knoxville, Tenn.; reappointment; Jan. 12, 1912, in Hillsboro, Wis.; Rep.; May 23.

U.S. ARMS CONTROL AND DISARMAMENT AGENCY

Director, $42,500—**Gerard C. Smith**; Washington, D.C.; lawyer; May 4, 1914, in New York, N.Y.; Feb. 7.

Deputy Director, $38,000—**Philip J. Farley**; Washington, D.C.; Deputy U.S. Representative to NATO; Aug. 6, 1916, in Berkeley, Calif.; Aug. 8.

U.S. INFORMATION AGENCY

Director, $42,500—**Frank Shakespeare**; Greenwich, Conn.; president, CBS International Division; April 9, 1925, in New York, N.Y.; Feb. 7.

Deputy Director, $38,000—**Henry Loomis**; Middleburg, Va.; partner, St. Vincent's Island Co.; April 19, 1919, in Tuxedo Park, Calif.; Rep.; April 3.

U.S. TARIFF COMMISSION

Member for the term expiring June 16, 1973, $36,000—**George M. Moore**; Silver Spring, Md.; minority counsel, House Post Office and Civil Service Committee; 1913 in LaGrange, Ky.; Rep.; Aug. 12.

Member for the term expiring June 16, 1975, $36,000—**Will E. Leonard Jr.**; Washington, D.C.; reappointment; Jan. 18, 1935, in Shreveport, La.; Dem.; June 17.

U.S. TAX COURT

Judge for the remainder of the term expiring June 2, 1972, $40,000—**William H. Quealy**; Arlington, Va.; minority counsel, House Ways and Means Committee; March 11, 1913, in New Orleans, La.; Rep.; Sept. 19.

VETERANS ADMINISTRATION

Administrator, $42,500—**Donald E. Johnson**; West Branch, Iowa; farm supplier; June 5, 1924, in Cedar Falls, Iowa; Rep.; June 19.

Judiciary

U.S. SUPREME COURT

Chief Justice of the United States, $62,500—**Warren E. Burger**; Arlington, Va.; associate judge, U.S. Court of Appeals for the District of Columbia; Sept. 17, 1907 in St. Paul, Minn.; Rep.; June 9.

U.S. CIRCUIT COURTS OF APPEALS

Judge for the Third Circuit, $42,500—**Arlin M. Adams**; Philadelphia, Pa.; lawyer; April 16, 1921, in Philadelphia, Pa.; Rep.; Oct. 1.

Judge for the Third Circuit, $42,500—**John J. Gibbons**; Newark, N.J.; lawyer; Dec. 8, 1924, in Newark; Rep.; Dec. 17.

Judge for the Fifth Circuit, $42,500—**George H. Carswell**; Tallahassee, Fla.; U.S. District Judge; Dec. 22, 1919, in Irwinton, Ga.; Rep.; June 19.

Judge for the Fifth Circuit, $42,500—**Charles Clark**; Jackson, Miss.; lawyer; Sept. 12, 1925, in Memphis, Tenn.; Dem.; Oct. 15.

Judge for the Fifth Circuit, $42,500—**Joe McDonald Ingraham**; Houston, Texas; U.S. District Judge for the Southern District of Texas; July 5, 1903, in Pawnee Co., Okla.; Rep.; Dec. 17.

Judge for the Sixth Circuit, $42,500—**Henry L. Brooks**; Louisville, Ky.; U.S. District Judge for the District of Ky.; Aug. 29, 1908 in Jackson, Tenn.; Rep.; Dec. 10.

Judge for the Ninth Circuit, $42,500—**John F. Kilkenny**; Portland, Ore.; U.S. District Judge; Oct. 26, 1901, in Hepner, Ore.; Rep.; Sept. 12.

Judge for the Ninth Circuit, $42,500—**Ozell M. Trask**; Phoenix, Ariz.; lawyer; July 4, 1909, in Wakita, Okla.; Rep.; Sept. 12.

Judge for the Ninth Circuit, $42,500—**Eugene A. Wright**; Seattle, Wash.; vice president, Pacific National Bank of Seattle; Rep.; Sept. 12.

(Continued on page 89)

Membership of Federal Regulatory Agencies

Atomic Energy Commission

(Five members appointed for five-year terms; no statutory limitation on political party membership)

Member	Party	Term Expires	Nominated By Nixon	Confirmed By Senate
Glenn T. Seaborg (C)	D	6/30/70		
*Theos J. Thompson	R	6/30/71	4/23/69	5/26/69
Wilfred E. Johnson	R	6/30/72		
James T. Ramey	D	6/30/73		
*Clarence E. Larson	R	6/30/74	6/30/69	8/8/69

Civil Aeronautics Board

(Five members appointed for six-year terms; not more than three members from one political party)

Member	Party	Term Expires	Nominated By Nixon	Confirmed By Senate
John G. Adams	R	12/31/70		
Whitney Gillilland	R	12/31/71		
Robert T. Murphy	D	12/31/72		
Joseph G. Minetti	D	12/31/73		
*Secor D. Browne (C)	R	12/31/74	9/12/69	10/3/69

Federal Communications Commission

(Seven members appointed for seven-year terms; not more than four members from one political party)

Member	Party	Term Expires	Nominated By Nixon	Confirmed By Senate
Kenneth A. Cox	D	6/30/70		
*Robert Wells	R	6/30/71	9/17/69	10/30/69
Robert T. Bartley	D	6/30/72		
Nicholas Johnson	D	6/30/73		
Robert E. Lee	R	6/30/74		
H. Rex Lee	D	6/30/75		
*Dean Burch (C)	R	6/30/76	9/17/69	10/30/69

Federal Maritime Commission

(Five members appointed for five-year term; not more than three members from one political party)

Member	Party	Term Expires	Nominated By Nixon	Confirmed By Senate
*Helen D. Bentley (C)	R	6/30/70	8/11/69	10/3/69
James F. Fanseen	R	6/30/71		
Ashton C. Barrett	D	6/30/72		
George H. Hearn	D	6/30/73		
**James V. Day	R	6/30/74	9/17/69	10/23/69

Federal Power Commission

(Five members appointed for five-year terms; not more than three members from one political party)

Member	Party	Term Expires	Nominated By Nixon	Confirmed By Senate
*John N. Nassikas (C)	R	6/22/70	5/19/69	6/17/69
Lawrence J. O'Connor Jr.	D	6/22/71		
Carl E. Bagge	R	6/22/72		
John A. Carver Jr.	D	6/22/73		
**Albert B. Brooke Jr.	R	6/22/74	6/23/69	10/23/69

Federal Reserve System, Board of Governors

(Seven members appointed for fourteen-year terms; no statutory limitation on political party membership, but not more than one member may be appointed from each Federal Reserve District. No member may be appointed to serve more than one full term.)

Member	Party	Term Expires	Nominated By Nixon	Confirmed By Senate
William McC. Martin Jr. (C)	D	1/31/70†		
Sherman J. Maisel	NA	1/31/72		
J. Dewey Daane	NA	1/31/74		
George W. Mitchell	D	1/31/76		
J. L. Robertson	NA	1/31/78		
Andrew F. Brimmer	D	1/31/80		
William W. Sherrill	D	1/31/82		

Federal Trade Commission

(Five members appointed for seven-year terms; not more than three members from one political party)

Member	Party	Term Expires	Nominated By Nixon	Confirmed By Senate
Philip Elman	I	9/25/70		
Mary G. Jones	R	9/25/73		
Paul Rand Dixon	D	9/25/74		
A. Everette MacIntyre	D	9/25/75		
*Caspar W. Weinberger (C)	R	9/25/76	10/3/69	11/19/69

Interstate Commerce Commission

(Eleven members appointed for seven-year terms; not more than six members from one political party)

Member	Party	Term Expires	Nominated By Nixon	Confirmed By Senate
Paul J. Tierney	R	12/31/69		
Virginia Mae Brown (C)	D	12/31/70		
Laurence K. Walrath	D	12/31/70		
Rupert L. Murphy	D	12/31/71		
John W. Bush	D	12/31/71		
Willard Deason	D	12/31/72		
Dale W. Hardin	R	12/31/72		
*Donald L. Jackson	R	12/31/73	2/20/69	3/13/69
George M. Stafford	R	12/31/73		
*Robert C. Gresham	R	12/31/74	9/25/69	11/19/69
Kenneth H. Tuggle	R	12/31/75		

National Labor Relations Board

(Five members appointed for five-year terms; no statutory limitation on political party membership)

Member	Party	Term Expires	Nominated By Nixon	Confirmed By Senate
Vacancy				
Frank W. McCulloch (C)	D	8/27/70		
Gerald A. Brown	D	8/27/71		
John H. Fanning	D	12/16/72		
Howard Jenkins Jr.	R	8/27/73		

National Mediation Board

(Three members appointed for three-year terms; not more than two members from one political party

Member	Party	Term Expires	Nominated By Nixon	Confirmed By Senate
Leverett Edwards (C)	D	7/1/70		
Francis A. O'Neill Jr.	R	7/1/71		
*George S. Ives	R	7/1/72	8/29/69	9/17/69

Securities and Exchange Commission

(Five members appointed for five-year terms; not more than three members from one political party)

Member	Party	Term Expires	Nominated By Nixon	Confirmed By Senate
Hugh F. Owens	D	6/5/70		
*A. Sydney Herlong Jr.	D	6/5/71	9/3/69	9/19/69
Richard B. Smith	R	6/5/72		
*James J. Needham	R	6/5/73	5/27/69	6/18/69
**Hamer H. Budge (C)	R	6/5/74	2/22/69	6/2/69

(C)—chairman.
 * Nixon appointment.
 ** Reappointed by Nixon; first appointed in a previous Administration.

†President Nixon Oct. 22 designated Arthur F. Burns (R) to succeed Martin as chairman upon the expiration of Martin's term.

HAYNSWORTH REJECTION FIRST MAJOR NIXON DEFEAT

President Nixon suffered his first major Congressional defeat when the Senate Nov. 21 by a 45-55 roll-call vote refused to confirm the President's nomination of Clement F. Haynsworth Jr. of South Carolina to be a Supreme Court Associate Justice.

Haynsworth thus became the 23rd man to be denied confirmation to the Court and the first to be formally rejected since 1930, when John J. Parker of North Carolina was rejected by a 39-41 vote. The nomination of Associate Justice Abe Fortas to be Chief Justice was blocked in 1968 by a filibuster.

Haynsworth, chief justice of the 4th Circuit Court of Appeals, was nominated by President Nixon Aug. 18 to fill the seat left vacant by the resignation of Fortas in May 1969.

The controversy over judicial ethics ignited by Fortas' resignation under fire for accepting an outside fee from the family foundation of a convicted stock manipulator was rekindled by opposition to Haynsworth's nomination.

Opponents of the nomination, led by Birch Bayh (D Ind.), said repeatedly that they did not question Haynsworth's honesty or integrity. They did question his sensitivity to the appearance of ethical impropriety and his judgment regarding participation in cases where his financial interests could be said to be involved, even indirectly.

Haynsworth was also opposed by labor and civil rights leaders, the same coalition which defeated the Court nomination of Parker in 1930, the only other man in the 20th century whose nomination was rejected outright by the Senate.

During Committee hearings in September and ensuing weeks, Haynsworth, his financial affairs, and his judicial record were scrutinized more thoroughly and extensively than those of any other Court nominee in history.

Demands for President Nixon to withdraw the nomination merely stiffened the President's determination to stand behind his nominee and to reassert his confidence in him. Considerable political pressure preceded the final vote, brought to bear on individual Senators by both opponents and advocates of the nomination.

The final vote divided generally along conservative and liberal lines, although there were some significant exceptions, with southern Democrats joining a majority of conservative and moderate Republicans in support of confirmation, opposed by northern Democrats and a majority of liberal Republicans. The vote showed 26 Republicans and 19 Democrats voting for confirmation, 17 Republicans and 38 Democrats voting against confirmation.

All three of the top Republican leaders in the Senate voted against confirmation: Minority Leader Hugh Scott (Pa.), Assistant Minority Leader Robert P. Griffin (Mich.) and Margaret Chase Smith (Maine), chairman of the Republican Conference.

Nixon Statement. Following the Senate's action, the White House Nov. 21 issued the following statement by President Nixon:

"An outstanding jurist, who would have brought great credit to the Supreme Court of the United States, has been rejected by the United States Senate.

"I deeply regret this action. I believe a majority of people in the nation regret it.

"Especially I deplore the nature of the attacks that have been made upon this distinguished man. His integrity is unimpeachable, his ability unquestioned. The Supreme Court needs men of his legal philosophy to restore the proper balance to that great institution.

"The nation is fortunate that Clement Haynsworth's ability and judgment will remain available to the judiciary through his continuance as Chief Judge of one of the largest and busiest Appellate Courts in the nation.

"When the Congress returns for its second session in January I will nominate another Associate Justice. The criteria I shall apply for this selection, as was the case with my nomination of Judge Haynsworth, will be consistent with my commitments to the American people before my election as President a year ago."

Haynsworth Comment. At his office in Greenville, S.C., Haynsworth Nov. 21 said, "The resolution is an unhappy one for me, but for our country's sake, I hope the debate will prove to have been a cleansing agent which will smooth the way for the President's next and later nominees."

Background

President Nixon Aug. 18 announced his nomination of Haynsworth to be an Associate Justice. Haynsworth was widely regarded as fitting Mr. Nixon's definition of a "strict Constitutional constructionist."

Civil rights enthusiasts argued that the 4th Circuit had been guilty of foot-dragging in school desegregation, especially in Virginia's Prince Edward County. Haynsworth dissented when his court ruled against Prince Edward County's resistance to desegregation, and again when the court ruled that hospitals which accepted federal funds could not segregate their facilities. His early opinions appeared to reflect a belief that giving students freedom of choice adequately fulfilled the Supreme Court's school desegregation mandate.

Organized labor said Haynsworth had a history of ruling against labor and charged him with conflict of interest in a 1963 case. With Haynsworth voting with the majority, the 4th Circuit Court that year held that the closing down of a textile plant in Darlington, S.C., by the Darlington Manufacturing Co. did not constitute an unfair labor practice. At the time of the ruling, Haynsworth owned stock in the Carolina Vend-A-Matic Company, which supplied vending services in plants owned by Deering Milliken Inc., of which the Darlington firm was a subsidiary.

Haynsworth also was criticized after it was learned he had purchased Brunswick Corporation stock between the time he had taken part in a decision in a case involving the company in 1967 and when the decision was formally announced in 1968.

Senate Action

The Senate Judiciary Committee held eight days of hearings in September on the Haynsworth nomination. The Committee Oct. 9 voted 10-7 to report the nomination. The report (Exec Rept 91-12) was filed Nov. 12.

The Senate Nov. 13 took up the nomination and on Nov. 21 by a 45-55 roll-call vote rejected the nomination. Debate ranged over much-reiterated arguments, both for and against the nominee, that had been heard before. Excerpts from the debate follow:

Stuart Symington (D Mo.): "I believe Judge Haynsworth to be an honest man. Nevertheless I am persuaded that the record of lack of care exercised in avoiding reasonable grounds for suspicion of impartiality should not serve as a stepping-stone to the Supreme Court."

James B. Pearson (R Kan.): "In the end one must confront the basic question, is the nominee an honest man? Although I know him only from the cold pages of the record of the hearings, the expressions of the committee report, and the evaluations of those who do know him, I cannot judge him to be dishonest. I accept his acts as unintentional indiscretions."

James O. Eastland (D Miss.), chairman of the Senate Judiciary Committee: "In his appearance before the Committee, Judge Haynsworth showed himself to be truthful, frank and candid.... With dignity, restraint and courage, he underwent an exhaustive interrogation without complaint. He withstood a trial-by-ordeal within the Committee and a trial-by-rumor without Committee with no trace of bitterness, or anger, or outrage which others felt for him."

Jacob K. Javits (R N.Y.): "I have found, on reviewing the written opinions of Judge Haynsworth, particularly in racial segregation cases, that...his views on the application of the Constitution to this most critical constitutional question of our time are so consistently out of date, so consistently insensitive to the centuries-old injustice which we as a nation have caused our black citizens to bear, that I could not support the introduction of Judge Haynsworth's judicial philosophy into the Nation's highest court."

Robert C. Byrd (D W.Va.): "Much of the opposition to this nomination comes from groups and blocs who... are opposed to the philosophy of Judge Haynsworth, so that the matter of conflict of interest, at least, may be considered a smokescreen."

Lee Metcalf (D Mont.): "In the light of Judge Haynsworth's record, it is plain that...the highest qualification for a seat on the Supreme Court is complete ideological identification with the reactionary tenets of the administration's southern strategy."

Edward W. Brooke (R Mass.): "The rejection of this nomination would be a personal tragedy for Judge Haynsworth. I regret that deeply. But his confirmation could be a collective tragedy for the Nation, and that risk is simply too real and too grave to accept."

"We cannot afford to fill the ninth seat on the Court with a man who enjoys anything less than the full faith and respect of those whom he serves. We cannot afford to weaken the reverence on which the Court's power is ultimately founded."

Ernest F. Hollings (D S.C.): "Would you please tell me...how can one smilingly say to everyone with super-courtesy and superdeference, charging that the fellow is a crook, and then saying 'Wait a minute—no, we are not questioning his honesty?' "

John J. Williams (R Del.): "For years I have been critical of federal judges' neglecting their judicial duties and directing their energies toward outside activities for the purpose of financial gain, and to confirm Judge Haynsworth...in the light of his record would, in my opinion, be

How Senate Voted

The following lists the votes of individual Senators on confirmation of Clement F. Haynsworth Jr. as Associate Justice of the Supreme Court:

Aiken (R Vt.) Y	Jordan (D N.C.) Y
Allen (D Ala.) Y	Jordan (R Idaho) N
Allott (R Colo.) Y	Kennedy (D Mass.) N
Anderson (D N.M.) N	Long (D La.) Y
Baker (R Tenn.) Y	McCarthy (D Minn.) N
Bayh (D Ind.) N	McClellan (D Ark.) Y
Bellmon (R Okla.) Y	McGee (D Wyo.) N
Bennett (R Utah) Y	McGovern (D S.D.) N
Bible (D Nev.) N	McIntyre (D N.H.) N
Boggs (R Del.) Y	Magnuson (D Wash.) N
Brooke (R Mass.) N	Mansfield (D Mont.) N
Burdick (D N.D.) N	Mathias (R Md.) N
Byrd (D Va.) Y	Metcalf (D Mont.) N
Byrd (D W.Va.) Y	Miller (R Iowa) N
Cannon (D Nev.) N	Mondale (D Minn.) N
Case (R N.J.) N	Montoya (D N.M.) N
Church (D Idaho) N	Moss (D Utah) N
Cook (R Ky.) Y	Mundt (R S.D.) Y
Cooper (R Ky.) N	Murphy (R Calif.) Y
Cotton (R N.H.) Y	Muskie (D Maine) N
Cranston (D Calif.) N	Nelson (D Wis.) N
Curtis (R Neb.) Y	Packwood (R Ore.) N
Dodd (D Conn.) N	Pastore (D R.I.) N
Dole (R Kan.) Y	Pearson (R Kan.) Y
Dominick (R Colo.) Y	Pell (D R.I.) N
Eagleton (D Mo.) N	Percy (R Ill.) N
Eastland (D Miss.) Y	Prouty (R Vt.) Y
Ellender (D La.) Y	Proxmire (D Wis.) N
Ervin (D N.C.) Y	Randolph (D W.Va.) N
Fannin (R Ariz.) Y	Ribicoff (D Conn.) N
Fong (R Hawaii) Y	Russell (D Ga.) Y
Fulbright (D Ark.) Y	Saxbe (R Ohio) N
Goldwater (R Ariz.) Y	Schweiker (R Pa.) N
Goodell (R N.Y.) N	Scott (R Pa.) N
Gore (D Tenn.) N	Smith (R Maine) N
Gravel (D Alaska) Y	Smith (R Ill.) N
Griffin (R Mich.) N	Sparkman (D Ala.) Y
Gurney (R Fla.) Y	Spong (D Va.) Y
Hansen (R Wyo.) Y	Stennis (D Miss.) Y
Harris (D Okla.) N	Stevens (R Alaska) Y
Hart (D Mich.) N	Symington (D Mo.) Y
Hartke (D Ind.) N	Talmadge (D Ga.) Y
Hatfield (R Ore.) N	Thurmond (R S.C.) Y
Holland (D Fla.) Y	Tower (R Texas) Y
Hollings (D S.C.) Y	Tydings (D Md.) N
Hruska (R Neb.) Y	Williams (D N.J.) N
Hughes (D Iowa) N	Williams (R Del.) N
Inouye (D Hawaii) N	Yarborough (D Texas) N
Jackson (D Wash.) N	Young (R N.D.) Y
Javits (R N.Y.) N	Young (D Ohio) N

placing a stamp of approval on such outside financial operations."

Pressures, Voting

Republican opponents ranged from conservatives such as John J. Williams (Del.) and Len B. Jordan (Idaho) to liberals such as Charles H. Percy (Ill.) and Mark O. Hatfield (Ore.). The top Republican leaders in the Senate—Hugh Scott (Pa.), the Minority Leader; Robert P. Griffin (Mich.), the party whip; Margaret Chase Smith, chairman of the Senate Republican Leadership Conference; and John J. Williams (Del.), chairman of the

GOP Committee on Committees—all voted against Haynsworth.

Sen. Ernest F. Hollings (D S.C.), Haynsworth's chief sponsor, told reporters after the vote, "We weren't in the ball park the last six weeks. You can't win if you can't get your leadership." Hollings said that "the White House told me to take Haynsworth around and introduce him and then they would get me a leader." Hollings said he told White House officials as long as two weeks before the vote that Haynsworth could not be confirmed.

Hatfield told *Congressional Quarterly* that lack of active support by the Senate's Republican leaders was one of the main factors leading to the Haynsworth defeat.

Scott said he did not announce his position prior to the vote so as not to "add to the burdens and increase the difficulties of the Administration. This I could not do as the party leader." Griffin, Mrs. Smith and Williams announced their opposition in advance.

Conservative Coalition. Most of the 26 Republican votes for Haynsworth came from the conservative and moderate wings of the party. Of the 19 Democrats who voted in favor of Haynsworth, 16 were from southern states. The three exceptions were: the two W.Va. Senators, Robert C. Byrd and Jennings Randolph, and Mike Gravel (Alaska). The 38 Democratic votes against Haynsworth included the two Missouri Senators, one from Tennessee, one from Oklahoma and one from Texas. The "nay" vote of Albert Gore (D Tenn.) was the only one of those five not publicly committed in advance. The other 33 Senators were from northern and western states.

Pressures. Several Republican Senators reported that in the days prior to the vote they had received political pressure from their home states. Much of the anti-Haynsworth pressure was attributed by the Senators to labor and civil rights groups that opposed the judge's court decisions. Much of the pro-Haynsworth pressure was attributed to the White House. The consensus of the Senators who reported receiving pressure was that direct Administration lobbying was low-keyed, while pressure from conservative state groups was more direct. Several Senators who reported pressure remained publicly uncommitted prior to the vote but voted against Haynsworth.

An aide to Sen. William B. Saxbe (R Ohio) said Attorney General John N. Mitchell and White House aide Bryce Harlow asked to meet with Saxbe about the vote, but there was "no arm twisting."

Percy reported that 10 of the 11 members of the Illinois GOP House delegation came to his office Nov. 19 and asked him to vote for Haynsworth.

Jordan said pressure from Republican groups in Idaho began after he confidentially told Mitchell he would vote against Haynsworth. An aide to Jordan said possible future opposition from Idaho Republicans was implied.

Freshman Sen. Robert W. Packwood (R Ore.) reported there were no unreasonable pressures for his vote. Aides to Packwood said that because the Senator supported the Safeguard antiballistic missile (ABM) authorization earlier in 1969 the Administration was less inclined to feel he "owed them something." Republicans Saxbe, Richard S. Schweiker (Pa.) and James B. Pearson (Kan.) all broke with the President on the ABM and reported receiving heavy pressure on the Haynsworth vote.

White House Liaison. Hollings said after the vote that President Nixon shortly should have gone to work on uncommitted Senators shortly after he submitted the nomination but that he let the opponents take the initiative. "I never talked to Harry Dent once," Hollings stated. He said he and Dent, a special assistant to the President, had not gotten along since Dent, a South Carolina Republican, had opposed Democrat Hollings for election.

CONFIRMATIONS *(Continued from p. 85)*

Judge for the District of Columbia Circuit, $42,500—**George E. MacKinnon**; Long Lake, Minn.; general counsel and vice president, Investors Mutual Corp.; April 22, 1906, in St. Paul, Minn.; Rep.; May 5.

Judge for the District of Columbia Circuit, $42,500—**Roger Robb**; Washington, D.C.; lawyer; July 7, 1907, in Bellows Falls, Vt.; Rep.; May 5.

U.S. COURT OF CUSTOMS AND PATENT APPEALS

Associate Judge, $42,500—**Donald E. Lane**; Washington, D.C.; commissioner, U.S. Court of Claims; June 10, 1909 in Chevy Chase, Md.; June 19.

U.S. DISTRICT COURTS

Judge for the Northern District of Alabama, $40,000—**Frank H. McFadden**; Birmingham, Ala.; lawyer; Nov. 20, 1925, in Oxford, Miss.; Rep.; Aug. 8.

Judge for the Northern District of California, $40,000—**Gerald S. Levin**; San Francisco, Calif.; judge, Superior Court of California; Jan. 9, 1906, in Danville, Ill.; Rep.; July 11.

Judge for the Eastern District of California, $40,000—**Philip C. Wilkins**; Sacramento, Calif.; lawyer; Jan. 27, 1913, in Sacramento; Rep.; Dec. 17.

Judge for the Central District of California, $40,000—**David W. Williams**; Los Angeles, Calif.; California state judge; March 20, 1910, in Atlanta, Ga.; Rep.; June 19.

Judge for the Northern District of Florida, $40,000—**David L. Middlebrooks Jr.**; Pensacola, Fla.; lawyer; June 27, 1926, in Pensacola; Rep.; Dec. 10.

Judge for the District of Montana, $40,000—**James F. Battin**; Billings, Mont.; Member, U.S. House of Representatives; Feb. 13, 1922, in Wichita, Kan.; Rep.; Feb. 25.

Judge for the District of New Jersey, $40,000—**George H. Barlow**; Trenton, N.J.; New Jersey State Judge; Jan. 4, 1921, in Trenton; Rep.; Dec. 17.

Judge for the District of New Jersey, $40,000—**Leonard I. Garth**; Paterson, N.J.; lawyer; April 7, 1921, in Brooklyn, N.Y.; Rep.; Dec. 17.

Judge for the District of Oregon, $40,000—**Alfred T. Goodwin**; Salem, Ore.; Associate Justice, Oregon Supreme Court; Aug. 29, 1923, in Bellingham, Wash.; Rep.; Dec. 17.

Judge for the Eastern District of Pennsylvania, $40,000—**John B. Hannum**; Unionville, Pa.; lawyer; March 9, 1915, in Chester, Pa.; Rep.; May 5.

Judge for the Middle District of Pennsylvania, $40,000—**R. Dixon Herman**; Harrisburg, Pa.; judge, Dauphin Co. Court of Common Pleas; Sept. 24, 1911, in Northumberland, Pa.; Rep.; Dec. 10.

Judge for the Western District of Virginia, $40,000—**H. Emory Widener Jr.**; Bristol, Va.; lawyer; April 30, 1923, in Abingdon, Va.; Rep.; July 11.

Judge for the District of Columbia, $40,000—**Barrington D. Parker**; Washington, D.C.; lawyer; Nov. 17, 1915, in Rosslyn, Va.; Rep.; Dec. 18.

Judge for the District of the Virgin Islands, $40,000—**Almeric L. Christian**; St. Thomas, V.I.; U.S. Attorney for the Virgin Islands; Nov. 23, 1919, in St. Croix, V.I.; Dem.; Aug. 8.

Judge for the District of Guam, $40,000—**Cristobal C. Duenas**; Agana, Guam; Judge, Guam Island Court; Sept. 12, 1920 in Agana; Rep.; Dec. 10.

PRESIDENT MAKES CHANGES IN GOVERNMENT MACHINERY

The President in 1969 reorganized some of the machinery of the Government on his own authority and took other steps that required no Congressional action, although some of his plans were subject to Congressional veto.

Reorganization Authority

President Nixon's first legislative request was for extension of Presidential authority to submit executive reorganization plans to Congress. The authority was first contained in the Reorganization Act of 1949, which allowed the President to reorganize executive agencies unless Congress vetoed the actions within 60 calendar days (excluding Congressional vacations).

President Johnson in 1968 requested a two-year extension of the authority. The House passed the measure, but the Senate took no action.

In 1969, the Senate passed President Nixon's extension request Feb. 28 by voice vote and without debate. The bill passed the House March 18 by a 334-44 roll-call vote.

Under the renewed authority, the President July 22 sent Reorganization Plan 1 of 1969 to Congress. The only such plan submitted during the year, it permitted the President to designate the chairman of the Interstate Commerce Commission (ICC) from among its members and gave the chairman the Commission's administrative authority. Previously, the chairmanship rotated annually among the 11 commissioners. The ICC was the only major regulatory agency for which the President could not designate the chairman. *(For text of message to Congress on plan, see p. 73-A.)*

Hearings were held on the plan Aug. 5 by the House Government Operations Subcommittee on Executive and Legislative Reorganization and Sept. 26 by the Senate Government Operations Subcommittee on Executive Reorganization. ICC Chairman Virginia Mae Brown and Dwight A. Ink, assistant director for executive management of the Bureau of the Budget, testified at both hearings in support of the plan.

No further Congressional action was taken on the plan, and it became effective Oct. 11.

Poverty Program Changes

In his first message to Congress, the President Feb. 19 proposed to shift four programs from the Office of Economic Opportunity (OEO) to other federal agencies: Head Start, health centers and the foster grandparents programs to the Department of Health, Education and Welfare (HEW), and the Job Corps to the Department of Labor. The Head Start and Job Corps shifts were delegations, meaning the President delegated operating responsibility for the programs to other agencies, effective July 1, 1969. Under a delegation, the program is still "coordinated" by the OEO and the authorization for the program is included in the OEO budget, but the program is actually run by the agency to which it is delegated. *(For text of message, see p. 39-A.)*

The health centers program and foster grandparents were to be transferred. To transfer the programs, the President had to submit specific legislative proposals. With the transfer of a program, OEO lost all control and direction of the program.

The President apparently changed his mind about health centers because in an Aug. 11 reorganization plan for OEO Mr. Nixon talked about a new Office of Health Services in OEO which would encompass the health centers program.

The foster grandparents program was transferred to the HEW Department under a provision in the Older Americans Act, which was cleared for the President's signature on Sept. 3.

The delegation of the Job Corps to the Department of Labor would become a transfer under the President's proposed Manpower Training Act. In that measure, the President recommended that all job-training programs under the OEO be completely transferred to the Labor Department. *(See below.)*

In Aug. 8 and 11 statements, the President announced additional changes in the operation of the OEO. The changes were: creation of a new Office of Program Development; revamping and strengthening the Office of Planning, Research and Evaluation; strengthening and upgrading the Office of Health Services and the Office of Legal Services; and creation of a new Office of Program Operations. He said the changes were aimed at turning the OEO into an innovator of experimental programs to take people out of poverty. *(For text of statements, see p. 81-A, 85-A; for story on poverty program, see p. 57.)*

President Nixon April 9 announced a new Office of Child Development was being set up in the Department of HEW. The new division would oversee Head Start, day care and other early childhood programs of the Children's Bureau.

The Nixon Administration April 11 announced the closing of 59 Job Corps centers around the country and the establishment in their place of 30 urban centers to train unskilled youth. The move drew strong criticism, especially from Members of Congress with centers in their states.

Manpower Training

President Nixon announced plans March 13 to reorganize manpower programs in the Department of Labor. The plans placed greater authority for all manpower programs with the Department's manpower administrator, streamlined procedures ranging from field offices to Washington, D.C., and established a single office to consolidate eight training programs and the job-placement and recruitment functions of the U.S. Employment Service which was to be eliminated.

The reorganization was intended, according to Administration officials, to reduce red tape for organizations developing manpower programs at the local level.

Regional administrators in eight geographic regions and the District of Columbia were to be given authority to approve and undertake job projects without prior clearance from regional directors, district offices and the former Work-Training Program in Washington.

The new office for training, job placement and recruitment was to be called the U.S. Training and Employment

Service. Among the programs incorporated into the unit were the Manpower Development and Training Program; New Careers; Operation Mainstream; Neighborhood Youth Corps; Work Incentive; Apprenticeship Outreach; Concentrated Employment; and Job Opportunities in the Business Sector (JOBS), administered in conjunction with the National Alliance of Businessmen.

President Nixon Aug. 12 sent Congress a message asking for a new manpower training act which ultimately would place most of the development responsibility in the hands of state and local governments. *(For text, see p. 78-A; for additional information on plan and Congressional action, see p. 58.)*

The President's plan would consolidate and expand activities presently under the OEO and manpower development training programs of the Department of Labor and use federal resources as a national planning agency.

A variety of manpower services—including on-the-job and institutional training, basic education and counseling and job placement—would be coordinated by a single agency at the federal planning level and its counterpart in the states.

Federal Pay Raises

President Nixon June 17 issued executive orders raising the pay of 2.3 million federal employees and nearly 3 million military personnel as of July 1. The raises were designed to make government and military employees' pay comparable with wage scales in private industry and were authorized by the 1967 federal pay raises bill (PL 90-206), which granted the President authority to implement raises on July 1, 1968, and July 1, 1969.

PL 90-206 also established a procedure permitting the President to issue proposed salary raises for Members of Congress and top officials of the Executive and Judicial Branches that would go into effect unless vetoed by either chamber within 30 days. The practice was put into effect in 1969 for the first time by President Johnson, who submitted proposed salary revisions in his fiscal 1970 Budget sent to Congress shortly before he left office.

Pacific Air Routes

President Nixon Jan. 24 rescinded a controversial decision of former President Johnson allocating new Pacific air routes among U.S. commercial airlines. Johnson critics had asserted that the route awards, approved Jan. 19, reflected political favoritism.

The Nixon action came hours before the deadline for airlines to file petitions for reconsideration of the awards. Petitions from at least 15 airlines reportedly had been received. In a letter to Chairman of the Civil Aeronautics Board (CAB) John H. Crooker, Mr. Nixon asked that the Board's recommendations, which had been the basis for the Johnson awards, be resubmitted for examination by the new Administration.

The airlines which would have benefited most from the Pacific routes awarded by Mr. Johnson were Trans World Airlines, Braniff and Continental. The airlines which would have found themselves the biggest losers reportedly were Eastern, Western and United.

In April, Mr. Nixon approved new routes to the Orient for Trans World Airlines, Pan American World Airways, Northwest Airlines and Flying Tiger Lines. Braniff, North-

west and Pan American lines lost previously awarded routes. On July 21, the President awarded the most controversial of the routes to American Airlines, following the CAB recommendation. Earlier the CAB and President Johnson had awarded the route to Continental Airlines.

Rail Strike Board

President Nixon Oct. 3 invoked the Railway Labor Act to delay a threatened nationwide railroad strike for 60 days. Also acting under the Act, he appointed an emergency board to study the dispute between a number of railroad and related unions and the National Railway Labor Conference, which represents railroad management.

Mr. Nixon did not invoke the Taft-Hartley Act, which permits the President to postpone a strike in other industries for 80 days.

Other Actions

In other major moves, the President:

• Jan. 23 established by Executive Order a Council for Urban Affairs to help him develop a national urban policy. It was called the domestic equivalent of the National Security Council and was chaired by the President. Daniel P. Moynihan, Presidential adviser on urban affairs, was named executive secretary. The other members were the Vice President, Attorney General and the Secretaries of Agriculture, Commerce, Labor, Health, Education and Welfare, Housing and Urban Development, and Transportation.

• Jan. 24 announced formation of a Cabinet Committee on Economic Policy to assist in long-range planning. It was to supplement the work of the "Quadriad" of economic policy makers (the director of the Bureau of the Budget, chairman of the Council of Economic Advisers, Treasury Secretary and chairman of the Federal Reserve Board). The President was the chairman of the committee. Other members included Vice President Spiro T. Agnew, Treasury Secretary David M. Kennedy, Secretary of Agriculture Clifford M. Hardin, Secretary of Commerce Maurice H. Stans, Secretary of Labor George P. Shultz, Budget Director Robert P. Mayo, Chairman Paul W. McCracken of the Council of Economic Advisers (CEA) and Arthur F. Burns, Counsellor to the President.

• Jan. 30, Feb. 3, 8, 10, and March 1 issued a long series of directives to various Executive Branch agencies requesting a wide range of studies.

• Feb. 5 said he and Postmaster General Winton M. Blount were abolishing the patronage system for appointing postmasters and rural letter carriers and providing for the positions to be filled instead by competitive examinations. *(See p. 63.)*

• Feb. 7 said he was revitalizing the National Security Council, that it would be the "principal forum" on policy, would meet regularly and would have several supporting committees and groups.

• Feb. 8 asked the Director of the Bureau of the Budget to direct Executive Branch departments and agencies to make public new statistics promptly.

• Feb. 14 by Executive Order created the Office of Intergovernmental Relations, to operate under the supervision of the Vice President, to strengthen federal, state and local relations.

• Feb. 14 provided for a Special Assistant to the President for Liaison with Former Presidents.

• Feb. 20 reassumed responsibility for oil import policies, which was delegated in 1963 by President Johnson to the Department of the Interior. The move relieved Interior Secretary Walter J. Hickel from potential conflict of interest problems.

• March 5 signed an Executive Order establishing the Office of Minority Business Enterprise in the Commerce Department and creating an Advisory Council for Minority Enterprise.

• March 24 issued a memorandum stating that only he could approve the use of "executive privilege" to withhold information from Congress. Similar memoranda were issued by Presidents Kennedy and Johnson after controversy arose in the Eisenhower Administration over the use of "executive privilege."

• March 27 and May 21 announced the establishment of 10 common regions and regional centers for five departments and agencies engaged in social or economic programs—the Departments of Labor; Health, Education and Welfare; Housing and Urban Development; and the Office of Economic Opportunity and the Small Business Administration. Regional offices were to be located in Boston, New York, Philadelphia, Atlanta, Chicago, Dallas-Fort Worth, Denver, San Francisco, Kansas City and Seattle. The President said decentralization of other Government departments and agencies would be studied.

• April 4 announced a relaxation of measures by the Johnson Administration that had restricted American investment abroad.

• April 8 announced he had directed Secretary of Housing and Urban Development George Romney to assemble a program to rehabilitate riot-damaged areas in 20 cities and said $9 million would be available for interim assistance.

• May 1 by Executive Order delegated to the Secretary of State the authority to approve or reject recommendations and actions of certain fisheries commissions.

• May 26 by Executive Order set up a national voluntary action program "to encourage and stimulate more widespread and effective voluntary action for solving public domestic problems." The order also established a Cabinet Committee on Voluntary Action. The Secretary of Housing and Urban Development was directed to encourage such programs, provide an information clearinghouse for voluntary action and make grants of seed money for stimulating the development of private voluntary action programs.

• July 9 ordered a 10-percent reduction in American direct-hire civilian personnel serving abroad in fiscal year 1970 and in certain U.S. military forces overseas. The move was taken to cut costs, help the balance of payments and reduce "the American presence overseas," the White House said.

• July 12 established a National Goals Research Staff within the White House made up of experts in data relating to social needs and trends. Leonard Garment, a special consultant to the President, was to direct it. Its purpose was to forecast social developments, assess alternatives and develop social indicators that "can reflect the present and future quality of American life, and the direction and rate of its change" and summarize the results of related research activities from many sources.

• Aug. 8 by Executive Order directed the head of each department and agency to establish "an affirmative program of equal employment opportunity."

• Sept. 4 directed all federal agencies to cut new contracts for Government construction by 75 percent immediately. He also urged state and local governments and businessmen to cut back on construction and directed the Secretaries of Labor and of Health, Education and Welfare to increase manpower training in the construction industry.

• Oct. 1 announced "advice" to the director of Selective Service, recommending that induction of graduate students be deferred until the end of the academic year.

• Nov. 26 by Executive Order implemented draft lottery system authorized by new law (PL 91-124).

Committees, Other Groups

The White House established a number of committees, task forces and other groups during the year. Most of them were assigned to study problems and formulate proposals for their solution. Among them were:

• The Cabinet Committee on Economic Policy, created by Executive Order Jan. 24.

• An interdepartmental ad hoc committee to review the supersonic transport program, announced Feb. 27.

• The Advisory Commission on an All-Volunteer Armed Force, appointed March 27.

• The President's Advisory Council on Executive Organization, announced April 5.

• The Richard Nixon Foundation, "for general educational and charitable purposes including the formation and construction of a Richard Nixon library and museum," announced May 12.

• The Environmental Quality Council and the Citizen's Advisory Committee on Environmental Quality, established May 29.

• The President's Committee on the Vietnam Veteran, appointed June 5.

• A nationwide system of Youth Advisory Committees on the Selective Service System, announced June 6.

• The Cabinet Committee on Construction, established Sept. 4.

• A Task Force on Business Taxation, headed by John H. Alexander of the President's former law firm, established Sept. 22.

• The Construction Industry Collective Bargaining Commission, established Sept. 22.

• A Task Force on Model Cities, established Sept. 24.

• A Task Force on Priorities in Higher Education, established Oct. 6.

• A Task Force on Science Policy, established Oct. 6.

• A Task Force on Problems of the Aging, established Oct. 10.

• A Task Force on Low-Income Housing, established Oct. 10.

• A Task Force on Oceanography, established Oct. 10.

• A Task Force on Economic Growth, established Oct. 15.

• A Task Force on Prisoner Rehabilitation, established Oct. 16.

• A Task Force on Urban Renewal, established Oct. 17.

• A Task Force on Highway Safety, established Oct. 23.

1969 PRESIDENTIAL NEWS CONFERENCES

JANUARY 27

Following is the complete text of President Nixon's first news conference. The Jan. 27 conference was televised live from the East Room of the White House.

THE PRESIDENT. Ladies and gentlemen, since this is my first press conference since the Inauguration, I can imagine there are a number of questions. Consequently, I will make no opening statement and we will go directly to your questions.

Mr. Cormier?

Legislative Program

Q. Do you plan to make your own State of the Union Message, and do you have a major legislative program to send to Congress this year?

THE PRESIDENT. I shall have a major legislative program to present to the Congress this year. Whether that would best be presented by a series of individual messages or a State of the Union Message, supplemented by some individual messages, is yet to be determined. I will make a determination within the next two weeks, after consultation with the Legislative Leaders.

Miss Thomas?

Vietnam Policy

Q. Mr. President, what is your peace plan for Vietnam?

THE PRESIDENT. I believe as we look at what is happening in negotiations in Paris, as far as the American side is concerned we are off to a good start. What now, of course, is involved is what happens on the other side.

We find that in Paris, if you read Ambassador Lodge's statement, we have been quite specific with regard to some steps that can be taken now on Vietnam. Rather than submitting a laundry list of various proposals, we laid down those things which we believe the other side should agree to and can agree to: The restoration of the demilitarized zone as set forth in the Geneva Conference of 1954; mutual withdrawal, guaranteed withdrawal, of forces by both sides; the exchange of prisoners. All of these are matters that we think can be precisely considered and on which progress can be made.

Now, where we go from here depends on what the other side offers in turn.

Relations With China

Q. Mr. President, now that you are President, could you be specific with us about what your plans are for improving relations with Communist China, and whether you think they will be successful or not?

THE PRESIDENT. Well, I have noted, of course, some expressions of interest on the part of various Senators and others in this country with regard to the possibility of admitting Communist China to the United Nations.

I also have taken note of the fact that several countries— including primarily Italy among the major countries—have indicated an interest in changing its policy and possibly voting to admit Communist China to the United Nations.

The policy of this country and this Administration at this time will be to continue to oppose Communist China's admission to the United Nations.

There are several reasons for that. First, Communist China has not indicated any interest in becoming a member of the United Nations.

Second, it has not indicated any intent to abide by the principles of the UN Charter, and to meet the principles that new members admitted to the United Nations are supposed to meet.

Finally, Communist China continues to call for expelling the Republic of China from the United Nations and the Republic of China has, as I think most know, been a member of the international community and has met its responsibilities without any question over these past few years.

Under these circumstances, I believe it would be a mistake for the United States to change its policy with regard to Communist China in admitting it to the United Nations.

Now, there is a second immediate point that I have noted. That is the fact that there will be another meeting in Warsaw. We look forward to that meeting. We will be interested to see what the Chinese Communist representatives have to say at that meeting, whether new changes of attitude on their part on major, substantive issues may have occurred.

Until some changes occur on their side, however, I see no immediate prospect of any change in our policy.

Urgent Problems

Q. Mr. President, what problems that you have to cope with do you feel require your most urgent attention now?

THE PRESIDENT. Mr. Kaplow, the major problems with which I have been concerned in this first week have been in the field of foreign policy, because there only the President can make some of the decisions.

The Security Council, as you ladies and gentlemen are aware, has had two very long meetings, and, in addition, I spent many long hours at night reading the papers, which involve the foreign policy of the United States.

This afternoon I will go to the Pentagon for my first major briefing by military officials on our military situation.

Going beyond that, however, I would say that the problems of our cities, which have been discussed at length at the Urban Affairs Council, and our economic problems, which were discussed at the meeting we had in the new Cabinet Committee on Economic Policy, require urgent attention.

It is very difficult to single one out and put it above the other. There are a number of problems which this Administration confronts; each requires urgent attention. The field of foreign policy will require more attention because it is in this field that only the President, in many instances, can make the decisions.

Nuclear Treaty, Arms Talks

Q. Mr. President, on foreign policy, nuclear policy, particularly, could you give us your position on the Nonproliferation Treaty and on starting missile talks with the Soviet Union.

THE PRESIDENT. I favor the Nonproliferation Treaty. The only question is the timing of the ratification of that treaty. That matter will be considered by the National Security Council, by my direction, during a meeting this week. I will also have a discussion with the leaders of both sides in the Senate and in the House on the treaty within this week and in the early part of next week. I will make a decision then as to whether this is the proper time to ask the Senate to move forward and ratify the treaty. I expect ratification of the treaty and will urge its ratification at an appropriate time, and, I would hope, an early time.

As far as the second part of your question, with regard to strategic arms talks, I favor strategic arms talks. Again, it is a question of not only when, but the context of those talks. The context of those talks is vitally important because we are here between two major, shall we say, guidelines.

On the one side, there is the proposition which is advanced by some that we should go forward with talks on the reduction of strategic forces on both sides; we should go forward with such talks, clearly apart from any progress on political settlement, and on the other side the suggestion is made that until we make progress on political settlements, it would not be wise to go forward on any reduction of our strategic arms, even by agreement with the other side.

It is my belief that what we must do is to steer a course between those two extremes. It would be a mistake, for example, for us to fail to recognize that simply reducing arms through mutual agreement—failing to recognize that that reduction will not, in itself, assure peace. The war which occurred in the Mid-East in 1967 was a clear indication of that.

What I want to do is to see to it that we have strategic arms talks in a way and at a time that will promote, if possible, progress on outstanding political problems at the same time—for example, on the problem of the Mid-East and on other outstanding problems in which the United States and the Soviet Union, acting together, can serve the cause of peace.

Middle East

Q. Mr. President, do you or your Administration have any plan outside the United Nations' proposal for achieving peace in the Middle East?

THE PRESIDENT. As you ladies and gentlemen are aware, the suggestion has been made that we have four-power talks. The suggestion has also been made that we use the United Nations as the primary forum for such talks. And it has also been suggested that the United States and the Soviet Union bilaterally should have talks on the Mid-East.

In addition to that, of course, the problem finally should be settled by the parties in the area. We are going to devote the whole day on Saturday to the Mid-East problem, just as we devoted the whole day this last Saturday on the problem of Vietnam.

We will consider on the occasion of that meeting the entire range of options that we have. I shall simply say at this time that I believe we need new initiatives and new leadership on the part of the United States in order to cool off the situation in the Mid-East. I consider it a powder keg, very explosive. It needs to be de-fused. I am open to any suggestions that may cool it off and reduce the possibility of another explosion, because the next explosion in the Mid-East, I think, could involve very well a confrontation between the nuclear powers, which we want to avoid.

I think it is time to turn to the left side now.

Budget Review

Q. Mr. President, could you tell us whether you have had a chance to examine the Johnson budget, and whether you see any hope for a reduction in the Johnson budget?

THE PRESIDENT. Yes, I have examined it. As far as hopes for reduction are concerned, the Director of the Bureau of the Budget has just Friday issued instructions to all of the departments to examine the budgets in their departments very closely and to give us recommendations as to where budget cuts might be made.

This is for two purposes: One, because we would like to cut the overall budget; and two, because we want to have room for some of the new programs that this Administration and the new approaches that this Administration would like to implement.

At this time I cannot say where and how the budget can be cut. I will say that we are taking a fresh look at all of the programs and we shall attempt to make cuts in order to carry out the objectives that I set forth during the campaign.

Vietnam Ceasefire

Q. Mr. President, do you consider it possible to have a cease fire in Vietnam so long as the Viet Cong still occupy Vietnamese territory?

THE PRESIDENT. I think that it is not helpful in discussing Vietnam to use such terms as "cease fire" because cease fire is a term of art that really has no relevance, in my opinion, to a guerrilla war.

When you are talking about a conventional war, then a cease fire agreed upon by two parties means that the shooting stops. When you have a guerrilla war, in which one side may not even be able to control many of those who are responsible for the violence in the area, the cease fire may be meaningless.

I think at this point this Administration believes that the better approach is the one that Ambassador Lodge, under our direction, set forth in Paris—mutual withdrawal of forces on a guaranteed basis by both sides from South Vietnam.

Nuclear Strategy

Q. Back to nuclear weapons, Mr. President. Both you and Secretary Laird have stressed, quite hard, the need for superiority over the Soviet Union. But what is the real meaning of that in view of the fact that both sides have more than enough already to destroy each other, and how do you distinguish the validity of that stance and the argument of Dr. Kissinger for what he calls "sufficiency"?

THE PRESIDENT. Here, again, I think the semantics may offer an inappropriate approach to the problem. I would say that with regard to Dr. Kissinger's suggestion of sufficiency, that that would meet, certainly, my guideline, and I think Secretary Laird's guideline, with regard to superiority.

Let me put it this way: When we talk about parity, I think we should recognize that wars occur, usually, when each side believes it has a chance to win. Therefore, parity does not necessarily assure that a war may not occur.

By the same token, when we talk about superiority, that may have a detrimental effect on the other side in putting it in an inferior position and, therefore, giving great impetus to its own arms race.

Our objective in this Administration, and this is a matter that we are going to discuss at the Pentagon this afternoon, and that will be the subject of a major discussion in the National Security Council within the month—our objective is to be sure that the United States has sufficient military power to defend our interests and to maintain the commitments which this Administration determines are in the interest of the United States around the world.

I think "sufficiency" is a better term, actually, than either "superiority" or "parity".

District of Columbia Crime

Q. Mr. President, you talked quite a bit during the campaign about crime in the District of Columbia. That crime has increased since January 1st, and I wondered how you proposed to deal with it.

THE PRESIDENT. Mr. Healy, it is a major problem in the District of Columbia, as I found when I suggested to the Secret Service I would like to take a walk yesterday. I had read Mary McCrory's column and wanted to try her cheesecake. But I find, of course, that taking a walk here in the District of Columbia, and particularly in the evening hours, is now a very serious problem, as it is in some other major cities.

One of the employees at the White House, just over the week end, was the victim of a purse snatching, which brings it very close to home.

Incidentally, I might point out in that case that my advisers tell me that by seeing that the area is better lighted, that perhaps the possibility of purse snatching and other crimes in the vicinity of the White House might be reduced. Therefore, we have turned on the lights in all of that area, I can assure you.

But to be quite specific with regard to the District of Columbia, it was not only a major commitment in the campaign; it is a major concern in the country. I noted an editorial in one of the major papers, The New York Times, for example, that Washington, D.C. was now a city of "fear and crime." That may go too far, but at least that was their judgment. All three of the Washington papers indicate great concern.

Consequently, I have on an urgent basis instructed the Attorney General to present to me a program to deal with crime in the District of Columbia, and an announcement of that program and also an announcement as to what we will ask the Congress to do, in addition to what we will do administratively, will be made at the end of this week.

LBJ Appointments, Air Routes

Q. Mr. President, why did you decide to withdraw all the appointments that had been sent to Capitol Hill by your predecessor, and can you tell us why you decided to cancel the decision, for the time, in the Pacific airline case?

THE PRESIDENT. Well, first, with regard to the appointments, I had two precedents to follow. Consequently, I took my choice. In the one instance, President Kennedy, as you will recall, did not withdraw the appointments of judgeships which he inherited from President Eisenhower. On the other hand, President Eisenhower had withdrawn all appointments and then proceeded to make new appointments, including some from the list that had been withdrawn.

I felt that the Eisenhower approach was the more efficient way to handle it.

I should point out that among those names that have been withdrawn, I already know that some will be reappointed. But I felt that the new Administration should examine the whole list and make its own decision with regard to whether the individuals that had been appointed would serve the interests of the Nation according to the guidelines that the new Administration was to lay down.

With regard to the action that had been taken by the previous Administration on the airlines, I received recommendations or, shall I say, requests on the part of both the Chairman of the House Foreign Affairs Committee and the Chairman of the Senate Foreign Relations Committee that this matter be returned to the White House for further examination.

As you know, the President has authority in this field only where it involves international matters. Under the circumstances, since both chairmen were members of the other party, and since also I had received suggestions from a number of other Congressmen, both Democratic and Republican, as well as Senators, that this should be re-examined, I brought it back for re-examination.

One other point that should be made: There is no suggestion, in asking for a re-examination of that decision, of impropriety or illegality, or improper influence. We will examine the whole situation, but particularly with regard to its impact on foreign relations.

Q. Mr. President, Ramsey Clark stated this morning that you gave President Johnson assurances through Attorney General Mitchell that you would not withdraw the traditional nominations of Mr. Poole and Mr. Byrne and several others. Could you comment on that, sir?

THE PRESIDENT. I remember exactly what did occur, and it may be that we did not have an exact meeting of the minds in the event that Ramsey Clark, former Attorney General Clark, had that understanding. What happened was that Ramsey Clark discussed this matter during the period between the election and the inauguration with Attorney General Mitchell. He asked Attorney General Mitchell to ask me whether I would object to action on the part of President Johnson in the event that he did submit these appointments to the Senate.

My reply was that I would not object to President Johnson submitting such names to the Senate just as I do not object to his action in the Trans-Pacific case or any other area. As you ladies and gentlemen are quite aware, I have scrupulously followed the line that we have one President at a time, and that he must continue to be President until he leaves office on January 20.

However, I did not have any understanding with the President directly, and no one, including Attorney General Mitchell, as far as I was concerned had any discretion to agree

to a deal that these nominations, having been made, would be approved by me. I have withdrawn them and now I am going to examine each one of them. As I have already indicated, I have decided that in at least some instances some of the names will be re-submitted.

TFX Contract

Q. Mr. President, in the last Administration, the McClellan Committee ran into a considerable problem in obtaining information on costs, performance and development on the TFX, F-111 contract. I wondered if you would open the records on this, and what your general view is with regard to dealing with Congressional committees?

THE PRESIDENT. I understand not only the McClellan Committee, but Mr. Mollenhoff did some examination in this field, too.

With regard to the TFX, and also with regard to all of the matters that you have referred to, this Administration will re-examine all past decisions where they are not foreclosed, where the re-examination is not foreclosed, by reason of what has gone before.

I will not, however, at this time, pre-judge what that examination will indicate. I believe that it is in the best interests of the nation, when a new Administration comes in, with a new team, that the President direct the new team, as I have directed it very strongly during this first week, to re-examine all decisions that may have been questioned, either by Senate committees or by responsible members of the press, or by other people in public or private life. This we are doing and this is one of the areas in which a re-examination is going forward.

Economic Policy

Q. Mr. President, inflation and rising prices are of great concern. What specific plans do you have to curb these?

THE PRESIDENT. In the meeting of the Cabinet Committee on Economic Policy, which I set up, one of the three new institutions I set up—I say three new institutions—if I might digress for a moment, I suppose the nation wonders what a President does in his first week and where is all the action that we have talked about. We have done a great deal, particularly in getting the machinery of Government set up which will allow us to move in an orderly way on major problems.

I do not believe, for example, that policy should be made, and particularly foreign policy should be made, by off the cuff responses in press conferences, or any other kind of conferences. I think it should be made in an orderly way. So it is with economic policy. That is why, in addition to the Cabinet committee, in addition to the Urban Affairs Council and a revitalized National Security Council for foreign affairs, we now have a Cabinet Committee on Economic Policy.

That Cabinet committee has considered the problem of inflation, and the problem is, first, that we are concerned about the escalation of prices to a rate of 4.8 percent, and we do not see, if present policies continue, any substantial reduction in that.

And, second, we are considering what actions can be taken which will not cause an unacceptable rise in unemployment. By unacceptable rise in unemployment, I want to emphasize that we believe it is possible to control inflation without increasing unemployment in, certainly, any substantial way.

I should make one further point. Unless we do control inflation, we will be confronted, eventually, with massive unemployment, because the history of economic affairs in other countries indicates that if inflation is allowed to get out of hand, eventually there has to be a bust and then unemployment comes. So what we are trying to do, without, shall we say, too much managing of the economy, is we are going to have some fine tuning of our fiscal and monetary affairs in order to control inflation.

One other point I should make in this respect: I do not go along with the suggestion that inflation can be effectively controlled by exhorting labor and management and industry to follow certain guidelines. I think that is a very laudable objective for labor and management to follow. But I think I am aware of the fact that the leaders of labor and the leaders of management, much as they might personally want to do what is in the best interest of the nation, have to be guided by the interests of the organizations that they represent.

So the primary responsibility for controlling inflation rests with the national administration, and its handling of fiscal and monetary affairs. That is why we will have some new approaches in this area. We assume that responsibility. We think we can meet it, that we can control inflation without an increase in unemployment.

Vietnam Settlement

Q. Mr. President, during the transition period in New York, several persons who conferred with you came away with the impression that you felt the Vietnam War might be ended within a year. Were these impressions correct?

THE PRESIDENT. I, of course, in my conversations with those individuals, and all individuals, have never used the term "six months," "a year," "two years," or "three years," because I do not think it is helpful in discussing this terribly difficult war, a war that President Johnson wanted to bring to an end as early as possible, that I want to bring to an end as early as possible.

I do not think it is helpful to make overly optimistic statements which, in effect, may impede and perhaps might make very difficult our negotiations in Paris. All that I have to say is this: that we have a new team in Paris, with some old faces, but a new team. We have new direction from the United States. We have a new sense of urgency with regard to the negotiations.

There will be new tactics. We believe that those tactics may be more successful than the tactics of the past.

I should make one further point, however. We must recognize that all that has happened to date is the settlement of the procedural problems, the size of the table, and who will sit at those tables.

What we now get to is really that hard, tough ground that we have to plow: the substantive issues as to what both parties will agree to; whether we are going to have mutual withdrawal; whether we are going to have self-determination by the people of South Vietnam without outside interference; whether we can have an exchange of prisoners.

This is going to take time, but I can assure you that it will have my personal attention. It will have my personal direction. The Secretary of State, my Adviser for National Security Affairs, the Secretary of Defense—all of us—will give it every possible attention and we hope to come up with some new approaches.

THE PRESS. Thank you, Mr. President.

FEBRUARY 6

Following is the complete text of President Nixon's Feb. 6 news conference, his second, held nine days after his first news conference.

THE PRESIDENT: Ladies and gentlemen, as you will note from a release from the Press Office, I will leave on the 23rd of this month for a trip to Europe which will take me to Brussels, to London, to Berlin and Bonn, to Rome and to Paris.

I will be accompanied on the trip by the Secretary of State, Mr. Rogers, and by my adviser for National Security Affairs, Dr. Kissinger.

The purpose of the trip I will describe as being a working trip rather than a protocol trip. I plan to see in each of the countries I visit the head of government, and in addition to that, I will have a visit with the members of our United States Delegation in Paris, headed by Ambassador Lodge, and will have a meeting with Pope Paul in Rome.

While I am in Brussels, I will see leaders of the NATO community. As far as the agenda is concerned for these meet-

ings, it is wide open. I have some ideas about the future of the European community which I will discuss, and I am sure that my colleagues in that community have some ideas that they will want to discuss.

I have requested that in addition to the usual group meetings which will take place, that I have an opportunity to have an individual, face-to-face meeting with each head of government, with no one present except a translator when needed.

As I look at this trip and what it may accomplish, I want to make very clear that this is only a first step in achieving a purpose that I have long felt to be vital to the future of peace for the United States and for the world. That is the strengthening and revitalizing of the American-European community.

This will be the first, I would hope, of several meetings of this type that will take place in the years ahead. I would trust that as a result of this meeting, and as a result of other meetings that will take place, this great alliance which, in my view, has been the greatest force for peace, to keep the peace, over the last 20 years—this great alliance which was brought together by a common fear 20 years ago—will be held together now and strengthened by a common sense of purpose.

I will now go to your questions. Mr. Smith?

Paris Talks

Q. Mr. President, in connection with your visit to Paris and your talks with Ambassador Lodge, do you see any possibility of your having any direct contact with the other side in these negotiations, specifically, the representatives of North Vietnam or the NLF?

THE PRESIDENT: Mr. Smith, I do not see any possibility of that kind of conversation at this time. I would not rule it out at some later time, if Ambassador Lodge and others who have responsibility for negotiation thought it were wise.

With Ambassador Lodge and his colleagues, I hope to get a complete report on the progress of the negotiations and also any recommendations that he or they may have with regard to new initiatives that we might take to make more progress than we have made.

I think we have made a good start in Paris, incidentally. I believe that we can now move forward to some substantive achievements.

Mr. Cormier?

Soviet Leaders

Q. Mr. President, looking beyond this trip, can you give us a clue of your attitude on the possibility of future meetings with Soviet leaders?

THE PRESIDENT: I believe that a meeting with Soviet leaders should take place at a future time. I should make clear that I think that where summitry is concerned, I take a dim view of what some have called instant summitry, particularly where there are very grave differences of opinion between those who are to meet.

I believe that a well prepared summit meeting, where we have on the table the various differences that we have, on which we can perhaps make progress, would be in our interest and in their interest, and it will be my intention after this trip is completed to conduct exploratory talks at various levels to see if such a meeting could take place.

I should point out, incidentally, that one of the reasons that this trip takes precedence is that I have long felt that before we have meetings of summitry with the Soviet leaders, it is vitally important that we have talks with our European allies, which we are doing.

Yes sir?

Vietnam Troops

Q. Mr. President, this morning South Vietnamese President Thieu said that the South Vietnamese army is capable of relieving a sizeable number of American troops in Vietnam. What is your understanding of sizeable, and do you think that there will actually be a reduction of the number of American troops?

THE PRESIDENT: Well, speaking personally, and also as the Commander of the Armed Forces, I do not want an American boy to be in Vietnam for one day longer than is necessary for our national interest. As our Commanders in the field determine that the South Vietnamese are able to assume a greater portion of the responsibility for the defense of their own territory, troops will come back. However, at this time, I have no announcements to make with regard to the return of troops.

I will only say that it is high on the agenda of priorities, and that just as soon as either the training program for South Vietnamese forces and their capabilities, the progress of the Paris peace talks, or other developments make it feasible to do so, troops will be brought back.

Yes, sir?

South Vietnamese

Q. Mr. President, on your trip to Paris, do you plan to see the South Vietnamese negotiators there? In that connection, a general question on the talks themselves: Do you think you can continue to separate the military issues from the political issues, and the political settlement of South Vietnam in the negotiations in Paris?

THE PRESIDENT: Well, Mr. Lisagor, that is one of the matters that I want to discuss with Ambassador Lodge, to get his judgment on that point. It is our view that at this time the separation of those two items is in our interest and in the interest of bringing progress in those talks.

Now, as far as meeting with the South Vietnamese leaders is concerned, we have no present plans to do so. If Ambassador Lodge advises that it would be wise to do so, such meetings will be scheduled. There will be enough time in the schedule for a meeting if he does suggest it.

Yes, sir?

UN Ambassador

Q. Mr. President, your nominee and now your Ambassador to the United Nations, Mr. Yost, has been under attack from some conservative groups, such as the Liberty Lobby, for his past associations with certain individuals, particularly including Alger Hiss. In light of your more than passing familiarity with the Hiss case, will you comment on these attacks on Mr. Yost and whether they should be given credence?

THE PRESIDENT: As far as Mr. Yost's background is concerned, I am completely aware of it because, of course, all of these matters are brought to my attention before appointments are made. But what I am looking to now is his capability to handle the problems of the future and not events that occurred over 20 years ago.

There is no question about his loyalty to this country. And I also think there is no question about his very good judgment on critical issues confronting the United States, particularly in the Mideast.

As I pointed out, he is one of our prime experts in the Mideast. He sat in on the National Security Council meetings when we discussed the Mideast and made some very valuable contributions.

Middle East

Q. Mr. President, on the Middle East, now that you have completed your review with the NSC, you spoke of the need for new initiatives, can you tell us what your policy is going to be now and what initiatives you do expect to take?

THE PRESIDENT: Mr. Bailey, our initiatives in the Mideast I think can well be summarized by that very word that you have used. What we see now is a new policy on the part of the United States in assuming the initiative. We are not going to stand back and rather wait for something else to happen.

We are going to assume it on what I would suggest five fronts.

We are going to continue to give our all-out support to the Jarring Mission. We are going to have bilateral talks at the United Nations, preparatory to the talks between the four powers. We shall have four-power talks at the United Nations. We shall also have talks with the countries in the area, with the Israelis and their neighbors, and, in addition, we want to go forward on some of the long range plans, the Eisenhower-Strauss plan for relieving some of the very grave economic problems in that area.

We believe that the initiative here is one that cannot be simply unilateral. It must be multilateral. And it must not be in one direction. We are going to pursue every possible avenue to peace in the Mideast that we can.

Mr. Semple?

Tax Reform

Q. Mr. President, how do you feel about the Johnson Administration's tax reform proposal that would exempt many poor families from paying any taxes at all, but would guarantee that wealthy families at least pay some minimum income tax? We are told that you are sending up a tax reform proposal and would like to get your opinion.

THE PRESIDENT: Tax reform has been a matter of discussion within Administration councils during the past week. In a discussion which I understand has already been widely publicized that I had with Chairman Mills of the Ways and Means Committee, and the ranking Republican, Mr. Byrnes, we went over the agenda and also the timetable as to when the proposals should come down.

The Secretary of the Treasury will have a preliminary announcement to make on tax reform tomorrow. He will make major tax reform recommendations to the Congress at a later time.

But at this time I do not want to indicate in advance the areas in which we are going to move. I will say that the two areas that you mentioned were considered and were discussed in the conference that we had here in the White House with the ranking members of the Ways and Means Committee.

Latin America

Q. Mr. President, would you please tell us how you plan to move in solving some of the problems of Latin America? Have you decided on your Assistant Secretary of State in that field?

THE PRESIDENT: I believe we have decided on the Assistant Secretary of State, but I am not yet prepared to make the announcement because the necessary clearances have not taken place.

May I make one thing very clear: I have noticed news stories to the effect that the job was going begging and we were unable to find a qualified man. We have several qualified people but the Secretary of State and I agree that this is an area of top priority. We think we need new initiatives with regard to the Alliance for Progress.

I would describe that in this way: I think the difficulty in the past, a well-intentioned difficulty, has been that we have been putting too much emphasis on what we are going to do for Latin America and not enough emphasis on what we are going to do with our Latin American friends. The new Assistant Secretary will attempt to remedy that and we shall attempt to develop new policies.

Sentinel System

Q. Mr. President, the Pentagon announced this morning that Secretary Laird had ordered a temporary halt in the construction of the Sentinel System, pending a high level review. Does that represent a change in policy on our part? Does it indicate that maybe we are getting somewhere with the Russians toward an agreement whereby neither one of us would have to build it?

THE PRESIDENT: Mr. Kaplow, answering the second part of your question first, there has been no progress with regard to the arms control talks with the Russians. I have made it clear in the appointment of Mr. Smith to that position that we are going to put emphasis on those talks, but I do believe we should go forward on settling some of the political differences at the same time.

As far as the decision on the Sentinel is concerned, Secretary Laird and his colleagues at the Defense Department will make decisions based on the security of the United States, and he will announce those decisions and justify them at this point.

Asia

Q. Mr. President, there has been some apprehension, sir, in Asia that your re-emphasis on U.S. relations with Europe would mean a lessening of U.S. interests in Asia. Would you comment on that, sir?

THE PRESIDENT: This gives me an opportunity to perhaps state my philosophy about emphasis on different parts of the world.

The reason that we have been discussing the Mideast a great deal lately is that it is an area of the world which might explode into a major war. Therefore, it needs immediate attention. That does not mean, however, that we are not going to continue to put attention on Latin America, on Africa, on Asia.

I think you could describe me best as not being a "half-worlder," with my eyes looking only to Europe or only to Asia, but one who sees the whole world. We live in one world and we must go forward together in this whole world.

Yes, sir?

China Threat

Q. Mr. President, you know the ABM system was planned originally to protect us against the threat of a nuclear attack by Red China early in the 1970s. Does your information indicate that there is any lessening of this threat, or greater, or just where do we stand on that?

THE PRESIDENT: First, I do not buy the assumption that the ABM system, the thin Sentinel system, as it has been described, was simply for the purpose of protecting ourselves against attack from Communist China.

This system, as are the systems that the Soviet Union have already deployed, adds to our over-all defense capability. I would further say that, as far as the threat is concerned, we do not see any change in that threat, and we are examining, therefore, all of our defense systems and all of our defense postures to see how we can best make them consistent with our other responsibilities.

Department of Peace

Q. Mr. President, as you are aware, I am sure, there has been discussion on the Hill about trying to set up a Department of Peace to include the Peace Corps and the Disarmament Agency and other organizations. I wondered about your reaction to that idea.

THE PRESIDENT: In fact, one of my task forces recommended a Department of Peace. I think, however, that derogates, and improperly downgrades, the role of the Department of State and the Department of Defense.

I consider the Department of State to be a Department of Peace. I consider the Department of Defense to be a Department of Peace, and I can assure you that at the White House level, in the National Security Council, that is where we coordinate all our efforts toward peace.

I think putting one department over here as a Department of Peace would tend to indicate that the other departments were engaged in other activities that were not interested in peace.

Cigarette Ads

Q. Mr. President, will you support the FCC proposal to ban cigarette advertising on radio and TV?

THE PRESIDENT: Well, as a non-smoker, it wouldn't pose any problems to me. I, however, have only had that FCC proposal brought to my attention by the late TV reports last night and the morning papers. I have not yet had an opportunity to evaluate it. After I have evaluated it, I will make an announcement as to my position.

School Desegregation

Q. Mr. President, there has been conflicting speculation about the extent to which your Administration will seek to advance school desegregation. Could you tell us what your policy will be on that, specifically including the so-called "freedom of choice" plan?

THE PRESIDENT: That was a subject, as you will recall from having covered me in the campaign, that I addressed myself to on several occasions.

First, as far as freedom of choice is concerned, freedom of choice must be defined in terms of what it does. If freedom of choice is found to be simply a subterfuge to perpetuate segregation, then funds should be denied to such a school system. If a freedom of choice plan, however, is found to be one which actually is bringing an end to segregation, then a freedom of choice plan, in my opinion, is appropriate and should receive funds.

As far as school segregation is concerned, I support the law of the land. I believe that funds should be denied to those districts that continue to perpetuate segregation. I think that what we have here is a very difficult problem, however, in implementing it. One is our desire, a desire that was emphasized by Dr. Allen, to keep our schools open, because education must receive the highest priority. The other is our desire to see to it that our schools are not segregated.

That is why I have, in discussing this with Secretary Finch, and with Dr. Allen, urged that before we use the ultimate weapon of denying funds and closing a school, let's exhaust every other possibility to see that local school districts do comply with the law.

Urban School Aid

Q. Mr. President, do you support Dr. Allen's statement of yesterday that he believes massive aid to urban schools is necessary?

THE PRESIDENT: Well, I support the proposition that there needs to be a massive infusion of assistance to education. Let me make one thing very clear in that respect, so that you can get my thinking directly. You will note yesterday that I supported a $10 million increase in the fund for the National Science Foundation, which will go to higher education.

I believe higher education needs more assistance, too. But at the present time the great need is in the area described by educators of "K through 12," kindergarten through 12th grade —preparing students in those years for the higher education which is now available to virtually every student who is capable of meeting the standards for getting into college.

As far as Dr. Allen's method of doing so, I do not believe that he, sophisticated as he is as the Superintendent of a State School System, would suggest that we go around the states. We cannot do that because the cities and the school systems within a state cannot exist without the state government.

However, the area of need is primarily in the city school systems. We will try to meet that problem as best we can.

Oil Pollution

Q. Mr. President, may I ask you two questions about the disaster in Santa Barbara. One, do Secretary Hickel's actions so far accord with your policies; and two, what implications does this disaster have for future conservation policy here?

THE PRESIDENT: Well, answering the second part of your question first, I have found that for 15 years we have not had any up-dating of our policies with regard to off-shore drilling. Secretary Hickel has now initiated a study within the Department for up-dating those regulations so that this kind of incident will not occur again.

With regard to the action that he has taken, I think he acted promptly in temporarily stopping the drilling and then insisting on very stringent requirements on the Union Oil Company and others involved so that this would not happen.

Looking to the future however, we have got to get at the source of the problem. That means very stringent regulations in off-shore drilling, because there isn't any question that if the companies involved will make the necessary expenditures in setting up their wells off-shore, there is minimal danger of this kind of an activity.

Labor Disputes

Q. Mr. President, we were told yesterday by the Congressional Leaders, that in dealing with labor disputes, like the dock strike, you preferred a permanent, long-range approach. And yet there seems to be real scepticism on the Hill that anything will be done. Can you give us your views currently on this?

THE PRESIDENT: Well, my view with regard to the dock strike is that for the White House to indicate publicly that we are going to do this and that generally has the effect of telling the parties to do nothing. For that reason, I think Secretary Schultz very properly is playing a mediating role but making it very clear that the primary responsibility is on the parties themselves.

Now, long range, I believe that the Taft-Hartley Act's provisions for national emergency strikes, which I helped to write along with other members of the Labor Committee 20 years ago, that those provisions are now outmoded. I do not believe we have enough options in dealing with these kinds of disputes and breakdowns. I have, therefore, asked the Department of Labor to develop some new approaches in this field, and we will submit them by legislation to this Congress.

Distrust Among Blacks

Q. Mr. President, do you agree with those who say that you and your Administration have a serious problem with distrust among the blacks, and whether you agree that it is one of your more serious problems or not could you tell us specifically what you are doing to deal with what some consider to be this distrust among the blacks?

THE PRESIDENT: I am concerned about this problem; and incidentally, let me make it very clear that those who have raised this question are not simply those who are political opponents. My Task Force on Education pointed up that I was not considered—I think the words they used—as a friend by many of our black citizens in America.

I can only say that, by my actions as President, I hope to rectify that. I hope that by what we do in terms of dealing with the problems of all Americans, it will be made clear that the President of the United States, as an elected official, has no state constituency. He has no Congressional constituency. He does not represent any special group. He represents all the people. He is the friend of all the people.

Putting it another way, as a lawyer, the President is the counsel for all the people of this country, and I hope that I can gain the respect and I hope eventually the friendship of black citizens and other Americans.

NSC-State Department

Q. Mr. President, there has been some confusion this week on the relationship between the National Security Council and the State Department. For example, the Assistant Secretary of State reporting to the NSC. Could you clarify that for us, please?

THE PRESIDENT: Yes. The Secretary of State is my chief foreign policy adviser and the chief agent of this Government in carrying out foreign policy abroad. As one of my very close friends, personally, he advises me independently as well as through the National Security Council.

The question has also, I know, been raised as to who makes the policy and the decisions? Are they made in the National Security Council or are they made in the State Department?

The answer is, neither place. The State Department advises the President. The National Security Council advises the President. The President has the authority to make decisions, and I intend to exercise that authority.

Import Quotas

Q. Mr. President, during the election campaign, sir, you said that you would seek international agreements to limit the import of certain textiles. Can you tell us when you plan to get around to doing that?

Also could you give us some idea as to what you feel about the growing feeling of protectionism in Congress?

THE PRESIDENT: Let me start at the second part of the question first. I believe that the interest of the United States and the interest of the whole world will best be served by moving toward freer trade rather than toward protectionism.

I take a dim view of this tendency to move toward quotas and other methods that may become permanent, whether they are applied here or by other nations abroad.

Second, as far as the textile situation is concerned, that is a special problem which has caused very great distress in certain parts of this country, and to a great number of wage earners, as well as those who operate our textile facilities.

For that reason, exploratory discussions have taken place and will be taking place with the major countries involved to see if we can handle this on a volunteer basis rather than having to go to a legislation which would impose quotas, and I think would turn the block back in our objective of trying to achieve freer trade.

Pueblo Seizure

Q. Mr. President, there has been a court of inquiry in the city of Coronado for several weeks now on the PUEBLO seizure. Do you think it is proper for the Navy, in effect, to be sitting in judgment of itself, or do you see any need for any kind of Presidential commission on this?

THE PRESIDENT: Well, as a Navy man, I know that the Navy has procedures which I think very adequately protect the rights of defendants in courts martial.

Second, I believe those procedures, from my investigation to date, have been very scrupulously followed.

Third, however, because of the great interest in this case, the Secretary of Defense has asked, as you know, Mr. Packard, the Deputy Secretary, to conduct a thorough investigation, not only of the handling of this case, but also an investigation as to how we can avoid this kind of an incident occurring in the future.

I also want to make it clear that I, as the Chief Executive of the Nation, will examine the whole record myself, both with regard to the individual guilt or innocence of the people involved, and also with regard to the even more important objective of seeing to it that this kind of incident can be avoided in the future.

Nonproliferation Treaty

Q. Mr. President, you have now asked the Senate to ratify the Nonproliferation Treaty. On your trip to Europe, do you have any hopes of trying to persuade particularly West Germany and France to move a little closer toward signing that treaty?

THE PRESIDENT: My view about asking other governments to follow our lead is this: They know what we think, and I am sure that matter will come up for discussion.

I will make it clear that I believe that ratification of the treaty by all governments, nuclear and non-nuclear, is in the interest of peace and in the interest of reducing the possibility of nuclear proliferation.

On the other hand, I do not believe that we gain our objectives through heavy-handed activities, publicly particularly, in attempting to get others to follow our lead. Each of these governments is a soverign government. Each has its own political problems. I think in the end, most of our friends in Western Europe will follow our lead. I will attempt to persuade, but I will not, certainly, attempt to use any blackmail or arm-twisting.

Appointment of Women

Q. Mr. President, in staffing your Administration, you have so far made about 200 high-level Cabinet and other policy position appointments, and of these only three have gone to women. Could you tell us, sir, whether we can expect a more equitable recognition of women's abilities, or are we going to remain a lost sex?

THE PRESIDENT: Would you be interested in coming into the Government?

Very seriously, I had not known that only three had gone to women, and I shall see that we correct that imbalance very promptly.

Czech Invasion

Q. On the Nonproliferation Treaty again, last fall during the campaign, Mr. President, you opposed ratification of the treaty because of the Soviet invasion of Czechoslovakia. Can you tell me, sir, how you feel that situation has changed since then?

THE PRESIDENT: It has changed in the sense that the number of Soviet forces in Czechoslovakia has been substantially reduced.

It has changed also in the sense that the passage of time tends somewhat to reduce the pent-up feelings that were then present with regard to the Soviet Union's actions.

I want to make it very clear that in asking the Senate to ratify the treaty, I did not gloss over the fact that we still very strongly disapproved of what the Soviet Union had done in Czechoslovakia and what it still is doing. But on balance, I considered that this was the time to move forward on the treaty, and have done so.

THE PRESS: Thank you, Mr. President.

MARCH 4

Following is the complete transcript of President Nixon's March 4 news conference, his third, held 26 days after his second conference.

THE PRESIDENT: Ladies and Gentlemen, as you know, the purpose of this unusually long Press Conference is to report to the American people on my trip to Europe.

Because I realize that there will probably be a number of questions, some of which may require some rather lengthy answers, I am going to make my opening statement quite brief.

A word about the purpose and also the limitations of a trip like this: I believe all of us in this room have no illusions about the limits of personal diplomacy in settling great differences and great general difficulties. A smile or handshake or an exchange of toasts or gifts or visits will not by themselves have effect where vital interests are concerned and where there are great differences.

On the other hand, I have learned that there is an intangible factor which does affect the relations between nations. I think it was perhaps best described by two of our visitors, those

with whom I was talking. One was in the case of Prime Minister Wilson. He used the term "mutual trust" when he welcomed me. The other, President de Gaulle, when he came to the American Embassy, used the term "confiance"—trust.

When there is trust between men who are leaders of nations there is a better chance to settle differences than when there is not trust. I think that one of the accomplishments of this trip is that we have established between the United States of America and the major nations of Europe—and I trust, other nations of Europe, as well—a new relationship of trust and confidence that did not exist before.

For example, as we look at the relations with France, they are different today than they were a week ago. How different they are, only time will tell. But that they are different and improved, I think, would be a fair assessment of that situation.

We can also say that as a result of this trip, the United States has indicated its continuing support of the Alliance—the Atlantic Alliance—and that we have also indicated our support of the concept and ideal of European unity.

In addition, we have indicated that we recognize our limitations insofar as European unity is concerned. Americans cannot unify Europe. Europeans must do so. And we should not become involved in differences among Europeans in which our vital interests are not involved.

Finally, a word that I think all of the American people will be gratified to hear. Sometimes we become rather disillusioned with our aid programs around the world, and we look back on our relations with Europe, particularly, and wonder if it was really worth all that we did immediately after World War II, in terms of the Marshall Plan and other programs.

Anyone who saw Europe as I did, in that period of devastation after World War II, when I visited all the countries except Belgium at that time, that I visited on this trip, and then saw it today, would realize that it was worth doing, because today a strong, prosperous, free Europe stands there, partly a result of our aid.

It could not have happened without our aid. It also, of course, could not have happened without their great efforts on their own behalf. And so, with that recognition, we now realize that this Alliance deserves our attention, should be the center of our concern, should not be taken for granted. It will not be. That will be a major objective of this Administration.

Now, as we go to your questions, I will take questions not only on the European trip, but any area of foreign policy, because on the trip I discussed with the leaders of Europe all areas of foreign policy, which was their desire and mine as well.

There will be only one ground rule. I know there will be great interest in what each of the leaders said to me and what I said to them. I will not divulge the content of these personal conversations, because if we are going to build confidence, we can't build confidence by breaking confidences.

We will go to the questions.

Summit

Q. Mr. President, we got the impression travelling with you that there was some relationship between your tour and a possible East-West summit at some future time. Could you relate the two?

THE PRESIDENT: Mr. Cormier, this tour was a condition precedent to an East-West summit at a later time. I have always indicated that before we had talks with those who have opposed us in the world, it was essential that we had clear understandings with our allies and friends.

I think at times in the past we have not had that kind of consultation. It was essential to have it on this trip. In every visit that I had, I discussed East-West relations with the leaders involved, discussed not only what our plans were, and what our policies might be, but got their views and their advice as to what programs they thought we should handle in any bilateral discussions we had with the Soviet Union.

Red China

Q. Mr. President, during the trip, and as recently as the conclusion of the trip Sunday night, you spoke of hoping that with greater unity with our allies, you would be able to develop new understanding with those who have opposed us on the other side of the world.

To follow up on Mr. Cormier's question, of whom are you speaking, sir? We assume the Russians. Are you thinking, for instance, you may be able to reach a better understanding with Red China?

THE PRESIDENT: Looking further down the road, we could think in terms of a better understanding with Red China. But being very realistic, in view of Red China's breaking off the rather limited Warsaw talks that were planned, I do not think that we should hold out any great optimism for any break-throughs in that direction at this time.

Certainly you are correct in assuming that in referring to those who oppose us in the world, I was referring primarily to the Soviet Union and to the talks that the United States would be having with the Soviet Union in a number of areas.

Europeans, I found, were greatly concerned by what they called the possibility of a U.S.-Soviet condominium, in which at the highest level the two superpowers would make decisions affecting their future without consulting them.

In fact, one statesman used the term Yalta. He said, "We don't want another Yalta on the part of the United States and the Soviet Union." Whether his assessment on the part of Yalta is correct or not is immaterial.

The fact about the United States and the Soviet Union making decisions will not happen as a result of this trip.

West Berlin

Q. Mr. President, will you assess for us, sir, the situation in West Berlin, how you see it, whether you think it has reached a crisis point, on the eve of the election?

THE PRESIDENT: The situation in West Berlin at the moment seems to have leveled off. I haven't seen the latest reports. I will have to look at the morning papers to see whether my projection at this point is correct, because it has changed hour from hour.

I believe that we have made our position quite clear to all the parties involved, as we should. We have made it clear to the West German Government, that if they went ahead with the election, that we would support them in that decision, or if they decided that they could gain concessions that they considered significant which would lead them to changing the place for the elections that we would support them in that move.

It is their decision and we are not trying to affect it one way or another. They have a right to have the elections there if they want. Also, we have indicated to the Soviets, the Soviet Ambassador, Mr. Dobrynin, both Mr. Rogers and I have pointed out that any harassment in West Berlin could jeopardize the progress that we see possible in other areas.

I have reported previously in a press conference that I felt that the Soviet Union did not want to see the West Berlin situation become a cause or even a pretext for any move which would be in retrogression insofar as our bilateral relations are concerned.

At this moment, based on the conversations that I have had myself with various European leaders and also the conversation that I and others have had with the representatives of the Soviet Union, I believe that the Soviet Union does not want to have the situation in West Berlin heated up to the point that it would jeopardize some, what they consider to be, more important negotiations at the highest level with the United States, and because those negotiations, in effect, are in the wings, I think I could predict that the Soviet Union will use its influence to cool off the West Berlin situation, rather than to heat it up.

Vatican Envoy

Q. Is it true, Mr. President, in your talks with Pope Paul at the Vatican there is any possibility that the United States might send an envoy to the Vatican as a permanent representative?

THE PRESIDENT: That possibility has been considered by the State Department and by me, because we have been concerned that we should have the very closest consultation and discussion with the Vatican. I found, for example, my conversations with Pope Paul extremely helpful. It was far ranging, and I received information and also counsel that I considered to be very important. I want that line of communication kept open. Whether we can have it kept open based on the present facilities that are available, I have not yet determined. The matter is still under study. But what is important is that the United States have with the Vatican close consultation on foreign policy matters in which the Vatican has a very great interest and very great influence.

Vietnam Offensive

Q. Mr. President, the Communist offensive in Vietnam has aroused speculation that your Administration is being tested, particularly as to the understanding that was reached last November 1, which led to the bombing halt. Would you give us your opinion of this, please?

THE PRESIDENT: Well, in speaking of the Communist offensive, I think it is important first to analyze what it is and what its purposes are compared with the offensive last year, and then see what that offensive means in terms of the violation of the understanding last October 31 or prior to October 31 at the time of the bombing halt.

When we look at the offensive, we find that in terms of the frequency of attacks it is approximately the same as the offensive of last year. In terms of intensity of attacks, it is less than that of last year. As far as the targets are concerned, it is primarily directed toward military targets, but there are also some very significant civilian targets. As far as the purposes are concerned, we can only guess, but three have been suggested, that it might be directed against the government of South Vietnam to break its morale and its back, that it might be directed against public opinion in the United States to put more pressure on the Administration to move more in the direction of North Vietnam's position at the Paris peace talks; or that it might be directed toward a military victory of sorts, if a military victory of sorts could be accomplished in Vietnam by the North Vietnamese against our forces there.

Now, this offensive has failed in all three of these areas. It has failed to achieve any significant military breakthrough. It has failed to break the back of the government of South Vietnam. Far from that, as a matter of fact, in terms of the pacification program, 700,000 were displaced by the Tet offensive last year, and only 25,000 have been displaced by this one. As far as this offensive affecting the United States and its negotiating position in Paris, it could have exactly the opposite effect. I think that therefore we must now analyze the offensive in terms of the understanding of October 31.

That understanding was to the effect that continued shelling, or attacks, on the cities, the major cities of South Vietnam, would be inconsistent with talks toward peace which would be productive in Paris.

Now, we are examining this particular offensive, examining it very carefully, to see whether its magnitude is in violation of that understanding. Technically, it could be said that it is in violation. Whether we reach the conclusion that the violation is so significant that it requires action on our part is a decision we will be reaching very soon if those attacks continue at their present magnitude.

As you know, Secretary Laird is going to South Vietnam tomorrow, and I have asked him to look into the situation and to give me a report after he has been there.

One other factor should be mentioned: I do not want to discount by this analysis the seriousness of these attacks, because the American casualty rate, I note, has doubled during the period of these attacks. Therefore, it is necessary for the American President, in analyzing the attacks, to think not only of the understanding with regard to the attacks on the cities, but also to his obligation to defend American fighting men in Vietnam.

We have not moved in a precipitate fashion, but the fact that we have shown patience and forebearance should not be considered as a sign of weakness. We will not tolerate a continuation of a violation of an understanding. But more than that, we will not tolerate attacks which result in heavier casualties to our men at a time that we are honestly trying to seek peace at the conference table in Paris. An appropriate response to these attacks will be made if they continue.

ABM System

Q. Mr. President, can you tell me if you, after your consultations overseas, have any reservations or have found any reservations on whether we should deploy an ABM system and whether you share any of the scientific reservations that have been expressed in this country?

THE PRESIDENT: The ABM system was not discussed in any detail in my conversations abroad. As far as the decision is concerned, there will be a meeting of the National Security Council tomorrow, which will be entirely devoted to an assessment of that system.

Then, during the balance of the week, I shall make some additional studies on my own involving the Defense Department and other experts whose opinions I value. I will make a decision and announce a decision on ABM at the first of next week.

Q. Mr. President, there have already been reports that you are already considering another trip abroad, maybe to Latin America or Israel. Can you tell us what your plans are?

THE PRESIDENT: I have no plans for foreign travel at this time. I have noted that several other travelers have committed me to trips abroad. I would like very much at an appropriate time to travel to Latin America again. I was there on a well-publicized trip with some of you in 1958. I was back there again at a less publicized one, but with a much more friendly welcome in 1967.

Such a trip, I think, would be valuable at a later time. But, as you know, Governor Rockefeller is going to Latin America to make an intensive study of our Alliance programs, a study which is vital because I think we need some changes in our Latin American policy.

Middle East

Q. Can you tell us whether or not, as a result of your talks with President de Gaulle while in Europe, you are now encouraged about prospects for maintaining peaceful conditions in the Middle East?

THE PRESIDENT: One of the tangible results that came out of this trip was substantial progress on the Middle East. Now, what that progress will be, and whether it reaches an eventual settlement, that is too early to predict.

But I know that when I met with you ladies and gentlemen of the press at an earlier time, the question was raised as to the four-power talks, and there were some who thought that I, and this Administration, was dragging its feet on going into four-power talks.

Frankly, I do not believe that the United States should go into any talks where the decks might be stacked against us. Now, as a result of the consultations that we had on this trip, the positions of our European friends, the British and the French, are now closer to ours than was the case before. We have a better understanding of their position; they have a better understanding of ours.

And also, we have had encouraging talks with the Soviet Ambassador. The Secretary of State and I have both talked with the Soviet Ambassador with regard to the Middle East. We will continue these bilateral consultations and if they continue at their present rate of progress, it seems likely that there will be four-power discussions in the United Nations on the Mideast.

Now, I should indicate also the limitations of such discussions and what can come out of them. The four powers, the Soviet Union, the United States, Great Britain and France cannot dictate a settlement in the Middle East. The time has passed in which great nations can dictate to smaller nations their future in which their vital interests are involved. This kind of assessment we are talking about, and the contributions that can be made to it, is limited in this respect.

The four powers can indicate those areas where they believe the parties directly involved in the Mideast could have profitable discussions. At the present time they are having no discussions at all.

Secondly, and this is even the more important part of it, from the four-power conference can come an absolute essential to any kind of a peaceful settlement in the Mideast, and that is a major power guarantee of the settlement, because we cannot expect the nation of Israel or the other nations in the area who think their major interests might be involved—we cannot expect them to agree to a settlement unless they think there is a better chance that it will be guaranteed in the future than has been the case in the past.

On this score then, we think that we have made considerable progress during the past week. We are cautiously hopeful that we can make more progress and move to the four-power talks very soon.

Response to Attacks

Q. Mr. President, have you considered an appropriate response if the attacks continue in South Vietnam? Would an appropriate response include resumption of the bombing in the North?

THE PRESIDENT: Mr. Wilson, that question is one that I have given thought to but it is one which I think should not be answered in this forum.

I believe that it is far more effective in their national policy to use deeds rather than words threatening deeds, in order to accomplish objectives.

I will only say in answer to that question that the United States has a number of options that we could exercise to respond. We have several contingency plans that can be put into effect.

I am considering all of those plans. We shall use whatever plan we consider is appropriate to the action to the other side. I will not indicate in advance, and I am not going to indicate publicly, and I am not going to threaten—I don't think that would be helpful—that we are going to start bombing the North or anything else.

I will only indicate that we will not tolerate a continuation of this kind of attack without some response that will be appropriate.

De Gaulle Talks

Q. Mr. President, mindful of your ground rule against revealing contents of your conversations with leaders, I ask you this question. Did the atmosphere of mutual trust generated in your long conversations with General de Gaulle give you any fresh indication, any fresh hope that France could be helpful in the future of NATO, and/or France could be helpful in settling the war in Vietnam, either directly or indirectly?

THE PRESIDENT: Well, on the first point, General de Gaulle said publicly, as you will note, what he has said in the past, that he supported the alliance.

He has withdrawn France's forces from the military side of the alliance but he supports the alliance, and he in his conversations backed that up very vigorously.

With regard to whether or not there is a possibility that France could move back into NATO in its military complex, I would not hold out at this time any hope that that might happen.

I would hold out, however, some hope that as our conversations continue, we can find a number of areas for mutual cooperation and consultation on the military side as well as in other respects.

I think that beyond that, it would not be appropriate to indicate what General de Gaulle's position is. As far as Vietnam is concerned, we did discuss it and whether it was Vietnam, or whether it was the Mideast, or whether it was U.S. relations with other countries where the French might be helpful, I received from General de Gaulle very encouraging indications that they would like to be helpful where we thought they could be helpful.

I wouldn't go beyond that, but I was very encouraged with the General's attitude. It was one of helpfulness in every respect on all of the major issues.

Kiesinger Talks

Q. Mr. President, in your conversations with Chancellor Kiesinger, do you believe that you convinced him that his government's reservations against joining in the Nuclear Non-Proliferation Treaty were not valid, and that joining in the treaty would be in West Germany's best interests?

THE PRESIDENT: I think it would be appropriate to say that the German Government has considerable difficulties with regard to ratification of the treaty—difficulties which we need to understand even though we may not agree with their position.

Their attitude as far as we are concerned is quite well known. They know that I have sent the treaty to the Senate, that the Senate will probably give its advice and consent and that we will ratify.

They know, too, my position, that it is not only in the interests of the United States but that I believe it is in the interests of all governments, including the West German Government, to ratify.

I did not put pressure on them, publicly or privately, and I will not put pressure on them publicly or privately. But I believe that since it is in their interest to ratify the treaty that after consideration without pressure the West German Government will at an appropriate time ratify the treaty.

Soviet Union

Q. Mr. President, you said in the recent past that you thought the United States might put some pressure, or use the Soviet Union, or seek to enlist the Soviet Union's help in Vietnam. I wonder if since you have become President you have moved in that respect, trying to get them to alleviate the situation or help solve it?

THE PRESIDENT: Mr. Lisagor, as you know, the Soviet Union is in a very delicate and sensitive position as far as Vietnam is concerned. I do not divulge any confidences from the Soviet Ambassador in indicating that is the case. You ladies and gentlemen have written it and you are correct, because here you have Communist China aiding North Vietnam. You also have the Soviet Union aiding North Vietnam. Each is vying for power in the Communist world and, therefore, what the Soviet Union does in the Vietnamese conflict is a very difficult decision for them as related to that objective—the objective of leadership in the Communist world. It is well known that the Soviet Union was helpful in terms of getting the Paris peace talks started, that the Soviet Union was helpful in working out the arrangement for the shape of the table, and I think I could say that based on the conversations that the Secretary of State and I have had with the Soviet Ambassador, I believe at this time that the Soviet Union shares the concern of many other nations in the world about the extension of the war in Vietnam, its continuing. They recognize that if it continues over a long period of time, the possibility of escalation increases. And I believe the Soviet Union would like to use what influence it could appropriately to help bring the war to a conclusion. What it can do, however, is something that only the Soviet Union would be able to answer to, and it would probably have to answer privately, not publicly.

International Trade

Q. Mr. President, can you tell us what international trade items came up in your trip to Europe; also, specifically could you tell us whether you discussed the problems of textile and steel imports to this country?

THE PRESIDENT: All international imports came up, and I discussed the problem of textiles and steel in all the countries involved. The Europeans are concerned about some of what they think are our restrictions in the trade area. For example, they talk about the American selling price, and they talk about the Buy American programs. I pointed out that many of our Congressional people, as well as American businessmen, were concerned about border taxes and other devices which we thought presented a problem.

I also pointed out in our conversations that there were 93 bills in the last session of the Senate alone which were introduced that would have called for quotas in the various products that you mentioned, and others as well, and that unless some voluntary restrictions or restraints were worked out on textiles particularly that the pressure for legislative quotas would be immense.

I also indicated that I favored freer trade rather than restrictions on trade, but that it would be very difficult to resist that kind of pressure in the event that some action were not taken to deal with the problem.

A final note in this respect: As we look at the whole trade pattern, I think we have to realize that we can not anticipate in the near future another big round of reductions of tariff barriers. We are going to do well if we can digest what we have on the plate. This is my view, and I found that was the view of our major European friends. I believe that we can make considerable progress in that area. Secretary Stans is going to Europe next month for the specific purpose of discussing trade problems with all of our European friends, with the hope that we can work out some of these differences.

Q. Mr. President, sir, I wonder if you think that the Soviets are anxious to bring the war to an end, or at least not prolong it, and I wonder if you have asked them if they will cut off their supplies to Hanoi?

THE PRESIDENT: We have had discussions, as I already indicated, with the Soviet Ambassador. I do not think it would be appropriate, however, to disclose our discussions with him any more than it is appropriate to disclose our discussions with others that we have dealt with that are supposed to be confidential in nature. I am sure that the Soviet Union is keenly aware of the fact that we would be greatly gratified by anything that they could do that could pull some of the support away from the government of North Vietnam. You could probably just guess as to what our conversations were, but I will not indicate what they were.

New Approaches

Q. Mr. President, Vice President Ky after meeting with you in Paris said you told him that you had new approaches to the war in Vietnam. Is that correct? And, if so, do you think it inappropriate to tell the American people about it at this time?

THE PRESIDENT: What I think Vice President Ky was referring to was new approaches not so much in the military field, but in terms of the diplomatic initiative. In our discussions with him, and also in our discussions with the American negotiating team, we discussed the approaches that might be made that would break the deadlock.

Now, with regard to the Paris negotiations, I think we can now say that we have neared the end of Phase 1, in which both parties have set out their positions in public forums. Those positions having been set out, we now come to Phase 2, in which we will have hard bargaining on the major points of difference. Our negotiating team has been given some instructions and will be given more with regard to a variety of approaches, approaches which, in some instances, will also be taken by the government of South Vietnam.

One point, incidentally, that I was very encouraged by was that Vice President Ky, speaking for his delegation, was most cooperative in indicating his desire to attempt to find and explore new approaches at the conference table, rather than simply resigning ourselves to a military decision.

Offensive Against Saigon

Q. Mr. President, you mentioned earlier that the offensive against Saigon might have as its objective an adverse effect upon American public opinion.

In the light of the experiences of your predecessor, do you feel that you could keep American public opinion in line if this war were to go on for months or even years?

THE PRESIDENT: Well, I trust that I am not confronted with that problem, when you speak of years. Our objective is to get this war over as soon as we can on a basis that will not leave the seeds of another war there to plague us in the future. We made, we think, some progress. We think that we are going to make some more.

As far as American public opinion is concerned, I think that the American people will support a President if they are told by the President why we are there, what our objectives are, what the costs will be, and what the consequences will be if we took another course of action. It will not be easy. The American people, I can say from having campaigned the country, are terribly frustrated about this war. They would welcome any initiative that they thought could appropriately bring it to an end on some responsible basis.

On the other hand, it is the responsibility of the President to examine all of the options that we have, and then if he finds that the course he has to take is one that is not popular, he has to explain it to the American people and gain their support.

I think I can perhaps be somewhat effective in explaining why we are there, and also in keeping the American people informed as negotiations go on. I intend to do so.

Troop Withdrawal

Q. Mr. President, President Thieu of South Vietnam has spoken publicly, sir, of the possibility of his expectation of withdrawing up to about 50,000 American troops in South Vietnam this year.

Do you see this possibility of a stage-by-stage withdrawal as a practicality?

THE PRESIDENT: The possibility of withdrawing troops is something that we have, as you know, been considering for sometime. There are no plans to withdraw any troops at this time or in the near future.

On the other hand, I have asked for a re-examination of our whole troop level in South Vietnam, and particularly a re-examination of the South Vietnamese effort and the training program of South Vietnamese forces. To the extent that South Vietnamese forces are able to take over a greater burden of the fighting and to the extent, too, that the level of the fighting may decrease, it may be possible to withdraw.

I do not, however, want to indicate at this time that we are going to withdraw 50,000 troops in the near future. I prefer to create the conditions, if we can, where withdrawal can take place and then announce it, rather than to hold up the promise and let people down when it doesn't happen.

Middle East

Q. Mr. President, on the basis of your conversations, can you foresee a condition under which the Israelis and the Arabs could sit at a negotiating table?

THE PRESIDENT: Not at this time, no. I think that we have to recognize that we are far away from the time when the Arabs and the Israeli can sit at the negotiating table. But I believe that by the time we very carefully go down this road of bilateral consultations first, four-power consultations—and incidentally, we are going to consult with the Israeli when they come here, Mr. Eban is going to be here, and there will be, I am sure, consultations on the other side as well—I think when we complete our course of action and come up, if we can, with a four-power recommendation for proceeding, that then it might be possible to bring both sides to a conference table.

Mr. Scali.

Negotiations With Soviet

Q. Mr. President, we were told during the trip that at the appropriate moment you were prepared to begin negotiations with the Soviet Union on a broad front and that these negotiations would include not only disarmament but other, possibly, political areas.

What problems do you think as ripe for discussion with the Soviets?

THE PRESIDENT: I should first indicate that talks already are going on with the Soviet Union in one sense. The discussions that the Secretary of State and I have had with Ambassador Dobrynin have been substantive and have been talks, in effect, with the Soviet Government, because he had consulted with his own government before he had his talk with me and with the Secreaty of State.

The talks on the Mideast would be the first subject in which bilateral as well as multilateral discussions could take place.

The possibility, also, of discussions on strategic arms. This is a possibility for the future.

Let me indicate where it stands now. We have completed our discussions with some of our European friends. We will have more discussions with them as we get our own position developed. We are going forward with the analysis of the American position of our strategic arms capabilities, of our conventional arms capabilities, so that when we have before us the decision as to whether we go into talks, we will know what our position will be.

Assuming that those studies go forward on schedule, and assuming that we make progress on some of these political areas, like the Mideast, then there is a possibility, a good possibility, that talks could go forward in that area.

I can see those as two areas, and there are others which could develop as well.

Soviet Mideast Policy

Q. Mr. President, I believe you have said, although I couldn't give you the direct quote, but the general assumption is that the Soviet Union is interested in peace in the Middle East. But how can this be reconciled with the fact that they have very quickly rearmed and fully rearmed the Arabs?

What evidence do we have, what proof do we have, that the Soviet Union is interested in fact in peace in the Middle East?

THE PRESIDENT: The Soviet Union's policy in the Mideast and Vietnam, and your question is quite perceptive from that standpoint, is ambivalent.

On the one hand, in Vietnam, they are heating up the war. They furnish 80 percent to 85 percent of the sophisticated military equipment for the North Vietnamese forces. Without that assistance, North Vietnam would not have the capability to wage the major war they are against the United States.

In the Mideast, without what the Soviet Union has done in rearming Israel's neighbors, there would be no crisis there that would require our concern.

On the other hand, at the same time that the Soviet Union has gone forward in providing arms for potential belligerents, potential belligerents in the one area and actual belligerents in the other, the Soviet Union recognizes that if these peripheral areas get out of control, the result could be a confrontation with the United States. And the Soviet Union does not want a confrontation with the United States, anymore than we want one with them, because each of us knows what a confrontation would mean.

I think it is that overwhelming fact, the fact that if the situation in the Mideast and Vietnam is allowed to escalate, it is that fact that it might lead to a confrontation that is giving the Soviet Union second thoughts, and leads me to what I would say the cautious conclusion at this point, that the Soviet Union will play possibly a peace-making role in the Mideast and even possibly in Vietnam.

I say a cautious conclusion because I base this only on talks that have taken place up to this time. But we are going to explore that road all the way that we can, because, let's face it, without the Soviet Union's cooperation the Mideast is going to continue to be a terribly dangerous area, if you continue to pour fuel on those fires of hatred that exist on the borders of Israel. And without the Soviet Union's cooperation it may be difficult to move as fast as we would like in settling the war in Vietnam.

Peru

Q. Mr. President, you mentioned earlier deeds rather than words in our international relations. In our relations with Peru and our problems there, is the United States prepared to take action should Peru not respond to our protest over the seizure of the oil company and attacks on fishing vessels?

THE PRESIDENT: What Peru has done in the seizure of our oil company is that under international law they have the right to expropriate a company but they also have the obligation to pay a fair amount for that expropriation.

It is the second point that is at issue, not the right to expropriate. Now if they do not take appropriate steps to provide for that payment, then under the law, the Hickenlooper Amendment, as you know well know, we will have to take appropriate action with regard to the sugar quota and also with regard to AID programs.

I hope that is not necessary because that would have a domino effect—if I can be permitted to use what is supposed to be an outworn term—a domino effect all over Latin America.

I feel, in my studies in recent days, that we are making some progress in attempting to get some steps taken by the Peruvian Government to deal with the expropriation matter in a fair way. If they do so then we don't have to go down that way.

De Gaulle Praise

Q. Mr. President, there are some people who think you were a little more fulsome in your praise of General de Gaulle than you were of the other European leaders.

Were you conscious of that? Do you have any background you can give us on that?

THE PRESIDENT: I try to have a policy of evenhandedness. I suppose that is a bad word, too—well, it is in the Mideast. In any event, I have the highest regard for all of the leaders that I met. I tried to speak of General de Gaulle with the proper respect that an individual with my background should have speaking to one with his.

After all, of the leaders of Europe, whether we agree or disagree with him, he is the giant, not only in his physical size but in his background and his great influence.

He deserved, I think, the words that I have spoken about him. But I can assure you that in speaking of Prime Minister Wilson, Dr. Kiesinger, President Saragat, and Prime Minister Rumor, I intended to speak of all of them with the same feeling and same affection.

Young People

Q. Mr. President, you demonstrated a great deal of interest in young people in your discussions both public and private abroad. Do you feel that those discussions have given you a better understanding of young people abroad, and are their problems similar to the problems of young people in this country?

THE PRESIDENT: Well, the problems differ, of course, in the different countries. I think that they are the same in one respect. The young people abroad, it seems, have somewhat the same problem of many young people here. They know what they are against, but they find difficulty in knowing what they are for. This is not unusual, because this is perhaps something that is common to young people generally, except that when we look to the revolutions of the past, the revolutionary movements, whether we agreed with those movements or not, there was something of a philosophy that the young people who supported the revolutions were for. All over Europe this seems to be the case. The younger generation is against the established institution, and against the way the universities are run, and yet not having a sense of purpose, a sense of direction, a sense of idealism.

I feel that that is part of the problem here in the United States, and I think that much of the responsibility rests not on the young people for not knowing what they are for, but on older people for not giving them the vision and the sense of purpose and the idealism that they should have.

In talking—and I talked with every leader about this, every one—all of us are concerned about it. All of us feel that we must find for this great western family of ours a new sense of purpose and idealism—one that young people will understand that they can be for.

That is not a satisfactory answer, because I am not able to describe it yet, but, believe me, we are searching for it.

Commitments

Q. Mr. President, there has been some concern in Congress about reports that a general in the Pentagon took the initiative in arranging for the United States to recognize a threat to Spain from North Africa. In your opinion, is this concern merited, and what is the policy of your Administration about the carving out of new commitments to other countries by the United States?

THE PRESIDENT: Well, I think as far as commitments are concerned, the United States has a full plate. I first do not believe that we should make new commitments around the world unless our national interests are very vitally involved. Secondly, I do not believe we should become involved in the quarrels of nations in other parts of the world unless we are asked to become involved and unless also we are vitally involved. I referred earlier to even the quarrels and divisions in Western Europe. I stayed out of most of those up to this point and I intend to in the future.

As far as this report is concerned, with regard to the General on the Spanish bases, I have checked into it, and no commitment has been made. My view is that none should be made. We will, of course, analyze it at the time to see whether our national, vital interests might require me to reassess it.

De Gaulle Conversations

Q. Mr. President, there were some interpretations some weeks ago about some of General de Gaulle's actions as his wanting to have Western Europe free of American influence. Did he address himself to this in talking with you? Did you get any deeper understanding of this?

THE PRESIDENT: I think, Mr. Kaplow, it would be not divulging a confidence to indicate that President de Gaulle completely disassociated his views which he expressed in great detail to us on the European Alliance and France's relation to it from any anti-American position.

He believes that Europe should have an independent position in its own right. And, frankly, I believe that, too. I think most Europeans believe that. I think the time when it served our interest to have the United States as the dominant partner in an alliance—that that time is gone.

We will be dominant because of our immense nuclear power and also because of our economic wealth. But on the other hand, the world will be a much safer place and, from our standpoint, a much healthier place economically, militarily and politically, if there were a strong European Community to be a balance, basically a balance between the United States and the Soviet Union, rather than to have this polarization of forces in one part of the world or another.

Now, as far as President de Gaulle's position is concerned, as I understand it, he has talked very eloquently on his desire to have European unity and a separate European identity. He has disagreed, however, with the proposals that currently are supported by most of the other European countries. He believes that it could better be worked out, as he indicated publicly, and he also indicated to me privately, through the major powers reaching an understanding rather than having it done through a basically convention or caucus of all the powers of Europe.

Summit Preconditions

Q. Mr. President, some of us have been under the impression that you attached important pre-conditions to summit talks with the Soviets, specifically some prior evidence or showing on their part that they were doing something to improve conditions in either the Middle East or Vietnam.

Have those impressions been false or has something happened to your own thinking in this area very recently?

THE PRESIDENT: No, I did not intend to leave the impression that we say to the Soviet Union that unless they do this we will not have talks that they want on strategic arms.

What I have, however, clearly indicated, is that I think their interests and ours would not be served by simply going down the road on strategic arms talks without, at the same time, making progress on resolving these political differences that could explode. Even assuming our strategic arms talks were successful, freezing arms at their present level, we could have a very devastating war. It is that point that I have been making.

I should also emphasize that I made this point to every European leader that I talked to, and every one of them—and I do not commit them to the position—every one of them understands the position, because the Europeans have a great sense of history. All of them recognize that most wars have come not from arms races, although sometimes arms races can produce a war, but they have come from political explosions.

Therefore, they want progress, for example, on Berlin; they want progress on the Mideast; they want progress on Vietnam, at the same time that they want progress on strategic arms talks.

So our attitude towards the Soviet is not a high-handed one of trying to tell them, "You do this or we won't talk." Our attitude is very conciliatory, and I must say that in our talks with the Soviet Ambassador, I think that they are thinking along this line now, too. If they are, we can make progress on several roads towards a mutual objective.

THE PRESS: Thank you.

MARCH 14

Following is the complete transcript of President Nixon's March 14 news conference, his fourth, held 10 days after his third conference.

THE PRESIDENT: Ladies and gentlemen, today I am announcing a decision which I believe is vital for the security and defense of the United States, and also in the interest of peace throughout the world.

Last year a program, the SENTINEL antiballistic missile program, was adopted. That program, as all listeners on television and radio and readers of newspapers know, has been the subject of very strong debate and controversy over the past few months.

After long study of all of the options available, I have concluded that the SENTINEL program previously adopted should be substantially modified. The new program that I have recommended this morning to the leaders, and that I announce today, is one that perhaps best can be described as a safeguard program.

It is a safeguard against any attack by the Chinese Communists that we can foresee over the next 10 years.

It is a safeguard of our deterrent system, which is increasingly vulnerable due to the advances that have been made by the Soviet Union since the year 1967 when the SENTINEL program was first laid out.

It is a safeguard also against any irrational or accidental attack that might occur of less than massive magnitude which might be launched from the Soviet Union.

The program also does not do some things which should be clearly understood. It does not provide defense for our cities, and for that reason the sites have been moved away from our major cities. I have made the decision with regard to this particular point because I found that there is no way, even if we were to expand the limited SENTINEL system which was planned for some of our cities to a so-called heavy or thick system—there is no way that we can adequately defend our cities without an unacceptable loss of life.

The only way that I have concluded that we can save lives, which is the primary purpose of our defense system, is to prevent war, and that is why the emphasis of this system is on protecting our deterrent, which is the best preventive for war.

The system differs from the previous SENTINEL system in another major respect. The SENTINEL system called for a fixed deployment schedule. I believe that because of a number of reasons, we should have a phase system. That is why, on an annual basis, the new safeguard system will be reviewed, and the review may bring about changes in the system based on our evaluation of three major points.

First, what our intelligence shows us with regard to the magnitude of the threat, whether from the Soviet Union or from the Chinese; and, second, in terms of what our evaluation is of any talks that we are having by that time, or may be having, with regard to arms control; and, finally because we believe that since this is a new system, we should constantly examine what progress has been made in the development of the technique to see if changes in the system should be made.

I should admit at this point that this decision has not been an easy one. None of the great decisions made by a President are easy. But it is one that I have made after considering all of the options, and I would indicate before going to your questions two major options that I have overruled.

One is moving to a massive city defense. I have already indicated why I do not believe that is, first, feasible, and there is another reason: Moving to a massive city defense system, even starting with a thin system and then going to a heavy system, tends to be more provocative in terms of making credible a first-strike capability against the Soviet Union. I want no provocation which might deter arms talks.

The other alternative, at the other extreme, was to do nothing, or to delay for six or twelve months, which would be the equivalent, really, of doing nothing, or, for example, going the road only of research and development.

I have examined those options. I have ruled them out because I have concluded that the first deployment of this system, which will not occur until 1973, that that first deployment is essential by that date if we are to meet the threat that our present intelligence indicates will exist by 1973.

In other words, we must begin now. If we delay a year, for example, it means that that first deployment will be delayed until 1975. That might be too late.

It is the responsibility of the President of the United States, above all other responsibilities, to think first of the security of the United States. I believe that this system is the best step that we can take to provide for that security.

There are, of course, other possibilities that have been strongly urged by some of the leaders this morning—for example that we could increase our offensive capability, our submarine force, or even our MINUTEMAN force or our bomber force. That I would consider to be, however, the wrong road because it would be provocative to the Soviet Union and might escalate an arms race.

This system is truly a safeguard system, a defensive system only. It safeguards our deterrent and under those circumstances can, in no way, in my opinion, delay the progress which I hope will continue to be made toward arms talks, which will limit arms, not only this kind of system, but particularly offensive systems.

We will now go to your questions.

Mr. Smith?

Vietnam War

QUESTION: Mr. President, the war in Vietnam has been intensifying recently, and if there has been any notable progress in Paris it has not been detectable publicly. Is your patience growing a little thin with these continued attacks, particularly such as came out of the DMZ today?

THE PRESIDENT: Mr. Smith, you may recall that on March 4 when I received a similar question, at an earlier stage of the attacks, I issued what was interpreted widely as a warning. It will be my policy as President to issue a warning only once, and I will not repeat it now. Anything in the future that is done will be done. There will be no additional warning.

As far as the Paris talks are concerned, I have noted the speculation in the press with regard to whether we will have, or should have, or are, for example, approving private talks going forward. I will not discuss that subject. I trust there will be private talks.

I think that is where this war will be settled—in private rather than in public. This is in the best interest of both sides, but public discussion of what I think is significant progress which is being made along the lines of private talks, I will not indulge in.

Mr. Cormier?

State of the Union

QUESTION: Mr. President, will you make your own State of the Union address, and what will your legislative program encompass?

THE PRESIDENT: I do not plan a State of the Union address in the traditional manner. I will, within approximately a month, however, state a general domestic program. By that time the program will be at the point that I think it should be completely summarized and set forth, not only for the Nation, as to what we have done, but particularly to the Congress as to what we expect for the balance. I would not want to anticipate now what will be in that program.

Congressional Criticism

QUESTION: Mr. President, there has been a great deal of criticism in Congress against deployment of any type of antiballistic defense system. What kind of reception do you think your proposal this morning will receive there?

THE PRESIDENT: It will be a very spirited debate, and it will be a very close vote. Debates in the field of national defense are often spirited and the votes are often close. Many of my friends in Congress who were there before I was there remarked that the vote on extending the draft in 1941 won by only one vote.

This might be that close. I think, however, that after the Members of the House and the Senate consider this program, which is a minimum program, and which particularly provides options to change in other directions if we find the threat is changed, or that the art has changed, our evaluation of the technique has changed, I think that we have a good chance of getting approval. We will, of course, express our views, and we hope that we will get support from the country.

Deployment

QUESTION: Mr. President, I understand that your first construction or deployment of antimissile systems would be around two MINUTEMAN retaliatory operations. Do you think that deploying around these two provides enough deterrent that would be effective?

THE PRESIDENT: Let me explain the difference between deploying around two MINUTEMAN bases and deploying around, say, 10 cities.

Where you are looking toward a city defense, it needs to be a perfect or near perfect system to be credible because, as I examine the possibility of even a thick defense of cities, I have found that even the most optimistic projections, considering the highest development of the art, would mean that we would still lose 30 million to 40 million lives. That would be less than half of what we would otherwise lose. But we would still lose 30 million to 40 million.

When you are talking about protecting your deterrent, it need not be perfect. It is necessary only to protect enough of the deterrent that the retaliatory second strike will be of such magnitude that the enemy would think twice before launching a first strike.

It has been my conclusion that by protecting two MINUTEMAN sites, we will preserve that deterrent as a credible deterrent, and that that will be decisive and could be decisive insofar as the enemy considering the possibility of a first strike.

Vietnam

QUESTION: Mr. President, there have been charges from Capitol Hill that you have stepped up the war in Vietnam. Have you?

THE PRESIDENT: I have not stepped up the war in Vietnam. I actually have examined not only the charges, but also examined the record. I discussed it at great length yesterday with Secretary Laird.

What has happened is this: For the past six months, the forces on the other side have been planning for an offensive, and for the past six months they not only have planned for an offensive, but they have been able, as a result of that planning, to have mounted a rather substantial offensive.

Under those circumstances, we had no other choice but to try to blunt the offensive. Had General Abrams not responded in this way, we would have suffered far more casualties than we have suffered, and we have suffered more than, of course, any of us would have liked to have seen.

The answer is that any escalation of the war in Vietnam has been the responsibility of the enemy. If the enemy de-escalates its attacks, ours will go down. We are not trying to step it up. We are trying to do everything that we can in the conduct of our war in Vietnam to see that we can go forward toward peace in Paris.

That is why my response has been measured, deliberate and, some think, too cautious. But it will continue to be that way, because I am thinking of those peace talks every time I think of a military option in Vietnam.

Tax Surcharge

QUESTION: Mr. President, your safeguard ABM system, I understand, would cost about $1 billion less in the coming fiscal year than the plan which President Johnson sent up. Would this give you the opportunity to reduce the surcharge or will the continued high level of taxation be needed for the economy?

THE PRESIDENT: That question will be answered when we see the entire budget. Secretary Laird will testify on the defense budget on Wednesday.

Incidentally, my understanding at this time, and I have seen the preliminary figures, is that the defense budget that Secretary Laird will present will be approximately $2½ billion less than that submitted by the previous Administration.

Whether after considering the defense budget and all of the other budgets that have been submitted, we then can move in the direction of either reducing the surcharge or move in the direction of some of our very difficult problems with regard to our cities, the problem of hunger and others—these are the options that I will have to consider at a later time.

Vietnam Casualties

QUESTION: Mr. President, last week you said that in the matter of Vietnam you would not tolerate heavier casualties and a continuation of the violation of the understanding without making an appropriate response.

Is what we are doing now in Vietnam in a military way that response of which you were speaking?

THE PRESIDENT: This is a very close decision on our part, one that I not only discussed with Secretary Laird yesterday, but that we will discuss more fully in the Security Council tomorrow.

I took no comfort out of the stories that I saw in the papers this morning to the effect that our casualties for the immediate past week went from 400 down to 300. That still is too high. What our response should be must be measured in terms of the effect on the negotiations in Paris. I will only respond as I did earlier to Mr. Smith's question. We issued a warning. I will not warn again. If we conclude that the level of casualties is higher than we should tolerate, action will take place.

Soviet Reaction

QUESTION: Mr. President, do you have reason to believe that the Russians will interpret your ABM decision today as not being an escalating move in the arms race?

THE PRESIDENT: As a matter of fact, Mr. Kaplow, I have reason to believe, based on the past record, that they would interpret it just the other way around.

First, when they deployed their own ABM system, and, as you know, they have 67 missile ABM sites deployed around Moscow, they rejected the idea that it escalated the arms race on the ground that it was defensive solely in character, and, second, when the United States last year went forward on the SENTINEL system, four days later the Soviet Union initiated the opportunity to have arms limitation talks.

I think the Soviet Union recognizes very clearly the difference between a defensive posture and an offensive posture.

I would also point this out, an interesting thing about Soviet military and diplomatic history: They have always thought in defensive terms, and if you read not only their political leaders, but their military leaders, the emphasis is on defense.

I think that since this system now, as a result of moving the city defense out of it, and the possibility of that city defense growing into a thick defense, I think this makes it so clearly defensive in character that the Soviet Union cannot interpret this as escalating the arms race.

Negotiations With Russia

QUESTION: Mr. President, last week at your press conference you mentioned negotiations with the Russians at the highest level being in the wind. Could you tell us if since then we have moved any closer to such a summit meeting?

THE PRESIDENT: I should distinguish between negotiations at what you call the highest level, and what I said was the highest level, and talks. Talks with the Soviet Union are going on at a number of levels at this time, on a number of subjects.

However, those talks have not yet reached the point where I have concluded, or where I believe they have concluded, that a discussion at the summit level would be useful. Whenever those talks, preliminary talks, do reach that point, I anticipate that a summit meeting would take place.

I do not think one will take place in the near future, but I think encouraging progress is being made toward the time when a summit talk may take place.

Johnson Holdovers

QUESTION: Mr. President, there have been several reports from your staff members that Kennedy and Johnson hold-over people who made policy have sown themselves into civil service status and this may mean some problem for you people in personnel. I wonder if this means that you will transfer a lot of these people or abolish jobs?

THE PRESIDENT: I have heard a lot from some of my Republican friends on Capitol Hill on this point, as well as from, of course, Republican leaders in the Nation. It seems that this is a rather common practice, when one Administration goes out and the other comes in. We will do what we think will best serve the interest of effective Government, and if the individual who has been frozen in can do the job, we are going to keep him.

However, we are moving some out, but we wouldn't do it through subterfuge. We will try to do it quite directly.

NATO

QUESTION: Mr. President, in your recent European trip, did you find any willingness on the part of our allies to increase their military and financial contribution to the alliance?

THE PRESIDENT: Well, that matter was discussed with all of our allies, and particularly will be a subject for discussion when we have the 20th Anniversary meeting of NATO here in April.

I think it might be potentially embarrassing to allies to suggest that we are urging them, any one specifically, to do one thing or another in this field. I think it is best for me to leave it in these terms:

Our allies do recognize the necessity to maintain NATO's conventional forces. They do recognize that they must carry their share or that the United States, and particularly our Congress, representing our people, will have much less incentive to carry our share. I believe they will do their share, but I think we are going to do the best through quiet conversation rather than public declaration.

Yes, sir?

Soviet Position

QUESTION: In any talks with the Soviet Union, would you be willing to consider abandoning the ABM program altogether if the Soviets showed a similar willingness or, indeed, if they showed a readiness to place limitations on offensive weapons?

THE PRESIDENT: Mr. Scali, I am prepared, in the event that we go into arms talks, to consider both offensive and defensive weapons. As you know, the arms talks, that at least preliminarily have been discussed, do not involve limitations or reduction. They involve only freezing where we are.

Your question goes to abandoning. On that particular point, I think it would take two, naturally, to make the agreement. Let's look at the Soviet Union's position with its defensive deployment of ABM's. Previously, that deployment was aimed only toward the United States. Today their radars, from our intelligence, are also directed toward Communist China.

I would imagine that the Soviet Union would be just as reluctant as we would be to leave their country naked against a potential Chinese Communist threat. So the abandoning of the entire system, particularly as long as the Chinese threat is there, I think neither country would look upon with much favor.

QUESTION: Mr. President, do you think these developments of the Soviet Union and the United States are compatible with the aims of the NPT?

THE PRESIDENT: I considered that problem, and I believe that they are compatible with the NPT. We discussed that in the leaders' meeting this morning and I pointed out that as we consider this kind of defensive system, which enables the United States of America to make its deterrent capability credible, that that will have an enormous effect in reducing the pressure on other countries who might want to acquire nuclear weapons.

That is the key point. If a country doesn't feel that the major country that has a nuclear capability has a credible deterrent, then they would move in that direction.

One other point I wish to make, and make an announcement with regard to the NPT: that I was delighted to see the Senate's confirmation or consent to the treaty, and this announcement—I hope President Johnson is looking. I haven't talked to him on the phone. I am going to invite President Johnson, if his schedule permits, to attend the ceremony when we will have the ratification of the treaty, because he started it in his Administration and I think he should participate when we ratify it.

Mr. Lisagor?

Campus Disorders

QUESTION: Mr. President, I wonder if I could turn to the campus disorders and unrest. They are continuing and we haven't had an opportunity to ask you your views of them. But particularly, would you favor the cutting off of Federal loans to the offenders?

THE PRESIDENT: Mr. Lisagor, I have asked the Attorney General and the Secretary of Health, Education, and Welfare to examine this problem, particularly in view of a Congressional report that 122 of the 540 who had been arrested at San Francisco State were direct recipients of Federal funds.

I will have a statement on that that I will be making either Monday or Tuesday, in detail. I would prefer not to go into it now.

Mr. Semple?

Response to Attacks

QUESTION: To follow up Mr. Bailey's question on Vietnam earlier, is there any evidence that your measured response to the enemy attacks in South Vietnam has produced or yielded any results in Paris or in the attitudes of the North Vietnamese leaders in Hanoi?

THE PRESIDENT: Our measured response has not had the effect of discouraging the progress, and it is very limited progress, toward talks in Paris. That is the negative side in answering your question.

As to whether or not a different response would either discourage those talks or might have the effect of even encouraging them is the decision that we now have to make.

Troop Levels

QUESTION: Mr. President, on Vietnam, in connection with Secretary Laird's visit, we have heard for some time predictions that American troop levels could be cut as the South Vietnamese capabilities improve, and again last week, while he was in Vietnam, we were getting similar reports from Saigon despite the high level of the fighting that is going on now.

Do you see any prospect for withdrawing American troops in any numbers soon?

THE PRESIDENT: Mr. Bailey, in view of the current offensive on the part of the North Vietnamese and the Viet Cong, there is no prospect for a reduction of American forces in the foreseeable future.

When we are able to reduce forces as a result of a combination of circumstances—the ability of the South Vietnamese to defend themselves in areas where we now are defending them; the

progress of the talks in Paris; or the level of enemy activity—when that occurs, I will make an announcement. But at this time there is no foreseeable prospect.

Mr. Theis?

Shelter Program

QUESTION: What effect, if any, will your safeguard program have on the shelter program? Can you tell us anything about your long-range plans?

THE PRESIDENT: Congressman Holifield in the meeting this morning strongly urged that the Administration look over the shelter program and he made the point that he thought it had fallen somewhat into disarray due to lack of attention over the past few years.

I have directed that General Lincoln, the head of the Office of Emergency Preparedness—I had directed him previously to conduct such a survey. We are going to look at the shelter program to see what we can do there in order to minimize American casualties.

De Gaulle

QUESTION: Mr. President, if I recall correctly, at the last press conference when you were discussing the meeting with General de Gaulle, and the Middle East situation, you said you were encouraged by what he told you, because he was moving closer to our position.

I wonder if you can tell us what our position is in the Middle East, and if it has changed significantly in the last year?

THE PRESIDENT: We have had bilateral talks not only with the French, but also with the Soviet Union, and with the British, preparatory to the possibility of four-power talks. I would not like to leave the impression that we are completely together at this point.

We are closer together than we were, but we still have a lot of yardage to cover. And until we make further progress in developing a common position, I would prefer not to lay out what our position is.

I don't think that would be helpful in bringing them to the position that we think is the right position.

THE PRESS: Thank you.

APRIL 18

Following is the complete transcript of President Nixon's April 18 news conference, his fifth, held five weeks after his fourth.

THE PRESIDENT: Won't you be seated, please?

Mr. Cormier?

Q: Mr. President, the question on all of our minds is where do we go from here with the incident of the shooting down of the plane? What further action do you contemplate diplomatically and militarily?

THE PRESIDENT: Mr. Cormier, first, I think a word with regard to the facts in this case: As was pointed out in the protest that was filed at Panmunjom yesterday and also in the Defense Department statement, the plane involved was an unarmed Constellation, propeller-driven.

The mission was a reconnaissance mission which at no time took the plane closer to the shores of North Korea than 40 miles. At the time the plane was shot down, all of the evidence that we have indicates that it was shot down approximately 90 miles from the shores of North Korea while it was moving outward, aborting the mission on orders that had been received. We knew this, based on our radar.

What is also even more important, the North Koreans knew it based on their radar. Therefore, this attack was unprovoked. It was deliberate. It was without warning. The protest has been filed. The North Koreans have not responded.

Now a word with regard to why we have such missions in the Sea of Japan. As you ladies and gentlemen are aware, there are 56,000 American troops stationed in South Korea. Those 56,000 men are the responsibility of the President of the United States as Commander-in-Chief.

In recent weeks and months, in fact, going back over the last two or three years but particularly in recent weeks and months, North Korea has threatened military action against South Korea and against our forces in South Korea. The number of incidents has increased.

It is the responsibility of the Commander-in-Chief to protect the security of those men. That is why, going back over 20 years and throughout the period of this Administration being continued, we have had a policy of reconnaissance flights in the Sea of Japan similar to this flight. This year we have had already 190 of these flights without incident, without threat, without warning at all.

Now the question is: What do we do about these flights in the future? They were discontinued immediately after this incident occurred.

I have today ordered that these flights be continued. They will be protected. This is not a threat; it is simply a statement of fact.

As the Commander-in-Chief of our Armed Forces I cannot and will not ask our men to serve in Korea, and I cannot and will not ask our men to take flights like this in unarmed planes without providing protection. That will be the case.

Looking to the future, as far as what we do will depend upon the circumstances. It will depend upon what is done as far as North Korea is concerned, its reaction to the protest, and also any other developments that occur as we continue these flights.

Mr. Smith?

Vietnam War

Q: Now that you have had about three months in a position of Presidential responsibility, do the chances of peace in Southeast Asia seem to come any closer at all, or has the situation, the outlook for peace, improved or deteriorated since your Inauguration?

THE PRESIDENT: Mr. Smith, the chances for peace in Southeast Asia have significantly improved since this Administration came into office. I do not claim that that has happened simply because of what we have done, although I think we have done some things that have improved those chances, and I am not trying to raise false hopes that peace is just around the corner, this summer or this fall.

But a number of developments clearly beyond the Paris talks have convinced me that the chances for bringing this war to a peaceful conclusion have significantly improved.

One factor that should be mentioned, that I note has not been covered perhaps as much as others, is the fact that South Korea has significantly improved its own capabilities. The way we can tell this has happened is that the South Korean President has taken an attitude with regard to the make-up of a government after peace comes that he wouldn't have even considered six months ago, and he has done this because South Korea—I am sorry; South Vietnamese forces. It is natural that you transplant these two words, I find, in discussing these two subjects—South Vietnamese forces are far better able to handle themselves militarily, and that program is going forward on a much more intensive basis than it was when this Administration came into office.

Second, political stability in South Vietnam has increased significantly since this Administration came into office. The trend has begun before, but it has continued and escalated since that time.

As a result of these two factors, it means that South Vietnam is able to make a peace which I think will give a better opportunity for negotiating room for their negotiators and ours at the Paris conference. That is one of the reasons for my feeling

somewhat optimistic, although we still have some hard ground to plow.

Q: To follow that up, then, are you considering now the unilateral withdrawal of American troops from South Vietnam?

THE PRESIDENT: I am not. If we are to have a negotiating position at the Paris peace talks, it must be a position in which we can negotiate from strength and discussion about unilateral withdrawal does not help that position. I will not engage in it, although I realize it might be rather popular to do so.

It is the aim of this Administration to bring men home just as soon as our security will allow us to do so. As I have indicated previously, there are three factors that we are going to take into consideration: The training of the South Vietnamese, their ability to handle their own defense, the level of fighting in South Vietnam, whether or not the offensive action of the enemy recedes, and progress in the Paris peace talks.

Looking to the future, I would have to say that I think there are good prospects that American forces can be reduced, but as far as that time is concerned, we have no plans to reduce our forces until there is more progress on one or all of the three fronts that I have mentioned.

Q: Mr. President—

THE PRESIDENT: Mr. Lisagor, yes.

Combat Casualties

Q: Can I ask you whether you have ordered that the level of American combat activity in South Vietnam be reduced in order to reduce the casualties?

THE PRESIDENT: No, Mr. Lisagor, the casualties have been reduced, as you have noted in your question, but the reason that American casualties are down is because the level of offensive action on the part of the enemy has receded.

An analysis—and I have studied this quite carefully because I have noted the great interest in this country on this subject as to whether or not the lower casualties are a result of our action or theirs, we find that the number of casualties has increased during the spring offensive. That offensive has at this time either run its course or is at a substantial lull. Because of that status at this time, our level of casualties is down.

I have not ordered or do not intend to order any reduction of our activity. We will do what is necessary to defend our position and to maintain the strength of our bargaining position in the Paris peace talks.

Q: Mr. President, do you forsee the possibility or the likelihood that after the Vietnam War ends; the 10 percent income tax surcharge will be continued indefinitely to help pay for what you call this country's compelling domestic needs?

THE PRESIDENT: No, I do not foresee that likelihood and that will not be the objective of this Administration. I indicated during the campaign that I thought that taxes were too high. I still believe that. And I believe that the surcharge, the so-called "war tax", which some describe it, that that tax should be reduced and removed just as soon as we are able to do so, either because of Vietnam or for other reasons.

I will also indicate that at this time the Administration's interim tax reform package will be submitted to the Congress early next week, either Monday or Tuesday. The Secretary of the Treasury, or the Treasury Department, is testifying on Tuesday. I have already approved the message. It will have some information on this and other matters that will be of interest to all of you. Mr. Theiss?

Missile Dispute

Q: Mr. President, it has been suggested that you may go directly to the country on the ABM issue to further clarify and support your case. Can you tell us of any plans you have in that direction, perhaps today?

THE PRESIDENT: No, I have no plans at this time to go to the country, as you have suggested. As a matter of fact, I consider a press conference as going to the country. I find that these conferences are rather well covered by the country, both by television, as they are today, and also by members of the press.

With regard to the ABM decision, however, I wish to emphasize again the point that I made when I announced that decision in this room a few weeks ago.

I made that decision after I considered all the options that were before me with regard to what was necessary to maintain America's defenses, and particularly the credibility of our national security and our diplomacy throughout the world.

I analyzed the nature of the threat. I found, for example, that even since the decision to deploy the ABM system called Sentinel in 1967, that the intelligence estimates indicated that the Soviet capabilities with regard to their SS-9's, their nuclear missiles, was 60 percent higher than we thought then; that their plans for nuclear submarines were 60 percent greater than we had thought then.

Under these circumstances, I had to make basically a command decision as to what the United States should do if we were to avoid falling into a second-class or inferior position vis-a-vis the Soviet Union.

I had a number of options. We could have increased our offensive forces in various directions. I determined that this limited defensive action, limited insofar as the Soviet Union is concerned, to defend our Minutemen missile sites, was the best action that could be taken.

I still believe that to be the case. I believe it is essential for the national security, and it is essential to avoid putting an American President, either this President or the next President, in the position where the United States would be second rather than first or at least equal to any potential enemy.

The other reason, and I emphasize this strongly, is that the Chinese Communists, according to our intelligence, have not moved as fast recently as they had over the past three to four years, but that, nevertheless, by 1973 or 1974 they would have a significant nuclear capability which would make our diplomacy not credible in the Pacific unless we could protect our country against a Chinese attack aimed at our cities.

The ABM system will do that, and the ABM safeguard system, therefore, has been adopted for that reason.

Consultation

Q: Mr. President, has there been any consultation with our allies or with Japan on sending armed planes along to guard the reconnaissance craft? Is it necessary?

THE PRESIDENT: There has been no consultation up to this point. I can only say in answer to that question that when I refer to protecting these flights, I am not going to go beyond that at this time, I am simply indicating that they will be protected.

If we think that consultation is necessary, we will have consultation.

ABM Views

Q: Mr. President, on the ABM issue, as you know, there are a number of Republican Senators who oppose your views on the ABM.

Do you think that they should support you because you are a Republican President even though they oppose the principle?

THE PRESIDENT: I certainly do not. I want to make it crystal-clear that my decision on ABM was not made on the basis of Republican versus Democrat. It was made on the basis of what I thought was best for the country.

I talked, for example, just yesterday, with Senator Cooper. He is one of those who opposes me as a Republican. He honestly and sincerely believes that this is not the best step to take.

I respect that belief, and I respect others who disagree with me on this. I also respect the beliefs of Senator Jackson, Speaker McCormack, Senator Stennis and Senator Russell, and a number of Democrats, who believe that this is the right step to take.

This issue will be fought out, as it should be fought out, on the basis of what is best for the Nation. It will not be fought out on partisan lines.

I am going to fight as hard as I can for it because I believe it is absolutely essential to the security of the country. But it is going to be fought on the basis of asking each Senator and Congressman to make his own decision, and I am confident, incidentally, that that decision will be in favor of the system when they know all the facts.

Q: Mr. President?

THE PRESIDENT: Yes, sir.

Tax Credit

Q: Democrats in the House have voted to repeal the seven percent investment tax credit. What is your position on this, sir?

THE PRESIDENT: The position of the Administration on this will be announced in the tax reform measure that will be submitted on Monday or Tuesday of next week. I will not discuss it further at this time.

Q: Mr. President?

THE PRESIDENT: Yes, sir, Mr. Scali.

Warheads

Q: Secretary Rogers said at a recent news conference that if and when we begin talks with the Soviets on missiles, one of the first questions to be asked them is why they find it necessary to build a big missile with a 25 megaton warhead.

Since the Russian decision to proceed to build such an enormous missile is one of the major factors in your going ahead with the ABM, the question is: Why are we waiting to ask that question for the beginning of negotiations? Why don't we ask it now?

THE PRESIDENT: Mr. Scali, in a sense I think Secretary Rogers probably asked the question by stating it as he did in a press conference. As you know, because you have covered these diplomatic matters for many years, in dealing with the Soviet Union or any other nation, this type of question is not always asked simply on a formal basis in a diplomatic conference.

Sometimes the best way to handle it is to state the position publicly. As far as Secretary Rogers' statement is concerned, I share his puzzlement as to why the Soviet Union is moving so heavily in this direction. As far as the Soviet Union's intentions are concerned, and I want to clarify one point that is made, the question as to their intentions is not something that I am going to comment upon. I don't know what their intentions are.

But we have to base our policy on their capabilities and when we project their SS-9 plans to 1972 or 1973, if we allow those plans to go forward without taking any action on our part, either offensively or defensively to counteract them, they will be substantially ahead of the United States in overall nuclear capability. We cannot allow that to happen.

I would remind the members of this press corps, I am here at a time when the United States faces a threat, not of the magnitude that President Kennedy faced at the time of the Cuban missile crisis, but I would remind the members of this press corps that at that time all of the professional experts agreed that the U.S. superiority was at least 4 to 1 and maybe 5 to 1, over the Soviet Union in terms of overall nuclear capability.

Now we don't have that today. That gap has been closed. We shall never have it again because it will not be necessary for us. Sufficiency, as I have indicated, is all that is necessary. But I do say this: I do not want to see an American President in the future, in the event of any crisis, have his diplomatic credibility be so impaired because the United States was in a second-class or inferior position. We saw what it meant to the Soviets when they were second. I don't want that position to be the United States' in the event of a future diplomatic crisis.

Soviet Role

Q: Mr. President, can you tell us what the Soviet role has been in the plane incident, and could you go beyond that and tell us what were some of the other elements that figured in your deliberations on how to properly respond to the downing of the plane?

THE PRESIDENT: The Soviet role in the plane incident, first, is one of being of assistance to the United States in recovering the debris and looking for survivors. We are most grateful to the Soviet Union for helping us in this respect.

Our intelligence and, of course, no one can be sure here, indicates that the Soviet Union was not aware that this attack was to be made. North Korea is not a nation that is predictable in terms of its actions. It is perhaps more than any other nation in the Communist bloc completely out of the control of either the Soviet Union or, for that matter, Communist China. That, at least, is our intelligence estimate at this time.

Now, as far as other matters that entered into this interim decision, and I emphasize it as an interim decision, I have concluded that the United States must face up to the fact that intelligence gathering—intelligence gathering that does not involve overflights, that does not involve interdiction of another nation's air space, or moving into its waters—here where intelligence people are involved, we recognize that they are necessarily subject to whatever action can or should be taken to another nation to defend itself.

But when planes of the United States, or ships of the United States, in intelligence gathering, are in international water or in international air space, they are not fair game. They will not be in the future. I state that as a matter of fact, and that was the basis for this interim decision.

NSF Appointment

Q: Mr. President, on the question of dissent on the ABM, can you tell us, sir, did you or did you not block the appointment of Dr. Long as head of the NSF because he disapproved of your position on the ABM?

THE PRESIDENT: Dr. Long's potential appointment was not discussed with me until after he had had a conversation with Dr. DuBridge on this matter.

The determination was made by members of the White House staff that his appointment, in view of his very sincere beliefs opposing the ABM, would not be in the best interests of the overall Administration position.

I wish to make it clear that we have vigorous dissent and discussion within our National Security Council on this and other matters. But to have at this time made an appointment of a man who quite honestly and quite sincerely—a man of eminent credentials, incidentally—disagreed with the Administration's position on a major matter of this sort, we thought this would be misunderstood. My staff thought that and, under the circumstances, I approved of their decision not to submit the recommendation to me.

Pueblo

Q: Mr. President, can you comment on the motives of the North Koreans in this attack and can you see any pattern in this attack and also the one on the PUEBLO?

THE PRESIDENT: The PUEBLO incident was quite different in two respects. One, there was some uncertainty for some time as to where the PUEBLO was. Present indications are that the PUEBLO was in international waters. But there was some uncertainty.

There was no uncertainty whatever as to where this plane was. We know what their radar showed. We, incidentally, know what the Russian radar showed. All three radars showed exactly the same thing.

Let me also say that there is no question of what they claim as their air space. Some of you, of course, know the confusion and, as a matter of fact, the confrontation we are having with Peru about the 200-mile limit. North Korea claims only 12 miles as its limit, so we were at least 28 miles away at the very closest point.

Also, with regard to the PUEBLO, in the case of the PUEBLO the North Koreans had warned and threatened the PUEBLO for a period of several weeks before they seized it. In the case of these flights, they have been going on, as I have indicated, for years, and during this Administration, without incident, 190 of them have occurred this year.

Under these circumstances, it was a completely surprise attack in every sense of the word and, therefore, did not give us the opportunity for protective action that I would have taken had it been threatened. Mr. Bailey?

Electoral Reform

Q: Mr. President, the House Judiciary Committee is going to report out an electoral reform bill providing for direct popular election of the President, perhaps with a provision delaying the effectiveness until after the next election. Will you support this?

THE PRESIDENT: Mr. Bailey, if the House and the Senate approve a direct election proposal for amending the Constitution, it will have my support. It is my judgment that that kind of a proposal will have far less chance to get the requisite number of States to approve it than the proposal that I favor, the proportional system. But my view is that, first, the present system must be modified. As far as I am concerned, the proportional system, the Congressional District system, or the direct election system would be preferable to the present system. That is my conviction as far as my judgment.

As to what the House and the Senate ought to do, I have expressed my view as to the practical political realities. If the Members of the House and Senate conclude that they can get the three-fourths of the States for the direct election system, and if they pass and can agree in conference that that is what they will approve, then that modification, that amendment, will have my enthusiastic support; however with some doubts as to whether it will succeed.

Civil Rights

Q: Mr. President, Roy Wilkins of the NAACP, on Wednesday, characterized the civil rights record of your Administration thus far as mixed, citing the textile mills case in the Department of Defense and also the resignation of Clifford Alexander.

How would you characterize your Administration's civil rights record?

THE PRESIDENT: The intent of our Administration is to enforce the laws of this land and to develop a coordinated program in which there will be standards that everybody will understand so that we will not be subject to this criticism of our record being mixed.

The reason for Roy Wilkins' criticism, and he has expressed this to me personally, too, the reason for it is well-founded as far as the implementation is concerned.

As all of you know, the number of agencies involved in civil rights compliance means that in these gray areas in which close cases come up, you will get different men coming up with different conclusions.

You mentioned the textile cases. The three South Carolina cases involved the Defense Department and Defense contracts and the compliance section interpreting how compliance could be obtained for that contractual provision.

The North Carolina case, which was brought by the Department of Justice, did not involve compliance with a Defense contractor but it involved a mill with no Government contracts and since compliance could not be negotiated, suit had to be brought.

That can be called mixed but nevertheless, I think you can see how that kind of result could be attained.

Soviet Union

Q: Mr. President, you have addressed yourself many times in the past, sir, to the danger and the consequences of aggression against our country by a minor military power.

It seems to me what we have seen developed here is a kind of new rules of warfare which we certainly have not agreed to and obviously the Soviet Union hasn't.

In your present circumstances, sir, can you tell us of some of the problems that you have faced in making a proper response?

THE PRESIDENT: The problems with regard to a proper response are quite obvious. The question as to what reaction we could expect not only from the party against whom we respond but other parties that might be involved, and also putting it in the larger context, how responding in one area might affect a major interest of the United States in another area, an area like Vietnam, Vietnam being the top priority area for us.

Now, in answering the question in that way, I do not want to leave the implication that the announcement of the renewal of and the continuation of reconnaissance flights is the final action that can or will be taken here.

Our action in this matter will be determined by what happens in the future.

Looking at the Soviet Union, it seems to me that had it not been for this incident the major story that I would have been asked about today would have been what happened in Czechoslovakia. I suppose that my reaction to that would be to condemn the Soviet Union for what it did.

The Soviet Union is aware of our disapproval of that action. All Americans, in fact, all people in the free world, see this as perhaps the final chapter in the great tragedy of the Czechoslovak people under Communist rule.

We hope it is not the final chapter. We hope that some vestiges of freedom will remain. Yet, the Soviet Union has acted there and acted quite decisively. They have to consider now, in terms of any future action, how that might affect their relations with the United States and with the Western World.

What I am trying to do in answering your question is to pose the problem that great powers confront when they take actions involving powers that are not in that league.

We must always measure our actions by that base.

THE PRESS: Thank you, Mr. President.

JUNE 19

Following is the complete transcript of President Nixon's June 19 news conference, his sixth since taking office.

THE PRESIDENT: Won't you be seated, please?
Mr. Smith.

Q: I ask this question against the background of a continually heating economy. Now with your tax package seemingly on its way through Congress, are you giving any concern to doing something else—some new moves against rising prices and the rising cost of living as they are reflected monthly in the federal indices?

THE PRESIDENT: Mr. Smith, it is true that we have rising prices, a rising cost of living, and also rising interest rates at 8½ percent at the last report. However, in looking at an economy, we find that there is usually a lead time of about six months from the time decisions are made on the economy from a fiscal standpoint within government and the effect of those decisions on it.

Now, this Administration has made some decisions—decisions in cutting the budget, decisions in asking for an extension of the surtax, and we expect it to be extended, and other decisions with regard to tightening of credit. We believe that the decisions that we have made will begin to have effect within a matter of two to three months. If our projection proves to be wrong, then we will have to look to other courses of action, because we cannot allow prices to continue to go up, interest to go up, and the other factors which you have described to continue.

Mr. Cormier.

Q: Could you tell us who you favor for Mayor of New York at this point?

THE PRESIDENT: I think the people of New York have had some difficulty in that respect.

I will follow the practice as President of the United States and as leader of the Republican Party of endorsing all Republican nominees. Therefore, I will endorse Senator Marchi and the other Republican nominees on the City ticket in New York.

However, I will also follow the practice that has been my practice during my entire political career of campaigning and participating in only National and State elections. I will not participate in, and I will not comment upon, city or local elections, including the election in New York.

Vietnam Peace

Q: Mr. President, on the Midway trip, we were told by an official of your Administration that he felt the time had come for substantive negotiations to begin at Paris. Do you agree with this assessment, and, if so, what evidence is there to point it up?

THE PRESIDENT: I agree with the conclusion that the time has come for some substantive negotiations in Paris. As far as evidence that such negotiations have begun, there is no substantial evidence, publicly, to report.

However, I am not pessimistic about the outcome. As you may recall when these questions were first raised, when the talks in Paris were beginning, I pointed out that it would be a long, hard road after we got over the procedural points.

When this Administration came in, all that had been decided was the shape of the table. Now we are down to substance. The two sides are far apart. But we believe that the time has come for a discussion of substance and we hope within the next two to three months to see some progress in substantive discussions.

Q: Mr. President, former Defense Secretary Clark Clifford has suggested that 100,000 American troops ought to be out by the end of this year and we ought to say that all ground troops will be out by the end of 1970. I wonder if you think that is a realistic timetable?

THE PRESIDENT: Well, I noted Mr. Clifford's comments in the magazine Foreign Affairs, and, naturally, I respect his judgment as a former Secretary of Defense.

I would point out, however, that for five years the Administration in which he was Secretary of Defense in the last part we had a continued escalation of the war, we had 500,000 Americans in Vietnam; we had 35,000 killed; we had over 200,000 injured.

And, in addition to that, we found that in the year, the full year, in which he was Secretary of Defense, our casualties were the highest of the whole five-year period and, as far as negotiations were concerned, all that had been accomplished, as I indicated earlier, was that we had agreed on the shape of the table.

This is not to say that Mr. Clifford's present judgment is not to be considered because of the past record. It does indicate, however, that he did have a chance in this particular respect, and did not move on it then.

I believe that we have changed that policy. We have started to withdraw forces. We will withdraw more. Another decision will be made in August. I will not indicate the number, because the number will depend upon the extent of the training of the South Vietnamese, as well as developments in Paris, and the other factors that I have mentioned previously.

As far as how many will be withdrawn by the end of this year, or the end of next year, I would hope that we could beat Mr. Clifford's timetable, just as I think we have done a little better than he did when he was in charge of our national defense.

Combat Orders

Q: Mr. President, Mr. Clifford goes on to urge that you order our military commanders to cease the policy of applying maximum military pressure against the enemy and switch, instead, to a policy of reducing the level of combat operations. Do you intend to issue any such instructions?

THE PRESIDENT: Mr. Scali, I have checked the situation with regard to our operations as compared with the enemy's since this Administration took over. I find that our casualties are in direct ratio to the level of enemy attacks.

We have not escalated our attacks. We have only responded to what the enemy has done.

As far as Mr. Clifford's suggestion is concerned, it implies that the United States is at the present time responsible for the level of fighting. It takes two in order to reduce the level of fighting, and I would only suggest that if the enemy now will withdraw forces, one-tenth of its forces, as we have withdrawn one-tenth of our combat forces, that would tend to reduce the level of fighting.

As far as the orders to General Abrams are concerned, they are very simply this: He is to conduct this war with a minimum of American casualties. I believe he is carrying out that order with great effectiveness in the field.

Q: Mr. President, have you had any response from the North Vietnamese or Viet Cong either in Paris or on the battlefield to the withdrawal of the first 25,000 American troops?

THE PRESIDENT: No, we have not.

Q: When and where do you expect to begin arms talks with the Soviet Union, and do you favor suspension of the testing of multiple warheads in the meantime?

THE PRESIDENT: We are just completing our own strategic review, and as a matter of fact, the National Security Council meeting dealing with our position on the SALT talks, as they are described—the first was held this last Friday, and the second will be held on Wednesday. Consultation with our allies will then proceed through the balance of June and through July.

We have set July 31st as a target date for the beginning of talks, and Secretary Rogers has so informed the Soviet Ambassador. We have not had a reply from them.

Assuming that our consultations are completed, and that the Soviets find this date is acceptable to them, I would say that sometime between July 31st and the 15th of August there would be a meeting. As far as the place of the meeting is concerned, it could be Vienna, it could be Geneva. We are open on that question.

Provisional Government

Q: Mr. President, the Viet Cong and/or Hanoi recently announced the creation of a new provisional government for South Vietnam. There have been many interpretive reports of what that may mean for the political stability or instability of South Vietnam and its portent on the international scene for progress toward peace. Could you give us an assessment of the new government?

THE PRESIDENT: The new government is simply a new name for the same activity that was there previously, the NLF or National Liberation Front, as it was called. There is no new blood in it. It has no capital. As a matter of fact, I do not know where Ambassadors would present their diplomatic credentials because it has no major city or town which it controls in South Vietnam.

As far as the changed situation is concerned, however, I would make this suggestion: President Thieu has offered to have internationally supervised elections to let the people of South Vietnam determine whether they want his government or some other government.

It would seem that if the provisional government which also claims to represent the people of South Vietnam really means that, that they would accede to this request and agree to internationally supervised elections.

As far as the United States is concerned, we will accept any decision that is made by the people of South Vietnam, but we think that the provisional government should join with the Government of South Vietnam, and any other political parties in South Vietnam, in participating in supervised elections.

Q: Mr. President, referring to an earlier question by Mr. Valeriani, do you regard further testing of MIRVs as an obstacle to reaching an arms control agreement?

THE PRESIDENT: I am sorry, Mr. Semple, I forgot the last part of his question. I am glad you brought it back.

As far as the further testing is concerned, this suggestion was made to me by Senator Brooke and by others in the Senate. I know that it is certainly a very constructive proposal insofar as they, themselves, are thinking about it. We are considering the

possibility of a moratorium on tests as part of any arms control agreement.

However, as far as any unilateral stopping of tests on our part, I do not think that would be in our interest. Only in the event that the Soviet Union and we could agree that a moratorium on tests could be mutually beneficial to us, would we be able to agree to do so.

Cease-fire Proposal

Q: Mr. President, several prominent Americans have urged you to propose a cease-fire in Vietnam as a means of reducing American casualties. Why does that idea not commend itself to you?

THE PRESIDENT: Well, the idea of a cease-fire, Mr. Lisagor, does commend itself to me. But I do not want us to cease and have the other side continue to fire, because, basically, as I have pointed out in a previous press conference, where we have a conventional war, cease-fire is very relevant; then we know that the guns have stopped firing.

In the case of a guerrilla war, unless you have an international force or some outside force to guarantee it, a cease fire is a grave disadvantage to those forces that are in place.

I should point out, however, that in my May 18th speech, I advocated supervised cease-fires. That is the position of this Administration. It is the position of Mr. Thieu.

We want cease-fires, but we want them supervised. We don't want us to cease fire and the other side to continue to kill our men.

Q: Mr. President, against the background of a controversy involving Mr. Hoover, J. Edgar Hoover, a controversy which revolves around electronic surveillance and in which one newspaper, at least, has called for his resignation, may I ask you two questions: One, does Mr. Hoover continue to enjoy your complete confidence; and, two, has there been any decision concerning his tenure?

THE PRESIDENT: Mr. Hoover does enjoy my complete confidence, and there has been no discussion with regard to his tenure as far as the future is concerned.

I should add, further, that with regard to the controversy on electronic surveillance, that I checked personally into the matter as to whether or not that surveillance which had been discussed had been conducted by him and the FBI, by themselves, or whether it had been, as is supposed to be the case, always approved by the Attorney General.

I found that it had always been approved by the Attorney General, as Mr. Hoover testified in 1964 and 1965. As far as this Administration is concerned, our attitude toward electronic surveillance is that it should be used very sparingly, very carefully; having in mind the rights of those who might be involved, but very effectively to protect the internal and external security of the United States.

Interest Rates

Q: Mr. President, sir, the small business people of this country are suffering and much more so now because of the high interest rates. I wonder if you have given any thought to organizing a Reconstruction Finance Corporation again?

THE PRESIDENT: I know that the high interest rates have caused great concern, particularly to the small business people.

I do not believe however, that a new RFC would necessarily be the approach that would be effective to deal with it. I think the way to get at high interest rates is to get at the cause, as I answered the earlier question put by Mr. Smith.

Q: What is your answer, sir, to the report presented to you yesterday by the group of Republican Senators on campus unrest?

THE PRESIDENT: It was a very thoughtful report by men who do not have the problem of the generation gap. They are young and vitally interested in these problems, and they gave me a lot of information that is essential for this Administration to have in mind as it develops a program to deal with campus unrest.

With regard to what our position is, I would like to point out, however, that I cannot support the legislative proposals in the House of Representatives which would simply cut off funds from any college or university in which there was a demonstration. This would be cutting off our nose to spite our face, and it would be just what the demonstrators wanted, because we do not want the Federal Government interfering in and responsible for discipline in every college and university in this country.

The responsibility for discipline in colleges and universities should be on the college administrators. That is why I have asked the Attorney General to develop, if he can, new legal remedies that might be available to college administrators to use where violence or lawlessness does occur on the campus. The responsibility should be theirs. The government's role should be to help them meet that responsibility.

HEW Controversy

Q: Mr. President, Secretary Finch very much wants Dr. John Knowles to be Assistant Secretary of Health. Evidently Senator Dirksen very much doesn't want him to be. Are you going to support your Secretary against your Senate Leader?

THE PRESIDENT: I have heard of this controversy from some people. As you well know, the President of the United States, under the Constitution, makes nominations with the advice and consent of the Senate. I have found in my short term of office that it is very easy to get advice and very hard to get consent.

But with regard to this particular matter, Secretary Finch has the responsibility for selecting those who will be his Assistant Secretaries. When he makes a recommendation, after he has made every effort to clear it with the Senators involved, I will support that recommendation.

Q: Mr. President, you expressed the hope earlier for substantive talks on Vietnam, perhaps in the next three months. I wonder, sir, in this process, and before elections are held in Vietnam, are we wedded, to whatever degree, to the government of President Thieu?

THE PRESIDENT: When you use the term "wedded to the government of President Thieu," I would not say that the United States, insofar as any government in the world is concerned, is wedded to it in the sense that we cannot take any course of action that that government does not approve.

On the other hand, I do not want to leave any doubt on this score: President Thieu is the elected President of Vietnam. He is cooperating with the United States in attempting to bring this war to a conclusion. He has made a very forthright offer and has supported our position that we have made, and I know will be making an offer of his own with regard to a political statement. Under those circumstances, there is no question about our standing with President Thieu.

I would also say further that insofar as our offers are concerned, we are not going to accede to the demands of the enemy that we have to dispose of President Thieu before they will talk. That would mean a surrender on our part, a defeat on our part, and turning South Vietnam to the tender mercies of those who have done a great deal of damage, to those in North Vietnam.

Policy Examination

Q: Mr. President, although not all of his recommendations were accepted, Mr. Clifford did reverse himself while in office, a rather rare thing for a public official to do. My question to you is perhaps somewhat philosophical: How do you keep from being locked in on a decision involving something as pressurized as Vietnam? How do you determine once a policy is adopted that it continues to be right?

THE PRESIDENT: This is one of my major concerns, and it is one of the reasons why I perhaps allow more controversy and,

frankly, even open dissent, as I note from reading all the newspapers, within our Administration than any in recent years.

I believe that a President must constantly re-examine the policies, and I am re-examining our policy on Vietnam every day. I am examining the military policy. I am examining the political policy, our diplomatic options, and I will not be frozen in.

With regard to my comment on Mr. Clifford, I do not mean to suggest that because he, in a very difficult position, was unable to do anything about it, that his words should not now be given some weight. They should be given some weight, and a man should be given credit for changing his mind if the facts have changed.

But I am only suggesting that, as I make up my own mind at this time, I have to look at the facts as they are presented to me today, and as they are presented to me today I think we are on the right road in Vietnam.

We have started toward the withdrawal that Mr. Clifford has advocated and, I hope, as I said earlier, that we will be able to beat his timetable and that we will not be in Vietnam as long as he suggests we will have to be there.

Q: Mr. President, your predecessor in office used to quite often solicit the advice of one of his predecessors, General Eisenhower, particularly with respect to foreign policy. Have you solicited Mr. Johnson's advice, and have you got any that is comparable to Clifford's, and does he back your policy?

THE PRESIDENT: I have talked to Mr. Johnson on the telephone, Mr. Potter, on two occasions, and he has been regularly briefed by members of the National Security Council, by Dr. Kissinger, and also by our Economic Advisers, and those briefings, of course, have provided an occasion for him to give his ideas to us. He has been very helpful in terms of advice and I think he will be more helpful in the future.

Mr. Kaplow?

Q: Mr. President, what do you make of the recent election results in the Mayors' races in Los Angeles, New York, and Minneapolis? What do you think the voters are saying?

THE PRESIDENT: Well, I think the snap reaction to the election in Los Angeles, which was understandable, may have been wrong. The snap reaction to that election, because it was a white man, was that it was simply a white-black vote.

And yet when you see Minneapolis, where there is only a four percent black constituency, coming up with a 62 percent vote for a candidate against the Republican candidate for Mayor, and then in New York City where you see conservative candidates, that is the label that has apparently been given to both of them, in both the Democratic and Republican primaries, winning over the liberal candidates, it seems to me we have to take a different view.

What I feel is this: I do not believe the great majority of the American people in our cities are anti-Negro. I do not believe they are anti-poor, or anti-welfare, or reactionary, or members of hate groups.

I do believe, however, this, and this is the message that comes through rather loud and clear from these elections: The American people in our cities, in our small towns, and in this country are fed up to here with violence and lawlessness and they want candidates who will take a strong stand against it. I think that is the message for the candidates in the future.

Q: Mr. President, the Surgeon General said today that your Administration faces what he called a crippling lack of leadership in its top health offices. You earlier indicated that you are staying out of the Dirksen-Ford controversy for now. Will there come a time when you feel that you must intervene as the nominating officer for those jobs?

THE PRESIDENT: I think that I can go even further than that. I will not have to intervene because Mr. Finch will make a decision on that next week.

National Commitments

Q: Mr. President, what do you think of the Fulbright proposal that would limit the Presidential power to act militarily in an emergency?

THE PRESIDENT: Well, I understand the sentiment behind the proposal. When I was a Member of the Senate and a Member of the House, I will have to admit that I felt that there should be more consultation with the Senate, and that Presidents should not have unlimited power to commit this Nation, militarily as well as politically.

On the other hand, as I now assume the responsibilities of power, I, of course, see it from a different vantage point. And for the President of the United States to have his hands tied in a crisis in the fast-moving world in which we live, would not be in the best interests of the United States.

As President, I intend to consult with the Senate, with Senator Fulbright and with his colleagues on the Foreign Relations Committee and the Armed Services Committee before taking any action whenever I can.

But look, for example, at President Eisenhower in 1958. He had to move very fast in order to save the situation in Lebanon. There was no time to consult, and also it would have tipped off the enemy.

Look at President Johnson when he sent in airplanes to save the missionaries in the Congo in 1964. He had to move fast. He had no time to consult.

I don't think a President of the United States should be tied down by a commitment which will not allow him to take the action that needs to be taken to defend American interests and to defend American lives where there is no time to consult.

Q: Mr. President, five months ago at your first news conference you described the Middle East as a dangerously explosive situation in need of defusing. In the five months since that time, do you think there has been any defusing that you can measure, or do you think the situation has become acutely worse?

THE PRESIDENT: I would have to admit that I see very little defusing. The situation is better only from the standpoint that we do have some four-power talks going, and we would trust that from those talks we might get some basis of communication between the two sides, and particularly that we might get all parties involved, including the Soviet Union, to use their influence to defuse a crisis. The talks will serve that interest if they serve no other interest.

Also in that connection, I would like to say that I, as you know, have met already with the King of Jordan, and I am hoping to meet sometime within the next month with the Prime Minister of Israel.

We intend to have bilateral talks, multilateral talks—anything that we can do—to attempt to defuse the situation.

Surtax Prospects

Q: Mr. President, you said earlier that you feel that the income surtax will be extended by the Congress. However, it expires in just 11 days. If the Congress does not act or does not act in time, what economic situation will you be faced with, and what realistic policy options will you be considering?

THE PRESIDENT: Despite the fact that the surtax will expire, and that has happened before, the Congress will pass a resolution which will allow the forms to go out and the collections to proceed. What is important is not that the Congress pass the tax before it expires, but that the general public and the world knows that the tax will eventually be passed. That has the psychological effect.

In my belief, due to the bipartisan support—and it has been really statesmanlike support that we received from the Democratic Leadership as well as the Republican Leadership—due to that support, it will pass the House and I then think will pass the Senate.

Q: Mr. President, due to Governor Rockefeller's difficulties on his Latin American jaunt, do you see any usefulness coming out of the trips, and could you tell us what it might be?

THE PRESIDENT: A great deal of usefulness. For example, in my conversations with President Lleras, the talking paper that President—Governor Rockefeller; a Freudian slip—the talking paper that Governor Rockefeller gave me was extremely helpful,

extremely helpful because it gave me the background of his conversation with President Lleras.

I would say further that the very fact that there are these rather explosive demonstrations indicates that such a trip was necessary. The United States can't be penned up within our borders simply because of the fear of demonstrations.

I remember very well when I planned my trip to Europe there were several editorials to the effect that I shouldn't take the trip because of the possibility of demonstrations. As those of you who were with me will remember, there were demonstrations in every major city which I visited. Yet the trip was worthwhile.

As far as I am concerned, I am very happy that Governor Rockefeller has made this trip. He is getting valuable information which we needed to get.

I would add one further thought: We must not interpret these demonstrations as reflecting the will of the people of Latin America. The few demonstrators, violent as they are, in Latin America, no more represent the 200 million people of Latin America than the Black Panthers represent the 11 million law abiding Negro citizens of this country. That is what we have to get across.

ABM Position

Q: Mr. President, when you proposed the Safeguard anti-ballistic system, you said it was vital to the interests of the United States. Nevertheless, reports persist that it is in trouble, the program is in trouble, in the Senate, and there is now talk of a possible compromise in our program. What is your position on Safeguard and what do you intend to do to win passage for the program?

THE PRESIDENT: On March 8th before I announced my decision on Safeguard, a story appeared in the *Washington Post* indicating that the count at that time was 20 Senators for it, 46 against it, with the rest undecided.

The latest count I have seen indicates that there are 50 or 51 for it, 46 against it and the rest undecided. We will win the fight on Safeguard. It will not be necessary to compromise.

I don't mean by that that every section of the bill as presented to the Armed Services Committee has to be kept as it is. That is up to the Committee and to the Chairman to work out.

But in recommending Safeguard, I did so based on intelligence information at that time. Since that time new intelligence information with regard to the Soviet success in testing multiple re-entry vehicles, that kind of information has convinced me that Safeguard is even more important. However we may argue about that intelligence, as to whether it has an independent guidance system as ours will have, there isn't any question but that it is a multiple weapon and its footprints indicate that it just happens to fall in somewhat the precise area in which our Minutemen silos are located.

This would mean that by the year 1973, in the event the Soviet Union goes forward with that program, that 80 percent of our Minutemen would be in danger. ABM is needed particularly in order to meet that eventuality.

THE PRESS: Thank you, Mr. President.

SEPTEMBER 26

Following is the complete text of President Nixon's Sept. 26 news conference, his seventh since taking office and the first since June 19.

THE PRESIDENT: Mr. Cormier.

Q: How do you feel about the various proposals to propose an arbitrary cut-off time on our military presence in Vietnam?

THE PRESIDENT: I have considered a number of those proposals within the Administration and, of course, have noted some of the references that have been made recently in the Senate in that regard. I know they were made with the best of intentions. However, it is my conclusion that if the Administration were to impose an arbitrary cut-off time, say the end of 1970, or the middle of 1971, for the complete withdrawal of American forces in Vietnam, that inevitably leads to perpetuating and continuing the war until that time and destroys any chance to reach the objective that I am trying to achieve of ending the war before the end of 1970 or before the middle of 1971.

I think this is a defeatist attitude, defeatist in terms of what it would accomplish. I do not think it is in the interest of the United States.

I also believe that even though these proposals, I know, are made with the best of intentions, they inevitably undercut and destroy the negotiating position that we have in Paris. We have not made significant progress in those negotiations. But any incentive for the enemy to negotiate is destroyed if he is told in advance that if he just waits for 18 months we will be out anyway. Therefore, I oppose that kind of arbitrary action.

Q: Mr. President?

THE PRESIDENT: Mr. Hensley.

Q: At the time or shortly after your appointment of Mr. Burger to the Supreme Court, it was said that you hoped, insofar as possible, to avoid appointments which would become controversial. The nomination of Judge Haynsworth has become controversial to a certain extent.

THE PRESIDENT: Yes, I understand.

Q: Has this become controversial enough to lead you to withdraw the nomination of Judge Haynsworth?

THE PRESIDENT: No, I do not intend to withdraw the nomination of Judge Haynsworth. I studied his record as it was submitted to me by the Attorney General before I sent the nomination to the Senate.

I have also noted in the various items that have been brought up during the course of his hearings in the Senate. I still have confidence in Judge Haynsworth's qualifications, in his integrity. I believe that the Senate should approve him. I believe it will. I believe that he will be a great credit to the Supreme Court when he becomes a member of that Court, I hope in the fall term.

Q: Mr. President?

THE PRESIDENT: Mr. Horner.

Q: What is your view, sir, concerning the student moratorium and other campus demonstrations being planned for this fall against the Vietnam war?

THE PRESIDENT: I have often said that there is really very little that we in Washington can do with regard to running the university and college campuses of this country. We have enough problems running the nation, the national problems.

Now, I understand that there has been and continues to be opposition to the war in Vietnam on the campuses, and also in the nation. As far as this kind of activity is concerned, we expect it. However, under no circumstances will I be affected whatever by it.

Q: Mr. President, does the "heartland" theory, which is outlined in the book, *The Emerging Republican Majority,* by an assistant of John Mitchell coincide with your own approach towards strengthening the party?

THE PRESIDENT: I regret to say, and I hope this does not discourage sales of the book, which I understand are quite good, that I have not read the book. My own views with regard to the Republican party have been often stated in backgrounders and also in public sessions.

I believe the Republican party should be a national party. I don't believe in writing off any section of the country. I have attempted to make our appeal nationally, to the South, to the North, the East, the West, and to all groups within the country.

To the extent that the book advocates theories that are inconsistent with that principle, of course, I would disagree with it.

Q: Mr. President, sir, many civil rights groups are saying that your policy on school desegregation amounts to a retreat from the Supreme Court decision of some years ago. Some even say this amounts to an effort to build a party base for the Republicans in the South.

Where do you stand on school segregation and how much more time do you think districts that haven't complied ought to have?

THE PRESIDENT: This is a very difficult problem. I would say first that we have had a lot of criticism from the South insofar as our integration and desegregation policies are concerned, as well as from the groups to which you refer.

It seems to me that there are two extreme groups. There are those who want instant integration and those who want segregation forever. I believe that we need to have a middle course on which we are embarked. I think it is correct.

As I evaluate the situation this year, I found that there are twice as many schools that are desegregated at the opening of this term as was the case at the opening of the term a year ago. I think that is progress.

Now one other point that should be made. I do not consider that it is a victory for integration when the Federal Government cuts off funds for a school and thereby for both black and white students in that school, denies them the education they should have. That is not a victory for anybody. It is a defeat for education.

I believe, therefore, that that particular device should be used as we currently are using it: only when it is absolutely necessary for the purpose of achieving our objective of desegregated education. We are for it, but we are going to avoid both extremes.

Q: You told an audience in Houston last fall that you opposed reduction of the oilmen's depletion allowance. Do you still oppose it?

THE PRESIDENT: As a matter of fact, I not only told the audience in Houston that, but that has been my position since I entered politics in California 22 years ago. It is still my position.

I believe that the depletion allowance is in the national interest because I believe it is essential to develop our resources when, as we look at the Mideast and other sections of the world, many of our oil supplies could be cut off in the event of a world conflict.

On the other hand, I am a political realist. I noted the action of the House of Representatives in reducing the depletion allowance. Also, my primary concern is to get tax reform. The tax reform which we submitted in April, which goes further than any tax reform in 25 years—we need that tax reform above everything else.

On some of the items that I recommended, the House did not follow my recommendations, and the same will be in the Senate. When the bill comes to my desk, I intend to sign that bill, even though it does not follow all of my recommendations— provided it does not require a revenue shortfall that is more than I believe the Nation can stand.

Q: Mr. President, can you tell us the reasons behind Russia's prolonged failure to respond to your proposal for prompt negotiations on strategic arms limitations?

THE PRESIDENT: We are trying to explore those reasons. Mr. Rogers met with Mr. Gromyko on Monday. He will meet with him again on next Monday. He has no answer except a suggestion—and I don't think I am divulging any confidences in this respect—that we may expect an answer in the near future and that it is likely to be a positive answer.

Now, why the answer has been delayed is a question really that would have to be asked of those who have control of policy in the Kremlin.

Q: Mr. President, would you please tell us when you are going to make some real, honest-to-goodness changes in personnel in these bureaucrats who have been in power through many generations who are still wasting the taxpayers' money and making errors on the war and policy and promoting their friends, who are unqualified, to high jobs? I refer particularly to the office in the Pentagon of Assistant Secretary of Defense, Barry J. Shillito.

THE PRESIDENT: I don't know the gentleman, but after that question, I am going to find out who he is.

Q: Mr. President, could you give us some insight into your thinking, sir, as to the difference between the situation that required Supreme Court Justice Fortas to resign and the recent disclosures concerning Judge Haynsworth?

THE PRESIDENT: Since the matter is still before the Senate committee, I am not going to comment on the specifics that are being considered by that committee.

I will simply stand on my statement that I was aware generally of Judge Haynsworth's background, of his financial status, before he was appointed. I had confidence then in his integrity. I think the Senate committee will overwhelmingly agree with that confidence.

Q: Mr. President, Congress has always taken a very dim view of the idea of automatically adjusting the social security benefits to the cost of living, as you proposed yesterday. As a political realist, do you think you can change their minds on this?

THE PRESIDENT: I am going to try. As far as that particular proposal is concerned, there are some who reach a different conclusion for a reason that all of us will understand. They believe that it is an automatic escalator as far as inflation is concerned, and discourages those fiscal policies that would control inflation by assuming that we are going to have to raise social security because we have to accept the idea we are always going to have inflation.

My view is different. I have found in examining this situation that where the Congress must always act to see to it that those on social security keep up with the rise in the cost of living, that the Congress tends to act either too late or with perhaps even over-reaction to the situation.

I believe this is the sensible, sound way to do it, and I think that it will be deflationary rather than inflationary in the long run.

Q: How are you doing, Mr. President, in your efforts to end the Vietnam war?

THE PRESIDENT: Not as well as I would hope. I will not be doing as well as I would hope until the war is ended. I would point, however, to some progress.

We point first to the fact that we have announced that 60,000 Americans will be returned from Vietnam.

We point, second, to the fact that as a result of that and other actions, that 50,000 Americans who otherwise might have been drafted before the end of the year will not be drafted.

In addition to that, we find that infiltration, which tells us a lot about the enemy's future capabilities, looking at the first nine months of this year, is two-thirds less than it was in the corresponding period last year.

We find that American casualties are down one-third from what they were over the same nine-month period last year.

We find also that on the negotiating front, that the United States has made a far-reaching and comprehensive peace offer, a peace offer which offers not only mutual withdrawal of forces, internationally guaranteed cease-fires, internationally supervised elections in which we will accept the result of those elections and the South Vietnamese will as well, even if it is a Communist government, and by making that offer we have reversed the whole tide of world public opinion.

I noted when I was at the UN that I found no significant criticism of the U.S. policy. Now is the time for Hanoi to make the next move. We certainly have made it.

There is one thing, however, which I should emphasize that is not negotiable. We will talk about anything else. What is not negotiable is the right of the people of South Vietnam to choose their own leaders without outside imposition, either by us or by anybody else. We believe that that limited goal must be one that we must insist on. We believe that it can be achieved and we believe that if we stay on this course and if we can have some more support in the Nation—we have a lot of support, but even more support in the Nation—for this steady course, that the enemy then will have the incentive to negotiate, recognizing that it isn't going to gain time; that it isn't going to wait us out.

Once the enemy recognizes that it is not going to win its objective by waiting us out, then the enemy will negotiate and we will end this war before the end of 1970. That is the objective we have.

Mr. Theis?

Q: Going back to Mr. Cormier's question about the Vietnam cut-off, Senator Goodell, who will be a candidate next year, is providing the vehicle for a new round of Senate hearings on this subject. Will this either embarrass you as a Republican President, or other Republican candidates next year?

THE PRESIDENT: Mr. Theis, I, of course, can't control the course of Senate hearings, particularly in the Foreign Relations Committee. On the other hand, as far as those hearings are concerned, I believe that a discussion in the Senate of this matter, an open discussion, in which all the consequences of this very well intentioned statement by Senator Goodell, all the consequences of it, the fact that it inevitably leads to the conclusion that the United States is going to be stuck in Vietnam until the end of 1970, that there is no hope of ending the war before then, that when that comes home, I think the Senate will overwhelmingly reject the Goodell proposition.

Mr. Lisagor?

Q: Mr. President, does the insistence upon self-determination in Vietnam as an indispensable condition mean that you will support the present Thieu regime there until there is a negotiated settlement or until there are elections to change that regime?

THE PRESIDENT: It means, Mr. Lisagor, that the Thieu regime is there because of the result of an election, and until the people of South Vietnam have another opportunity to vote, I think that the United States should not reverse that election mandate. That is the answer that I think is only appropriate under the circumstances.

THE PRESIDENT: Mr. Loory?

Q: Going back to your response to the school desegregation question, it is now 15 years since the Supreme Court made its decision. How much longer do you think school desegregation should be allowed to exist anywhere in the country?

THE PRESIDENT: Only as long as it is absolutely necessary to achieve two goals—to achieve the goal of desegregated schools without, at the same time, irreparably damaging the goal of education now for the hundreds of thousands of black and white students who otherwise would be harmed if the move toward desegregation closes their schools.

Q: Mr. President, in connection with the school desegregation, one of the most controversial cases has been the action that the Government took in Mississippi in deciding to ask for a further postponement of some of the school integration there.

There have been published reports that Senator John Stennis of Mississippi informed the Administration that if the school integration went through there, he might not be able to handle the Administration's defense bill, and that you, yourself, made the decision.

Would you tell us whether these reports are true, whether Senator Stennis did so inform the Administration and your connection, if any, with this Mississippi case?

THE PRESIDENT: Senator Stennis did speak to me, along with several other representatives from Mississippi, with regard to his concern on this problem. But anybody who knows Senator Stennis and anybody who knows me, would know that he would be the last person to say, "Look, if you don't do what I want in Mississippi, I am not going to do what is best for this country."

He did not say that, and under no circumstances, of course, would I have acceded to it.

With regard to the action in Mississippi, that action was taken by this Administration because it was felt that better than cutting off the funds with the disastrous effect on the black and white students affected by that, the better course was the one that we did take—the one which gave more time to achieve desegregation without impairing education.

Q: There has been growing concern, sir, about deepening U.S. involvement in the combat in Laos. If you confirm that, would you also say where this runs counter to your new Asian policy?

THE PRESIDENT: There are no American combat forces in Laos. At the present time, we are concerned by the North

Vietnamese move into Laos. There are 50,000 North Vietnamese there at the present time, and more perhaps are coming.

As you know, the American participation in Laos is at the request of the neutralist government, which was set up in accordance with the 1962 Accords, which were agreed to, incidentally, by Hanoi, Peking and the Soviet Union. That was during the Administration of President Kennedy, negotiated by Mr. Harriman.

We have been providing logistical support and some training for the neutralist government in order to avoid Laos falling under Communist domination. As far as American power in Laos is concerned, there are none there at the present time on a combat basis.

Q: Mr. President?

THE PRESIDENT: Mr. Potter.

Q: You say there are no combat forces in Laos. How do you regard the airmen who bomb the Ho Chi Minh Trail from bases in Thailand and Vietnam? Would you regard those as combat forces?

THE PRESIDENT: When we consider the situation in Laos, I think President Kennedy in his first major television speech, which we all remember, in 1962, put it very well. He pointed out that Laos was potentially the key to what would happen in Thailand as well as in Vietnam, and the balance of Southeast Asia.

Now, Laos relates very much to Vietnam, because the Ho Chi Minh Trail runs through Laos. It is necessary, under those circumstances, that the United States take cognizance of that, and we do have aerial reconnaissance; we do have perhaps some other activities. I won't discuss those other activities at this time.

Q: Mr. President, yesterday in Chicago, your Assistant Secretary of Labor, Mr. Fletcher, tried to hold some hearings about getting more blacks into the construction unions, and he was prevented from doing so.

I wonder if you could tell us, first of all, your reaction to that specific situation in Chicago, and, secondly, your general feeling about getting more blacks into the trade unions?

THE PRESIDENT: Relating first to the second part of the question, it is essential that black Americans, all Americans, have an equal opportunity to get into the construction unions. There is a shortage in construction workers.

The interests of the nation requires this, apart from the matters of simple justice which are involved.

Second, in this respect, we have, as you know, the Philadelphia Plan. We have had our problems in Pittsburgh which are presently being discussed through our mediation, at least discussed, although it is still a very volatile situation. And now, of course, we have the problem in Chicago.

We intend to continue through the Department of Labor to attempt to make progress in this field, because in the long run, we cannot have construction unions which deny the right of all Americans to have those positions.

America needs more construction workers, and, of course, all Americans are entitled to an equal right to be a member of a union.

Q: Mr. President, on the subject of inflation, a number of economists have said that they do not believe the Administration can take the steam out of the economy without exerting pressure on specific price increases, such as the auto increase, the steel price increase, and the others.

Are you considering taking such steps, or do you feel that the corner has already been turned in the battle on inflation?

THE PRESIDENT: I would take those steps if history told me they would work. I would point out, however, that the previous Administration tried, through jawboning, as it is called, to put the blame on business for price increases; the blame on labor for wage increases.

In 1966, the guidelines died. They died because when Government, which is the primary agent for increasing prices, fails to do its job, Government asking labor and management to do theirs, it simply won't work. It is hypocritical, it is dishonest,

but most important, it is ineffective, because since 1966, as you will note, 1966, 1967, 1968, despite all of the calling of the people to the White House, telling them to hold prices down, hold wages down, prices continued to escalate.

Now, we have attacked the source of the budget. We have cut the budget by $7 billion. We have monetary restraints. We have asked for an extension of the surtax rather than its complete elimination. And these basic policies, which go to the core of the problem, are beginning to work, as Mr. McCracken pointed out in his speech in Detroit on Monday.

Now that the Government has set the example, I believe that labor and management would be well advised to follow the example. I am not job owning and telling them to reform themselves, when we refuse to reform ourselves. But I do say this: That labor and management, labor that asks for exhorbitant wage increases, management that raises prices too high, will be pricing themselves out of the market.

Anybody who bets on a continuing inflation will lose that bet, because our Government policies are beginning to work and we are going to stick to those policies until we cut the cost in the rise of living.

Q: Mr. President, my question concerns the draft, sir. The National Council to Repeal the Draft contends that your draft cut is a fraud, because the summer draft calls were inflated to allow for a pre-planned cut.

Would you comment, please?

THE PRESIDENT: I don't consider that charge as one of merit. I know of no inflation in the summer draft calls. I would also point out the fact that when you look at the statistics with regard to the withdrawal of our forces from Vietnam, with regard to the reduction of our forces around the world, it is quite obvious that we don't need as many through the draft. That is why we did it, and not for the reason suggested here.

Q: Mr. President, does the change of leadership in Hanoi, brought about by the death of Ho Chi Minh, show any sign at all to you, sir, of any change of intent either in combat or in Paris, on the part of the enemy?

THE PRESIDENT: Not yet, and we would expect nothing yet. Each of our systems of government has a problem. The major problem in the Communist system of government is the problem of succession. The North Vietnamese are going through that.

Immediately after a change of leadership, there is a tendency for uncertainty and rigidity as the contest for power goes on. We think that is going on within North Vietnam at the present time. However, looking to the future, as new leaders emerge, as they look at the consequences of past policy and the prospects for future policy, and as long as the United States holds to its course, I think the prospects for a possible change are there.

I am not predicting it. I am not trying to raise false hopes. I am only suggesting that since there is new leadership, we can expect perhaps some re-evaluation of policy.

Q: Mr. President, when do you plan to make Governor Rockefeller's report on Latin America public, and what is the main thrust of his recommendations to you?

THE PRESIDENT: During the time that I have been in Washington, and a few of you—not many—have been in Washington longer than I, in and out, I have found that we have had at least eight reports on Latin America.

In talking to my friends in the Diplomatic Corps, they have begged me, "Please don't study us," because they have said, "All you do is study us and make headlines with the words and then have no action."

Now, when I set up the Rockefeller Task Force, I made one commitment to him, to which he completely agreed: that he would make the report to me, and what we would try to do is to make our actions make the news rather than the words make the news.

I have already met with Governor Rockefeller. There are some very exciting recommendations in his report which we are going to adopt. I am going to meet with him for an extended visit tomorrow at Camp David, along with the Assistant Secretary of State for Latin America, Mr. Meyer.

Then later in the month—I mean later in October—we will be making a major new procurement on Latin American policy, and a number of the Rockefeller recommendations will be in that announcement.

Q: Mr. President, two weeks ago today you had a major meeting with your top advisers and people directly involved in the Vietnam effort. I don't think we have had a report, as such, on that meeting. I wonder if there was a focus such as the death of Ho Chi Minh, or just what was it all about?

THE PRESIDENT: Naturally, much of what was discussed in that meeting could not be appropriately discussed in a public forum like this. We looked over the military situation, the political situation in South Vietnam, and naturally we speculated privately, and I would never speculate publicly, as to what might happen with the change of leadership.

We did determine, however, that there were some good signs on the horizon—the failure of the enemy to be able to launch a summer offensive which everybody had predicted, the fact that the infiltration rate was down by two-thirds, which means that the possibility of an offensive this fall has receded.

We took note of that, and the fact that this Vietnamization program, despite some problems, was moving forward. Political and economic stability in the South, despite some significant problems, was going forward.

All of these matters were taken into consideration. Generally, I would not like to leave the impression that this was an overly optimistic report, because I believe in looking at Vietnam and all of our problems in a very realistic, down-to-earth manner.

But I would say this: I think we are on the right course in Vietnam. We are on a course that is going to end this war. It will end much sooner if we can have to an extent, to the extent possible in this free country, a united front behind very reasonable proposals. If we have that united front, the enemy then will begin to talk, because the only missing ingredient to escalating the time when we will end the war is the refusal of the enemy in Paris to even discuss our proposals. The moment that they start discussing those proposals, then that means that we can bring the war to a conclusion sooner than if we just continue on our present course.

THE PRESS: Thank you very much.

OCTOBER 20

Following is the complete text of President Nixon's news conference on Judge Clement F. Haynsworth, held Oct. 20 in the President's office. The White House described it as an "informal meeting with members of the White House press corps."

THE PRESIDENT: Ron Ziegler has suggested that it might be useful to members of the press if from time to time on a specific subject I brief the press myself and then take questions so you can follow through on that subject.

You may recall that I did this on the occasion of the Chief Justice Burger subject and it seems to me that this type of procedure is one that we can follow.

I want also to say that as far as those who are here for television and radio, you, of course, can only comment on this because we do not have sound and do not have film. But we will have ready, I understand, on December 15th, the new press room in the West Wing. When that is available we shall have this kind of a briefing session on a subject-by-subject basis in that room so that those who want to get sound or film can get it. We won't do it always that way. Sometimes we will do it this way, but I think that will be a very useful way to do it.

It will be a very nice room. I was there this morning and it is coming along very well.

This morning this will be on the record and a transcript will be made available to you when we finish.

This morning I have selected as a subject one you have been asking Ron about over the past several weeks, the Haynsworth matter.

In discussing that matter, I want to give you my own thinking with regard to the nomination of Judge Haynsworth, where it stands at the present time, and what my evaluation of the charges that have been made against him is.

You may recall that when I nominated Judge Haynsworth, I said that he was the man, of all the Circuit judges in the country, and a Chief Judge, with 12 years experience, that he was the man I considered to be, by age, experience, background, philosophy, the best qualified to serve on the Supreme Court at this time.

Three weeks ago at a press conference I not only had one question on this matter, as I recall, two. I reiterated that position, and today, after having had an opportunity to evaluate all the charges that have been made in the past three weeks I reaffirm my support of Judge Haynsworth and in reaffirming it I reaffirm it with even greater conviction.

I say with greater conviction because when a man has been through the fire, when he has had his entire life and its entire record exposed to the glare of investigation, which, of course, any man who is submitted for confirmation to the Senate should expect to have, and in addition to that, when he has had to go through what I believe to be a vicious character assassination, if after all that he stands up and comes through as a man of integrity, a man of honesty, and a man of qualifications, then that even more indicates that he deserves the support of the President of the United States who nominated him in the first place, and also the votes of the Senators who will be voting on his nomination.

I would like to touch upon perhaps three or four of the major points that have been raised: they are technical points, as many of you who have been studying the case will know.

I should say I have some experience in investigations myself, and I have studied this case completely in every respect.

I have read the income tax returns, the financial statements, all the charges that have been made by various Senators, and the answers that have been made on the Senate floor by Judge Marlow Cook, by Senator Allott, and also the evaluation, of course, of the Department of Justice.

Based on that examination, I personally now have made and concluded, now that all the evidence is in, there are four or five points, perhaps, that are worth discussing, but more if you want to bring them up in your question.

The charge is made that Judge Haynsworth should have disqualified himself in six cases involving litigants who were customers of a company in which he owned stock. I have examined those cases and that charge. I agree completely with the American Bar Association, with Judge Sobeloff who conducted an investigation of this matter in 1963 and 1964, and also with John Frank, the leading authority on conflict of interest, when he said that not only did Judge Haynsworth have no requirement to disqualify himself; he had a responsibility to sit in these cases because in not one of these instances or cases named did Judge Haynsworth use his influence in any way in behalf of the company in which he owned stock, and in no instance was there any indication that he was influenced whatever in decisions by that stock-ownership.

If you want to spread this out just a bit, if we were to apply that kind of a standard to all Federal Court judges across this country, I would say that perhaps half of them would have to be impeached, and some in the Supreme Court, because carrying it to the ridiculous end result, if a judge owned stock in U.S. Steel, U.S. Steel has customers, a great number of them, and most of those customers or a great number of them get to the Supreme Court or the Circuit Court of Appeals.

So the judge should not disqualify himself because customers of a company he happens to own stock in are in the court. This charge has no substance.

The second major charge is that Judge Haynsworth had a substantial interest in litigation which he decided as a member of the Circuit Court of Appeals.

Let me be quite precise. The law refers not to a substantial interest in the company or the litigant, but a substantial interest in the case. Of course, that is the proper standard to apply.

In this case, I find that the Senator from Indiana who made the charges cited six cases, and these six cases represent perhaps one of the most glaring examples of sloppy staff work that I have seen in the years of seeing what can happen in such cases. Two of the cases were mistakes, of course, and on the others the question of a substantial interest has been, again, reduced to an absurdity.

In the Brunswick case, it is now found, as Judge Marlow Cook pointed out—and he was a judge before he became a Senator, as you know—Judge Haynsworth would have profited by $5.00, at the most, probably $4.92, the exact figure, if the litigant had recovered all the amount that was involved in the case.

In the Grace case, which involved, incidentally, a parent-subsidiary relationship, Judge Haynsworth's stock would have been reduced in value by 48 cents as a result of the decision that he made.

As an indication of the staff work in this case, one of the other reasons was the Greenville Hotel case.

It is true that Judge Haynsworth did have an interest in the Greenville Hotel. It appeared that years ago as an attorney he was a director for the hotel. Being a director of the hotel he was issued a share of stock in the hotel corporation.

Then after he became a judge, he received a stock dividend of 15 cents, a check which was mailed to him. The judge, of course, returned the check, thinking it was a joke. The company returned it to him. So Judge Haynsworth recorded 15 cents on his income tax return.

Then there is another group of cases that have been raised. That is that Judge Haynsworth should have disqualified himself in those cases involving former clients of his law firm. I should say his former law firm. The law is quite clear here. A judge does not have responsibility and should not disqualify himself in cases involving clients of his former law firm unless that relationship has been very close to the client and has continued close, and also, in point of time, unless the relationship has continued. In other words, the passage of time and the closeness of the relationship is a factor to be considered.

In all of the cases, the 12 which were raised in hearings involving the former clients, it appeared that Judge Haynsworth was beyond suspicion, and, as a matter of fact, not only should not have disqualified himself but had a duty to sit, in my opinion.

Now the Bobby Baker matter. This is guilt by association and character assassination of the very worst type. Judge Haynsworth knew Bobby Baker. He saw him last ten years ago. Many of you gentlemen of the press know I used to see him quite often when he was a Clerk to the Majority. He had three contacts with him. He had no influence on Bobby Baker, and Bobby Baker had no influence on him.

The so-called business deals in which they were partners have been completely laid before the Senate Committee, and any suggestion of improper influence has been discounted by Senator Williams, who is kind of a bull on these matters.

I should say, incidentally, while we are talking, I knew Bobby Baker very well myself, too, as the Presiding Officer of the Senate. He was Clerk to the Majority.

One of the members of my staff, Rose Mary Woods, pointed up something I had forgotten. As a matter of fact, Bobby Baker's wife served as a stenographer on my staff for several months when I was a Senator from California.

The fact that I knew him does not make me guilty by association. The fact that Judge Haynsworth along with others knew him, Senator Hollings and others, does not make him guilty by association.

On this particular point, I stand very firmly against the use of that tactic.

Now I will go to something a little more fundamental because this involves the decision as to what Senators should consider as they determine whether they confirm a judge for the Supreme Court, or, for that matter, any court.

The question is raised, and one Senator, Senator Magnuson, I thought quite candidly and honestly faced up to this question.

He said he did not raise any question with regard to Judge Haynsworth's impropriety charges, but that he simply disagreed with his philosophy on certain matters, civil rights and labor law.

That is a ground which a Senator can give for rejecting, perhaps, Judge Haynsworth. I do not believe it is a proper ground. I would agree with those Senators, many of whom are now opposing Judge Haynsworth, who, in the Marshall confirmation, categorically said that a judge's philosophy was not a proper basis for rejecting him from the Supreme Court.

Looking back over the history of the cases, as I said when you were here before on the Burger matter, among my heroes of the Court is Louis Brandeis. If philosophy were a test for him he would have been ruled out because he was too liberal.

Another was Charles Evans Hughes. If philosophy had been a test for him he would have been ruled out because he was too conservative in representing the business interests.

If you want to go back and read what really can happen in cases of this sort, I would suggest you read the debate over Louis Brandeis and also the confirmation of Charles Evans Hughes, in which they poured on him all the filth they could possibly amass because of his connection with insurance companies. Also like Judge Haynsworth, he had represented various other interests.

As far as philosophy is concerned, I would be inclined to agree with the writer for the *St. Louis Post-Dispatch* who said he thought Judge Haynsworth was a man with a razor sharp mind and a middle of the road record on the major issues.

But if Judge Haynsworth's philosophy leans to the conservative side, in my view that recommends him to me. I think the Court needs balance, and I think that the Court needs a man who is conservative—and I use the term not in terms of economics, but conservative, as I said of Judge Burger, conservative in respect of his attitude towards the Constitution.

It is the Judge's responsibility, and the Supreme Court's responsibility, to interpret the Constitution and interpret the law, and not to go beyond that in putting his own socio-economic philosophy into decisions in a way that goes beyond the law, beyond the Constitution.

Now the final point, and this one is one that troubles, I think, many people who are not prejudiced against Judge Haynsworth because he is a Southerner or because of his civil rights record, or because of his labor record.

It is this: At this time in our history, it is very important to have a man that is beyond reproach.

An editorial in the *Washington Post*, I thought quite a thoughtful editorial, was quite candid in saying that the charges against him on the ethical side were not warranted, or at least were not with the foundation they should be, but because a doubt had been raised, that the name should be withdrawn.

I just want to say categorically here I shall never accept that philosophy with regard to Judge Haynsworth.

The appearance of impropriety, some say, is enough to disqualify a man who served as judge or in some other capacity. That would mean that anybody who wants to make a charge can thereby create the appearance of impropriety, raise a doubt, and that then his name should be withdrawn.

That isn't our system. Under our system, a man is innocent until he is proven guilty.

Judge Haynsworth, when the charges were made, instead of withdrawing his name, as he could—and, incidentally, if he now asks for his name to be withdrawn I would not do so—Judge Haynsworth, when the charges were made, openly came before the committee, answered all the questions, and submitted his case to the committee, and now to the full Senate.

I have examined the charges. I find that Judge Haynsworth is an honest man. I find that he has been, in my opinion as a lawyer, a lawyer's lawyer and a judge's judge. I think, he will be a great credit to the Supreme Court, and I am going to stand by him until he is confirmed. I trust he will be.

Q: Mr. President, how much of this attack on Judge Haynsworth do you think is an attack, an end run attempt to get at you?

THE PRESIDENT: I have read some of the spec stories on that but I am not going to be involved in that.

The Brandeis case was not a very proud moment in the history of the United States Senate. There was anti-Semitism in it and there was also a very strong partisan attitude towards Woodrow Wilson.

The Hughes debate was not a proud moment. There were a lot of partisan considerations that entered into it. This was a great man and a great Chief Justice, as was Judge Brandeis.

I don't think the Parker nomination was a very happy moment either.

I don't hold any brief for any one of these men in terms of philosophy. I don't agree with them, but no lawyer agrees with every other lawyer on everything. But in Judge Parker's case it was not proper to turn down a man because he was a Southerner.

It is not proper to turn down a man because he is a Southerner, because he is a Jew, because he is a Negro or because of his philosophy. The question is what kind of a lawyer is he? What is his attitude toward the Constitution? Is he a man of integrity? Is he a man that will call the great cases that come before him as he sees them, and in this case will provide the balance that his great court needs? I think Judge Haynsworth does that.

Q: Mr. President, it has been suggested, and I wonder what you think of the idea, that every member of the Federal Judiciary holding a lifetime appointment, to avoid this kind of trouble, place their investments perhaps in some kind of a blind trust or perhaps in some kind of fund.

THE PRESIDENT: Bill, as you noticed, Judge Haynsworth said he would put his stocks into trust. I suppose the American Bar Association or, for that matter, the Senate, or the Congress, could lay down some sort of a rule about that to really meet the problem.

I don't happen to think that blind trusts, particularly in the public mind, are going to remove these questions. That is one of the reasons, as a matter of fact, before I came to office, I disposed of every stock I owned. I own nothing but real estate.

Q: What would you say, Mr. President, when people say you selected Haynsworth in large part because of political obligations?

THE PRESIDENT: I selected Judge Haynsworth for the reasons that I mentioned. I was looking for a man, first, who, like Judge Burger, had broad experience as an Appeals judge, a Court of Appeals judge—that is the next highest court to the Supreme Court—who was the right age, and who also had a philosophy for the Constitution similar to my own because that is what a President is expected to do. As far as a political obligation is concerned, I had no political obligation to select Judge Haynsworth or Judge Burger. In fact, my acquaintance with Judge Haynsworth can only be casual. If he would walk into this room, I am afraid I wouldn't recognize him.

Q: Can you tell me on what you base your confidence in the confirmation, Mr. President?

THE PRESIDENT: The Senate is a body in which time and discussion work on the side of fairness and justice. That sounds like a cliche, I suppose.

As a former member of the Senate it is perhaps a self-serving statement. But I am convinced that when Senators read the record, as I did, not just the editorials but the record, the evidence, and as they study every one of these cases—and believe me, I have studied every one of them—if I had found one case where there was a serious doubt I would have had him removed because I want that court to be above reproach.

If the Senators do that, I believe a majority of the Senators will vote for Judge Haynsworth's confirmation.

Let me say this too: It is not a partisan matter.

To answer your earlier question, sure, there is some partisanship, I suppose. That is perhaps part of the game, and perhaps with some Republicans. I am not questioning their motives.

All I ask is that every Senator should look very carefully into this record because he has to make the decision that I had to make.

Let me be quite candid. There were those, good friends of mine, who came to me a few weeks ago suggesting I withdraw Judge Haynsworth's nomination due to the fact that a doubt had been raised and that politically it was going to be very difficult to wield.

I had to consider then whether because charges had been made without proof, and whether there was a doubt, whether I would then take upon my hands the destruction of a man's whole life, to destroy his reputation, to drive him from the bench and public service.

I did not do so, and I think that as Senators consider what they will be doing as they vote on this matter, as they consider the evidence, they will realize that they are dealing here with an honest man, a man who has laid all the facts before them, a man who is qualified to serve on the Supreme Court, and I think they will conclude as I did that there is no dishonor in connection with him.

Q: Senator Griffin is one of the men you referred to and he has studied his record, case by case.

How do you account for Senator Griffin's point of view?

THE PRESIDENT: I hope he will study it further. I trust that after he studies it more, he will change his mind.

Q: One of the things that has happened in the Haynsworth case is that there has been a piecemeal revelation of details.

Is there a problem in our government, a problem of confidence with Congress and with judges, that we do not have a more comprehensive disclosure law?

THE PRESIDENT: The matter of piecemeal disclosure is because the critics have chosen to make the charges this way.

Some Senators were worried about when the other shoe would drop. I saw the other shoe and it wasn't even a slipper. We wondered why Senator Bayh wouldn't debate Senator Hollings. Senator Bayh is a very articulate man. But after reading the record I know why. He was well advised not to debate.

THE PRESS: Thank you, Mr. President.

DECEMBER 8

Following is the complete text of President Nixon's Dec. 8 news conference, his eighth since taking office and the first since Sept. 26.

THE PRESIDENT: Won't you be seated. Mr. Smith.

Q: Mr. President, do you see any signs of the Vietnam war cooling off?

THE PRESIDENT: Well, looking over the long period, yes—as far as recent weeks are concerned, since my speech of Nov. 3, no significant change. When we compare the situation with regard to infiltration and casualties this year with last year, there is a great difference. Looking to the future, if that situation continues, I believe that we can see that the Vietnam war will come to a conclusion regardless of what happens at the bargaining table. It will come to a conclusion as a result of the plan that we have instituted on which we are embarked for replacing American troops with Vietnamese forces. Mr. Cornell.

Q: In your opinion, was what happened at My Lai a massacre, an alleged massacre, or what was it? And what do you think can be done to prevent things like that? If it was a massacre, do you think it was justifiable on military or other grounds?

THE PRESIDENT: Well, trying to answer all of those questions and sorting it out, I would start first with this statement: What appears was certainly a massacre, under no circumstances was it justified. One of the goals we are fighting for in Vietnam is to keep the people from South Vietnam from having imposed upon them a government which has atrocity against civilians as one of its policies. We cannot ever condone or use atrocities against civilians in order to accomplish that goal.

Now when you use the word "alleged," that is only proper in terms of the individuals involved. Under our system a man is not guilty until proven be be so. There are several individuals involved here who will be tried by military courts. Consequently, we should say "alleged" as far as they are concerned until they are proven guilty.

As far as this kind of activity is concerned, I believe that it is an isolated incident. Certainly within this Administration we are doing everything possible to find out whether it was isolated and so far our investigation indicates that it was.

As far as the future is concerned, I would only add this one point: looking at the other side of the coin, we have 1,200,000 Americans who have been in Vietnam. Forty thousand of them have given their lives. Virtually all of them had helped the people of Vietnam in one way or another. They built roads and schools. They built churches and pagodas. The Marines alone this year have built over 250,000 churches, pagodas and temples for the people of Vietnam. Our soldiers in Vietnam and sailors and airmen this year alone contributed three-quarters of a million dollars to help the people of South Vietnam.

Now this record of generosity, of decency, must not be allowed to be smeared and slurred because of this kind of incident. That is why I am going to do everything I possibly can to see that all of the facts in this incident are brought to light and that those who are charged, if they are found guilty, are punished. Because if it is isolated, it is against our policy and we shall see to it that what these men did, if they did it, does not smear the decent men that have gone to Vietnam, in my opinion, in a very important cause.

Q: Vice President Agnew, in recent weeks, has made two speeches in which he has criticized the news media, broadcasting in particular. What, if anything, in those speeches is there with which you disagree?

THE PRESIDENT: Before this audience?

The Vice President does not clear his speeches with me, just as I did not clear my speeches with President Eisenhower. However, I believe that the Vice President rendered a public service in talking in a very dignified and courageous way about a problem that many Americans are concerned about; that is, the coverage by news media, and particularly the television news media, of public figures.

Let me be quite precise. He did not advocate censorship. On the contrary, he advocated that there should be free expression. He did not oppose bias. On the contrary, he recognized, as I do, that there should be opinion. Let me say on that score that I don't want a bunch of intellectual enuchs, either writing the news or talking about the news. I like excitement in the news, whether it is on television or whether it is in the columns. He did say, and perhaps this point should be well taken, that television stations might well follow the practice of newspapers, of separating news from opinion. When opinion is expressed, label it so, but don't mix the opinion in with reporting of the news.

It seems to me these were useful suggestions. Perhaps the networks disagreed with the criticisms. But I would suggest that they should be just as dignified and just as reasonable in answering the criticisms as he was in making them. Mr. Bailey.

Q: Sir, if the final version of the tax reform bill now pending in Congress includes the Senate-adopted $800 exemption provision and the 15-percent Social Security increase, can you sign it?

THE PRESIDENT: No. Mr. Theis?

Q: May I go back to Mr. Cornell's question to ask in the light of the My Lai incident, would you prefer a civilian commission, something other than a military inquiry in this case?

THE PRESIDENT: Mr. Theis, I do not believe that a civilian commission at this time would be useful. I believe that the matter now is in the judicial process, and that a civilian commission might be, and very properly could be, used by the defendant's attorneys as having prejudiced their rights.

Now, if it should happen that the judicial process, as set up by the military under the new law passed by Congress, does not prove to be adequate in bringing this incident completely before the public, as it should be brought before the public, then I would consider a commission, but not at this time.

Q: Mr. President, today Secretary of Defense Laird is reported to have said that you would be expected to announce a further troop cutback from Vietnam later this month, probably below 40,000 men. Also, today, Senator George Aiken is reported as having said that you have already withdrawn or ordered withdrawn another 9,000 that were not announced. Could you give us your thinking on the prospects and the substance of both of those reports?

THE PRESIDENT: As I indicated in my speech on television on Nov. 3, the reports from Vietnam with regard to infiltration, with regard to casualties, and with regard to the training of South Vietnamese, indicate more progress on all fronts than we had anticipated when we started our troop scheduled withdrawal in June. There will be a troop cut with a replacement by South Vietnamese later this month, I would say within the next two to three weeks. As far as the number is concerned, the number is still under consideration. It will depend on the events and our analysis of the events between now and the time I make the announcement.

Q: Sir, there are two flagrant instances of intimidation and harassment and threats against Pentagon personnel who may have divulged information to Congress and to the public about cost overruns and mismanagements and irregular industrial alliances.

These two instances are related because some of the same people are involved. I refer, one, to the Gestapo-like interrogation of Pentagon personnel to see who leaked information to Sarah McClendon for news stories. This involves Barry Shillito and Edward Sheridan. I also refer to the firing of A. Ernest Fitzgerald whose divulgement of cost overruns saved the American people $2 billion. His greatest critics were Dr. Robert Moot and Barry Shillito. Can you do something about this, please, sir?

THE PRESIDENT: Miss McClendon, I better, after the way you put this question.

Q. Mr. President, last week the White House Conference on Food and Nutrition strongly recommended approval of a bill which has passed the Senate to reform the food stamp program that was blocked in the House and another bill which would reform the school lunch program which has passed the House but is blocked in the Senate.

Your Administration is reported to be lobbying against both bills. Will you follow the recommendations of your White House Conference, and what course of action will you take?

THE PRESIDENT: I favor the approach that our Administration has put before the Congress as being the more responsible approach on both scores. I will, of course, consider the recommendations of the White House conference, which will be made to me at my request within approximately 30 days.

There is another recommendation by the White House conference which I, unfortunately, cannot give really sympathetic consideration to, and that is the one recommending a $5,400 minimum for a family of four in America. That would cost approximately $70 billion to $80 billion in taxes, or $70 billion to $80 billion in increased prices. I do not say that to discredit the conference. I simply say that all of us in this country want to end hunger in the United States. All of us want the poor to have a minimum floor, and that minimum to be as high as possible.

All of us, for example, want Social Security to be higher. But when I consider all of these matters, I have to think also of this fact: The fact that I, as President, am the one who has the primary responsibility for the cost of living in this country.

Referring a moment ago to the tax question, it would be very easy for me to sign a bill which reduces taxes. But if I sign the kind of bill which the Senate is about to pass, I would be reducing taxes for some of the American people and raising the prices for all the American people. I will not do that.

Q: How fair do you think news media have been in reporting on you and on Vice President Agnew and on your Administration generally?

THE PRESIDENT: Generally, I think the news media has been fair. I have no complaints about, certainly, the extent of the coverage that I have received.

I also will have no complaints just so long as the news media allows, as it does tonight, an opportunity for me to be heard directly by the people and then the television commentators to follow me. I will take my chances. Miss Thomas.

Q: Do you think that the wife of the Attorney General, like the Vice President, has rendered a public service by her statements on protest movements and on their political activities?

THE PRESIDENT: Well, now, Miss Thomas, I decided when this Administration came to Washington that I would take the responsibility for answering for my own personal family and for my Cabinet family, but that each Cabinet member would answer for his family. So I will leave that question to the Attorney General. Mr. Semple.

Q: To broaden that a little bit, on Nov. 3 you called for support for your policies in Vietnam. You since received a response that some of your aides feel is gratifying. My question is, however, have you not with the ehlp of Vice President Agnew, and I am referring to some of his recent speeches, purchased the support at the cost of alienating a sizable segment of the American public and risking polarization of the country?

THE PRESIDENT: Mr. Semple, one of the problems of leadership is to take a position. I like to be liked, I don't like to say things that everybody doesn't agree with.

When peace marchers come to Washington it would be very easy to say that I agree with them and I will do what they want. But a President has to do what he considers to be right, right for the people, right, for example, in pursuing a just peace and not just peace for our time, for a little time.

I believe that I pursued that path. I do not believe that that is a disservice to the public interest, because I believe that sometimes it is necessary to draw the line clearly, not to have enmity against those who disagree, but to make it clear that there can be no compromise where such great issues as self-determination and freedom and a just peace are involved.

Q: Will you assess for us how you see now the prospects of a special session of Congress during the Christmas holidays?

THE PRESIDENT: Well, I have had some conversations with some of the Members of the House and Senate since I indicated to the Republican leaders that I might call that session.

I would say the jury is still out. The House is moving much more speedily. The Senate has begun to move more speedily. If the present Congress continues at this rate, it may be that we can all have some vacation after Christmas. But if they do not pass the appropriation bills as I indicated, I will have to call a special session as much as I would not want to do so.

Q: The United States today asked for a postponement in the SALT talks, the Strategic Arms Talks. Can you tell us why and assess the talks for us, please?

THE PRESIDENT: Well, the postponement does not have any long-range significance. It is only for the purpose of developing positions in a proper way. As far as the progress is concerned, I would say it is encouraging. I say that somewhat cautiously, because I would not want to leave out the hope that we would have an agreement within a matter of weeks or even months.

But it is encouraging because both sides are presenting positions in a very serious way and are not trying to make propaganda out of their positions. Both sides, I believe, therefore, want a limitation on strategic arms. As long as this is the case, there is a chance for an agreement.

Now, it is going to take some time, because what is involved here, as distinguished from the test ban, as distinguished from the nonproliferation treaty, both of which were important, but which were basically peripheral issues, here you have the basic security of the United States of America and the Soviet Union involved. Therefore, both must bargain hard. But I believe the progress to date has been good. The prospects are better than I anticipated they would be when the talks began.

Q: Mr. President, as the Vietnamization process moves along, are there any circumstances, such as, perhaps, a series of defeats by the South Vietnamese army, that might lead you to want to reverse the process of troop withdrawals and increase our troops in Vietnam?

THE PRESIDENT: I do not anticipate that at this time. I want to make it, of course, clear, that we do not anticipate that there will not be troubles. The enemy still has the capability of launching some offensive actions. Not, certainly, the capability

that it had a year ago. It is much less because their infiltration has been less. But the present prognosis that I think I can make is this: That we can go forward with our troop withdrawal program and that any action that the enemy takes, either against us or the South Vietnamese can be contained within that program.

Q: Mr. President, is there any truth in the reports that have been rather persistent for the last couple of weeks that we paid Thailand something like a billion dollars for their cooperation in Vietnam? In that connection, where do our allies, like Thailand, South Korea, and their troops fit into our withdrawal program?

THE PRESIDENT: Well, first, with regard to the second part of the question, both Thailand and South Korea have no intention, at least none that has been indicated to us, of withdrawing forces at the time that we are withdrawing ours, because we have a much greater commitment there than they have. Second, with regard to the billion dollars that allegedly has been paid to Thailand, the amount is, of course, far less than that. But quite candidly, yes, the United States is subsidizing the Thai troops. We also are subsidizing the South Korean troops. We are doing exactly what we did in western Europe immediately after World War II when we subsidized virtually all of western Europe due to the fact they could not maintain forces themselves for their own cefense. These are newly developing countries. They are unable to maintain their forces for their own defense. Therefore, we think that subsidy is correct. I can only say this, it seems to me it makes a great deal of sense. The Thais are in Vietnam as volunteers, and if they are willing to go there are volunteers, I would much rather pay out some money to have them there than to have American men fighting there in their place.

Q: Since Ambassador Lodge resigned, you have not named a successor as Chief Negotiator. Is this in effect downgrading the Paris talks, because they have been nonproductive?

THE PRESIDENT: No. Mr. Habib is a very competent career diplomat, and he will be able to discuss anything that is brought up seriously by the other side. We are simply waiting for a serious proposal.

Q: Considering how things have gone in Paris, how do you now rate the chances of a negotiated settlement of the war?

THE PRESIDENT: Not good. Quite candidly, I would like to say that they were good, but looking at the present situation, the enemy's line continues to be hard.

Their proposals are quite frivolous, as the ones by the VC today, and I do not anticipate any progress on the negotiating front at this time. But I put in this one condition: As our program for Vietnamization continues to work, and as it becomes apparent, as I believe it increasingly will, that it will succeed, I think the pressures for the enemy then to negotiate a settlement will greatly increase, because once we are out and the South Vietnamese are there, they will have a much harder individual to negotiate with than they had when we were there.

Q: Before the Supreme Court ordered immediate school integration, you said you preferred a middle road policy, that is between segregation forever and instant integration. What is your policy now?

THE PRESIDENT: To carry out what the Supreme Court has laid down. I believe in carrying out the law even though I may have disagreed as I did in this instance with the degree that the Supreme Court eventually came down with. But we will carry out the law.

Q: A question on your broad philosophy on the tax problem that we are all struggling with. You have often pointed out that this is a very rich country and there are some people who argue that the American people can tax themselves whenever they want to and when they are prepared to make the sacrifice in order to provide the very substantial sums that are necessary for the very big problems at home, the cities, getting their housing program rolling and so forth, and that we might very well do it now and get on with the job because the end of the Vietnam war apparently is not going to release very substantial amounts of fresh funds. Could you comment on this rather hair-shirted approach to the tax program?

THE PRESIDENT: It is a very complicated but very fundamental question. I would put it briefly in answer in this way: Approximately 35 to 37 percent of the total income of the United States goes to taxes, that is in federal, state and local taxes. I believe that amount is high enough. I believe that when a nation takes a substantially larger portion of the national income than that for taxes, that then that nation loses its character as a free, private enterprice economy and turns over and becomes primarily a state-controlled and oriented economy.

Therefore, while I believe that the United States can afford what it needs to do in many fields, including the environment and others that I will be touching upon in the State of the Union, I do not want to see a substantial increase in the tax burden as a percentage of our gross national income. Mr. Lisagor.

Q: Mr. President, getting back to the Congress for a moment, House Democratic Leader Carl Albert today said that the Administration spokesmen have issued misleading statements about the Congress in an effort to undermine public confidence in it. He went on to say, and I quote him as saying it is the fault of the Administration for delays, obfuscations and confusion and lack of leadership on the part of the Administration. Would you care to comment?

THE PRESIDENT: Well, that sounds like a pretty good political statement by Mr. Albert. I can understand why he is the Majority Leader and might find it necessary to make that statement. However, I think he knows, as all of you know, for six months we have had a major crime control package before the Congress with no action. For months we have had other programs in a number of fields there without action. This Congress has the worst record in terms of appropriations bills of any Congress in history. Now let me say I am a defender of the Congress, and, having said all of this, I am a defender of Carl Albert. I like him and I want to continue to work with him and I don't want to answer that question any further at this point. All right.

Q: I have two related questions, sir. Why have you only had three full-dress news conferences in six months? And what is your reaction to the general philosophy among some of us in the press that the press is not doing its job, if it doesn't hold the Administration, any Administration, to account without, shall we say coziness?

THE PRESIDENT: Well, I don't think I have had any problem with regard to the press holding me to account in my political lifetime. I think if I could paraphrase Winston Churchill's statement made in 1914, I have always derived a great deal of benefit from criticism and I have never known when I was short of it. Now as far as the press conferences are concerned, I try to have press conferences when I think there is a public interest—not just a press interest or my interest, but the public interest in having them—and also to use various devices. As you know, I have had conferences in my office. I had a conference in Guam. I have also made three major television addresses in prime time. If I considered that the press and the public needs more information than I am giving through press conferences, I will have more. I welcome the opportunity to have them. I am not afraid of them—just as the press is not afraid of me.

Q: Mr. President, will our Vietnam involvement be reduced in your Administration to the point where it will command no more public attention than, say, Korea does now?

THE PRESIDENT: That is certainly our goal and I think we are well on the way to achievement of that goal. We have a plan for the reduction of American forces in Vietnam, for removing all combat forces from Vietnam, regardless of what happens in the negotiations. That plan is going forward. As I will report to the nation, when I announce the troop withdrawal two or three weeks from now, I believe that developments since my Nov. 3 speech have been on schedule.

Q: Mr. President, what limits do you put on what the people of the United States ought to know about the war that is going on in Laos, and the American involvement in it?

THE PRESIDENT: The public interest. As far as I am concerned, the people of the United States are entitled to know everything that they possibly can with regard to any involvement of the United States abroad. As you know, and in answer to a question I think Mr. Potter asked at the last press conference, I pointed out what were the facts. There are no American combat troops in Laos. Our involvement in Laos is solely due to the request of Souvanna Phouma, the neutralist prime minister, who was set up there in Laos, as a result of the Laos negotiations and accords that were arranged by Governor Harriman during the Kennedy Administration. We are attempting to uphold those accords and we are doing that despite the fact that North Vietnam has 50,000 troops in Laos. We are also, as I have publicly indicated and as you know, interdicting the Ho Chi Minh Trail as it runs through Laos. Beyond that, I don't think the public interest would be served by any further discussion. All right.

Q: Mr. President, Budget Director Mayo said recently that uncontrolled federal spending is likely to push the fiscal '71 budget beyond the $200 billion mark and that the eventual elimination of the surtax could produce a deficit that year. I have two questions: Do you foresee the possibility of a deficit in '71 and, if that is the prospect, will you recommend continuing the surtax beyond June 30?

THE PRESIDENT: The answer to the second question is that I do not intend to recommend the continuation of the surtax beyond June 30.

With regard to the first part of the question, only by use of the Presidential veto and by impounding funds are we going to be able to avoid the kind of a situation that Director Mayo has described. But I can assure you that I intend to use all the powers of the Presidency to stop the rise in the cost of living.

Q: Mr. President, the enemy's infiltration has been up recently in Vietnam. Could you give us your assessment of this, specifically whether you think he is replacing losses, or building up for an offensive, and what significance could this fact have in terms of your own plans for troop reduction?

THE PRESIDENT: It has great significance because, as I have pointed out, enemy infiltration, the fact that it was down, is one of the reasons that we have been able to go forward with our troop withdrawal programs. However, I have been analyzing these reports week by week. The figures that we got two weeks ago seem to have been inflated. The inflation rate is not as great as we thought then. It is higher than it was a few months ago. It is still lower than it was a year ago. We do not consider the infiltration significant enough to change our troop withdrawal plans. Now, something may occur in the next two to three weeks that may give me a different view on that, but at this time that would be my observation.

Q: Mr. President, a move is underway in the House, and it is supported by the Republican leadership, to change the structure of the antipoverty program, to give the Governors a veto over programs in their States. What is your position on that?

THE PRESIDENT: I support the Director of OEO. He has asked for a two-year extension. He has pledged to reform the OEO, and I think he should be given the chance to reform it.

I hope he is able to work out with the leadership in the House, most of whom are Republicans in this instance, who want the changes, and some Democrats, and be able to work out some kind of accommodation with them. But, of course, I support my director that I have appointed.

Q: Getting back to the polarization question, Mr. President, your Administration has been charged with the failure to reach the young people, both those who protest and march and those who don't. Have you any specific plans for reaching the young people of this country?

THE PRESIDENT: I think you reach the young people more by talking to them as adults than talking to them as young people. I like to treat them as adults. I like to talk to them.

I was rather encouraged by the number of letters and calls I received with regard to my Vietnam speech from young people. They didn't all agree. But at least they had listened, they had paid attention. I know a way not to reach them, and that is to try to pick number one as far as the football teams are concerned.

THE PRESS: Thank you, Mr. President.

President Richard M. Nixon's Inaugural Address

Stresses Peace, Unity, and a 'Just and Abundant Society'

Following is a complete transcript of President Nixon's Jan. 20 Inaugural Address.

Senator Dirksen, Mr. Chief Justice, Mr. Vice President, President Johnson, Vice President Humphrey, My Fellow Americans—and my fellow citizens of the world community:

I ask you to share with me today the majesty of this moment. In the orderly transfer of power, we celebrate the unity that keeps us free.

Each moment in history is a fleeting time, precious and unique. But some stand out as moments of beginning, in which courses are set that shape decades or centuries.

This can be such a moment.

Forces now are converging that make possible, for the first time, the hope that many of man's deepest aspirations can at last be realized. The spiraling pace of change allows us to contemplate, within our own lifetime, advances that once would have taken centuries.

In throwing wide the horizons of space, we have discovered new horizons on earth.

For the first time, because the people of the world want peace, and the leaders of the world are afraid of war, the times are on the side of peace.

Eight years from now America will celebrate its 200th Anniversary as a nation. Within the lifetime of most people now living, mankind will celebrate that great new year which comes only once in a thousand years—the beginning of the Third Millennium.

What kind of a nation we will be, what kind of a world we live in, whether we shape the future in the image of our hopes, is ours to determine by our actions and our choices.

Peace

The greatest honor history can bestow is the title of peacemaker. This honor now beckons America—the chance to help lead the world at last out of the valley of turmoil and onto that high ground of peace that man has dreamed of since the dawn of civilization.

If we succeed, generations to come will say of us now living that we mastered our moment, that we helped make the world safe for mankind.

This is our summons to greatness.

I believe the American People are ready to answer this call.

The second third of this century has been a time of proud achievement. We have made enormous strides in science and industry and agriculture. We have shared our wealth more broadly than ever. We have learned at last to manage a modern economy to assure its continued growth.

We have given freedom new reach. We have begun to make its promise real for black as well as for white.

We see the hope of tomorrow in the youth of today. I know America's youth. I believe in them. We can be proud that they are better educated, more committed, more passionately driven by conscience than any generation in our history.

No people has ever been so close to the achievement of a just and abundant society, or so possessed of the will to achieve it. And because our strengths are so great, we can afford to appraise our weaknesses with candor and to approach them with hope.

Standing in this same place a third of a century ago, Franklin Delano Roosevelt addressed a nation ravaged by depression and gripped in fear. He could say in surveying the nation's troubles: "They concern, thank God, only material things."

Our crisis today is in reverse.

We have found ourselves rich in goods, but ragged in spirit; reaching with magnificent precision for the moon, but falling into raucous discord on earth.

We are caught in war, wanting peace. We are torn by division, wanting unity. We see around us empty lives, wanting fulfillment. We see tasks that need doing, waiting for hands to do them.

To a crisis of the spirit, we need an answer of the spirit.

And to find that answer, we need only look within ourselves.

When we listen to "the better angels of our nature," we find that they celebrate the simple things, the basic things—such as goodness, decency, love, kindness.

"To Lower Our Voices"

Greatness comes in simple trappings.

The simple things are the ones most needed today if we are to surmount what divides us, and cement what unites us.

To lower our voices would be a simple thing.

In these difficult years, America has suffered from a fever of words; from inflated rhetoric that promises more than it can deliver; from angry rhetoric that fans discontents into hatreds; from bombastic rhetoric that postures instead of persuading.

We cannot learn from one another until we stop shouting at one another—until we speak quietly enough so that our words can be heard as well as our voices.

For its part, government will listen. We will strive to listen in new ways—to the voices of quiet anguish, the voices that speak without words, the voices of the heart—to the injured voices, the anxious voices, the voices that have despaired of being heard.

Those who have been left out, we will try to bring in.

Those left behind, we will help to catch up.

For all of our people, we will set as our goal the decent order that makes progress possible and our lives secure.

As we reach toward our hopes, our task is to build on what has gone before—not turning away from the old, but turning toward the new.

In this past third of a century, government has passed more laws, spent more money, initiated more programs, than in all our previous history.

In pursuing our goals of full employment, better housing, excellence in education; in rebuilding our cities and improving our rural areas; in protecting our environment and enhancing the quality of life; in all these and more, we will and must press urgently forward.

We shall plan now for the day when our wealth can be transferred from the destruction of war abroad to the urgent needs of our people at home.

The American dream does not come to those who fall asleep.

Limits of Government

But we are approaching the limits of what government alone can do.

Our greatest need now is to reach beyond government, to enlist the legions of the concerned and the committed.

What has to be done, has to be done by government and people together or it will not be done at all. The lesson of past agony is that without the people we can do nothing; with the people we can do everything.

To match the magnitude of our tasks, we need the energies of our people—enlisted not only in grand enterprises, but more importantly in those small, splendid efforts that make headlines in the neighborhood newspaper instead of the national journal.

With these, we can build a great cathedral of the spirit— each of us raising it one stone at a time, as he reaches out to his neighbor, helping, caring, doing.

I do not offer a life of uninspiring ease. I do not call for a life of grim sacrifice. I ask you to join in a high adventure— one as rich as humanity itself, and exciting as the times we live in.

The essence of freedom is that each of us shares in the shaping of his own destiny.

Until he has been part of a cause larger than himself, no man is truly whole.

The way to fulfillment is in the use of our talents. We achieve nobility in the spirit that inspires that use.

As we measure what can be done, we shall promise only what we know we can produce, but as we chart our goals, we shall be lifted by our dreams.

No man can be fully free while his neighbor is not. To go forward at all is to go forward together.

This means black and white together, as one nation, not two. The laws have caught up with our conscience. What remains is to give life to what is in the law: to insure at last that all are born equal in dignity before God, all are born equal in dignity before man.

As we learn to go forward together at home, let us also seek to go forward together with all mankind.

Let us take as our goal: where peace is unknown, make it welcome; where peace is fragile, make it strong; where peace is temporary, make it permanent.

Era of Negotiation

After a period of confrontation, we are entering an era of negotiation.

Let all nations know that during this Administration our lines of communication will be open.

We seek an open world—open to ideas, open to the exchange of goods and people, a world in which no people, great or small, will live in angry isolation.

We cannot expect to make everyone our friend, but we can try to make no one our enemy.

Those who would be our adversaries, we invite to a peaceful competition—not in conquering territory or extending dominion, but in enriching the life of man.

As we explore the reaches of space, let us go to the new worlds together—not as new worlds to be conquered, but as a new adventure to be shared.

With those who are willing to join, let us cooperate to reduce the burden of arms, to strengthen the structure of peace, to lift up the poor and the hungry.

But to all those who would be tempted by weakness, let us leave no doubt that we will be as strong as we need to be for as long as we need to be.

Over the past 20 years, since I first came to this Capital as a freshman Congressman, I have visited most of the nations of the world. I have come to know the leaders of the world, and the great forces, the hatreds, the fears that divide the world.

I know that peace does not come through wishing for it— that there is no substitute for days and even years of patient and prolonged diplomacy.

I also know the people of the world.

I have seen the hunger of a homeless child, the pain of a man wounded in battle, the grief of a mother who has lost her son. I know these have no ideology, no race.

I know America. I know the heart of America is good.

I speak from my own heart, and the heart of my country, the deep concern we have for those who suffer, and those who sorrow.

I have taken an oath today in the presence of God and my countrymen to uphold and defend the Constitution of the United States. To that oath I now add this sacred commitment: I shall consecrate my office, my energies, and all the wisdom I can summon to the cause of peace among nations.

The American Spirit

Let this message be heard by strong and weak alike:

The peace we seek—the peace we seek to win—is not victory over any other people, but the peace that comes "with healing in its wings"; with compassion for those who have suffered; with understanding for those who have opposed us; with the opportunity for all the peoples of this earth to choose their own destiny.

Only a few short weeks ago we shared the glory of man's first sight of the world as God sees it, as a single sphere reflecting light in the darkness.

As the Apollo Astronauts flew over the moon's gray surface on Christmas eve, they spoke to us of the beauty of earth— and in that voice so clear across the lunar distance, we heard them invoke God's blessing on its goodness.

In that moment, their view from the moon moved poet Archibald MacLeish to write: "To see the earth as it truly is, small and blue and beautiful in that eternal silence where it floats, is to see ourselves as riders on the Earth together, brothers in that bright loveliness in the eternal cold—brothers who know now they are truly brothers."

In that moment of surpassing technological triumph, men turned their thoughts toward home and humanity—seeing in that far perspective that man's destiny on earth is not divisible; telling us that however far we reach into the cosmos, our destiny lies not in the stars but on earth itself, in our own hands, in our own hearts.

We have endured a long night of the American spirit. But as our eyes catch the dimness of the first rays of dawn, let us not curse the remaining dark. Let us gather the light.

Our destiny offers not the cup of despair, but the chalice of opportunity. So let us seize it not in fear, but in gladness— and, "riders on the Earth together," let us go forward, firm in our faith, steadfast in our purpose, cautious of the dangers; but sustained by our confidence in the will of God and the promise of man.

URBAN AFFAIRS COUNCIL

Following is the complete text of President Nixon's statement on signing the executive order creating the Council on Urban Affairs Jan. 23

The establishment of the President's Urban Affairs Council is an historic occasion in American Government. Half a century ago the Census of 1920 revealed that a majority of Americans had come to live in cities. But only decades later did the American National Government begin to respond to this changed reality. By 1960, 70% of the population was urban and today probably 73% is.

For all this, the American National Government has responded to urban concerns in a haphazard, fragmented, and often woefully shortsighted manner (as when the great agricultural migrations from the rural South were allowed to take place with no adjustment or relocation arrangements whatever). What we have never had is a policy: coherent, consistent positions as to what the National Government would hope to see happen; what it will encourage, what it will discourage.

Having a policy in urban affairs is no more a guarantor of success than having one in foreign affairs. But it is a precondition of success. With the creation of the Urban Affairs Council we begin to establish that precondition: the formulation and implementation of a national urban policy.

NONPROLIFERATION TREATY

Following is the complete text of President Nixon's Feb. 5 message to the Senate urging approval of the Treaty on Non-proliferation of Nuclear Weapons.

TO THE SENATE OF THE UNITED STATES:

After receiving the advice of the National Security Council, I have decided that it will serve the national interest to proceed with the ratification of the Treaty on Non-Proliferation of Nuclear Weapons. Accordingly, I request that the Senate act promptly to consider the Treaty and give its advice and consent to ratification.

I have always supported the goal of halting the spread of nuclear weapons. I opposed ratification of the Treaty last fall in the immediate aftermath of the Soviet invasion of Czechoslovakia. My request at this time in no sense alters my condemnation of that Soviet action.

I believe that ratification of the Treaty at this time would advance this Administration's policy of negotiation rather than confrontation with the USSR.

I believe that the Treaty can be an important step in our endeavor to curb the spread of nuclear weapons and that it advances the purposes of our Atoms for Peace program which I have supported since its inception during President Eisenhower's Administration.

In submitting this request I wish to endorse the commitment made by the previous Administration that the United States will permit the International Atomic Energy Agency to apply its safeguards to all nuclear activities in the United States, exclusive of those activities with direct national security significance.

I also reiterate our willingness to join with all Treaty parties to take appropriate measures to insure that potential benefits from peaceful applications of nuclear explosions will be made available to non-nuclear-weapon parties to the Treaty.

Consonant with my purpose to "strengthen the structure of peace," therefore, I urge the Senate's prompt consideration and positive action on this Treaty.

D.C. PROPOSALS

Following is a partial text of President Nixon's Jan. 31 statement on recommendations for Washington, D.C.

Responsibility begins at home.

The District of Columbia is the Federal City, and the Federal Government cannot evade its share of responsibility for the conditions of life in the District.

For many who live here, those conditions have become intolerable. Violent crimes in the District have increased by almost three times in the last 8 years; only 2 days ago, the local newspapers carried a report that armed robberies had more than doubled in the past year alone.

This violence—raw, vicious violence, hurting most of all those who are poor and work hard—is the surface manifestation of far deeper troubles.

These troubles have been long building. In part, Washington today is reaping a whirlwind sown long since by rural poverty in the South, by failures in education, by racial prejudice, and by the sometimes explosive strains of rapid social readjustments.

Because its roots are deep and closely woven, crime in the District cannot be brought under control overnight. Neither can poverty be ended or hatred eliminated or despair overcome in a year. But we can begin.

In the 11 days since the new administration took office, I have asked the departments and agencies concerned to make an intensive study—as a matter of first priority—of actions that

could be taken now toward curbing crime and improving the conditions of life in the city of Washington.

I wish I could report that we had produced a magic formula that would end crime and sweep away despair overnight. We have not. I have determined on a number of actions and recommendations which will provide a start.

These include:

—A swift start on restoring those areas devastated nearly 10 months ago.

—A package of proposals that can at least help toward restoring the safety of life and property.

—A commitment to give the people of the District of Columbia the voice they legitimately should have in the public policies that affect their lives.

Before detailing these measures I would like to make two points, both of which may help set the measures themselves in perspective.

I am pleased to report, first, that Mayor Washington and I, together with key members of our respective administrations, have established the basis for what I confidently expect will be the most effective cooperation yet achieved in the relations between the federal and city governments.

The basic framework within which we both intend to operate is one of local initiative and responsibility, and fullest possible federal support—not only in terms of the necessary money, but also by involving the vast array of technical assistance available from within the federal departments and agencies head-quartered here.

Second, the great majority of these actions and recommendations are in the fields of crime control and the administration of justice. I recognize full well that crime and violence are only part of the complex interweave of problems the District faces, and that in the long run crime itself also requires much more far-reaching and subtle approaches. But the rapidly mounting urgency of the crime crisis in the District marks immediate, direct anticrime measures as the first-priority task.

There is another reason for this early and urgent emphasis. Crime in America today is both a primary local responsibility and a primary national concern. Here in the District, the Federal Government bears a special responsibility and has a unique opportunity. By searching for new ways of applying the resources of the Federal Government in the war against crime here, we may discover new ways of advancing the war against crime elsewhere....

Crime

A meaningful assault on crime requires action on a broad array of fronts. But in the midst of a crime crisis, immediate steps are needed to increase the effectiveness of the police and to make justice swifter and more certain.

Toward these ends and as a beginning, I have taken or will propose action in 12 major areas.

1. The Courts of the District of Columbia

I am asking Congress to provide 10 more judges for the courts of the District of Columbia. I will ask later for more additional judges as they become necessary upon the reorganization of the District of Columbia court system.

As an interim measure, I would hope that the existing visiting judges program would be expanded in the District. The Chief Judge of the District of Columbia circuit here has diligently sought the services of visiting judges. I will encourage and aid him in his effort to obtain the services of more judges.

To improve the administration of justice in the District, I have directed the Attorney General to consult with the bench, the bar and the various interested groups, to assist in the drafting of appropriate legislation providing for a reorganization and restructuring of our present court system toward the eventual goal of creating one local court of general, civil, criminal, and juvenile jurisdiction for the District of Columbia. It is consistent with my support for home rule to urge the creation of a local court system similar to that of the states and other large municipalities.

To perform with full effectiveness, a modern court needs modern computer and management techniques. I have asked the Attorney General to offer his department's assistance to the study groups in the District that are presently seeking to apply such techniques in the court system.

I have asked the Attorney General to submit specific recommendations for such additional court house personnel, including United States Marshals, court clerks, probation officers, law clerks, and bailiffs, as are necessary to support not only the present judges but the additional judges that will be requested.

2. United States Attorney's Office

The chronic under staffing of the prosecutor's office has long hampered the efficient administration of justice in the District. It is widely recognized that a ratio of at least two prosecutors for each judge is needed. To achieve that goal, 20 new Assistant U.S. Attorneys are required immediately. With the creation of 10 additional judgeships and the contemplated court reorganization, another 20 prosecutors will be required. Consequently I am recommending the authorization of 40 more Assistant U.S. Attorneys.

A comprehensive reorganization of the Office of the U.S. Attorney is imperative. This should include a restructuring of the office to provide for two-man prosecutor teams in important cases; the development of specialized functions for technical cases such as frauds and other economic crimes; and the creation of a special "violent crimes unit" to handle such crimes as armed bank robberies on a priority basis, as is presently being tried experimentally. In addition, greater emphasis is needed on developing policy guidelines and training programs. On January 14, $120,000 was awarded by the National Institute of Law Enforcement and Criminal Justice for a special study committee. Included in its study is an examination of the prosecutor's office, with a view toward recommending improvements in its operation. I strongly support this study and have instructed the Attorney General to make available the resources of the Department of Justice to assist the committee and to facilitate reorganization found desirable.

In addition, I will seek authorization for the hiring of law clerks and sufficient other personnel for the proper staffing of the U.S. Attorney's office—and for the hiring and use of trained investigators, who are necessary to the effective functioning of the prosecutor's office.

3. Courthouse Facilities

The local courts already are overflowing the existing Court of General Sessions buildings. Judges are sitting in three different buildings, and some in temporary courtrooms. With the creation of additional judges and the eventual transfer of greatly expanded jurisdiction to the local courts, a new courthouse complex becomes a pressing necessity. $100,000 has already been utilized for planning for a new courthouse and $3.5 million has been appropriated for site selection. But we must have these facilities now. Consequently, I am vigorously endorsing the requests presently pending before the Congress for $1,240,000 to be used to complete acquisition and for additional planning. The administration will fully support the Mayor in such additional requests as are needed to speed the building program. Meanwhile, I have instructed the General Services Administration to assist in providing temporary facilities.

4. Bail Reform and the Bail Agency

Problems arising out of the operation of the Bail Reform Act of 1966 are now being considered by the Congress. But substantial changes in this area are needed quickly. Increasing numbers of crimes are being committed by persons already indicted for earlier crimes, but free on pretrial release. Many are now being arrested two, three, even seven times for new offenses while awaiting trials. This requires that a new provision be made in the law, whereby dangerous hard core recidivists

could be held in temporary pretrial detention when they have been charged with crimes and when their continued pretrial release presents a clear danger to the community.

Additionally, crimes committed by persons on pretrial release should be made subject to increased penalties.

Insufficient staffing of the Bail Agency is one of the contributors to crime by those on pretrial release. I support immediate lifting of the ceiling that now constricts the Agency's funding. I will seek appropriations for an initial expansion of the agency from 13 to 35 permanent positions. If the pretrial release system is to protect the rights of the community, the agency must have the capacity for adequate investigation and supervision.

5. The District of Columbia Department of Corrections

As the local government is painfully aware, the existing facilities and programs of the Department of Corrections are woefully inadequate. On January 16, 1969, the Director of the Bureau of Prisons submitted a comprehensive report to Mayor Washington identifying the deficiencies and making a number of recommendations. I join with the Mayor in urging immediate implementation of those recommendations, and I will offer whatever Federal assistance is possible in doing so.

All who have studied the problem agree that far-reaching changes are needed in the penal facilities and programs serving the District. I will press vigorously for accomplishment of the needed reforms.

6. Office of Public Defender

The recent bail reform hearings before the Senate Judiciary Subcommittee on Constitutional Rights have emphasized the important contributions skilled defense counsel can make toward expediting criminal trials.

Too often, inexperienced lawyers who are appointed to represent indigent defendants complicate and delay the trial process by their unfamiliarity with the law and criminal practice. Experience has shown that professional public defenders, on the other hand, not only better safeguard the rights of defendants, but also speed the process of justice. The Legal Aid Agency in the District is a pilot project which has given every indication of great success if properly supported. I believe the time has come to convert this project into a full-fledged public defender program. To make this project possible, I will support the Legal Aid Agency's 1970 budget request for $700,000 to allow an increase in its staff from 22 to 34 attorneys and to assume responsibility for a successful project in offender rehabilitation. This would allow it to become a full-fledged public defender's office with the capacity to represent almost half of the indigent adult and juvenile defendants in the District.

7. The Metropolitan Police Department

There is no deterrent to crime quite so effective as the public presence of policemen. Several immediate steps are needed to bolster and improve the local police force in the District of Columbia.

The first step is more effective recruitment. Despite diligent recruitment efforts, the police force has hundreds of unfilled vacancies. I have pledged to the Mayor the assistance and full support of this administration to improve the recruitment process. I will sponsor the establishment of a procedure by which the District can draw upon the experience of other cities. Imaginative and innovative approaches may be necessary.

But even bringing the department up to its presently authorized strength will not secure adequate public protection in these troubled times. Consequently, I am recommending to the Mayor that he request authorization of an additional 1,000 police officers for the District, and I will support such a request....

8. Director of Public Safety

The potential of this office is great. It is presently vacant. The Mayor informs me that he is diligently searching for the right man to fill the job. I have offered the Mayor this administration's resources to assist him in selecting the best possible Director.

9. Citizen Participation

Increased citizen involvement is essential to any program of crime control and prevention; it is also in keeping with the American tradition. I strongly support the Mayor in his plan to appoint a Criminal Justice Coordinating Committee patterned after similar successful programs in other large cities....

10. Narcotics

Although the narcotics traffic in the District of Columbia is apparently not dominated by organized crime it has become an acute and growing problem. It is a direct cause of much of the District's crime, by driving the narcotic user to commit crime to support his "habit." Many armed robberies, assaults, and bank holdups are directly related to narcotics use.

Consequently, I have instructed the U.S. Bureau of Narcotics and Dangerous Drugs to increase significantly its role in the District of Columbia in enforcing the narcotic and dangerous drug laws. The Bureau has assured me that they will also increase their cooperation with the Metropolitan Police Department in enforcement, training, and in making available additional laboratory facilities and expert and technical assistance.

I have also directed the Bureau and the Department of Justice to seek more effective application of the civil commitment provisions of the Narcotics Rehabilitation Act of 1966 which has not yet been widely used.

11. Juvenile Crime

In recent years the median age of those charged with crime has been ominously dropping. The National Commission on Violence warned this month: "The key to much of the violence in our society seems to lie with the young. Our youth account for an ever-increasing percentage of crime, greater than their increasing percentage of the population.... It may be here, with tomorrow's generation, that much of the emphasis of our studies and the national response should lie."

I strongly support the city government's efforts to draft a new Juvenile Code, and I am making available technical assistance by federal authorities. The Department of Justice is already cooperating with the Corporation Counsel and other local officials on the project.

Under the proposed court reorganization, the now isolated and undernourished Juvenile Court would be brought into the new District of Columbia court of general jurisdiction. Thus juveniles would have the advantage of the comprehensive facilities of the new court, including family services and probation assistance....

12. New Attention to the District

The Attorney General has created a new post within the Justice Department, that of Associate Deputy Attorney General for the Administration of Criminal Justice, with one of the new official's special and continuing responsibilities that of helping improve the administration of justice in the District of Columbia....

District Representation

For more than 20 years I have supported home rule for the District of Columbia. I continue to support home rule, but I consider the timing of that effort the key, as is proven by its past history of failure. For the present, I will seek within the present system to strengthen the role of the local government in the solution of local problems.

Beyond this, I will press for Congressional representation for the District. In accordance both with my own conviction and with the platform pledge of my party, I will support a constitutional amendment to give the 850,000 people of the District at last a voting representative in Congress.

Adding an amendment to our Constitution, however, is a long and difficult process. As an interim measure, I will press this year for legislation that would give the District a non-voting delegate. The District is a federal city, but it should not be a federal colony. Nearly 200 years ago, the people of America confronted the question of taxation without representation. It was not acceptable then; it hardly is justifiable today....

REORGANIZATION MESSAGE

Following is the complete text of President Nixon's Jan. 30 message to Congress requesting extension of the President's authority to transmit reorganization plans.

TO THE CONGRESS OF THE UNITED STATES:

New times call for new ideas and fresh approaches. To meet the needs of today and tomorrow, and to achieve a new level of efficiency, the Executive Branch requires flexibility in its organization.

Government organization is created to serve, not to exist; as functions change, the organization must be ready to adapt itself to those changes.

Ever since the Economy Act of 1932, the Congress has recognized the need of the President to modernize the Federal Government continually. During most of that time, the Congress has provided the President the authority to reorganize the Executive Branch.

The current reorganization statute—Chapter 9 of Title 5 of the United States Code—is derived from the Reorganization Act of 1949. That law places upon the President a permanent responsibility "from time to time to examine the organization of all agencies" and "to determine what changes therein are necessary" to accomplish the purposes of the statute. Those purposes include promoting the better execution of the laws, cutting expenditures, increasing efficiency in Government operations, abolishing unnecessary agencies and eliminating duplication of effort. The law also authorizes the President to transmit reorganization plans to the Congress to make the changes he considers necessary.

Unfortunately, the authority to transmit such plans expired on December 31, 1968. The President cannot, therefore, now fulfill his reorganization responsibilities. He is severely limited in his ability to organize and manage the Executive Branch in a manner responsive to new needs.

I, therefore, urge that the Congress promptly enact legislation to extend for at least two years the President's authority to transmit reorganization plans.

This time-tested reorganization procedure is not only a means for curtailing ineffective and uneconomical Government operations, but it also provides a climate that enables good managers to manage well.

Under the procedure, reorganization plans are sent to the Congress by the President and generally take effect after 60 days unless either House passes a resolution of disapproval during that time. In this way the President may initiate improvements, and the Congress retains the power of review.

This cooperative executive-legislative approach to reorganization has shown itself to be sensible and effective for more than three decades, regardless of party alignments. It is more efficient than the alternative of passing specific legislation to achieve each organizational change. The cooperative approach is tested; it is responsive; it works.

Reorganization authority is the tool a President needs to shape his Administration to meet the new needs of the times, and I urgently request its extension.

POVERTY MESSAGE

Following is the complete text of President Nixon's Feb. 19 message on his plans for reorganizing the war on poverty.

TO THE CONGRESS OF THE UNITED STATES:

The blight of poverty requires priority attention. It engages our hearts and challenges our intelligence. It cannot and will not be treated lightly or indifferently, or without the most searching examination of how best to marshal the resources available to the Federal Government for combatting it.

At my direction, the Urban Affairs Council has been conducting an intensive study of the nation's antipoverty programs, of the way the antipoverty effort is organized and administered, and of ways in which it might be made more effective.

That study is continuing. However, I can now announce a number of steps I intend to take, as well as spelling out some of the considerations that will guide my future recommendations.

The Economic Opportunity Act of 1964 is now scheduled to expire on June 30, 1970. The present authorization for appropriations for the Office of Economic Opportunity runs only until June 30, 1969. I will ask Congress that this authorization for appropriations be extended for another year. Prior to the end of the Fiscal Year, I will send Congress a comprehensive proposal for the future of the poverty program, including recommendations for revising and extending the Act itself beyond its scheduled 1970 expiration.

How the work begun by OEO can best be carried forward is a subject on which many views deserve to be heard—both from within Congress, and among those many others who are interested or affected, including especially the poor themselves. By sending my proposals well before the Act's 1970 expiration, I intend to provide time for full debate and discussion.

In the maze of antipoverty efforts, precedents are weak and knowledge uncertain. These past years of increasing Federal involvement have begun to make clear how vast is the range of what we do not yet know, and how fragile are projections based on partial understanding. But we have learned some lessons about what works and what does not. The changes I propose will be based on those lessons and those discoveries, and rooted in a determination to press ahead with antipoverty efforts even though individual experiments have ended in disappointment.

From the experience of OEO, we have learned the value of having in the Federal Government an agency whose special concern is the poor. We have learned the need for flexibility, responsiveness, and continuing innovation. We have learned the need for management effectiveness. Even those most thoroughly committed to the goals of the antipoverty effort recognize now that much that has been tried has not worked.

The OEO has been a valuable fount of ideas and enthusiasm, but it has suffered from a confusion of roles.

New Role of OEO

OEO's greatest value is as an initiating agency—devising new programs to help the poor, and serving as an "incubator" for these programs during their initial, experimental phases. One of my aims is to free OEO itself to perform these functions more effectively, by providing for a greater concentration of its energies on its innovative role.

Last year, Congress directed that special studies be made by the Executive Branch of whether Head Start and the Job Corps should continue to be administered directly by OEO, or whether responsibility should be otherwise assigned.

Section 309 of the Vocational Education Amendments of 1968 provides:

"The President shall make a special study of whether the responsibility for administering the Head Start program established under the Economic Opportunity Act of 1964 should continue to be vested in the Director of the Office of Economic Opportunity, should be transferred to another agency of the Government, or should be delegated to another such agency pursuant to the provisions of section 602(d) of the aforementioned Economic Opportunity Act of 1964, and shall submit the findings of this study to the Congress not later than March 1, 1969."

I have today submitted this study to the Congress. Meanwhile, under the Executive authority provided by the Economic Opportunity Act, I have directed that preparations be made for the delegation of Head Start to the Department of Health, Education and Welfare. Whether it should be actually transferred is a question I will take up in my later, comprehensive message, along with my proposals for a permanent status and organizational structure for OEO. Pending a final decision by the Secretary of HEW on where within the department responsibility for Head Start would be lodged, it will be located directly within the Office of the Secretary.

In order to provide for orderly preparation, and to ensure that there is no interruption of programs, I have directed that this delegation be made effective July 1, 1969. By then the summer programs for 1969 will all have been funded, and a new cycle will be beginning.

I see this delegation as an important element in a new national commitment to the crucial early years of life.

Head Start is still experimental. Its effects are simply not known—save of course where medical care and similar services are involved. The results of a major national evaluation of the program will be available this Spring. It must be said, however, that preliminary reports on this study confirm what many have feared: the long-term effect of Head Start appears to be extremely weak. This must not discourage us. To the contrary it only demonstrates the immense contribution the Head Start program has made simply by having raised to prominence on the national agenda the fact—known for some time, but never widely recognized—that the children of the poor mostly arrive at school age seriously deficient in the ability to profit from formal education, and already significantly behind their contemporaries. It also has been made abundantly clear that our schools as they now exist are unable to overcome this deficiency.

In this context, the Head Start Follow-Through Program already delegated to HEW by OEO, assumes an even greater importance.

In recent years, enormous advances have been made in the understanding of human development. We have learned that intelligence is not fixed at birth, but is largely formed by the environmental influences of the early formative years. It develops rapidly at first, and then more slowly; as much of that development takes place in the first four years as in the next thirteen. We have learned further that environment has its greatest impact on the development of intelligence when that development is proceeding most rapidly—that is, in those earliest years.

This means that many of the problems of poverty are traceable directly to early childhood experience—and that if we are to make genuine, long-range progress, we must focus our efforts much more than heretofore on those few years which may determine how far, throughout his later life, the child can reach.

Recent scientific developments have shown that this process of early childhood development poses more difficult problems than had earlier been recognized—but they also promise a real possibility of major breakthroughs soon in our understanding of this process. By placing Head Start in the Department of HEW, it will be possible to strengthen it by association with a wide range of other early development programs within the department, and also with the research programs of the National Institutes of Health, the National Institute of Mental Health, and the National Institute of Child Health and Human Development.

Much of our knowledge is new. But we are not on that ground absolved from the responsibility to respond to it. So crucial is the matter of early growth that we must make a national commitment to providing all American children an opportunity for healthful and stimulating development during the first five years of life. In delegating Head Start to the Department of HEW, I pledge myself to that commitment.

Job Corps

The Vocational Education Amendments of 1968 directed the Commissioner of Education to study the Job Corps in relation to state vocational education programs. I have directed the Secretaries of Labor and of Health, Education, and Welfare, and the Assistant Secretary of Labor for Manpower, to work with the Acting Commissioner of Education in preparing such a report for submission to Congress at the earliest opportunity.

One of the priority aims of the new Administration is the development by the Department of Labor of a comprehensive manpower program, designed to make centrally available to the unemployed and the under-employed a full range of Federal job training and placement services. Toward this end, it is essential that the many Federal manpower programs be integrated and coordinated.

Therefore, as a first step toward better program management, the Job Corps will be delegated to the Department of Labor.

For the Department, this will add another important manpower service component. For the Job Corpsmen, it will make available additional training and service opportunities. From the standpoint of program management, it makes it possible to coordinate the Job Corps with other manpower services, especially vocational education, at the point of delivery.

The Department of Labor already is deeply involved in the recruitment, counseling and placement of Job Corpsmen. It refers 80 percent of all male and 45 percent of all female enrollees; it provides job market information, and helps locate Job Corpsmen in the areas of greatest opportunity.

This delegation will also be made effective on July 1, 1969; and the Departments of Interior and Agriculture will continue to have operating responsibility for the Job Corps centers concerned primarily with conservation.

I have directed that preparations be made for the transfer of two other programs from OEO to the Department of Health, Education, and Welfare: Comprehensive Health Centers, which provide health service to the residents of poor neighborhoods, and Foster Grandparents program. In my judgment, these can be better administered at present, or in the near future, within the structure of the Department.

In making these changes, I recognize that innovation costs money—and that if OEO is to continue its effectiveness as an innovating agency, adequate funds must be made available on a continuing basis. Moreover, it is my intent that Community Action Agencies can continue to be involved in the operation of programs such as Head Start at the local level, even though an agency other than OEO has received such programs, by delegation, at the national level. It also is my intent that the vital Community Action Programs will be pressed forward, and that in the area of economic development OEO will have an important role to play, in cooperation with other agencies, in fostering community-based business development.

One of the principal aims of the Administration's continuing study of the antipoverty effort will be to improve its management effectiveness. When poverty-fund monies are stolen, those hurt most are the poor—whom the monies were meant to help. When programs are inefficiently administered, those hurt most again are the poor. The public generally, and the poor especially, have a right to demand effective and efficient management. I intend to provide it.

Efficiency Goal

I expect that important economies will result from the delegation of the Job Corps to the Department of Labor, and we shall continue to strive for greater efficiency, and especially for greater effectiveness in Head Start.

A Concentrated Management Improvement Program initiated in OEO will be intensified. Under this program selected Community Action Agencies will be required to take steps to devise improvements in such areas as organizational structure, financial and accounting systems, personnel training and work scheduling. Standards will be applied under the "management improvement program" to evaluate the operations of Community Action Agencies. We intend to monitor these programs actively in order to ensure that they are achieving high-level effectiveness and that they are being administered on an orderly basis.

In the past, problems have often arisen over the relationship of State, county and local governments to programs administered by OEO. This has particularly been the case where the State and local officials have wanted to assume greater responsibility for the implementation of the programs but for various reasons have been prevented from doing so.

I have assigned special responsibility for working out these problems to the newly-created Office of Intergovernmental Relations, under the supervision of the Vice President.

I have directed the Urban Affairs Council to keep the antipoverty effort under constant review and evaluation, seeking new ways in which the various departments can help and better ways in which their efforts can be coordinated.

My comprehensive recommendations for the future of the poverty program will be made after the Urban Affairs Council's own initial study is completed, and after I have reviewed the Comptroller General's study of OEO ordered by Congress in 1967 and due for submission next month.

Meanwhile, I would stress this final thought: If we are to make the most of experimental programs, we must frankly recognize their experimental nature and frankly acknowledge whatever shortcomings they develop. To do so is not to belittle the experiment, but to advance its essential purpose: that of finding new ways, better ways, of making progress in areas still inadequately understood.

We often can learn more from a program that fails to achieve its purpose than from one that succeeds. If we apply those lessons, then even the "failure" will have made a significant contribution to our larger purposes.

I urge all those involved in these experimental programs to bear this in mind—and to remember that one of the primary goals of this Administration is to expand our knowledge of how best to make real progress against those social ills that have so stubbornly defied solution. We do not pretend to have all the answers. We are determined to find as many as we can.

The men and women who will be valued most in this administration will be those who understand that not every experiment succeeds, who do not cover up failures but rather lay open problems, frankly and constructively, so that next time we will know how to do better.

In this spirit, I am confident that we can place our antipoverty efforts on a secure footing—and that as we continue to gain in understanding of how to master the difficulties, we can move forward at an accelerating pace.

RICHARD NIXON

ELECTORAL COLLEGE MESSAGE

Following is the complete text of President Nixon's Feb. 20 message to Congress on electoral reform.

TO THE CONGRESS OF THE UNITED STATES:

One hundred and sixty-five years ago, Congress and the several states adopted the Twelfth Amendment to the United States Constitution in order to cure certain defects—underscored by the election of 1800—in the electoral college method of choosing a President. Today, our presidential selection mechanism once again requires overhaul to repair defects spotlighted by the circumstances of 1968.

The reforms that I propose are basic in need and desirability. They are changes which I believe should be given the earliest attention by the Congress.

I have not abandoned my personal feeling, stated in October and November 1968, that the candidate who wins the most popular votes should become President. However, practicality demands recognition that the electoral system is deeply rooted in American history and federalism. Many citizens, especially in our smaller states and their legislatures, share the belief stated by President Johnson in 1965 that "our present system of computing and awarding electoral votes by States is an essential counterpart of our Federal system and the provisions of our Constitution which recognize and maintain our nation as a union of states." I doubt very much that any constitutional amendment proposing abolition or substantial modification of the electoral vote system could win the required approval of three-quarters of our fifty states by 1972.

For this reason, and because of the compelling specific weaknesses focused in 1968, I am urging Congress to concentrate its attention on formulating a system that can receive the requisite Congressional and State approval.

I realize that experts on constitutional law do not think alike on the subject of electoral reform. Different plans for reform have been responsibly advanced by Members of Congress and distinguished private groups and individuals. These plans have my respect and they merit serious consideration by the Congress.

I have in the past supported the proportional plan of electoral reform. Under this plan the electoral vote of a state would be distributed among the candidates for President in proportion to the popular vote cast. But I am not wedded to the details of this plan or any other specific plan. I will support any plan that moves toward the following objectives: first, the abolition of individual electors; second, allocation to Presidential candidates of the electoral vote of each State and the District of Columbia in a manner that may more closely approximate the popular vote than does the present system; third, making a 40% electoral vote plurality sufficient to choose a President.

The adoption of these reforms would correct the principal defects in the present system. I believe the events of 1968 constitute the clearest proof that priority must be accorded to electoral college reform.

Next, I consider it necessary to make specific provision for the eventuality that no Presidential slate receives 40% or more of the electoral vote in the regular election. Such a situation, I believe, is best met by providing that a run-off election between the top two candidates shall be held within a specified time after the general election, victory going to the candidate who receives the largest popular vote.

We must also resolve some other uncertainties: First, by specifying that if a Presidential candidate who has received a clear electoral vote plurality dies before the electoral votes are counted, the Vice-President-elect should be chosen President. Second, by providing that in the event of the death of the Vice-President-elect, the President-elect should, upon taking office, be required to follow the procedures otherwise provided in the Twenty-Fifth Amendment for filling the unexpired term of the Vice-President. Third, by giving Congress responsibility, should

both the President-elect and Vice-President-elect die or become unable to serve during this interim, to provide for the selection—by a new election or some other means—of persons to serve as President and Vice-President. And finally, we must clarify the situation presented by the death of a candidate for President or Vice-President prior to the November general election.

Many of these reforms are noncontroversial. All are necessary. Favorable action by Congress will constitute a vital step in modernizing our electoral process and reaffirming the flexible strength of our constitutional system.

RICHARD NIXON

DEBT MESSAGE

Following is the complete text of President Nixon's Feb. 24 message requesting the Congress to raise the limit on the public debt.

TO THE CONGRESS OF THE UNITED STATES:

When I took office as President of the United States, the public debt subject to limit was $364.2 billion—only $800 million below the statutory ceiling of $365 billion. Available projections indicated that borrowings needed to provide the Government with minimum cash balances essential for its operations would place the debt subject to limit at or above the legal ceiling by mid-April.

These projections have now been reviewed and updated on the basis of the latest revenue and expenditure flows. They continue to show inadequate leeway under the debt limit to meet all anticipated cash requirements through the middle of April. These facts permit me only one prudent course of action. I must ask the Congress to revise the debt limit before mid-April. The new limit should provide a reasonable margin for contingencies.

President Johnson foresaw the possible need for such action when he stated in his fiscal year 1970 Budget that "It may be necessary...within the next few months to raise the present debt limit."

Continuing high interest rates may add several hundred million dollars to the 1969 expenditures estimated by President Johnson. Other possible increases in outlays, including farm price support payments and a wide variety of past commitments in other programs—such as highways—may be greater than was estimated by the outgoing Administration.

All department and agency heads are now reviewing their programs in a determined effort to reduce costs. But we should not let our hopes for success in this effort deter us from the necessary action on the debt limit. Such cost reductions can have only a minor effect on expenditures in the next month or two, and it is in early March and again in early April that the Treasury will be faced with the heaviest drain on its resources.

Moreover, even if the Budget surpluses for fiscal years 1969 and 1970 were to prove somewhat larger than estimated in the January Budget, the present debt limit would be inadequate for fiscal year 1970. Thus even if an immediate increase in the debt limit could be avoided, an increase cannot be postponed very far into the next fiscal year. My predecessor also noted this fact when he presented his Budget for fiscal year 1970.

The apparent paradox of a need for a higher debt limit in years of anticipated budget surplus is explained mainly by the fact that the fiscal year 1969 and 1970 surpluses reflect substantial surpluses in Government trust funds—projected at $9.4 billion in fiscal year 1969 and $10.3 billion in fiscal year 1970. These surpluses in the trust funds provide cash to the Treasury, but only through the medium of investment in special Treasury issues. The consequent increase in such special issues is subject to the debt limit, under present definitions. Hence, the debt subject to limit will rise even though borrowing from the public will decline.

In addition, we must acknowledge the seasonal pattern in Treasury receipts. Net cash requirements prior to the mid-April tax date are regularly very substantial, while after that date the Treasury will be repaying a large amount of debt on a net basis.

While a small, temporary increase in the debt limit might prevent the undue restrictiveness of the present limit in the months immediately ahead, I urge that we now direct our attention to the future, and at least through fiscal year 1970.

I believe that the Congress should now enact a debt limit which will serve the needs of our Nation both for the balance of this fiscal year and for the foreseeable future.

In doing so, I also believe that the Congress should take this occasion to redefine the debt subject to limit to bring it into accord with the new unified Budget concept developed by a distinguished Commission that was headed by the present Secretary of the Treasury and included leaders from both Houses of Congress, officials of the previous Administration, and distinguished private citizens. The recommendations of this Commission largely have been adopted in the last two Budget presentations and in the new form of Congressional budget scorekeeping. These have been major forward steps toward better public understanding of the budget. The concept of the debt limit should also be redefined as suggested in the Commission's report.

Under the unified Budget concept, attention is focused on the total receipts and expenditures of the Federal Government, including the trust funds. The surplus or deficit thus reflects the net of revenue and expenditure transactions between the Federal Government and the public, and the net debt transactions between the Government and the public are thus the relevant basis for a proper understanding of the Federal borrowing requirements. To conform fully with this Budget presentation, only those Federal obligations which are held by the public—all debt except that held by Federally-owned agencies and by the trust funds—should be subject to the statutory limit on the public debt. Debt of Federally-owned agencies held by the public would be included as well as direct Treasury debt.

This change would in no way affect the integrity of the trust funds. This Administration recognizes, as the Commission on Budget Concepts emphasized, the firm obligation of the Government to maintain proper, separate accounting for the trust funds. This can and will be done without including obligations held by the trust funds in the total debt subject to the debt limit.

I therefore propose that the Congress establish a new debt limit defined to accord with the unified Budget concept. On this basis, a limit of $300 billion should be adequate to permit efficient and responsible handling of the Government's financing for the foreseeable future. This compares with an outstanding debt on the unified Budget concept of $293.7 billion on January 21, 1969.

On the present public debt limit concept, the debt outstanding on January 21, 1969 was $364.2 billion as compared with the current debt limit of $365 billion. An increase in that limit to approximately $382 billion would correspond in the next fiscal year to the $300 billion limit I am proposing on the unified budget basis.

RICHARD NIXON

POSTMASTERS

Following is the complete text of President Nixon's Feb. 25 message to Congress on patronage in the Post Office Department.

TO THE CONGRESS OF THE UNITED STATES:

Reform of the postal system is long overdue.

The postal service touches the lives of all Americans. Many of our citizens feel that today's service does not meet today's needs, much less the needs of tomorrow. I share this view.

In the months ahead, I expect to propose comprehensive legislation for postal reform.

If this long-range program is to succeed, I consider it essential, as a first step, that the Congress remove the last vestiges of political patronage in the Post Office Department.

Accordingly, I urge the Congress promptly to enact legislation that would:

—eliminate the present statutory requirement for Presidential appointment and Senatorial confirmation of postmasters of first, second, and third-class post offices;

—provide for appointment of all postmasters by the Postmaster General in the competitive civil service; and

—prohibit political considerations in the selection or promotion of postal employees.

Such legislation would make it possible for future postmasters to be chosen in the same way that career employees have long been chosen in the other executive departments. It would not, however, affect the status of postmasters now in office.

Adoption of this proposal by the Congress would assure all of the American people—and particularly the more than 750,000 dedicated men and women who work in the postal service—that future appointments and promotions in this important department are going to be made on the basis of merit and fitness for the job, and not on the basis of political affiliations or political influence.

The tradition of political patronage in the Post Office Department extends back to the earliest days of the Republic. In a sparsely populated country, where postal officials faced few of the management problems so familiar to modern postmasters, the patronage system may have been a defensible method of selecting jobholders. As the operation of the postal service has become more complex, however, the patronage system has become an increasingly costly luxury. It is a luxury that the nation can no longer afford.

In the past two decades, there has been increasing agreement that postmaster appointments should be made on a nonpolitical basis. Both the first and second Hoover Commissions emphasized the need for such action. So did the recent President's Commission on Postal Organization, headed by Frederick R. Kappel. President Harry S. Truman and many members of Congress from both political parties have proposed legislation designed to take politics out of postal appointments. In the 90th Congress, the Senate, by a vote of 75 to 9, passed a bill containing a provision that would have placed postal appointments on a merit basis. Forty-two such bills were introduced in the House of Representatives during the 90th Congress.

The overwhelmingly favorable public comment that followed my recent announcement of our intention to disregard political consideration in selecting postmasters and rural carriers suggests that the American people are more than ready for legislative action on this matter. The time for such action is now at hand.

The benefits to be derived from such legislation are, I believe, twofold.

First, the change would expand opportunities for advancement on the part of our present postal employees. These are hard-working and loyal men and women. In the past, many of them have not received adequate recognition or well-deserved promotions for reasons which have had nothing to do with their fitness for higher position or the quality of their work. For reasons of both efficiency and morale, this situation must be changed.

Secondly, I believe that over a period of time the use of improved professional selection methods will improve the level of competence of those who take on these important postal responsibilities.

I would not request this legislation without also presenting a plan which insures that the new selection process will be effectively and impartially administered. The Postmaster General has such a plan.

He is creating a high level, impartial national board to assist him in the future selection of postmasters for the 400 largest post offices in the country. Regional boards, also made up of exceptionally well-qualified citizens, will perform a similar task in connection with the selection of other postmasters. First consideration will be given to the promotion, on a competitive basis, of present postal employees.

The Postmaster General has also initiated action to improve the criteria by which postmasters are selected. The revised criteria will emphasize managerial competence, human relations sensitivity, responsiveness to customer concerns, an understanding of labor relations and other important qualities.

Proposals for additional legislation dealing with the selection process will be included in the broad program for postal reform that the Postmaster General is now preparing.

Some of the needs of the Post Office clearly require extensive study before detailed solutions can be proposed. Other problems can and should be dealt with now. One objective which can be met promptly is that of taking politics out of the Post Office and I strongly recommend the swift enactment of legislation that will allow us to achieve that goal. Such legislation will be an important first step "towards postal excellence."

RICHARD NIXON

MINE SAFETY MESSAGE

Following is the complete text of President Nixon's March 3 message on coal mine safety.

TO THE CONGRESS OF THE UNITED STATES:

The workers in the coal mining industry and their families have too long endured the constant threat and often sudden reality of disaster, disease and death. This great industry has strengthened our nation with the raw material of power. But it has also frequently saddened our nation with news of crippled men, grieving widows and fatherless children.

Death in the mines can be as sudden as an explosion or a collapse of a roof and ribs, or it comes insidiously from pneumoconiosis or "black lung" disease. When a miner leaves his home for work, he and his family must live with the unspoken but always present fear that before the working day is over, he may be crushed or burned to death or suffocated. This acceptance of the possibility of death in the mines has become almost as much a part of the job as the tools and the tunnels.

The time has come to replace this fatalism with hope by substituting action for words. Catastrophes in the coal mines are not inevitable. They can be prevented, and they must be prevented.

To these ends, I have ordered the following actions to advance the health and safety of the coal mine workers:

—Increase substantially the number of inspectors, and improve coal mine inspections and the effectiveness of staff performance and requirements.
—Revise the instructions to the mine inspectors so as to reflect more stringent operating standards.
—Initiate an in-depth study to reorganize the agency charged with the primary responsibility for mine safety so that it can meet the new challenges and demands.
—Expand research activities with respect to pneumoconiosis and other mine health and safety hazards.
—Extend the recent advances in human engineering and motivational techniques, and enlarge and intensify education and training functions, for the improvement of health and safety in coal mines to the greatest degree possible.
—Establish cooperative programs between management and labor at the *mine level* which will implement health and safety efforts at the site of the mine hazards.

—Encourage the coordination of Federal and State inspections, in order to secure more effective enforcement of the present safety requirements.
—Initiate grant programs to the States, as authorized but not previously invoked, to assist the States in planning and advancing their respective programs for increased health and safety in the coal mines.

In addition to these immediate efforts under existing law, I am submitting to the Congress legislative proposals for a comprehensive new program to provide a vigorous and multi-faceted attack on the health and safety dangers which prevail in the coal mining industry.

These proposals would:
—Modernize a wide range of mandatory health and safety standards, including new provisions for the control of dust, electrical equipment, roof support, ventilation, illumination, fire protection, and other operating practices in underground and surface coal mines engaged in commerce.
—Authorize the Secretary of the Interior to develop and promulgate any additional or revised standards which he deems necessary for the health and safety of the miners.
—Provide strict deterrents and enforcement measures and, at the same time, establish equitable appeal procedures to remedy any arbitrary and unlawful actions.
—Recruit and carefully train a highly motivated corps of coal mine inspectors to investigate the coal mines, and to enforce impartially and vigorously the broad new mandatory standards.
—Improve Federal-State inspection plans.
—Substantially increase, by direct action, grants and contracts, the necessary research, training, and education for the prevention and control of occupational diseases, the improvement of State workmen's compensation systems, and the reduction of mine accidents.

These legislative proposals, together with other steps already taken or to be taken are essential to meet our obligation to the Nation's coal miners, and to accomplish our mission of eliminating the tragedies which have occurred in the mines.

These proposals are not intended to replace the voluntary and enlightened efforts of management and labor to reduce coal mine hazards, while efforts are the touchstone to any successful health and safety program. Rather, these measures would expand and render uniform by enforceable authority the most advanced of the health and safety precautions undertaken and potentially available in the coal mining industry.

I urge the immediate adoption by Congress of this legislation.

RICHARD NIXON

SURTAX MESSAGE

Following is the complete text of President Nixon's March 26 message requesting extension of the 10-percent surtax.

TO THE CONGRESS OF THE UNITED STATES:

Clearly this Nation must come to grips with the problem of an inflation that has been allowed to run into its fourth year. This is far too long, and it has already caused substantial distortions in our economy.

Inflation is a form of economic aggression against the very young and the very old, the poor and the thrifty. It is these Americans who are largely defenseless against the kind of price increases for food, clothing, medicine, housing and education that have swept over the Nation in the last few years.

Government has two major instruments for dealing with this problem. One is monetary policy, which should continue its program of restraint. The other is fiscal policy—the management of the Federal budget—which must turn away from budgets which have propelled the inflation, and turn instead to one with a strong surplus that will help to curb it.

The prospect of a thin budget surplus or a return to deficits would again nudge monetary policy off course. The result, as always, would be further increases in interest rates, a dangerously overheated economic engine, and the threat of accelerating the advance of the price level. Because the problem of inflation was neglected far too long, we cannot risk even a neutral budget policy of narrow balance.

Only a combined policy of a strong budget surplus and monetary restraint can now be effective in cooling inflation, and in ultimately reducing the restrictive interest rates forced on us by past policies. This is fundamental economics, and we intend to deal with fundamentals.

We are determined to keep faith with America's wage earners, farmers and businessmen. We are committed to take every necessary action to protect every American's savings and real income from further loss to inflation.

The budget for the year beginning July 1, 1969, submitted in January, estimates the surplus at $3.4 billion. However, current examination of this budget reveals that some of its estimates of expenditures were low. For example, interest on the Federal debt will be far more than was estimated. This, along with such items as an underestimate of farm price support payments and a substantial overestimate of offshore oil lease receipts, means that a current analysis of the budget submitted in January shows a reduction in the surplus of $1.3 billion for this fiscal year and $1.7 billion for the fiscal year 1970.

Thus, half of the projected 1970 surplus has disappeared before the year begins. Similarly, more than half of this year's projected surplus of $2.4 billion will not be realized—and for the same reasons.

On the matter of cutting expenditures:

To produce a budget that will stop inflation, we must cut expenditures while maintaining revenues. This will not be easy. Dealing with fundamentals never is.

I intend to submit budget revisions which will reduce Federal spending in fiscal 1970 significantly below the amount recommended in January, even before those previous figures have been adjusted to reflect current conditions.

On the matter of maintaining revenues:

I am convinced that the path of responsibility requires that the income tax surcharge, which is expected to yield $9-1/2 billion, be extended for another year. As I have said before, the surcharge is a temporary tax that must be ended as soon as our commitments in Southeast Asia and economic conditions permit. Because of budget and economic conditions, I reaffirm my support of the recommendation President Johnson made last January that the surcharge be extended, and I am transmitting to the Congress a request that this be done.

In addition, the scheduled reductions in the telephone and passenger car excise taxes must be postponed, and user charges equal in revenue yield to those now in the budget should be enacted. Together, these will produce close to $1 billion in revenue next year.

On the question of tax reform, this Administration remains committed to a more equitable and more efficient tax structure. In the coming month, the first specific proposals of that reform will be coming up to the Congress from the Treasury Department.

Taken together, these actions to reduce spending and maintain revenues will produce the strong budget surplus urgently needed to meet the inflationary threat.

Moreover, by proving Government's serious intent to counter the upward spiral of prices and wages, we will create conditions which will encourage the private sector to stop assuming a high rate of inflation in long-range planning.

Courageous Government action will modify the inflationary psychology which now afflicts business, labor and consumers generally. It is particularly hard on small business, and those of modest means in the management of their incomes and savings.

This ordering of our economic house—distasteful as it is in many respects—will do much to slow down the rise in the cost of living, help our seriously weakened position in international trade, and restore the sound basis for our on-going prosperity.

RICHARD NIXON

BANK HOLDING COMPANIES

Following is the complete text of President Nixon's March 24 statement on bank holding companies.

The Secretary of the Treasury, with my approval, has today transmitted to the Congress proposed legislation on the further regulation of bank holding companies.

Legislation in this area is important because there has been a disturbing trend in the past year toward erosion of the traditional separation of powers between the suppliers of money—the banks—and the users of money—commerce and industry.

Left unchecked, the trend toward the combining of banking and business could lead to the formation of a relatively small number of power centers dominating the American economy. This must not be permitted to happen; it would be bad for banking, bad for business, and bad for borrowers and consumers.

The strength of our economic system is rooted in diversity and free competition; the strength of our banking system depends largely on its independence. Banking must not dominate commerce or be dominated by it.

To protect competition and the separation of economic powers, I strongly endorse the extension of Federal regulation to one-bank holding companies and urge the Congress to take prompt and appropriate action.

BURGER NOMINATION

Following is a partial text of President Nixon's announcement May 21 of appointment of Judge Warren Earl Burger as Chief Justice of the United States.

This announcement is one that I have considered for many months, since I knew that I would have the responsibility even before I became President. I say this with due respect of the great responsibilities held by all the Members of the Cabinet here, I believe that the most important nomination that a President of the United States makes during his term of office is that of Chief Justice of the United States....

When we consider what a Chief Justice has in the way of influence on his age and the ages after him, I think it could fairly be said that our history tells us that our Chief Justices have probably had more profound and lasting influence on their times and on the direction of the Nation than most Presidents have had. You can see, therefore, why I consider this decision to be so important....

I have known him for 21 years and I would evaluate him as being qualified intellectually, qualified from the standpoint of judicial temperament, qualified from the standpoint of his legal philosophy, and above all, qualified because of his unquestioned integrity throughout his private and public life.

I am very proud tonight to nominate as the 15th Chief Justice of the United States, Judge Warren Burger.

PRESIDENT LISTS PLANS FOR DOMESTIC LEGISLATION

Following is the complete text of President Nixon's April 14 message to Congress on his domestic legislative program.

TO THE CONGRESS OF THE UNITED STATES:

As the members of Congress know, I have had under consideration the question of whether to send to the Congress this year a message on the State of the Union. I have decided against doing so. However, to assist Congress in formulating its plans, I would like to indicate at this time some of the principal legislative proposals that I will be sending in the weeks immediately ahead, and to report on the development of Administration plans and priorities as they relate to domestic programs.

The first twelve weeks of the new Administration have been devoted intensively to the pursuit of peace abroad, and to the development of new structures and new programs for the pursuit of progress at home.

Peace has been the first priority. It concerns the future of civilization; and even in terms of our domestic needs themselves, what we are able to do will depend in large measure on the prospects for an early end to the war in Viet Nam.

At the same time, the first days of this Administration have afforded us a unique opportunity to study the nation's domestic problems in depth, and to overhaul and re-tool the complex machinery of the Executive Office.

A systematic review of domestic programs and policies has led to a series of recommendations which I will begin sending to Congress this week. Among those recommendations will be:

—An increase in Social Security benefits, to take account of the rise in living costs.

—New measures to combat organized crime, and to crack down on racketeers, narcotics traffickers and peddlers of obscenity.

—A program of tax credits, designed to provide new incentives for the enlistment of additional private resources in meeting our urgent social needs.

—A program to increase the effectiveness of our national drive for equal employment opportunity.

—A comprehensive reorganization of the Post Office Department.

—A program for the District of Columbia, including home rule and Congressional representation.

—A start on sharing the revenues of the Federal Government, so that other levels of government where revenue increases lag behind will not be caught in a constant fiscal crisis.

—A far-reaching new program for development of our airways and airports, and our mass transit systems.

—A comprehensive labor and manpower program, including job training and placement, improvements in unemployment insurance, and proposals to help guarantee the health and safety of workers.

—Reform of the tax structure. The burden of taxation is great enough without permitting the continuance of unfairness in the tax system. New legislation will be proposed to prevent several specific abuses this year, and plans will be set in motion for a comprehensive revision of our tax structure by 1970, the first since 1954.

The legislative proposals of the next few weeks are beginning. They form part of a responsible approach to our goal of managing constructive change in America.

This is not law we seek in order to have it "on the books," but law that we need in action. It is designed, not to look appealing in the record, but to take effect in our lives.

It will be the goal of this Administration to propose only legislation that we know we can execute once it becomes law. We have deliberated long and hard on each of these measures,

in order to be sure we could make it work. Merely making proposals takes only a typewriter; making workable proposals takes time. We have taken this time.

In other areas, where more time is needed, we will take more time. I urge the Congress to join with this Administration in this careful approach to the most fundamental issues confronting our country. Hasty action or a seeking after partisan advantage either by the Congress or Executive Branch can only be self-defeating and aggravate the very ills we seek to remedy.

For example, one area of deep concern to this Administration has to do with the most dependent constituency of all: the child under five. I have announced a commitment to the first five years of life as one of the basic pledges of this Administration. Head Start was one promising idea for bettering the environment and nutrition of young children; there also are many others. We have already begun enlarging the scope of our commitment in this vital field, including the establishment of an Office of Child Development within the Department of Health, Education, and Welfare. We hope that this enlarging commitment will be accompanied by an enlarging of the base of knowledge on which we act. We are not beginning with "massive" programs that risk tripping over their own unreadiness. Rather, our proposals will include step-by-step plans, including careful projections of funding requirements. Equally important, though Federally supported, they will embrace a network of local programs that will enlist voluntary participation.

These legislative proposals are, of course, being prepared within the context of other Administration actions which bear on domestic program development.

On taking office, I could see that whether measured in terms of its ability to respond, to decide or to implement, the Executive Branch simply was not structured to meet the emerging needs of the 1970s. Therefore my first moves were organizational.

The National Security Council was revitalized. The Urban Affairs Council was created, so that the problems of our cities could be approached in the broader perspective they now require. A Cabinet Committee on Economic Policy was established, to bring greater coherence to the management of our nation's economic prosperity. The system of Federal regional offices was reorganized so that, for the first time, related agencies will have common regional headquarters and common regional boundaries. An Office of Inter-governmental Relations was set up, to smooth the coordination of Federal, State and local efforts.

In specific operational areas, we removed postmasterships from politics, started an overhaul of the Office of Economic Opportunity and its programs, and streamlined the administration of the various manpower programs.

One purpose of this early emphasis on organizational activity was to get the decision-making process in order before moving to the major decisions.

At the same time, I sent more than 100 directives to the heads of the various departments and agencies, asking their carefully considered recommendations on a wide range of domestic policy issues. The budget was submitted to an intensive review, and throughout the Administration we addressed ourselves to the critical question of priorities.

One priority that has emerged clearly and compellingly is that we must put a halt, swiftly, to the ruinous rise of inflationary pressures. The present inflationary surge, already in its fourth year, represents a national self-indulgence we cannot afford any longer. Unless we save the dollar, we will have nothing left with which to save our cities—or anything else. I have already outlined certain steps that will be required:

—Continuation of the monetary policies the Federal Reserve authorities are now pursuing.

—A reduction of fiscal year 1970 expenditures by $4 billion below the best current estimate of the budget expenditures recommended by the last Administration.

—Continuation of the income tax surcharge for another year.

—Postponing of the scheduled reductions in telephone and passenger car excise taxes.

—Enactment of user charges equal in revenue to those now in the budget.

—An increase in postal charges.

These steps are not pleasant medicine. Medicine to combat inflation is never pleasant. But we can no longer delay taking it.

Another priority is the control of crime. On January 31, I announced a detailed plan for combatting crime in the District of Columbia, recognizing that the Federal city should be made a model of law observance and law enforcement. The crime-control package soon to be submitted to Congress will make clear the Federal Government's commitment, nationwide, to assisting local authorities in protecting the lives, rights and property of their citizens.

An equally pressing priority is the entire complex of needs that we commonly group under the heading, "the problems of the cities"—but which in fact reach beyond the cities, and include the distresses of rural America as well.

Our policy review has strengthened my conviction that in approaching these problems, America needs a new direction—not a turning away from past goals, but a clear and determined turn toward new means of achieving those goals.

One example is hunger and malnutrition. The failure of past efforts to combat these problems has been made shockingly clear. Our new programs will be both vigorous and innovative.

Another example is welfare. Our studies have demonstrated that tinkering with the present welfare system is not enough. We need a complete re-appraisal and re-direction of programs which have aggravated the troubles they were meant to cure, perpetuating a dismal cycle of dependency from one generation to the next. Therefore, I will be submitting to Congress a program providing for the reform of the welfare system.

In the field of social legislation, we now have a hodge-podge of programs piled on programs, in which too often the pressure to perpetuate ill-conceived but established ones has denied needed resources to those that are new and more promising.

We have learned that too often government's delivery systems have failed: though Congress may pass a law, or the President may issue an order, the intended services never reach the intended recipients. Last week, for example, in announcing a $200 million program for rebuilding riot-torn areas, I noted that after two, three and even four years nothing had been done, and cited this as evidence of the growing impotence of government. The crucial point here is that whereas in the past, "leave it to the states" was sometimes a signal for inaction by design, now "leave it to Washington" has become too often a signal for inaction by default. We have to design systems that go beyond "commitment," and guarantee performance.

If there is one thing we know, it is that the Federal Government cannot solve all the nation's problems by itself; yet there has been an over-shift of jurisdiction and responsibility to the Federal Government. We must kindle a new partnership between government and people, and among the various levels of government.

Too often, Federal funds have been wasted or used unwisely—for example, by pouring them into direct grants, when more money could have been made available at less cost by the use of incentives to attract private funds.

The programs I will submit have been drawn with those principles in mind. Among their aims are:

—To supplement Federal funds with private funds, through the use of "seed money" devices such as tax credits and loan guarantees.

—To enlist the great, vital voluntary sector more fully, using the energies of those millions of Americans who are able and eager to help in combatting the nation's ills.

—To help rebuild state and local institutions, so that they both merit and gain a greater measure of confidence on the part of their own citizens.

—To streamline the administration of Federal programs, not only for efficiency and economy, but to improve the certainty of delivery and to cut away the clouds of confusion that now surround not only their operation, but often their purposes.

—To make maximum use of the new knowledge constantly being gained, as, for example, in our commitment to the first five years of life.

These programs will not carry extravagant promises. The American people have seen too many promises, too many false hopes raised, too much substitution of the easy slogan for the hard performance.

Neither will they carry large price tags for the coming fiscal year. We must recognize, however, that in the long run progress will not come cheaply; and even though the urgency of controlling inflation dictates budget cuts in the short run, we must be prepared to increase substantially our dollar investment in America's future as soon as the resources become available.

This Administration will gladly trade the false excitement of fanfare for the abiding satisfaction of achievement. Consolidation, coordination and efficiency are not ends in themselves; they are necessary means of making America's government responsive to the legitimate demands for new departures.

Quietly, thoughtfully, but urgently, the members of this Administration have moved in these first few months to redirect the course of the nation. I am confident of the direction, and convinced that the time to take it has come.

RICHARD NIXON

FISCAL 1970 BUDGET STATEMENT

Following is the complete text of President Nixon's April 12 statement on the Federal Budget for fiscal 1970.

The Administration's first full review of the federal budget for the fiscal year 1970 is now complete. As a result, beginning next week I shall send a series of budget amendments to the Congress. Amendments for most agencies will go forward within a few days. The over-all totals are now being made available.

The budget that we inherited from the previous Administration in January stated the estimated expenditures for the fiscal year 1970 at $195.3 billion. Our examination of that budget reveals that some of these estimates—notably those for interest on the federal debt and farm price support payments—are those turning out to be too low. After making the necessary adjustments to cover these underestimated items, we find that the actual expenditures budget submitted by the previous Administration is $196.9 billion.

I am proposing new reductions in federal spending of $4 billion, reducing the over-all spending figures for the coming fiscal year to $192.9 billion. I am also recommending to the Congress cuts totalling $5.5 billion in appropriations requests and other budget authority—thereby reducing significantly the future spending obligations of the Federal Government.

Our proposals mean not only a substantial cutback in the spending of tax dollars in the coming year, but a substantial reduction in claims against future tax dollars and future budgets. With this approach, we believe we have made a necessary and significant beginning toward bringing the federal budget under closer Presidential control; we have taken the reins firmly in hand.

We recognize, however, the responsibility for budget control is a continuing one. For the past eight years—the sole exception being the current year—our government has run an uninterrupted string of budget deficits. Our actions now, we believe, have brought an end to the era of the chronic budget deficit.

As a result of this review and these cutbacks, we are proposing the largest budget surplus in eighteen years—and the fourth largest in our history—a surplus of $5.8 billion dollars for fiscal year 1970.

We believe that a surplus of this magnitude will speak louder than any words to the business and labor communities in this country and to the world that the United States is determined to bring a halt to the inflationary spiral which has seriously affected our economy these last four years.

In the last thirty-six months, inflation has seriously eroded the value of every pay raise won by the average wage earner; it has done unquestionable harm to the economic welfare of the very poor in our society and those millions of Americans living on pensions and Social Security; it has weakened our international payments position; it has sapped foreign and domestic confidence in the American dollar.

Inflation is the most disguised and least just of all the taxes that can be imposed; and we intend to lift that hidden tax off the backs of an over-taxed people.

These reductions in spending cannot be achieved effortlessly, or without making some very difficult decisions as to our priorities. But they can be achieved by an Administration and a Congress dedicated to eliminating the crushing burden of inflation and committed to the responsible control of the federal budget. They can be achieved if this government is willing to impose upon itself the same new discipline that inflation and rising taxes have imposed upon the American wage earner and his family.

Some of the decreases in the budget will require legislation; others will result from smaller appropriation requests; still others will come from executive actions that I have directed be taken. In sum, these reductions constitute my best judgment as to where to reduce this budget to bring the acceleration of federal spending under control.

But even in the wake of these cuts—which we believe to be in the best interest of all Americans—great resources remain at our disposal to do the work that needs to be done in our society.

For example, I am proposing for fiscal year 1970 a level of spending for our domestic problems $6 1/2 billion higher than the figure for the fiscal year 1969.

This Administration will never turn its back upon the growing needs of the American people. That is why domestic spending in the coming year—even after these cuts—will far exceed that for any other year in American history.

We have come into office convinced that there are better ways than the old ways to solve new problems; and we intend to explore these more hopeful approaches.

With regard to specific cuts, the Secretary of Defense has already identified reductions in defense budget outlays of $1.1 billion. We believe these cuts will enhance our economic security without risk to our national security. Information with regard to other specific cuts will be released by the Bureau of the Budget on Tuesday.

As part of the budget review, I have directed that a substantial reduction be made in the level of federal employment recommended by the preceding Administration. As a result, full-time employment in the executive branch, by the close of the coming fiscal year, will be more than 45,000 below that recommended in the January budget.

These reductions will not be made "across the board," but selectively, since manpower for vital needs such as crime control will have to be increased.

Consistent with these objectives, I will ask Congress for repeal of Section 201 of the Revenue and Expenditure Control Act, which imposes restrictions on hiring in the executive branch. I am in full accord with the objective of that legislation. However, that objective is best achieved, not through some arbitrary limitation, but through leadership determined to reduce personnel and willing to make the difficult decisions as to where the cuts should come.

Just as we have made the judgments as to where the federal budget should be cut, so we ask for the authority to determine those areas where the reduction of personnel can most beneficially be made.

Although the officials of this Administration have worked long and hard conducting this review of federal expenditures and employment, the 1970 budget is not yet a finished effort. Conditions affecting the budget change constantly.

What will remain constant, however, is our determination to rein in this rising cost of living and to spend the tax dollars of the American people with a full awareness of the personal effort and labor they represent.

RICHARD NIXON

POSTAL RATES

Following is the complete text of President Nixon's April 24 message to Congress on raising postal rates.

TO THE CONGRESS OF THE UNITED STATES:

The Post Office Department faces a record deficit in Fiscal Year 1970, one which will reach nearly $1.2 billion. This unhappy fact compels me to recommend to the Congress that it increase postal rates for first, second, and third class mail.

The increases that I am proposing will reduce the postal deficit in Fiscal Year 1970 by over $600 million. If rates were not raised, that sum would have to be added to the already considerable burdens of our taxpayers. But if these recommendations are adopted, the costs of postal service will be borne more adequately by those who use the service most.

That is the way it should be if the Post Office is to become an example of sound business practices. That is also what the law requires. The Postal Policy Act stipulates that postal rates should produce revenue which is approximately equal to the cost of operating the postal establishment—after the costs of such special public services as the Congress may designate are deducted. It is in accordance with both general principle and specific law, then, that I make the following recommendations:

1. First class mail—I propose that the rates for letters and postcards be increased one cent, to seven and six cents respectively, on July 1, 1969. Air mail postage rates would remain unchanged.

2. Second class mail—The rates for newspapers and magazines which circulate outside the county in which they are published would go up by 12 percent on July 1, 1970. This increase would constitute an addition to the 8 percent increase for second class mail which is already scheduled to take effect on January 1 of next year.

3. Third class mail—Bulk rates are already scheduled for increase on July 1, 1969. I suggest that there be a further increase on January 1, 1970, so that the overall level at that time would be some 16 percent above present levels. Further, I recommend that the minimum single piece third class rate be increased by one cent on July 1, 1969.

I regret the need to raise postal rates. I can suggest, however, that these increases can help our country achieve two important goals. First, the proposal can help in our efforts to control inflation by bringing federal revenues and expenditures into better balance. Secondly, rate increases will make it easier for the Postmaster General and his associates to provide better postal service. After carefully reviewing the fiscal 1970 Post Office budget submitted by the previous administration, we have been able to achieve reductions of net outlays equal to $140 million. A comprehensive review of all postal operations is now underway; modern management techniques are being introduced and efficiency is being increased.

Further improvements will take time—and during that time it is essential that financial pressures should not impair or reduce available services.

I would add one further comment: this Administration is determined that the cycle of greater and greater postal deficits and more and more rate increases will be broken. The only way to break that cycle is through effective, long-range reforms in the way the postal system operates. Some of these reforms can be implemented by the Postmaster General; others will require

Congressional action. We will be submitting specific proposals for such reform to the Congress within the next forty-five days.

Postal reform will not be achieved easily; there are always many obstacles to even the most necessary change. But we remain confident that we can, with your cooperation, move boldly toward our three goals: better postal service, improved working conditions for all employees, and a reduction of the recent pressure for frequent increases in postal rates.

Proposed legislation to effect the revenue increases which I have recommended here will be sent to the Congress shortly.

RICHARD NIXON

TEXT OF PRESIDENTIAL MESSAGE ON TAX REFORMS

Following is the complete text of President Nixon's April 21 message to Congress on tax reform.

TO THE CONGRESS OF THE UNITED STATES:

Reform of our Federal income tax system is long overdue. Special preferences in the law permit far too many Americans to pay less than their fair share of taxes. Too many other Americans bear too much of the tax burden.

This Administration, working with the Congress, is determined to bring equity to the Federal tax system. Our goal is to take important first steps in tax reform legislation during this session of the Congress.

The economic overheating which has brought inflation into its fourth year keeps us from moving immediately to reduce Federal tax revenues at this time. Inflation is itself a tax—a cruel and unjust tax that hits hardest those who can least afford it. In order to "repeal" the tax of inflation, we are cutting budget spending and have requested an extension of the income tax surcharge.

Although we must maintain total Federal revenues, there is no reason why we cannot lighten the burden on those who pay too much, and increase the taxes of those who pay too little. Treasury officials will present the Administration's initial group of tax reform proposals to the Congress this week. Additional recommendations will be made later in this session. The overall program will be equitable and essentially neutral in its revenue impact. There will be no substantial gain or loss in Federal revenue, but the American taxpayer who carries more than his share of the burden will gain some relief.

Much concern has been expressed because some citizens with incomes of more than $200,000 pay no Federal income taxes. These people are neither tax dodgers nor tax cheats. Many of them pay no taxes because they make large donations to worthy causes, donations which every taxpayer is authorized by existing law to deduct from his income in figuring his tax bill.

But where we can prevent it by law, we must not permit our wealthiest citizens to be 100% successful at tax avoidance. Nor should the Government limit its tax reform only to apply to these relatively few extreme cases. Preferences built into the law in the past—some of which have either outlived their usefulness or were never appropriate—permit many thousands of individuals and corporate taxpayers to avoid their fair share of Federal taxation.

A number of present tax preferences will be scaled down in the Administration's proposals to be submitted this week. Utilizing the revenue gained from our present proposals, we suggest tax reductions for lower-income taxpayers. Further study will be necessary before we can propose changes in other preferences and as these are developed we will recommend them to the Congress.

Specifically, the Administration will recommend:

• Enactment of what is in effect a "minimum income tax" for citizens with substantial incomes by setting a 50% limitation on the use of the principal tax preferences which are subject to change by law.

This limit on tax preferences would be a major step toward assuring that all Americans bear their fair share of the Federal tax burden.

• Enactment of a "low income allowance," which will remove more than 2,000,000 of our low income families from the Federal tax rolls and assure that persons or families in poverty pay no Federal income taxes.

This provision will also benefit students and other young people. For example, the person who works in the summer or throughout the year and earns $1,700 in taxable income—and now pays $117 in Federal income taxes—would pay nothing.

The married couple—college students or otherwise—with an income of $2,300 and current taxes of $100 would pay nothing.

A family of four would pay no tax on income below $3,500—the cutoff now is $3,000.

The "low income allowance," if enacted by the Congress, will offer genuine tax relief to the young, the elderly, the disadvantaged and the handicapped.

Other tax reform proposals would also help workers who change jobs by liberalizing deductions for moving expenses and would reduce specific preferences in a number of areas:

• Taxpayers who have certain nontaxable income or other preferences would have their nonbusiness deductions reduced proportionately.

• Certain mineral transactions (so-called "carved out" mineral production payments and "ABC" transactions) would be treated in a way that would stop artificial creation of net operating losses in these industries.

• Exempt organizations, including private foundations, would come under much stricter surveillance.

• The rules affecting charitable deductions would be tightened —but only to screen out the unreasonable and not stop those which help legitimate charities and therefore the nation.

• The practice of using multiple subsidiaries and affiliated corporations to take undue advantage of the lower tax rate on the first $25,000 of corporate income would be curbed.

• Farm losses, to be included in the "limitation on tax preferences," would be subject to certain other restrictions in order to curb abuses in this area.

I also recommend that the Congress repeal the 7% investment tax credit effective today.

This subsidy to business investment no longer has priority over other pressing national needs.

In the early 60's, America's productive capacity needed prompt modernization to enable it to compete with industry abroad. Accordingly, Government gave high priority to providing tax incentives for this modernization.

Since that time, American business has invested close to $400 billion in new plant and equipment, bringing the American economy to new levels of productivity and efficiency. While a vigorous pace of capital formation will certainly continue to be needed, national priorities now require that we give attention to the need for general tax relief.

Repeal of the investment tax credit will permit relief to every taxpayer through relaxation of the surcharge earlier than I had contemplated.

The revenue effect of the repeal of the investment tax credit will begin to be significant during calendar year 1970. Therefore,

I recommend that investment tax credit repeal be accompanied by extension of the full surcharge only to January 1, 1970, with a reduction to 5% on January 1. This is a reappraisal of my earlier recommendation for continuance of the surcharge until June 30, 1970 at a 10% rate. If economic and fiscal conditions permit, we can look forward to elimination of the remaining surtax on June 30, 1970.

I am convinced, however, that reduction of the surtax without repeal of the investment tax credit would be imprudent.

The gradual increase in Federal revenues resulting from repeal of the investment tax credit and the growth of the economy will also facilitate a start during fiscal 1971 in funding two high-priority programs to which this Administration is committed:

• Revenue sharing with State and local governments.

• Tax credits to encourage investment in poverty areas and hiring and training of the hard-core unemployed.

These proposals, now in preparation, will be transmitted to the Congress in the near future.

The tax reform measures outlined earlier in this message will be recommended to the House Ways and Means Committee by Treasury officials this week. This is a broad and necessary program for tax reform. I urge its prompt enactment.

But these measures, sweeping as they are, will not by themselves transform the U.S. tax system into one adequate to the long-range future. Much of the current tax system was devised in depression and shaped further in war. Fairness calls for tax reform now; beyond that, the American people need and deserve a simplified Federal tax system, and one that is attuned to the 1970's.

We must reform our tax structure to make it more equitable and efficient; we must redirect our tax policy to make it more conducive to stable economic growth and responsive to urgent social needs.

That is a large order. Therefore, I am directing the Secretary of the Treasury to thoroughly review the entire Federal tax system and present to me recommendations for basic changes, along with a full analysis of the impact of those changes, no later than November 30, 1969.

Since taxation affects so many wallets and pocketbooks, reform proposals are bound to be controversial. In the debate to come on reform, and in the even greater debate on redirection, the nation would best be served by an avoidance of stereotyped reactions. One man's "loophole" is another man's "incentive." Tax policy should not seek to "soak" any group or give a "break" to any other—it should aim to serve the nation as a whole.

Tax dollars the Government deliberately waives should be viewed as a form of expenditure, and weighed against the priority of other expenditures. When the preference device provides more social benefit than Government collection and spending, that "incentive" should be expanded; when the preference is inefficient or subject to abuse, it should be ended.

Taxes, often bewailed as inevitable as death, actually give life to the people's purpose in having a Government: to provide protection, service and stimulus to progress.

We shall never make taxation popular, but we can make taxation fair.

RICHARD NIXON

TEXT OF PRESIDENT NIXON MESSAGE ON ORGANIZED CRIME

Following is the complete text of President Nixon's April 23 message on organized crime.

TO THE CONGRESS OF THE UNITED STATES:

Today, organized crime has deeply penetrated broad segments of American life. In our great cities, it is operating prosperous criminal cartels. In our suburban areas and smaller cities, it is expanding its corrosive influence. Its economic base is principally derived from its virtual monopoly of illegal gambling, the numbers racket, and the importation of narcotics. To a large degree, it underwrites the loan sharking business in the United States and actively participates in fraudulent bankruptcies. It encourages street crime by inducing narcotic addicts to mug and rob. It encourages housebreaking and burglary by providing efficient disposal methods for stolen goods. It quietly continues to infiltrate and corrupt organized labor. It is increasing its enormous holdings and influence in the world of legitimate business. To achieve his end, the organized criminal relies on physical terror and psychological intimidation, on economic retaliation and political bribery, on citizen indifference and governmental acquiescence. He corrupts our governing institutions and subverts our democratic processes. For him, the moral and legal subversion of our society is a life-long and lucrative profession.

Many decent Americans contribute regularly, voluntarily and unwittingly to the coffers of organized crime—the suburban housewife and the city slum dweller who place a twenty-five cent numbers bet; the bricklayer and college student who buy a football card; the businessman and the secretary who bet illegally on a horse.

Estimates of the "take" from illegal gambling alone in the United States run anywhere from $20 billion, which is over 2% of the nation's gross national product, to $50 billion, a figure larger than the entire federal administrative budget for fiscal year 1951. This wealth is but one yardstick of the economic and political power held by the leaders of organized crime who operate with little limitation or restriction within our society.

Organized crime's victims range all across the social spectrum—the middle-class businessman enticed into paying usurious loan rates; the small merchant required to pay protection money; the white suburbanite and the black city dweller destroying themselves with drugs; the elderly pensioner and the young married couple forced to pay higher prices for goods. The most tragic victims, of course, are the poor whose lack of financial resources, education and acceptable living standards frequently breed the kind of resentment and hopelessness that make illegal gambling and drugs an attractive escape from the bleakness of ghetto life.

Background

For two decades now, since the Attorney General's Conference on Organized Crime in 1950, the Federal effort has slowly increased. Many of the nation's most notorious racketeers have been imprisoned or deported and many local organized crime business operations have been eliminated. But these successes have not substantially impeded the growth and power of organized criminal syndicates. Not a single one of the 24 Cosa Nostra families has been destroyed. They are more firmly entrenched and more secure than ever before.

It is vitally important that Americans see this alien organization for what it really is—a totalitarian and closed society operating within an open and democratic one. It has succeeded so far because an apathetic public is not aware of the threat it poses to American life. This public apathy has permitted most organized criminals to escape prosecution by corrupting officials, by intimidating witnesses and by terrorizing victims into silence.

As a matter of national "public policy," I must warn our citizens that the threat of organized crime cannot be ignored or tolerated any longer. It will not be eliminated by loud voices and good intentions. It will be eliminated by carefully conceived, well-funded and well-executed action plans. Furthermore, our action plans against organized crime must be established on a long-term basis in order to relentlessly pursue the criminal syndicate. This goal will not be easily attained. Over many decades, organized crime has extended its roots deep into American society and they will not be easily extracted. Our success will first depend on the support of our citizens who must be informed of the dangers that organized crime poses. Success also will require the help of Congress and of the State and local governments.

This Administration is urgently aware of the need for extraordinary action and I have already taken several significant steps aimed at combating organized crime. I have pledged an unstinting commitment, with an unprecedented amount of money, manpower and other resources to back up my promise to attack organized crime. For example—I have authorized the Attorney General to engage in wiretapping of organized racketeers. I have authorized the Attorney General to establish 20 Federal racketeering field offices all across the nation. I have authorized the Attorney General to establish a unique Federal-State Racket Squad in New York City. I have asked all Federal agencies to cooperate with the Department of Justice in this effort and to give priority to the organized crime drive. I have asked the Congress to increase the fiscal 1970 budget by $25 million, which will roughly double present expenditures for the organized crime effort.

In addition, I have asked the Congress to approve a $300 million appropriation in the 1970 budget for the Law Enforcement Assistance Administration. Most of these funds will go in block grants to help State and local law enforcement programs and a substantial portion of this assistance money will be utilized to fight organized crime. I have had discussions with the State Attorneys General and I have authorized the Attorney General to cooperate fully with the States and local communities in this national effort, and to extend help to them with every means at his disposal. Finally, I have directed the Attorney General to mount our Federal anti-organized crime offensive and to coordinate the Federal effort with State and local efforts where possible.

Assistance to States, Local Governments

Through the Law Enforcement Assistance Administration, and other units of the Department of Justice, the Attorney General has already taken some initial steps:

1. A program is being established so that State and local law enforcement people can exchange recent knowledge on the most effective tactics to use against organized crime at the local level.

2. The Justice Department is furnishing technical assistance and financial help in the training of investigators, prosecutors, intelligence analysts, accountants, statisticians—the professional people needed to combat a sophisticated form of criminal activity.

3. The Justice Department is encouraging municipalities and States to reexamine their own laws in the organized crime area. We are also encouraging and assisting in the formation of State-wide organized crime investigating and prosecuting units.

4. A computerized organized crime intelligence system is being developed to house detailed information on the personalities and activities of organized crime nationally. This system will also serve as a model for State computer intelligence systems which will be partially funded by the Federal Government.

5. We are fostering cooperation and coordination between States and between communities to avoid a costly duplication of effort and expense.

6. We are providing Federal aid for both State and local public information programs designed to alert the people to the nature and scope of organized crime activity in their communities.

These actions are being taken now. But the current level of Federal activity must be dramatically increased, if we expect progress. More men and money, new administrative actions, and new legal authority are needed.

Expanded Budget

There is no old law or new law that will be useful without the necessary manpower for enforcement. I am therefore, as stated, asking Congress to increase the Fiscal Year 1970 budget for dealing with organized crime by $25 million. This will roughly double the amount spent in the fight against organized crime during Fiscal Year 1969, and will bring the total Federal expenditures for the campaign against organized crime to the unprecedented total of $61 million. I urge Congress to approve our request for these vital funds.

Reorganization of Crime Effort

I have directed the newly appointed Advisory Council on Executive Organization to examine the effectiveness of the Executive Branch in combating crime—in particular, organized crime.

Because many departments and agencies of the Executive Branch are involved in the organized crime effort, I believe we can make lasting improvement only if we view this matter in the full context of executive operations.

Federal Racketeering Field Offices

The focal center of the Federal effort against organized crime is the Department of Justice. It coordinates the efforts of all of the Federal agencies. To combine in one cohesive unit a cadre of experienced Federal investigators and prosecutors, to maintain a Federal presence in organized crime problem areas throughout the nation on a continuing basis, and to institutionalize and utilize the valuable experience that has been gained by the "Strike Forces" under the direction of the Department of Justice, the Attorney General has now established Federal Racketeering Field Offices in Boston, Brooklyn, Buffalo, Chicago, Detroit, Miami, Newark, and Philadelphia. These offices bring together, in cohesive single units, experienced prosecutors from the Justice Department, Special Agents of the FBI, investigators of the Bureau of Narcotics and Dangerous Drugs, the finest staff personnel from the Bureau of Customs, the Securities and Exchange Commission, the Internal Revenue Service, the Post Office, the Secret Service and other Federal offices with expertise in diverse areas of organized crime.

The Racketeering Field Offices will be able to throw a tight net of Federal law around an organized crime concentration and through large scale target investigations, we believe we can obtain the prosecutions that will imprison the leaders, paralyze the administrators, frighten the street workers and, eventually, paralyze the whole organized crime syndicate in any one particular city. The Attorney General plans to set up at least a dozen additional field offices within the next two years.

Federal-State Racket Squad

Investigations of the national crime syndicate, La Cosa Nostra, show its membership at some 5,000, divided into 24 "families" around the nation. In most cities organized crime activity is dominated by a single "family"; in New York City, however, the lucrative franchise is divided among five such "families."

To deal with this heavy concentration of criminal elements in the nation's largest city, a new Federal-State Racket Squad is being established in the Southern District of New York. It will include attorneys and investigators from the Justice Department as well as from New York State and city. This squad will be directed by the Department of Justice, in conjunction with a supervisory council of officials from State and local participating agencies, who will formulate policy, devise strategy and oversee tactical operations. Building on the experience of this special Federal-State Racket Squad, the Attorney General will be working with State and local authorities in other major problem areas to determine whether this concept of governmental partnership should be expanded to those areas through the formation of additional squads.

New Legislation

From his studies in recent weeks, the Attorney General has concluded that new weapons and tools are needed to enable the Federal Government to strike both at the Cosa Nostra hierarchy and the sources of revenue that feed the coffers of organized crime. Accordingly the Attorney General will ask Congress for new laws, and I urge Congress to act swiftly and favorably on the Attorney General's request.

Witness Immunity

First, we need a new broad general witness immunity law to cover all cases involving the violation of a Federal statute. I commend to the Congress for its consideration the recommendations of the National Commission on Reform of Federal Criminal Laws. Under the Commission's proposal, a witness could not be prosecuted on the basis of anything he said while testifying, but he would not be immune from prosecution based on other evidence of his offense. Furthermore, once the government has granted the witness such immunity, a refusal then to testify would bring a prison sentence for contempt. With this new law, government should be better able to gather evidence to strike at the leadership of organized crime and not just the rank and file. The Attorney General has also advised me that the Federal Government will make special provisions for protecting witnesses who fear to testify due to intimidation.

Wagering Tax Amendments

We shall ask for swift enactment of S 1624 or its companion bill HR 322, sponsored by Senator Roman Hruska of Nebraska and Congressman Richard Poff of Virginia respectively. These measures would amend the wagering tax laws and enable the Internal Revenue Service to play a more active and effective role in collecting the revenues owed on wagers; the bills would also increase the Federal operator's tax on gamblers from $50 annually to $1,000.

Corruption

For most large scale illegal gambling enterprises to continue operations over any extended period of time, the cooperation of corrupt police or local officials is necessary. This bribery and corruption of government closest to the people is a deprival of one of a citizen's most basic rights. We shall seek legislation to make this form of systematic corruption of community political leadership and law enforcement a federal crime. This law would enable the Federal Government to prosecute both the corruptor and the corrupted.

Illegal Gambling Businesses

We also shall request new legislation making it a Federal crime to engage in an illicit gambling operation, from which five or more persons derive income, which has been in operation more than thirty days, or from which the daily "take" exceeds $2,000. The purpose of this legislation is to bring under Federal jurisdiction all large-scale illegal gambling operations which involve or affect inter-state commerce. The effect of the law will be to give the Attorney General broad latitude to assist local and state government in cracking down on illegal gambling, the wellspring of organized crime's financial reservoir.

This Administration has concluded that the major thrust of its concerted anti-organized crime effort should be directed against gambling activities. While gambling may seem to most Americans to be the least reprehensible of all the activities of organized crime, it is gambling which provides the bulk of the revenues that eventually go into usurious loans, bribes of police and local officials, "campaign contributions" to politicians, the wholesale narcotics traffic, the infiltration of legitimate businesses, and to pay for the large stables of lawyers and accountants and assorted professional men who are in the hire of organized crime.

Gambling income is the lifeline of organized crime. If we can cut it or constrict it, we will be striking close to its heart.

Procedural Laws

With regard to improving the procedural aspects of the criminal law as it relates to the prosecution of organized crime, the Attorney General has been working with the Senate Subcommittee on Criminal Laws and Procedures to develop and perfect S 30, the "Organized Crime Control Act of 1969." As Attorney General Mitchell indicated in his testimony on that bill, we support its objectives. It is designed to improve the investigation and prosecution of organized crime cases, and to provide appropriate sentencing for convicted offenders. I feel confident that it will be a useful new tool.

Development of New Laws

Finally, I want to mention an area where we are examining the need for new laws: the infiltration of organized crime into fields of legitimate business. The syndicate-owned business, financed by illegal revenues and operated outside the rules of fair competition of the American market-place, cannot be tolerated in a system of free enterprise. Accordingly, the Attorney General is examining the potential application of the theories underlying our anti-trust laws as a potential new weapon.

The injunction with its powers of contempt and seizure, monetary fines and treble damage actions, and the powers of a forfeiture proceeding, suggest a new panoply of weapons to attack the property of organized crime rather than the unimportant persons (the fronts) who technically head up syndicate-controlled businesses. The arrest, conviction and imprisonment of a Mafia lieutenant can curtail operations, but does not put the syndicate out of business. As long as the property of organized crime remains, new leaders will step forward to take the place of those we jail. However, if we can levy fines on their real estate corporations, if we can seek treble damages against their trucking firms and banks, if we can seize the liquor in their warehouses, I think we can strike a critical blow at the organized crime conspiracy.

Clearly, the success or failure of any ambitious program such as I have outlined in this Message depends on many factors. I am confident the Congress will supply the funds and the requested legislation, the States and communities across the country will take advantage of the Federal capability and desire to assist and participate with them, and the Federal personnel responsible for programs and actions will vigorously carry out their mission.

RICHARD NIXON

TEXT OF NIXON MESSAGE ON D.C. REORGANIZATION

Following is the complete text of President Nixon's April 28 message on the reorganization of the District of Columbia.

TO THE CONGRESS OF THE UNITED STATES:

Carved out of swampland at our country's birth, the Nation's Capital city now sets a new test of national purpose. This was a city that men dared to plan—and build by plan—laying out avenues and monuments and housing in accordance with a common rational scheme. Now we are challenged once again to shape our environment: to renew our city by rational foresight and planning, rather than leaving it to grow swamp-like without design.

At issue is whether the city will be enabled to take hold of its future: whether its institutions will be reformed so that its government can truly represent its citizens and act upon their needs.

Good government, in the case of a city, must be local government. The Federal Government has a special responsibility for the District of Columbia. But it also bears toward the District the same responsibility it bears toward all other cities: to help local government work better, and to attempt to supplement local resources for programs that city officials judge most urgent.

My aim is to increase the responsibility and efficiency of the District of Columbia's new government, which has performed so ably during its first perilous years. Early in this Administration, we recommended proposals that would increase the effectiveness of local law enforcement and provide the resources needed by local officials to begin revitalizing the areas damaged during the civil disturbance. Those proposals, however, cover only a part of the program which will be essential for the District Government to respond to the wishes of its people.

I now present the second part of this program, worked out in close consultation with the District Government, and based upon the needs articulated by the Mayor and the City Council.

This program will provide:

• An orderly mechanism for achieving self-government in the District of Columbia.

• Representation in Congress.

• Added municipal authority for the City Council and the Mayor.

• Additional top management positions to bring new talents and leadership into the District Government.

• A secure and equitable source of Federal funds for the District's budget.

• An expanded rapid rail transit system, linking the diverse segments of our Capital's metropolitan region.

The Federal Government bears a major responsibility for the welfare of our Capital's citizens in general. It owns much of the District's land and employs many of its citizens. It depends on the services of local government. The condition of our Capital city is a sign of the condition of our nation—and is certainly taken as such by visitors, from all the states of the Union, and from around the globe.

However, this Federal responsibility does not require Federal rule. Besides the official Washington of monuments and offices, there is the Washington of 850,000 citizens with all the hopes and expectations of the people of any major city, striving and sacrificing for a better life—the eighth largest among the cities of our country.

Self-Government. Full citizenship through local self-government must be given to the people of this city: The District Government cannot be truly responsible until it is made responsible to those who live under its rule. The District's citizens should not be expected to pay taxes for a government which they have no part in choosing—or to bear the full burdens of citizenship without the full rights of citizenship.

I therefore ask Congress to create a Commission on Self-Government for the District of Columbia, to be charged with submitting to Congress and the President a proposal for establishing meaningful self-government in the District.

In order for any government to be accountable to the people, responsibilities must be clearly pinpointed, and officials must have the powers they need to carry out their responsibilities. The Commission would recommend how best to augment and allocate the legislative and executive authorities with respect to governing the city.

The members of this Commission would be partly appointed by the President, partly designated by the Congress, and partly chosen in a city-wide election by the citizens of the District. They would be given an adequate but strictly defined time period to formulate their plan. I would hope that the Commission would be established promptly, so that its report could be submitted to Congress and the President in time for the 1970 legislative session. With adequate funding, they would be able to draw on the wisdom of consultants throughout the country—men who know firsthand the art of the possible, as well as those who study government—in addition to their own staff.

The Commission members must give thorough consideration to the many alternative plans for self-government which have been presented over the years. But they must also make use of new knowledge we have gained about the problems of existing local governments around the country—in finance, management, urban development, citizen participation and many other areas. They must seek the sentiment of the District's citizens from the earliest stages of their work.

There also is a Federal interest that must be respected. The normal functions of the Federal agencies must be guaranteed and their vital operations protected. There must be continued Federal jurisdiction over public buildings and monuments and assurance of well-being for the men and women who work in them or come to visit. The rights of the national government must be protected, at the same time as the rights of the city's residents are secured. There must be respect for the responsibilities with regard to the District which the Constitution places in the Congress.

To establish a new government in so diverse and active a city as the District is certainly no easy task. There are dangers in setting up new governments, as well as opportunities. Congress has been rightly concerned that the plan for self-government must insure responsible elections, effective executive leadership, protection of individual liberty and safeguards for District of Columbia employees. Self-government must be extended in a timely and orderly manner.

It is especially important that the Commission go beyond the issue of self-government as such, and concern itself with the effective functioning of government in the District of Columbia. Under the existing governmental structure the City Council finds itself without the powers to deal with many crucial problems because of the conflicting and divided authorities that now reside in independent agencies.

But there is no cause for delay: Self-government has remained an unfulfilled promise for far too long. It has been energetically supported by the past four Presidents—Harry S. Truman, Dwight D. Eisenhower, John F. Kennedy, and Lyndon B. Johnson. The Senate approved measures to provide it during the 81st, 82nd, 84th, and 86th Congresses. We owe the present lack of local elections to the Reconstruction period, when Congress rescued the District from bankruptcy but suspended the voting franchise. Congress established the Commission form of government in 1874 as a temporary "receivership," but the Commissioners' government persisted for over 90 years—and today, even after reorganization in 1967, the District remains under Federal control.

The history of failure for self-government proposals shows the need for a new plan strong enough to stand up against the old questions or criticisms. Myriad different plans have been offered—and will be offered again this year. But each will have its own doubters as well as its supporters. A Commission must examine all of them, combining old and new ideas in a proposal that will at last win the broad-based respect necessary for final acceptance, and that will carry the authority of a disinterested group of men whose vocation is government—jurists, political leaders and scholars, as well as other citizens, investing the wisdom of their life's work in a truly new government.

Recognizing both the solemn right of the District's citizens to self-government and the Federal interest, I ask Congress to act promptly on proposed legislation to establish a Commission on Self-Government for the District of Columbia, which will be transmitted shortly.

Congressional Representation. I also urge Congress to grant voting representation in Congress to the District of Columbia. It should offend the democratic senses of this nation that the 850,000 citizens of its Capital, comprising a population larger than eleven of its states, have no voice in the Congress.

I urge that Congress approve, and the States ratify, an amendment to the Constitution granting to the District at least one representative in the House of Representatives, and such additional representatives in the House as the Congress shall approve, and to provide for the possibility of two Senators. Until such an amendment is approved by Congress and ratified by the States, I recommend that Congress enact legislation to provide for a non-voting House delegate from the District.

City Council and Mayor. While working for self-government and Congressional Representation for the future, I recommend that Congress take certain measures this session to strengthen the present District Government, in both authority and efficiency.

The Reorganization Plan which established the present government left to Congress many mundane muncipal functions which are burdensome chores to it but important functions for good local government. At present, Congress must allot a portion of its legislative calendar to setting ordinances for the District of Columbia, in effect performing the duties of a local City Council for the Capital. It thus deals with matters which are of little or no importance to the nation as a whole—the setting of a fee, for example, to redeem a dog from the city pound. The concerns of the District are frequently shunted aside to allow for higher-priority legislative business. "No policy can be worse than to mingle great and small concerns," argued Augustus Woodward, one of the founders of our city, when Congress considered establishing a territorial form of government in 1800. "The latter become absorbed in the former; are neglected and forgotten."

Legislation will be proposed to transfer a number of specific authorities to the District Government—including authority to change various fees for user charges now fixed by statute, waive license fees for new businesses, for persons whose businesses have been burnt out in a civil disturbance, and modernize the licensing of various businesses, occupations and professions.

In addition, I recommend that the Mayor be given certain local responsibilities now exercised by Federal departments or agencies. Reorganization plans will be submitted in the coming weeks to transfer local functions now operated by the Federal Government—and frequently paid for by the District—to the Executive Branch of the District Government. Local services should be operated by local government. Such responsibilities are only an extra burden for the Federal departments, which should rightly devote their energies to the welfare of the entire nation.

I will also submit other reorganization plans to transfer certain independent or quasi-independent District agencies to the Mayor's jurisdiction. These actions will strengthen the executive direction of the City's administration and complement the continuing reorganization and strengthening of the District's administrative structure.

Granting new authority to the Mayor and City Council would in no way prejudice the ultimate form or degree of self-government. It would provide them with powers which any good local government, however chosen, should exercise. By initiating this process now, we thus build the strength of local institutions even as we make them more responsible, formally, to their citizens.

Civil Servants. Good government is the product of able and dedicated people working together. The District Government needs the very best urban managers and experts this nation has to direct the Capital's growth and apply its resources, and it must be able to attract such public servants at realistic salary rates.

Adding to the number of top management positions is vital to the effective carrying out of District Government reorganization—the creation of new departments recently announced by the Mayor, and other steps planned for the future. Such reorganization, streamlining the chain of command, is one of the most promising achievements of the Mayor's first years.

Accordingly, I urge Congress to enact legislation to increase the number of supergrade positions available to the District Government.

Federal Payment. The District of Columbia cannot achieve strong and efficient government unless it has ample and dependable sources of financing. Sound financing can be achieved only if the Federal Government pays its appropriate share.

I therefore recommend that the Congress authorize a Federal payment formula, fixing the Federal contribution at 30 percent of local tax and other general fund revenues.

This formula would equitably reflect the Federal interest in the District of Columbia at this time with respect to:

• the 217,000 Federal employees who work in the District, about one-third of the local work force.

• the more than 10 million Americans who visit their nation's Capital each year.

• the embassies and nationals of the foreign governments.

• the land and buildings owned by the Federal Government which cannot be taxed but comprise more than 40 percent of the District's land value.

Enactment of a formula approach would be a significant step toward effective government in the District. It would tie the level of Federal aid to the burden of local taxes on the District's citizens. It would also provide the District with a predictable estimate for use in the annual budget process, thus allowing it to plan its expenditures more accurately and imaginatively for the growing needs of its population. A similar formula, dealing with District borrowing authorization, was enacted by the Congress more than a year ago—and has already proven its worth in improved budgetary planning.

The proposed Federal payment formula would not involve an automatic expenditure of Federal funds. The Federal payment would still have to be appropriated by Congress.

By authorizing the Federal payment at 30 percent of all District general fund revenues, the Congress would allow a payment of $120 million in fiscal 1970, an increase of $30 million above the present fixed authorization. This payment is incorporated in the District's 1970 budget request.

Transportation. The National Capital needs and deserves a mass transit system that is truly metropolitan, unifying the central city with the surrounding suburbs. As a part of its responsibility for the National Capital Region, the Federal Government should support deliberate action, based upon effective planning, to meet the future transportation needs of the Region. The surrounding areas in Maryland and Virginia, as Congress rightly recognized, include the most rapidly growing areas of population and job opportunities, potentially of rich benefit to the inner city.

Mass transit must be part of a balanced transportation network. A subway will not relieve local governments of the duty to modernize and improve their highway systems and other forms of transportation, so that all citizens have an adequate choice as to how they travel. Clearly, the impasse that has arisen between proponents of road and rail transportation in the Washington metropolitan area has contributed little to the progress of either. There are, however, hopeful signs that a fair and effective settlement of these issues will be reached in the near future. It is in the interest of all those involved—central city dwellers, suburbanites, shoppers, employees, and visitors alike—that this be done.

The Washington Metropolitan Area Transit Authority, in consultation with the District Government and other local jurisdictions, has prepared legislation which would extend the presently authorized 25-mile rapid rail transit system to a 97-mile regional system. The expanded system would provide rapid transit between the downtown and outlying areas. It would facilitate the free flow of resources and labor, and would benefit all eight jurisdictions involved in its planning and approval.

The proposed legislation fulfills the Congressional mandate in a 1966 Act, which directed the Washington Metropolitan Area Transportation Authority to plan, develop, finance and provide for the operation of a full regional rapid rail system for the National Capital area.

The 97-mile system would relieve downtown congestion; increase employment; make educational, cultural and recreational facilities more accessible; reduce air pollution; stimulate business, industry, and tourism; broaden tax bases; and promote orderly urban development of the Nation's Capital.

The cost of the expanded system is estimated to be some $2.5 billion. Fare box receipts would pay for $835 million. The remaining cost of $1.7 billion (the net project cost) would be divided equitably among all the governments concerned on a 2/3-1/3 sharing basis between Federal and local governments.

The local governments concerned have already passed bond referenda or taken other appropriate action to finance their contributions of $347 million. But action by Congress is needed to authorize grants sufficient to cover the $1.1 billion Federal (2/3) share of the net project cost and capital contributions of $216 million for the District's portion of the local (1/3) share.

I urge that Congress promptly appropriate the necessary authorizing legislation for the 97-mile system.

Pennsylvania Avenue. Finally, we come to the Washington that so many millions flock to visit; the Washington that stands as a proud physical symbol of our Nation's liberties and its hopes.

Pennsylvania Avenue should be one of the great Avenues of our Republic—as in the original vision of our Capital City—and will be so if the Pennsylvania Avenue Commission presses forward with its present plans. Already, in accordance with the Commission's plans, construction of the Presidential Building at 12th Street has been completed; construction is continuing on the new Capitol Reflecting Pool, as well as buildings for the Federal Bureau of Investigation and the Labor Department. Planning is going forward for the Federal Triangle, a new Municipal Center at Judiciary Square, and an extension of the National Gallery. Our ultimate goal must be the Avenue of L'Enfant's Plan, a grand route connecting the Congress and the President's House, the vital center of the City, monumental in importance but designed for the Citizens of this Nation to enjoy at all hours for work or pleasure. I will encourage the development of this plan and submit legislation at the appropriate time.

One of the most significant additions to Pennsylvania Avenue will be an international center for scholars, to be established as a living memorial to Woodrow Wilson in the area just north of the National Archives. There could hardly be a more appropriate memorial to a President who combined a devotion to scholarship with a passion for peace. The District has long sought, and long needed, a center for both men of letters and men of affairs. This should be, as it was first proposed, "an institution of learning that the 22nd Century will regard as having influenced the 21st."

The renewal of Pennsylvania Avenue is an enterprise which two Presidents have supported. Their vision was the great vision of Pierre L'Enfant, George Washington, and Thomas Jefferson, whose plans embodied the ageless ideal of a Capital City. It is a vision which links Presidents, as it links the citizens of the District, in the love of this city. And I am proud to join them.

Capital Planning. It is a noble aim—this planning of a Capital City. It encompasses a drive which must apply to areas of rebuilding beyond a single Avenue, and to areas of need beyond physical renovation. It infuses our knowledge of human want with a new urgency. It tests our vision of man, and of the future of his cities.

I ask the Congress, and the American people, to join in this great enterprise knowing that if we govern with wisdom in this Capital City, it will be a proud symbol of the quality of American life and the reach of America's aspirations.

RICHARD NIXON

GRANT CONSOLIDATION

Following is the complete text of President Nixon's April 30 message to Congress requesting authority to consolidate certain federal-aid grants.

TO THE CONGRESS OF THE UNITED STATES:

In the administration of federal programs, one of the principal needs today is to improve the delivery systems: to ensure that the intended services actually reach the intended recipients, and that they do so in an efficient, economical and effective manner.

As grant-in-aid programs have proliferated, the problems of delivery have grown more acute. States, cities, and other recipients find themselves increasingly faced with a welter of overlapping programs, often involving multiple agencies and diverse criteria. This results in confusion at the local level, in the waste of time, energy and resources, and often in frustration of the intent of Congress.

As a major step toward improved administration of these programs, I urge that Congress enact a Grant Consolidation Act.

Under our present fragmented system, each one of a group of closely related categorical grants is encumbered with its own individual array of administrative and technical requirements. This unnecessarily complicates the planning process; it discourages comprehensive planning; it requires multiple applications, and multiple bookkeeping both by the federal agencies and by state and local governments.

The legislation I propose would be patterned in part after procedures used successfully for the past 20 years to reorganize Executive Branch functions. It would give the President power to initiate consolidation of closely related federal assistance programs, and to place consolidated programs under the jurisdiction of a single agency. However, it would give either House of Congress the right to veto a proposed consolidation within 60 days, and it would establish stringent safeguards against possible abuse.

In order to make consolidation possible, it would be necessary in many cases to make changes in the statutory terms and conditions under which individual programs would be administered. Formulas, interest rates, eligibility requirements, administrative procedures, and other terms and conditions of the various programs being consolidated would have to be brought into harmony. The proposed legislation would empower the President to do this in drawing up his consolidation plans—but only within carefully defined limits. For example:

• Only programs in closely related functional areas could be consolidated.

• Terms and conditions could be changed only to the extent necessary to achieve the purposes of the consolidation plan.

• In setting new terms and conditions, the President would be limited by the range of those already provided in the programs being consolidated. Thus, if a program providing for a 10-percent state matching share were being merged with one providing a 20-percent matching share, he would have to propose a matching share between 10 and 20 percent.

• No consolidation plan could continue any program beyond the period authorized by law for its existence.

• No plan could provide assistance to recipients not already eligible under one of the programs being merged.

• Responsibility for the consolidated program could not be vested in an agency or office not already responsible for one of those being merged.

The effect of these limits would be to safeguard the essential intent of Congress in originally establishing the various programs; the effect of consolidation would be to carry out that intent more effectively and more efficiently.

The number of separate federal assistance programs has grown enormously over the years.

When the Office of Economic Opportunity set out to catalogue federal assistance programs, it required a book of more than 600 pages even to set forth brief descriptions. It is an almost universal complaint of local government officials that the web of programs has grown so tangled that it often becomes impermeable. However laudable each may be individually, the total effect can be one of government paralysis.

If these programs are to achieve their intended purposes, we must find new ways of cutting through the tangle.

Passage of the Grant Consolidation Act would not be a substitute for other reforms necessary in order to improve the delivery of federal services, but it is an essential element. It would be another vital step in the administrative reforms undertaken already, such as establishing common regional boundaries for federal agencies, creating the Urban Affairs Council and the Office of Intergovernmental Relations, and beginning a streamlining of administrative procedures for federal grant-in-aid programs. Its aim, essentially, is to help make more certain the delivery and more manageable the administration of a growing complex of federal programs, at a time when the problems they address increasingly cross the old jurisdictional lines of departments and agencies.

This proposal would permit rapid action, initiated by the President, while preserving the power to Congress to disapprove such action. It would benefit the intended beneficiaries of the programs involved; it would benefit state and local governments, which now have to contend with a bewildering array of rules and jurisdictions; and it would benefit the American taxpayer, who now bears the cost of administrative inefficiencies.

RICHARD NIXON

TEXT OF PRESIDENT'S MESSAGE ON OBSCENITY

Following is the complete text of President Nixon's May 2 message on the mailing of obscene and pornographic materials.

TO THE CONGRESS OF THE UNITED STATES:

American homes are being bombarded with the largest volume of sex-oriented mail in history. Most of it is unsolicited, unwanted, and deeply offensive to those who receive it. Since 1964, the number of complaints to the Post Office about this salacious mail has almost doubled. One hundred and forty thousand letters of protest came in during the last nine months alone, and the volume is increasing. Mothers and fathers by the tens of thousands have written to the White House and the Congress. They resent these intrusions into their homes, and they are asking for federal assistance to protect their children against exposure to erotic publications.

The problem has no simple solution. Many publications dealing with sex—in a way that is offensive to many people—are protected under the broad umbrella of the First Amendment prohibition against any law "abridging the freedom of speech, or of the press."

However, there are constitutional means available to assist parents seeking to protect their children from the flood of sex-oriented materials moving through the mails. The Courts have not left society defenseless against the smut peddler; they have not ruled out reasonable government action.

Cognizant of the constitutional strictures, aware of recent Supreme Court decisions, this Administration has carefully studied the legal terrain of this problem.

We believe we have discovered some untried and hopeful approaches that will enable the federal government to become a full partner with states and individual citizens in drying up a primary source of this social evil. I have asked the Attorney General and the Postmaster General to submit to Congress three new legislative proposals.

The first would prohibit outright the sending of offensive sex materials to any child or teenager under 18. The second would prohibit the sending of advertising designed to appeal to a prurient interest in sex. It would apply regardless of the age of the recipient. The third measure complements the second by providing added protection from the kind of smut advertising now being mailed, unsolicited, into so many homes.

Protecting Minors. Many states have moved ahead of the federal government in drawing distinctions between materials considered obscene for adults and materials considered obscene for children. Some of these states, such as New York, have taken substantial strides toward protecting their youth from materials that may not be obscene by adult standards but which could be damaging to the healthy growth and development of a child. The United States Supreme Court has recognized, in repeated decisions, the unique status of minors and has upheld the New York statute. Building on judicial precedent, we hope to provide a new measure of federal protection for the young.

I ask Congress to make it a federal crime to use the mails or other facilities of commerce to deliver to anyone under 18 years of age material dealing with a sexual subject in a manner unsuitable for young people.

The proposed legislation would not go into effect until the sixth month after passage. The delay would provide mailers of these materials time to remove from their mailing lists the names of all youngsters under 18. The federal government would become a full partner with parents and states in protecting children from much of the interstate commerce in pornography. A first violation of this statute would be punishable by a maximum penalty of five years in prison and a $50,000 fine; subsequent violations carry greater penalties.

Prurient Advertising. Many complaints about salacious literature coming through the mails focus on advertisements. Many of these ads are designed by the advertiser to appeal exclusively to a prurient interest. This is clearly a form of pandering.

I ask the Congress to make it a federal crime to use the mails, or other facilities of commerce, for the commercial exploitation of a prurient interest in sex through advertising.

This measure focuses on the intent of the dealer in sex-oriented materials and his methods of marketing his materials. Through the legislation we hope to impose restrictions on dealers who flood the mails with grossly offensive advertisements intended to produce a market for their smut materials by stimulating the prurient interest of the recipient. Under the new legislation, this form of pandering could bring a maximum penalty of 5 years imprisonment, and a fine of $50,000 for a first offense and 10 years and a fine of $100,000 for subsequent offenses.

Invasion of Privacy. There are other erotic, sex-oriented advertisements that may be constitutionally protected but which are, nonetheless, offensive to the citizen who receives them in his home. No American should be forced to accept this kind of advertising through the mails.

In 1967 Congress passed a law to help deal with this kind of pandering. The law permits an addressee to determine himself whether he considers the material offensive in that he finds it "erotically arousing or sexually provocative." If the recipient deems it so, he can obtain from the Postmaster General a judicially enforceable order prohibiting the sender from making any further mailings to him or his children, and requiring the mailer to delete them from all his mailing lists.

More than 170,000 persons have requested such orders. Many citizens, however, are still unaware of this legislation, or do not know how to utilize its provisions. Accordingly, I have directed the Postmaster General to provide every Congressional office with pamphlets explaining how each citizen can use this law to protect his home from offensive advertising. I urge Congress to assist our effort for the widest possible distribution of these pamphlets.

This pandering law was based on the principle that no citizen should be forced to receive advertisements for sex-oriented matter he finds offensive. I endorse that principle and believe its application should be broadened.

I therefore ask Congress to extend the existing law to enable a citizen to protect his home from any intrusion of sex-oriented advertising regardless of whether or not a citizen has ever received such mailings.

This new stronger measure would require mailers and potential mailers to respect the expressed wishes of those citizens who do not wish to have sex-oriented advertising sent into their homes. These citizens will put smut-mailers on notice simply by filing their objections with a designated postal authority. To deliberately send such advertising to their homes would be an offense subject to both civil and criminal penalties.

As I have stated earlier, there is no simple solution to this problem. However, the measures I have proposed will go far toward protecting our youth from smut coming through the mails; they will place new restrictions upon the abuse of the postal service for pandering purposes; they will reinforce a man's right to privacy in his own home. These proposals, however, are not the whole answer.

The ultimate answer lies not with the government but with the people. What is required is a citizens' crusade against the obscene. When indecent books no longer find a market, when pornographic films can no longer draw an audience, when obscene plays open to empty houses, then the tide will turn. Government can maintain the dikes against obscenity, but only people can turn back the tide.

RICHARD NIXON

FOOD ASSISTANCE PROPOSALS

Following is the complete text of President Nixon's May 6 message to Congress proposing food assistance programs for the needy.

TO THE CONGRESS OF THE UNITED STATES:

We have long thought of America as the most bounteous of nations. In our conquest of the most elemental of human needs, we have set a standard that is a wonder and aspiration for the rest of the world. Our agricultural system produces more food than we can consume, and our private food market is the most effective food distribution system ever developed. So accustomed are most of us to a full and balanced diet that, until recently, we have thought of hunger and malnutrition as problems only in far less fortunate countries.

But in the past few years we have awakened to the distressing fact that despite our material abundance and agricultural wealth, many Americans suffer from malnutrition. Precise factual descriptions of its extent are not presently available, but there can be no doubt that hunger and malnutrition exist in America, and that some millions may be affected.

That hunger and malnutrition should persist in a land such as ours is embarrassing and intolerable. But it is an exceedingly complex problem, not at all susceptible to fast or easy solutions. Millions of Americans are simply too poor to feed their families properly. For them, there must be first sufficient food income. But this alone would only begin to address the problem for what matters finally is what people buy with the money they have. People must be educated in the choosing of proper foods. All of us, poor and non-poor alike, must be reminded that a proper diet is a basic determinant of good health. Our private food industry has made great advances in food processing and packaging, and has served the great majority of us very well. But these advances have placed great burdens on those who are less well off and less sophisticated in the ways of the modern marketplace. We must therefore work to make the private food market serve these citizens as well, by making nutritious foods widely available in popular forms. And for those caught in the most abject poverty, special efforts must be made to see that the benefits of proper foods are not lost amidst poor health and sanitary conditions.

The Council for Urban Affairs has for the past three months been studying the problem of malnutrition in America, and has assessed the capacities of our present food and nutrition programs. As a result of the Council's deliberations, I am today prepared to take the following actions:

Family Food Programs. The Federal Government presently provides food assistance to nearly seven million needy Americans through the Food Stamp and Direct Distribution programs. Though these programs have provided welcome and needed assistance to these persons, both programs are clearly in need of revision.

The present Food Stamp program can be greatly improved. I shall in a short period of time submit to the Congress legislation which will revise the Food Stamp program to:

- provide poor families enough food stamps to purchase a nutritionally complete diet. The Department of Agriculture estimates this to be $100 per month for a typical family of four.
- provide food stamps at no cost to those in the very lowest income brackets.
- provide food stamps to others at a cost of no greater than 30% of income.
- ensure that the Food Stamp program is complementary to a revised welfare program, which I shall propose to the Congress this year.
- give the Secretary of Agriculture the authority to operate both the Food Stamp and Direct Distribution programs con-

currently in individual counties, at the request and expense of local officials. This will permit the Secretary to assist counties wishing to change from Direct Distribution to Food Stamps, and to meet extraordinary or emergency situations.

It will not be possible for the revised program to go into effect until sometime after the beginning of the calendar year 1970, that is to say after the necessary legislative approval and administrative arrangements have been made. The requested appropriations will then permit the establishment of the revised program in all current Food Stamp counties before the end of the fiscal year, as well as a modest expansion into Direct Distribution counties, and some counties with no current programs.

This program, on a full year basis, will cost something in excess of $1 billion per year. (Precise estimates will only become available over time.) This will be in addition to the $1.5 billion for food for the hungry which I have requested for the forthcoming fiscal year, making a total program of $2.5 billion. In the meantime, $270 million is being reprogrammed within the forthcoming budget to permit the program to begin as soon as legislative and administrative arrangements can be made and other necessary measures taken.

While our long-range goal should be to replace direct food distribution with the revised Food Stamp program, the Direct Distribution program can fill many short-range needs. Today there are still over 440 counties without any Family Food Assistance program, and this Administration shall establish programs in each of these counties before July 1970. The Direct Distribution program will be used in most of these counties. In these and other Direct Distribution counties, the most serious criticism of the program will be met by ensuring that all counties offer the full range of available foods.

To strengthen both current Family Food Assistance programs, efforts will proceed on a high priority basis to establish more distribution points, prompter and simpler certification, financing arrangements, mailing of food stamps, and appeal mechanisms.

Special Supplemental. Serious malnutrition during pregnancy and infancy can impair normal physical and mental development in children. Special effort must be made to protect this vulnerable group from malnutrition.

The Special Package program, which provides needy women and mothers with packages of especially nutritious foods, was designed to meet this need. But the program has encountered logistical problems which have severely limited its success. I am therefore directing that a substantial portion of the Fiscal Year 1970 budget for this program be used to establish pilot programs that make use of the private food market. Under these programs, needy pregnant women and mothers of infants will be issued vouchers, redeemable at food and drug stores for infant formulas and other highly nutritious special foods. If such a program seems workable, and the administrative problems are resolved, the program will be expanded later on the basis of that experience.

Administration. I am directing the Urban Affairs Council to consider the establishment of a new agency, the Food and Nutrition Service, whose exclusive concern will be the administration of the Federal Food programs. Presently the food programs are operated in conjunction with numerous other unrelated programs. The creation of a new agency will permit greater specialization and concentration on the effective administration of the food programs.

Private Sector. I shall shortly announce a White House Conference on Food and Nutrition, involving executives from the nation's leading food processing and food distribution companies and trade unions. I shall ask these men to advise me on how the private food market might be used to improve the nutritional status of all Americans, and how the government food programs could be improved. I shall also call on these

men to work with the advertising industry and the Advertising Council, to develop an educational advertising and packaging campaign to publicize the importance of good food habits.

Inter-Agency Efforts. Although most of the current food and nutrition programs are administered by the Department of Agriculture, other agencies are critically involved. I am therefore establishing a sub-Cabinet working committee of the Urban Affairs Council to promote coordination between the food and nutrition programs and other health, educational and anti-poverty programs.

At the present time, I am directing the Secretary of Health, Education and Welfare and the Director of the Office of Economic Opportunity to take a number of immediate steps.

I am asking the Secretary of HEW to:

- work with state agencies to ensure that the Medicaid program is fully coordinated with the Special Package and pilot voucher programs for pregnant women and infants, so that vitamin and mineral products can be made available to those diagnosed as suffering from nutrient deficiencies.

- expand the National Nutrition Survey, presently being conducted by the Public Health Service, to provide us with our first detailed description of the extent of hunger and malnutrition in our country.

- initiate detailed research into the relationship between malnutrition and mental retardation.

- encourage emphasis by medical schools on training for diagnosis and treatment of malnutrition and malnutrition-related diseases.

The Office of Economic Opportunity, with its exclusive commitment to the problems of poverty and its unique "outreach" among the poor themselves, has an especial role to play. I am asking the Director of OEO to:

- work with the Secretaries of Agriculture and HEW to establish a greatly expanded role for the Community Action Agencies in delivering food stamps and commodity packages. Volunteers working in the VISTA program will also aid in the delivery and outreach process, supplementing the efforts of the Agricultural Extension Service.

- redirect OEO funds into the Emergency Food and Health Service program to increase its food, health, and sanitation services for our most depressed areas. Presently, health and sanitary conditions in many of our most depressed counties are so poor that improved food services alone would have little impact on the nutritional health of the population. The Emergency Food and Health Service has provided invaluable services in aiding these areas, and its good work should be substantially expanded.

More is at stake here than the health and well-being of 16 million American citizens who will be aided by these programs and the current Child Food Assistance programs. Something very like the honor of American democracy is at issue. It was half a century ago that the "fruitful plains" of this bounteous land were first called on to a great work of humanity, that of feeding a Europe exhausted and bleeding from the First World War. Since then on one occasion after another, in a succession of acts of true generosity—let those who doubt that find their counterpart in history—America has come to the aid of one starving people after another. But the moment is at hand to put an end to hunger in America itself for all time. I ask this of a Congress that has already splendidly demonstrated its own disposition to act. It is a moment to act with vigor; it is a moment to be recalled with pride.

RICHARD NIXON

POSTAL REFORM TEXT

Following is the complete text of President Nixon's May 27 message proposing the legislation to transfer functions of the Post Office to a Government-owned corporation.

TO THE CONGRESS OF THE UNITED STATES:

Total reform of the nation's postal system is absolutely essential.

The American people want dependable, reasonably priced mail service, and postal employees want the kind of advantages enjoyed by workers in other major industries. Neither goal can be achieved within the postal system we have today.

The Post Office is not keeping pace with the needs of our expanding population or the rightful aspirations of our postal workers.

Encumbered by obsolete facilities, inadequate capital, and outdated operation practices, the Post Office Department is failing the mail user in terms of service, failing the taxpayer in terms of cost, and failing the postal worker in terms of truly rewarding employment. It is time for a change.

Two years ago, Lawrence F. O'Brien, then Postmaster General, recognized that the Post Office was in "a race with catastrophe," and made the bold proposal that the postal system be converted into a government-owned corporation. As a result of Mr. O'Brien's recommendations, a Presidential commission was established to make a searching study of our postal system. After considering all the alternatives, the Commission likewise recommended a government corporation. Last January, President Johnson endorsed that recommendation in his State of the Union message.

One of my first actions as President was to direct Postmaster General Winton M. Blount to review that proposal and others. He has made his own first-hand study of the problems besetting the postal service, and after a careful analysis has reported to me that only a complete reorganization of the postal system can avert the steady deterioration of this vital public service.

I am convinced that such a reorganization is essential. The arguments are overwhelming and the support is bipartisan. Postal reform is not a partisan political issue, it is an urgent national requirement.

Employee Opportunities. For many years the postal worker walked a dead-end street. Promotions all too often were earned by the right political connections rather than by merit. This Administration has taken steps to eliminate political patronage in the selection of postal employees; but there is more—much more—that must be done.

Postal employees must be given a work environment comparable to that found in the finest American enterprises. Today, particularly in our larger cities, postal workers labor in crowded, dismal, old fashioned buildings that are little short of disgraceful. Health services, employee facilities, training programs and other benefits enjoyed by the worker in private industry and in other federal agencies are, all too often, unavailable to the postal worker. In an age when machines do the heavy work for private companies, the postal worker still shoulders, literally, the burden of the nation's mail. That mail fills more than a billion sacks a year; and the men and women who move those sacks need help.

Postal employees must have a voice in determining their conditions of employment. They must be given a stake in the quality of the service the Department provides the public; they must be given a reason for pride in themselves and in the job they do. The time for action is now.

Rising Deficits and Rates. During all but seventeen years since 1838, when deficit financing became a way of life for the Post Office, the postal system has cost more than it has earned.

In this fiscal year, the Department will drain over a billion dollars from the national treasury to cover the deficit incurred in operating the Post Office. Over the last decade, the tax money used to shore up the postal system has amounted to more than eight billion dollars. Almost twice that amount will be diverted from the Treasury in the next ten years if the practices of the past are continued. We must not let that happen.

The money to meet these huge postal deficits comes directly out of the taxpayer's pocket—regardless of how much he uses the mails. It is bad business, bad government, and bad politics to pour this kind of tax money into an inefficient postal service. Every taxpayer in the United States—as well as every user of the mails—has an important stake in seeing that the Federal Government institutes the kind of reform that is needed to give the nation a modern and well managed postal system. Without such a system Congress will either have to raise postage rates far above any level presently contemplated, or the taxpayers will have to shoulder the burden of paying postal deficits the like of which they have never seen before.

Neither alternative is acceptable. The nation simply cannot afford the cost of maintaining an inefficient postal system. The will of the Congress and the will of the people is clear. They want fast, dependable and low-cost mail service. They want an end to the continuing cycle of higher deficits and increasing rates.

Quality Service. The Post Office is a business that provides a vital service which its customers, like the customers of a private business, purchase directly. A well managed business provides dependable service; but complaints about the quality of postal service under existing procedures are widespread. While most mail ultimately arrives at its destination, there is no assurance that important mail will arrive on time; and late mail—whether a birthday card or a proxy statement—is often no better than lost mail.

Delays and breakdowns constantly threaten the mails. A complete breakdown in service did in fact occur in 1966 in one of our largest cities, causing severe economic damage and personal hardship. Similar breakdowns could occur at any time in many of our major post offices. A major modernization program is essential to insure against catastrophe in the Post Office.

A modern postal service will not mean fewer postal workers. Mail volume—tied as it is to economic activity—is growing at such a rate that there will be no cutback in postal jobs even with the most dramatic gains in postal efficiency. Without a modernized postal system, however, more than a quarter of a million new postal workers will be needed in the next decade simply to move the growing mountain of mail. The savings that can be realized by holding employment near present levels can and should mean more pay and increased benefits for the three quarters of a million men and women who will continue to work in postal service.

Politics Out. While the work of the Post Office is that of a business enterprise, its organization is that of a political department. Traditionally it has been run as a Cabinet agency of the United States Government—one in which politics has been as important as efficient mail delivery. Under the present system, those responsible for managing the postal service do not have the authority that the managers of any enterprise must have over prices, wages, location of facilities, transportation and procurement activities and personnel policy.

Changes in our society have resulted in changes in the function of the Post Office Department. The postal system must be given a non-political management structure consistent with the job the postal system has to perform as a supplier of vital services to the public. Times change, and now is the time for change in the postal system.

I am, therefore, sending to the Congress reform legislation entitled the Postal Service Act of 1969.

Proposed New Law. The reform that I propose represents a basic and sweeping change in direction; the ills of the postal service cannot be cured by partial reform.

The Postal Service Act of 1969 provides for:

• removal of the Post Office from the Cabinet
• creation of an independent Postal Service wholly owned by the Federal Government

- new and extensive collective bargaining rights for postal employees
- bond financing for major improvements
- a fair and orderly procedure for changing postage rates, subject to Congressional review
- regular reports to Congress to facilitate Congressional oversight of the postal system
- a self-supporting postal system.

The new government-owned corporation will be known as the United States Postal Service. It will be administered by a nine-member board of directors selected without regard to political affiliation. Seven members of the board, including the chairman, will be appointed by the President with the advice and consent of the Senate. These seven members will select a full-time chief executive officer, who will join with the seven others to select a second full-time executive who will also serve on the board.

Employees will retain their Civil Service annuity rights, veterans' preference, and other benefits.

The Postal Service is unique in character. Therefore, there will be, for the first time in history, true collective bargaining in the postal system. Postal employees in every part of the United States will be given a statutory right to negotiate directly with management over wages and working conditions. A fair and impartial mechanism—with provision for binding arbitration—will be established to resolve negotiating impasses and disputes arising under labor agreements.

For the first time, local management will have the authority to work with employees to improve local conditions. A modernization fund adequate to the needs of the service will be available. The postal worker will finally take his rightful place beside the worker in private industry.

The Postal Service will become entirely self-supporting, except for such subsidies as Congress may wish to provide for specific public service groups. The Postal Service, like the Tennessee Valley Authority and similar public authorities, will be able to issue bonds as a means of raising funds needed for expansion and modernization of postal facilities and other purposes.

Proposals for changes in classes of mail or postage rates will be heard by expert rate commissioners, who will be completely independent of operating management. The Board of the Postal Service will review determinations made by the Rate Commissioners on rate and classification questions, and the Presidentially appointed members of the board will be empowered to modify such determinations if they consider it in the public interest to do so.

Congress will have express authority to veto decisions on rate and classification questions.

The activities of the Postal Service will be subject to Congressional oversight, and the Act provides for regular reports to Congress. The Postal Service and the rules by which it operates can, of course, be changed by law at any time.

Toward Excellence. Removing the postal system from politics and the Post Office Department from the Cabinet is a sweeping reform.

Traditions die hard and traditional institutions are difficult to abandon. But tradition is no substitute for performance, and if our postal system is to meet the expanding needs of the 1970s, we must act now.

Legislation, by itself, will not move the mail. This must be done by the three-quarters of a million dedicated men and women who today wear the uniform of the postal service. They must be given the right tools—financial, managerial and technological—to do the job. The legislation I propose today will provide those tools.

There is no Democratic or Republican way of delivering the mail. There is only the right way.

This legislation will let the postal service do its job the right way, and I strongly recommend that it be promptly considered and promptly enacted.

RICHARD NIXON

FOREIGN AID

Following is the complete text of President Nixon's May 28 message to Congress on foreign aid.

TO THE CONGRESS OF THE UNITED STATES:

Americans have for many years debated the issues of foreign aid largely in terms of our own national self-interest. Certainly our efforts to help nations feed millions of their poor help avert violence and upheaval that would be dangerous to peace. Certainly our military assistance to allies helps maintain a world in which we ourselves are more secure. Certainly our economic aid to developing nations helps develop our own potential markets overseas. And certainly our technical assistance puts down roots of respect and friendship for the United States in the court of world opinion.

These are all sound, practical reasons for our foreign aid programs. But they do not do justice to our fundamental character and purpose. There is a moral quality in this nation that will not permit us to close our eyes to the want in this world, or to remain indifferent when the freedom and security of others are in danger.

We should not be self-conscious about this. Our record of generosity and concern for our fellow men, expressed in concrete terms unparalleled in the world's history, has helped make the American experience unique. We have shown the world that a great nation must also be a good nation. We are doing what is right to do.

A Fresh Approach. This Administration has intensively examined our programs of foreign aid. We have measured them against the goals of our policy and the goal of our conscience. Our review is continuing, but we have come to this central conclusion: U.S. assistance is essential to express and achieve our national goals in the international community—a world order of peace and justice.

But no single government, no matter how wealthy or well-intentioned, can by itself hope to cope with the challenge of raising the standard of living of two-thirds of the world's people. This reality must not cause us to retreat into helpless, sullen isolation. On the contrary, this reality must cause us to redirect our efforts in four main ways:

We must enlist the energies of private enterprise, here and abroad, in the cause of economic development. We must do so by stimulating additional investment through businesslike channels, rather than offering ringing exhortations.

We must emphasize innovative technical assistance, to ensure that our dollars for all forms of aid go further, and to plant the seeds that will enable other nations to grow their own capabilities for the future.

We must induce other advanced nations to join in bearing their fair share—by contributing jointly to multilateral banks and the United Nations, by consultation and by the force of our example, and by effective coordination of national and multilateral programs in individual countries.

We must build on recent successes in furthering food production and family planning.

To accomplish these goals, this Administration's foreign aid proposals will be submitted to the Congress today. In essence, these are the new approaches:

1. Enlisting Private Enterprise. I propose the establishment of the Overseas Private Investment Corporation.

The purpose of the Corporation is to provide businesslike management of investment incentives now in our laws so as to contribute to the economic and social progress of developing nations. The majority of the Board of Directors, including its President, will be drawn from private life and have business experience.

Venture capital seeks profit, not adventure. To guide this capital to higher-risk areas, the Federal Government presently offers a system of insurance and guaranties. Like the Federal Housing Administration in the housing field here at home, the Overseas Private Investment Corporation will be able to place the credit of the United States Government behind the insurance and guaranties which the Corporation would sell to U.S. private investors.

The Corporation will also have a small direct lending program for private developmental projects. It will carry out investment survey and development activities. And it will undertake for AID some of the technical assistance required to strengthen private enterprise abroad. The financial performance of OPIC will be measurable: It is expected to break even or to show a small profit. The Overseas Private Investment Corporation will give new direction to U.S. private investment abroad. As such, it will provide new focus to our foreign assistance effort.

Simultaneously, I propose a mandate for the Agency for International Development to direct a growing part of its capital, technical and advisory assistance to improving opportunities for local private enterprise in developing countries— on farms as well as in commerce and industry.

We do not insist that developing countries imitate the American system. Each nation must fashion its own institutions to its own needs. But progress has been greatest where governments have encouraged private enterprise, released bureaucratic controls, stimulated competition and allowed maximum opportunity for individual initiative. AID's mandate will be directed to this end.

2. Expanding Technical Assistance. I propose a strong new emphasis on technical assistance.

Over one-fifth of the funds requested for fiscal year 1970 are for technical assistance activities. Imaginative use of these funds at the points where change is beginning can have a gradual but pervasive impact on the economic growth of developing nations. It can make our dollars for all forms of aid go further.

Technical assistance takes many forms. It includes the adaptation of U.S. technical knowledge to the special needs of poor countries, the training of their people in modern skills, and the strengthening of institutions which will have lives and influence of their own. The main emphases of technical assistance must be in agriculture, education and in family planning. But needs must also be met in health, public administration, community action, public safety and other areas. In all of these fields, our aim must be to raise the quality of our advisory, training and research services.

Technical assistance is an important way for private U.S. organizations to participate in development. U.S. technical assistance personnel serving abroad must increasingly come from private firms, universities and colleges and non-profit service groups. We will seek to expand this broad use of the best of our American talent.

AID is preparing plans to reorganize and revitalize U.S. technical assistance activities. A new Technical Assistance Bureau headed by an Assistant Administrator will be created within AID to focus on technical assistance needs and ensure effective administration of these activities. The bureau will devise new techniques, evaluate effectiveness of programs, and seek out the best qualified people in our universities and other private groups.

To make it possible to carry through these plans most effectively, I am requesting a two-year funding authorization for this part of the AID program.

3. Sharing the Assistance Effort. I propose that we channel more of our assistance in ways that encourage other advanced nations to fairly share the burden of international development.

This can be done by: increasing jointly our contributions to international development banks; increasing jointly our contributions to the United Nations technical assistance program; acting in concert with other advanced countries to share the cost of aid to individual developing countries.

Most development assistance—from other advanced nations as well as the United States—is provided directly from one country to another. That is understandable. Such bilateral programs provide assistance in accordance with each country's own standards, make the source more visible to the recipient's people and can reflect historical political ties.

But assistance through international development banks and the United Nations is approaching a fifth of total worldwide aid for development and should be expanded. Multilateral programs cushion political frictions between donors and recipients and bring the experience of many nations to bear on the development problem. Moreover, they explicitly require shared contributions among the advanced nations. This calls for funds in addition to those which I am proposing today.

I appreciate the prompt response by the Congress to my earlier proposal authorizing the United States to join with others in the second replenishment of the International Development Association. I urge early passage of appropriations for this contribution so that we may meet our pledge.

I reaffirm my request for appropriations in fiscal 1970 of $20 million for the ordinary capital of the Asian Development Bank, and $300 million for our scheduled contribution to the Fund for Special Operations of the Inter-American Development Bank.

In separate legislation I will submit a new proposal for a U.S. contribution of $25 million to the Special Fund of the Asian Development Bank in FY 1970. I am convinced that a fairly-shared Special Fund, to enable the Bank to provide concessional financing for priority needs, is a necessary supplement to the Bank's ordinary lending facilities. The United States should join with other donor countries in establishing this Special Fund, and strengthen the Bank so that it can better deal with Asia's current development problems and future needs.

The United States will consult with the management of the African Development Bank and with other potential donors, to identify the most appropriate way we can support the objectives of African development and assist in meeting the needs of that continent.

Today's proposed legislation includes a 43 percent increase in the U.S. contribution to multilateral technical assistance through the United Nations Development Program. Our contribution will be on the same sharing basis as in the past.

4. Furthering Food Production and Family Planning. This Administration, while moving in the new directions I have outlined, will apply the lessons of experience in our foreign aid programs. One basic lesson is the critical importance of releasing the brakes on development caused by low agricultural productivity. A few years ago, mass starvation within a decade seemed clearly possible in many poor nations. Today they stand at least on the threshold of a dramatic breakthrough in food production. The combination of the new "miracle" seeds for wheat and rice, aid-financed fertilizer, improved cultivation practices, and constructive agriculture policies shows what is possible. They also demonstrate the potential for success when foreign aid, foreign private investment and domestic resources in developing countries join together in a concerted attack on poverty.

The experience of this decade has also shown that lower rates of population growth can be critical for speeding up economic development and social progress. An increasing number of countries have adopted national family planning programs to attack the problem. At least another decade of sustained hard work will be needed if we are to win the battle between economic development and population. But our assistance to voluntary family planning programs and support for the work of the United Nations and other international organizations in this field must continue to have high priority, as will our support of efforts to increase food production.

Another important lesson is that our aid programs need better means of continuous management inspection. We are creating a new position of Auditor-General in the Agency for International Development. His job will be to make sure that AID's funds are used for their intended purpose and that AID's operations are managed as tightly and efficiently as possible. He will report directly to the AID Administrator.

Legislative and Budget Requests. The proposed legislation revises that part of the present Foreign Assistance Act which deals with economic aid, to reflect the priorities of this Administration. The proposals are designed to accomplish the following: create the Overseas Private Investment Corporation and authorize its programs for an initial five years; strengthen AID's mandate to use official aid to stimulate private initiative in development; expand the role of technical assistance under consolidated legislation and a two-year authorization.

The proposed budget includes new appropriation of $2,210 million for AID, $138 million below the January budget request of the previous Administration. In addition, the budget includes $75 million to augment existing reserves for guaranties to be issued by the proposed Overseas Private Investment Corporation.

The appropriation request for economic assistance will support these regional programs: for Latin America, $605 million; for the Near East and South Asia, $625 million; for Africa, $186 million; for East Asia, $234 million; and for Vietnam, $440 million.

In order to protect the U.S. balance of payments at the same time we are providing assistance abroad, goods and services will be purchased in the United States wherever practicable. Over 90 percent of all AID expenditures and virtually all purchases of goods will be made in the United States. The remaining funds that are spent abroad are mainly for living expenses of U.S. personnel and for other local expenditures in support of technical assistance programs.

For military assistance, the proposed budget includes $375 million, the same as in the January budget. Maintenance of a climate of international security still calls for military strength sufficient to deter aggression. Seventy-seven percent of the total amount available for the military assistance program will be allocated to four of our long-standing allies—Korea, the Republic of China, Turkey and Greece. The balance of the request will be used to provide modest amounts of training and equipment to 44 other countries where our security and foreign policy interests are partially met by this form of assistance. We are negotiating a renewal of our base agreement with Spain. If these negotiations succeed, we shall then need to request an amendment to this authorization asking for additional funds to cover our year's needs for Spain.

The United States will continue to provide military assistance from the U.S. Armed Services budget to Vietnam, Laos and Thailand.

I am also asking in separate legislation for $275 million for credit necessary to facilitate the purchase of essential military equipment by countries now able to buy all or a growing part of their defense requirements. These funds will be returned to the United States during the next few years as the purchasing countries meet their repayment obligations.

Planning for the 70s. I believe these proposals for fiscal year 1970 are sound—and necessary to make clearly desirable improvements in our foreign aid program. But we need to learn more about the role which foreign assistance can play in the development process, and the relationship between development and overall U.S. foreign policy.

I am therefore establishing a task force of private citizens to make a comprehensive review of the entire range of U.S. aid activities, to consider proposals of the United Nations bodies and international commissions, and to help me determine what our national policies should be toward the developing countries in the decade of the 1970s. I will look to the task force's report in developing the program next year, in my response to the Javits Amendment to the Foreign Assistance Act and in considering the recommendations of the internationally sponsored Pearson Commission report to be published in the fall.

Toward a World of Order. Foreign aid cannot be viewed in isolation. That is a statement with a double meaning, each side of which is true.

If we turn inward, if we adopt an attitude of letting the underdeveloped nations shift for themselves, we would soon see them shift away from the values so necessary to international stability. Moreover, we would lose the traditional concern for humanity which is so vital a part of the American spirit.

In another sense, foreign aid must be viewed as an integral part of our overall effort to achieve a world order of peace and justice. That order combines our sense of responsibility for helping those determined to defend their freedom; our sensible understanding of the mutual benefits that flow from cooperation between nations; and our sensitivity to the desires of our fellow men to improve their lot in the world.

In this time of stringent budgetary restraint, we must stimulate private investment and the cooperation of other governments to share with us in meeting the most urgent needs of those just beginning to climb the economic ladder. And we must continue to minimize the immediate impact on our balance of payments.

This request for foreign economic and military assistance is the lowest proposed since the program began. But it is about 900 million dollars more than was appropriated last year. I consider it necessary to meet essential requirements now, and to maintain a base for future action.

The support by the Congress of these programs will help enable us to press forward in new ways toward the building of respect for the United States, security for our people and dignity for human beings in every corner of the globe.

RICHARD NIXON

DRAFT MESSAGE TEXT

Following is a partial text of President Nixon's May 13 message on revision of the draft system.

TO THE CONGRESS OF THE UNITED STATES:

For almost two million young men who reach the age of military service each year—and for their families—the draft is one of the most important facts of life. It is my conviction that the disruptive impact of the military draft on individual lives should be minimized as much as possible, consistent with the national security. For this reason I am today asking the Congress for authority to implement important draft reforms.

Ideally, of course, minimum interference means no draft at all. I continue to believe that under more stable world conditions and with an armed force that is more attractive to volunteers, that ideal can be realized in practice. To this end, I appointed, on March 27, 1969, an Advisory Commission on an All-Volunteer Armed Force. I asked that group to develop a comprehensive plan which will attract more volunteers to military service, utilize military manpower in a more efficient way, and eliminate conscription as soon as that is feasible. I look forward to receiving the report of the Commission this coming November.

Under present conditions, however, some kind of draft will be needed for the immediate future. As long as that is the case, we must do everything we can to limit the disruption caused by the system and to make it as fair as possible. For one's vision of the eventual does not excuse his inattention to the immediate. A man may plan to sell his house in another year, but during that year he will do what is necessary to make it livable.

Accordingly, I will ask the Congress to amend the Military Selective Service Act of 1967, returning to the President the power which he had prior to June 30, 1967, to modify call-up procedures. I will describe below in some detail the new procedures which I will establish if Congress grants this authority. Essentially, I would make the following alterations:

• Change from an oldest-first to a youngest-first order of call, so that a young man would become less vulnerable rather than more vulnerable to the draft as he grows older.

• Reduce the period of prime draft vulnerability—and the uncertainty that accompanies it—from seven years to one year, so that a young man would normally enter that status during the time he was nineteen years old and leave it during the time he was twenty.

• Select those who are actually drafted through a random system. A procedure of this sort would distribute the risk of call equally—by lot—among all who are vulnerable during a given year, rather than arbitrarily selecting those whose birthdays happen to fall at certain times of the year or the month.

• Continue the undergraduate student deferment, with the understanding that the year of maximum vulnerability would come whenever the deferment expired.

• Allow graduate students to complete, not just one term, but the full academic year during which they are first ordered for induction.

• In addition, as a step toward a more consistent policy of deferments and exemptions, I will ask the National Security Council and the Director of Selective Service to review all guidelines, standards and procedures in this area and to report to me their findings and recommendations.

I believe these reforms are essential. I hope they can be implemented quickly.

Any system which selects only some from a pool of many will inevitably have some elements of inequity. As its name implies, choice is the very purpose of the Selective Service System. Such choices cannot be avoided so long as the supply of men exceeds military requirements. In these circumstances, however, the Government bears a moral obligation to spread the risk of induction equally among those who are eligible.

Moreover, a young man now begins his time of maximum vulnerability to the draft at age nineteen and leaves that status only when he is drafted or when he reaches his twenty-sixth birthday. Those who are not called up are nevertheless vulnerable to call for a seven year period. For those who are called, the average age of induction can vary greatly. A few years ago, when calls were low, the average age of involuntary induction was nearly twenty-four. More recently it has dropped to just about twenty. What all of this means for the average young man is a prolonged time of great uncertainty.

The present draft arrangements make it extremely difficult for most young people to plan intelligently as they make some of the most important decisions of their lives, decisions concerning education, career, marriage, and family....

My specific proposals, in greater detail, are as follows:

• **A "youngest-first" order of call.** Under my proposal, the government would designate each year a "prime age group," a different pool of draft eligibles for each consecutive twelve-month period. (Since that period would not necessarily begin on January 1, it would be referred to as a "selective service year.") The prime age group for any given selective service year would contain those registrants who were nineteen years old when it began. Those who received deferments or exemptions would rejoin the prime age group at the time their deferment or exemption expired. During the first year that the new plan was in operation, the prime age group would include all eligible men from nineteen to twenty-six, not deferred or exempt, so that no one would escape vulnerability simply because of the transition.

• **Limited vulnerability.** Each individual would experience maximum vulnerability to the draft only for the one selective service year in which he is in the prime age group. At the end of the twelve-month period—which would normally come sometime during his twentieth year—he would move on to progressively less vulnerable categories and an entirely new set of registrants would become the new prime age group. Under this system, a young man would receive an earlier and more decisive answer to his question, "Where do I stand with the draft?" and he could plan his life accordingly.

• **A random selection system.** Since more men are classified as available for service each year than are required to fill current or anticipated draft calls, Selective Service Boards must have some way of knowing whom to call first, whom to call second, and whom not to call at all. There must be some fair method of determining the sequence of induction for those available for service in the prime age group.

In my judgment, a fair system is one which randomizes by lot the order of selection. Each person in the prime age group should have the same chance of appearing at the top of the draft list, at the bottom, or somewhere in the middle. I would therefore establish the following procedure:

At the beginning of the third month after Congress grants this authority, the first of a sequence of selective service years would begin. Prior to the start of each selective service year, the dates of the 365 days to follow would be placed in a sequence determined by a random method. Those who spend the following year in the pool would take their place in the draft sequence in the same order that their birthdays come up on this scrambled calendar. Those born on June 21st, for example, might be at the head of the list, followed by those born on January 12th, who in turn might be followed by those born on October 23rd. Each year, a new random order would be established for the next year's draft pool. In turn those who share the same birthday would be further distributed, this time by the first letter of their last names. But rather than systematically discriminating against those who come at the front of the alphabet, the alphabet would also be scrambled in a random manner.

Once a person's place in the sequence was determined, that assignment would never change. If he were granted a deferment or exemption at age nineteen or twenty, he would re-enter the prime age group at the time his deferment or exemption expires, taking the same place in the sequence that he was originally assigned.

While the random sequence of induction would be nationally established, it would be locally applied by each draft board to meet its local quota. In addition to distributing widely and evenly the risk of induction, the system would also aid many young men in assessing the likelihood of induction even before the classification procedure is completed. This would reduce uncertainty for the individual registrant and, particularly in time of low draft calls, simplify the task of the draft boards.

• **Undergraduate student deferments.** I continue to believe in the wisdom of college deferments. Permitting the diligent student to complete his college education without interruption by the draft is a wise national investment. Under my proposal, a college student who chooses to take a student deferment would still receive his draft sequence number at the time he first enters the prime age group. But he would not be subject to induction until his deferment ended and he re-entered a period of maximum vulnerability.

• **Graduate student induction.** I believe that the induction of men engaged in graduate study should be postponed until the end of the full academic year during which they are first called to military service. I will ask the National Security Council to consider appropriate advice to the Director of the Selective Service to establish this policy. At present, graduate students are allowed to delay induction only to the end of a semester. This often means that they lose valuable time which has been invested in preparation for general examinations or other degree requirements. It can also jeopardize some of the financial arrangements which they made when they planned on a full year of schooling. Induction at the end of a full academic year will provide a less damaging interruption and will still be consistent with Congressional policy.

At the same time, however, the present policy against general graduate deferments should be continued, with exceptions only for students in medical and allied fields who are subject to a later special draft. We must prevent the pyramiding of student deferments—undergraduate and graduate—into a total exemption from military service. For this reason the postponement of induction should be possible only once for each graduate student.

• **A review of guidelines.** The above measures will reduce the uncertainty of young men as to when and if they may be called for service. It is also important that we encourage a consistent administration of draft procedures by the more than 4,000 local boards around the country. I am therefore requesting the National Security Council and the Director of Selective Service to conduct a thorough review of our guidelines, standards and procedures for deferments and exemptions, and to report their findings to me by December 1, 1969. While the autonomy of local boards provides valuable flexibility and sensitivity, reasonable guidelines can help to limit geographic inequities and enhance the equality of the entire System. The 25,000 concerned citizens who serve their country so well on these local boards deserve the best possible framework for their decisions....

I am hopeful that we can soon restore the principle of no draft in peacetime. But until we do, let us be sure that the operation of the Selective Service System is as equitable and as reasonable as we can make it. By drafting the youngest first, by limiting the period of vulnerability, by randomizing the selection process, and by reviewing deferment policies, we can do much to achieve these important interim goals. We should do no less for the youth of our country.

RICHARD NIXON

TEXT OF NIXON MESSAGE ON PLAN TO ATTACK DRUG ABUSE

Following is the complete text of President Nixon's July 14 message to Congress on combating drug abuse.

TO THE CONGRESS OF THE UNITED STATES:

Within the last decade, the abuse of drugs has grown from essentially a local police problem into a serious national threat to the personal health and safety of millions of Americans.

A national awareness of the gravity of the situation is needed; a new urgency and concerted national policy are needed at the Federal level to begin to cope with this growing menace to the general welfare of the United States.

Between the years 1960 and 1967, juvenile arrests involving the use of drugs rose by almost 800 percent; half of those now being arrested for the illicit use of narcotics are under 21 years of age. New York City alone has records of some 40,000 heroin addicts, and the number rises between 7,000 and 9,000 a year. These official statistics are only the tip of an iceberg whose dimensions we can only surmise.

The number of narcotics addicts across the United States is now estimated to be in the hundreds of thousands. Another estimate is that several million American college students have at least experimented with marihuana, hashish, LSD, amphetamines, or barbiturates. It is doubtful that an American parent can send a son or daughter to college today without exposing the young man or woman to drug abuse. Parents must also be concerned about the availability and use of such drugs in our high schools and junior high schools.

The habit of the narcotics addict is not only a danger to himself, but a threat to the community where he lives. Narcotics have been cited as a primary cause of the enormous increase in street crimes over the last decade.

As the addict's tolerance for drugs increases, his demand for drugs rises, and the cost of his habit grows. It can easily reach hundreds of dollars a day. Since an underworld "fence" will give him only a fraction of the value of goods he steals, an addict can be forced to commit two or three burglaries a day to maintain his habit. Street robberies, prostitution, even the enticing of others into addiction to drugs—an addict will reduce himself to any offense, any degradation in order to acquire the drugs he craves.

However far the addict himself may fall, his offenses against himself and society do not compare with the inhumanity of those who make a living exploiting the weakness and desperation of their fellow men. Society has few judgments too severe, few penalties too harsh for the men who make their livelihood in the narcotics traffic.

It has been a common oversimplification to consider narcotics addiction, or drug abuse, to be a law enforcement problem alone. Effective control of illicit drugs requires the cooperation of many agencies of the Federal and local and State governments; it is beyond the province of any one of them alone. At the Federal level, the burden of the national effort must be carried by the Departments of Justice, Health, Education, and Welfare, and the Treasury. I am proposing ten specific steps as

this Administration's initial counter-moves against this growing national problem.

Federal Legislation. To more effectively meet the narcotic and dangerous drug problems at the Federal level, the Attorney General is forwarding to the Congress a comprehensive legislative proposal to control these drugs. This measure will place in a single statute, a revised and modern plan for control. Current laws in this field are inadequate and outdated.

I consider the legislative proposal a fair, rational and necessary approach to the total drug problem. It will tighten the regulatory controls and protect the public against illicit diversion of many of these drugs from legitimate channels. It will insure greater accountability and better recordkeeping. It will give law enforcement stronger and better tools that are sorely needed so that those charged with enforcing these laws can do so more effectively. Further, this proposal creates a more flexible mechanism which will allow quicker control of new dangerous drugs before their misuse and abuse reach epidemic proportions. I urge the Congress to take favorable action on this bill.

In mid-May the Supreme Court struck down segments of the marihuana laws and called into question some of the basic foundations for the other existing drug statutes. I have also asked the Attorney General to submit an interim measure to correct the constitutional deficiencies of the Marihuana Tax Act as pointed out in the Supreme Court's recent decision. I urge Congress to act swiftly and favorably on the proposal to close the gap now existing in the Federal law and thereby give the Congress time to carefully examine the comprehensive drug control proposal.

State Legislation. The Department of Justice is developing a model State Narcotics and Dangerous Drugs Act. This model law will be made available to the fifty State governments. This legislation is designed to improve State laws in dealing with this serious problem and to complement the comprehensive drug legislation being proposed to Congress at the national level. Together these proposals will provide an interlocking trellis of laws which will enable government at all levels to more effectively control the problem.

International Cooperation. Most of the illicit narcotics and high-potency marihuana consumed in the United States is produced abroad and clandestinely imported. I have directed the Secretary of State and the Attorney General to explore new avenues of cooperation with foreign governments to stop the production of this contraband at its sources. The United States will cooperate with foreign governments working to eradicate the production of illicit drugs within their own frontiers. I have further authorized these Cabinet officers to formulate plans that will lead to meetings at the law enforcement level between the United States and foreign countries now involved in the drug traffic either as originators or avenues of transit.

Suppression Of Illegal Importation. Our efforts to eliminate these drugs at their point of origin will be coupled with new efforts to intercept them at their point of illegal entry into the United States. The Department of the Treasury, through the Bureau of Customs, is charged with enforcing the nation's smuggling laws. I have directed the Secretary of the Treasury to initiate a major new effort to guard the nation's borders and ports against the growing volume of narcotics from abroad. There is a recognized need for more men and facilities in the Bureau of Customs to carry out this directive. At my request, the Secretary of the Treasury has submitted a substantial program for increased manpower and facilities in the Bureau of Customs for this purpose which is under intensive review.

In the early days of this Administration, I requested that the Attorney General form an inter-departmental Task Force to conduct a comprehensive study of the problem of unlawful trafficking in narcotics and dangerous drugs. One purpose of the Task Force has been to examine the existing programs of law enforcement agencies concerned with the problem in an effort to improve their coordination and efficiency. I now want to report that this Task Force has completed its study and has a recommended plan of action, for immediate and long-term implementation, designed to substantially reduce the illicit trafficking in narcotics, marihuana and dangerous drugs across United States borders. To implement the recommended plan, I have directed the Attorney General to organize and place into immediate operation an "action task force" to undertake a frontal attack on the problem. There are high profits in the illicit market for those who smuggle narcotics and drugs into the United States; we intend to raise the risks and cost of engaging in this wretched traffic.

Suppression of National Trafficking. Successful prosecution of an increased national effort against illicit drug trafficking will require not only new resources and men, but also a redeployment of existing personnel within the Department of Justice.

I have directed the Attorney General to create, within the Bureau of Narcotics and Dangerous Drugs, a number of special investigative units. These special forces will have the capacity to move quickly into any area in which intelligence indicates major criminal enterprises are engaged in the narcotics traffic. To carry out this directive, there will be a need for additional manpower within the Bureau of Narcotics and Dangerous Drugs. The budgetary request for FY 1970 now pending before the Congress will initiate this program. Additional funds will be requested in FY 1971 to fully deploy the necessary special investigative units.

Education. Proper evaluation and solution of the drug problem in this country has been severely handicapped by a dearth of scientific information on the subject—and the prevalence of ignorance and misinformation. Different "experts" deliver solemn judgments which are poles apart. As a result of these conflicting judgments, Americans seem to have divided themselves on the issue, along generational lines.

There are reasons for this lack of knowledge. First, widespread drug use is a comparatively recent phenomenon in the United States. Second, it frequently involves chemical formulations which are novel or age-old drugs little used in this country until very recently. The volume of definitive medical data remains small—and what exists has not been broadly disseminated. This vacuum of knowledge—as was predictable—has been filled by rumors and rash judgments, often formed with a minimal experience with a particular drug, sometimes formed with no experience or knowledge at all.

The possible danger to the health or well-being of even a casual user of drugs is too serious to allow ignorance to prevail or for this information gap to remain open. The American people need to know what dangers and what risks are inherent in the use of the various kinds of drugs readily available in illegal markets today. I have therefore directed the Secretary of Health, Education, and Welfare, assisted by the Attorney General through the Bureau of Narcotics and Dangerous Drugs, to gather all authoritative information on the subject and to compile a balanced and objective educational program to bring the facts to every American—especially our young people.

With this information in hand, the overwhelming majority of students and young people can be trusted to make a prudent judgment as to their personal course of conduct.

Research. In addition to gathering existing data, it is essential that we acquire new knowledge in the field. We must know more about the short and long-range effects of the use of drugs being taken in such quantities by so many of our people. We need more study as well to find the key to releasing men from the bonds of dependency forged by any continued drug abuse.

The National Institute of Mental Health has primary responsibility in this area, and I am further directing the Secretary of Health, Education, and Welfare to expand existing efforts to acquire new knowledge and a broader understanding in this entire area.

Rehabilitation. Considering the risks involved, including those of arrest and prosecution, the casual experimenter with drugs of any kind must be considered, at the very least, rash and foolish. But the psychologically dependent regular users and the physically addicted are genuinely sick people. While this sickness cannot excuse the crimes they commit, it does help to explain them. Society has an obligation both to itself and to these people to help them break the chains of their dependency.

Currently, a number of federal, state and private programs of rehabilitation are being operated. These programs utilize separately and together, psychiatry, psychology and "substitute drug" therapy. At this time, however, we are without adequate data to evaluate their full benefit. We need more experience with them and more knowledge. Therefore, I am directing the Secretary of Health, Education, and Welfare to provide every assistance to those pioneering in the field, and to sponsor and conduct research on the Federal level. This Department will act as a clearinghouse for the collection and dissemination of drug abuse data and experience in the area of rehabilitation.

I have further instructed the Attorney General to insure that all Federal prisoners, who have been identified as dependent upon drugs, be afforded the most up-to-date treatment available.

Training Program. The enforcement of narcotics laws requires considerable expertise, and hence considerable training. The Bureau of Narcotics and Dangerous Drugs provides the bulk of this training in the Federal Government. Its programs are extended to include not only its own personnel, but State and local police officers, forensic chemists, foreign nationals, college deans, campus security officers, and members of industry engaged in the legal distribution of drugs.

Last year special training in the field of narcotics and dangerous drug enforcement was provided for 2,700 State and local law enforcement officials. In fiscal year 1969 we expanded the program an estimated 300 percent in order to train some 11,000 persons. During the current fiscal year we plan to redouble again that effort—to provide training to 22,000 State and local officers. The training of these experts must keep pace with the rise in the abuse of drugs, if we are ever to control it.

Local Law Enforcement Conferences. The Attorney General intends to begin a series of conferences with law enforcement executives from the various States and concerned Federal officials. The purposes of these conferences will be several: first, to obtain firsthand information, more accurate data, on the scope of the drug problem at that level; second, to discuss the specific areas where Federal assistance and aid can best be most useful; third, to exchange ideas and evaluate mutual policies. The end result we hope will be a more coordinated effort that will bring us visible progress for the first time in an alarming decade.

These then are the first ten steps in the national effort against narcotic marihuana and other dangerous drug abuse. Many steps are already underway. Many will depend upon the support of the Congress. I am asking, with this message, that you act swiftly and favorably on the legislative proposals that will soon be forthcoming, along with the budgetary requests required if our efforts are to be successful. I am confident that Congress shares with me the grave concern over this critical problem, and that Congress will do all that is necessary to mount and continue a new and effective federal program aimed at eradicating this rising sickness in our land.

RICHARD NIXON

AIR TRANSPORTATION TEXT

Following is the text of President Nixon's June 16 message to Congress on airports and air transportation.

TO THE CONGRESS OF THE UNITED STATES:

Preparing for the Future of Air Transportation. Years of neglect have permitted the problems of air transportation in America to stack up like aircraft circling a congested airport.

The purpose of air transportation is to save time. This purpose is not served when passengers must wait interminably in terminals; when modern jet aircraft creep at five miles per hour in a long line waiting for takeoff; when it takes longer to land than it takes to travel between cities; or when it takes longer for the air traveler to get to an airport than it does to fly to his destination.

In the 10th year of the jet age, more intercity passenger miles were accounted for by air than by any other mode of common carriage. In 1968, scheduled airlines logged over 150 million passenger trips, triple that of a decade ago; at the same time, the non-airline aircraft fleet almost doubled and the use of air freight quintupled. That rate of increase is likely to continue for the next decade—but it can be accommodated only if we prepare for it now.

The growth in the next decade must be more orderly. It must be financed more fairly. It must be kept safe. And it must not permit congestion and inadequate facilities to defeat the basic purpose of air transportation: to save time.

Air travel is a convenience hundreds of thousands of people take for granted—a means of commerce that millions depend upon for their goods and services. In a nation as large as ours and in a world grown suddenly small, flight has become a powerful unifying force. The ability to transport people and products by air—safely, surely and efficiently—is a national asset of great value and an international imperative for trade and travel.

That ability is being challenged today by insufficiencies in our nation's airports and airways. The demand for aviation services is threatening to exceed the capacity of our civil aviation system. Unless relieved, this situation will further compromise the convenience of air transportation, erode its efficiency and—ultimately—require more regulation if the enviable safety record of the airplane as a means of public and private transportation is to be preserved.

The challenge confronting us is not one of quality, or even of technology. Our air traffic control system is the best in the world; our airports among the finest anywhere. But we simply do not have the capacity in our airways and airports ample to our present needs or reflective of the future.

Accordingly, the Secretary of Transportation is submitting to the Congress today legislative proposals to provide the resources necessary to the air transportation challenges facing us. These proposals are responsive to the short-term as well as the long-range opportunities for civil aviation progress.

Improving Our Airways. To provide for the expansion and improvement of the airway system, and for a high standard of safety, this Administration proposes that the program for construction of airways facilities and equipment be increased to about $250 million annually for the next ten years. This is in sharp contrast to the average of $93 million appropriated in each of the past ten years, and is responsive to the substantial expansion in the operation and maintenance of the air traffic system in the next decade.

While this will provide for the needs of the '70s, development for the 1980s and beyond cannot be neglected. Technology is moving rapidly and its adaptation to provide future solutions must keep pace. Consequently, this program includes a provision for a doubling of development funds.

Building and Improving Airports. The proposed airport program consists of both an expanded planning effort and the provision of additional Federal aid for the construction and improvement of airports. The airport systems planning we contem-

plate at both the Federal and local level will begin a new era of Federal, State and local cooperation in shaping airport development to meet national and local needs.

I propose Federal aid for airport development in fiscal 1970 of $180 million and in fiscal 1971 of $220 million, with continued expansion leading to a total of two and one-half billion dollars in the next ten years. Together with matching grants on a 50-50 basis with State and local governments, this strongly increased program will permit financing of five billion dollars in new and expanded airfield facilities.

The proposed fiscal year 1970 program of $180 million would help finance the development of airfield facilities, the conduct of airport systems planning, and airport planning and development activities carried on by States.

Of the $180 million:

- $140 million would be available for grants to air carrier and general aviation airports, with a primary objective of alleviating congestion in the most heavily used air terminals.
- $25 million in grants would be available to aid in the development of airfields used solely by general aviation.
- $10 million would be available in grants to planning agencies to assist them in conducting airport systems planning.
- $5 million would be available for grants to States to carry on airport planning and development activities.

Airport terminal buildings are a responsibility of local airport authorities. The Administration's legislative proposal suggests ways in which those authorities can meet that responsibility.

Improving the Environment of Transportation. In all planning for airways and airports, it will be the policy of this Administration to consider the relation of air transportation to our total economic and social structure.

For example, existing jetports are adding to the noise and air pollution in our urban areas. New airports become a nucleus for metropolitan development. These important social and conservation considerations must be taken into greater account in future air systems development.

In addition, airport planners must carefully consider the opportunity for business growth and the availability of labor supply. The presence of airport facilities is both a follower of and a harbinger of business and job development.

Most important, government at all levels, working with industry and labor, must see to it that all aviation equipment and facilities are responsive to the needs of the traveler and the shipper and not the other way around. Transportation to airports, whether by public conveyance or private vehicle, is as much a part of a traveler's journey as the time he spends in the air, and must never be viewed as a separate subject. A plane travels from airport to airport, but a person travels from door to door. I have directed the Secretary of Transportation to give special attention to all the components of a journey in new plans for airways and airports improvements.

Financing Air Transportation Facilities. The Federal Government must exert new leadership in the development of transportation, in the integration of the various modes, and in supporting programs of national urgency.

However, the added burden of financing future air transportation facilities should not be thrust upon the general taxpayer. The various users of the system, who will benefit from the developments, should assume the responsibility for the costs of the program. By apportioning the costs of airways and airports improvements among all the users, the progress of civil aviation should be supported on an equitable, pay-as-we-grow basis.

At present, the Treasury obtains revenues, generally regarded as airways user charges, from airline passengers who pay a five per cent tax on the tickets they buy, and from the operators of aircraft who pay a tax at the effective rate of two cents a gallon on aviation gasoline. The revenues obtained from these taxes are not applied directly to airways expenditures. They are either earmarked for other purposes or go into the general fund of the Treasury.

I propose that there be established a revised and expanded schedule of taxes as follows, the revenues from which would be placed in a Designated Account in the Treasury to be used only to defray costs incurred in the airport and airway programs:

- A tax of eight percent on airline tickets for domestic flights
- A tax of $3 on passenger tickets for most international flights, beginning in the United States
- A tax of five per cent on air freight waybills
- A tax of nine cents a gallon on all fuels used by general aviation.

This new tax schedule would generate about $569 million in revenues in fiscal year 1970, compared with the revenues of $295 million under existing taxes.

To sum up:

- For the airline passenger, the proposed legislation would save his time and add to his safety.
- For the air shipper, it would expedite the movement of his goods, thereby permitting him to improve his services.
- For the private aircraft owner, it would provide improved facilities and additional airports.
- For the airline, it would permit greater efficiencies and enable the carrier to expand its markets by providing greater passenger convenience.

In short, the airways and airports system which long ago came of age will come to maturity. Those who benefit most will be those who most bear its cost, and the nation as a whole will gain from aviation's proven impetus to economic growth.

The revenue and expenditure programs being proposed are mutually dependent and must be viewed together. We must act to increase revenues concurrently with any action to authorize expenditures; prudent fiscal management will not permit otherwise.

These proposals are necessary to the safety and convenience of a large portion of our mobile population, and I recommend their early enactment by the Congress.

RICHARD NIXON

NATIONAL DEFENSE TEXT

Following is the text of President Nixon's June 4 speech on national defense as prepared for delivery at the Air Force Academy, Colorado Springs.

For each of you, and for your parents and your countrymen, this is a moment of quiet pride.

After years of study and training, you have earned the right to be saluted.

But the members of the graduating class of the Air Force Academy are beginning their careers at a difficult moment in military life.

On a fighting front, you are asked to be ready to make unlimited sacrifice in a limited war.

On the home front, you are under attack from those who question the need for a strong national defense, and indeed see a danger in the power of the defenders.

You are entering the military service of your country when the nation's potential adversaries abroad were never stronger and your critics at home were never more numerous.

It is open season on the armed forces. Military programs are ridiculed as needless if not deliberate waste. The military profession is derided in some of the best circles. Patriotism is considered by some to be a backward, unfashionable fetish of the uneducated and unsophisticated. Nationalism is hailed and applauded as a panacea for the ills of every nation—except the United States.

This paradox of military power is a symptom of something far deeper that is stirring in our body politic. It goes beyond the dissent about the war in Vietnam. It goes behind the fear of the "military industrial complex."

The underlying questions are really these:

What is America's role in the world? What are the responsibilities of a great nation toward protecting freedom beyond its shores? Can we ever be *left* in peace if we do not actively assume the burden of *keeping* the peace?

When great questions are posed, fundamental differences of opinion come into focus. It serves no purpose to gloss over these differences, or to try to pretend they are mere matters of degree.

One school of thought holds that the road to understanding with the Soviet Union and Communist China lies through a downgrading of our own alliances and what amounts to a unilateral reduction of our arms—as a demonstration of our "good faith."

They believe that we can be conciliatory and accommodating only if we do not have the strength to be otherwise. They believe America will be able to deal with the possibility of peace only when we are unable to cope with the threat of war.

Those who think that way have grown weary of the weight of free world leadership that fell upon us in the wake of World War II, and they argue that we are as much responsible for the tensions in the world as any adversary we face.

They assert that the United States is blocking the road to peace by maintaining its military strength at home and its defense forces abroad. If we would only reduce our forces, they contend, tensions would disappear and the chances for peace brighten.

America's presence on the world scene, they believe, makes peace abroad improbable and peace in our society impossible.

We should never underestimate the appeal of the isolationist school of thought. Their slogans are simplistic and powerful: "Charity begins at home." "Let's first solve our own problems and then we can deal with the problems of the world."

This simple formula touches a responsive chord with many an over-burdened taxpayer. It would be easy to buy some popularity by going along with the new isolationists. But it would be disastrous for our nation and the world.

I hold a totally different view of the world, and I come to a different conclusion about the direction America must take.

Imagine what would happen to this world if the American presence were swept from the scene. As every world leader knows, and as even the most outspoken of America's critics will admit, the rest of the world would be living in terror.

If America were to turn its back on the world, a deadening form of peace would settle over this planet—the kind of peace that suffocated freedom in Czechoslovakia.

The danger to us has changed, but it has not vanished. We must revitalize our alliances, not abandon them.

We must rule out unilateral disarmament. In the real world that simply will not work. If we pursue arms control as an end in itself, we will not achieve our end. The adversaries in the world today are not in conflict because they are armed. They are armed because they are in conflict, and have not yet learned peaceful ways to resolve their conflicting national interests.

The aggressors of this world are not going to give the United States a period of grace in which to put our domestic house in order—just as the crises within our society cannot be put on a back burner until we resolve the problem of Vietnam.

Programs solving our domestic problems will be meaningless if we are not around to enjoy them. Nor can we conduct a successful policy of peace abroad if our society is at war with itself at home.

There is no advancement for Americans at home in a retreat from the problems of the world. America has a vital national interest in world stability, and no other nation can uphold that interest for us.

We stand at a crossroad in our history. We shall reaffirm our aspiration to greatness or we shall choose instead to withdraw into ourselves. The choice will affect far more than our foreign policy; it will determine the quality of our lives.

A nation needs many qualities, but it needs faith and confidence above all. Skeptics do not build societies; the idealists are the builders. Only societies that believe in themselves can rise to their challenges. Let us not, then, pose a false choice between meeting our responsibilities abroad and meeting the needs of our people at home. We shall meet both or we shall meet neither.

This is why my disagreement with the skeptics and the isolationists is fundamental. They have lost the vision indispensable to great leadership. They observe the problems that confront us; they measure our resources; and they despair. When the first vessels set out from Europe for the New World, these men would have weighed the risks, and stayed behind. When the colonists on the Eastern seaboard started across the Appalachians to the unknown reaches of the Ohio Valley, these men would have calculated the odds, and stayed behind.

Our current exploration of space makes the point vividly: Here is testimony to man's vision and man's courage. The journey of the astronauts is more than a technical achievement; it is a reaching-out of the human spirit. It lifts our sights; it demonstrates that magnificent conceptions can be made real.

They inspire us and at the same time teach us true humility. What could bring home to us more the limitations of the human scale than the hauntingly beautiful picture of our earth seen from the moon?

Every man achieves his own greatness by reaching out beyond himself. So it is with nations. When a nation believes in itself—as Athenians did in their golden age, as Italians did in the Renaissance—that nation can perform miracles. Only when a nation means something to itself can it mean something to others.

That is why I believe a resurgence of American idealism can bring about a modern miracle—a world order of peace and justice.

I know that every member of this graduating class is, in that sense, an idealist.

In the years to come, you may hear your commitment to America's responsibility in the world derided as a form of militarism. It is important that you recognize that strawman issue for what it is: The outward sign of a desire by some to turn America inward—to have America turn away from greatness.

I am not speaking about those responsible critics who reveal waste and inefficiency in our defense establishment, who demand clear answers on procurement policies, who want to make sure a new weapons system will truly add to our defense. On the contrary, you should be in the vanguard of that movement. Nor do I speak of those with sharp eyes and sharp pencils who are examining our post-Vietnam planning with other pressing national priorities in mind. I count myself as one of those.

As your Commander-in-Chief, I want to relay to you as future officers of our armed forces some of my thoughts on these issues of national moment.

I worked closely with President Eisenhower. I know what he meant when he said "...we must guard against the acquisition of unwarranted influence, whether sought or unsought, by the military industrial complex."

Many people conveniently forget that he followed that warning with another: "We must also be alert to the equal and opposite danger that public policy could itself become the captive of a scientific-technological elite."

And in that same Farewell Address, President Eisenhower made quite clear the need for national security. As he put it: "a vital element in keeping the peace is our military establishment. Our arms must be mighty, ready for instant action, so that no potential aggressor may be tempted to risk his own destruction."

The American defense establishment should never be a sacred cow, nor should the American military be anybody's scapegoat.

America's wealth is enormous but it is not limitless. Every dollar available to the Federal Government has been taken from the American people in taxes. A responsible government has a duty to be prudent when it spends the people's money. There is no more justification for wasting money on unnecessary military hardware than there is for wasting it on unwarranted social programs.

There can be no question that we should not spend "unnecessarily" for defense. But we must also not confuse our priorities.

The question in defense spending is "how much is necessary?" The President of the United States is the man charged with making that judgment. After a complete review of our foreign and defense policies I have submitted requests to the Congress for military appropriations—some of them admittedly controversial. These requests represent the minimum I believe essential for the United States to meet its current and long-range obligations to itself and to the free world. I have asked only for those programs and those expenditures that I believe are necessary to guarantee the security of this country and to honor our obligations. I will bear the responsibility for these judgments. I do not consider my recommendations infallible. But if I have made a mistake, I pray that it is on the side of too much and not too little. If we do too much, it will cost us our money; if we do too little, it may cost us our lives.

Mistakes in military policy can be irretrievable. Time lost in this age of science can never be regained. I have no choice in my decisions but to come down on the side of security. History has dealt harshly with those nations who have taken the other course.

In that spirit, let me offer this credo for the defenders of our nation:

I believe that we must balance our need for survival as a nation with our need for survival as a people. Americans, soldiers and civilians, must remember that defense is not an end in itself—it is a way of holding fast to the deepest values known to civilized man.

I believe that our defense establishment will remain the servant of our national policy of bringing about peace in this world, and that those in any way connected with the military must scrupulously avoid even the appearance of becoming the master of that policy.

I believe that every man in uniform is a citizen first and a serviceman second, and that we must resist any attempt to isolate or separate the defenders from the defended. In this regard, those who agitate for the removal of the ROTC from college campuses only contribute to an unwanted militarism.

I believe that the basis for decisions on defense spending must be what do we need for our security" and not "what will this mean for business and employment." The Defense Department must never be considered a modern-day WPA: There are far better ways for government to help ensure a sound prosperity and high employment.

I believe that moderation has a moral significance only in those who have another choice. The weak can only plead magnanimity and restraint gain moral meaning coming from the strong.

I believe that defense decisions must be made on the hard realities of the offensive capabilities of our adversaries, and not on our fervent hopes about their intentions. With Thomas Jefferson, we can prefer "the flatteries of hope" to the gloom of despair, but we cannot survive in the real world if we plan our defense in a dream world.

I believe we must take risks for peace—but calculated risks, not foolish risks. We shall not trade our defenses for a disarming smile or honeyed words. We are prepared for new initiatives in the control of arms, in the context of other specific moves to reduce tensions around the world.

I believe that America is not about to become a Garrison State, or a Welfare State, or a Police State—because we will defend our values from those forces, external or internal, that would challenge or erode them.

And I believe this above all: That this nation shall continue to be a source of world leadership and a source of freedom's strength, in creating a just world order that will bring an end to war.

Let me conclude with a personal word.

A President shares a special bond with the men and women of the nation's armed services. He feels that bond strongly at moments like these, facing all of you who have pledged your lives, your fortunes and your sacred honor to the service of your country. He feels that bond most strongly when he presents a Medal of Honor to an 8-year-old boy who will not see his father again. Because of that bond, let me say this to you now:

In the past generation, since 1941, this nation has paid for fourteen years of peace with fourteen years of war. The American war dead of this generation has been far greater than all of the preceding generations of Americans combined. In terms of human suffering, this has been the costliest generation in the two centuries of our history.

Perhaps this is why my generation is so fiercely determined to pass on a different legacy. We want to redeem that sacrifice. We want to be remembered, not as the generation that suffered, but as the generation that was tempered in its fire for a great purpose: to make the kind of peace that the next generation will be able to keep.

This is a challenge worthy of the idealism which I know motivates every man who will receive his diploma today.

I am proud to have served in America's armed forces in a war which ended before members of this class were born.

It is my deepest hope and my belief that each of you will be able to look back on your career with pride, not because of the wars in which you served but because of the peace and freedom which your service made possible for America and the world.

NIXON ASKS FOR BROADER UNEMPLOYMENT COVERAGE

Following is the complete text of President Nixon's July 8 message to Congress on unemployment insurance.

TO THE CONGRESS OF THE UNITED STATES:

The best time to strengthen our unemployment insurance system is during a period of relatively full employment.

The Secretary of Labor is sending to the Congress today proposed legislation to extend unemployment insurance to 4,800,000 workers not now covered; to end the shortsighted restrictions that stand in the way of needed retraining efforts; and to add a federal program automatically extending the duration of benefits in periods of high unemployment.

There are three principles to be considered as we move to make the unemployment insurance system responsive to our times.

• Unemployment insurance is an earned benefit. When a man covered by unemployment insurance is working, the employer pays a tax on his wages to insure against the day when the employee may be between jobs. That insurance is like a mandatory fringe benefit; it is insurance bought in the employee's behalf, and the worker therefore is entitled to the benefits he receives when he is unemployed. Accordingly, there is no demeaning of human dignity, no feeling of being "on the dole," when the insured worker receives benefits due.

• Unemployment insurance is one of the foremost examples of creative federal-state partnership. Although the system was created by federal law, most decisions about the nature of the program are left to the states, which administer the system with state employees. This makes the system far more flexible and attuned to local needs and special circumstances of local economies.

• Unemployment insurance is an economic stabilizer. If, for example, the economy were ever to slow and unemployment were to rise, this program automatically would act to sustain personal income. This would help prevent a downturn from gathering momentum resulting from declines in purchasing power. When employment is at a high level, and greater stimulation of consumer demand is unwanted, relatively little money flows into the economy from unemployment insurance.

With these principles in mind, I am making these recommendations for both federal and state action:

1. We should act together to extend unemployment protection to more employees, including many highly vulnerable to layoffs who are not now covered.

2. The states should make certain that workers throughout the United States receive enough money for a long enough period of time to sustain them while they seek new jobs.

3. We should end the restrictions imposed by almost half the states on payments to unemployed workers undergoing retraining and, instead, follow the lead of those states which encourage retraining.

4. We should better protect the investment made on behalf of the insured by seeing to it that the funds are paid only to those who should receive them.

5. We should increase the responsiveness of the system to major changes in national economic conditions.

6. We should strengthen the financing of the system which presently discriminates against the low-wage worker and the steady employer.

Protecting More Employees. Over 57 million workers are protected by unemployment insurance. However, almost 17 million are not covered: more than half of these are employees of state and local governments. The last extension of coverage was enacted during the Eisenhower Administration, when 6 million additional workers were included; there is a clear social need today to cover as many more employees as we can.

I propose that an additional 4.8 million workers be covered by unemployment insurance. These include:

—1,600,000 workers in small firms with less than four employees;
—400,000 on large farms employing four or more workers in each of 20 weeks;
—200,000 in agricultural processing activities;
—1,800,000 in non-profit organizations;
—600,000 in state hospitals and universities;
—200,000 salesmen, delivery tradesmen, and others who are not currently defined as employees.

These 4,800,000 workers are in real need of protection against unemployment. Many of them are low wage workers with little job security and no prospect of termination pay if they are laid off.

The present gaps in coverage work a disproportionate hardship on minority workers, since a higher percentage of the 4,800,000 are nonwhite, compared to the entire labor force.

To cushion the immediate impact of this extension on employers, I recommend that states be permitted to lower the tax rates on newly covered employers until such time as a record of employment experience can be compiled to determine what their true rate should be.

With the passage of this legislation, the majority of those remaining uncovered will be employees of state and local governments. I urge the states and localities to take action, in the light of their local circumstances, to include their own employees in unemployment insurance coverage.

Making Benefits Adequate. The basic purpose of the Unemployment Insurance Program is to pay weekly benefits high enough to prevent a severe cut in a worker's standard of living when he is between jobs. The principle is generally accepted that it takes at least 50 percent of the worker's wage to meet this purpose.

Almost every state subscribes to this general principle, but benefit ceilings in their legislation have in fact made this principle largely ineffective, especially for the family breadwinner. At least two out of five claimants currently fail to get a benefit equal to one-half their wages.

In 1954, President Eisenhower recommended to states that they provide a maximum high enough to permit the great majority of covered workers to receive one-half their wages. This means that at least 80 percent of insured workers should be able to receive a benefit of one-half their wages in unemployed.

Men are most adversely affected by the limit on weekly benefits. In one large industrial state, for example, only 23 percent of the men receive benefits equal to as much as one-half their weekly wages.

If the program is to fulfill its role, it is essential that the benefit maximum be raised. A maximum of two-thirds of the average wage in the state would result in benefits of 50 percent in wages to at least 80 percent of insured workers.

Up to now, the responsibility for determining benefit amounts has been the responsibility of the states. There are advantages in states having that freedom. However, the overriding consideration is that the objective of adequate benefits be achieved. I call upon the states to act within the next two years to meet this goal, thereby averting the need for federal action.

Encouraging Retraining. During the present decade, many manpower programs were launched in the United States. We have seen how unemployed workers can be equipped with new skills and started on new careers. When the decade began, only three states permitted workers who enrolled in retraining programs to continue to receive benefit payments. All the rest disqualified them upon entry into training.

During the early 1960's, many states recognized the potential of training for employment rehabilitation, and by 1969 twenty-five states, plus Puerto Rico and the District of Columbia, had removed such restrictive requirements.

However, twenty-five states continue to discourage retraining by denying benefits to workers in such programs on the theory that they are not "available for work." On the contrary, the workers are trying to keep themselves available by learning new techniques and technologies, and government should certainly stop penalizing them for doing something that government, business and labor all want to encourage.

I propose a requirement that the remaining states permit workers to continue to receive benefits while enrolled in training programs designed to increase their employability.

Protecting the Insurance System. We must also be sure that benefits are going only to those people the system is designed to protect. The funds must not be dissipated.

The unemployment insurance system is designed to protect workers whose attachment to the labor force is more than casual. A worker's attachment is measured by both his past employment history and his present situation. He must be ready, willing and able to work and trying to find work while he is claiming benefits; and he must have had at least a certain amount of employment in the recent past. Generally, from fourteen to twenty weeks of work is required, depending on the employment patterns of the state and the minimum duration of benefits.

A few states, however, measure past employment by a flat dollar amount. This discriminates against the low-wage worker, because it means he must work for a longer period to be eligible. Also, it permits other high wage workers to become eligible on the basis of very short seasonal work. I recommend that a standard based on a minimum period of 15 weeks' employment be required as a condition of benefit eligibility, and that no flat dollar amount be permitted as the only yardstick.

The unemployment tax we require employers to pay was never intended to supplement strike funds to be used against them. A worker who chooses to exercise his right to strike is not involuntarily unemployed.

In two states, workers on strike are paid unemployment insurance benefits after a certain period. This is not the purpose of the unemployment insurance system.

I propose a requirement that this practice of paying unemployment insurance benefits to workers directly engaged in a strike be discontinued.

Improving Responsiveness to Economic Conditions. Difficult times are far less likely to occur in nations that take the

trouble to prepare for them. The presence of a strong, anti-recessionary arsenal will in itself help prevent the need for its ever being used.

In normal times, the duration of benefit payments may be adequate. Most state programs now provide around twenty-six weeks of benefits; for the great majority of claimants, this is enough to see them through to another job. However, if the economy were ever to falter, the number of persons exhausting benefits would grow rapidly.

In each of the last two periods of high unemployment, the President proposed, and the Congress enacted, legislation to extend the duration of benefits temporarily. However, while this process was taking place, many workers were without income, and the economy was exposed to sharp declines in personal income due to unemployment.

I am proposing legislation that would automatically extend the length of time benefits are paid in all states when the national jobless rate of those covered by insurance equals or exceeds 4.5 percent for three consecutive months. If periods of high unemployment were ever to occur, individuals would receive benefits for an additional period up to 13 weeks; this extension would end when the national unemployment rate of those in the system (currently 2.2%) fell back below 4.5%, and when the number exhausting their benefits in a three-month period dropped below 1% of those covered. These additional payments would be financed out of that portion of the unemployment tax that is now retained by the Federal Government.

Strengthening and Reforming Financing. We must enable the Federal Government to finance its share of the improvements proposed in this message, along with the costs of administering the Employment Security System. In addition, there will be a need to improve the ability of states to finance the higher benefit levels I am urging.

I propose that the taxable wage base be raised over a five-year period to $6,000 and thereafter be reviewed periodically to make certain the adequacy of financing.

In the majority of states, the taxable wage base for the Unemployment Insurance Tax is the first $3,000 of wages—exactly what it was three decades ago. In that same period, average wages in employment covered by the system have increased almost five-fold. The low tax base places obstacles in the way of hiring low-wage workers because a substantially higher proportion of their wage is taxed. In addition, the impact of the tax tends to encourage use of overtime rather than adding workers.

The higher base will have the desirable effect of allocating costs more equitably among employers. Particularly at the state level, overall benefit costs will represent a lower percent of taxable wages, and allow rates to reflect employer experience more accurately.

Unemployment insurance was begun as an answer to the human need for sustenance of the unemployed workingman seeking another job. It was designed to reduce the element of economic panic in job-hunting.

But as we move now to extend that insurance and meet that need more fully, we discover—not quite by accident—the bonus of serendipity. Here is insurance purchased through a tax on the employers of America in behalf of their employees that can be a potent counter to a downturn in the business cycle. This proves that well-conceived social legislation can be a great boon to business and to all Americans affected by the state of the economy.

The success of this system can be a great example in the relationship between the states and the Federal Government.

The Federal Government brought this unemployment insurance system into being—but the states have rightly adopted it as their own. The Federal Government has traditionally established minimum coverage—but many states have expanded that coverage to fit their own needs.

Now the federal-state system of unemployment insurance should move to provide adequate benefits in accordance with the goal that has been set and with full recognition of the diversity of economic conditions among states. Such action is most important to protect the individual and to achieve the anti-recessionary potential of unemployment insurance.

The federal and state actions recommended will help advance the economy of each state and in protecting the economy of the nation. In human terms, the recommended changes will

better enable a worker to weather the adversity of unemployment and to find a suitable job.

I urge that the Congress and the states enact the legislation proposed to carry out these improvements.

RICHARD NIXON

NIXON PROPOSES COMMISSION ON POPULATION GROWTH

Following is the complete text of President Nixon's July 18 message to Congress on population problems.

TO THE CONGRESS OF THE UNITED STATES:

In 1830 there were one billion people on the planet earth. By 1930 there were two billion, and by 1960 there were three billion. Today the world population is three and one-half billion persons.

These statistics illustrate the dramatically increasing rate of population growth. It took many thousands of years to produce the first billion people; the next billion took a century; the third came after thirty years; the fourth will be produced in just fifteen.

If this rate of population growth continues, it is likely that the earth will contain over seven billion human beings by the end of this century. Over the next thirty years, in other words, the world's population could double. And at the end of that time, each new addition of one billion persons would not come over the millennia nor over a century nor even over a decade. If present trends were to continue until the year 2000, the eighth billion would be added in only five years and each additional billion in an even shorter period.

While there are a variety of opinions as to precisely how fast population will grow in the coming decades, most informed observers have a similar response to all such projections. They agree that population growth is among the most important issues we face. They agree that it can be met only if there is a great deal of advance planning. And they agree that the time for such planning is growing very short. It is for all these reasons that I address myself to the population problem in this message, first to its international dimensions and then to its domestic implications.

In the Developing Nations. It is in the developing nations of the world that population is growing most rapidly today. In these areas we often find rates of natural increase higher than any which have been experienced in all of human history. With their birth rates remaining high and with death rates dropping sharply, many countries of Latin America, Asia, and Africa now grow ten times as fast as they did a century ago. At present rates, many will double and some may even triple their present populations before the year 2000. This fact is in large measure a consequence of rising health standards and economic progress throughout the world, improvements which allow more people to live longer and more of their children to survive to maturity.

As a result, many already impoverished nations are struggling under a handicap of intense population increase which the industrialized nations never had to bear. Even though most of these countries have made rapid progress in total economic growth—faster in percentage terms than many of the more industrialized nations—their far greater rates of population growth have made development in per capita terms very slow. Their standards of living are not rising quickly, and the gap between life in the rich nations and life in the poor nations is not closing.

There are some respects, in fact, in which economic development threatens to fall behind population growth, so that the quality of life actually worsens. For example, despite considerable improvements in agricultural technology and some dramatic increases in grain production, it is still difficult to feed these added people at adequate levels of nutrition. Protein malnutrition is widespread. It is estimated that every day some 10,000 people—most of them children—are dying from diseases of which malnutrition has been at least a partial cause. Moreover, the physical and mental potential of millions of youngsters is not realized because of a lack of proper food. The promise for increased produc-

tion and better distribution of food is great, but not great enough to counter these bleak realities.

The burden of population growth is also felt in the field of social progress. In many countries, despite increases in the number of schools and teachers, there are more and more children for whom there is no schooling. Despite construction of new homes, more and more families are without adequate shelter. Unemployment and underemployment are increasing and the situation could be aggravated as more young people grow up and seek to enter the work force.

Nor has development yet reached the stage where it brings with it diminished family size. Many parents in developing countries are still victimized by forces such as poverty and ignorance which make it difficult for them to exercise control over the size of their families. In sum, population growth is a world problem which no country can ignore, whether it is moved by the narrowest perception of national self-interest or the widest vision of a common humanity.

International Cooperation. It is our belief that the United Nations, its specialized agencies, and other international bodies should take the leadership in responding to world population growth. The United States will cooperate fully with their programs. I would note in this connection that I am most impressed by the scope and thrust of the recent report of the Panel of the United Nations Association, chaired by John D. Rockefeller III. The report stresses the need for expanded action and greater coordination, concerns which should be high on the agenda of the United Nations.

In addition to working with international organizations, the United States can help by supporting efforts which are initiated by other governments. Already we are doing a great deal in this field. For example, we provide assistance to countries which seek our help in reducing high birthrates—provided always that the services we help to make available can be freely accepted or rejected by the individuals who receive them. Through our aid programs, we have worked to improve agricultural production and bolster economic growth in developing nations.

As I pointed out in my recent message on Foreign Aid, we are making important efforts to improve these programs. In fact, I have asked the Secretary of State and the Administrator of the Agency for International Development to give population and family planning high priority for attention, personnel, research, and funding among our several aid programs. Similarly, I am asking the Secretaries of Commerce and Health, Education, and Welfare and the Directors of the Peace Corps and the United States Information Agency to give close attention to population matters as they plan their overseas operations. I also call on the Department of Agriculture and the Agency for International Development to investigate ways of adapting and extending our agricultural experience and capabilities to improve food production and distribution in developing countries. In all of these international efforts, our programs should give further recognition to the important resources of private organizations and university research centers. As we increase our population and family planning efforts abroad, we also call upon other nations to enlarge their programs in this area.

Prompt action in all these areas is essential. For high rates of population growth, as the report of the Panel of the United Nations Association puts it, "impair individual rights, jeopardize national goals, and threaten international stability."

In the United States. For some time population growth has been seen as a problem for developing countries. Only recently has it come to be seen that pressing problems are also posed for advanced industrial countries when their populations increase at the rate that the United States, for example, must now anticipate. Food supplies may be ample in such nations, but social supplies—the capacity to educate youth, to provide privacy and living space, to maintain the processes of open, democratic government—may be grievously strained.

In the United States our rate of population growth is not as great as that of developing nations. In this country, in fact, the growth rate has generally declined since the eighteenth century. The present growth rate of about one percent per year is still significant, however. Moreover, current statistics indicate that the fertility rate may be approaching the end of its recent decline.

Several factors contribute to the yearly increase, including the large number of couples of childbearing age, the typical size of American families, and our increased longevity. We are rapidly reaching the point in this country where a family reunion, which has typically brought together children, parents, and grandparents, will instead gather family members from *four* generations. This is a development for which we are grateful and of which we can be proud. But we must also recognize that it will mean a far larger population if the number of children born to each set of parents remains the same.

In 1917 the total number of Americans passed 100 million, after three full centuries of steady growth. In 1967—just half a century later—the 200 million mark was passed. If the present rate of growth continues, the third hundred million persons will be added in roughly a thirty-year period. This means that by the year 2000, or shortly thereafter, there will be more than 300 million Americans.

This growth will produce serious challenges for our society. I believe that many of our present social problems may be related to the fact that we have had only fifty years in which to accommodate the second hundred million Americans. In fact, since 1945 alone some 90 million babies have been born in this country. We have thus had to accomplish in a very few decades an adjustment to population growth which was once spread over centuries. And it now appears that we will have to provide for a third hundred million Americans in a period of just 30 years.

The great majority of the next hundred million Americans will be born to families which looked forward to their birth and are prepared to love them and care for them as they grow up. The critical issue is whether social institutions will also plan for their arrival and be able to accommodate them in a humane and intelligent way. We can be sure that society will not be ready for this growth unless it begins its planning immediately. And adequate planning, in turn, requires that we ask ourselves a number of important questions.

Where, for example, will the next hundred million Americans live? If the patterns of the last few decades hold for the rest of the century, then at least three quarters of the next hundred million persons will locate in highly urbanized areas. Are our cities prepared for such an influx? The chaotic history of urban growth suggests that they are not and that many of their existing problems will be severely aggravated by a dramatic increase in numbers. Are there ways, then, of readying our cities? Alternatively, can the trend toward greater concentration of population be reversed? Is it a desirable thing for example, that half of all the counties in the United States actually lost population in the 1950's, despite the growing number of inhabitants in the country as a whole? Are there ways of fostering a better distribution of the growing population?

Some have suggested that systems of satellite cities or completely new towns can accomplish this goal. The National Commission on Urban Growth has recently produced a stimulating report on this matter, one which recommends the creation of 100 new communities averaging 100,000 people each, and ten new communities averaging at least one million persons. But the total number of people who would be accommodated if even this bold plan were implemented is only twenty million—a mere one-fifth of the expected thirty-year increase. If we were to accommodate the full 100 million persons in new communities, we would have

to build a new city of 250,000 persons each month from now until the end of the century. That means constructing a city the size of Tulsa, Dayton, or Jersey City every thirty days for over thirty years. Clearly, the problem is enormous, and we must examine the alternative solutions very carefully.

Other questions also confront us. How, for example, will we house the next hundred million Americans? Already economical and attractive housing is in very short supply. New architectural forms, construction techniques, and financing strategies must be aggressively pioneered if we are to provide the needed dwellings.

What of our natural resources and the quality of our environment? Pure air and water are fundamental to life itself. Parks, recreational facilities, and an attractive countryside are essential to our emotional well-being. Plant and animal and mineral resources are also vital. A growing population will increase the demand for such resources. But in many cases their supply will not be increased and may even be endangered. The ecological system upon which we now depend may seriously deteriorate if our efforts to conserve and enhance the environment do not match the growth of the population.

How will we educate and employ such a large number of people? Will our transportation systems move them about as quickly and economically as necessary? How will we provide adequate health care when our population reaches 300 million? Will our political structures have to be reordered, too, when our society grows to such proportions? Many of our institutions are already under tremendous strain as they try to respond to the demands of 1969. Will they be swamped by a growing flood of people in the next thirty years? How easily can they be replaced or altered?

Finally we must ask: how can we better assist American families so that they will have no more children than they wish to have? In my first message to Congress on domestic affairs, I called for a national commitment to provide a healthful and stimulating environment for all children during their first five years of life. One of the ways in which we can promote that goal is to provide assistance for more parents in effectively planning their families. We know that involuntary childbearing often results in poor physical and emotional health for all members of the family. It is one of the factors which contribute to our distressingly high infant mortality rate, the unacceptable level of malnutrition, and the disappointing performance of some children in our schools. Unwanted or untimely childbearing is one of several forces which are driving many families into poverty or keeping them in that condition. Its threat helps to produce the dangerous incidence of illegal abortion. And finally, of course, it needlessly adds to the burdens placed on all our resources by increasing population.

None of the questions I have raised here is new. But all of these questions must now be asked and answered with a new sense of urgency. The answers cannot be given by government alone, nor can government alone turn the answers into programs and policies. I believe, however, that the Federal Government does have a special responsibility for defining these problems and for stimulating thoughtful responses.

Perhaps the most dangerous element in the present situation is the fact that so few people are examining these questions from the viewpoint of the whole society. Perceptive businessmen project the demand for their products many years into the future by studying population trends. Other private institutions develop sophisticated planning mechanisms which allow them to account for rapidly changing conditions. In the governmental sphere, however, there is virtually no machinery through which we can develop a detailed understanding of demographic changes and bring that understanding to bear on public policy. The Federal Government makes only a minimal effort in this area. The efforts of state and local governments are also inadequate. Most importantly, the planning which does take place at some levels is poorly understood at others and is often based on unexamined assumptions.

In short, the questions I have posed in this message too often go unasked, and when they are asked, they seldom are adequately answered.

Commission on Population Growth. It is for all these reasons that I today propose the creation by Congress of a Commission on Population Growth and the American Future.

The Congress should give the Commission responsibility for inquiry and recommendations in three specific areas.

First, the probable course of population growth, internal migration and related demographic developments between now and the year 2000.

As much as possible, these projections should be made by regions, states, and metropolitan areas. Because there is an element of uncertainty in such projections, various alternative possibilities should be plotted.

It is of special importance to note that, beginning in August of 1970, population data by county will become available from the decennial census, which will have been taken in April of that year. By April 1971, computer summaries of first-count data will be available by census tract and an important range of information on income, occupations, education, household composition, and other vital considerations will also be in hand. The Federal Government can make better use of such demographic information than it has done in the past, and state governments and other political subdivisions can also use such data to better advantage. The Commission on Population Growth and the American Future will be an appropriate instrument for this important initiative.

Second, the resources in the public sector of the economy that will be required to deal with the anticipated growth in population.

The single greatest failure of foresight—at all levels of government—over the past generation has been in areas connected with expanding population. Government and legislatures have frequently failed to appreciate the demands which continued population growth would impose on the public sector. These demands are myriad: they will range from pre-school classrooms to post-doctoral fellowships; from public works which carry water over thousands of miles to highways which carry people and products from region to region; from vest pocket parks in crowded cities to forest preserves and quiet lakes in the countryside. Perhaps especially, such demands will assert themselves in forms that affect the quality of life. The time is at hand for a serious assessment of such needs.

Third, ways in which population growth may affect the activities of Federal, state and local government.

In some respects, population growth affects everything that American government does. Yet only occasionally do our governmental units pay sufficient attention to population growth in their own planning. Only occasionally do they consider the serious implications of demographic trends for their present and future activities.

Yet some of the necessary information is at hand and can be made available to all levels of government. Much of the rest will be obtained by the Commission. For such information to be of greatest use, however, it should also be interpreted and analyzed and its implications should be made more evident. It is particularly in this connection that the work of the Commission on Population Growth and the American Future will be as much educational as investigative. The American public and its governing units are not as alert as they should be to these growing challenges. A responsible but insistent voice of reason and foresight is needed. The Commission can provide that voice in the years immediately before us.

The membership of the Commission should include two members from each house of the Congress, together with knowledgeable men and women who are broadly representative of our society. The majority should be citizens who have demonstrated a capacity to deal with important questions of public policy. The membership should also include specialists in the biological, social, and environmental sciences, in theology and law, in the arts and in engineering. The Commission should be empowered to create advisory panels to consider subdivisions of its broad subject area and to invite experts and leaders from all parts of the world to join these panels in their deliberations.

The Commission should be provided with an adequate staff and budget, under the supervision of an executive director of exceptional experience and understanding.

In order that the Commission will have time to utilize the initial data which results from the 1970 census, I ask that it be established for a period of two years. An interim report to the President and Congress should be required at the end of the first year.

Other Government Activities. I would take this opportunity to mention a number of additional government activities dealing with population growth which need not await the report of the Commission.

First, increased research is essential. It is clear, for example, that we need additional research on birth control methods of all types and the sociology of population growth. Utilizing its Center for Population Research, the Department of Health, Education, and Welfare should take the lead in developing, with other federal agencies, an expanded research effort, one which is carefully related to those of private organizations, university research centers, international organizations, and other countries.

Second, we need more trained people to work in population and family planning programs, both in this country and abroad. I am therefore asking the Secretaries of State, Labor, Health, Education, and Welfare, and Interior along with the Administrator of the Agency for International Development and the Director of the Office of Economic Opportunity to participate in a comprehensive survey of our efforts to attract people to such programs and to train them properly. The same group—in consultation with appropriate state, local, and private officials—should develop recommendations for improvements in this area. I am asking the Assistant to the President for Urban Affairs to coordinate this project.

Third, the effects of population growth on our environment and on the world's food supply call for careful attention and immediate action. I am therefore asking the Environmental Quality Council to give careful attention to these matters in its deliberations. I am also asking the Secretaries of Interior, Agriculture, and Health, Education, and Welfare to give the highest priority to research into new techniques and to other proposals that can help safeguard the environment and increase the world's supply of food.

Fourth, it is clear that the domestic family planning services supported by the Federal Government should be expanded and better integrated. Both the Department of Health, Education, and Welfare and the Office of Economic Opportunity are now involved in this important work, yet their combined efforts are not adequate to provide information and services to all who want them. In particular, most of an estimated five million low income women of childbearing age in this country do not now have adequate access to family planning assistance, even though their wishes concerning family size are usually the same as those of parents of higher income groups.

It is my view that no American woman should be denied access to family planning assistance because of her economic condition. I believe, therefore, that we should establish as a national goal the provision of adequate family planning services within the next five years to all those who want them but cannot afford them. This we have the capacity to do.

Clearly, in no circumstances will the activities associated with our pursuit of this goal be allowed to infringe upon the religious convictions or personal wishes and freedom of any individual, nor will they be allowed to impair the absolute right of all individuals to have such matters of conscience respected by public authorities.

In order to achieve this national goal, we will have to increase the amount we are spending on population and family planning. But success in this endeavor will not result from higher expenditures alone. Because the life circumstances and family planning wishes of those who receive services vary considerably, an effective program must be more flexible in its design than are many present efforts. In addition, programs should be better coordinated and more effectively administered. Under current legislation, a comprehensive State or local project must assemble a patchwork of funds from many different sources—a time-consuming and confusing process. Moreover, under existing legislation, requests for funds for family planning services must often compete with requests for other deserving health endeavors.

But these problems can be overcome. The Secretary of Health, Education, and Welfare—whose Department is responsible for the largest part of our domestic family planning services—has developed plans to reorganize the major family planning service activities of this agency. A separate unit for these services will be established within the Health Services and Mental Health Administration. The Secretary will send to Congress in the near future legislation which will help the Department implement this important program by providing broader and more precise legislative authority and a clearer source of financial support.

The Office of Economic Opportunity can also contribute to progress in this area by strengthening its innovative programs and pilot projects in the delivery of family planning services to the needy. The existing network of OEO-supported community groups should also be used more extensively to provide family planning assistance and information. I am asking the Director of the Office of Economic Opportunity to determine the ways in which his Agency can best structure and extend its programs in order to help achieve our national goal in the coming years.

As they develop their own plans, the Secretary of Health, Education, and Welfare and the Director of the Office of Economic Opportunity should also determine the most effective means of coordinating all our domestic family planning programs and should include in their deliberations representatives of the other agencies that share in this important work. It is my intention that such planning should also involve state and local governments and private agencies, for it is clear that the increased activity of the Federal Government in this area must be matched by a sizeable increase in effort at other levels. It would be unrealistic for the Federal Government alone to shoulder the entire burden, but this Administration does accept a clear responsibility to provide essential leadership.

For the Future. One of the most serious challenges to human destiny in the last third of this century will be the growth of the population. Whether man's response to that challenge will be a cause for pride or for despair in the year 2000 will depend very much on what we do today. If we now begin our work in an appropriate manner, and if we continue to devote a considerable amount of attention and energy to this problem, then mankind will be able to surmount this challenge as it has surmounted so many during the long march of civilization.

When future generations evaluate the record of our time, one of the most important factors in their judgment will be the way in which we responded to population growth. Let us act in such a way that those who come after us—even as they lift their eyes beyond earth's bounds—can do so with pride in the planet on which they live, with gratitude to those who lived on it in the past, and with continuing confidence in its future.

RICHARD NIXON

TEXT ON ICC REORGANIZATION

Following is the complete text of President Nixon's July 22 message to Congress on reorganization of the Interstate Commerce Commission.

TO THE CONGRESS OF THE UNITED STATES:

The Interstate Commerce Commission, oldest of the Federal regulatory agencies, has jurisdiction over 17,000 carriers—rail and motor, water and pipeline, express companies and freight forwarders. Its decisions help shape the scope and character of the Nation's transportation system.

But, as important as the Commission is, as extensive as its jurisdiction is, it is hampered by:

1. Lack of continuity: The Chairman of the Commission serves only a year, selected by annual rotation from among the eleven Commissioners. In no other major Federal regulatory agency is the President without the power to designate the Chairman.

2. Lack of leadership: The Chairman does not have vested in him by law the executive and administrative functions of the Commission. As a result there is no firm and clear legal responsibility for the management of the Commission's day-to-day affairs.

To change this situation, I am sending to the Congress today Reorganization Plan No. 1 of 1969, prepared in accordance with chapter 9 of title 5 of the United States Code.

Continuity. The Chairman of the Interstate Commerce Commission is the Commission's spokesman, its key link to other agencies and the industry, the supervisor of its staff, and director of its internal operations. Yet today, despite the need for sustained leadership, the Chairman of this Agency serves only one year. I know of no modern business that would tolerate the practice of annually rotating its chief executive.

To provide the necessary continuity of leadership in the conduct of the Commission's administrative affairs, I propose that the President be authorized to designate the Chairman of the Commission from among its members. This principle of good management has already been taken with respect to most other major Federal regulatory agencies. The time has come to apply it to the Interstate Commerce Commission.

Leadership. The administrative powers of the Chairman must be strengthened.

In 1961, the Commission delegated its administrative powers to its Chairman. However, unless and until the administrative powers are vested in the Chairman by law, statutory authority will remain dispersed among the Commissioners.

Almost 20 years ago the Hoover Commission emphasized that "administration by a plural executive is universally regarded as inefficient." It then recommended that all administrative responsibility be assigned the chairmen of these regulatory agencies.

That recommendation is as sound today as it was then. It has already been applied to almost every other major Federal regulatory agency. I propose that administrative authority be vested in the Chairman of the Interstate Commerce Commission.

In sum, the reorganization plan provides continuity of leadership and vests responsibility for internal administrative functions in a chairman designated by the President, with safeguards to ensure that the Commission retains full control over policy and the direction of its regulatory programs. This does not affect the statutory provisions governing the exercise of quasi-legislative and quasi-judicial powers by the Commission and its employees to whom it has delegated the responsibility of hearing and deciding cases.

Each reorganization included in the plan is necessary to accomplish one or more of the purposes set forth in section 901 (a) of title 5 of the United States Code. In particular, the plan is responsive to section 901 (a) (1), "to promote the better execution of the laws, the more effective management of the Executive Branch and of its agencies and functions, and the expeditious administration of the public business;" and section 901 (a) (3), "to increase the efficiency of the operations of the Government to the fullest extent practicable." This plan will help achieve those ends.

This plan should result in more efficient operation of the Commission. To itemize or aggregate resulting expenditure reductions under the plan is not practicable. I shall continue to explore other ways to make the Commission structure more effective.

I strongly recommend that the Congress permit this necessary reorganization plan to become effective.

RICHARD NIXON

PRESIDENT CALLS FOR NATIONAL JOB SAFETY STANDARDS

Following is the complete text of President Nixon's Aug. 6 message to Congress on occupational safety.

TO THE CONGRESS OF THE UNITED STATES:

Technological progress can be a mixed blessing. The same new method or new product which improves our lives can also be the source of unpleasantness and pain. For man's lively capacity to innovate is not always matched by his ability to understand his innovations fully, to use them properly, or to protect himself against the unforeseen consequences of the changes he creates.

The side effects of progress present special dangers in the workplaces of our country. For the working man and woman, the by-products of change constitute an especially serious threat. Some efforts to protect the safety and health of the American worker have been made in the past both by private industry and by all levels of government. But new technologies have moved even faster to create newer dangers. Today we are asking our workers to perform far different tasks from those they performed five or fifteen or fifty years ago. It is only right that the protection we give them is also up-to-date.

There has been much discussion in recent months about the quality of the environment in which Americans live. It is important to note in this regard that during their working years most American workers spend nearly a quarter of their time at their jobs. For them, the quality of the workplace is one of the most important of environmental questions. The protection of that quality is a critical matter for government attention.

Few people realize the extent of needless illness, needless injury, and needless death which results from unsafe or unhealthy working conditions. Every now and then a major disaster—in a factory or an office building or a mine—will dramatize certain occupational hazards. But most such dangers are realized under less dramatic circumstances. Often, for example, a threat to good health will build up slowly over a period of many years. To such situations, the public gives very little attention. Yet the cumulative extent of such losses is great.

Consider these facts. Every year in this country, some 14,000 deaths can be attributed to work-related injuries or illnesses. Because of accidents or diseases sustained on the job, some 250 million man-days of labor are lost annually. The most important consequence of these losses is the human tragedy which results when an employee—often the head of a family—is struck down. In addition, the economy loses millions of dollars in unrealized production and millions more must be used to pay workmen's compensation benefits and medical expenses. It is interesting to note that in the last five years, the number of man-days lost because of work-related injuries has been 10 times the number lost because of strikes.

What have we done about this problem? The record is haphazard and spotty. For many decades, governmental responsibility for safe workplaces has rested with the states. But the scope and effectiveness of state laws and state administration varies widely and discrepancies in the performances of state programs appear to be increasing. Moreover, some states are fearful that stricter standards will place them at a disadvantage with other states.

Many industries and businesses have made commendable progress in protecting worker health and safety on their own. Some, in fact, have managed to reduce the frequency of accidents by as much as 80 or 90 percent, demonstrating what can be accomplished with the proper effort. But such voluntary successes are not yet sufficiently widespread.

There are some other positive signs. Collective bargaining agreements often include safety and health provisions; many professional organizations have suggested voluntary standards; groups like the National Safety Council have worked to promote better working conditions. But the overall record is still uneven and unsettling.

The federal role in occupational safety and health has thus far been limited. A few specific industries have been made subject to special federal laws and limited regulations have been applied to workers in companies who hold certain government contracts. In my message to Congress last March on Coal Mine Safety, I outlined an important area in which further specific federal action is imperative. But something broader is also needed, I believe. I am therefore recommending a new mechanism through which safety and health standards for industry in general can be improved.

The comprehensive Occupational Safety and Health Act which the Secretary of Labor will soon transmit to the Congress will correct some of the important deficiencies of earlier approaches. It will go beyond the limited "accident" orientation of the past, giving greater attention to health considerations, which are often difficult to perceive and which have often been overlooked. It will separate the function of setting safety and health standards from the function of enforcing them. Appropriate procedures to guarantee due process of law and the right to appeal will be incorporated. The proposal will also provide a flexible mechanism which can react quickly to the new technologies of tomorrow.

Under the suggested legislation, maximum use will be made of standards established through a voluntary consensus of industry, labor, and other experts. No standard will be set until the views of all interested parties have been heard. This proposal would also encourage stronger efforts at the state level, sharing enforcement responsibility with states which have adequate programs. Greater emphasis will also be given to research and education, for the effects of modern technologies on the physical well-being of workers are complex and poorly understood. The Public Health Service has done some important groundwork in the field of occupational health, but we still need much more information and understanding.

Our specific recommendations are as follows:

1. Safety and health standards will be set by a new National Occupational Safety and Health Board. The five members of the Board will be appointed by the President with the advice and consent of the Senate to five-year terms; one member of the Board will change each year. At least three members of the Board must have technical competence in the field of occupational safety and health.

The Board will have the power to promulgate standards which have been established by nationally-recognized public or private standard-setting organizations. Thousands of these standards have been carefully worked out over the years; the Board will adopt such a "national consensus standard" when the standard-setting organization possesses high technical competence and considers the views of all interested parties in making its decisions.

If the Secretary of Labor (in matters of safety) or the Secretary of Health, Education and Welfare (in matters of health) objects to any such "national consensus standard," they may bring that objection before the Board. The Board can then set a new standard after giving the matter a full public hearing. When national consensus standards do not exist, the Board will have the power to break new ground after full hearings. If the Secretary of Labor or the Secretary of Health, Education and Welfare object to the Board's action, they can delay its implementation until at least three of the Board members reconfirm their original decision.

2. The Secretary of Labor will have the initial role in enforcing the standards which the Board establishes. The Secretary will ask employers whom he believes to be in violation of the standards to comply with them voluntarily; if they fail to do so, he can bring a complaint before the Occupational Safety and Health Board which will hold a full hearing on the matter. If the Board determines that a violation exists, it shall issue appropriate orders which the Secretary of Labor can then enforce

through the court system. In emergency situations, the Secretary can go directly to the courts and petition for temporary relief.

3. The state governments will be encouraged to submit plans for expanding and improving their own occupational safety and health programs. Federal grants will be available to pay up to 90 percent of the cost of developing such plans. When a State presents a plan which provides at least as much protection to the worker as the federal plan, then the federal standard administration will give way to the state administration, with the Federal Government assuming up to 50 percent of that state's costs.

4. The Secretary of Health, Education and Welfare, will be given the specific assignment of developing and carrying out a broad program of study, experiment, demonstration, education, information, and technical assistance—as further means of promoting better safety and health practices in the workplace. The Secretary will be required to submit a comprehensive report to the President and the Congress, including an evaluation of the program and further recommendations for its improvement.

5. A National Advisory Committee on Occupational Safety and Health will be established to advise the Secretary of Labor and the Secretary of Health, Education and Welfare in the administration of the Act.

Three years ago, following its study of traffic and highway safety, the Congress noted that modern technology had brought with it new driving hazards, and accordingly, it enacted the National Traffic and Motor Vehicle Act and the Highway Safety Act. With the advent of a new workplace technology, we must now give similar attention to workplace safety and health.

The legislation which this Administration is proposing can do much to improve the environment of the American worker. But it will take much more than new government efforts if we are to achieve our objectives. Employers and employees alike must be committed to the prevention of accident and disease and alert to every opportunity for promoting that end. Together the private and public sectors can do much that we cannot do separately.

RICHARD NIXON

WELFARE REFORM MESSAGE

Following is the complete text of President Nixon's Aug. 11 welfare reform message to Congress. (For text of Mr. Nixon's Aug. 8 nationally televised speech on welfare and other reforms, see p. 75-A.)

TO THE CONGRESS OF THE UNITED STATES:

A measure of the greatness of a powerful nation is the character of the life it creates for those who are powerless to make ends meet.

If we do not find the way to become a working nation that properly cares for the dependent, we shall become a welfare state that undermines the incentive of the working man.

The present welfare system has failed us—it has fostered family breakup, has provided very little help in many states and has even deepened dependency by all too often making it more attractive to go on welfare than to go to work.

I propose a new approach that will make it more attractive to go to work than to go on welfare, and will establish a nationwide minimum payment to dependent families with children.

I propose that the Federal Government pay a basic income to those American families who cannot care for themselves in whichever state they live.

I propose that dependent families receiving such income be given good reason to go to work by making the first 60 dollars a month they earn completely their own, with no deductions from their benefits.

I propose that we make available an addition to the incomes of the "working poor," to encourage them to go on working and to eliminate the possibility of making more from welfare than from wages.

I propose that these payments be made upon certification of income, with demeaning and costly investigations replaced by simplified reviews and spot checks and with no eligibility requirement that the household be without a father. That present requirement in many states has the effect of breaking up families and contributes to delinquency and violence.

I propose that all employable persons who choose to accept these payments be required to register for work or job training and be required to accept that work or training, provided suitable jobs are available either locally or if transportation is provided. Adequate and convenient day care would be provided children wherever necessary to enable a parent to train or work. The only exception to this work requirement would be mothers of preschool children.

I propose a major expansion of job-training and day-care facilities, so that current welfare recipients able to work can be set on the road to self-reliance.

I propose that we also provide uniform federal payment minimums for the present three categories of welfare aid to adults—the aged, the blind and the disabled.

This would be total welfare reform—the transformation of a system frozen in failure and frustration into a system that would work and would encourage people to work.

Accordingly, we have stopped considering human welfare in isolation. The new plan is part of an over-all approach which includes a comprehensive new Manpower Training Act and a plan for a system of revenue sharing with the states to help provide all of them with necessary budget relief. Messages on manpower training and revenue sharing will follow this message tomorrow and the next day, and the three should be considered as parts of a whole approach to what is clearly a national problem.

Need for New Departures. A welfare system is a success when it takes care of people who cannot take care of themselves and when it helps employable people climb toward independence.

A welfare system is a failure when it takes care of those who can take care of themselves, when it drastically varies payments in different areas, when it breaks up families, when it perpetuates a vicious cycle of dependency, when it strips human beings of their dignity.

America's welfare system is a failure that grows worse every day.

First, it fails the recipient: In many areas, benefits are so low that we have hardly begun to take care of the dependent. And there has been no light at the end of poverty's tunnel. After four years of inflation, the poor have generally become poorer.

Second, it fails the taxpayer: Since 1960, welfare costs have doubled and the number on the rolls has risen from 5.8 million to over 9 million, all in a time when unemployment was low. The taxpayer is entitled to expect government to devise a system that will help people lift themselves out of poverty.

Finally, it fails American society: By breaking up homes, the present welfare system has added to social unrest and robbed millions of children of the joy of childhood; by widely varying payments among regions, it has helped to draw millions into the slums of our cities.

The situation has become intolerable. Let us examine the alternatives available:

• We could permit the welfare momentum to continue to gather speed by our inertia; by 1975 this would result in 4 million more Americans on welfare rolls at a cost of close to $11 billion a year, with both recipients and taxpayers shortchanged.

• We could tinker with the system as it is, adding to the patchwork of modifications and exceptions. That has been the approach of the past, and it has failed.

• We could adopt a "guaranteed minimum income for everyone," which would appear to wipe out poverty overnight. It would also wipe out the basic economic motivation for work and place an enormous strain on the industrious to pay for the leisure of the lazy.

• Or we could adopt a totally new approach to welfare, designed to assist those left far behind the national norm and provide all with the motivation to work and a fair share of the opportunity to train.

This Administration, after a careful analysis of all the alternatives, is committed to a new departure that will find a solution for the welfare problem. The time for denouncing the old is over; the time for devising the new is now.

Recognizing the Practicalities. People usually follow their self-interest.

This stark fact is distressing to many social planners who like to look at problems from the top down. Let us abandon the ivory tower and consider the real world in all we do.

In most states, welfare is provided only when there is no father at home to provide support. If a man's children would be better off on welfare than with the low wage he is able to bring home, wouldn't he be tempted to leave home?

If a person spent a great deal of time and effort to get on the welfare rolls, wouldn't he think twice about risking his eligibility by taking a job that might not last long?

In each case, welfare policy was intended to limit the spread of dependency; in practice, however, the effect has been to increase dependency and remove the incentive to work.

We fully expect people to follow their self-interest in their business dealings; why should we be surprised when people follow their self-interest in their welfare dealings? That is why we propose a plan in which it is in the interest of every employable person to do his fair share of work.

The Operation of the New Approach. We would assure an income foundation throughout every section of America for all parents who cannot adequately support themselves and their children. For a family of four with less than $1,000 income, this payment would be $1,600 a year; for a family of four with $2,000 income, this payment would supplement that income by $960 a year.

Under the present welfare system, each state provides "Aid to Families with Dependent Children," a program we propose to replace. The Federal Government shares the cost, but each state establishes key eligibility rules and determines how much income support will be provided to poor families. The result has been an uneven and unequal system. The 1969 benefits average for a family of four is $171 a month across the nation, but individual state averages range from $263 down to $39 a month.

A new federal minimum of $1,600 a year cannot claim to provide comfort to a family of four, but the present low of $468 a year cannot claim to provide even the basic necessities.

The new system would do away with the inequity of very low benefit levels in some states, and of state-by-state variations in eligibility tests, by establishing a federally financed income floor with a national definition of basic eligibility.

States will continue to carry an important responsibility. In 30 states the federal basic payment will be less than the present levels of combined federal and state payments. These states will be required to maintain the current level of benefits, but in no case will a state be required to spend more than 90 percent of its present welfare cost. The Federal Government will not only provide the "floor," but it will assume 10 percent of the benefits now being paid by the states as their part of welfare costs.

In 20 states, the new payment would exceed the present average benefit payments, in some cases by a wide margin. In these states, where benefits are lowest and poverty often the most severe, the payments will raise benefit levels substantially. For five years, every state will be required to continue to spend at least half of what they are now spending on welfare, to supplement the federal base.

For the typical "welfare family"—a mother with dependent children and no outside income—the new system would provide a basic national minimum payment. A mother with three small children would be assured an annual income of at least $1,600.

For the family headed by an employed father or working mother, the same basic benefits would be received, but $60 per month of earnings would be "disregarded" in order to make up

the costs of working and provide a strong advantage in holding a job. The wage-earner could also keep 50 percent of his benefits as his earnings rise above that $60 per month. A family of four, in which the father earns $2,000 in a year, would receive payments of $960, for a total income of $2,960.

For the aged, the blind and the disabled, the present system varies benefit levels from $40 per month for an aged person in one state to $145 per month for the blind in another. The new system would establish a minimum payment of $65 per month for all three of these adult categories, with the Federal Government contributing the first $50 and sharing in payments above that amount. This will raise the share of the financial burden borne by the Federal Government for payments to these adults who cannot support themselves, and should pave the way for benefit increases in many states.

For the single adult who is not handicapped or aged, or for the married couple without children, the new system would not apply. Food stamps would continue to be available up to $300 per year per person, according to the plan I outlined last May in my message to the Congress on the food and nutrition needs of the population in poverty. For dependent families there will be an orderly substitution of food stamps by the new direct monetary payments.

• The new approach would end the blatant unfairness of the welfare system.

In over half the states, families headed by unemployed men do not qualify for public assistance. In no state does a family headed by a father working full-time receive help in the current welfare system, no matter how little he earns. As we have seen, this approach to dependency has itself been a cause of dependency. It results in a policy that tends to force the father out of the house.

The new plan rejects a policy that undermines family life. It would end the substantial financial incentives to desertion. It would extend eligibility to all dependent families with children, without regard to whether the family is headed by a man or a woman. The effects of these changes upon human behavior would be an increased will to work, the survival of more marriages, the greater stability of families. We are determined to stop passing the cycle of dependency from generation to generation.

The most glaring inequity in the old welfare system is the exclusion of families who are working to pull themselves out of poverty. Families headed by a non-worker often receive more from welfare than families headed by a husband working full-time at very low wages. This has been rightly resented by the working poor, for the rewards are just the opposite of what they should be.

• The new plan would create a much stronger incentive to work.

For people now on the welfare rolls, the present system discourages the move from welfare to work by cutting benefits too fast and too much as earnings begin. The new system would encourage work by allowing the new worker to retain the first $720 of his yearly earnings without any benefit reduction.

For people already working, but at poverty wages, the present system often encourages nothing but resentment and an incentive to quit and go on relief where that would pay more than work. The new plan, on the contrary, would provide a supplement that will help a low-wage worker—struggling to make ends meet—achieve a higher standard of living.

For an employable person who just chooses not to work, neither the present system nor the one we propose would support him, though both would continue to support other dependent members in his family.

However, a welfare mother with preschool children should not face benefit reductions if she decides to stay home. It is not our intent that mothers of preschool children must accept work. Those who can work and desire to do so, however, should have the opportunity for jobs and job training and access to day-care centers for their children; this will enable them to support themselves after their children are grown.

A family with a member who gets a job would be permitted to retain all of the first $60 monthly income, amounting to $720 per year for a regular worker, with no reduction of federal payments. The incentive to work in this provision is obvious. But there is another practical reason: Going to work costs money. Expenses such as clothes, transportation, personal care, Social Security taxes and loss of income from odd jobs amount to substantial costs for the average family. Since a family does not begin to add to its net income until it surpasses the cost of working, in fairness this amount should not be subtracted from the new payment.

After the first $720 of income, the rest of the earnings will result in a systematic reduction in payments.

I believe the vast majority of poor people in the United States prefer to work rather than have the government support their families. In 1968, 600,000 families left the welfare rolls out of an average caseload of 1,400,000 during the year, showing a considerable turnover, much of it voluntary.

However, there may be some who fail to seek or accept work, even with the strong incentives and training opportunities that will be provided. It would not be fair to those who willingly work, or to all taxpayers, to allow others to choose idleness when opportunity is available. Thus, they must accept training opportunities and jobs when offered, or give up their right to the new payments for themselves. No able-bodied person will have a "free ride" in a nation that provides opportunity for training and work.

• The bridge from welfare to work should be buttressed by training and child-care programs. For many, the incentives to work in this plan would be all that is necessary. However, there are other situations where these incentives need to be supported by measures that will overcome other barriers to employment.

I propose that funds be provided for expanded training and job development programs so that an additional 150,000 welfare recipients can become jobworthy during the first year.

Manpower training is a basic bridge to work for poor people, especially people with limited education, low skills and limited job experience. Manpower training programs can provide this bridge for many of our poor. In the new manpower training proposal to be sent to the Congress this week, the interrelationship with this new approach to welfare will be apparent.

I am also requesting authority, as a part of the new system, to provide child care for the 450,000 children of the 150,000 current welfare recipients to be trained.

The child care I propose is more than custodial. This Administration is committed to a new emphasis on child development in the first five years of life. The day care that would be part of this plan would be of a quality that will help in the development of the child and provide for its health and safety, and would break the poverty cycle for this new generation.

The expanded child-care program would bring new opportunities along several lines: opportunities for the further involvement of private enterprise in providing high quality child-care service; opportunities for volunteers; and opportunities for training and employment in child-care centers of many of the welfare mothers themselves.

I am requesting a total of $600 million additional to fund these expanded training programs and child-care centers.

• The new system will lessen welfare red tape and provide administrative cost savings. To cut out the costly investigations so bitterly resented as "welfare snooping," the federal payment will be based upon a certification of income, with spot checks sufficient to prevent abuses. The program will be administered on an automated basis, using the information and technical experience of the Social Security Administration, but, of course, will be entirely separate from the administration of the Social Security trust fund.

The states would be given the option of having the Federal Government handle the payment of the state supplemental benefits on a reimbursable basis, so that they would be spared their present administrative burdens and so a single check could be sent to the recipient. These simplifications will save money and eliminate indignities; at the same time, welfare fraud will be detected and lawbreakers prosecuted.

• This new departure would require a substantial initial investment, but will yield future returns to the nation. This transformation of the welfare system will set in motion forces that will lessen dependency rather than perpetuate and enlarge it. A more productive population adds to real economic growth without inflation. The initial investment is needed now to stop the momentum of work-to-welfare and to start a new momentum in the opposite direction.

The costs of welfare benefits for families with dependent children have been rising alarmingly the past several years, increasing from $1 billion in 1960 to an estimated $3.3 billion in 1969, of which $1.8 billion is paid by the Federal Government and $1.5 billion is paid by the states. Based on current population and income data, the proposals I am making today will increase federal costs during the first year by an estimated $4 billion, which includes $600 million for job training and child-care centers.

The "start-up costs" of lifting many people out of dependency will ultimately cost the taxpayer far less than the chronic costs—in dollars and in national values—of creating a permanent underclass in America.

From Welfare to Work. Since this Administration took office, members of the Urban Affairs Council, including officials of the Department of Health, Education and Welfare, the Department of Labor, the Office of Economic Opportunity, the Bureau of the Budget and other key advisers have been working to develop a coherent, fresh approach to welfare, manpower training and revenue sharing.

I have outlined our conclusions about an important component of this approach in this message; the Secretary of HEW will transmit to the Congress the proposed legislation after the summer recess.

I urge the Congress to begin its study of these proposals promptly so that laws can be enacted and funds authorized to begin the new system as soon as possible. Sound budgetary policy must be maintained in order to put this plan into effect— especially the portion supplementing the wages of the working poor.

With the establishment of the new approach, the Office of Economic Opportunity will concentrate on the important task of finding new ways of opening economic opportunity for those who are able to work. Rather than focusing on income support activities, it must find means of providing opportunities for individuals to contribute to the full extent of their capabilities and of developing and improving those capabilities.

This would be the effect of the transformation of welfare into "workfare," a new work-rewarding system:

For the first time, all dependent families with children in America, regardless of where they live, would be assured of minimum standard payments based upon uniform and single eligibility standards.

For the first time, the more than 2 million families who make up the "working poor" would be helped toward self-sufficiency and away from future welfare dependency.

For the first time, training and work opportunity with effective incentives would be given millions of families who would otherwise be locked into a welfare system for generations.

For the first time, the Federal Government would make a strong contribution toward relieving the financial burden of welfare payments from state governments.

For the first time, every dependent family in America would be encouraged to stay together, free from economic pressure to split apart.

These are far-reaching effects. They cannot be purchased cheaply or by piecemeal efforts. This total reform looks in a new direction; it requires new thinking, a new spirit and a fresh dedication to reverse the downhill course of welfare. In its first year, more than half the families participating in the program will have one member working or training.

We have it in our power to raise the standard of living and the realizable hopes of millions of our fellow citizens. By providing an equal chance at the starting line, we can reinforce the traditional American spirit of self-reliance and self-respect.

RICHARD NIXON

TEXT OF MANPOWER MESSAGE

Following is the complete text of President Nixon's August 12 message to Congress on manpower training.

TO THE CONGRESS OF THE UNITED STATES:

A job is one rung on the ladder of a lifelong career of work.

That is why we must look at manpower training with new eyes: as a continuing process to help people to get started in a job and to get ahead in a career.

"Manpower training" is one of those phrases with a fine ring and an imprecise meaning. Before a fresh approach can be taken, a clear definition is needed.

Manpower training means: (1) making it possible for those who are unemployed or on the fringes of the labor force to become permanent, full-time workers; (2) giving those who are now employed at low income the training and the opportunity they need to become more productive and more successful; (3) discovering the potential in those people who are now considered unemployable, removing many of the barriers now blocking their way.

Manpower training, in order to work on all rungs of the ladder, requires the efficient allocation by private enterprise and Government of these human resources. We must develop skills in a place, in a quantity and in a way to ensure that they are used effectively and constantly improved.

Today, Government spends approximately $3 billion in a wide variety of manpower programs, with half directly devoted to job training; private enterprise spends much more on job training alone. The investment by private industry—given impetus by the profit motive as well as a sense of social responsibility—is the fundamental means of developing the nation's labor force. But the Government's investment has failed to achieve its potential for many reasons, including duplication of effort, inflexible funding arrangements and an endless ribbon or red tape. For example:

• A jobless man goes to the local skill training center to seek help. He has the aptitudes for training in blue collar mechanical work, but no suitable training opportunities are available. At the same time, vacancies exist in a white collar New Careers project and in the Neighborhood Youth Corps. But the resources of these programs cannot be turned over to the training program that has the most local demand.

• A 17-year-old boy wants to take job training. The only manpower program available to him is the Job Corps, but its nearest camp is hundreds of miles away. With no other choice, he leaves home; within 30 days he had become homesick or feels his family needs him; he drops out of the Corps and has suffered "failure" which reinforces his self-image of defeat.

• A big-city Mayor takes the lead in trying to put together a cohesive manpower program for the entire labor market area—tying together jobless workers in the inner city with job openings outside the "beltway." He finds it difficult to assemble a coherent picture of what's going on. Manpower programs funded by different agencies follow different reporting rules, so that the statistics cannot be added up. Moreover, there is no single agency which maintains an inventory of all currently operating manpower programs. He knows that help is available—but where does he turn?

• An unemployed high school drop-out in a small town wants to learn a trade in the electronics field. His local employment office tells him that there is not enough demand in his town for qualified technicians to warrant setting up a special training class in a local public school. He is also told that "administrative procedures" do not lend themselves to the use of a local

private technical institute which offers the very course he wants. This youngster walks the streets and wonders what happened to all those promises of "equal opportunity."

This confused state of affairs in the development of human resources can no longer be tolerated. Government exists to serve the needs of people, not the other way around. The idea of creating a set of "programs," and then expecting people to fit themselves into those programs, is contrary to the American spirit; we must redirect our efforts to tailor government aid to individual need.

This government has a major responsibility to make certain that the means to learn a job skill and improve that skill are available to those who need it.

Manpower training is central to our commitment to aid the disadvantaged and to help people off welfare rolls and onto payrolls. Intelligently organized, it will save tax dollars now spent on welfare, increase revenues by widening the base of the taxpaying public, and—most important—lift human beings into lives of greater dignity.

I propose a comprehensive new Manpower Training Act that would pull together much of the array of federal training services and make it possible for state and local government to respond to the needs of the individual trainee.

The nation must have a manpower system that will enable each individual to take part in a sequence of activities—tailored to his unique needs—to prepare for and secure a good job. The various services people need are afforded in laws already on the books. The need today is to knit together all the appropriate services in one readily available system. By taking this step we can better help the disadvantaged gain control and direction of their own lives.

A first step was taken in this direction in March when I announced the reorganization of the Manpower Administration of the U.S. Department of Labor. This reorganization consolidated the agencies that had fragmented responsibility for carrying out most of the nation's manpower training program. We must now complete the job by streamlining the statutory framework for our manpower training efforts.

In specific terms, the Act which I propose would:

1. Consolidate major manpower development programs administered by the Department of Labor—namely, the Manpower Development and Training Act and Title I-A (Job Corps) and I-B (Community Work and Training Program) of the Economic Opportunity Act. These programs, operated in conjunction with strengthened state manpower agencies, will provide training activities in a cohesive manpower services system. The Office of Economic Opportunity, without major manpower operational responsibilities, will continue its role in research work and program development working with the Department of Labor in pioneering new manpower training approaches.

2. Provide flexible funding of manpower training services so that they can be sensitive to and focused on local needs; this will ensure the most efficient use of available resources.

3. Decentralize administration of manpower services to states and metropolitan areas, as governors and mayors evidence interest, build managerial capacity, and demonstrate effective performance. This process will take place in three stages. First, a state will administer 25 percent of the funds apportioned to it when it develops a comprehensive manpower planning capability; second, it will exercise discretion over 66-2/3 percent when it establishes a comprehensive Manpower Training Agency to administer the unified programs; and, third, it will administer 100 percent when the state meets objective standards of exemplary performance in planning and carrying out its manpower service system.

The proposed Act will assure that equitable distribution of the manpower training dollars is made to the large metropolitan areas and to rural districts, working through a state grant system.

By placing greater reliance on state and local elected officials, the day-to-day planning and administration of manpower programs will become more responsive to individual job training needs. A dozen states have already taken steps to reshape administrative agencies and to unify manpower and related programs.

To qualify for full participation under the proposed Act, each state and the major cities in a state would unify its manpower administration under state and local prime sponsors. These agencies would administer the programs funded by the Federal Government; be responsible for other state and local activities to help people secure employment; help employers find manpower; and work in close liaison with state and local vocational education, vocational rehabilitation and welfare programs, for which leadership will be provided at the national level by the Department of Health, Education, and Welfare.

In addition, the state and local prime sponsors would establish advisory bodies, including employees, employers and representatives of the local populations to be served, to assist in developing local policy. In this manner, the units of government would be able to benefit continually from the experience and counsel of the private sector.

4. Provide more equitable allowances for trainees, simplifying the present schedule to provide an incentive for a trainee to choose the training best suited to his own future, and not the training that "pays" most.

As an incentive to move from welfare rolls to payrolls, the allowance to welfare recipients who go into training would be increased to $30 per month above their present welfare payments. These increased training allowances carefully dovetail into the work incentives outlined in my message to the Congress regarding the transformation of the welfare system. As the welfare recipient moves up the ladder from training to work, the first $60 per month of earnings would result in no deductions from federally-financed payments.

5. Create a career development plan for trainees, tailored to suit their individual capabilities and ambitions.

Eligible applicants—in general, those over 16 who need training—would be provided a combination of services that would help them to train, to find work, and to move on up the ladder. These services will include counseling, basic vocational education, medical care, work experience, institutional and on-the-job training, and job referral. Manpower services will also be available for those who are presently employed but whose skill deficiencies hold them in low-income, dead-end jobs.

6. Establish a National Computerized Job Bank to match job seekers with job vacancies. It would operate in each state, with regional and national activities undertaken by the Secretary of Labor, who would also set technical standards.

The computers of the Job Bank would be programmed with constantly changing data on available jobs. A job seeker would tell an employment counselor his training or employment background, his skills and career plans, which could be matched with a variety of available job options. This would expand the potential worker's freedom of choice and help him make best use of his particular talents.

7. Authorize the use of the comprehensive manpower training system as an economic stabilizer. If rising unemployment were ever to suggest the possibility of a serious economic downturn, a counter-cyclical automatic "trigger" would be provided. Appropriations for manpower services would be increased by 10 percent if the national unemployment rate equals or exceeds 4.5 percent for three consecutive months. People without the prospect of immediate employment could use this period to enhance their skills—and the productive capacity of the nation. I proposed a similar measure in my message to the Congress on expansion of the unemployment insurance system.

The proposed comprehensive Manpower Training Act is a good example of a new direction in making federalism work. Working together, we can bring order and efficiency to a tangle of federal programs.

We can answer a national need by decentralizing power, setting national standards, and assigning administrative responsibility to the states and localities in touch with community needs.

We can relate substantial federal-state manpower efforts to other efforts in welfare reform, tax sharing and economic opportunity, marshaling the resources of the departments and agencies involved to accomplish a broad mission.

We can meet individual human needs without encroaching on personal freedom, which is perhaps the most exciting challenge to government today.

With these proposals, which I strongly urge the Congress to enact, we can enhance America's human resources. By opening up the opportunity for manpower training on a large scale, we build a person's will to work; in so doing, we build a bridge to human dignity.

RICHARD NIXON

REVENUE SHARING TEXT

Following is the complete text of President Nixon's Aug. 13 message to Congress on revenue sharing.

TO THE CONGRESS OF THE UNITED STATES:

If there is a single phenomenon that has marked the recent history of nations, large and small, democratic and dictatorial, it has been rise of the central government.

In the United States, revenues of the Federal Government have increased 90-fold in 36 years. The areas of our national life where the Federal Government has become a dominant force have multiplied.

The flow of power from the cities and states to Washington accelerated in the Depression years, when economic life in America stagnated and an energetic national government seemed the sole instrument of national revival. World War II brought another and necessary expansion of the Federal Government to marshal the nation's energies to wage war on two sides of the world.

When the war ended, it appeared as though the tide would be reversed. But the onset of the Cold War, the needs of a defeated and prostrate Europe, the growing danger and then the reality of conflict in Asia and later, the great social demands made upon the Federal Government by millions of citizens, guaranteed the continued rapid growth and expansion of federal power.

Today, however, a majority of Americans no longer supports the continued extension of federal services. The momentum for federal expansion has passed its peak; a process of deceleration is setting in.

The cause can be found in the record of the last half decade. In the last five years the Federal Government enacted scores of new federal programs; it added tens of thousands of new employees to the federal payrolls; it spent tens of billions of dollars in new funds to heal the grave social ills of rural and urban America. No previous half decade had witnessed domestic federal spending on such a scale. Yet, despite the enormous federal commitment in new men, new ideas and new dollars from Washington, it was during this very period in our history that the problems of the cities deepened rapidly into crises.

The problems of the cities and the countryside stubbornly resisted the solutions of Washington; and the stature of the Federal Government as America's great instrument of social progress has suffered accordingly—all the more so because the Federal Government promised so much and delivered so little. The loss of faith in the power and efficacy of the Federal Government has had at least one positive impact upon the American people. More and more, they are turning away from the central government to their local and state governments to deal with their local and state problems.

As the Federal Government grew in size and power, it became increasingly remote not only from the problems it was supposed to solve, but from the people it was supposed to serve. For more than three decades, whenever a great social change was needed, a new national program was the automatic and inevitable response. Power and responsibility flowed in greater and greater measure from the state capitals to the national capital.

Furthermore, we have hampered the effectiveness of local government by constructing a federal grant-in-aid system of staggering complexity and diversity. Many of us question the efficiency of this intergovernmental financial system which is based on the federal categorical grant. Its growth since the end of 1962 has been near explosive. Then there were 53 formula grant and 107 project grant authorizations—a total of 160. Four years later, on Jan. 1, 1967, there were 379 such grant authorizations.

While effective in many instances, this rapid growth in federal grants has been accompanied by:

• Overlapping programs at the state and local level.

• Distortion of state and local budgets.

• Increased administrative costs.

• Program delay and uncertainty.

• A decline in the authority and responsibility of chief executives, as grants have become tied to functional bureaucracies.

• Creation of new and frequently competitive state and local governmental institutions.

Another inevitable result of this proliferation of federal programs has been a gathering of the reins of power in Washington. Experience has taught us that this is neither the most efficient nor effective way to govern; certainly it represents a radical departure from the vision of federal-state relations the nation's founders had in mind.

This Administration brought into office both a commitment and a mandate to reverse the trend of the last three decades—a determination to test new engines of social progress. We are committed to enlist the full potential of the private sector, the full potential of the voluntary sector and the full potential of the levels of government closer to the people.

This week, I am sending to Congress for its approval for fiscal year 1971 legislation asking that a set amount of federal revenues be returned annually to the states to be used as the states and their local governments see fit — without federal strings.

Because of budget stringencies, the initial fund set aside to start the program will not be great—$500 million. The role of the Federal Government will be redefined and redirected. But it is my intention to augment this fund annually in the coming years so that in the fiscal year beginning in mid-1975, $5 billion in federal revenues will be returned to the states without federal strings. Ultimately, it is our hope to use this mechanism to so strengthen state and local government that by the end of the coming decade, the political landscape of America will be visibly altered, and states and cities will have a far greater share of power and responsibility for solving their own problems. The role of the Federal Government will be redefined and redirected toward those functions where it proves itself the only or the most suitable instrument.

The fiscal case for federal assistance to states and localities is a strong one. Under our current budget structure, federal revenues are likely to increase faster than the national economy. At the local level, the reverse is true. State and local revenues, based heavily on sales and property taxes, do not keep pace with economic growth, while expenditures at the local level tend to exceed such growth. The result is a "fiscal mismatch," with potential federal surpluses and local deficits.

The details of this revenue-sharing program were developed after close consultation with Members of the Congress, governors, mayors and county officials. It represents a successful effort to combine the desirable features of simplicity and equity with a need to channel funds where they are most urgently needed and efficiently employable.

The program can best be described by reviewing its four major elements.

First, the size of the total fund to be shared will be a stated percentage of personal taxable income—the base on which fed-

eral individual income taxes are levied. For the second half of fiscal year 1971, this will be one-third of one percent of personal taxable income; for subsequent fiscal years this percentage will rise to a regular, constant figure. In order to provide for the assured flow of federal funds, a permanent appropriation will be authorized and established for the Treasury Department, from which will be automatically disbursed each year an amount corresponding to the stipulated percentage.

Second, the allocation of the total annual fund among the 50 states and the District of Columbia will be made on the basis of each state's share of national population, adjusted for the state's revenue effort.

The revenue effort adjustment is designed to provide the states with some incentive to maintain (and even expand) their efforts to use their own tax resources to meet their needs. A simple adjustment along these lines would provide a state whose revenue effort is above the national average with a bonus above its basic per capita portion of revenue sharing.

Third, the allocation of a state's share among its general units of local government will be established by prescribed formula. The total amount a state will share with all its general political subdivisions is based on the relative roles of state and local financing in each state. The amount which an individual unit of general local government will receive is based on its share of total local government revenue raised in the state.

Several points should be noted about these provisions for distribution of a state's portion of revenue sharing.

• The distribution will be made by the state.

• The provisions make allowance for state-by-state variations and would tend to be neutral with respect to the current relative fiscal importance of state and local governments in each state.

• In order to provide local flexibility, each state is authorized to develop an alternative distribution plan, working with its local governments.

Fourth, administrative requirements are kept at a minimum. Each state will meet simple reporting and accounting requirements.

While it is not possible to specify for what functions these federally shared funds will provide—the purpose of this program being to leave such allocation decisions up to the recipient units of government—an analysis of existing state and local budgets can provide substantial clues. Thus, one can reasonably expect that education, which consistently takes over two-fifths of all state and local general revenues, will be the major beneficiary of these new funds. Another possible area for employment of shared funds, one most consistent with the spirit of this program, would be for intergovernmental cooperation efforts.

This proposal marks a turning point in federal-state relations, the beginning of decentralization of governmental power, the restoration of a rightful balance between the state capitals and the national capital.

Our ultimate purposes are many: To restore to the states their proper rights and roles in the federal system with a new emphasis on and help for local responsiveness; to provide both the encouragement and the necessary resources for local and state officials to exercise leadership in solving their own problems; to narrow the distance between people and the government agencies dealing with their problems; to restore strength and vigor to local and state governments; to shift the balance of political power away from Washington and back to the country and the people.

This tax-sharing proposal was pledged in the campaign; it has long been a part of the platform of many men in my own political party—and men in the other party as well. It is integrally related to the national welfare reform. Through these twin approaches we hope to relieve the fiscal crisis of the hard-pressed state and local governments and to assist millions of Americans out of poverty and into productivity.

RICHARD NIXON

TEXT OF PRESIDENT'S WELFARE-'WORKFARE' SPEECH

Following is the complete text of President Nixon's Aug. 8 speech on public welfare and other reforms.

As you know, I returned last Sunday night from a trip around the world—a trip that took me to eight countries in nine days.

The purpose of this trip was to help lay the basis for a lasting peace, once the war in Vietnam is ended. In the course of it, I also saw once again the vigorous efforts so many new nations are making to leap the centuries into the modern world.

Here in the United States, we are more fortunate. We have the world's most advanced industrial economy, the greatest wealth ever known to man and the fullest measure of freedom ever enjoyed by any people anywhere.

Yet we, too, have an urgent need to modernize our institutions—and our need is no less than theirs.

We face an urban crisis, a social crisis—and at the same time, a crisis of confidence in the capacity of government to do its job.

A third of a century of centralizing power and responsibility in Washington has produced a bureaucratic monstrosity, cumbersome, unresponsive and ineffective.

A third of a century of social experiment has left us a legacy of entrenched programs that have outlived their time or outgrown their purposes.

A third of a century of unprecedented growth and change has strained our institutions and raised serious questions about whether they are still adequate to the times.

It is no accident, therefore, that we find increasing skepticism—and not only among the young, but among citizens everywhere—about the continuing capacity of government to master the challenges we face.

Nowhere has the failure of government been more tragically apparent than in its efforts to help the poor, and especially in its system of public welfare.

Target: Reform

Since taking office, one of my first priorities has been to repair the machinery of government and put it in shape for the 1970s. I have made many changes designed to improve the functioning of the Executive Branch. I have asked Congress for a number of important structural reforms: among others, a wideranging postal reform, a comprehensive draft reform, a reform of the unemployment insurance and antihunger programs and reform of the present confusing hodge-podge of federal grants-in-aid. Last April 21 I sent Congress a message asking for a package of major tax reforms, including both the closing of loopholes and the removal of more than 2 million low-income tax-paying families from the tax rolls entirely. I am glad Congress is acting now on tax reform; I hope it acts soon on the other reforms as well.

The purpose of all these reforms is to eliminate unfairness; to make government more effective as well as more efficient; and to bring an end to its chronic failure to deliver the service that it promises.

My purpose tonight, however, is not to review the past record, but to present a new set of reforms—a new set of proposals—a new and drastically different approach to the way in which government cares for those in need, and to the way the responsibilities are shared between the state and federal governments.

I have chosen to do so in a direct report to the people because these proposals call for public decisions of the first importance; because they represent a fundamental change in the nation's approach to one of its most pressing social problems; and because, quite deliberately, they also represent the first major reversal of the trend toward ever more centralization of government in Washington. After a third of a century of power flowing from the people and the states to Washington, it is time for a New Federalism in which power, funds and responsibility will flow from Washington to the states and to the people.

During last year's election campaign, I often made a point that touched a responsive chord wherever I traveled.

I said that this nation became great, not because of what government did for people, but because of what people did for themselves.

It aims at getting everyone able to work off welfare rolls and onto payrolls.

It aims at ending the unfairness in a system that has become unfair to the welfare recipient, unfair to the working poor and unfair to the taxpayer.

This new approach aims to make it possible for people—wherever in America they live—to receive their fair share of opportunity. It aims to ensure that people receiving aid, and who are able to work, contribute their fair share of productivity.

This new approach is embodied in a package of four measures: first, a complete replacement of the present welfare system; second, a comprehensive new job training and placement program; third, a revamping of the Office of Economic Opportunity; and fourth, a start on the sharing of the federal tax revenues with the states.

Next week—in three messages to the Congress and one statement—I will spell out in detail what these measures contain. Tonight I want to explain what they mean, what they are intended to achieve and how they are related.

Welfare

Whether measured by the anguish of the poor themselves or by the drastically mounting burden on the taxpayer, the present welfare system has to be judged a colossal failure.

Our states and cities find themselves sinking in a welfare quagmire as caseloads increase, as costs escalate and as the welfare system stagnates enterprise and perpetuates dependency. What began on a small scale in the depression 30s has become a monster in the prosperous 60s. The tragedy is not only that it is bringing states and cities to the brink of financial disaster, but also that it is failing to meet the elementary human, social and financial needs of the poor.

It breaks up homes. It often penalizes work. It robs recipients of dignity. And it grows.

Benefit levels are grossly unequal—for a mother with three children, they range from an average of $263 a month in one state down to an average of $39 in another state. So great an inequality is wrong; no child is "worth" more in one state than in another. One result of this inequality is to lure thousands more into already overcrowded inner cities, as unprepared for city life as they are for city jobs.

The present system creates an incentive for desertion. In most states, a family is denied welfare payments if a father is present—even though he is unable to support his family. In practice, this is what often happens: a father is unable to find a job at all, or one that will support his children. To make the children eligible for welfare, he leaves home—and the children are denied the authority, the discipline and the love that come with having a father in the house. This is wrong.

The present system often makes it possible to receive more money on welfare than on a low-paying job. This creates an incentive not to work; it also is unfair to the working poor. It is morally wrong for a family that is working to try to make ends meet to receive less than the family across the street on welfare. This has been bitterly resented by the man who works, and rightly so—the rewards are just the opposite of what they should be. Its effect is to draw people off payrolls and onto welfare rolls—just the opposite of what government should be doing. To put it bluntly and simply—any system which makes it more profitable for a man not to work than to work, and which encourages a man to desert his family rather than stay with his family, is wrong and indefensible.

We cannot simply ignore the failures of welfare or expect them to go away. In the past eight years, 3 million more people have been added to the welfare rolls—all in a period of low unemployment. If the present trend continues, another 4 million will have joined the welfare rolls by 1975. The financial cost will be crushing; the human cost will be suffocating.

I propose that we abolish the present welfare system and adopt in its place a new family assistance system. Initially, this new system would cost more than welfare. But unlike welfare, it is designed to correct the condition it deals with and thus to lessen the long-range burden.

Under this plan, the so-called "adult categories" of aid—aid to the aged, the blind and disabled—would be continued and a national minimum standard for benefits would be set, with the Federal Government contributing to its cost and also sharing the cost of additional state payments above that amount.

But the program now called "Aid to Families with Dependent Children"—the program we normally think of when we think of "welfare"—would be done away with completely. The new family assistance system I propose in its place rests essentially on three principles: equality of treatment, a work requirement and a work incentive.

Its benefits would go to the working poor as well as the nonworking; to families with dependent children headed by a father as well as to those headed by a mother; and a basic federal minimum would be provided, the same in every state.

I propose that the Federal Government build a foundation under the income of every American family with dependent children that cannot care for itself—wherever in America that family may live.

For a family of four now on welfare, with no outside income, the basic federal payment would be $1,600 a year. States could add to that amount, and most would do so. In no case would anyone's present level of benefits be lowered. At the same time, this foundation would be one on which the family itself could build. Outside earnings would be encouraged, not discouraged. The new worker could keep the first $60 a month of outside earnings with no reduction in his benefits, and beyond that his benefits would be reduced by only 50 cents for each dollar earned.

By the same token, a family head already employed at low wages could get a family assistance supplement; those who work would no longer be discriminated against. A family of five in which the father earns $2,000 a year—which is the hard fact of life for many families—would get family assistance payments of $1,260 for a total income of $3,260. A family of seven earning $3,000 a year would have its income raised to $4,360.

Thus, for the first time, the government would recognize that it has no less of an obligation to the working poor than to the nonworking poor; and for the first time, benefits would be scaled in such a way that it would always pay to work.

With such incentives, most recipients who can work will want to work. This is part of the American character.

But what of the others—those who can work but choose not to? The answer is very simple.

Under this proposal, everyone who accepts benefits must also accept work or training provided suitable jobs are available, either locally or at some distance if transportation is provided. The only exceptions would be those unable to work and mothers of preschool children. Even mothers of preschool children, however, would have the opportunity to work—because I am also proposing along with this a major expansion of day-care centers to make it possible for mothers to take jobs by which they can support themselves and their children.

This national floor under incomes for working or dependent families is not a "guaranteed income." Under the guaranteed income proposal, everyone would be assured a minimum income, regardless of how much he was capable of earning, regardless of what his need was, regardless of whether or not he was willing to work.

During the Presidential campaign last year I opposed such a plan. I oppose it now and will continue to oppose it. A guaran-

teed income would undermine the incentive to work; the family assistance plan increases the incentive to work. A guaranteed income establishes a right without responsibilities; family assistance recognizes a need and establishes a responsibility. It provides help to those in need and in turn requires that those who receive help work to the extent of their capabilities. There is no reason why one person should be taxed so that another can choose to live idly.

In states that now have benefit levels above the federal floor, family assistance would help ease the states' financial burdens. But in 20 states—those in which poverty is most widespread—the new federal floor would be above present average benefit levels and would mean a leap upward for many thousands of families that cannot care for themselves.

Manpower Training

Next, let me turn to the job training proposals that are part of our full opportunity concept. America prides itself on being the "land of opportunity." I deeply believe in this ideal.

Full opportunity means the chance for upward mobility on every rung of the economic ladder—and for every American, no matter what his handicaps of birth.

The cold, hard truth is that a child born to a poor family has far less chance to make a good living than a child born to a middle-income family.

He is born poor, fed poorly; and if his family is on welfare, he starts life in an atmosphere of handout and dependency; often he receives little preparation for work and less inspiration. The wonder of the American character is that so many have the spark and drive to fight their way up. But for millions of others, the burden of poverty in early life stifles that spark.

The new family assistance would provide aid for needy families; it would establish a work requirement and a work incentive; but these in turn require effective programs of job training and job placement—including a chance to qualify, not just for any jobs, but for good jobs that provide both additional self-respect and full self-support.

Therefore, I am also sending a message to Congress calling for a complete overhaul of the nation's manpower training services.

The Federal Government's job training programs have been a terrible tangle of confusion and waste. They are overcentralized, over-categorized; with good reason, many young people wonder why the Federal Government cannot take money out of one program that has too few applicants and use it instead to expand another that has too many. They wonder why they have to accept training programs they have no interest in instead of ones they care about. They want to be treated as human beings, not cogs in a machine.

To remedy the confusion, arbitrariness and rigidity of the present system, the new Manpower Training Act would basically do three things:

• It would pull together the jumble of programs that currently exist and equalize standards of eligibility.

• It would provide flexible funding—so that federal money would follow the demands of labor and industry and flow into those programs that people most want and need.

• It would decentralize administration, gradually moving it away from the Washington bureaucracy and turning it over to states and localities.

In terms of its symbolic importance, I can hardly overemphasize this last point. For the first time, applying the principles of the New Federalism, administration of a major established federal program would be turned over to the states and local governments, recognizing that they are in a position to do the job better.

For years, thoughtful Americans have talked of the need to decentralize government. The time has come to begin.

Federal job training programs have grown to vast proportions, costing more than a billion dollars a year. Yet they are essentially local in character. As long as the Federal Government continues to bear the cost, they can perfectly well be run by states and localities—and that way they can better be adapted to specific state and local needs.

What I propose is not a sudden dumping of these programs on unprepared local authorities, but rather a careful, phased transfer, with benchmarks of readiness and incentives for performance. If states and localities decline to pick up the responsibility, the Federal Government will continue to manage the programs. If they try and fail, the Federal Government can resume the responsibility. We should trust the American capacity for self-government enough to try. The only way to bring about decentralization is to do it, and this is the place to begin.

The Manpower Training Act will have other provisions specifically designed to help move people off welfare rolls and onto payrolls.

• A computerized job bank would be established, to match jobseekers with job vacancies.

• For those on welfare, a $30-a-month bonus would be offered as an incentive to go into job training.

• For heads of families now on welfare, 150,000 new training slots would be opened.

• As I mentioned previously, greatly expanded day-care center facilities would be provided for the children of welfare mothers who choose to work. However, these would be day-care centers with a difference. There is no single ideal to which this Administration is more firmly committed than to the enriching of a child's first five years of life, and thus helping lift the poor out of misery at a time when a lift can help the most. Therefore, these day-care centers would offer more than custodial care; they would also be devoted to the development of vigorous young minds and bodies. As a further dividend, the day-care centers would offer employment to many welfare mothers themselves.

Office Of Economic Opportunity

One common theme running through my proposals tonight is that of providing full opportunity for every American. A second theme is that of trying to equip every American to play a productive role. A third is the need to make government itself workable—which means reshaping, reforming, innovating.

The Office of Economic Opportunity is an innovative agency—and thus it has a vital place in our efforts to develop new programs and apply new knowledge. But in order to do effectively what it can do best, OEO itself needs reorganization.

In the past, OEO suffered from a confusion of roles and from a massive attempt to do everything at once, with the same people performing many conflicting functions: coordinating old programs, doing new research, setting up demonstration projects, evaluating results and serving as advocates for the poor. As a result, inefficiency, waste and resentment too often clouded the record of even its best accomplishments.

This Administration has made a thorough study of OEO. We have assigned it a leading role in the effort to develop and test new approaches to the solving of social problems. OEO is to be a laboratory agency, where new ideas for helping people are tried on a pilot basis. When these prove successful, they can be "spun off" to operating departments or agencies—just as the agency, for example, "spun off" the weather satellite and the communications satellite when these proved successful. Then OEO will be free to concentrate on breaking even newer ground.

OEO has a broad charter: not only to help make opportunity real but to search out ways of making institutions more responsive and to get behind the effects of poverty to the causes of poverty. These goals are fundamental commitments of this Administration.

The OEO reorganization to be announced next week will stress its innovative role. It also will stress accountability, a clear separation of functions and a tighter, more effective organization of field operations.

Revenue Sharing

We come now to a proposal which I consider profoundly important to the future of our federal system of shared responsibilities. As we look ahead to the 1970s and the 1980s, it also is vital in terms of ensuring that states and localities can continue to do their part in dealing with the kinds of social problems I have been discussing tonight.

When we speak of poverty or jobs or opportunity, or making government more effective or getting it closer to the people, it brings us directly to the financial plight   our states and cities.

We can no longer have effective government on any level unless we have it on all levels. There is too much to be done for the cities to do it alone or for the states to do it alone—or for Washington to do it alone.

For a third of a century, power and responsibility have flowed toward Washington—and Washington has taken for its own the best sources of revenue.

We intend to reverse this tide, and to turn back to the states a greater measure of responsibility—not as a way of avoiding problems but as a better way of solving problems. Along with this should go a share of federal revenues. I shall propose to the Congress next week that a set portion of the revenues from federal income taxes be remitted directly to the states—with a minimum of federal restrictions on how those dollars are to be used and with a requirement that a percentage of them be channeled through for the use of local governments.

The funds provided under this program will not be great in the first year. But the principle will have been established, and the amounts will increase as our budgetary situation improves.

As we look ahead to the complex tasks of the 70s; as we contemplate the diversity of this vast and varied country, it is clear beyond question that effective, responsive government will require not one center of power, but many. This start on revenue sharing is a step toward the New Federalism. It is a gesture of faith in America's states and localities and in the principles of democratic self-government.

With this revenue-sharing proposal, we follow through on a commitment I made in the last campaign; we follow through on a mandate which the electorate gave us last November—after nearly 40 years of moving power from the states to Washington, we begin in America a decade of decentralization, a shifting of power away from the center whenever it can be used better locally.

In recent years, we all have concentrated a great deal of attention on what we commonly call the "crisis of the cities." These proposals I have made are addressed in part to that, but they also are focused much more broadly.

They are addressed to the crisis of government—to adapting its structures and making it manageable.

They are addressed to the crisis of poverty and need—which is rural as well as urban. This Administration is committed to full opportunity on the farm as well as in the city; to a better life for rural America; to ensuring that government is responsive to the needs of rural America. These proposals will advance those goals.

I have discussed these four matters together, because together they make both a package and a pattern. They should be studied together, debated together, seen in perspective.

These proposals will be controversial. They also are expensive. Let us face that fact frankly and directly.

The first-year costs of the new family assistance program, including the child-care centers and job training, would be $4 billion. I deliberated long and hard over whether we could afford such an outlay. I decided in favor of it for two reasons: because the costs would not begin until fiscal 1971, when I expect the funds to be available; and because I concluded that this is a reform we cannot afford not to undertake. The cost of continuing the present system, in financial as well as human terms, is staggering if projected into the 1970s.

Revenue sharing would begin in the middle of fiscal 1971, at a half-year cost of a half billion dollars. This cuts into the federal budget, but it represents relief for the equally hard-pressed states. It would help curb the rise in state and local taxes.

Over-all, we would be spending more—in the short run—to help people who now are poor and who now are unready for work or unable to find work.

I see it this way: Every businessman and every working man knows what "start-up costs" are. They are a heavy investment made in early years in the expectation that they will more than pay for themselves in future years.

The investment in these proposals is a human investment; it also is a "start-up cost" in turning around our dangerous decline into welfarism. We cannot produce productive people with the antiquated, wheezing, over-loaded machine we now call the welfare system.

If we fail to make this investment in work incentives now, if we merely try to patch up the system here and there, we will only be pouring good money after bad in ever-increasing amounts.

If we do invest in this modernization, the heavily burdened taxpayer at least will see the light at the end of the tunnel. And the man who now looks ahead only to a lifetime of dependency will see hope for a life of work and pride and dignity.

In the final analysis, we cannot talk our way out of poverty; we cannot legislate our way out of poverty; but this nation can work its way out of poverty. What America needs now is not more welfare but more "workfare."

The task of this government, the great task of our people, is to provide the training for work, the incentive to work, the opportunity to work and the reward for work. Together, these measures are a first long step in that direction.

For those in the welfare system today, or struggling to fight their way out of poverty, these measures offer a way to independence through the dignity of work.

For those able to work, these measures provide new opportunities to learn work and to find work.

For the working poor—the forgotten poor—these measures offer a fair share in the assistance given to the poor.

The new system establishes a direct link between the government's willingness to help the needy and the willingness of the needy to help themselves.

It removes the present incentive not to work and substitutes an incentive to work; it removes the present incentive for families to break apart and substitutes an incentive for families to stay together.

It removes blatant inequities, injustices and indignities of the welfare system.

It establishes a basic federal floor so that children in any state can have at least the minimum essentials of life.

Together, these measures cushion the impact of welfare costs on states and localities, many of which have found themselves in fiscal crisis as costs have spiraled.

They bring reason, order and purpose into a tangle of overlapping programs and show that government can be made to work.

Poverty will not be defeated by a stroke of a pen signing a check; it will not be reduced to nothing overnight with slogans or ringing exhortations.

Poverty is not only a state of income. It is also a state of mind and a state of health. Poverty must be conquered without sacrificing the will to work, for if we take the route of the permanent handout, the American character will itself be impoverished.

In my recent trip around the world, I visited countries in all stages of economic development; countries with different social systems, different economic systems, different political systems.

In all of them, however, I found that one event had caught their imagination and lifted their spirits almost beyond measure: The trip of Apollo to the moon and back. On that historic day when the astronauts set foot on the moon, the spirit of Apollo 11 truly swept the world—a spirit of peace and brotherhood and adventure and a spirit that thrilled to the knowledge that man had dreamed the impossible, dared the impossible and done the impossible.

Abolishing poverty, putting an end to dependency—like reaching for the moon a generation ago, that may be impossible. But in the spirit of Apollo, we can lift our sights and marshal our best efforts. We can resolve to make this the year, not that we reached the goal, but that we turned the corner: From a dismal cycle of dependency toward a new birth of independence; from despair toward hope; from an ominously mounting impotence of government toward a new effectiveness of government—and toward a full opportunity for every American to share the bounty of this rich land.

TRANSPORTATION TEXT

Following is the complete text of President Nixon's Aug. 7 message to Congress about transportation development.

TO THE CONGRESS OF THE UNITED STATES:

Public transportation has suffered from years of neglect in America. In the last 30 years urban transportation systems have experienced a cycle of increasing costs, decreasing funds for replacements, cutbacks in service and decrease in passengers.

Transit fares have almost tripled since 1945; the number of passengers has decreased to one-third the level of that year. Transit industry profits before taxes have declined from $313 million in 1945 to $25 million in 1967. In recent years 235 bus and subway companies have gone out of business. The remaining transit companies have progressively deteriorated. Today they give their riders fewer runs, older cars and less service.

Local governments, faced with demands for many pressing public services and with an inadequate financial base, have been unable to provide sufficient assistance.

This is not a problem peculiar to our largest cities alone. Indeed, many of our small and medium-sized communities have seen their bus transportation systems simply close down.

When the nation realized the importance and need for improved highways in the last decade, the Congress responded with the Highway Act of 1956. The result has been a magnificent federally aided highway system. But highways are only one element in a national transportation policy. About a quarter of our population lack access to a car. For these people—especially the poor, the aged, the very young and the handicapped—adequate public transportation is the only answer.

Moreover, until we make public transportation an attractive alternative to private car use, we will never be able to build highways fast enough to avoid congestion. As we survey the increasing congestion of our roads and strangulation of our central cities today, we can imagine what our plight will be when our urban population adds 100 million people by the year 2000.

We cannot meet future needs by concentrating development on just one means of transportation. We must have a truly balanced system. Only when automobile transportation is complemented by adequate public transportation can we meet those needs.

The Public Transportation Program. I propose that we provide $10 billion out of the general fund over a 12-year period to help in developing and improving public transportation in local communities. To establish this program, I am requesting contract authorization totaling $3.1 billion for the first five years starting with a first year authorization of $300 million and rising to $1 billion annually by 1975. Furthermore, I am asking for a renewal of this contract authorization every two years so that the outstanding contract authorization will never be for a shorter period than three years. Over the 12-year period, $9.5 billion is programmed for capital investments and $500 million for research and development.

The program which I am recommending would help to replace, improve and expand local bus, rail and subway systems.

It would help to develop and modernize subway tracks, stations and terminals; it would help to build and improve rail train tracks and stations, new bus terminals and garages.

The program would authorize assistance to private as well as public transit systems so that private enterprise can continue to provide public services in urban transportation. It would give state governments an opportunity to comment on project applications in order to improve intergovernmental coordination. It would require local public hearings before any major capital construction is undertaken. And it would permit localities to acquire rights-of-way in advance of system construction in order to reduce future dislocation and costs.

Fares alone cannot ordinarily finance the full cost of public transit systems, including the necessary capital investments. Higher fares usually result in fewer riders, taking much of the "mass" out of mass transit and defeating the social and economic purpose of the system.

One problem with most transit systems operating today is that they rely for revenues on people who must use them and make no appeal to those who have a choice of using them or not. Thus we have the self-defeating cycle of fewer riders, higher fares, lower revenues, worse facilities and still fewer riders.

The way to break that cycle is to make public transit truly attractive and convenient. In this way, more riders will provide more revenues, and fares can be kept down while further efficiencies can be introduced.

In addition to assistance for capital improvements, I am proposing substantial research and technology efforts into new ways of making public transit an attractive choice for owners of private cars. These would include:

• Advanced bus and train design to permit easier boarding and dismounting.

• Improved interiors in bus and trains for increased convenience and security for riders.

• New traffic control systems to expedite the flow of buses over streets and highways.

• Tracked air-cushioned vehicles and automated transit.

• Flexible bus service based on computer-forecast demands.

• New bus propulsion systems which would reduce noise and air pollution as well as cost.

• Systems such as moving sidewalks and capsules to transport people for short distances within terminals, and other major activity.

In summary, this public transportation program I am recommending would give state and local governments the assurance of federal commitment necessary both to carry out long-range planning and to raise their share of the costs. It would meet the challenge of providing resources that are adequate in amount, and it would assure adequate duration of their availability.

The bus rider, train commuter and subway user would have better service. The car driver would travel on less congested roads. The poor would be better able to get to work, to reach new job opportunities and to use training and rehabilitation centers. The centers of big cities would avoid strangulation and the suburbs would have better access to urban jobs and shops.

Most important, we as a nation would benefit. The nation which has sent men to the moon would demonstrate that it can meet the transportation needs of the city as well.

RICHARD NIXON

TEXT ON OEO REORGANIZATION

Following is the complete text of President Nixon's Aug. 11 statement on the reorganization of the Office of Economic Opportunity.

We live in an exciting and difficult time. We possess great strength and skill; yet we are often unable to harness our strength in the service of our ideals. We sense new possibilities for unlocking the full potential of every individual; yet our institutions too often are unresponsive to our needs. We dream of what we might be able to make of our society; but we have not yet learned to achieve that dream.

Our nation will attain its social objectives, I believe, only if we develop a new spirit of adventure in their pursuit. We must become pioneers in reshaping our society even as we have become pioneers in space. We must show a new willingness to take risks for progress, a new readiness to try the untried.

Such an innovative spirit should characterize all of our institutions and all agencies of government. But it is in the Office of Economic Opportunity that social pioneering should be a specialty. It is the OEO that should act as the "R and D" arm for government's social programs.

When I sent a message to the Congress on OEO last February, I offered several preliminary comments about the agency. Since that time, the new director of the office has made a thorough review of its operations. On the basis of our discussions, I have reached a number of further conclusions about the direction of OEO and the way it does its work.

The following are among the specific changes in OEO which I am announcing today:

• Creation of a new Office of Program Development.

• Revamping and strengthening the Office of Planning, Research and Evaluation.

• Strengthening and upgrading the Office of Health Services and the Office of Legal Services.

• Creation of a new Office of Program Operations to improve the administration of activities in the field.

These and other specific changes, in turn, are based on a number of general principles which will help set new directions for OEO.

Setting New Directions

It has been said frequently in the past few weeks that if our country can marshal resources so effectively that we can travel to the moon, then we should also use our power and knowledge to better advantage in solving social problems on our own planet. I share this view. But if we are to make a better response to social challenges, then we will have to act with the same clear commitment to well-defined goals, the same freedom to undertake bold experiments, the same managerial discipline and the same spirit of teamwork that has characterized our accomplishments in space.

This Administration believes that every American should have the opportunity to participate in our nation's economic life to the full extent of his abilities. The Office of Economic Opportunity will make this objective its highest priority. It will address itself to unanswered and difficult questions: What determines an individual's capacity for growth and achievement? What can be done to awaken this capacity and develop it? How can we be sure that these capacities, when they are available, will be fully used and properly rewarded?

It is important that OEO concentrate its energies on causes rather than symptoms, that it help people become productive participants in the economy rather than focusing on the conduct of income support or other ameliorative activities. These latter functions should belong instead to efforts such as the new family assistance program, a revised unemployment compensation system, improved plans for food distribution and various benefit payment programs.

We see today a healthy determination on the part of our people to continuously examine and update national priorities so that the energy and resources of our country can be properly allocated to solve domestic problems. But our people have also learned that the challenge of bringing unproductive people into active economic roles is more difficult than many had thought. We know now that the amount of money we spend in this effort will mean little unless the approach is right. The Office of Economic Opportunity will help us develop needed new approaches to this problem. It will translate our general commitment to provide full opportunity to all Americans into specific programs which will help us use our resources to the greatest effect.

The freedom to try out a wide variety of ideas, to test them fully both in theory and in practice, to move boldly on several fronts, to thoroughly master and carefully apply the results of this experimental process—these are capacities which are as instrumental to social progress as they are to advances in science.

Since OEO is to be the cutting edge by means of which government moves into unexplored areas, the experimental temper will be vital to its success. The agency should marshal the most creative minds in the country, both to ask new questions and find new answers. It should be free to take creative risks. It should set up a variety of demonstration projects, carefully test their effectiveness and systematically assess the results.

Just as NASA developed weather satellites and communication satellites and then spun them off, transferring them to the Department of Commerce and to COMSAT, so OEO should concentrate on the experimental stage of domestic programs. When a program has proven successful in the domestic area, it too may be transferred to other agencies or other levels of the government or even to the private sector if that seems desirable. This approach will leave OEO free to break still newer ground.

Too often the lines of responsibility in OEO programs have been badly blurred; too often there has been no method for determining whether a program has succeeded or failed and what is responsible for failure and success. Too often the same individuals or groups, at both the national and local level, have found themselves wearing many hats: coordinating old programs, doing new research, setting up demonstration projects, evaluating results and serving as advocates before the government on behalf of the poor. Precisely because each of these functions is important, each should be assigned to specific offices wherever that is possible, and they, in turn, should be held strictly accountable for the way in which their work is performed.

Finally, our social programs will require a greater sense of common endeavor among our people. Close cooperation between the private sector and government, for example, can be a key in assisting the economically disadvantaged as it has been a key to success in space. Moreover, we should be certain that the fears or suspicions which sometimes separate races or economic groups are diminished by our activities and not accentuated. We must avoid words and actions which drive people apart and emphasize instead the common stake of all Americans in extending economic opportunity.

These are some of the new directions which will define the scope of OEO and give new focus to its work. The specific organizational reforms we are making in the agency will help us move in these new directions; they will make OEO a stronger and more flexible instrument in the struggle for human dignity.

Specific Reforms

1. Office of Program Development. This new unit will be responsible for most of the experimental efforts which OEO will now emphasize and will include within it both totally new programs and some existing activities which previously were distributed throughout the agency. The Office of Program Development will seek new ways of bringing services to the poor, helping them to increase their skills, educate their children, improve their homes, protect their health and develop their communities. It will try to find new methods of increasing their business and employment opportunities.

2. Office of Planning, Research and Evaluation. The Office of Planning, Research and Evaluation will be reorganized and strengthened. Reporting straight to the director, it will have responsibility for reviewing existing social programs, for comparing the results of projects with the objectives which have been set for them, for commenting on the adequacy with which both programs and objectives are formulated and for recommending alterations in existing programs as well as new experiments. It will seek to establish more precise standards for measuring performance than OEO has used in the past. The Office of Planning, Research and Evaluation will provide a regular source for that independent ap-

praisal of federal social programs which often is not available at present.

3. Office of Health Services. A strengthened Office of Health Services will also report directly to the Director of OEO. Many of the problems of the poor are the product of ill health and many have serious medical consequences. We have already begun to develop new mechanisms for helping the poor pay medical costs. But now we must further improve our methods for delivering health services so that all the poor will have ready access to doctors, diagnosis, treatment and hospital care. The Neighborhood Health Center Program is one experimental effort which is working in this direction; OEO will initiate other activities in this area. The 1970 budget will also show increases in food and nutrition programs, family planning services and other health-related activities.

4. Office of Legal Services. The Office of Legal Services will also be strengthened and elevated so that it reports directly to the director. It will take on central responsibility for programs which help provide advocates for the poor in their dealings with social institutions. The sluggishness of many institutions—at all levels of society—in responding to the needs of individual citizens is one of the central problems of our time. Disadvantaged persons in particular must be assisted so that they fully understand the lawful means of making their needs known and having those needs met. This goal will be better served by a separate Legal Services Program, one which can test new approaches to this important challenge.

5. Office of Program Operations. More attention must be given to the way in which OEO policies are carried out at the local, state and regional level. A new Office of Program Operations will work to improve the quality of field operations; it will be able to define more clearly the purposes for which grants and contracts are given and to apply higher standards of effective management. Training and technical assistance funds for those who run OEO-supported programs will be increased. We also plan to raise allocations to state Economic Opportunity offices.

It is particularly important that the management of community action agencies be improved. The goals of community action are desirable ones and the work of these agencies deserves our support. Unfortunately, many of these local agencies have suffered from a proliferation of duties and from a confusion of roles. While some progress has been made in correcting these problems, the activities of community action agencies must be further clarified and such agencies must more clearly assign priorities among their various functions.

One of the important strengths of the community action program has been its ability to involve local citizens in planning and carrying out its projects. This value should not be lost. Community organizations, close to the people, can play an important role in delivering government programs on a local and individual level.

Other Programs

Following the belief that the Office of Economic Opportunity should be an innovative agency, this Administration has already moved the Job Corps to the Department of Labor and the Head Start Program to the Department of Health, Education and Welfare. In addition, I am suggesting in my Manpower Training proposals that several OEO-funded manpower programs which have been administered by the Department of Labor be transferred to that Department. These are ongoing programs which have passed the trial stage and should now be seen as parts of our established manpower strategy.

Some proven programs which are national in scope should, however, remain in OEO because they can help us develop new experiments and because of the agency's special identification with the problems of the poor. The VISTA program is one example; it will make a greater effort to attract people with specific technical and professional skills to its ranks.

Mankind is presently entering a new era of exploration and fulfillment. We are able to move beyond the limits which once confined us, both in our travels beyond this planet and in our efforts to shape our life upon it. Now we must use this ability to explore on earth, as we have explored in space, with intelligence and courage, recognizing always how little we really know and how far we still must go.

I believe that the goal of full economic opportunity for every American can be realized. I expect the Office of Economic Opportunity to play a central role in that achievement. With new organizational structures, new operating procedures and a new sense of precision and direction, OEO can be one of the most creative and productive offices in the Government. For here much of our social pioneering will be done. Here will begin many of our new adventures.

SOCIAL SECURITY MESSAGE TEXT

Following is the complete text of President Nixon's Sept. 25 message to Congress on Social Security.

TO THE CONGRESS OF THE UNITED STATES:

This nation must not break faith with those Americans who have a right to expect that Social Security payments will protect them and their families.

The impact of an inflation now in its fourth year has undermined the value of every Social Security check and requires that we once again increase the benefits to help those among the most severely victimized by the rising cost of living.

I request that the Congress remedy the real losses to those who now receive Social Security benefits by increasing payments by 10 per cent.

Beyond that step to set right today's inequity, I propose that the Congress make certain once and for all that the retired, the disabled and the dependent never again bear the brunt of inflation. The way to prevent future unfairness is to attach the benefit schedule to the cost of living.

This will instill new security in Social Security. This will provide peace of mind to those concerned with their retirement years, and to their dependents.

By acting to raise benefits now to meet the rise in the cost of living, we keep faith with today's recipients. By acting to make future benefit raises automatic with rises in the cost of living, we remove questions about future years; we do much to remove this system from biennial politics; and we make fair treatment of beneficiaries a matter of certainty rather than a matter of hope.

In the 34 years since the Social Security program was first established, it has become a central part of life for a growing number of Americans. Today approximately 25 million people are receiving cash payments from this source. Three-quarters of these are older Americans; the Social Security check generally represents the greater part of total income. Millions of younger people receive benefits under the disability or survivor provisions of Social Security.

Almost all Americans have a stake in the soundness of the Social Security system. Some 92 million workers are contributing to Social Security this year. About 80 per cent of Americans of working age are protected by disability insurance and 95 per cent of children and mothers have survivorship insurance protection. Because the Social Security program is an essential part of life for so many Americans, we must continually re-examine the program and be prepared to make improvements.

Aiding in this Administration's review and evaluation is the Advisory Council on Social Security which the Secretary of Health, Education and Welfare appointed in May. For example, I will look to this Council for recommendations in regard to working women; changing work patterns and the increased contributions of working women to the system may make present law unfair to them. The recommendations of this council and of other advisers, both within the Government and outside of it, will be important to our planning. As I indicated in my message to the Congress on April 14, improvement in the Social Security program is a major objective of this Administration.

There are certain changes in the Social Security program, however, for which the need is so clear that they should be made without awaiting the findings of the Advisory Council. The purpose of this message is to recommend such changes.

• I propose an across-the-board increase of 10% in Social Security benefits, effective with checks mailed in April 1970, to make up for increases in the cost of living.

• I propose that future benefits in the Social Security system be automatically adjusted to account for increases in the cost of living.

• I propose an increase from $1680 to $1800 in the amount beneficiaries can earn annually without reduction of their benefits, effective January 1, 1971.

• I propose to eliminate the one-dollar-for-one-dollar reduction in benefits for income earned in excess of $2880 a year and replace it by a one dollar reduction in benefits for every two dollars earned, which now applies at earnings levels between $1680 and $2880, also effective January 1, 1971.

• I propose to increase the contribution and benefit base from $7800 to $9000, beginning in 1972, to strengthen the system, to help keep future benefits to the individual related to the growth of his wages, and to meet part of the cost of the improved program. From then on, the base will automatically be adjusted to reflect wage increases.

• I propose a series of additional reforms to ensure more equitable treatment for widows, recipients above age 72, veterans, for persons disabled in childhood and for the dependent parents of disabled and retired workers.

I emphasize that the suggested changes are only first steps, and that further recommendations will come from our review process.

The Social Security system needs adjustment now so it will better serve people receiving benefits today, and those corrections are recommended in this message. The system is also in need of long-range reform, to make it better serve those who contribute now for benefits in future years, and that will be the subject of later recommendations.

The Benefit Increase. With the increase of 10 percent, the average family benefit for an aged couple, both receiving benefits, would rise from $170 to $188 a month. Further indication of the impact of a 10 per cent increase on monthly benefits can be seen in the following table:

	Present Minimum	New Minimum	Present Maximum	New Maximum
Single Person (A man retiring at age 65 in 1970)	$55.00	$61.00	$165.00	$181.50
Married Couple (Husband retiring at age 65 in 1970)	$82.50	$91.50	$247.50	$272.30

The proposed benefit increases will raise the income of more than 25 million persons who will be on the Social Security rolls in April 1970. Total budget outlays for the first full calendar year in which the increase is effective will be approximately $3 billion.

Automatic Adjustments. Benefits will be adjusted automatically to reflect increases in the cost of living. The uncertainty of adjustment under present laws and the delay often encountered when the needs are already apparent is unnecessarily harsh to those who must depend on Social Security benefits to live.

Benefits that automatically increase with rising living costs can be funded without increasing Social Security tax rates so long as the amount of earnings subject to tax reflects the rising level of wages. Therefore, I propose that the wage base be automatically adjusted so that it corresponds to increases in earnings levels.

These automatic adjustments are interrelated and should be enacted as a package. Taken together they will depoliticize, to a certain extent, the Social Security system and give a greater stability to what has become a cornerstone of our society's social insurance system.

Reforming the System. I propose a series of reforms in present Social Security law to achieve new standards of fairness. These would provide:

• An increase in benefits to a widow who begins receiving her benefit at age 65 or later. The benefit would increase the current 82½% of her husband's benefit to a full 100%. This increased benefit to widows would fulfill a pledge I made a year ago. It would provide an average increase of $17 a month to almost three million widows.

• Non-contributory earnings credits of about $100 a month for military service from January 1957 to December 1967. During that period, individuals in military service were covered under Social Security but credit was not then given for "wages in kind"—room and board, etc. A law passed in 1967 corrected this for the future, but the men who served from 1957 (when coverage began for servicemen) to 1967 should not be overlooked.

• Benefits for the aged parents of retired and disabled workers. Under present law, benefits are payable only to the dependent parents of a worker who has died; we would extend this to parents of workers who are disabled or who retire.

• Child's insurance benefits for life if a child becomes permanently disabled before age 22. Under present law, a person must have become disabled before age 18 to qualify for these benefits. The proposal would be consistent with the payment of child's benefit to age 22 so long as the child is in school.

• Benefits in full paid to persons over 72, regardless of the amount of his earnings in the year he attains that age. Under present law, he is bound by often confusing tests which may limit his exemption.

• A fairer means of determining benefits payable on a man's earnings record. At present, men who retire at age 62 must compute their average earnings through three years of no earnings up to age 65, thus lowering the retirement benefit excessively. Under this proposal, only the years up to age 62 would be counted, just as is now done for women, and three higher-earning years could be substituted for low-earning years.

Changes in the Retirement Test. A feature of the present Social Security law that has drawn much criticism is the so-called "retirement test," a provision which limits the amount that a beneficiary can earn and still receive full benefits. I have been much concerned about this provision, particularly about its effects on incentives to work. The present retirement test actually penalizes Social Security beneficiaries for doing additional work or taking a job at higher pay. This is wrong.

In my view, many older people should be encouraged to work. Not only are they provided with added income, but the country retains the benefit of their skills and wisdom; they, in turn, have the feeling of usefulness and participation which employment can provide.

This is why I am recommending changes in the retirement test. Raising the amount of money a person can earn in a year without affecting his Social Security payments—from the present $1680 to $1800—is an important first step. But under the approach used in the present retirement test, people who earned more than the exempt amount of $1680, plus $1200, would continue to have $1 in Social Security benefits withheld for every $1 they received in earnings. A necessary second step is to eliminate from present law the requirement that when earnings reach $1200 above the exempt amount, Social Security benefits will be reduced by a full dollar for every dollar of added earnings until all his benefits are withheld; in effect, we impose a tax of more than 100% on these earnings.

To avoid this, I would eliminate this $1 reduction for each $1 earned and replace it with the same $1 reduction for each $2 earned above $3000. This change will reduce a disincentive to increased employment that arises under the retirement test in its present form.

The amount a retired person can earn and still receive his benefits should also increase automatically with the earnings level. It is sound policy to keep the exempt amount related to changes in the general level of earnings.

These alterations in the retirement test would result in added benefit payments of some $300 million in the first full calendar year. Approximately one million people would receive this money—some who are now receiving no benefits at all and some who now receive benefits but who would get more under this new arrangement. These suggestions are not by any means the solution to all the problems of the retirement test, however, and I am asking the Advisory Council on Social Security to give particular attention to this matter.

Contribution and Benefit Base. The contribution and benefit base—the annual earnings on which Social Security contributions are paid and that can be counted toward Social Security benefits—has been increased several times since the Social Security program began. The further increase I am recommending—from its present level of $7800 to $9000 beginning January 1, 1972—will produce approximately the same relationship between the base and general earnings levels as that of the early 1950s. This is important since the goal of Social Security is the replacement, in part, of lost earnings; if the base on which contributions and benefits are figured does not rise with earnings increases, then the benefits deteriorate. The future benefit increases that will result from the higher base I am recommending today would help to prevent such deterioration. These increases would, of course, be in addition to those which result from the 10% across-the-board increase in benefits that is intended to bring them into line with the cost of living.

Financing. I recommend an acceleration of the tax rate scheduled for hospital insurance to bring the hospital insurance trust fund into actuarial balance. I also propose to decelerate the rate schedule of the old-age, survivors and disability insurance trust funds in current law. These funds taken together have a long-range surplus of income over outgo, which will meet much of the cost. The combined rate, known as the "social security contribution," already scheduled by statute, will be decreased from 1971 through 1976. Thus, in 1971 the currently scheduled rate of 5.2% to be paid by employees would become 5.1%, and in 1973 the currently scheduled rate of 5.65% would become 5.1%. The actuarial integrity of the two funds will be maintained, and the ultimate tax rates will not be changed in the rate schedules which will be proposed.

The voluntary supplementary medical insurance (SMI) of title XVIII of the Social Security Act, often referred to as part B Medicare coverage, is not adequately financed with the current $4 premium. Our preliminary studies indicate that there will have to be a substantial increase in the premium. The Secretary of Health, Education and Welfare will set the premium rate in December for the fiscal year beginning July 1970, as he is required to do by statute.

To meet the rising costs of health care in the United States, this Administration will soon forward a Health Cost Control proposal to the Congress. Other administrative measures are already being taken to hold down spiraling medical expenses.

In the coming months, this Administration will give careful study to ways in which we can further improve the Social Security program. The program is an established and important American institution, a foundation on which millions are able to build a more comfortable life than would otherwise be possible—after their retirement or in the event of disability or death of the family earner.

The recommendations I propose today, which I urge the Congress to adopt, will move the cause of Social Security forward on a broad front.

We will bring benefit payments up to date.

We will make sure that benefit payments stay up to date, automatically tied to the cost of living.

We will begin making basic reforms in the system to remove inequities and bring a new standard of fairness in the treatment of all Americans in the system.

And we will lay the groundwork for further study and improvement of a system that has served the country well and must serve future generations more fairly and more responsively.

RICHARD NIXON

NIXON ASKS 'WORKING PARTNERSHIP' TO ENACT PROGRAM

Following is the complete text of President Nixon's Oct. 13 message to Congress calling for action on his legislative program.

TO THE CONGRESS OF THE UNITED STATES:

In the nine months since Inauguration, a number of issues have arisen clearly calling for the Congress and the Administration to work together.

One such issue was the extension of the surtax, where our economic security was involved. Another was authority to build the Safeguard ballistic missile defense, where the national safety was the issue. On both occasions, when the time came to be counted, Congress subordinated partisan concerns and voted the country's interest.

The continuance of this working partnership between a Congress heavily Democratic and a Republican Administration, on occasions where great issues are involved, is imperative for the good of our country. I hope this partnership will survive the "spirit of party" that grows more evident weekly in the national capital. Yet, in recent days, the call to partisan combat has grown more compelling.

I am aware that members of the Administration have criticized the Democratic-controlled Congress for "dragging its feet" in the enactment of legislation, for holding hearings thus far on only half the Administration proposals before it, for having enacted but a single appropriations bill for fiscal 1970, a full quarter of the way through the fiscal year. From Capitol Hill there have come similar charges—that the Administration has been laggard in proposing legislation, that the Executive Departments have been slow in giving the Congress the reports it has requested, that some of the most far-reaching Administration proposals have only lately been sent to the Congress, and so cannot be acted upon by the end of the year.

If a working partnership between men of differing philosophies and different parties is to continue, then candor on both sides is required. There may be merit in both charges; neither the Democratic Congress nor the Republican Administration is without fault for the delay of vital legislation.

But, in my view, the American people are not interested in political posturing between the Executive Branch and Capitol Hill. We are co-equal branches of government, elected not to maneuver for partisan advantage, but to work together to find hopeful answers to problems that confound the people all of us serve.

Both the President and Congress have been commissioned by the same American people, for a limited time, to achieve objectives upon which the great majority agree. For our part, we are willing to travel more than half-way to work with Congress to accomplish what needs to be done. The time for staking out political claims will come soon enough.

Let us resolve, therefore, to make the legislative issue of the 1970 campaign the question of who deserves greater credit for the 91st Congress' record of accomplishment, not which of us should be held accountable because it did nothing. The country is not interested in what we say, but in what we do—let us roll up our sleeves and go to work. Before us are urgent legislative priorities.

The legislative program of this Administration differs fundamentally from that of previous administrations. We do not seek more and more of the same. We were not elected to pile new resources and manpower on the top of old programs. We were elected to initiate an era of change. We intend to begin a decade of government reform such as this nation has not witnessed in half a century. Some months ago, a Washington columnist wrote in some pessimism that if ours is not to be an age of revolution then it must become an age of reform. That is the watchword of this Administration: Reform.

Reform Of The Draft. I have asked Congress to make the most extensive changes in the way we select young men for military service since the draft became an accepted feature of American life. We have the administrative power—and we will exercise it if Congress fails to act—to make far-reaching reforms in the selective service system, reducing the period of prime vulnerability for young Americans from seven years to 12 months. However, we need Congressional approval to shift from the inequitable requirement of choosing the "oldest first" to the more just method of random selection. I asked Congress five months ago for this power; I ask again today. Basic fairness to our young people is the prime reason for this recommendation. I see no reason why this vital piece of legislation cannot be enacted *now*.

Reform Of The Welfare System. Last summer I asked Congress to make the most sweeping changes in the American system of welfare since the beginning of the New Deal. Last week legislation went to Congress outlining the proposals I have made for a new family assistance system to replace the demeaning and bankrupt system that now exists.

Under the present system, sometimes a father must desert his wife and children to make them eligible for benefits. Under the present system, some mothers with three children must survive with only $39 a month for the entire family to live on.

The family assistance system is built on a different set of principles. It provides incentives for families to stay together. It provides economic rewards for men and women on welfare who enter training programs and search out jobs. It provides a floor under income that assures the minimum necessary for food and clothing and shelter.

The present system has led this country into a morass. It has laid a heavier and heavier burden on the American taxpayer. It has loaded the relief rolls with more and more families even in times of rising prosperity and low unemployment. I ask that Congress begin hearings on the new family assistance system at once. The welfare system should be abandoned as quickly as we can discard it and a new system established in its place.

Reform Of The Tax Code. In April I recommended to Congress the most comprehensive set of tax reforms in many years. Subsequently the House of Representatives responded with an even more far-reaching proposal of its own. The national momentum behind tax reform—to make the code more fair and equitable, to shift part of the burden from those who have borne too much for too long to the shoulders of others who have not carried their fair share—must not be allowed to dribble away while a partisan wrangle goes on over who deserves the political credit. We will give Congress as much assistance and as many hours of labor as it requires to enact extensive and responsible reform in this calendar year.

I do ask, however, that Congress, in acting on this major reform, not compromise this Administration's effort to combat the most unjust tax of all, inflation. Specifically, I ask that Congress not convert this historic tax reform legislation into a sharp tax reduction that would unbalance the Federal Budget and neutralize our campaign to halt the rising cost of living. I ask again that Congress repeal the seven percent investment tax credit, and extend for another six months the income tax surcharge at one-half the present rate. To fail to take these steps would be an abdication by Congress of its vital role in controlling inflation.

Revenue Reform. For the first time in the history of this government, we have recommended a national policy of permanent sharing of the federal income tax revenues with the states and lesser political units in the country. For years, political students and leaders have contended that governments at the state, county and local levels have lost their creativity and lost the capacity to respond because they lack access to the great source of growing revenues available to the Federal Government. I have recommended that Congress set aside a rising portion of federal revenues each year and transmit them directly back to the states and communities to spend as they see fit and not as Washington sees fit. This concept has been debated by both parties and recommended by their majorities for years. The time has come to move it off the plain of discussion to make it a reality. I urge the Congress to move.

Postal Reform. For more than a decade the American people have complained increasingly of the rising cost of postal service accompanied step by step with declining service. Today the United States postal system is inferior to that of many countries of Western Europe; it is grossly inadequate to the needs of our society. The nation has known this for years. I have acted in that knowledge—recommending that the existing postal system be scrapped, that a government-owned corporation replace the United States Post Office, that business principles replace partisanship in its management, and that merit of performance—rather than political affiliation—be the new criteria for appointment and advancement. Three years ago this month the Chicago postal system, a microcosm of the national system, collapsed under a flood of mail. The rapid delivery of mail is not a partisan issue. Distinguished leaders, of both parties, have endorsed the precise reform I have recommended. There is no reason why the Congress cannot enact the most complete reform of the United States Post Office in the nation's history—by the close of this session.

I am aware of the setback which postal reform sustained in a House Committee on October 8. That action must be reversed. I shall persist in behalf of both the taxpayers and the mail users in this country to press for this urgently needed reform. I still believe enactment should come by the end of this session of the 91st Congress.

Here I must again urge responsible Congressional action, and promptly, on the proposed increase in postal rates for all three classes of mail. When this Administration entered office in January, it confronted a deficit in the postal budget for fiscal year 1970 of more than $1.2 billion. We are already three months into that fiscal year—and this deficit is being underwritten by the taxpayers, rather than the users of the postal service, who should rightly bear the cost. I recognize that such a measure is hardly a political delight. Yet it is required in the interest of equity and fiscal integrity. I request the Congress to face up to this task.

Manpower Reform. The history of the 1960s chronicles an intense political debate that has resulted in the old centralism of the thirties losing converts to the new federalism of the seventies. More and more progressive men in both parties have become convinced from the failures of programs run from Washington that important areas of government decision-making must be returned to the regions and locales where the problems exist.

I have attempted to take that conclusion out of the forum of debate and into the arena of action—Congress. I have recommended that management of a federal program—the multi-billion dollar manpower training program—be consolidated, and turned over in a three-stage operation to the states and communities to run in a way that fits the needs of the immediate areas involved. No reform of this magnitude has been attempted since centralism became the dominant national trend at the depths of the depression. This recommendation represents the beginning of a revitalized federalism, the gradual transfer of greater power and responsibility for the making of government decisions to governments closest to the people. I urge swift Congressional action.

Social Security Reform. I have requested an across-the-board increase of ten percent in Social Security benefits to compensate elderly Americans for the losses they are suffering because of an inflation they could do nothing either to prevent or avoid. In addition, I have proposed a new reform, an escalator in Social Security to ensure that benefits will rise correspondingly whenever the cost of living goes up. When this reform is enacted, never again will those Americans least able to afford it be made to bear the brunt of inflation. These necessary steps can and should be taken by Congress before the end of this year.

One word of caution. I know the political temptations here. Why not balloon the benefits now, far above 10 percent, for political rewards in 1970? I remind the Congress that it is long since time that we stopped the political over-reactions which fuel the inflation that robs the poor, the elderly, and those on fixed incomes. I urge Congress to hold to this ten percent figure—and let the new escalator protect older Americans against the possibility of future inflation.

A second reform I have proposed is to alter the system of Social Security to encourage and reward the workers who want to go on working past age 65—rather than discourage them. I ask Congress to enact this measure without delay.

Reform Of The Grant-In-Aid System. Among the first major pieces of legislation I asked of Congress was authority to make uniform the requirements for participation in many grant-in-aid programs that have proliferated in the last five years. If we are granted the power to draw these programs together, to group them by function—setting far more simple regulations—then states and communities will participate more and Congress' original purposes will be better served. We need that authority *now*. I know of no reason for delay.

Electoral Reform. While I originally favored other methods of reforming the electoral college system, I have strongly endorsed the direct popular election plan approved by the House. I hope the Senate will concur so that final favorable action can be completed before the end of this session. This must be done if we are to have this needed reform amended to the Constitution in time for the Presidential election of 1972.

D.C. Government Reform. For years there has been broad support for granting the people of Washington, D.C. the same right to Congressional representation other Americans have always prized, and the right to conduct their public business themselves. The federal city has been a federal colony far too long. Months ago I presented to Congress a program to bring about the orderly transfer of political power to the people of this community. I recommended a constitutional amendment giving the District of Columbia at least one Representative in the House and such additional Representatives as Congress may approve, and providing for the possibility of two United States Senators. I urged Congress further to grant the city one non-voting Congressional representative in the interim, and recommended creation of a commission to prepare and present to Congress and the President a program to improve the efficiency and competence of the District Government—looking to the day of complete self-government. Favorable action has been taken by the Senate. I ask this work be completed before the end of the year.

OEO Reform. I have provided the Office of Economic Opportunity with a new director, a new structure, and added responsibilities as the research and development arm of the nation's effort to deal with the problems of the poor. OEO is now strengthening its present operating programs, including the Community Action Agencies, VISTA, Legal Services, Neighborhood Health Centers, Family Planning, Emergency Food, Rural, Older Persons, Indian and Migrant Programs. In addition, there is new emphasis on research, the evaluation of existing federal social programs, and developing and testing new approaches in community and economic development, manpower and education, to assist the poor to move into the economic life of the nation. I have asked for a two-year extension of the existing legislation, without crippling amendments. I believe that a reformed OEO has a major and continuing role to play in our national life. Here again, there is no need or justification for further delay.

In recent years the Federal Government has suffered a precipitous decline in public confidence. The reason can be found in the chronic gap that exists between the publicity and promise attendant to the launching of a new federal program—and that program's eventual performance. If confidence in government is to be restored, the gap must be closed.

This is the purpose of the foregoing proposals and great goal of this Administration—not to establish some new arithmetical record for the number of programs proposed, but to do more than other Administrations have done—to devise new approaches, to make the worthy old programs work, and to make old institutions responsive.

It is for this that we prize the mechanics and engineers of government who retool and improve its machinery as much as we do the planners and the idea men who develop new programs and new agencies. There is little publicity and less glamor in the labor of the mechanics and engineers of government but, with billions in tax dollars invested in scores and scores of on-going federal programs, the need is certainly greater. Let us together make Government's performance and responsiveness more commensurate with its size.

Reform Of Foreign Aid. Our foreign aid program, sent to Congress in May, differs from earlier programs in three significant ways. First, it would place greater emphasis on technical assistance, especially in the areas of agriculture, education and family planning, where the return would be greatest when measured in terms of national and human development. Second, the new program would create an Overseas Private Investment Corporation to provide a greater thrust for the channeling of private investment to the low-income countries. Third, it would increase the share of our assistance contributed through multilateral institutions.

I know of the economic miracles which foreign aid has helped create in Western Europe and in parts of Asia. I know also that our program is far from perfect. With this in mind, I have recently appointed a Presidential Task Force on International Development, charged with proposing new approaches to aid for the 1970s.

One fundamental question must be faced as Congress prepares to vote on this issue: will we in the United States live out our lives in comparative affluence, while denying reasonable help to those who are our neighbors in the world community and who are struggling to help themselves achieve a better life? To enable us to answer this question positively, I have requested $2.7 billion—the smallest request in the history of the U.S. aid program but an amount vitally needed to maintain our relationship with the developing world.

In addition to the reforms already cited, I have made other recommendations that call for new commitments by the Federal Government, and offer more hopeful avenues of progress than the paths of the past.

Specifically, I have asked Congress to:

• Establish a national computer Job Bank, which would enable the unemployed and the employer to come together through a computer matching system. The bank would have "branches" in every major labor market in the country. No longer would men have to go without work solely because they did not know where to find jobs.

• Commit this country to the most extensive improvement of the nation's air facilities in history. Under this program, the annual federal appropriation for improving air facilities will rise from $93 million a year—the average of the last decade—to $250 million annually over the next decade. I have proposed further aid for airport development of $2.5 billion dollars in federal funds in the next ten years to be matched dollar-for-dollar by the states and local governments. This will mean an added $5 billion in funds for airport development. It will mean a running start on the national effort to build for the doubling of airline traffic expected by 1975 and its tripling by 1980.

• Commit this country to the redevelopment of the nation's deteriorating public transportation system by providing an unprecedented measure of federal support. In the six-year period ending with fiscal 1970, some $800 million will have been authorized by Congress to aid the nation's deteriorating public transit industry. I have proposed raising that commitment to $3.1 billion over the next five years and to a total of $10 billion over the next twelve.

• Enact the most extensive improvements in the federal-state unemployment system in a decade, with coverage extended to an additional 4.8 million workers, mostly low-income, with an automatic extension of benefits to workers during times of high unemployment.

• Enact the strongest mine health and safety bill in history; one which empowers the Secretary of the Interior to upgrade health and safety standards for coal mines as the technology develops.

• Establish a national occupational health and safety board, with power to set standards to protect workers.

• Empower the Equal Employment Opportunity Commission to bring suit in a Federal District Court to enforce federal laws against discrimination.

• Ban literacy tests as a prerequisite for voting throughout the United States.

New Initiatives

The Hungry. For many years, in this richest of societies, we have heard rumors of malnourished children and hungry men and women. Now we know these rumors are true. This realization has prompted us to a commitment—that we eliminate every vestige of hunger and malnutrition from America. I have asked Congress to help us assure that every American family will have a nutritionally complete diet; I have asked that the poorest members of our national community be provided with food stamps free of cost.

The Senate has shown a willingness to join in this commitment and has acted with dispatch. I urge the House to move so as not to prolong any further the day when this ancient curse of malnutrition and hunger is eliminated in this most modern of nations.

Population. There is a widely recognized correlation between population growth and poverty in the under-developed nations of the world. I have asked Congress to support our endorsement of those individuals and organizations seeking voluntary answers to this global question in other lands.

To approach this question as it applies at home, I have called on Congress to create a national commission to undertake now a study of how the nation is to provide for the 100 million new Americans expected before the turn of the century.

Beyond this, I have asked that a new philosophy become American government policy. We will interfere with no American's freedom of choice; we will infringe upon no one's religious convictions; but we shall not deny to any American woman the family planning assistance she may desire but cannot afford. That is the goal I ask Congress to support.

The Control Of Crime

There is no greater need in this free society than the restoration of the individual American's freedom from violence in his home and on the streets of his city or town. Control and reduction of crime are among the first and constant concerns of this Administration. But we can do little more unless and until Congress provides more tools to do the job. No crisis is more urgent in our society. No subject has been the matter of more legislative requests from this Administration. Yet, not a single one of our major recommendations on crime has been acted upon favorably. I have not even received yet the budget appropriation for the Department of Justice for this fiscal year which is three months old. In light of the rising crime statistics in the country—and in the nation's capital—I again call upon Congress to become a full-fledged ally in this national campaign.

Organized Crime. To intensify the national effort against organized crime I have asked for an arsenal of new legal weapons:

• A doubling of existing resources for the organized crime effort;

• Authority for Justice Department agents to enter any community and shut down large-scale gambling operations;

• A modern general witness immunity statute under which witnesses in federal criminal cases could be compelled to testify under threat of a prison sentence for contempt;

• Finally, because organized crime would shrivel up without its enormous gambling resources, and because illegal gambling on a large scale cannot go on without cooperation of corrupt law enforcements, I have asked Congress to make corruption of local authorities who are tied in with such gambling operations a federal crime. I must stress the great urgency of these measures. Let the Congress act—*now*.

D.C. Crime. To deal with the increase in crime in the District of Columbia I have asked for an expansion and strengthening of the entire system of law enforcement and criminal justice, including a fundamental reorganization of the courts. I have stressed the urgent need for more police, more judges, more prosecutors, more courtroom space, a new public defender's office, better penal and rehabilitation facilities and reform in the procedures for dealing with juvenile offenders. Crime in the District of Columbia continues to rise to new records with each month. We cannot contain or control it with existing resources; we need more men and money; we need a speedier trial system and, as important as any other measure, the power to keep hard-core criminal repeaters in the District of Columbia off the streets, so they are not committing five and six crimes before they are ever brought to trial. The Congress should act—*now*.

Narcotics. In the federal effort against the illicit narcotics trade, I have submitted a major revision of all federal narcotics laws and requested more men and money to deal with a

problem that long ago outstripped the capacity of government at every level. Existing manpower and resources are stretched to their elastic limits—they are demonstrably inadequate. We have to have the cooperation of Congress to attack this terrible problem. Let's get at it—*now*.

Pornography. To prevent the use of the nation's postal system for the mailing of unsolicited sex-oriented materials to families that do not want the material and to children to whom it might do psychological harm, I offered three legislative proposals that will protect American citizens from the barrages of the filth peddlers, and will also be consistent with the decisions of the U.S. Supreme Court interpreting the First Amendment. These bills are still in Congress. I ask that they be promptly enacted.

These are among my major legislative proposals in these first nine months in office. I believe they speak directly to the needs of a nation in distress. I can see no legitimate reason why—with good will and cooperation between us—we cannot make the great majority of these urgently needed programs law before the end of the year. We should have all of them—as well as the others now pending—on the statute books well before the 91st Congress enters the history books.

To that end, I again pledge the cooperation of this Administration.

RICHARD NIXON

NIXON PROPOSES PLAN TO REBUILD MERCHANT FLEET

Following is the complete text of President Nixon's Oct. 23 Merchant Marine message to Congress.

TO THE CONGRESS OF THE UNITED STATES:

The United States Merchant Marine—the fleet of commercial ships on which we rely for our economic strength in time of peace and our defense mobility in time of war—is in trouble.

While only one-fourth of the world's merchant ships are more than 20 years old, approximately three-fourths of American trading vessels are at least that antiquated. In the next four years, much of our merchant fleet will be scrapped. Yet we are now producing only a few new ships a year for use in our foreign trade. Building costs for American vessels are about twice those in foreign shipyards and production delays are excessive. Operating expenses also are high by world standards, and labor-management conflicts have been costly and disruptive.

Both Government and industry share responsibility for the recent decline in American shipping and shipbuilding. Both Government and industry must now make a substantial effort to reverse that record. We must begin immediately to rebuild our merchant fleet and make it more competitive. Accordingly, I am announcing today a new maritime program for this nation, one which will replace the drift and neglect of recent years and restore this country to a proud position in the shipping lanes of the world.

Our program is one of challenge and opportunity. We will challenge the American shipbuilding industry to show that it can rebuild our Merchant Marine at reasonable expense. We will challenge American ship operators and seamen to move toward less dependence on Government subsidy. And, through a substantially revised and better administered Government program, we will create the opportunity to meet that challenge.

The need for this new program is great since the old ways have not worked. However, as I have frequently pointed out, our budget constraints at this time are also significant. Our program, therefore, will be phased in such a way that it will not increase subsidy expenditures during the rest of fiscal year 1970 and will require only a modest increase for fiscal year 1971. We can thus begin to rebuild our fleet and at the same time meet our fiscal responsibilities.

The Shipbuilding Industry

Our shipbuilding program is designed to meet both of the problems which lie behind the recent decline in this field: low production rates and high production costs. Our proposals would make it possible for shipbuilders to build more ships and would encourage them to hold down the cost of each vessel. We believe that these two aspirations are closely related. For only as we plan a major long-range building program can we encourage builders to standardize ship design and introduce mass production techniques which have kept other American products competitive in world markets. On the other hand, only if our builders are able to improve their efficiency and cut their costs can we afford to replace our obsolescent merchant fleet with American-built vessels. These cost reductions are essential if our ship operators are to make capital investments of several billion dollars over the next ten years to build new, high-technology ships.

Our new program will provide a substantially improved system of construction differential subsidies, payments which reimburse American shipbuilders for that part of their total cost which exceeds the cost of building in foreign shipyards. Such subsidies allow our shipbuilders—despite their higher costs—to sell their ships at world market prices for use in our foreign trade. The important features of our new subsidy system are as follows:

1. We should make it possible for industry to build more ships over the next 10 years, moving from the present subsidy level of about ten ships a year to a new level of thirty ships a year.

2. We should reduce the percentage of total costs which are subsidized. The Government presently subsidizes up to 55 percent of a builder's total expenses for a given vessel. Leaders of the shipbuilding industry have frequently said that subsidy requirements can be reduced considerably if they are assured a long-term market. I am therefore asking that construction differential subsidies be limited to 45 percent of total costs in fiscal year 1971. That percentage should be reduced by 2 percent in each subsequent year until the maximum subsidy payment is down to 35 percent of total building expenses.

We are confident that the shipbuilding industry can meet this challenge. If the challenge is not met, however, then the

Administration's commitment to this part of our program will not be continued.

3. Construction differential subsidies should be paid directly to shipbuilders rather than being channeled through shipowners as is the case under the present system. A direct payment system is necessary if our program is to encourage builders to improve designs, reduce delays, and minimize costs. It will also help us to streamline subsidy administration.

4. The multi-year procurement system which is now used for other government programs should be extended to shipbuilding. Under this system, the Government makes a firm commitment to build a given number of ships over a specified and longer period of time, a practice which allows the industry to realize important economies of scale and to receive lower subsidies.

5. The increased level of ship construction will require a corresponding increase in the level of federally insured mortgages. Accordingly, we should increase the ceiling on our present mortgage insurance programs from $1 billion to $3 billion.

6. We should extend construction differential subsidies to bulk carriers, ships which usually carry ore, grain, or oil and which are not covered by our present subsidy program.

7. A Commission should be established to review the status of the American shipbuilding industry, its problems, and its progress toward meeting the challenge we have set forth. The Commission should report on its findings within three years and recommend any changes in Government policy which it believes are desirable.

The Ship Operating Industry

My comments to this point have related to the building of merchant vessels. The other arm of our maritime policy is that which deals with the operation of these ships. Here, too, our new program offers several substantial improvements over the present system.

1. Operating differential subsidies should be continued only for the higher wage and insurance costs which American shipping lines experience. Subsidies for maintenance and repair and for subsistence should be eliminated. Instead of paying the difference between the wages of foreign seamen and actual wages on American ships, however, the Government should compare foreign wages with prevailing wage levels in several comparable sectors of the American economy. A policy which ties subsidies to this wage index will reduce subsidy costs and provide an incentive for further efficiencies. Under this system, the operator would no longer lose in subsidies what he saves in costs. Nor would he continue to be reimbursed through subsidies when his wage costs rise to higher levels.

2. At the same time that we are reducing operating subsidies, it is appropriate that we eliminate the "recapture" provisions of the Merchant Marine Act of 1936. These provisions require subsidized lines to pay back to the Government a portion of profits. If the recapture provisions are removed, the purpose for which they were designed will be largely accomplished by corporate taxes, which were at much lower rates when these provisions were instituted. We will also save the cost of administering recapture provisions.

3. Many bulk carriers presently receive indirect operating subsidies from the Government because of the statutory requirement that certain Government cargos must be shipped in United States vessels at premium rates. When the Department of Agriculture ships grain abroad, for example, it pays higher rates out of its budget than if it were allowed to ship at world market rates. We will propose a new, direct subsidy system for such carriers, thus allowing us to phase out these premium freight rates and reduce the costs of several nonmaritime Government programs.

4. Ship operators now receiving operating differential subsidies are permitted to defer federal tax payments on reserve funds set aside for construction purposes. This provision should be extended to include all qualified ship operators in the foreign trade, but only for well-defined ship replacement programs.

5. Past Government policies and industry attitudes have not been conducive to cooperation between labor and management. Our program will help to improve this situation by ending the uncertainty that has characterized our past maritime policy. Labor and management must now use this opportunity to find ways of resolving their differences without halting operations. If the desired expansion of merchant shipping is to be achieved, the disruptive work stoppages of the past must not be repeated.

6. The larger capital investment necessary to construct a modern and efficient merchant fleet requires corresponding port development. I am therefore directing the Secretary of Commerce and the Secretary of Transportation to work with related industries and local governments in improving our port operations. We must take full advantage of technological advances in this area and we should do all we can to encourage greater use of intermodal transportation systems, of which these high-technology ships are only a part.

Equal Employment Opportunities

The expansion of American merchant shipbuilding which this program makes possible will provide many new employment opportunities. All of our citizens must have equal access to these new jobs. I am therefore directing the Secretary of Commerce and the Secretary of Labor to work with industry and labor organizations to develop programs that will insure all minority groups their rightful place in this expansion.

Research and Development

We will also enlarge and redirect the maritime research and development activities of the Federal Government. Greater emphasis will be placed on practical applications of technological advances and on the coordination of federal programs with those of industry.

The history of American commercial shipping is closely intertwined with the history of our country. From the time of the Colonial fishing sloops, down through the great days of the majestic clipper ships, and into the new era when steam replaced the sail, the venturesome spirit of maritime enterprise has contributed significantly to the strength of the nation.

Our shipping industry has come a long way over the last three centuries. Yet, as one of the great historians of American seafaring, Samuel Eliot Morrison, has written: "all her modern docks and terminals and dredged channels will avail nothing, if the spirit perish that led her founders to 'trye all ports.'" It is that spirit to which our program of challenge and opportunity appeals.

It is my hope and expectation that this program will introduce a new era in the maritime history of America, an era in which our shipbuilding and ship operating industries take their place once again among the vigorous, competitive industries of this nation.

RICHARD NIXON

CAMPUS UNREST

Following is a partial text of President Nixon's April 29 address to the Chamber of Commerce of the United States.

...I have decided to speak briefly on a subject of very great concern to all of you, of very great concern to me, and I will say to all Americans at this time. I refer to the problems of education in the very broadest sense in the United States....

That is the problem of what I would call the new revolutionary spirit and new revolutionary actions that are taking place on the campuses of many of our colleges and universities and also that may begin to take place, and also are taking place, I understand, in some of the high schools of this country.

Now I am not going to speak to that problem in the way that you might usually expect. It is easy to be against some of the actions that have occurred. All of us are concerned by those actions. We are against them. The question is to refine our discussions to some simple issues and some simple principles. I am going to state some opinions now that are my own.

Some will not agree with me. But I think they are opinions that are in accord with the great traditions of free education in America. I think they need to be stated by the President of the United States and if you share them, I hope that when you go back to your communities you will state them and I would hope also to the extent that you have opportunities in official or other capacities, school boards, or as trustees, or faculty members, if you are that, you will be able, perhaps, to implement it.

First, with regard to that great problem of dissent on the college and university campuses, let us recognize that this is a very healthy force when we consider it at its best. We do not want, in America, an educational system which becomes ingrown, stultified, loses the ability to develop the new ideas to keep pace with the change in our very fast-changing society.

Consequently, we can be thankful today that we do have a younger generation, which is as I have often said, with all of the faults that we may see in it, the best-educated younger generation that we have ever had; more deeply motivated than any that we have ever had; one that deeply cares about America, about our system, and about our educational system. We may not agree with them, but they do care.

Now having said that, I now indicate what I think are some principles in which dissent must properly be expressed. One is this: As far as our colleges and universities are concerned, I think that young people, students, are correct in asking that they have a voice; a voice in determining what the courses should be, a voice in determining what the rules should be. But then I say that while they should have a voice, under no circumstances should they be given control of the colleges and universities....

Look to the countries to the south of us, our closest neighbors, our closest friends—very proud countries, many great and old universities. Those universities, most of them, went through a revolution similar to ours 100 years ago.

The students won. They won not only a voice, but they won control in many of those universities, the right to hire and fire the professors and to determine the courses. And the result is that the educational system as far as higher education is concerned, in Latin America generally, is one of the most inferior in the world. I say let us not let it happen here in the United States of America.

So our answer here is not to deny the voice. We must listen, and certainly where that voice expresses views that ought to be implemented, we should implement them. But on the other hand, remember that it is the responsibility of faculties, boards and trustees, to provide the leadership for educational institutions.

Then we come to the second point: That is the method of dissent. Here again, we have some fine lines that need to be drawn and some principles that we must have in mind.

There are those who believe that any means are justified, if the end is worthwhile. And all of us, again, if we remember the past, will, of course, agree that we can never adopt that principle, because when we adopt that principle of any means to the end, the end eventually becomes the means.

So we look at our college campuses and our university campuses today and we see some things which concern us. We see, first, the dissent. That we accept, we welcome, and we encourage, provided it is the peaceful kind of dissent within the rules of an institution and of our society.

And, second, we also—and I presently today proclaim as I have previously the principle that we do not want to have the Federal Government of this country running our institutions. We do not want them interfering with our colleges and our universities. It is their responsibility to provide education in an independent, free way in the American tradition.

But, third, we have another factor that we must face. That is this: When we find situations in numbers of colleges and universities which reach the point where students in the name of dissent and in the name of change terrorize other students and faculty members, when they rifle files, when they engage in violence, when they carry guns and knives in the classrooms, then I say it is time for faculties, boards of trustees and school administrators to have the backbone to stand up against this kind of situation.

What I am simply suggesting here is this: We do not want government control of our great educational institutions. We want to have that freedom which comes from the independence of a great university and college community. But as we look at the situation today, I think all of those who have a responsibility for providing educational leadership must recognize that there can be no compromise with lawlessness and no surrender to force if free education is to survive in the United States of America....

NIXON CALLS FOR NATIONAL UNITY ON VIETNAM

Following is the complete text of President Nixon's Nov. 3 speech on Vietnam policies.

Good evening, my fellow Americans:

Tonight I want to talk to you on a subject of deep concern to all Americans and to many people in all parts of the world—the war in Vietnam.

I believe that one of the reasons for the deep division about Vietnam is that many Americans have lost confidence in what their Government has told them about our policy. The American people cannot and should not be asked to support a policy which involves the overriding issues of war and peace unless they know the truth about that policy.

Tonight, therefore, I would like to answer some of the questions that I know are on the minds of many of you listening to me.

How and why did America get involved in Vietnam in the first place?

How has this Administration changed the policy of the previous Administration?

What has really happened in the negotiations in Paris and on the battlefront in Vietnam?

What choices do we have if we are to end the war?

What are the prospects for peace?

Let me begin by describing the situation I found when I was inaugurated on January 20.

- The war had been going on for four years.
- 31,000 Americans had been killed in action.

- The training program for the South Vietnamese was behind schedule.
- 540,000 Americans were in Vietnam with no plans to reduce the number.
- No progress had been made at the negotiations in Paris and the United States had not put forth a comprehensive peace proposal.
- The war was causing deep division at home and criticism from many of our friends as well as our enemies abroad.

In view of these circumstances there were some who urged I end the war at once by ordering the immediate withdrawal of all American forces.

From a political standpoint this would have been a popular and easy course to follow. After all, we became involved in the war while my predecessor was in office. I could blame the defeat which would be the result of my action on him and come out as the peacemaker. Some put it quite bluntly: This was the only way to avoid allowing Johnson's war to become Nixon's war.

But I had a greater obligation than to think only of the years of my Administration and the next election. I had to think of the effect of my decision on the next generation and on the future of peace and freedom in America and in the world.

Let us all understand that the question before us is not whether some Americans are for peace and some Americans are against peace. The question at issue is not whether Johnson's war becomes Nixon's war.

The great question is: How can we win America's peace?

Let us turn now to the fundamental issue. Why and how did the United States become involved in Vietnam in the first place?

Fifteen years ago, North Vietnam, with the logistical support of Communist China and the Soviet Union, launched a campaign to impose a Communist government on South Vietnam by instigating and supporting a revolution.

In response to the request of the government of South Vietnam, President Eisenhower sent economic aid and military equipment to assist the people of South Vietnam in their efforts to prevent a Communist takeover. Seven years ago, President Kennedy sent 16,000 military personnel to Vietnam as combat advisors. Four years ago, President Johnson sent American combat forces to South Vietnam.

Now, many believe that President Johnson's decision to send American combat forces to South Vietnam was wrong. And many others—I among them—have been strongly critical of the way the war has been conducted.

But the question facing us today is—now that we are in the war, what is the best way to end it?

In January, I could only conclude that the precipitate withdrawal of American forces from Vietnam would be a disaster not only for South Vietnam but for the United States and for the cause of peace.

For the South Vietnamese, our precipitate withdrawal would inevitably allow the Communists to repeat the massacres which followed their takeover in the North 15 years before.

• They then murdered more than 50,000 people and hundreds of thousands more died in slave labor camps.

• We saw a prelude of what would happen in South Vietnam when the Communists entered the city of Hue last year. During their brief rule, there was a bloody reign of terror in which 3,000 civilians were clubbed, shot to death and buried in mass graves.

• With the sudden collapse of our support, these atrocities of Hue would become the nightmare of the entire nation—and particularly for the million and a half Catholic refugees who fled to South Vietnam when the Communists took over in the North.

For the United States, this first defeat in our nation's history would result in a collapse of confidence in American leadership, not only in Asia but throughout the world.

Three American Presidents have recognized the great stakes involved in Vietnam and understood what had to be done.

In 1963, President Kennedy, with his characteristic eloquence and clarity, said, "we want to see a stable government there carrying on the struggle to maintain its national independence. We believe strongly in that. We're not going to withdraw from that effort. In my opinion for us to withdraw from that effort would mean a collapse not only of South Vietnam, but Southeast Asia, so we're going to stay there."

President Eisenhower and President Johnson expressed the same conclusion during their terms of office.

For the future of peace, precipitate withdrawal would thus be a disaster of immense magnitude.

A nation cannot remain great if it betrays its allies and lets down its friends.

Our defeat and humiliation in South Vietnam would without question promote recklessness in the councils of those great powers who have not yet abandoned their goals of world conquest.

This would spark violence wherever our commitments help maintain peace—in the Middle East, in Berlin, eventually even in the Western Hemisphere.

Ultimately, this would cost more lives.

It would not bring peace but more war.

For these reasons, I rejected the recommendation that I should end the war by immediately withdrawing all our forces. I chose instead to change American policy on both the negotiating front and the battlefront.

In order to end a war fought on many fronts, I initiated a pursuit for peace on many fronts.

In a television speech on May 14, in a speech before the United Nations and on a number of other occasions, I set forth our peace proposals in great detail.

• We have offered the complete withdrawal of all outside forces within one year.

• We have proposed a cease-fire under international supervision.

• We have offered free elections under international supervision with the Communists participating in the organization and conduct of the elections as an organized political force. The Saigon government has pledged to accept the result of the elections.

We have not put forth our proposals on a take-it-or-leave-it basis. We have indicated that we are willing to discuss the proposals that have been put forth by the other side. We have declared that anything is negotiable except the right of the people of South Vietnam to determine their own future. At the Paris peace conference, Ambassador Lodge has demonstrated our flexibility and good faith in 40 public meetings.

Hanoi has refused even to discuss our proposals. They demand our unconditional acceptance of their terms, which are that we withdraw all American forces immediately and unconditionally and that we overthrow the government of South Vietnam as we leave.

We have not limited our peace initiatives to public forums and public statements. I recognized, in January, that a long and bitter war like this usually cannot be settled in a public forum. That is why in addition to the public statements and negotiations I have explored every possible private avenue that might lead to a settlement.

Tonight I am taking the unprecedented step of disclosing to you some of our other initiatives for peace—initiatives we undertook privately and secretly because we thought that we thereby might open a door which publicly would be closed.

I did not wait for my inauguration to begin my quest for peace.

Soon after my election through an individual who is directly in contact on a personal basis with the leaders of North Vietnam I made two private offers for a rapid, comprehensive settlement. Hanoi's replies called in effect for our surrender before negotiations.

Since the Soviet Union furnishes most of the military equipment for North Vietnam, Secretary of State Rogers, my assistant for national security affairs, Dr. Kissinger, Ambassador Lodge, and I, personally, have met on a number of occasions with representatives of the Soviet government to enlist their assistance in getting meaningful negotiations started. In addition we have had extended discussions directed toward that same end with representatives of other governments which have diplomatic relations with North Vietnam. None of these initiatives have to date produced results.

In mid-July, I became convinced that it was necessary to make a major move to break the deadlock in Paris talks. I spoke directly in this office, where I am now sitting, with an individual who had known Ho Chi Minh on a personal basis for 25 years. Through him I sent a letter to Ho Chi Minh.

I did this outside of the usual diplomatic channels with the hope that with the necessity of making statements for propaganda removed, there might be constructive progress toward bringing the war to an end. Let me read from that letter:

"Dear Mr. President:

"I realize that it is difficult to communicate meaningfully across the gulf of four years of war. But precisely because of this gulf, I wanted to take this opportunity to reaffirm in all solemnity my desire to work for a just peace. I deeply believe that the war in Vietnam has gone on too long and delay in bringing it to an end can benefit no one—least of all the people of Vietnam....

"The time has come to move forward at the conference table toward an early resolution of this tragic war. You will find us forthcoming and open-minded in a common effort to bring the blessing of peace to the brave people of Vietnam. Let history record that at this critical juncture, both sides turned their face toward peace rather than toward conflict and war."

I received Ho Chi Minh's reply on August 30, three days before his death. It simply reiterated the public position North Vietnam had taken in the Paris talks and flatly rejected my initiative.

The full text of both letters is being released to the press.

In addition to the public meetings I referred to, Ambassador Lodge has met with Vietnam's chief negotiator in Paris in 11 private meetings.

We have taken other significant initiatives which must remain secret to keep open some channels of communication which may still prove to be productive.

But the effect of all the public, private and secret negotiations which have been undertaken since the bombing halt a year ago and since this Administration came into office on January 20, can be summed up in one sentence—

No progress whatever has been made except agreement on the shape of the bargaining table. Now who is at fault?

It has become clear that the obstacle in negotiating an end to the war is not the President of the United States. And it is not the South Vietnamese.

The obstacle is the other side's absolute refusal to show the least willingness to join us in seeking a just peace. It will not do so while it is convinced that all it has to do is to wait for our next concession, and the next, until it gets everything it wants.

There can now be no longer any question that progress in negotiation depends only on Hanoi's deciding to negotiate, to negotiate seriously.

I realize that this report on our efforts on the diplomatic fronts is discouraging to the American people, but the American people are entitled to know the truth—the bad news as well as the good news, where the lives of our young men are involved.

Now let me turn, however, to a more encouraging report on another front.

At the time we launched our search for peace I recognized we might not succeed in bringing an end to the war through negotiation. I, therefore, put into effect another plan to bring peace—a plan which will bring the war to an end regardless of what happens on the negotiating front.

It is in line with a major shift in U.S. foreign policy which I described in my press conference at Guam on July 25. Let me briefly explain what has been described as the Nixon Doctrine—a policy which not only will help end the war in Vietnam, but which is an essential element of our program to prevent future Vietnams.

We Americans are a do-it-yourself people. We are an impatient people. Instead of teaching someone else to do a job, we like to do it ourselves. And this trait has been carried over into our foreign policy.

In Korea and again in Vietnam, the United States furnished most of the money, most of the arms and most of the men to help the people of those countries defend their freedom against the Communist aggression.

Before any American troops were committed to Vietnam, a leader of another Asian country expressed this opinion to me when I was traveling in Asia as a private citizen. He said, "When you are trying to assist another nation defend its freedom, U.S. policy should be to help them fight the war but not to fight the war for them."

Well, in accordance with this wise counsel, I laid down in Guam three principles as guidelines for future American policy toward Asia:

First, the United States will keep all of its treaty commitments.

Second, we shall provide a shield if a nuclear power threatens the freedom of a nation allied with us or of a nation whose survival we consider vital to our security.

Third, in cases involving other types of aggression, we shall furnish military and economic assistance when requested in accordance with our treaty commitments. But we shall look to the nation directly threatened to assume the primary responsibility of providing the manpower for its defense.

After I announced this policy, I found that the leaders of the Philippines, Thailand, Vietnam, South Korea, and other nations which might be threatened by Communist aggression, welcomed this new direction in American foreign policy.

The defense of freedom is everybody's business—not just America's business. And it is particularly the responsibility of the people whose freedom is threatened. In the previous Administration, we Americanized the war in Vietnam. In this Administration, we are Vietnamizing the search for peace.

The policy of the previous Administration not only resulted in our assuming the primary responsibility for fighting the war but even more significantly did not adequately stress the goal of strengthening the South Vietnamese so that they could defend themselves when we left.

The Vietnamization Plan was launched following Secretary Laird's visit to Vietnam in March. Under the plan, I ordered first a substantial increase in the training and equipment of South Vietnamese forces.

In July, on my visit to Vietnam, I changed General Abrams' orders so that they were consistent with the objectives of our new policies. Under the new orders, the primary mission of our troops is to enable the South Vietnamese forces to assume the full responsibility for the security of South Vietnam.

Our air operations have been reduced by over 20 percent.

And now we have begun to see the results of this long overdue change in American policy in Vietnam.

• After five years of Americans going into Vietnam, we are finally bringing American men home. By December 15, over 60,000 men will have been withdrawn from South Vietnam—including 20 percent of all of our combat forces.

• The South Vietnamese have continued to gain in strength. As a result they have been able to take over combat responsibilities from our American troops.

Two other significant developments have occurred since this Administration took office.

• Enemy infiltration, infiltration which is essential if they are to launch a major attack, over the last three months is less than 20 percent of what it was over the same period last year.

• Most important—United States casualties have declined during the last two months to the lowest point in three years.

Let me now turn to our program for the future.

We have adopted a plan which we have worked out in cooperation with the South Vietnamese for the complete withdrawal of all U.S. combat ground forces, and their replacement by South Vietnamese forces on an orderly scheduled timetable. This withdrawal will be made from strength and not from weakness. As South Vietnamese forces become stronger, the rate of American withdrawal can become greater.

I have not and do not intend to announce the timetable for our program. There are obvious reasons for this decision which I am sure you will understand. As I have indicated on several occasions, the rate of withdrawal will depend on developments on three fronts.

• One of these is the progress which can be or might be made in the Paris talks. An announcement of a fixed timetable for our withdrawal would completely remove any incentive for the enemy to negotiate an agreement.

• They would simply wait until our forces had withdrawn and then move in.

The other two factors on which we will base our withdrawal decisions are the level of enemy activity and the progress of the training program of the South Vietnamese forces. I am glad to be able to report tonight progress on both of these fronts has been greater than we anticipated when we started the program in June for withdrawal. As a result, our timetable for withdrawal is more optimistic now than when we made our first estimates in June. This clearly demonstrates why it is not wise to be frozen in on a fixed timetable.

We must retain the flexibility to base each withdrawal decision on the situation as it is at that time rather than on estimates that are no longer valid.

Along with this optimistic estimate, I must—in all candor—leave one note of caution.

If the level of enemy activity significantly increases we might have to adjust our timetable accordingly.

However, I want the record to be completely clear on one point.

At the time of the bombing halt just a year ago, there was some confusion as to whether there was an understanding on the part of the enemy that if we stopped the bombing of North Vietnam they would stop the shelling of cities in South Vietnam. I want to be sure that there is no misunderstanding on the part of the enemy with regard to our withdrawal program.

We have noted the reduced level of infiltration, the reduction of our casualties, and are basing our withdrawal decisions partially on those factors.

If the level of infiltration or our casualties increase while we are trying to scale down the fighting, it will be the result of a conscious decision by the enemy.

Hanoi could make no greater mistake than to assume that an increase in violence will be to its advantage. If I conclude that increased enemy action jeopardizes our remaining forces in Vietnam, I shall not hesitate to take strong and effective measures to deal with that situation.

This is not a threat. This is a statement of policy which as Commander-in-Chief of our Armed Forces I am making in meeting my responsibility for the protection of American fighting men wherever they may be.

My fellow Americans, I am sure you recognize from what I have said that we really only have two choices open to us if we want to end this war.

I can order an immediate, precipitate withdrawal of all Americans from Vietnam without regard to the effects of that action.

Or we can persist in our search for a just peace through a negotiated settlement if possible, or through continued implementation of our plan for Vietnamization if necessary—a plan in which we will withdraw all of our forces from Vietnam on a schedule in accordance with our program, as the South Vietnamese become strong enough to defend their own freedom.

I have chosen the second course.

It is not the easy way.

It is the right way.

It is a plan which will end the war and serve the cause of peace—not just in Vietnam but in the Pacific and in the world.

In speaking of the consequences of a precipitate withdrawal, I mentioned that our allies would lose confidence in America.

Far more dangerous, we would lose confidence in ourselves. The immediate reaction would be a sense of relief that our men were coming home. But as we saw the consequences of what we had done, inevitable remorse and divisive recrimination would scar our spirit as a people.

We have faced other crises in our history and have become stronger by rejecting the easy way out and taking the right way in meeting our challenges. Our greatness as a nation has been our capacity to do what had to be done when we knew our course was right.

I recognize that some of my fellow citizens disagree with the plan for peace I have chosen. Honest and patriotic Americans have reached different conclusions as to how peace should be achieved.

In San Francisco a few weeks ago, I saw demonstrators carrying signs reading: "Lose in Vietnam, bring the boys home."

Well, one of the strengths of our free society is that any American has a right to reach that conclusion and to advocate that point of view. But as President of the United States, I would be untrue to my oath of office if I allowed the policy of this nation to be dictated by the minority who hold that point of view and who try to impose it on the nation by mounting demonstrations in the street.

For almost 200 years, the policy of this nation has been made under our Constitution by those leaders in the Congress and in the White House selected by all of the people. If a vocal minority, however fervent its cause, prevails over reason and the will of the majority this nation has no future as a free society.

And now I would like to address a word if I may to the young people of this nation who are particularly concerned, and I understand why they are concerned about this war.

I respect your idealism.

I share your concern for peace.

I want peace as much as you do.

There are powerful personal reasons I want to end this war. This week I will have to sign 83 letters to mothers, fathers, wives and loved ones of men who have given their lives for America in Vietnam. It is very little satisfaction to me that this is only one-third as many letters as I signed the first week in office. There is nothing I want more than to see the day come when I do not have to write any of those letters.

I want to end the war to save the lives of those brave young men in Vietnam.

But I want to end it in a way which will increase the chance that their younger brothers and their sons will not have to fight in some future Vietnam someplace in the world.

And I want to end the war for another reason. I want to end it so that the energy and dedication of you, our young people, now too often directed into bitter hatred against those responsible for the war, can be turned to the great challenges of peace, a better life for all Americans, a better life for all people on this earth.

I have chosen a plan for peace. I believe it will succeed.

If it does not succeed, what the critics say now won't matter. Or, if it does succeed, what the critics say now won't matter. If it does not succeed, anything I say then won't matter.

I know it may not be fashionable to speak of patriotism or national destiny these days. But I feel it is appropriate to do so on this occasion.

Two hundred years ago this nation was weak and poor. But even then, America was the hope of millions in the world. Today we have become the strongest and richest nation in the world. The wheel of destiny has turned so that any hope the world has for the survival of peace and freedom will be determined by whether the American people have the moral stamina and the courage to meet the challenge of free world leadership.

Let historians not record that when America was the most powerful nation in the world we passed on the other side of the road and allowed the last hopes for peace and freedom of millions of people to be suffocated by the forces of totalitarianism.

And so tonight—to you, the great silent majority of my fellow Americans—I ask for your support.

I pledged in my campaign for the Presidency to end the war in a way that we could win the peace. I have initiated a plan of action which will enable me to keep that pledge.

The more support I can have from the American people, the sooner that pledge can be redeemed; for the more divided we are at home, the less likely the enemy is to negotiate at Paris.

Let us be united for peace. Let us also be united against defeat. Because let us understand: North Vietnam cannot defeat or humiliate the United States. Only Americans can do that.

Fifty years ago, in this room and at this very desk, President Woodrow Wilson spoke words which caught the imagination of a war-weary world. He said, "This is the war to end wars." His dream for peace after World War I was shattered on the hard realities of great power politics and Woodrow Wilson died a broken man.

Tonight I do not tell you that the war in Vietnam is the war to end wars. But I do say this:

I have initiated a plan which will end this war in a way that will bring us closer to that great goal to which Woodrow Wilson and every American President in our history has been dedicated—the goal of a just and lasting peace.

As President I hold the responsibility for choosing the best path to that goal and then leading the nation along it.

I pledge to you tonight that I shall meet this responsibility with all of the strength and wisdom I can command in accordance with your hopes, mindful of your concerns, sustained by your prayers.

Thank you and good night.

RICHARD NIXON

NIXON PROPOSES 'BILL OF RIGHTS' FOR CONSUMERS

Following is the complete text of President Nixon's Oct. 30 message on consumer affairs.

TO THE CONGRESS OF THE UNITED STATES:

Consumerism—Upton Sinclair and Rachel Carson would be glad to know—is a healthy development that is here to stay.

That does not mean that *caveat emptor*—"let the buyer beware"— has been replaced by an equally harsh *caveat venditor* —"let the seller beware." Nor does it mean that government should guide or dominate individual purchasing decisions.

Consumerism in the America of the '70s means that we have adopted the concept of "buyer's rights."

I believe that the buyer in America today has the right to make an intelligent choice among products and services.

The buyer has the right to accurate information on which to make his free choice.

The buyer has the right to expect that his health and safety is taken into account by those who seek his patronage.

The buyer has the right to register his dissatisfaction, and have his complaint heard and weighed, when his interests are badly served.

This "Buyer's Bill of Rights" will help provide greater personal freedom for individuals as well as better business for everyone engaged in trade.

The program I am outlining today represents the most significant set of Presidential recommendations concerning consumer interests in our history. Specifically, I propose:

• A new Office of Consumer Affairs in the Executive Office of the President with new legislative standing, an expanding budget, and greater responsibilities. This will give every American consumer a permanent voice in the White House.

• A new Division of Consumer Protection in the Department of Justice, to act as a consumer advocate before federal regulatory agencies in judicial proceedings and in government councils.

• A new consumer protection law which would be enforced by the Department of Justice and United States Attorneys across the land. Such a law would also better enable consumers either as individuals or as a class to go into court to obtain redress for the damages they suffer.

• Expanded powers for a revitalized Federal Trade Commission, to enable it to protect consumers promptly and effectively.

• A newly activated National Commission on Consumer Finance to investigate and report on the state of consumer credit.

• Expanded consumer education activities, including government review of product-testing processes, a new *Consumer Bulletin*, and the release of certain government information regarding consumer products.

• Stronger efforts in the field of food and drug safety, including a thorough reexamination of the Food and Drug Administration and a review of the products on the "generally regarded as safe" list.

• Other reforms, including an expansion of consumer activities in the Office of Economic Opportunity and greater efforts to encourage the strengthening of state and local programs.

To their credit, producers and sellers have generally become far more responsible with the passing years, but even the limited abuses which occur now have greater impact. Products themselves are more complicated; there is more about them that can go wrong and less about them that can be readily understood by laymen. Mass production and mass distribution systems mean that a small error can have a wide effect; the carelessness of one producer can bring harm or disappointment to many. Moreover, the responsibility for a particular problem is far more difficult to trace than was once the case, and even when responsibility for an error can be assigned, it is often difficult to lodge an effective complaint against it.

All too often, the real advantages of mass production are accompanied by consumer alienation; many an average buyer is intimidated by seemingly monolithic organizations, and frequently comes to feel alone and helpless in what he regards as a cruelly impersonal marketplace. In addition, many of the government's efforts to help the consumer are still geared to the problems of past decades; when it is able to act at all, government too often acts too slowly.

Fortunately, most businessmen in recent years have recognized that the confidence of the public over a long period of time is an important ingredient for their own success and have themselves made important voluntary progress in consumer protection. At the same time, buyers are making their voices heard more often, as individuals and through consumer organizations. These trends are to be encouraged and our governmental programs must emphasize their value. Government consumer programs, in fact, are a complement to these voluntary efforts. They are designed to help honest and conscientious businessmen by discouraging their dishonest or careless competitors.

New Office of Consumer Affairs. One of the central roles in present government efforts in the consumer rights field is performed by the President's Special Assistant for Consumer Affairs and those who work with her. This position has been created by Presidential order rather than by statute, however, and it is neither as visible nor as effective as it should be. It is important that both the prestige and the responsibility of this office be strengthened.

I am therefore asking the Congress to establish within the Executive Office of the President a new Office of Consumer Affairs to play a leading role in the crusade for consumer justice. This Office and its director would have central responsibility for coordinating all federal activities in the consumer protection field, helping to establish priorities, to resolve conflicts, to initiate research, and to recommend improvements in a wide range of government programs. The Office would advise the President on consumer matters and would alert other government officials to the potential impact of their decisions on the consumers' interests. It would receive complaints from individual consumers and refer them to appropriate agencies or to the businesses concerned.

The new Office of Consumer Affairs would not work solely within the Executive Branch of the government, however; it would continue to carry out other assignments which the Special Assistant to the President for Consumer Affairs now performs. For example, when called upon, it would assist in the legislative process, testifying at Congressional hearings, and consulting with individual Congressmen. It would aid schools and media in educating the public in consumer skills. The new Office will continue the constructive interchange of information which the Special Assistant has established with businesses and industries, and carry forward its assistance to state and local consumer protection programs.

As I will explain in greater detail later in this message, I am also asking the Special Assistant for Consumer Affairs to undertake specific surveillance responsibilities in the area of product safety, to review the government's policy concerning the release of its own information on consumer products, and to publish a new *Consumer Bulletin* on a regular basis. When the new Office of Consumer Affairs is established, it would take over these and related duties.

A new Office of Consumer Affairs would be a focal point for a wide variety of government efforts to aid people who buy. I urge the Congress to grant it the legislative standing and the added resources necessary to do this work effectively.

Consumer Protection. A second important structural reform which I am recommending is the establishment by statute of a new Consumer Protection Division in the Department of Justice. This Division would be headed by an Assistant Attorney General and would be staffed by lawyers and economists. It would be adequately financed and given appropriate investigative power so that it could effectively ascertain consumer needs and advance consumer causes. The head of the new Division would act, in effect, as the consumers' lawyer, representing the consumer interest before federal agencies, in judicial proceedings and in government councils.

I also propose that Congress arm this new Consumer Protection Division with a new law—one which would prohibit a broad, but clearly defined, range of frauds and deceptions. The legislation I will propose will be of sufficient scope to provide substantial protection to consumers and of sufficient specificity to give the necessary advance notice to businessmen of the activities to be considered illegal.

The role of the new Assistant Attorney General for Consumer Protection would be similar to that of the Assistant Attorney General who heads the Antitrust Division in the Department of Justice. Just as the Antitrust Division enforces the antitrust laws and intervenes in various governmental proceedings to preserve competition, so the Consumer Protection Division would enforce consumer rights and intervene in agency proceedings to protect the consumer. In enforcing these rights, the Assistant Attorney General for Consumer Protection would also have the assistance of United States Attorneys throughout the country. Their power to take quick and effective action under the new statute would be particularly important for protecting low-income families who are frequently victimized by fraudulent and deceptive practices.

Effective representation of the consumer does not require the creation of a new federal department or independent agency, but it does require that an appropriate arm of the government be given the tools to do an effective job. In the past a lone Justice Department lawyer—the Consumer Counsel—has attempted to carry out a portion of this task. Our proposal asks that the new Division of Consumer Protection be adequately staffed and independently funded, as is the Antitrust Division, so that it can vigorously represent the interests of the consumer and enforce the newly proposed legislation.

The new Assistant Attorney General and his Division would, of course, work closely with the Office of Consumer Affairs, the Federal Trade Commission and state and local law enforcement agencies.

Consumers in the Federal Courts. Present federal law gives private citizens no standing to sue for fraudulent or deceptive practices and state laws are often not adequate to their problems. Even if private citizens could sue, the damage suffered by any one consumer would not ordinarily be great enough to warrant costly, individual litigation. One would probably not go through a lengthy court proceeding, for example, merely to recover the cost of a household appliance.

To correct this situation, I will recommend legislation to give private citizens the right to bring action in a federal court to recover damages, upon the successful termination of a government suit under the new consumer protection law.

This measure will, for the first time, give consumers access to the federal courts for violation of a federal law concerning fraudulent and deceptive practices, without regard to the amount in controversy. Under federal court rules, consumers would have the right to sue as a class and not only as individuals. In other words, a group of people could come into court together if they could show that the act in question affected all of them. This is a significant consideration, for it would allow a number of citizens to divide among themselves the high costs of bringing a law suit. Although each person's individual damage might be small, the cumulative effect of a class complaint could be significant and in some circumstances could provide a significant deterrent to expensive fraud or deception. At the same time, the fact that private action must follow in the wake of a successful government action will prevent harassment of legitimate businessmen by unlimited nuisance lawsuits.

The Federal Trade Commission. The problems of the American consumer first became a central matter of federal concern in the late years of the nineteenth century and the early years of the twentieth. One of the important elements in the government's response at that time was the establishment in 1914 of the Federal Trade Commission, an independent body which was designed to play a leading role in the fight against unfair and deceptive trade practices. While new legislation has given the FTC additional and more specific duties, there has been increasing public concern over the Commission's ability to meet all of its many responsibilities. I believe the time has now come for the reactivation and revitalization of the FTC.

The chairman-designate of the FTC has assured me that he intends to initiate a new era of vigorous action as soon as he is confirmed by the Senate and takes office. A report prepared at my request by a commission of the American Bar Association should help considerably in this effort, for it presents a valuable description of the problems which face the FTC and the ways in which they can be remedied. I urge the FTC to give serious consideration to these recommendations. I have also asked the Bureau of the Budget to help with the revitalization process by supervising an even more detailed management study of this Commission.

I am particularly hopeful that a number of specific improvements in the FTC can be quickly accomplished. For example, the Commission should immediately begin to process its business more rapidly so that it can reduce its unacceptably large backlog of cases. I also believe that it should seek out new information on consumer problems through more energetic field investigations, rather than waiting for complaints to come in through its mailrooms or from other government agencies. This initiative could begin with pilot field projects in a limited number of cities, as the ABA task force has suggested. Whatever the strategy, I would hope that it could be accomplished through a more efficient use of existing personnel and finances; if that proves impossible, added funds should later be appropriated for this purpose.

Administrative reforms will provide only part of the answer, however. I believe the Commission should also consider the extent to which Section 5 of the Federal Trade Commission Act, broadly interpreted, may be used more effectively to cope with contemporary consumer problems. This is the section which gives the Commission its legislative mandate to move against unfair or deceptive practices. The language of this section might well provide an appropriate instrument for policing more effectively some of the more prevalent abuses described by the ABA task force study.

Even if the Commission does apply Section 5 more broadly, however, there remains a question about its jurisdiction which the Congress should promptly resolve. Past FTC enforcement activities have been inhibited by a Supreme Court decision of some twenty-five years ago, holding that activities "affecting" interstate commerce were not subject to FTC jurisdiction since the language of the law was limited to activities "in" interstate commerce. This means that there is a doubt at present concerning the FTC's ability to consider many unfair and deceptive practices which have a nationwide impact but are local in terms of their actual operation.

I am therefore recommending that the Congress amend Section 5 so as to permit the FTC to take action concerning consumer abuses which "affect" interstate commerce, as well as those which are technically "in" interstate commerce. This amendment would make it clear that the FTC has a jurisdiction consistent with that of several other federal agencies and commissions. The purpose of the amendment is to clarify FTC jurisdiction over cases which have true national significance; it should not be interpreted in a way which burdens the Commission with a large number of cases which are of only local importance.

One of the most important obstacles to the present effectiveness of the FTC is its inability to seek an injunction against an unfair or deceptive business practice. The result of this inability is an unacceptable delay between the time a harmful practice is discovered and the time it is ended. Often two years will pass between the time the FTC agrees to hear a complaint and the time it issues its final order and another two years may pass while the order is reviewed by the courts.

I recommend that the Congress remedy this situation by giving to the Federal Trade Commission the power to seek and obtain from the federal courts a preliminary injunction against consumer practices which are unfair or deceptive. The judicial process includes safeguards which will assure that this authority is fairly used. Courts will retain their usual discretion to grant or deny an injunction in the light of all the consequences for both the accused and the plaintiff. Parties will, of course, retain their right to a fair hearing before any injunction is issued.

National Commission on Consumer Finance. The buying public and businessmen alike have been concerned in recent years about the growth of consumer credit. Twenty-five years ago the total consumer credit outstanding was only 5.7 billion dollars; today it is 110 billion dollars. The arrangements by which the credit is provided are subject to government supervision and regulation, an assignment which has recently become increasingly complex and difficult. For this reason a National Commission on Consumer Finance was established by law in 1968. It was instructed to review the adequacy and the cost of consumer credit and to consider the effectiveness with which the public is protected against unfair credit practices.

The National Commission on Consumer Finance should begin its important work immediately. I will therefore announce shortly the names of three new members of the Commission, including a new chairman, and I will ask the Congress for a supplemental appropriation to finance the Commission's investigations during the current fiscal year. I look forward to receiving the report of the National Commission on Consumer Finance in January of 1971.

Consumer Education. No matter how alert and resourceful a purchaser may be, he is relatively helpless unless he has adequate, trustworthy information about the product he is considering and *knows what to make of that information.* The fullest product description is useless if a consumer lacks the understanding or the will to utilize it.

This Administration believes that consumer education programs should be expanded. Our study of existing consumer education efforts in both the public schools and in adult education programs has been funded by the Office of Education and will report its results in the near future.

The Special Assistant to the President for Consumer Affairs is focusing many of the resources of her office on educational projects. One new project which I am asking that office to undertake is the preparation and publication, on a regular basis, of a new *Consumer Bulletin.* This publication will contain a selection of items which are of concern to consumers and which now appear in the daily government journal, *The Federal Register.* The material it presents, which will include notices of hearings, proposed and final rules and orders, and other useful information, will be translated from its technical form into language which is readily understandable by the layman.

The government can help citizens do a better job of product evaluation in other ways as well. First, I recommend that Congress authorize the Federal Government to review the standards for evaluation which are used by private testing laboratories and to publish its findings as to their adequacy, working through appropriate scientific agencies such as the National Bureau of Standards. Laboratories presently issue quality endorsements, of one kind or another, for a wide variety of products. Some of these endorsements have meaning, but others do not. It would be most helpful, I believe, if the testing procedures on which these endorsements were based were evaluated by government experts. Manufacturers whose products had been tested under government-evaluated testing standards would be allowed to advertise the fact. If no testing standard existed or if the standard in use was found to be inadequate, then the appropriate agency would be authorized to develop a new one.

Secondly, I propose that we help the consumer by sharing with him some of the knowledge which the government has accumulated in the process of purchasing consumer items for its own use. Government agencies, such as the General Services Administration and the Department of Defense, have developed their own extensive procedures for evaluating the products they buy—products which range from light bulbs and detergents to tires and electric drills. As a result of this process, they have developed considerable purchasing expertise; in short, they know what to look for when they are buying a given product. They know, for example, what general types of paint are appropriate for certain surfaces; they know what "check-points" to examine when a piece of machinery is being purchased. The release of such information could help all of our people become more skillful consumers. I am therefore asking my Special Assistant for Consumer Affairs to develop a program for disseminating general information of this sort and to carry on further studies as to how the skill and knowledge of government purchasers can be shared with the public in a fair and useful manner.

Food and Drugs. The surveillance responsibilities of the Food and Drug Administration extend not only to food and drugs themselves, but also to cosmetics, therapeutic devices, and other products. Both the structure and the procedures of the FDA must be fully adequate to this sizeable and sensitive assignment, which is why this Administration has made the FDA the subject of intensive study.

I have asked the Secretary of Health, Education and Welfare to undertake a thorough reexamination of the FDA, and I expect that this review will soon produce a number of important reforms in the agency's operations. This study is taking up several central questions: What further financial and personnel resources does the FDA require? Are laboratory findings communicated as promptly and fully as is desirable to high Administration officials and to the public? What should be the relationship of the FDA to other scientific arms of the government? What methods can bring the greatest possible talent to bear on the critical questions the FDA considers?

There are a number of actions relating to FDA concerns which should be taken promptly, even while our study of that institution continues. For example, I have already asked the Secretary of Health, Education and Welfare to initiate a full review of food additives. This investigation should move as fast as our resources permit, reexamining the safety of substances which are now described by the phrase, "generally recognized as safe" (GRAS). Recent findings concerning the effects of cyclamate sweeteners on rats underscore the importance of continued vigilance in this field. The major suppliers and users of cyclamates have shown a sense of public responsibility during the recent difficulties and I am confident that such cooperation from industry will continue to facilitate this investigation.

I also recommend that the Congress take action which would make possible, for the first time, the rapid identification of drugs and drug containers in a time of personal emergency. When overdosage or accidental ingestion of a drug presently occurs, a physician is often unable to identify that drug without elaborate laboratory analysis. Many manufacturers are already working to remedy this problem on a voluntary basis by imprinting an identification number on every drug capsule and container they produce. As many in the industry have urged, this simple process should now be required of all drug producers, provided they are given suitable time to adjust their production machinery.

Another important medical safety problem concerns medical devices—equipment ranging from contact lenses and hearing aids to artificial valves which are implanted in the body. Certain minimum standards should be established for such devices; the government should be given additional authority to require premarketing clearance in certain cases. The scope and nature of any legislation in this area must be carefully considered, and the Department of Health, Education and Welfare is undertaking a thorough study of medical device regulation. I will receive the results of that study early in 1970.

The Office of Economic Opportunity. The problems which all American consumers encounter are experienced with particular intensity by the poor. With little purchasing experience to rely upon and no money to waste, poorer citizens are the most frequent and most tragic victims of commercial malpractices. The Office of Economic Opportunity is therefore establishing its own Division of Consumer Affairs to help focus and improve its already extensive consumer activities for poorer Americans. The nationwide network of community action agencies can be one instrument for extending consumer education into this area.

States and Localities. An important segment of consumer abuses can be handled most effectively at the state and local level, we believe, provided that each state has a strong consumer protection statute and an effective mechanism for enforcing it. Several states set examples for the Federal Government in this field; every state should be encouraged to explore the need for an adequately financed Division of Consumer Protection as a part of its state attorney general's office. Both the Special Assistant for Consumer Affairs and the Federal Trade Commission can do much to help states and localities to improve their consumer protection activities. The codification of state consumer protection laws which the Special Assistant is now conducting promises to be a useful part of the states in this effort.

Guarantees and Warranties. Consumers are properly concerned about the adequacy of guarantees and warranties on the goods they buy. On Jan. 8, 1969, a task force recommended that the household appliance industry disclose more fully the terms of the warranties it provides. It recommended that if, at the end of one year, voluntary progress had not occurred, then legislative action should be considered.

In order to evaluate the industry's recent progress, I am today reactivating that task force. It will be chaired by my Special Assistant for Consumer Affairs and will include representatives from the Department of Commerce, the Department of Labor, the Federal Trade Commission, the Department of Justice and the Council of Economic Advisors. I am asking the task force to make its report by the end of this year and to comment on the need for guarantee and warranty legislation in the household appliance industries and in other fields.

Product Safety. The product safety area is one which requires further investigation and further legislation, as the hearings of the National Commission on Product Safety have already demonstrated. I am asking my Special Assistant for Consumer Affairs to provide continued surveillance in the area of product safety, particularly after June 30, 1970, when the National Commission on Product Safety is scheduled to complete its work. And I am also instructing the appropriate agencies of the government to consult with the Commission and to prepare appropriate safety legislation for submission to Congress.

Finally, I am asking the Congress to require that any government agency, in any written decision substantially affecting the consumer's interest, give due consideration to that interest and express in its opinion the manner in which that interest was taken into account. I would also note that the major review which will be conducted this December by the White House Conference on Food, Nutrition and Health will provide further welcome advances in the protection and education of the American consumer.

Interest in consumer protection has been an important part of American life for many decades. It was in the mid-1920s, in fact, that two of the leading consumer advocates of the day, Stuart Chase and F. J. Schlink reached the following conclusion: "The time has gone—possibly forever—," they wrote, "when it is possible for each of us to become informed on all the things we have to buy. Even the most expert today can have knowledge of only a negligible section of the field. What sense then in a specialized industrial society if each individual must learn by trial and error again and forever again?" It was clear at that time and it is clear today, that the consumer needs expert help. The consumer has received some of that needed help through the years, from a variety of sources, private and public.

Our program is a part of that tradition. Its goal is to turn the buyer's Bill of Rights into a reality, to make life in a complex society more fair, more convenient and more productive for all our citizens. Our program is fair to businessmen and good for business, since it encourages everyone who does business to do an even better job of providing quality goods and services. Our action is intended to foster a just marketplace—a marketplace which is fair both to those who sell and those who buy.

RICHARD NIXON

TRADE POLICY TEXT

Following is the complete text of President Nixon's Nov. 18 message to Congress on trade policy.

TO THE CONGRESS OF THE UNITED STATES:

For the past 35 years, the United States has steadfastly pursued a policy of freer world trade. As a nation, we have recognized that competition cannot stop at the ocean's edge. We have determined that American trade policies must advance the national interest—which means they must respond to the whole of our interests, and not be a device to favor the narrow interest.

This Administration has reviewed that policy and we find that its continuation is in our national interest. At the same time, however, it is clear that the trade problems of the 1970s will differ significantly from those of the past. New developments in the rapidly evolving world economy will require new responses and new initiatives.

As we look at the changing patterns of world trade, three factors stand out that require us to continue modernizing our own trade policies:

First, world economic interdependence has become a fact. Reductions in tariffs and in transportation costs have internationalized the world economy just as satellites and global television have internationalized the world communications network. The growth of multinational corporations provides a dramatic example of this development.

Second, we must recognize that a number of foreign countries now compete fully with the United States in world markets.

We have always welcomed such competition. It promotes the economic development of the entire world to the mutual benefit of all, including our own consumers. It provides an additional stimulus to our own industry, agriculture and labor force. At the same time, however, it requires us to insist on fair competition among all countries.

Third, the traditional surplus in the U.S. balance of trade has disappeared. This is largely due to our own internal inflation and is one more reason why we must bring that inflation under control.

The disappearance of the surplus has suggested to some that we should abandon our traditional approach toward freer trade. I reject this argument not only because I believe in the principle of freer trade, but also for a very simple and pragmatic reason: any reduction in our imports produced by U.S. restrictions not accepted by our trading partners would invite foreign reaction against our own exports—all quite legally. Reduced imports would thus be offset by reduced exports, and both sides would lose. In the longer term, such a policy of trade restriction would add to domestic inflation and jeopardize our competitiveness in world markets at the very time when tougher competition throughout the world requires us to improve our competitive capabilities in every way possible.

In fact, the need to restore our trade surplus heightens the need for further movement toward freer trade. It requires us to persuade other nations to lower barriers which deny us fair access to their markets. An environment of freer trade will permit the widest possible scope for the genius of American industry and agriculture to respond to the competitive challenge of the 1970s.

Fourth, the less developed countries need improved access to the markets of the industrialized countries if their economic development is to proceed satisfactorily. Public aid will never be sufficient to meet their needs, nor should it be. I recently announced that, as one step toward improving their market access, the United States would press in world trade forums for a liberal system of tariff preferences for all developing countries. International discussions are now in progress on the matter and I will not deal with it in the trade bill I am submitting today. At the appropriate time, I will submit legislation to the Congress to seek authorization for the United States to extend preferences and to take any other steps toward improving the market access of the less developed countries which might appear desirable and which would require legislation.

The Trade Act of 1969

The trade bill which I am submitting today addresses these new problems of the 1970s. It is modest in scope, but significant in its impact. It continues the general drive toward freer world trade. It also explicitly recognizes that, while seeking to advance world interests, U.S. trade policies must also respect legitimate U.S. interests, and that to be fair to our trading partners does not require us to be unfair to our own people. Specifically:

• It restores the authority needed by the President to make limited tariff reductions.

• It takes concrete steps toward the increasingly urgent goal of lowering non-tariff barriers to trade.

• It recognizes the very real plight of particular industries, companies and workers faced with import competition, and provides for readier relief in these special cases.

• It strengthens GATT—the General Agreement on Tariffs and Trade—by regularizing the funding of United States participation.

While asking enactment of these proposals now, the trade program I will outline in this message also includes setting preparations under way for the more ambitious initiatives that will later be needed for the long-term future.

Tariff Reduction. I recommend that the President be given authority to make modest reductions in U.S. tariffs.

The President has been without such authority for over two years. This authority is not designed to be used for major tariff negotiations, but rather to make possible minor adjustments that individual circumstances from time to time require—as, for example, when it becomes necessary to raise the duty on an article as the result of an "escape clause" action or when a statutory change is made in tariff classification. Our trading partners are then entitled to reasonable compensation, just as we would be entitled to receive it from them in reverse circumstances. Lack of this authority exposes our exports to foreign retaliation. Therefore, the bill would provide to the President, through June 30, 1973, the authority to reduce tariffs by limited amounts.

Non-Tariff Barriers. The time has come for a serious and sustained effort to reduce non-tariff barriers to trade. These non-tariff barriers have become increasingly important with the decline in tariff protection and the growing interdependence of the world economy. Their elimination is vital to our efforts to increase U.S. exports.

As a first step in this direction, I propose today that the United States eliminate the American Selling Price system of customs valuation.

Although this system applies only to a very few American products—mainly benzenoid chemicals—it is viewed by our principal trading partners as a major symbol of American protectionism. Its removal will bring reciprocal reductions in foreign tariffs on U.S. chemical exports, and a reduction in important foreign non-tariff barriers—including European road taxes, which discriminate against our larger automobiles, and the preferential treatment on tobacco extended by the United Kingdom to the countries of the Commonwealth. Beyond this, its removal will unlock the door to new negotiations on the entire range of non-tariff barriers. Because of the symbolic importance our trading partners attach to it, the American Selling Price system has itself become a major barrier to the removal of other barriers.

Essentially, the American Selling Price system is a device by which the value of imports for tariff purposes is set by the price of competitive American products instead of the actual price of the foreign product, which is the basis of tariff valuation for all

other imports. The extraordinary protection it provides to these few products has outlived its original purposes. The special advantage it gives particular producers can no longer justify its heavy cost in terms of the obstacles it places in the way of opening foreign markets to American exports.

Reducing or eliminating other non-tariff barriers to world trade will require a great deal of detailed negotiating and hard bargaining.

Unlike tariffs, approaches to the reduction of non-tariff barriers are often difficult to embody in prior delegation of authority. Many—both here and abroad—have their roots in purely domestic concerns that are only indirectly related to foreign trade, and many arise from domestic laws.

Many would require specific legislative actions to accomplish their removal—but the nature of this action would not finally be clear until negotiation had shown what was possible.

This presents a special opportunity for Congress to be helpful in achieving international agreements in this vital area.

I would welcome a clear statement of Congressional intent with regard to non-tariff barriers to assist in our efforts to obtain reciprocal lowering of such barriers.

It is not my intention to use such a declaration as a "blank check." On the contrary, I pledge to maintain close consultation with the Congress during the course of any such negotiations, to keep the Congress fully informed on problems and progress, and to submit for Congressional consideration any agreements which would require new legislation. The purpose of seeking such an advance declaration is not to bypass Congress, but to strengthen our negotiating position.

In fact, it is precisely because ours is a system in which the Executive cannot commit the Legislative Branch that a general declaration of legislative intent would be important to those with whom we must negotiate.

At the same time, I urge private interests to work closely with the government in seeking the removal of these barriers. Close cooperation by the private sector is essential, because many non-tariff barriers are subtle, complex and difficult to appraise.

Aid for Affected Industries. Freer trade brings benefits to the entire community, but it can also cause hardship for parts of the community. The price of a trade policy from which we all receive benefits must not fall unfairly on the few—whether on particular industries, on individual firms or on groups of workers. As we have long recognized, there should be prompt and effective means of helping those faced with adversity because of increased imports.

The Trade Act of 1969 provides significant improvements in the means by which U.S. industry, firms, and workers can receive assistance from their government to meet injury truly caused by imports.

This relief falls into two broad categories: 1) the escape clause, which is industry-wide; and 2) adjustment assistance, which provides specific aid to particular firms or groups of workers.

These improvements are needed because the assistance programs provided in the Trade Expansion Act of 1962 have simply not worked.

Escape Clause. The escape clause provisions of the 1962 Act have proved so stringent, so rigid, and so technical that in not a single case has the Tariff Commission been able to justify a recommendation for relief. This must be remedied. We must be able to provide, on a case-by-case basis, careful and expedited consideration of petitions for relief, and such relief must be available on a fair and reasonable basis.

I recommend a liberalization of the escape clause to provide, for industries adversely affected by import competition, a test that will be simple and clear: relief should be available whenever increased imports are the primary cause of actual or potential serious injury. The increase in imports should not—as it now is—have to be related to a prior tariff reduction.

While making these escape clause adjustments more readily obtainable, however, we must ensure that they remain what they are intended to be: temporary relief measures, not permanent features of the tariff landscape. An industry provided with temporary escape-clause relief must assume responsibility for improving its competitive position. The bill provides for regular reports on these efforts, to be taken into account in determining whether relief should be continued.

Adjustment Assistance. With regard to adjustment assistance for individual firms and groups of workers, the provisions of the Trade Expansion Act of 1962 again have not worked adequately.

The Act provides for loans, technical assistance and tax relief for firms, and readjustment allowances, relocation and training for workers. This direct aid to those individually injured should be more readily available than tariff relief for entire industries. It can be more closely targeted; it matches the relief to the damage; and it has no harmful side effects on overall trade policy.

I recommend that firms and workers be considered eligible for adjustment assistance when increased imports are found to be a substantial cause of actual or potential serious injury.

Again, the increase in imports would not have to be related to a prior tariff reduction. The "substantial cause" criterion for adjustment assistance would be less stringent than the "primary cause" criterion for tariff relief.

I also recommend two further changes in existing adjustment provisions:

• That the Tariff Commission continue to gather and supply the needed factual information, but that determinations of eligibility to apply for assistance be made by the President.

• That adjustment assistance be made available to separate units of multi-plant companies and to groups of workers in them, when the injury is substantial to the unit but not to the entire parent firm.

With these modifications, plus improved administrative procedures, our program of assistance to import-injured firms and workers can and will be made to work. Taken together, they will remedy what has too long been a serious shortcoming in our trade programs.

These changes in our escape clause and adjustment assistance programs will provide an adequate basis for government help in cases where such help is justified in the overall national interest. They will thus help us move away from protectionist proposals, which would reverse the trend toward interdependence, and toward a constructive attack on the existing trade barriers of others.

The textile import problem, of course, is a special circumstance that requires special measures. We are now trying to persuade other countries to limit their textile shipments to the United States. In doing so, however, we are trying to work out with our trading partners a reasonable solution which will allow both domestic and foreign producers to share equitably in the development of the U.S. market.

Such measures should not be misconstrued, nor should they be allowed to turn us away from the basic direction of our progress toward freer exchange.

Fair Treatment of U.S. Exports. By nature and by definition, trade is a two-way street. We must make every effort to ensure that American products are allowed to compete in world markets on equitable terms. These efforts will be more successful if we have the means to take effective action when confronted with illegal or unjust restrictions on American exports.

Section 252 of the Trade Expansion Act of 1962 authorizes the President to impose duties or other import restrictions on the products of any nation that places unjustifiable restrictions on U.S. agricultural products. I recommend that this authority be expanded in two ways:

• By extending the existing authority to cover unfair actions against all U.S. products, rather than only against U.S. agricultural products.

• By providing new authority to take appropriate action against nations that practice what amounts to subsidized competition in third-country markets, when that subsidized competition unfairly affects U.S. exports.

Any weapon is most effective if its presence makes its use unnecessary. With these new weapons in our negotiating arsenal, we should be better able to negotiate relief from the unfair restrictions to which American exports still are subject.

Strengthening GATT. Ever since its beginning in 1947, U.S. participation in GATT—the General Agreement on Tariffs and Trade—has been financed through general contingency funds rather than through a specific appropriation.

GATT has proved its worth. It is the international organization we depend on for the enforcement of our trading rights, and toward which we look as a forum for the important new negotiations on non-tariff barriers which must now be undertaken.

I recommend specific authorization for the funding of our participation in GATT, thus both demonstrating our support and regularizing our procedures.

For the Long-Term Future

The trade bill I have submitted today is a necessary beginning. It corrects deficiencies in present policies; it enables us to begin the 1970s with a program geared to the start of that decade.

As we look further into the Seventies, it is clear that we must reexamine the entire range of our policies and objectives.

We must take into account the far-reaching changes which have occurred in investment abroad and in patterns of world trade. I have already outlined some of the problems which we will face in the 1970s. Many more will develop—and also new opportunities will emerge.

Intense international competition, new and growing markets, changes in cost levels, technological developments in both agriculture and industry, and large-scale exports of capital are having profound and continuing effects on international production and trade patterns. We can no longer afford to think of our trade policies in the old, simple terms of liberalism vs. protectionism. Rather, we must learn to treat investment, production, employment and trade as interrelated and interdependent.

We need a deeper understanding of the ways in which the major sectors of our economy are actually affected by international trade.

We have arrived at a point at which a careful review should also be made of our tariff structure itself—including such traditional aspects as its reliance upon specific duties, the relationships among tariff rates on various products, and adapting our system to conform more closely with that of the rest of the world.

To help prepare for these many future needs, I will appoint a Commission on World Trade to examine the entire range of our trade and related policies, to analyze the problems we are likely to face in the 1970s, and to prepare recommendations on what we should do about them. It will be empowered to call upon the Tariff Commission and the agencies of the Executive Branch for advice, support and assistance, but its recommendations will be its own.

By expanding world markets, our trade policies have speeded the pace of our own economic progress and aided the development of others. As we look to the future, we must seek a continued expansion of world trade, even as we also seek the dismantling of those other barriers—political, social and ideological—that have stood in the way of a freer exchange of people and ideas, as well as of goods and technology.

Our goal is an open world. Trade is one of the doors to that open world. Its continued expansion requires that others move with us, and that we achieve reciprocity in fact as well as in spirit.

Armed with the recommendations and analyses of the new Commission on World Trade, we will work toward broad new policies for the 1970s that will encourage that reciprocity, and that will lead us, in growing and shared prosperity, toward a world both open and just.

RICHARD NIXON

TEXT OF PRESIDENT'S SPEECH ON VIETNAM PEACE PROPOSALS

Following is the complete text of President Nixon's May 14 speech offering proposals to end the Vietnam war.

Good evening, my fellow Americans.

I have asked for this television time tonight to report to you on our most difficult and urgent problem—the war in Vietnam.

Since I took office four months ago, nothing has taken so much of my time and energy as the search for a way to bring lasting peace to Vietnam. I know that some believe I should have ended the war immediately after the inauguration by simply ordering our forces home from Vietnam.

This would have been the easy thing to do. It might have been a popular move. But I would have betrayed my solemn responsibility as President of the United States if I had done so.

I want to end this war. The American people want to end this war. The people of South Vietnam want to end this war. But we want to end it permanently so that the younger brothers of our soldiers in Vietnam will not have to fight in the future in another Vietnam someplace else in the world.

The fact that there is no easy way to end the war does not mean that we have no choice but to let the war drag on with no end in sight.

For four years American boys have been fighting and dying in Vietnam. For 12 months our negotiators have been talking with the other side in Paris. And yet the fighting goes on. The destruction continues. Brave men still die.

The time has come for some new initiatives. Repeating the old formulas and the tired rhetoric of the past is not enough. When Americans are risking their lives in war, it is the responsibility of their leaders to take some risks for peace.

I would like to report to you tonight on some of the things we have been doing in the past four months to bring true peace, and then I would like to make some concrete proposals to speed that day.

Our first step began before inauguration. This was to launch an intensive review of every aspect of the nation's Vietnam policy. We accepted nothing on faith, we challenged every assumption and every statistic. We made a systematic, serious examination of all the alternatives open to us. We carefully considered recommendations offered both by critics and supporters of past policies.

From the review, it became clear at once that the new Administration faced a set of immediate operational problems.

• The other side was preparing for a new offensive.

• There was a wide gulf of distrust between Washington and Saigon.

• In eight months of talks in Paris, there had been no negotiations directly concerned with a final settlement.

Therefore, we moved on several fronts at once.

We frustrated the attack which was launched in late February. As a result, the North Vietnamese and the Viet Cong failed to achieve their military objectives.

We restored a close working relationship with Saigon. In the resulting atmosphere of mutual confidence, President Thieu and his government have taken important initiatives in the search for a settlement.

We speeded up the strengthening of the South Vietnamese forces. I am glad to report tonight, that as a result, General Abrams told me on Monday that progress in the training program had been excellent, and that apart from any developments that may occur in the negotiations in Paris, that time is approaching when South Vietnamese forces will be able to take over some of the fighting fronts now being manned by Americans.

In weighing alternate courses, we have had to recognize that the situation as it exists today is far different from what it was two years ago or four years ago or ten years ago.

One difference is that we no longer have the choice of not intervening. We have crossed that bridge. There are now more than a half million American troops in Vietnam and 35,000 Americans have lost their lives.

We can have honest debate about whether we should have entered the war in Vietnam. We can have honest debate about how the war has been conducted. But the urgent question today is what to do now that we are there.

Against that background, let me discuss first what we have rejected, and second, what we are prepared to accept.

We have ruled out attempting to impose a purely military solution on the battlefield.

We have also ruled out either a one-sided withdrawal from Vietnam, or the acceptance in Paris of terms that would amount to a disguised American defeat.

When we assumed the burden of helping defend South Vietnam, millions of South Vietnamese men, women and children placed their trust in us. To abandon them now would risk a massacre that would shock and dismay everyone in the world who values human life.

Abandoning the South Vietnamese people, however, would jeopardize more than lives in South Vietnam. It would threaten our long-term hopes for peace in the world. A great nation cannot renege on its pledges. A great nation must be worthy of trust.

When it comes to maintaining peace, "prestige" is not an empty word. I am not speaking of false pride or bravado—they should have no place in our policies. I speak, rather, of the respect that one nation has for another's integrity in defending its principles and meeting its obligations.

If we simply abandoned our effort in Vietnam, the cause of peace might not survive the damage that would be done to other nations' confidence in our reliability.

Another reason for not withdrawing unilaterally stems from debates within the Communist world between those who argue for a policy of containment or confrontation with the United States, and those who argue against it.

If Hanoi were to succeed in taking over South Vietnam by force—even after the power of the United States had been engaged—it would greatly strengthen those leaders who scorn negotiation, who advocate aggression, who minimize the risks of confrontation with the United States. It would bring peace now but it would enormously increase the danger of a bigger war later.

If we are to move successfully from an era of confrontation to an era of negotiation, then we have to demonstrate—at the point at which confrontation is being tested—that confrontation with the United States is costly and unrewarding.

Almost without exception, the leaders of non-Communist Asia have told me that they would consider a one-sided American withdrawal from Vietnam to be a threat to the security of their own nations.

In determining what choices would be acceptable, we have to understand our essential objective in Vietnam. What we want is very little, but very fundamental. We seek the opportunity for the South Vietnamese people to determine their own political future without outside interference.

Let me put it plainly: What the United States wants for South Vietnam is not the important thing. What North Vietnam wants for South Vietnam is not the important thing. What is important is what the people of South Vietnam want for South Vietnam.

The United States has suffered over a million casualties in four wars in this century. Whatever faults we may have as a nation, we have asked nothing for ourselves in return for those sacrifices. We have been generous toward those whom we have fought. We have helped our former foes as well as our friends in the task of reconstruction. We are proud of this record, and we bring the same attitude in our search for a settlement in Vietnam.

In this spirit, let me be explicit about several points:

• We seek no bases in Vietnam.

• We seek no military ties.

• We are willing to agree to neutrality for South Vietnam if that is what the South Vietnamese people freely choose.

• We believe there should be an opportunity for full participation in the political life of South Vietnam by all political elements that are prepared to do so without the use of force or intimidation.

• We are prepared to accept any government in South Vietnam that results from the free choice of the South Vietnamese people themselves.

• We have no intention of imposing any form of government upon the people of South Vietnam, nor will we be a party to such coercion.

• We have no objection to reunification, if that turns out to be what the people of North Vietnam and the people of South Vietnam want: we ask only that the decision reflect the free choice of the people concerned.

At this point, I would like to add a personal word based on many visits to South Vietnam over the past five years. This is the most difficult war in America's history, fought against a ruthless enemy. I am proud of our men who have carried the terrible burden of this war with dignity and courage, despite the division and opposition to the war in the United States. History will record that never have America's fighting men fought more bravely for more unselfish goals than our men in Vietnam. It is our responsibility to see that they have not fought in vain.

In pursuing our limited objective, we insist on no rigid diplomatic formula. Peace could be achieved by a formal negotiated settlement. Peace could be achieved by an informal understanding, provided that the understanding is clear, and that there were adequate assurances that it would be observed. Peace on paper is not as important as peace in fact.

This brings us to the matter of negotiations.

We must recognize that peace in Vietnam cannot be achieved overnight. A war that has raged for many years will require detailed negotiations and cannot be settled by a single stroke.

What kind of a settlement will permit the South Vietnamese people to determine freely their own political future? Such a settlement will require the withdrawal of all non-South Vietnamese forces, including our own, from South Vietnam, and procedures for political choice that give each significant group in South Vietnam a real opportunity to participate in the political life of the nation.

To implement these principles, I reaffirm now our willingness to withdraw our forces on a specified timetable. We ask only that North Vietnam withdraw its forces from South Vietnam, Cambodia and Laos into North Vietnam, also in accordance with a timetable.

We include Cambodia and Laos to ensure that these countries would not be used as bases for a renewed war. Our offer provides for a simultaneous start on withdrawal by both sides; for agreement on a mutually acceptable timetable; and for the withdrawal to be accomplished quickly.

The North Vietnamese delegates have been saying in Paris that political issues should be discussed along with military issues, and there must be a political settlement in the South. We do not dispute this, but the military withdrawal involves outside forces, and can, therefore, be properly negotiated by North Vietnam and the United States, with the concurrence of its allies.

The political settlement is an internal matter which ought to be decided among the South Vietnamese themselves, and not imposed by outsiders. However, if our presence at these political negotiations would be helpful, and if the South Vietnamese concerned agreed, we would be willing to participate, along with the representatives of Hanoi, if that also were desired.

Recent statements by President Thieu have gone far toward opening the way to a political settlement. He has publicly declared his government's willingness to discuss political solution with the National Liberation Front, and has offered free elections. This was a dramatic step forward, a reasonable offer that could lead to a settlement. The South Vietnamese government has offered to talk without preconditions. I believe the other side should also be willing to talk without preconditions.

The South Vietnamese government recognizes, as we do, that a settlement must permit all persons and groups that are prepared to renounce the use of force to participate freely in the political life of South Vietnam. To be effective, such a settlement would require two things: First, a process that would allow the South Vietnamese people to express their choice; and, second, a guarantee that this process would be a fair one.

We do not insist on a particular form of guarantee. The important thing is that the guarantees should have the confidence of the South Vietnamese people, and that they should be broad enough and strong enough to protect the interests of all major South Vietnamese groups.

This, then, is the outline of the settlement that we seek to negotiate in Paris. Its basic terms are very simple: Mutual withdrawal of non-South Vietnamese forces from South Vietnam, and free choice for the people of South Vietnam. I believe that the long-term interests of peace require that we insist on no less, and that the realities of the situation require that we seek no more.

And now, to make very concrete what I have said, I propose the following specific measures, which seem to me consistent with the principles of all parties. These proposals are made on the basis of full consultation with President Thieu.

• As soon as agreement can be reached, all non-South Vietnamese forces would begin withdrawals from South Vietnam.

• Over a period of twelve months, by agreed-upon stages, the major portions of all U.S., Allied, and other non-South Vietnamese forces would be withdrawn. At the end of this twelve month period, the remaining U.S., Allied and other non-South Vietnamese forces would move into designated base areas and would not engage in combat operations.

• The remaining U.S. and Allied forces would complete their withdrawals as the remaining North Vietnamese forces were withdrawn and returned to North Vietnam.

• An international supervisory body, acceptable to both sides, would be created for the purpose of verifying withdrawals, and for any other purposes agreed upon between the two sides.

• This international body would begin operating in accordance with an agreed timetable and would participate in arranging supervised cease-fires in Vietnam.

• As soon as possible after the international body was functioning, elections would be held under agreed procedures and under the supervision of the international body.

• Arrangements would be made for the release of prisoners of war on both sides at the earliest possible time.

• All parties would agree to observe the Geneva Accords of 1954 regarding South Vietnam and Cambodia, and the Laos Accords of 1962.

I believe this proposal for peace is realistic, and takes account of the legitimate interests of all concerned. It is consistent with President Thieu's six points. It can accommodate the various programs put forth by the other side. We and the government of South Vietnam are prepared to discuss its details with the other side.

Secretary Rogers is now in Saigon and he will be discussing with President Thieu how, together, we may put forward these proposed measures most usefully in Paris. He will, as well, be consulting with our other Asian allies on these measures while on his Asian trip. However, I would stress that these proposals are not offered on a take-it-or-leave-it basis. We are quite willing to consider other approaches consistent with our principles.

We are willing to talk about anybody's program—Hanoi's four points, the NLF's 10 points—provided it can be made consistent with the very few basic principles I have set forth here.

Despite our disagreement with several of its points, we welcome the fact that the NLF has put forward its first comprehensive program. We are studying that program carefully. However, we cannot ignore the fact that immediately after the offer, the scale of enemy attacks stepped up and American casualties in Vietnam increased.

Let me make one point clear. If the enemy wants peace with the United States, that is not the way to get it.

I have set forth a peace program tonight which is generous in its terms. I have indicated our willingness to consider other proposals. But no greater mistake could be made than to confuse flexibility with weakness or of being reasonable with lack of resolution. I must also make clear, in all candor, that if the needless suffering continues, this will affect other decisions. Nobody has anything to gain by delay.

Reports from Hanoi indicate that the enemy has given up hope for a military victory in South Vietnam, but is counting on a collapse of American will in the United States. There could be no greater error in judgment.

Let me be quite blunt. Our fighting men are not going to be worn down; our mediators are not going to be talked down; and our allies are not going to be let down.

My fellow Americans, I have seen the ugly face of war in Vietnam. I have seen the wounded in field hospitals—American boys, South Vietnamese boys, North Vietnamese boys. They were different in many ways—the color of their skins, their religions, their races, some were enemies, some were friends.

But the differences were small, compared with how they were alike. They were brave men, and they were so young. Their lives—their dreams for the future—had been shattered by a war over which they had no control.

With all the moral authority of the office which I hold, I say that America could have no greater and prouder role than to help to end this war in a way which will bring nearer that day in which we can have a world order in which people can live together in peace and friendship.

I do not criticize those who disagree with me on the conduct of our peace negotiations. And I do not ask unlimited patience from a people whose hopes for peace have too often been raised and then cruelly dashed over the past four years.

I have tried to present the facts about Vietnam with complete honesty, and I shall continue to do so in my reports to the American people.

Tonight, all I ask is that you consider those facts, and, whatever our differences, that you support a program which can lead to a peace we can live with and a peace we can be proud of. Nothing could have a greater effect in convincing the enemy that he should negotiate in good faith than to see the American people united behind a generous and reasonable peace offer.

In my campaign for the Presidency, I pledged to end this war in a way that would increase our chances to win true and lasting peace in Vietnam, in the Pacific, and in the world. I am determined to keep that pledge. If I fail to do so, I expect the American people to hold me accountable for that failure.

But while I will never raise false expectations, my deepest hope, as I speak to you tonight, is that we shall be able to look back on this day, at this critical turning point when American initiative moved us off dead center and forward to the time when this war would be brought to an end and when we shall be able to devote the unlimited energies and dedication of the American people to the exciting challenges of peace.

Thank you, and good night.

ELECTORAL REFORM STATEMENT

Following is the complete text of President Nixon's Sept. 30 statement in support of the proposed constitutional amendment for direct election of the President. (For message, see p. 41-A.)

In February of this year I committed this Administration to support any reform of the electoral system that removed its most negative features. I said I would support any amendment approved by Congress that would make three specific reforms in the current system—one, eliminate the problem of the "faithless elector," two, make a 40 percent margin adequate for victory, and three, reform the system so that the electoral outcome more closely reflects the popular outcome.

It was my judgment then that the approach most likely to prevail in the country would be the proportional distribution method. I thought it had the best chance of being approved by the Congress and by three-fourths of the States.

Now there is an entirely new factor to be considered if we are to have electoral reform with all necessary speed. The House of Representatives has overwhelmingly supported the direct election approach. It is clear that unless the Senate follows the lead of the House, all opportunity for reform will be lost this year and possibly for years to come.

Accordingly, because the ultimate goal of electoral reform must prevail over differences as to how best to achieve that goal, I endorse the direct election approach and urge the Senate also to adopt it. While many Senators may prefer a different method, I believe that contrary views are now a luxury—that the need for electoral reform is urgent and should be our controlling consideration. I hope, therefore, that two-thirds of the Senate will approve the House-passed amendment as promptly as possible so that all of us together can then urge the States also to give their approval.

ENVIRONMENTAL QUALITY COUNCIL

Following is the text of President Nixon's May 29 statement creating the Environmental Quality Council and Citizens' Advisory Committee on Environmental Quality.

"The conservation of our natural resources and their proper use constitute the fundamental problem which underlies almost every other problem of our national life," Theodore Roosevelt said in 1907. When men talked about conservation in his time, they usually singled out the wildlands, plant and animal life, and valuable minerals, for in these areas they saw the threat of scarcity. Resources such as the air or the water or the countryside itself were of less concern, for the supply and the quality of such things seemed invulnerable.

I am sure that Roosevelt and his associates of sixty and more years ago would be most surprised if they knew that in our time technological development threatens the availability of good air and good water, of open space and even quiet neighborhoods. Yet that is exactly what is happening. Each day we receive new evidence of the declining quality of the American environment.

Because the quality of American environment is threatened as it has not been threatened before in our history, I am creating today, by Executive order, the Environmental Quality Council. This new body will be a Cabinet-level advisory group which will provide the focal point for this administration's efforts to protect all of our natural resources.

The Council, the structure of which in some respects parallels that of the National Security Council and the Urban Affairs Council, will have as its Executive Secretary the Science Advisor to the President, Dr. Lee A. DuBridge. My Executive order also creates a 15-member Citizens' Advisory Committee on Environmental Quality, which will be chaired by Laurance S. Rockefeller.

I am asking the new Council, with the assistance of the Citizens' Advisory Committee, to examine the full range of variables which affect environmental quality. I expect the group to review existing policies and programs and to suggest ways of improving them. Its members must project the impact of new technologies and encourage scientific developments which will help us protect our resources.

I am hopeful that the Environmental Quality Council will foster greater cooperation in this problem area between our Government and the governments of other nations, between the various levels of American government, and between governmental and relevant nongovernmental organizations.

Finally, I would suggest that this new body must anticipate new problems even as it focuses on present ones. It is not enough that it provide answers to the questions we are asking today. It must also pose the new questions which will face us tomorrow.

The deterioration of the environment is in large measure the result of our inability to keep pace with progress. We have become victims of our own technological genius. But I am confident that the same energy and skill which gave rise to these problems can also be marshaled for the purpose of conquering them. Together we have damaged the environment and together we can improve it.

As I said during last fall's campaign: "We need a high standard of living, but we also need a high quality of life....We need a strategy of quality for the seventies to match the strategy of quantity of the past." I am pleased to announce the creation of the Environmental Quality Council, for I believe it will provide us with that strategy and will give us the means for implementing it.

NIXON URGES SUPPORT FOR 'NEW FEDERALISM,' 'NEW REALISM'

Following is the complete text of President Nixon's Sept. 1 speech as prepared for delivery to the National Governors' Conference, Colorado Springs, Colo.

We are meeting here tonight at a time of great and fundamental change in America—of changes more far-reaching than have ever before been seen in the span of a single lifetime.

These changes summon all of us—the Federal Government, the states, the counties, cities and towns, each person everywhere—to an adventure in human advancement.

We stand on the threshold of a time when the impossible becomes possible—a time when we can choose goals that, a generation ago, would have seemed as unreachable as the moon, and reach them.

The Spirit of Apollo gave us a brief, glittering glimpse of how far we can stretch. Thousands of minds, thousands of hands, all were marshaled in selfless dedication in achieving a great human dream—and the dream came true.

Today, we in America can afford to dream—but we have to put drive behind those dreams.

This requires that we turn—now—to a new strategy for the '70s—one that enables us to command our own future by commanding the forces of change.

Only seven years from now, in 1976, America will celebrate its 200th birthday as a nation. So let us look ahead to that great anniversary in the Spirit of Apollo—and discover in ourselves a new Spirit of '76.

Let us resolve that what we can do, we will do.

When a great nation confronts its shortcomings, not angrily, but analytically; when it commits its resources, not wantonly, but wisely; when it calms its hatreds, masters its fears and draws together in a spirit of common endeavor, then the forces of progress are on the march.

The central race in the world today is neither an arms race nor a space race. It is the race between man and change. The central question is whether we are to be the master of events or the pawn of events.

If we are to win this race, then our first need is to make government itself governable.

When the new Administration took office last January, we confronted a set of hard and unpleasant facts. I cite these not in a partisan way; they are not the fault of any one Administration or any one party. Rather, they are part of our common experience as a people, the result of an accumulating failure of government over the years to come to grips with a future that soon overtook it.

We confronted a legacy of federal deficits that has added $58 billion to the burden of public debt in the past 10 years.

We confronted an inflationary spiral that had gone out of control, that has raised consumer prices 18 percent in the last 5 years, 26 percent in the last 10 years and that threatened to destroy the dollar unless we acted promptly and forcibly to curb it.

We confronted the fact that state and local governments were being crushed in a fiscal vise, squeezed by rising costs, rising demands for services and exhaustion of revenue sources.

We confronted the fact that in the past five years the Federal Government alone spent more than a quarter of a trillion dollars on social programs—more than $250 billion. Yet far from solving our problems, these expenditures had reaped a harvest of dissatisfaction, frustration and bitter division.

Never in human history has so much been spent by so many for such a negative result. The cost of the lesson has been high, but we have learned that it is not only what we spend that matters; it is the way we spend it.

Beyond this, we confronted a collapse of confidence in government itself, a mounting distrust of all authority that stemmed in large measure from the increasing inability of government to deliver its services or to keep its promises.

As Professor Peter Drucker has written, "There is mounting evidence that government is big rather than strong; that it is fat and flabby rather than powerful; that it costs a great deal but does not achieve much. There is mounting evidence also that the citizen less and less believes in government and is increasingly disenchanted with it. Indeed, government is sick— and just at the time when we need a strong, healthy and vigorous government."

The problem has not been a lack of good intentions, and not merely a lack of money. Methods inherited from the '30s proved out of date in the '60s. Structures put together in the '30s broke down under the load of the '60s.

Overly centralized, over-bureaucratized, the Federal Government became unresponsive as well as inefficient.

In their struggle to keep up, states and localities found the going increasingly difficult.

In the space of only 10 years, state and local expenditures rose by two and a half times—from $44 billion in 1958 to $108 billion in 1968.

States alone have had to seek more than 200 tax rate increases in the past years. Nearly four-fifths of the state legislatures that convened in 1969 have found themselves considering requests for even higher taxes.

You know and I know that simply piling tax on tax is not the long-range solution to the problems we face together.

We have to devise a new way to make our revenue system meet the needs of the '70s—to put the money where the problems are and to get a dollar's worth of return for a dollar spent. Our new strategy for the '70s begins with the reform of the government:

● Overhauling its structure.

● Pruning out those programs that have failed or that have outlived their time.

● Ensuring that its delivery systems actually deliver the intended services to the intended beneficiaries.

● Gearing its programs to the concept of social investment.

● Focusing its activities not only on tomorrow, but on the day after tomorrow.

This must be a cooperative venture among governments at all levels, because it centers on what I have called the "New Federalism"—in which power, funds and authority are channeled increasingly to those governments closest to the people.

The essence of the New Federalism is to help regain control of our national destiny by returning a greater share of control to state and local authorities.

This in turn requires constant attention to raising the quality of government at all levels.

The new strategy for the '70s also requires a strategy for peace—and I pledge to you tonight that we will have an effective strategy for peace.

This means maintaining defense forces strong enough to keep the peace—while not allowing wasteful expenditures to drain away resources we need for progress.

It means limiting our commitments abroad to those we can prudently and realistically keep. It means helping other free nations maintain their own security, but not rushing in to do for them what they can and should do for themselves.

It does not mean laying down our leadership. It does not mean abandoning our allies. It does mean forging a new structure of world stability in which the burdens as well as the benefits are fairly shared—a structure that does not rely on the strength of one nation, but that draws strength from all nations.

An effective strategy for peace makes possible an effective strategy for meeting our domestic needs. To place this new domestic strategy in concrete terms, let me cite a few examples of changes we in the new Administration have made or proposed since taking office.

We have proposed the first major reform of welfare in the history of welfare.

This would abolish the discredited Aid to Families With Dependent Children program and launch in its place a new system that for the first time would ensure a minimum income for every family with dependent children—and at the same time provide a coordinated structure of work requirements, incentives and training designed to move people off the welfare rolls and onto payrolls.

Some object to these proposals—understandably—as seeming to favor one region over another, or because they give the rich states less than the poorer states. We rejected these arguments because we are one country. We must think in terms of the people and their needs—wherever they are. We must meet our problems where the problems are. Unless we act to meet the problems of human need in the places where they exist, the troubles of rural America today will be the troubles of urban America tomorrow.

Consider the name of this nation: the United States of America. We establish minimum national standards because we are united; we encourage local supplements because we are a federation of states; and we care for the unfortunate because this is America.

We have proposed the first major restructuring of food programs for the needy in the history of the food programs.

For years, food programs were designed as much to get rid of surplus commodities as to feed hungry people. For the first time, we have proposed that every American family shall have the resources, in food stamps, commodities and other assistance, to obtain a minimum nutritious diet, with free food stamps for those with very low incomes.

We have declared the first five years of a child's life to be a period of special and specific federal concern.

New knowledge recently acquired has shown that these earliest, formative years are crucial to a child's later development. Yet with only random exceptions, no provision had previously been made to ensure the welfare of children during these years. With an eye to the next generation, we have made it our business to fill that void.

We have proposed the first major reform of the income tax system in nearly two decades, to remove millions of the poor from the tax rolls entirely, to close loopholes that have allowed many of the rich to escape taxation and to make the entire structure more balanced and more equitable.

We have proposed the most fundamental reform of the unemployment insurance system in the history of unemployment insurance.

The system established in the '30s has been allowed to fall far behind its presumed level of benefits, has failed to stay abreast of new possibilities for providing extended benefits in periods of economic recession and has continued to leave millions of workers uncovered. The reform we have proposed meets each of these issues.

We have proposed the first reform in the fiscal structure of federalism since the 1930s.

In proposing to begin the sharing of federal tax revenues with the states—to be spent as the states see fit—we are putting our money where our principles are. The power to tax is the power to destroy; but the sharing of tax revenues provides the power to build.

We have proposed, for the first time in history, a comprehensive and effective delegation of federal programs to state and local management.

The Comprehensive Manpower Act would turn over to state and local direction a major federal program which clearly has to be nationwide in scope, and federally funded, but which can most effectively be managed at the state and local level.

We have begun the first over-all reform of the organization of the Federal Government since the Hoover Commission.

By establishing common headquarters and common regional boundaries for the various federal agencies, we have made decentralized administration possible—and made it possible for governors and mayors to do their business with those agencies at one time and in one place. We have proposed consolidation of closely related federal grant programs. The manpower programs of the Department of Labor have been overhauled into a coherent, effective system for delivering skills to those who need them and matching workers with job vacancies. A President's Advisory Council on Executive Organization has been established to provide over-all and specific recommendations for improved effectiveness.

For the first time, machinery has been created to raise the problems of the cities and the problems of the environment to the level of formal, inter-departmental, Cabinet-level concern, with the creation of the Urban Affairs Council and the Council on Environmental Quality.

For the first time, machinery has been created within the White House for a coordinated system of forward planning of needs and resources. With establishment of the National Goals Research Staff, we have built into the budgetary and program operations of the National Government a systematic assessment of future needs and the resources available for meeting them.

There is another reform I have asked, and to which I attach special priority as a matter of high principle: reform of the draft.

Until peacetime conditions make a shift to an all-volunteer armed force possible—while the draft remains necessary—it is imperative that we make it as nearly fair as possible and that we reduce to a minimum the unnecessarily long period of uncertainty that now hangs over the lives of millions of our young people.

The 24 major legislative requests I have sent to Congress have also included proposals ranging from an overhaul of foreign aid to the most wide-ranging reform of the postal service in history; from a new program of mass transit aid to new measures for the combating of narcotics, pornography and organized crime.

Taken together, these measures are sweeping in their implications; they also represent fundamental new directions in national policy.

They represent a comprehensive, concerted effort to make government work; to make it work fairly; to make it responsive; and to gear it to the early anticipation of emerging needs, rather than belated response to crises that could have been avoided.

Let us look at these measures in a larger framework.

Exactly four months from today, we will enter the decade of the '70s. And as we look ahead toward that 200th anniversary of American independence in 1976, we have a target to shoot for.

What kind of a nation we will be on that momentous anniversary is ours to determine by what we do or fail to do.

As conditions are changing, so we must change.

If we are to make our choices effective, we need the machinery to translate wish into reality.

The reforms I have proposed in these legislative recommendations are not partisan changes. They are positive changes. They have no special constituency of region or class or interest group. Their constituency is tomorrow.

It already is painfully clear that many hard choices will have to be made. Dreams of unlimited billions of dollars being released once the war in Vietnam ends are just that—dreams. True, there will be additional money—but the claims on it already are enormous. There should be no illusion that what some call the "peace and growth dividend" will automatically solve our national problems or release us from the need to establish priorities.

There are hard budget and tax decisions ahead. These involve your interests, as Governors; they involve the interests of all of us, as citizens.

In order to find the money for new programs, we will have to trim it out of old ones.

This is one reason why I regard the reforms I have proposed as essential. We can no longer afford the luxury of inefficiency. We cannot count on good money to bail us out from a bad idea.

Equally important, continued improvement of governments at the state and local levels is essential to make these new concepts work.

If the delegation of funds and authority to state and local governments under the Comprehensive Manpower Act is successful, this can be a model for other programs. But we can only toss the ball; the states and localities have to catch it and carry it.

I am confident that you can.

For a long time, the phrase "states' rights" was often used as an escape from responsibility—as a way of avoiding a problem rather than of meeting a problem.

But that time has passed.

The plain fact of the matter is that as we look ahead to the '70s, we can see one thing with startling clarity: there is far more that needs to be done than any one unit of government, or any one level of government, could possibly hope to do by itself. If the job is to be done, a greater part of it must be done by states and localities themselves, and by the people themselves.

I can assure you of this: we are not simply going to tell you the states have a job to do; we are going to help you find the resources to do it.

We are not simply going to lecture you on what you should do. We are going to examine what we can do together.

One of the key points I want to make tonight is, in a sense, very similar to one that I made on my recent visits to our NATO partners and to our friends in Asia. Washington will no longer try to go it alone; Washington will no longer dictate without consulting. A new day has come, in which we recognize that partnership is a two-way street, and if the partnership is to thrive that street has to be traveled—both ways.

This poses a new challenge to the states—not only to administer programs, but to devise programs; not only to employ resources, but to choose the things for which they should be employed.

But in my talks with many Governors and other state officials, I have found them ready to rise to that challenge. I have become convinced that the states today are ready for a new role.

The quality of state and local government already is markedly improving.

As one healthy indicator of the states' determination to improve still further, I would cite especially the recent trend toward higher pay for state legislators and other state and local officials. Their responsibilities are growing heavier. We should be willing to pay for the performance that we rightly ask.

The New Federalism also recognizes the role of people—of individuals doing, caring, sharing. The concept of voluntary action, of community action, of people banding together in a spirit of neighborliness to do those things which they see must be done, is deeply rooted in America's character and tradition. As we have swept power and responsibility to Washington, we have undercut this tradition. Yet when it comes to helping one another, Washington can never bring to the task the heart that neighbors can. Washington can never bring the sensitivity to local conditions, or the new sense of self-importance a person feels when he finds that some one person cares enough to help.

In encouraging a new birth of voluntary action, I intend to look not only to the Federal Government but also to the states for inspiration and encouragement. Each state has had its own pattern of experience, its own examples of how people have successfully helped people. By sharing these examples, they can be multiplied.

As we look toward 1976 and beyond, our range of possible choices is breathtaking: how we manage our growing abundance, how we make real our ideals of full opportunity, how we clean up our air and water, how we balance our systems of transportation, how we expand our systems of education and health care—and the list could go on, almost indefinitely.

As only one dimension of the new tasks we face, the best estimates are that America's population will increase by 100 million between now and the year 2000. That means that thirty years from now, there will be half again as many people as there are today. It means that in this short span of time we have to build the equivalent of 50 cities the size of Philadelphia.

Or to put it another way, the Committee on Urban Growth Policy has recommended that we should begin planning now for 100 new cities averaging 100,000 in population and 10 new cities averaging a million each—yet even if we did this, it would accommodate only 20 percent of the added population we have to plan for by the year 2000.

Yet the other side of this coin of challenge is an enormous opportunity.

Growth on such an heroic scale offers an unprecedented opportunity to shape that growth so that our cities and communities enhance man himself.

More than anything else, it is these new tasks of the future—not the distant future, but the immediate future—that give urgency to the need to reform government today.

We can command the future only if we can manage the present.

The reforms I have proposed are designed to make this possible.

Only if we clean out the unnecessary can we focus on the necessary.

Only if we stop fighting the battles of the '30s can we take on the battles of the '70s.

These reforms represent a New Federalism; a new humanism; a new realism.

They are based not on theoretical abstractions, but on the hard experience of the past third of a century.

They are addressed to the real problems of real people in a real world—and to the needs of the next third of a century.

They represent not an end, but a beginning—the beginning of a new era in which we confound the prophets of doom and make government an instrument for casting the future in the image of our hopes.

That task requires the best efforts of all of us together.

It requires the best thinking of all of us together, as we choose our goals and devise the means of their achievement.

But the future that beckons us holds greater promise than any man has ever known. These reforms are steps in the direction of that promise—and as we take them, let us do so confident in the strength of America and firm in our faith that we can chart our destiny in the abundant spirit of a great and resourceful people. This spirit has been our strength. Marshaled in a new Spirit of '76, giving force to our purposes and direction to our efforts, it can be our salvation.

VOLUNTARY ACTION

Following is the complete text of President Nixon's April 30 statement on voluntary action in helping to solve the nation's problems.

One of the great, distinguishing characteristics of the American people is their readiness to join together in helping one another. The principle of voluntary action is not something lately grafted onto America's ways; it goes back as far as the nation's founding.

Today, we find that the nation has grown enormously in wealth, and that its wealth is more widely distributed than ever before. Yet need persists: human need, personal need, which government can help to meet but which it cannot meet alone. The very magnitude of everything, government included, increases the need for that direct, human dimension that only the concerned individual can provide. More than ever, America needs the enlistment of the energies and resources of its people—not as substitutes for government action, but as supplements to it. People can reach where government cannot; people can do what government cannot. Today, more than ever, America needs the hearts and hands of its people, joined in those common enterprises, small as well as large, that are the mark of caring and the cement of community.

There is no lack of will. Millions of Americans stand ready to serve and to help, eager to know what they can do and how they can do it. One of the chief aims of this Administration is to help in matching up the willing hands with the tasks that need doing.

Voluntary efforts already are contributing enormously to our national well-being, but they have had neither the assistance nor the recognition that they deserve.

In the past, government has sometimes been the jealous competitor of private efforts. From now on, it will offer encouragement and support.

Toward this end, I have taken or am taking four preliminary steps:

• On the Government side of the effort, I will, by Executive Order, form a Cabinet Committee on Voluntary Action. Its chairman will be Secretary Romney of the Department of Housing and Urban Development, who scored impressive successes in stimulating voluntary action during his terms as Governor of Michigan. Its other members will be the Secretaries of Commerce, of Labor, of Agriculture, and of Health, Education, and Welfare, the Attorney General and the director of the Office of Economic Opportunity.

• I have asked Secretary Romney to establish an Office of Voluntary Action in his Department.

• I have asked Max M. Fisher of Detroit to serve as my special consultant on voluntary action and to work with Secretary Romney and the Cabinet Committee. Mr. Fisher has brought together small groups of private leaders for informal consultation on the most effective means by which the Government can assist in stimulating voluntary activities. He will have continuing responsibility for the important aspect of this program which involves nongovernmental organizations and individuals. Mr. Fisher is currently chairman of the New Detroit Committee, the United Foundation of Detroit, and president of the United Jewish Appeal.

• I have directed the Secretary of Housing and Urban Development to establish a clearinghouse for information on voluntary programs and on government programs designed to foster voluntary action. Eventually this clearinghouse will be a function of the private sector.

The Cabinet Committee will report directly to the Cabinet and the President. It will foster cooperation among the various Departments and agencies on programs related to voluntary action and will seek to promote more widespread reliance on and recognition of voluntary activities. In addition, it will serve voluntary organizations by providing a focal point through which they can better make their needs and concerns known to the Administration, and by clearing away governmental roadblocks to the effective employment of voluntary resources. It will be a prime mover in developing new federal initiatives for encouraging voluntary action.

The Office of Voluntary Action in the Department of Housing and Urban Development will seek the development and implementation of voluntary action programs for solving problems of urban living and poverty. It will provide for the development and operation of the information clearinghouse, and will make use of both Government vehicles and nongovernment channels to help expand and multiply innovative voluntary action programs. Consistent with law, it will coordinate federal voluntary action programs for dealing with urban and poverty problems. It will cooperate with private groups and citizens, and will be available to assist Mr. Fisher.

Mr. Fisher is already counseling with representatives of a wide range of different kinds of private and voluntary organizations:

• Private social service, health and welfare organizations.
• Private economic organizations—business, labor and agriculture.
• Fraternal service, professional and religious organizations.
• Foundations.
• Civic and community organizations.
• Youth, women's and minority group organizations.
• Communications media and their organizations.

Representatives of state and local governments will also be consulted, because of their own great potential for stimulating voluntary action.

The response of the groups Mr. Fisher has consulted with thus far has been enthusiastic. Many of them have offered to make staff available full time to work with the Office of Voluntary Action during its initial stages.

The information clearinghouse will fill a need long recognized but never met. It will serve government, private organizations and individuals.

At one time or another, millions of Americans have asked themselves or others, "What can I do? How can I help?" One of the chief aims of this new effort will be to make answers readily available. It is a remarkable and little-appreciated fact that for practically every one of the great social ills that plague us, solutions have been found somewhere—*by citizen volunteers,* who have devised programs that actually work in their own community. In nearly every case, the experience can be helpful to those who are concerned with similar problems elsewhere.

The four steps I have outlined today are a beginning. As we consider further steps, we will develop them in the closest possible collaboration with the leaders of voluntary activities themselves. All of us involved in this effort are keenly aware that this is an area in which Government initiatives must not be imposed, and that a too-tight federal embrace could smother the voluntary principle. I will not allow that to happen. Our effort will be to assist, not to control; to encourage, not to coerce.

Our aim is not to substitute federal leadership for the dedicated private leadership that already exists in our voluntary organizations. Rather, we will seek to help in every way possible in order that these groups can better realize their larger ambitions for public service.

Within the limits of this caution, however, I am convinced that an enriched partnership—a creative partnership—is possible.

The measure of a government's performance is not only its capacity to deliver services to its citizens, but also its capacity to inspire them to contribute their own efforts.

From the time our nation's first settlers struggled together against a wilderness, voluntary action for mutual help and community betterment has been a hallmark of the American way. Free men and women have worked with one another and aided one another. That spirit is vigorously alive today, and the encouragement of that spirit is needed if our nation is to become what it has the capacity to be.

NIXON ANNOUNCES 50,000 VIETNAM TROOP REDUCTION

Following is the text of President Nixon's Dec. 15 televised progress report to the nation on Vietnam.

Good evening, my fellow Americans.

I have asked for this television time tonight to give you a progress report on our plan to bring a just peace in Vietnam, which I described in my television address on November 3.

As you will recall, I said then that we were proceeding in our pursuit for peace on two fronts—a peace settlement through negotiation, or if that fails, ending the war through Vietnamization, a plan we have developed with the South Vietnamese for the complete withdrawal first of all U.S. combat ground forces and eventually of other forces and their replacement by South Vietnamese forces on an orderly scheduled timetable.

I must report to you tonight with regret that there has been no progress whatever on the negotiating front since November 3. The enemy still insists on a unilateral, precipitate withdrawal of American forces and on a political settlement which would mean the imposition of a Communist government on the people of South Vietnam against their will, and defeat and humiliation for the United States.

This we cannot and will not accept.

Typical of their attitude is their absolute refusal to talk about the fate of the American prisoners they hold and their refusal even to supply their names so as to ease the anguish of their loved ones in the United States. This cruel indefensible action is a shocking demonstration of the inflexible attitude they have taken on all issues at the negotiating table in Paris.

But despite their attitude, we shall continue to participate in the Paris talks and to seek a negotiated peace—one which is fair, fair to North Vietnam, fair to the United States, but most important, fair to the people of South Vietnam. Because as I have indicated, anything is negotiable except the right of the people of South Vietnam to determine their own fate.

As you know, Ambassador Lodge has had to leave his assignment in Paris because of personal reasons. I have designated Philip Habib, one of our most experienced foreign service officers who has been participating in the negotiations for over 18 months, as the acting head of our delegation with the personal rank of Ambassador. He has been given full authority to discuss any proposal that will contribute to a just peace.

Let me turn now to the progress of our plan for Vietnamization and our troop withdrawal program.

When I announced this program in June, I said that the rate of withdrawal would depend on three criteria—progress in the Paris negotiations, progress in the training of South Vietnamese forces and the level of enemy activity.

Now, while there has been no progress on the negotiating front, I have a much more favorable report to give to you tonight with regard to the training of South Vietnamese forces.

First, let me share with you how I reached this conclusion. In making decisions, I believe a President should listen not only to those who tell him what he wants to hear, but to those who tell him what he needs to hear. It is more important to get independent judgments from individuals who are expert on the factors to be considered but who are not directly involved in the operations themselves. This is particularly essential when the lives of American men are involved.

Several months ago I read a book by Sir Robert Thompson, a British expert who was one of the major architects of the victory over the Communist guerillas who attempted to take over Malaya in the 1950s. In his book which was published just as this Administration took office, he was very pessimistic about the conduct of the war in Vietnam. He particularly noted the failure to prepare the South Vietnamese to take over their responsibilities for their own defense.

On October 7 I met with Mr. Thompson and asked him to go to Vietnam and give me a firsthand, candid and completely independent report on the situation there. After five weeks of intensive investigation he gave me his report on December 3.

His full report, which makes several very constructive recommendations, must remain confidential since it bears on the security of our men. But let me read to you from his summary on his findings.

"I was very impressed by the improvement in the military and political situation in Vietnam as compared with all previous visits and especially in the security situation, both in Saigon and the rural areas.

"A winning position in the sense of obtaining a just peace (whether negotiated or not) and of maintaining an independent, non-Communist South Vietnam has been achieved but we are not yet through. We are in a psychological period where the greatest need is confidence, a steady application of the 'do it yourself' concept with continuing U.S. support in the background will increase the confidence already shown by many South Vietnam leaders."

Mr. Thompson's report, which I would describe as cautiously optimistic, is in line with my own attitude and with reports I have received from other observers and from our own civilian and military leaders in Vietnam.

There is one disturbing new development, however, with regard to enemy activity. Enemy infiltration has increased substantially. It has not yet reached the point where our military leaders believe the enemy has developed the capability to mount a major offensive, but we are watching the situation closely to see whether it could develop to that extent.

Now for the decision. Taking all these developments into consideration, I am announcing tonight a reduction in our troop ceiling of 50,000 more U.S. troops by April 15 next year. This means that the ceiling which existed when I took office on January 20 has now been reduced by 115,500 men. This reduction has been made with approval of the government of South Vietnam, and in consultation with the other nations which have combat forces in Vietnam.

Now there are some who believe that to continue our withdrawals at a time when enemy infiltration is increasing is a risk we should not take. However, I have consistently said we must take risks for peace. And in that connection, let me remind the leaders in Hanoi that if their infiltration and the level of enemy activity increases while we are reducing our forces they also will be running a risk. I repeat the statement I made in my speech on Nov. 3.

"Hanoi could make no greater mistake than to assume that an increase in violence will be to its advantage. If I conclude that increased enemy action jeopardizes our remaining forces in Vietnam, I shall not hesitate to take strong and effective measures to deal with that situation."

This reduction in our forces is another orderly step in our plan for peace in Vietnam.

• It marks further progress toward turning over the defense of South Vietnam to the South Vietnamese.

• And it is another clear sign of our readiness to bring an end to the war and to achieve a just peace.

Before concluding this report, I wish to express my appreciation to the great number of people from all over the nation who have indicated their support for our program for a just peace since my speech on November 3.

This support was particularly underlined by the action of the House of Representatives and the Congress in which a majority of both Democrats and Republicans voted overwhelmingly 334 to 55 for a resolution supporting the plan for peace which I announced on November 3.

The leaders in Hanoi have declared on a number of occasions that division in the United States would eventually bring them the victory they cannot win over our fighting men in Vietnam. This demonstration of support by the American people for our plan to bring a just peace has dashed those hopes.

Hanoi should abandon its dream of military victory.

It is time for them to join us in serious negotiations.

There is nothing to be gained by delay.

If Hanoi is willing to talk seriously they will find us flexible and forthcoming.

I am glad that I was able to report tonight some progress in reaching our goal of a just peace in Vietnam. After five years of increasing the number of Americans in Vietnam, we are bringing American men home.

Our casualties continue to be at the lowest rate in three years. But I want you to know that despite this progress, I shall not be satisfied until we achieve the goal we all want—an end to the war on a just and lasting basis.

This is the fifth Christmas when Americans will be fighting in a war far away from home.

I know that there is nothing the American people want more and there is nothing I want more than to see the day come when the Christmas message of "Peace on Earth, Good Will to Men" will be not just an eloquent ideal but a reality for Americans and for all others who cherish peace and freedom throughout the world.

Your continued support of our plan for peace will greatly strengthen our hopes that we can achieve that great goal.

LATIN AMERICAN TEXT

Following is the text of President Nixon's Oct. 31 address to the Inter-American Press Association.

As we stand here on this 25th Anniversary meeting of the Inter-American Press Association, I should like to be permitted some personal comments before I then deliver my prepared remarks to you.

I have learned that this is the first occasion in which the remarks of the President of any one of the American nations has been carried and is being carried live by Telstar to all the nations in the hemisphere. We are proud that it is before the Inter-American Press Association.

I am sure that those of you, and I know that most of you here are members and publishers of the newspaper profession, will not be jealous if this is on television tonight.

Also, I am very privileged to appear before this organization again. I was reminded it was 15 years ago that I, as Vice President, addressed the organization in New Orleans. It is good to be with you tonight, and particularly as the outgoing president is an old friend, Mr. Edwards from Santiago. The new president is also an old friend, Mr. Copley from San Diego—sister cities, one in the Northern Hemisphere of the Americas and the other in the Southern Hemisphere.

There is one other remark that Mrs. Edwards brought eloquently to my attention as we heard that magnificent rendition by the Army Corps of "America the Beautiful." She said, "That is for all of us. We are all Americans in this room."

It is in that spirit that I want to address my remarks tonight to our partnership in the Americas. In doing so, I wish to place before you some suggestions for reshaping and reinvigorating that partnership.

Often we in the United States have been charged with an overweening confidence in the rightness of our own prescriptions, and occasionally we have been guilty of the charge. I intend to correct that. Therefore, my words tonight are meant as an invitation by one partner for further interchange, for increased communication, and above all for new imagination in meeting our shared responsibilities.

For years, we in the United States have pursued the illusion that we alone could remake continents. Conscious of our wealth and technology, seized by the force of good intentions, driven by habitual impatience, remembering the dramatic success of the Marshall Plan in postwar Europe, we have sometimes imagined that we knew what was best for everyone else and that we could and should make it happen. Well, experience has taught us better.

It has taught us that economic and social development is not an achievement of one nation's foreign policy, but something deeply rooted in each nation's own traditions.

It has taught us that aid that infringes pride is no favor to any nation.

It has taught us that each nation, and each region, must be true to its own character.

What I hope we can achieve, therefore, is a more mature partnership in which all voices are heard and none is predominant—a partnership guided by a healthy awareness that give-and-take is better than take-it-or-leave-it.

My suggestions this evening for new directions toward a more balanced relationship come from many sources.

First, they are rooted in my personal convictions. I have seen the problems of this hemisphere. As those in this room know, I have visited every nation in this hemisphere. I have seen them at first hand. I have felt the surging spirit of those nations—determined to break the grip of outmoded structures, yet equally determined to avoid social disintegration. Freedom—justice—a chance for each of our people to live a better and more abundant life—these are goals to which I am unshakeably committed, because progress in our hemisphere is not only a practical necessity, it is a moral imperative.

Second, these new approaches have been substantially shaped by the report of Governor Rockefeller, who, at my request and at your invitation, listened perceptively to the voices of our neighbors and incorporated their thoughts into a set of foresighted proposals.

Third, they are consistent with thoughts expressed in the Consensus of Vina del Mar, which we have studied with great care.

Fourth, they have benefited from the counsel of many persons in government and out, in this country and throughout the hemisphere.

And, finally, basically, they reflect the concern of the people of the United States for the development and progress of a hemisphere which is new in spirit, and which—through our efforts together—we can make new in accomplishment.

Tonight, I offer no grandiose promises and no panaceas.

I do offer action.

The actions I propose represent a new approach. They are based on five principles:

* First, a firm commitment to the inter-American system, to the compacts which bind us in that system—as exemplified by the Organization of American States and by the principles so nobly set forth in its charter.

* Second, respect for national identity and national dignity, in a partnership in which rights and responsibilities are shared by a community of independent states.

* Third, a firm commitment to continued United States assistance for hemispheric development.

* Fourth, a belief that the principal future pattern of this assistance must be U.S. support for Latin American initiatives, and that this can best be achieved on a multi-lateral basis within the inter-American system.

* Finally, a dedication to improving the quality of life in this new world of ours—to making people the center of our concerns, and to helping meet their economic, social and human needs.

We have heard many voices from the Americas in these first months of our new Administration—voices of hope, voices of concern, and some voices of frustration.

We have listened.

These voices have told us they wanted fewer promises and more action. They have told us that the United States aid programs seemed to have helped the United States more than Latin America. They have told us that our trade policies were insensitive to the needs of other American nations. They have told us that if our partnership is to thrive, or even to survive, we must recognize that the nations of the Americas must go forward in their own way, under their own leadership.

Now it is not my purpose here tonight to discuss the extent to which we consider the various charges that I have listed right or wrong. But I recognize the concerns. I share many of them. What I propose tonight is, I believe, responsive to those concerns.

The most pressing concerns center on economic development —and especially on the policies by which aid is administered and by which trade is regulated.

In proposing specific changes tonight, I mean these as examples of the actions I believe are possible in a new kind of partnership in the Americas.

Our partnership should be one in which the United States lectures less and listens more. It should be one in which clear, consistent procedures are established to ensure that the shaping of the future of the nations in the Americas reflects the will of those nations.

I believe this requires a number of changes.

To begin with, it requires a fundamental change in the way in which we manage development assistance in the hemisphere.

That is why I propose that a multilateral inter-American agency be given an increasing share of responsibility for development assistance decisions. CIAP—the Inter-American Committee for the Alliance for Progress—could be given this new function. Or an entirely new agency could be created within the system.

Whatever the form, the objective would be to evolve an effective multilateral framework for bilateral assistance, to provide the agency with an expert international staff and, over time, to give it major operational and decision-making responsibilities.

The other American nations themselves would thus jointly assume a primary role in setting priorities within the hemisphere, in developing realistic programs, in keeping their own performance under critical review.

One of the areas most urgently in need of new policies is the area of trade. In my various trips to the Latin American countries and other American countries, I have found that this has been uppermost on the minds of the leaders for many, many years. In order to finance their import needs and to achieve self-sustaining growth, the other American nations must expand their exports.

Most Latin American exports now are raw material and foodstuffs. We are attempting to help the other countries of the hemisphere to stabilize their earnings from these exports, to increase them as time goes on.

Increasingly, however, those countries will have to turn more toward manufactured and semi-manufactured products for balanced development and major export growth. Thus they need to be assured of access to the expanding markets of the industrialized world. In order to help achieve this, I have determined to take the following major steps:

• First, to lead a vigorous effort to reduce the non-tariff barriers to trade maintained by nearly all industrialized countries against products of particular interest to Latin America and other developing countries.

• Second, to support increased technical and financial assistance to promote Latin American trade expansion.

• Third, to support the establishment, within the inter-American system, of regular procedures for advance consultation on trade matters. United States trade policies often have a very heavy impact on our neighbors. It seems only fair that in the more balanced relationship we seek, there should be full consultation within the hemisphere family before decisions affecting its members are taken, not after.

• Finally, and most important, in world trade forums, I believe it is time to press for a liberal system of generalized tariff preferences for all developing countries, including Latin America. We will seek adoption by all of the industrialized nations of a scheme with broad product coverage and with no ceilings on preferential imports. We will seek equal access to industrial markets for all developing countries, so as to eliminate the discrimination against Latin America that now exists in many countries. We will also urge that such a system eliminate the inequitable "reverse preferences" that now discriminate against Western Hemisphere countries.

There are three other important economic issues that directly involve the new partnership concept, and which a number of our partners have raised. They raised them with me and raised them

with Governor Rockefeller, with the Secretary of State and others in our Administration.

These are "tied" loans, debt service and regional economic integration.

For several years now, virtually all loans made under United States aid programs have been "tied"—that is, as you know, they have been encumbered with restrictions designed to maintain United States exports, including a requirement that the money be spent on purchases in the United States.

These restrictions have been burdensome for the borrowers. They have impaired the effectiveness of the aid. In June, I ordered the most cumbersome restrictions removed.

In addition, I announce tonight that I am now ordering that effective Nov. 1, loan dollars sent to Latin America under AID be freed to allow purchases not only here, but anywhere in Latin America.

As a third step, I am also ordering that all other onerous conditions and restrictions on U.S. assistance loans be reviewed, with the objective of modifying or eliminating them.

If I might add a personal word, this decision on freeing AID loans is one of those things that people kept saying ought to be done but could not be done. In light of our own balance of payments problems, there were compelling arguments against it. I can assure you that within the Administration we had a very vigorous session on this subject. But I felt, and the rest of my colleagues within the Administration felt, that the needs of the Hemisphere had to come first, so I simply ordered it done, showing our commitment in actions rather than only in words. This will be our guiding principle in the future.

We have present many Members of the House and Senate here tonight. I am sure they realize that there are not too many occasions that the President can accomplish something by just ordering it to be done.

The growing burden of external debt service has increasingly become a major problem of future development. Some countries find themselves making heavy payments in debt service which reduce the positive effects of development aid. Therefore, tonight I suggest that CIAP might appropriately urge the international financial organizations to recommend possible remedies.

We have seen a number of moves in the Americas toward regional economic integration, such as the establishment of the Central American Common Market, the Latin American and Caribbean Free Trade Areas, and the Andean Group. The decisions on how far and how fast this process of integration goes, of course, are not ours to make. But I do want to stress this: We in the United States stand ready to help in this effort if our help is requested and is needed.

On all of these matters, we look forward to consulting further with our hemisphere neighbors and partners. In a major related move, I am also directing our representatives to invite CIAP, as a regular procedure, to conduct a periodic review of U.S. economic policies as they affect the other nations of the hemisphere, and to consult with us about them.

Similar reviews are now made of the other hemisphere countries' policies, as you are aware, but the United States has not previously opened its policies to such consultation. I believe that true partnership requires that we should, and henceforth, if our partners so desire, as I gather from your applause you do, we shall.

I would like to turn now to a vital subject in connection with economic development in the hemisphere, namely, the role of private investment. Clearly, each government in the Americas must make its own decision about the place of private investment, domestic and foreign, in its development process. Each must decide for itself whether it wishes to accept or forego the benefits that private investment can bring.

For a developing country, constructive foreign private investment has the special advantage of being a prime vehicle for the transfer of technology. And certainly, from no other source is so much investment capital available, because capital, from government to government on that basis, is not expansible. In fact, it tends to be more restricted, whereas, private capital can be greatly expanded.

As we have seen, however, just as a capital-exporting nation cannot expect another country to accept investors against its will, so must a capital-importing country expect a serious impairment of its ability to attract investment funds when it acts against existing investments in a way which runs counter to commonly accepted norms of international law and behavior. Unfortunately, and perhaps unfairly, such acts in one of the Americas affect investors in the entire region.

We will not encourage U.S. private investment where it is not wanted or where local conditions face it with unwarranted risks. But I must state my own strong belief, and it is this: I think that properly motivated private enterprise has a vitally important role to play in social as well as economic development in all of the nations. We have seen it work in our own country. We have seen it work in other countries, whether they are developing or developed, other countries that lately have been recording the world's most spectacular rates of economic growth.

Referring to a completely other area of the world, exciting stories of the greatest growth rates are those that have turned toward more private investment, rather than less. Japan we all know about, but the story is repeated in Korea, Taiwan, Malaysia, Singapore and Thailand.

In line with this belief, we are examining ways to modify our direct investment controls in order to help meet the investment requirements of developing nations in the Americas and elsewhere. I have further directed that our aid programs place increasing emphasis on assistance to locally-owned private enterprise. I am also directing that we expand our technical assistance for establishing national and regional capital markets.

As we all have seen, in this age of rapidly advancing science, the challenge of development is only partly economic. Science and technology increasingly hold the key to our national futures. If the promise of this final third of the 20th Century is to be realized, the wonders of science must be turned to the service of man.

In the Consensus of Vina del Mar, we were asked for an unprecedented effort to share our scientific and technical capabilities.

To that request we shall respond in a true spirit of partnership.

This I pledge to you tonight: The nation that went to the moon in peace for all mankind is ready, ready to share its technology in peace with its nearest neighbors.

Tonight, I have discussed with you a new concept of partnership. I have made a commitment to act. I have been trying to give some examples of actions we are prepared to take.

But as anyone familiar with government knows, commitment alone is not enough. There has to be the machinery to ensure an effective follow-through.

Therefore, I am also directing a major re-organization and upgrading of the United States Government structure for dealing with Western Hemisphere affairs.

As a key element of this—and this is one of those areas where the President cannot do it, and he needs the approval of the Congress—but as a key element of this, I have ordered preparation of a legislative request, which I will submit to the Congress, raising the rank of the Assistant Secretary of State for Inter-American Affairs to Under Secretary—thus giving the hemisphere special representation.

I know that many in this room, fifteen years ago urged that upon me, and I see Mr. Pedro Beltran here particularly applauding. He urged it upon me just a few years ago, too.

I trust we will be able, through the new Under Secretary of State, to do a more effective job with regard to the problems of the hemisphere, and the new Under Secretary will be given authority to coordinate all United States Government activities in the hemisphere, so that there will be one window for all of those activities.

And now, my friends, in the American family, I turn to a sensitive subject. Debates have long raged, raged in the United States and elsewhere, as to what our attitude should be toward the various forms of government within the inter-American system.

Let me sum up my own views, very candidly.

First, my own country lives by a democratic system which has preserved its form for nearly two centuries. It has its problems. But we are proud of our system. We are jealous of our liberties. We hope that eventually most, perhaps all, of the world's people will share what we believe to be the blessings of a genuine democracy.

We are aware that most people today in most countries of the world do not share those blessings.

I would be less than honest if I did not express my concern over examples of liberty compromised, of justice denied or of rights infringed.

Nevertheless, we recognize that enormous, sometimes explosive, forces for change are operating in Latin America. These create instabilities, and bring changes in governments. On the diplomatic level, we must deal realistically with governments in the inter-American system as they are. We have, of course, we in this country, a preference for democratic procedures, and we hope that each government will help its own people to move forward toward a better, a fuller and a freer life.

In this connection, however, I would stress one other point. We cannot have a peaceful community of nations if one nation sponsors armed subversion in another's territory. The Ninth Meeting of American Foreign Ministers clearly enunciated this principle. The "export" of revolution is an intervention which our system cannot condone, and a nation like Cuba which seeks to practice it can hardly expect to share in the benefits of this community.

And now, finally, a word about what all this can mean—not just for the Americas, but for the world.

Today, the world's most fervent hope is for a lasting peace in which life is secure, progress is possible and freedom can flourish. In each part of the world we can have lasting peace and progress only if the nations directly concerned take the lead themselves in achieving it, and in no part of the world can there be a true partnership if one partner dictates its direction.

I can think of no assembly of nations better suited than ours to point the way in developing such a partnership. A successfully progressing Western Hemisphere, here in this new world, demonstrating in action mutual help and mutual respect, will be an example for the world. Once again, by this example, we will stand for something larger than ourselves.

For three quarters of a century, many of us have been linked together in the Organization of American States and its predecessors in a joint quest for a better future. Eleven years ago, Operation Pan America was launched as a Brazilian initiative. More recently, we have joined in a noble Alliance for Progress, whose principles still guide us. Now I suggest our goal for the 70s should be a decade of Action for Progress for the Americas.

As we seek to forge a new partnership, we must recognize that we are a community of widely diverse peoples. Our cultures are different. Our perceptions are often different. Our emotional reactions are often different. May it always be that way. What a dull world it would be if we were all alike. Partnership—mutuality—these do not flow naturally. We have to work at them.

Understandably, perhaps, a feeling has arisen in many Latin American countries that the United States really "no longer cares."

My answer to that is very simple.

We do care. I care. I have visited most of your countries, as I have said before. I have met most of your leaders. I have talked with your people. I have seen your great needs as well as your great achievements.

And I know this, in my heart as well as in my mind: If peace and freedom are to endure in this world, there is no task more urgent than lifting up the hungry and the helpless, and putting flesh on the dreams of those who yearn for a better life.

Today, we in this American community share an historic opportunity.

As we look together down the closing decades of the century, we see tasks that summon the very best that is in us. But those tasks are difficult, precisely because they do mean the difference between despair and fulfillment for most of the 600 million people who will live in Latin America in the year 2000. Those lives are our challenge. Those lives are our hope. And we could ask no prouder reward than to have our efforts crowned by peace, prosperity and dignity in the lives of those 600 million human beings—in Latin America and in the United States—each so precious, each so unique—our children and our legacy.

CHEMICAL-BIOLOGICAL WARFARE

Following is the text of President Nixon's Nov. 25 statement on biological warfare weapons.

Soon after taking office I directed a comprehensive study of our chemical and biological defense policies and programs. There had been no such review in over fifteen years. As a result, objectives and policies in this field were unclear and programs lacked definition and direction.

Under the auspices of the National Security Council, the Departments of State and Defense, the Arms Control and Disarmament Agency, the Office of Science and Technology, the Intelligence Community and other agencies worked closely together on this study for over six months. These government efforts were aided by contributions from the scientific community through the President's Scientific Advisory Committee.

This study has now been completed and its findings carefully considered by the National Security Council. I am now reporting the decisions taken on the basis of this review.

Chemical Warfare Program. As to our chemical warfare program, the United States:

• Reaffirms its oft-repeated renunciation of the first use of lethal chemical weapons.

• Extends this renunciation to the first use of incapacitating chemicals.

Consonant with these decisions, the Administration will submit to the Senate, for its advice and consent to ratification, The Geneva Protocol of 1925 which prohibits the first use in war of "asphyxiating, poisonous or other Gases and Bacteriological Methods of Warfare." The United States has long supported the principles and objectives of this Protocol. We take this step toward formal ratification to reinforce our continuing advocacy of international constraints on the use of these weapons.

Biological Research Program. Biological weapons have massive, unpredictable and potentially uncontrollable consequences. They may produce global epidemics and impair the health of future generations. I have therefore decided that:

• The U.S. shall renounce the use of lethal biological agents and weapons, and all other methods of biological warfare.

• The U.S. will confine its biological research to defensive measures such as immunization and safety measures.

• The DOD has been asked to make recommendations as to the disposal of existing stocks of bacteriological weapons.

In the spirit of these decisions, the United States associates itself with the principles and objectives of the United Kingdom Draft Convention which would ban the use of biological methods of warfare. We will seek, however, to clarify specific provisions of the draft to assure that necessary safeguards are included.

Neither our association with the Convention nor the limiting of our program to research will leave us vulnerable to surprise by an enemy who does not observe these rational restraints. Our intelligence community will continue to watch carefully the nature and extent of the biological programs of others.

These important decisions, which have been announced today, have been taken as an initiative toward peace. Mankind already carries in its own hands too many of the seeds of its own destruction. By the examples we set today, we hope to contribute to an atmosphere of peace and understanding between nations and among men.

STUDENT RIOTERS

Following is the complete text of President Nixon's March 22 statement on campus disorders.

This week the Secretary of Health, Education and Welfare has sent a letter to the presidents of the institutions of higher education in the nation calling attention to the provisions enacted in law by the 90th Congress which provide for the withdrawal of various forms of federal support to students found guilty of violation of criminal statutes in connection with campus disorders.

He did this in the exercise of his responsibility as the Cabinet officer chiefly charged with the routine enforcement of federal laws pertaining to education. However, the state of our campuses have for some time been anything but routine.

I should like to take this occasion to make some more general comments which I hope may be of some assistance in moderating the present turmoil.

First, a measure of perspective is in order with regard to the action of the previous Congress. The new regulations are moderate, and they are justified. It is one of the oldest of the practices of universities and colleges that privileges of various kinds are withdrawn from students judged to have violated the rules and regulations of their institution. Congress has done no more than to withdraw federal assistance from those students judged, not by university regulations, but by courts of law, to have violated criminal statutes. Almost by definition, given the present tactics of disruption, anyone so convicted may fairly be assumed to have been assaulting the processes of free inquiry which are the very life of learning. Any society that will not protect itself against such assault exhibits precious little respect for intellect, compared to which the issue of public order is very near to *de minimis*.

For there is a second issue, of far greater concern to me, and, as I believe, to the Congress, to the American people generally, and the faculties and students of American colleges and universities especially. That is the preservation of the integrity, the independence, and the creativity of our institutions of higher learning.

Freedom—intellectual freedom—is in danger in America. The nature and content of that danger is as clear as any one thing could be. Violence—physical violence, physical intimidation—is seemingly on its way to becoming an accepted, or at all events a normal and not to be avoided element in the clash of opinion within university confines. Increasingly it is clear that this violence is directed to a clearly perceived and altogether too conceivable objective: not only to politicize the student bodies of our educational institutions, but to politicize the institutions as well. Anyone with the least understanding of the history of freedom will know that this has invariably meant not only political disaster to those nations that have submitted to such forces of obfuscation and repression, but cultural calamity as well. It is not too strong a statement to declare that this is the way civilizations begin to die.

The process is altogether too familiar to those who would survey the wreckage of history. Assault and counter assault, one extreme leading to the opposite extreme; the voices of reason and calm discredited. As Yeats foresaw: "Things fall apart; the centre cannot hold..." None of us has the right to suppose it cannot happen here.

The first thing to do at such moments is to reassert first principles. The Federal Government cannot, should not—must not—enforce such principles. That is fundamentally the task and the responsibility of the university community. But any may state what these principles are, for they are as widely understood as they are cherished.

First, that universities and colleges are places of excellence in which men are judged by achievement and merit in defined areas. The independence and competence of the faculty, the commitment, and equally the competence of the student body, are matters not to be compromised. The singular fact of American society—the fact which very likely distinguishes us most markedly from any other nation on earth, is that in the untroubled pursuit of an application of this principle we have created the largest, most democratic, most open system of higher learning in history. None need fear the continued application of those principles; but all must dread their erosion. The second principle—and I would argue, the only other—is that violence or the threat of violence may never be permitted to influence the actions or judgments of the university community. Once it does the community, almost by definition, ceases to be a university.

It is for this reason that from time immemorial expulsion has been the primary instrument of university discipline. Those who would not abide by the rules of the community of learning have simply been required to leave it, for any other form of coercion would cause that community to change its fundamental nature.

The difficulty of this moment, as of most times when fundamental principles are challenged, is that many of those posing the challenges, and even more of those supporting them, are responding to very basic problems. To reassert, in the face of student protest, the first principles of academic freedom, while ignoring the issues that are foremost in the minds of those students, is less than inglorious: it is slothful, and dishonest, an affront to those principles and in the end futile.

Students today point to many wrongs which must be made right:

—We have seen a depersonalization of the educational experience. Our institutions must reshape themselves lest this turns to total alienation.

—Student unrest does not exist in a vacuum but reflects a deep and growing social unrest affecting much of our world today. Self-righteous indignation by society will solve none of this. We must resolve the internal contradictions of our communities.

—There must be university reform including new experimentation in curricula such as ethnic studies, student involvement in the decision-making process and a new emphasis in faculty teaching.

I have directed the Department of Health, Education and Welfare to launch new initiatives toward easing tensions in our educational community.

This Administration will always be receptive to suggestions for constructive reform. But the forces of separation and nonreason must be replaced by vigorous, persuasive and lawful efforts for constructive change.

BALANCE OF PAYMENTS

Following is the complete text of President Nixon's April 4 statement on measures to improve the balance of payments.

In my fiscal message to the Congress on March 26, I called for a strong budget surplus and monetary restraint to curb an inflation that has been allowed to run into its 4th year. This is fundamental economics, and I pointed out that we intend to deal with fundamentals.

Similarly, the problem of regaining equilibrium in the U.S. balance of payments cannot be solved with expedients that postpone the problem to another year. We shall stop treating symptoms and start treating causes, and we shall find our solutions in the framework of freer trade and payments.

Fundamental economics call for:

—creating the conditions that make it possible to rebuild our trade surplus.

—ultimate dismantling of the network of direct controls which may seem useful in the short run but are self-defeating in the long run.

The U.S. balance of payments showed a surplus last year. But this surplus included an unusually high and probably unsustainable capital inflow. Our trade surplus, which reached a peak

of $6.5 billion in the mid-sixties, declined sharply and all but disappeared.

That trade surplus must be rebuilt, and it can only be rebuilt by restoring stable and noninflationary economic growth to the U.S. economy. Inflation has drawn in a flood of imports while it has diminished our competitiveness in world markets and thus dampened our export expansion.

This is why our program of fiscal and monetary restraint is as necessary for our external trade as for restoring order in our domestic economy.

Building on the solid base of a healthy, noninflationary economy—a base that only the fundamentals of fiscal and monetary restraint now can restore—we are planning a sustained effort in several key areas:

—*In export expansion,* we have tentatively set an export goal of $50 billion to be achieved by 1973. This compares with 1968 exports of about $34 billion. This is primarily the task of American private enterprise, but government must help to coordinate the effort and offer assistance and encouragement. We must also call on the productivity and ingenuity of American industry to meet the competitive challenge of imported goods.

—*In trade policies,* we will be working with our major trading partners abroad to insure that our products receive a fair competitive reception.

—*In defense activities,* we will also work with our friends abroad to ensure that the balance of payments burden of providing for the common defense is shared fairly.

—*In travel,* we will encourage more foreign travel to the United States. Here, as in other areas, we will be relying heavily on the support of the private community. We seek no restrictions on the American tourists' freedom to travel.

—*In international investment,* we will review our own regulations and tax policy to assure that foreign investment in the U.S. is not discouraged; for example, we move now to eliminate from our laws the prospective taxation of interest on foreign-held bank deposits.

—*In the international financial area,* we will be continuing to work with our friends abroad to strengthen and improve the international monetary system. An expanding world economy will require growing levels of trade with adequate levels of reserves, and effective methods by which countries can adjust their payments imbalances. In particular, we look forward to ratification by the International Monetary Fund members of the special drawing rights plan and its early activation.

I am confident that measures in these areas, coupled with the cooling of the economy through fiscal-monetary restraint, will move us in an orderly manner toward true balance-of-payments equilibrium. Accordingly, I have begun, gradually but purposefully, to dismantle the direct controls which only mask the underlying problem.

Specifically:

First, I have today signed an Executive order reducing the effective rate of the interest equalization tax from 1-1/4 percent to 3/4 of 1 percent. This measure was designed to close a large gap—which has now narrowed—between foreign and domestic interest rates. I shall, however, request the Congress to extend the President's discretionary authority under the interest equalization tax for 18 months beyond its scheduled expiration in July.

Second, I have approved a recommendation to relax somewhat the foreign direct investment program of the Department of Commerce. This means that most firms investing abroad will have substantially more freedom in planning these investments.

Third, I have been informed by Chairman Martin of modifications in the Federal Reserve program which will provide more flexibility for commercial banks, particularly smaller and medium-sized banks, to finance U.S. exports.

These are prudent and limited steps that recognize the realities of our present balance-of-payments situation.

The distortions created by more than 3 years of inflation cannot be corrected overnight. Nor can the dislocations resulting from a decade of balance-of-payments deficits be corrected in a short time.

But the time for restoring the basis of our prosperity is long overdue. We shall continually direct America's economic policy, both foreign and domestic, at correcting the root causes of our problems, rather than covering them over with a patchwork quilt of controls.

By facing up to fundamental economic needs, the inflationary tide and the trade tide can be turned and the U.S. dollar continued strong and secure.

INFLATION

Following is the complete text of President Nixon's Oct. 17 radio-address on inflation.

Today I would like to share my thoughts with you about a problem that worries millions of Americans—high prices that just keep getting higher.

All across this land, hard working men and women look at paychecks that say they have had a raise. But they wonder why those bigger checks just don't buy any more than their lower paychecks bought four years ago.

All across this land, men and women in their retirement, who depend on insurance and on Social Security and on their life savings, look at their monthly checks and wonder why they just can't seem to make ends meet anymore.

And all across this land, housewives wonder why they have to pay 66 cents a pound, and in some areas more, for hamburger that cost 53 cents four years ago; people who are ill want to know why in those four years the cost of one day in a hospital has gone from $27 to $48; children who pay a nickel for a candy bar want to know why that bar is only half as big as it used to be.

When it comes to rising prices, it seems to most people that there is no end in sight. Many Americans are upset, and many are even angry about this, and they have a right to be—because the ever-rising cost of food and clothing and rent robs them of their savings, cheats them of the vacations and those necessary extras that they thought they had been working for.

Now, why does everything cost so much? And what can we do to hold down the upward climb of prices?

Living Cost Denounced

For five long years, you have heard politicians and economists denouncing "the high cost of living." Back in 1966 and '67, when prices rose by three percent a year, everyone said how bad that was; and then in 1968, when prices speeded up by four percent, everyone agreed something ought to be done; and now, when momentum has carried the rise to nearly six percent, the same heads are shaking.

You might begin to wonder: If a rising cost of living has so many enemies, why has it been allowed to grow so fast? For years, in political speeches, the high cost of living has been as safe to denounce as the man-eating shark; but after the speeches were over, nobody seemed to do anything about it.

Now, there was a very simple reason why your cost of living got out of hand: the blame for the spiral of wages and prices falls fundamentally on the past policies of your Government.

The Federal Government spent a lot more than it raised in taxes. Some of that spending was on the war in Vietnam, some of the spending was on new social programs, but the total spending was very heavy.

Now we are paying for all that red ink—not only in higher taxes, but in higher prices for everything you buy. To put it bluntly, the frequent failure to balance the Federal Budget over the past five years has been the primary cause for unbalancing the family budgets of millions of Americans.

So today I want to tell you what we have been doing to make it easier for you to balance your family budget. I want you to know what results we are beginning to see, to understand the meaning of the news about the economy you will be reading in the coming months. And finally, I want to suggest what the American people—what you—can do together to hold down the cost of living.

When this Administration took office nine months ago, we decided that we were going to stop talking about higher prices and we were going to start doing something about them. We knew that some sophisticated investors could make out fairly well in a time of skyrocketing prices, but that the average family bore the brunt of the high cost of living, and the family on a fixed income was being driven right up the wall.

And so, to meet the real needs of most Americans, we began a steady effort to take the upward pressure off your cost of living.

Of course, there was a faster way available to bring prices down—many people suggested that we slam on the brakes hard and fast, and bring about a recession. But that kind of shock treatment is harsh and unnecessary—we want to level things off, not shake them up and down.

Steps Administration Took

Step by step we took those measures necessary to get our nation's house in order.

Step one was to cut federal spending, which more than anything else was pushing your prices up. We cut proposed federal spending by more than $7 billion. We have taken it out of defense, we are cutting back on construction, we are squeezing it out of many other departmental budgets.

Now, we have been selective in these cuts, recognizing urgent national and social needs, but hardly anything has escaped some reduction. One area that was not cut, and I am sure you will agree with this decision, was the Department of Justice, which has fallen far behind in the war against crime—a war we are determined to win.

Next, working with the Congress, we proposed to phase out the tax surcharge over the course of a year. We could not afford to let the surtax lapse in the middle of 1969, because that would have driven up the prices you pay for everything.

And, also, we have supported our central banking system in its policy of keeping money hard to borrow. When too much money is borrowed, this money is simply used to bid prices up higher.

Now, let's face it: Holding down Government spending and holding up the tax rate, and making it harder for people to get credit, is not the kind of policy that makes friends for people in politics. We have asked the American people to take some bitter medicine. We believe that the American people are mature enough to understand the need for it.

Medicine Is Working

Well, here we are, nine months later, and I can report to you that the medicine has begun to work. There will be no overnight cure, but we are on the road to recovery from the disease of runaway prices.

Let me be careful not to mislead anyone: Prices are still going up. They may continue to do so for awhile—a five year momentum is not easy to stop. But now prices are no longer increasing faster and faster—the increases not only have slackened, but the rates of increase are actually down. Without shock treatment, we are curing the causes of the rising cost of living.

For some time to come, you will be reading about how some business is not doing very well. Sales may be sluggish in department stores; new housing, which this nation needs, has declined; the production of our industry has edged down for the first time in a year.

Ordinarily, this is bad news. But today, these declines are evidence that our policy of curbing the rising cost of living is beginning to take hold.

We must be realistic; as we gently, but firmly, apply the brakes, we are going to experience some "slowing pains." Just like growing pains, these are a healthy development—but they are painful, nevertheless.

My point very simply is this: We have undertaken a policy that is slowing down the rise in prices. Unfortunately, some industries and some individuals will feel this necessary adjustment more directly than others. But difficult though it may be, and unpopular though it may become when the water gets choppier, by curbing inflation we do what is best for all the American people.

Just as we must be realistic, we must be compassionate; we must keep a close watch on the rate of unemployment. Now, there are some who say that a high rate of unemployment can't be avoided.

Will Resist Unemployment

I don't agree. In our leveling-off process, we intend to do everything we can to resist increases in unemployment, to help train and place workers in new jobs, to cushion the effects of readjustment.

For example, we have overhauled and modernized our job training programs. We have proposed reforms extending unemployment insurance to millions not now covered, with higher benefits paid over longer periods to those in the system. We have proposed a computer job bank to match workers with hundreds of thousands of vacant jobs, which exist all over this country.

The nation must dedicate itself to the ideal of helping every man who is looking for a job to find a job. Today, about 96 percent of the work force is employed. We want it to be more. But we cannot effectively and fairly make it more by ignoring the widespread hardship that a runaway cost of living imposes on so many Americans.

Now that we have begun to detect the signs of success in slowing down, what can you expect your Government to do next?

First, let me tell you what we are not going to do.

We are not going to change our game plan at the end of the first quarter of the game, particularly at a time that we feel that we are ahead. We are not going to turn away from treating basic causes to start treating symptoms alone.

No Controls or Guidelines

In other words, we are not considering wage or price controls. My own first job in Government was with the old Office of Price Administration at the beginning of World War II. And from personal experience, let me just say this: Wage and price controls are bad for business, bad for the working man, and bad for the consumer. Rationing, black markets, regimentation—that is the wrong road for America, and I will not take the nation down that road.

Nor are we considering putting the Government into the business of telling the working man how much he should charge for his services or how much the businessman should charge for his goods. Those are called "guidelines." They collapsed back in 1966 because they failed to get to the root of the problem.

What we are going to do is based on total realism.

This weekend, I am sending a letter to a cross-section of leaders in labor and business across America calling their attention to the latest facts of economic life.

I am asking them to take a hard look at what Government has done in these nine months—not just our words, but our deeds. And I am asking them to base their own future plans on the basis of working and selling in a country that is not fooling about slowing down the rise in the cost of living.

Instead of relying on our jawbone, we have put some backbone in Government's determination to hold the line for the consumer. We are going to continue to exercise that backbone in the face of criticism by a lot of powerful special interests. You can rely on that. And, most important, you can make your plans on the basis that price rises are going to be slowed down.

As working men and businessmen get that message—as they see that Government is willing to live up to its responsibilities

for doing what is needed to hold down prices—we can expect to see a new responsibility in the decisions of labor and management. By responding to the changed conditions, they will be following their self-interest and helping the national interest as well.

Today, I have laid out our strategy to take the pressure off the prices you pay. There is a good reason for spelling out the strategy right now, at the beginning of a turning point in the struggle.

You see, there is a secret weapon that we intend to use in the battle against rising prices. That secret weapon is the confidence of the American people.

In recent years, that confidence in our ability to slow down the upward spiral has been missing. More and more, a paralyzing fatalism has crept into our view of prices. Too many of us have made the mistake of accepting ever-higher prices as inevitable and, as a result, we have planned on higher and higher prices. And what we expected—we got.

Only our secret weapon of American confidence in ourselves will get us out of that vicious circle.

More than a generation ago, in the depths of the depression, an American President told you—over this medium of radio—that the only thing we had to fear was fear itself.

Only Fear Is Fatalism

Today, in a prosperity endangered by a speed-up of prices, the only thing we have to fear is fatalism—that destructive habit of shrugging our shoulders and resigning ourselves to a hopeless future on a wage-price treadmill.

I say to my fellow Americans today: The runaway cost of living is not a cross we are obliged to bear. It can be brought under control. It is being slowed by firm and steady action that deals with its root causes.

And as you plan for your own future on the assumption that the rise in prices will indeed slow down, you will be bringing our secret weapon into play. Your confidence in the strength of our economy, your confidence in the determination of America to win this battle—that is what will turn the tide.

On that note of confidence, let me issue this call:

I call upon the Congress to extend the surtax at half rate, five percent, from January 1 to June 30 of next year. Also I call upon the Congress, when it passes tax reform legislation, which I have recommended, which is greatly needed, that it do so in a way that we not have a net tax reduction of a size that will help push up prices that the consumer has to pay.

Call on Congressmen

I call upon Americans to urge their Congressmen to pass those measures of manpower training and unemployment insurance that I have proposed—measures that would help make it easier for people to adjust to change.

And I call for your support in our policy of holding down federal spending so that we are able to continue setting an example with a responsible budget for the next year, fiscal 1971.

I call upon the American people to urge their state and local governments to cooperate in postponing spending that can appropriately be delayed.

I call upon labor's leadership and labor's rank and file to base their wage demands on the new prospect of a return toward price stability.

I call upon businessmen to base their investment and price decisions on that new economic climate, keeping in mind it is in their private interest to be realistic in their planning and to help build a strong economy.

I call upon all Americans to bear the burden of restraint in their personal credit and purchasing decisions, so as to reduce the pressures that help drive prices out of sight.

I am convinced that Americans will answer this call.

I am convinced that a new confidence will be felt in this country when we match the strength of our resources with the strength of our resolution.

The dollar you earn should stay worth a dollar. The dollar you save should stay worth a dollar. This is no impossible dream—this is something you are entitled to.

The cost of living affects the quality of life. Together we are going to improve the quality of life—and together, we are going to succeed in slowing down the rise in your cost of living.

POSTMASTERS

Following is a partial text of President Nixon's Feb. 5 remarks to newsmen on the new postal appointment policy.

...As most of you who have covered Washington know, from the beginning of this Republic, as a matter of fact, even before the Constitution was adopted when Benjamin Franklin was the Postmaster General, during the Articles of the Confederation, postmasters have always been the subject of patronage.

The Party in power had the right to appoint the postmasters and the Party out of power, of course, was waiting until the time when it would get that right as a result of winning an election.

It has been generally agreed by experts who have examined the operations of the Post Office Department that this had a detrimental effect on morale in the career service and that it also might have had a very detrimental effect on the efficiency of the operations of the Department....

As far as the second objective is concerned, by bringing the Postmaster General into this position, a man with immense success in the business community, and a team I would say among all the Cabinet teams one of the best that I have in the whole government, we think that we have moved toward efficient operation of the Department.

The first responsibility of taking politics out of the appointment of postmasters is one that is not only mine, but it is one in which we have to have the support of the members of our Party in Congress....

Consequently, I have made the decision, which has been recommended by the Postmaster General, that beginning now postmasters will be appointed on a merit basis without the usual political clearance which has been the case for the 190 years or more that this Nation has been a nation, and even before that time....

ARTS, HUMANITIES TEXT

Following is the complete text of President Nixon's Dec. 10 message to Congress on the arts and humanities.

TO THE CONGRESS OF THE UNITED STATES:

Americans have long given their first concerns to the protection and enhancement of Life and Liberty; we have reached the point in our history when we should give equal concern to "the Pursuit of Happiness."

This phrase of Jefferson's, enshrined in our Declaration of Independence, is defined today as "the quality of life." It encompasses a fresh dedication to protect and improve our environment, to give added meaning to our leisure and to make it possible for each individual to express himself freely and fully.

The attention and support we give the arts and the humanities—especially as they affect our young people—represent a **vital part of our commitment to enhancing the quality of life** for all Americans. The full richness of this nation's cultural life need not be the province of relatively few citizens centered in a few cities; on the contrary, the trend toward a wider appreciation of the arts and a greater interest in the humanities should be strongly encouraged, and the diverse culture of every region and community should be explored.

America's cultural life has been developed by private persons of genius and talent and supported by private funds from audiences, generous individuals, corporations and foundations. The Federal Government cannot and should not seek to substitute public money for these essential sources of continuing support.

However, there is a growing need for federal stimulus and assistance—growing because of the acute financial crisis in which many of our privately-supported cultural institutions now find themselves, and growing also because of the expanding opportunity that derives from higher educational levels, increased leisure and greater awareness of the cultural life. We are able now to use the nation's cultural resources in new ways—ways that can enrich the lives of more people in more communities than has ever before been possible.

Need and opportunity combine, therefore, to present the Federal Government with an obligation to help broaden the base of our cultural legacy—not to make it fit some common denominator of official sanction, but rather to make its diversity and insight more readily accessible to millions of people everywhere.

Therefore, *I ask the Congress to extend the legislation creating the National Foundation on the Arts and Humanities beyond its termination date of June 30, 1970, for an additional three years.*

Further, *I propose that the Congress approve $40,000,000 in new funds for the National Foundation in fiscal 1971 to be available from public and private sources. This will virtually double the current year's level.*

Through the National Foundation's two agencies—the National Endowment for the Arts and the National Endowment for the Humanities—the increased appropriation would make possible a variety of activities:

• We would be able to bring more productions in music, theatre, literature readings and dance to millions of citizens eager to have the opportunity for such experiences.

• We would be able to bring many more young writers and poets into our school system, to help teachers motivate youngsters to master the mechanics of self-expression.

• We would be able to provide some measure of support to hard-pressed cultural institutions, such as museums and symphony orchestras, to meet the demands of new and expanding audiences.

• We would begin to redress the imbalance between the sciences and the humanities in colleges and universities, to provide more opportunity for students to become discerning as well as knowledgeable.

• We would be able to broaden and deepen humanistic research into the basic causes of the divisions between races and generations, learning ways to improve communication within American society and bringing the lessons of our history to bear on the problems of our future.

In the past five years, as museums increasingly have transformed themselves from warehouses of objects into exciting centers of educational experience, attendance has almost doubled; in these five years, the investment in professional performing arts has risen from 60 million dollars to 207 million dollars and attendance has tripled. State arts agencies are now active in 55 states and territories; the total of state appropriations made to these agencies has grown from $3.6 million in 1967 to $7.6 million this year. These state agencies, which share in federal-state partnership grants, represent one of the best means for the National Endowment to protect our cultural diversity and to encourage local participation in the arts.

In this way, federal funds are used properly to generate other funds from state, local and private sources. In the past history of the Arts Endowment, every dollar of federal money has generated three dollars from other sources.

The Federal Role. At a time of severe budget stringency, a doubling of the appropriation for the arts and humanities might seem extravagant. However, I believe that the need for a new impetus to the understanding and expression of the American idea has a compelling claim on our resources. The dollar amounts involved are comparatively small. The federal role would remain supportive, rather than primary. And two considerations mark this as a time for such action:

• Studies in the humanities will expand the range of our current knowledge about the social conditions underlying the most difficult and far-reaching of the nation's domestic problems.

We need these tools of insight and understanding to target our larger resources more effectively on the solution of the larger problems.

• The arts have attained a prominence in our life as a nation and in our consciousness as individuals, that renders their health and growth vital to our national well-being. America has moved to the forefront as a place of creative expression. The excellence of the American product in the arts has won worldwide recognition. The arts have the rare capacity to help heal divisions among our own people and to vault some of the barriers that divide the world.

Our scholars in the humanities help us explore our society, revealing insights in our history and in other disciplines that will be of positive long-range benefit.

Our creative and performing artists give free and full expression to the American spirit as they illuminate, criticize and celebrate our civilization. Like our teachers, they are an invaluable national resource.

Too many Americans have been too long denied the inspiration and the uplift of our cultural heritage. Now is the time to enrich the life of the mind and to evoke the splendid qualities of the American spirit.

Therefore, I urge the Congress to extend the authorization and increase substantially the funds available to the National Foundation for the Arts and Humanities. Few investments we could make would give us so great a return in terms of human understanding, human satisfaction and the intangible but essential qualities of grace, beauty and spiritual fulfillment.

RICHARD NIXON

MINORITY ENTERPRISE COUNCIL

Following is a partial text of President Nixon's Oct. 13 remarks to the Advisory Council for Minority Enterprise:

...And what we want to do is to enlist this power, this creative power that all of you have, because I know the backgrounds of so many of you—how you started with very little and then built the business enterprises which have so much.

We want that creative power enlisted in a very high risk enterprise.

...You all know that any business is a risk. You all know that a small business is a much bigger risk. And it is certainly no secret that a minority small business is the biggest risk of all....

But all of us know that the bigger the risk is, the bigger the potential gain is, whether it is in betting on a contest—the higher the odds, if you win, the greater the gain.

That is why in this whole field of minority business enterprise, much of which will begin small but can eventually grow until it is big, you have such a challenge—a challenge that we want to work with you on. Because, while the risk is great, the risk of minority enterprise, for reasons that are no fault of the minorities, while the risk is great, the risk of small business, because small business does not have the capital that big business has, it doesn't have the talent that big business has, nevertheless, it can be done. And it will be done provided we can add this extra ingredient of the talent and the ability that is represented in this room, not only by you, individually, but by all the people in your companies.

...And, I suppose, too, that at a meeting like this, the real question is "Was it necessary? Was the trip necessary? Was the meeting necessary?" And the question also is raised, "Can we really come forth from this meeting with something new that will change America—change it for the better?"

...I spoke to the point that it was not enough simply to see that all people in this country had an equal opportunity to get a job—and that is an enterprise that many of you as businessmen have contributed to enormously—but that it was necessary for every individual in America to be able not only to get a job, but to have a chance to become an owner or a manager, to have a piece of the action in private enterprise in this country.

And, frankly, there are a lot of people that are skeptical about that. There are a lot of people who believe that this is

so long away in the future, it is so much of a dream, that the concentration should be almost exclusively on the area of jobs.

I don't think that is enough. We don't want a minority that is a class apart simply as job holders. We want a group of people who not only can be employees, but who can honestly feel that they have an equal chance to go up, to go up from that job, that employee status, to become an owner and a manager—as a matter of fact, to become what the people in this room are, people who are eminently successful.

You know you wouldn't have had the chance, those of you who came from small beginnings to the big businesses that many of you represent, you wouldn't have had it unless you had a helping hand along the way.

What we are simply saying here today is, we need your help, the Government needs your help. A lot of people who won't have that chance need your help in order to get this program moving and to provide opportunity for literally hundreds of thousands at the beginning, and we hope millions in the end, of Americans to proudly stand up and have the dignity that comes from not simply being part of an organization, being an employee, but from being an owner and a manager just as those in this room, for the most part, are....

STATEMENT TO MOON

Following is the complete text of President Nixon's July 20 conversation with Apollo 11 Astronauts Neil A. Armstrong and Edwin E. Aldrin Jr. after they had landed on the moon:

THE PRESIDENT: Neil and Buzz, I am talking to you by telephone from the Oval Room at the White House. This certainly has to be the most historic telephone call ever made from the White House.

I just can't tell you how proud we all are of what you have done. For every American this has to be the proudest day of our lives. For people all over the world I am sure that they, too, join with Americans in recognizing what an immense feat this is.

Because of what you have done the heavens have become a part of man's world. As you talk to us from the Sea of Tranquility, it inspires us to redouble our efforts to bring peace and tranquility to earth.

For one priceless moment in the whole history of man all of the people on this earth are truly one—one in their pride in what you have done and one in our prayers that you will return safely to earth.

ARMSTRONG: Thank you, Mr. President. It is a great honor and privilege for us to be here representing not only the United States, but men of peaceable nations, men with an interest and a curiosity, and men with a vision for the future. It is an honor for us to be able to participate here today.

THE PRESIDENT: Thank you very much and I look forward, all of us look forward to seeing you on the *Hornet* on Thursday.

ARMSTRONG: Thank you. We look forward to that very much, sir.

OAS ASSEMBLY

Following are excerpts of President Nixon's April 14 remarks to the Organization of American States Assembly:

...I think there has been a tendency, in examining the relations of the United States with our friends to the South, to smother the problems that we have with fine slogans, beautiful rhetoric, and sometimes with a abrazos.

I think there is a place for a fine slogan and always there is a place for eloquent language. And I would not underplay, certainly, the importance of that kind of relationship on a dignified basis between nations and the leaders of nations.

But at the present time, the problems we confront in this hemisphere are too serious to be glossed over simply by the usual slogans and the words and the gestures of the past. What we need is a new policy. What we need are new programs. What we need are new approaches.

I would like to describe those policies today, not with a new slogan, because I have none—none that I think would be appropriate to the challenge that we face.

But I would like to describe our approach in this way: Sometimes the new Administration has been described as an open Administration. I hope we can live up to that particular description. But if I were to set forth the objectives for our approach to the problems of this hemisphere, it would be these words: I want our policies to be ones which are derived from open eyes, open ears, open minds, and open hearts.

Let me be specific on each of those particular items. When I speak of open eyes, I mean that it is necessary for us to look at our common problems without any of the prejudices that we may have had in the past and without being imprisoned with the policies of the past or without perpetuating the mistakes of the past.

The President of this organization has referred to Governor Rockefeller and the trip that he will be taking—or several trips, I should say— to this hemisphere in the months ahead.

On that trip, as Governor Rockefeller will tell each of the Ambassadors assembled here today, he is going with open eyes and open ears. He is not going there to tell the people in the various countries that he will visit what the United States wants them to do. But he is going there to listen to them and to hear what they believe we can do together.

I think there has been too much of a tendency in the past for the discussion to get down to this point: What will the United States do for Latin America?

The question, otherwise, I think should be put—and this is the approach of the Rockefeller mission, it is the approach of the new Secretary of State, the new Assistant Secretary of State, Charles Meyer. Our approach is this: Not what do we do for Latin America, what do we do with Latin America? What do we do together?

We want, therefore, to have open eyes and we also have open ears. We want to hear from our friends in each of the countries represented what you think is wrong with our policy, but also what you think you can do with us to develop a better policy. And we, fortunately, approach this problem with no pre-conceived notions as to the policies of the past.

One of the reasons that we must also have open minds is that there sometimes is a tendency to become wedded to a program because it has a popular connotation. I speak of the Alliance for Progress, the great concept.

And as I examined the effect of the Alliance for Progress on my last trip to Latin America in which I covered most of the countries in that Continent in 1967, I saw many areas where the Alliance for Progress had done much good.

On the other hand, when I looked at the over-all statistics as to what has happened to the rate of growth in Latin America during the period of the Alliance for Progress as compared with the period immediately preceding the Alliance, and when I compared that rate of growth with the rates of growth in other areas of the world, I found a very disconcerting result.

And it very simply is this: The rate of growth is not fast enough. It has been approximately the same during the period of the Alliance as it was before the Alliance. But even more significant, the rate of growth in Latin America over-all, and of course there are some individual countries that are far ahead, but over-all the rate of growth is less than the rate of growth in non-Communist Asia, and it is less, even, than the rate of growth in Communist Eastern Europe.

This is a result which we cannot tolerate. We must do better. We must find the ways and the means whereby we can move forward together in a more effective way.

And that is why I emphasize that we will have open eyes and open ears and open minds in attempting to find the answer...

I want you to know that we do consider the problems of this Hemisphere to be of the highest priority. We do consider that whatever progress we have made has not been enough and for that reason we come here today asking your assistance in working with us so that we can find better solutions for those problems that we mutually have throughout the Hemisphere...

NIGERIAN CIVIL WAR

Following is the complete text of President Nixon's Feb. 22 statement on naming a special coordinator of U.S. relief to civilian victims of the Nigerian civil war:

I know that I speak for all Americans in expressing this nation's deep anguish for the terrible human suffering in the Nigerian civil war. It is tragic enough to watch a military conflict between peoples who once lived together in peace and developing prosperity. But that tragedy has been compounded, and the conscience of the world engaged by the starvation threatening millions of innocent civilians on both sides of the battle.

Immediately after taking office, I directed an urgent and comprehensive review of the relief situation. The purpose was to examine every possibility to enlarge and expedite the flow of relief. This very complex problem will require continuing study. I am announcing, however, the following initial conclusions of the review:

1. The Red Cross and the Voluntary Agencies are now feeding nearly 1 million people in areas of the war zone controlled by the Federal Military Government of Nigeria. They fully expect the numbers will grow in magnitude over the coming months. This, therefore, will require additional support for the international relief effort from donor countries, and of course the continued cooperation of Federal authorities.

2. There is widely conflicting information on future food requirements within the Biafran-controlled area, where the relief operation is feeding an estimated two million persons. The United States Government therefore is urgently seeking a comprehensive, internationally conducted survey of food needs in that area.

3. Whatever the results of such a survey, it is already clear that the present relief effort is inadequate to the need in the Biafran-controlled area. The major obstacle to expanded relief is neither money, food, nor means of transport. The main problem is the absence of relief arrangements acceptable to the two sides which would overcome the limitations posed by the present hazardous and inadequate nighttime airlift.

4. The efforts of outside governments to expand relief are greatly complicated by the political and military issues that divide the contestants. Unfortunately, the humanitarian urge to feed the starving has become enmeshed in those issues and stands in danger of interpretation by the parties as a form of intervention. But surely it is within the conscience and ability of man to give effect to his humanitarianism without involving himself in the politics of the dispute.

5. It is in this spirit that U.S. policy will draw a sharp distinction between carrying out our moral obligations to respond effectively to humanitarian needs and involving ourselves in the political affairs of others. The U.S. will not shrink from this humanitarian challenge but, in cooperation with those of like mind, will seek to meet it.

With the above conclusions in view, I am pleased to announce that Secretary of State Rogers has today appointed Mr. Clarence Clyde Ferguson, Jr., a distinguished American civic leader and Professor of Law at Rutgers University, as Special Coordinator on relief to civilian victims of the Nigerian civil war. He will be charged with assuring that the U.S. contributions to the international relief effort are responsive to increased needs to the maximum extent possible and that they are effectively utilized. In so doing, he will give particular attention to ways and means by which the flow of relief can be increased to the suffering on both sides of the battle line. He will, of course, work closely with the ICRC and other international relief agencies, the Organization of African Unity, donor governments, and with the parties to the conflict.

The Special Coordinator will not seek and will not accept a charge to negotiate issues other than those directly relevant to relief.

Nevertheless, the U.S. earnestly hopes for an early negotiated end to the conflict and a settlement that will assure the protection and peaceful development of all the people involved.

18-NATION CONFERENCE

Following is the complete text of President Nixon's March 15 letter to Ambassador Gerard C. Smith, head of the U.S. delegation to the conference of the 18-Nation Disarmament Committee meeting in Geneva:

In view of the great importance which I attach to the work of the Eighteen-Nation Disarmament Conference in Geneva, I wish to address directly to you, as the new Director of the Arms Control and Disarmament Agency and the head of our delegation, my instructions regarding the participation of the United States in this conference.

The fundamental objective of the United States is a world of enduring peace and justice, in which the differences that separate nations can be resolved without resort to war.

Our immediate objective is to leave behind the period of confrontation and to enter an era of negotiation.

The task of the delegation of the United States to the disarmament conference is to serve these objectives by pursuing negotiations to achieve concrete measures which will enhance the security of our own country and all countries.

The new Administration has now considered the policies which will help us to make progress in this endeavor.

I have decided that the Delegation of the United States should take these positions at the Conference.

First, in order to assure that the seabed, man's latest frontier, remains free from the nuclear arms race, the United States delegation should indicate that the United States is interested in working out an international agreement that would prohibit the implacement or fixing of nuclear weapons or other weapons of mass destruction on the seabed. To this end, the United States delegation should seek discussion of the factors necessary for such an international agreement. Such an agreement would, like the Antarctic Treaty and the Treaty on Outer Space which are already in effect, prevent an arms race before it had a chance to start. It would ensure that this potentially useful area of the world remained available for peaceful purposes.

Second, the United States supports the conclusion of a comprehensive test ban adequately verified. In view of the fact that differences regarding verification have not permitted achievement of this key arms control measure, efforts must be made towards greater understanding of the verification issue.

Third, the United States delegation will continue to press for an agreement to cut off the production of fissionable materials for weapons purposes and to transfer such materials to peaceful purposes.

Fourth, while awaiting the United Nations Secretary General's study on the effects of chemical and biological warfare, the United States delegation should join with other delegations in exploring any proposals or ideas that could contribute to sound and effective arms control relating to these weapons.

Fifth, regarding more extensive measures of disarmament, both nuclear and conventional, the United States delegation should be guided by the understanding that actual reduction of armaments, and not merely limiting their growth or spread, remains our goal.

Sixth, regarding the question of talks between the United States and the Soviet Union on the limitation of strategic arms, the United States hopes that the international political situation will evolve in a way which will permit such talks to begin in the near future.

In carrying out these instructions, the United States delegation should keep in mind my view that efforts toward peace by all nations must be comprehensive. We cannot have realistic hopes for significant progress in the control of arms if the policies of confrontation prevail throughout the world as the rule of international conduct. On the other hand, we must attempt to exploit every opportunity to build a world of peace—to find areas of accord—to bind countries together in cooperative endeavors.

A major part of the work of peace is done by the Eighteen-Nation Disarmament Committee. I expect that all members of the United States delegation will devote that extra measure of determination, skill, and judgment which this high task merits.

I shall follow closely the progress that is made and give my personal consideration to any problems that arise whenever it would be helpful for me to do so.

Please convey to all your colleagues my sincere wishes for success in our common endeavor. Over the years, their achievements at the Eighteen-Nation Disarmament Conference have been outstanding. I am confident that in the future our efforts, in cooperation with theirs, will be equal to any challenge and will result in progress for the benefit of all.

STATEMENT ON PRISON REFORM

Following is the text of President Nixon's Nov. 1 statement on prison and correctional reform:

Nineteen out of every twenty persons who are sent to prison eventually return to society. What happens to them while they are in confinement is a tremendously important question for our country.

Are they effectively rehabilitated? In some instances, the answer is yes. But in an appalling number of cases, our correctional institutions are failing.

According to recent studies, some forty percent of those who are released from confinement later return to prison. Or, to put it another way, a sizeable proportion of serious crimes are committed by persons who have already served a jail sentence. Eight out of every ten offenders sampled in a recent FBI study had at least one prior arrest and seven out of ten had a prior conviction. Of those charged with burglary, auto theft or armed robbery, between sixty and seventy percent had been arrested two or more times in the preceding seven years.

For youthful offenders, the picture is even darker. The repeater rates are greater among persons under twenty than over and there is evidence that our institutions actually compound crime problems by bringing young delinquents into contact with experienced criminals.

A nation as resourceful as ours should not tolerate a record of such futility in its correctional institutions. Clearly, our rehabilitative programs require immediate and dramatic reform. As a first step in that reform, I have today issued a broad directive to the Attorney General, asking him to take action to improve our correctional efforts in thirteen specific ways. He will report to me on his progress after six months and will at that time make such further recommendations as he believes are necessary.

The primary purpose of my directive is to improve the Federal corrections system. If this goal can be speedily accomplished, then the Federal system can serve as a model for State and local reform. The Federal Government will make every effort to help the States and localities make needed improvements, providing them with information, technical aid, and funds. We will also encourage greater cooperation and coordination between government and the private sector and among all the various units of government. I have specifically asked that our rehabilitative programs give greater attention to the special problems of distinct categories of offenders, such as juveniles, women, narcotics and alcoholic addicts, the mentally ill, and hard-core criminals. Closely supervised parole work release and probationary projects should be accelerated, as should our basic research into rehabilitative methods.

Thirteen Point Program. The thirteen specific concerns of my directive are as follows:

1. To end the crisis-oriented, stop-gap nature of most reform efforts, I have asked the Attorney General to develop a ten-year plan for reforming our correctional activities.

2. I have directed that explorations begin on the feasibility of pooling the limited resources of several governmental units in order to set up specialized treatment facilities. Several counties within a State or several States can often accomplish together what none of them could accomplish alone. Regional cooperation could be especially helpful in dealing with women offenders who are so few in number that their treatment in local institutions is often inefficient and inadequate, with hard-core criminals who require close supervision and particularly secure quarters, and with the mentally ill and narcotics and alcoholic addicts who need extensive medical treatment.

3. It is a tragic fact that juveniles comprise nearly a third of all offenders who are presently receiving correctional treatment and that persons under the age of twenty-five comprise half of that total. Yet our treatment facilities are least adequate for these same age groups. This is the reason that so many young offenders are thrown in with older criminals. I have asked the Attorney General to give special emphasis to programs for juvenile offenders—including group homes, modern diagnostic and treatment centers, and new probation mechanisms. This effort should be closely coordinated with the Department of Health, Education and Welfare.

4. We must expedite the design and construction of the long-planned Federal psychiatric study and treatment facility for mentally disturbed and violent offenders. Since the late 1950s, this project has been delayed by a series of administrative problems. It should be delayed no longer, for our understanding of mentally disturbed offenders is distressingly inadequate.

5. Federal law, like many State laws, has never been adequately concerned with the problem of the mental incompetent who is accused of a crime, sentenced for a crime, or found innocent because of his mental condition. I do not believe, for example, that present law adequately protects the civil rights of the accused mental incompetent. Nor does the disposition of such cases always give adequate protection to society. We need a comprehensive study of this matter, one which takes up both the Constitutional and the medical problems involved. A new law should be drafted which could not only serve the Federal jurisdiction but which might aid State authorities who have similar problems.

6. A great number of existing city and county jails are antiquated and overcrowded. Correctional experts believe that the local jail concept should be replaced with a comprehensive, community-oriented facility which would bring together a variety of detention efforts, adult and juvenile court diagnostic services, treatment programs both for those who are incarcerated and for those on supervisory release, and the half-way house concept. Pilot projects along these lines have already been designed for New York City and Chicago. They should be given the highest priority and available funds should wherever possible, be used to encourage other centers of this sort.

7. Ninety percent of convicted criminals and accused persons held in custody are housed in State or local institutions. The Federal Government should do all it can to help the States and localities carry this burden through programs of technical and financial aid. This Federal assistance should be especially directed toward the development of parole and probation programs and other alternatives to incarceration.

8. The lack of adequate public money for Federal and State prisons suggests that we should look to the private sector for supplementary assistance. Private industry can help rehabilitate criminals in many ways, such as retraining and hiring those who have served time. Voluntary agencies and professional organizations can also help those who are released from jail, tutoring them in new skills, helping them locate jobs, advising them as they readjust to civilian society, and cooperating with the courts in their probationary programs. A number of industries and volunteer organizations have already started successful programs of this sort; their example should be used to stimulate broader private efforts.

9. An adequate corrections system is only as effective as those who run it. Unfortunately too many rehabilitative programs are staffed with untrained personnel. I am therefore asking the Department of Justice to significantly expand its existing training programs for those who work in correctional institutions, both newcomers and experienced employees. The Justice Department's informal efforts to disseminate information should also be expanded.

10. I have asked the Attorney General to establish a task force which will make recommendations concerning a unified Federal corrections system. The various stages or rehabilitation are often poorly coordinated at present. The offender cannot proceed in an orderly manner from confinement to work release to release under supervision and finally to an unsupervised release. The unification of the various programs involved could bring to this process the coordination and sense of progression it badly needs.

11. Our experience with so-called "half-way houses," institutions which offer a mediating experience between prison and complete return to society, has been most successful to this point. The per capita cost of operating half-way houses are not significantly higher than that of maintaining a man in prison, and the rate of recidivism among those who leave half-way houses is lower than among those who return directly to society—after confinement. I am asking the Attorney General to prepare legislation which would expand the half-way house program to include a greater number of convicted offenders, specifically, those on parole and probation who cannot participate in the program at present. The Department of Justice will also assist States and localities in establishing and expanding half-way house projects.

12. Many correctional programs are based more on tradition and assumption than on theories which have been scientifically tested. Few of our programs have been closely studied to see just what results they bring. Clearly the poor record of our rehabilitative efforts indicates that we are doing something wrong and that we need extended research both on existing programs and on suggested new methods. I have asked the Attorney General to marshall the combined resources of the Department of Justice in a major new research effort.

13. Correctional programs have proliferated in recent years with little or no effort at consolidation or coordination. Among the Federal agencies presently involved in correctional activities are the Bureau of Prisons, the Board of Parole, the Office of the Pardon Attorney and the Law Enforcement Assistance Administration—all at the Department of Justice. Also involved are the Social and Rehabilitation Service, the Office of Education and the Public Health Service of the Department of Health, Education and Welfare. The Manpower Administration of the Department of Labor and the Office of Economic Opportunity also play major roles.

If all these efforts are to be effectively coordinated then some one authority must do the coordinating. I have asked the Attorney General to take on that assignment.

A Word to the Concerned Citizen. Many millions of words have been written about the crime crisis in our country. Surely it is among the most severe domestic crises of our times. Its successful solution will require the best efforts of the government at every level and the full cooperation of our citizens in every community.

One of the areas where citizen cooperation is most needed is in the rehabilitation of the convicted criminal. Men and women who are released from prison must be given a fair opportunity to prove themselves as they return to society. We will not insure our domestic tranquility by keeping them at arms length. If we turn our back on the ex-convict, then we should not be surprised if he again turns his back on us.

None of our vocational education programs, our work-release efforts, our half-way houses, or our probation and parole systems will succeed if the community to which an offender returns is unwilling to extend a new opportunity. Unions, civic groups, service clubs, labor organizations, churches and employers in all fields can do a great deal to fight crime by extending a fair chance to those who want to leave thier criminal records behind them and become full and productive members of society.

INDEX

1969 Nixon News Conferences, Messages, Major Statements

M

Magnuson, Warren G., 29-A
Manpower Training, 45-A, 78-A, 82-A, 90-A, 108-A, 118-A
Marchi, John J., 21-A
Marihuana, 63-A
Mass Transit. *See* Transportation.
McClellan, John L., 3-A
McCormack, John W., 19-A
McCrory, Mary, 2-A
Medicare, 88-A
Merchant Marine, 92-A
Messages, Statements and Speeches
  Airports and Air Transport, 65-A
  Apollo 11 astronauts, 120-A
  Arts and humanities, 119-A
  Asia policy (Nixon Doctrine), 96-A
  Balance of payments, 116-A
  Bank Holding Companies, 44-A
  Budget, 47-A
  Burger Nomination, 44-A
  Campus unrest, 93-A, 115-A
  Chemical-biological warfare, 115-A
  Consumer Affairs, 98-A
  Crime, 49-A
  Disarmament Committee; letter, 122-A
  District of Columbia, 36-A, 52-A
  Draft Revision, 61-A
  Drug Abuse, 63-A
  Electoral College reform, 41-A
  Environmental Quality, 106-A
  Federal-Aid Grant Consolidation, 54-A
  Food aid, 56-A, 91-A
  Foreign Aid, 59-A
  Guam, 96-A
  Inaugural, 34-A
  Inflation, 117-A
  Interstate Commerce Commission, 73-A
  Job Safety, 74-A
  Latin America, 112-A; OAS Assembly, 120-A
  Legislative Program, 45-A, 89-A
  Manpower Training, 78-A
  Merchant Marine, 92-A
  Mine Safety, 43-A
  Minority enterprise, 120-A
  National Defense, 66-A
  New Federalism (Natl. Governors' Conf.), 107-A
  Nigerian civil war, 121-A
  Nonproliferation Treaty, 36-A
  Obscene Materials, 55-A
  OEO Reorganization, 85-A
  Population, 70-A
  Postal matters, 42-A, 47-A, 55-A, 58-A, 119-A
  Poverty, 39-A
  Prison reform, 122-A
  Public Debt, 41-A
  Reorganization Plans, 38-A
  Revenue sharing, 79-A
  Social Security, 87-A
  Taxation, 43-A, 48-A
  Trade Policy, 101-A
  Transportation, 84-A
  Unemployment Insurance, 68-A
  Urban Affairs Council, 35-A
  Vietnam, May 14, 104-A; Nov. 3, 94-A; troop reduction, Dec. 15, 111-A
  Voluntary action, 110-A
  Welfare Reform, 75-A, 81-A
Meyer, Charles A., 27-A, 121-A
Middle East
  News conferences, 6-A, 10-A, 12-A, 17-A, 24-A
  Policy statement, 5-A
  Strategic arms talks, 2-A
  U.S. commitments, 95-A
  U.S. economic aid, 61-A

Military Assistance, 61-A
Mine Safety, 43-A, 91-A
Minneapolis Election, 23-A
Minority Enterprise Council, 120-A
Missiles and Missile Defense Systems
  ABM, 5-A, 10-A, 14-A, 15-A, 16-A, 18-A, 19-A, 24-A
  ABM and Red China threat, 6-A, 14-A, 16-A, 19-A
  Minuteman, 15-A, 24-A
  Soviet, 16-A, 19-A, 24-A
Mississippi, 26-A
Mitchell, John N., 3-A, 32-A
Mollenhoff, Clark R., 3-A
Monetary Policy. *See* Balance of Payments. Budget.
Moon. *See* Apollo.
Moot, Robert, 31-A
Morrison, Samuel Eliot, 93-A
My Lai Incident, 30-A, 31-A

N

Narcotics, 38-A, 63-A, 92-A, 99-A
National Commission on Consumer Finance, 98-A, 100-A
National Commission on Product Safety, 101-A
National Commission on Reform of Federal Criminal Laws, 51-A
National Commission on Urban Growth, 71-A
National Commission on Violence, 38-A
National Computerized Job Bank, 79-A, 83-A, 91-A
National Defense. *See* Armament and Defense.
National Foundation on the Arts and Humanities, 119A
National Goals Research Staff, 108-A
National Liberation Front, 4-A, 22-A, 105-A, 106-A
National Nutrition Survey, 57-A
National Occupational Safety and Health Board, 74-A
National Science Foundation, 6-A, 20-A
National Security Council
  ABM, 10-A
  Relationship with State Dept. and President, 7-A
  Revitalized, 3-A, 45-A
  SALT talks, 1-A, 22-A
Natural Resources, 106-A
Navy, U.S., 7-A
New Federalism, 81-A, 107-A
New Realism, 109-A
New York City Election, 21-A, 23-A
News Conferences. *See also* subject headings, e.g. Arms Control. Vietnam. etc.
  January 27, 1-A
  March 4, 8-A
  March 14, 14-A
  April 18, 17-A
  June 19, 21-A
  September 26, 24-A
  October 20, 28-A
  December 8, 30-A
News Conferences, Frequency of, 33-A
News Media, 31-A, 33-A
Nigeria, 121-A
Nixon Doctrine, 96-A
Nominations and Appointments
  Assistant Secretary (Under Secretary) of State for Latin America, 5-A, 27-A
  Burger, Warren Earl, 44-A
  DuBridge, Lee A., 106-A
  Fisher, Max M., 110-A

Haynsworth, Clement F., 25-A
HEW Dept., 23-A
Holdovers with Civil Service status, 16-A
Johnson appointments withdrawn, 3-A
Judgeships, 3-A
National Science Foundation head, 20-A
Rockefeller, Laurance S., 106-A
Smith, Gerard C., 6-A
Women, 8-A
Yost, Charles W., 5-A

Nonproliferation Treaty. *See* Arms Control.
North Atlantic Treaty Organization, 10-A, 16-A

O

O'Brien, Lawrence F., 58-A
Obscenity, 55-A, 92-A
Occupational Safety, 74-A, 91-A
Office of Child Development, 45-A
Office of Consumer Affairs, 98-A
Office of Economic Opportunity
  Consumer activities, 98-A, 99-A, 100-A
  Family planning, 70-A, 73-A
  Food programs, 57-A
  Governors' veto power, 33-A
  Reform of, 39-A, 40-A, 45-A, 83-A, 85-A, 90-A
Office of Inter-governmental Relations, 45-A, 55-A
Oil
  Aviation fuel tax, 66-A
  Depletion allowance, 25-A
  Peru, 13-A
  Pollution, off-shore drilling, 6-A
Organization of African Unity, 121-A
Organization of American States, 112-A, 120-A
Overseas Private Investment Corp., 59-A, 61-A, 91-A

P

Patronage, 42-A, 58-A, 119-A
Paul VI (Pope), 4-A, 9-A
Peace: Inaugural Address, 34-A; April 14 message, 45-A; New Federalism speech, 108-A
Peace Department, 6-A
Pearson Commission Report, 61-A
Peru, 13-A
Philadelphia Plan, 27-A
Poff, Richard, 51-A
Police, 37-A, 38-A, 92-A
Political Patronage, 42-A, 58-A, 119-A
Poole, Cecil F., 3-A
Population and Family Planning, 60-A, 70-A, 91-A
Population Research, Center for, 72-A
Pornography, 55-A, 92-A
Post Office Department, 42-A, 45-A, 46-A, 47-A, 58-A, 90-A, 119-A; obscene mail, 55-A
Poverty Program, 31-A, 33-A, 39-A, 75-A, 81-A, 85-A
Presidency, 7-A, 20-A, 41-A, 90-A, 106-A
Presidential Task Force on International Development, 91-A
President's Advisory Council on Executive Organization, 108-A
President's Commission on Postal Organization, 42-A
President's Scientific Advisory Committee, 115-A
President's Urban Affairs Council, 35-A, 39-A, 108-A
Press Conferences. *See* News Conferences.

PB-49710
5-02

39301

DATE DUE